McCall's
NO TIME TO COOK
Meals in Minutes

By the Food Editors of McCall's
Edited by Dorcas A. Comstock and
Elaine Prescott Wonsavage

Newfield Publications

McCall's Magazine

Barbara Chernetz, *Food Editor*
Mary B. Johnson, *Senior Food Editor*

McCall's No Time To Cook

Production Editor
Barbara Jean Dooley

Contributing Writers
Home Economists
Meg Beutel, Donna Johnson,
Ruth Pomeroy

Contributing Editor
Mary J. Norton

Editorial Coordinator
Dawn Therrien

Designer
Barbara Marks

NY TIMES Women's Magazines
Book Publishing & Licensing

Carol A. Guasti, *Editorial Director*
Christopher Cavanaugh, *Managing*
Editor

CONTENTS

SIX
30-MINUTE MEALS
195

SEVEN
ONE-DISH MEALS
235

EIGHT
EASY, ELEGANT
ENTERTAINING
271

NINE
HOLIDAY
CELEBRATIONS
327

NO TIME TO COOK

◆

I just have no time to cook! Probably no other statement more accurately reflects the effect of today's hectic schedules on the way we live. But just because there's less time to devote to cooking doesn't mean that we're willing to accept less in terms of food variety, wholesomeness and excitement. On the contrary, today's busy cooks expect—no, demand—recipes and menus that deliver the utmost in convenience, great taste and quality.

And that's just what you can expect from this creative new cookbook researched, developed, tested and compiled with you, the contemporary cook, in mind. You'll first discover basic timesaving techniques to make the most of every minute spent in the kitchen. The remaining sections offer a culinary collage of sensational quick-to-fix recipes, delectably delicious do-aheads, freeze-ahead favorites, no-fuss, no-cook delights, step-by-step 30-minute menus, simple single-dish meals, elegantly easy entertaining for any occasion and fast 'n' festive fare for holiday celebrations.

So whenever you feel there's no time to cook, reach for this book and get ready to enjoy some wonderful quick-to-fix food—and some spare time too!

ONE

TIMESAVING KITCHEN TECHNIQUES

♦

Picture this: Two people in identical kitchens about to prepare the same meal. As the minutes pass, we see Pat engaged in a frantic game of beat-the-clock, searching for a measuring cup for the sour cream that was never purchased for the misplaced Stroganoff recipe clipped from a magazine. Jay, however, has the Stroganoff cooking, the table nicely set, and even has enough time to sit and relax. What does Jay know that Pat doesn't? Many of the basic planning tips and work-saving tricks contained in the next pages! From kitchen-organization techniques and handy charts of ingredient substitutions and measures to freeze-ahead hints and smart shopping strategies, you'll discover all the simple "secrets" to help you become the best—and quickest cook possible!

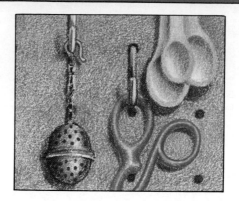

THE WELL-ORGANIZED KITCHEN

Whether small or large, newly designed or ancient, any kitchen works better when it's organized for space and time efficiency. Here are some ideas to help you organize equipment, utensils and food storage for quick-and-easy access.

DRAWERS

♦ Organize kitchen drawers where you keep small utensils with dividers, baskets and plastic drawer organizers. Separate small utensils from large, and those frequently used from those used occasionally. If drawer space is limited, hang small tools from a pegboard attached to a wall.

♦ Keep measuring spoons and cups in one definite location in a drawer, preferably next to the stove or mixing center. That way they'll be within easy reach and you'll be more likely to use them when following a recipe.

♦ Keep pretty placemats, napkins and color-coordinated candles together in a drawer. This way you can pull them out in a jiffy for unexpected company or to add a special touch to an everyday meal.

♦ For barbecues, keep all "outdoor" utensils together in a drawer (or basket tucked into a spare closet) for spur-of-the-moment barbecues or picnics.

CABINETS

♦ Spices should never be stored close to the kitchen range. Heat quickly robs spices of their flavor and color. Instead, store them in a cabinet within easy reach, but as far from the stove as possible. Invest in an inexpensive plastic turntable that fits into the cabinet or a wire rack that hangs on the cabinet door—this allows for quick selection of any spice and makes inventory-taking a snap.

♦ Look *under* your cabinets and you'll discover a space-saving bonanza! Make it the new home of a roll of paper towels on a decorative holder, an electric can opener, a coffee maker, plus a host of other compact kitchen equipment.

♦ Baking equipment is often difficult and awkward to store because of the many shapes and sizes of pie and cake pans, baking sheets and muffin tins. Try storing them vertically in a dish drainer that fits into a cabinet.

♦ Instead of placing dishes on top of one another in a cabinet, make use of sturdy plastic-coated shelf-stackers. They're sturdy enough to hold several dinner plates on top, leaving enough space underneath to stack smaller plates, bowls and cups. No more juggling to get to those plates—and less chance of chipping or breaking your dinnerware!

DAVID SCHULZ

COUNTERS

♦ Keep wooden spoons and cooking utensils in a jar or crock on the counter: It puts them right at your fingertips and adds a decorative touch too!

♦ If counter space is limited (and it usually is), keep out only those appliances essential to everyday living: the coffee maker, toaster oven, electric can opener, for example. Look for space-saving appliances that can be mounted under cabinets to make the most of counter space. Appliances used less frequently should be kept in cabinets or closets where they can be reached easily.

♦ Keep a large cutting board on a counter by the sink to save time and steps in a multitude of food-preparation activities.

♦ If you don't have a dishwasher or just don't use it every day, make space in a cabinet for the dish drainer and board to be put away. It frees up valuable counter space and gives a tidy look to the kitchen. If cabinet space is really limited, invest in a folding plastic or wooden drainer that can be hung on the wall.

♦ Well-sharpened knives are a cook's most valuable tools. Keep them in a holder or rack on the counter or on a magnetic bar above the counter. They should never be jumbled in a drawer where the edges can be nicked or damaged—or where a searching hand may be cut.

♦ Stackable canisters for flour, sugar, coffee and tea save room on counters.

PANTRY

♦ Group similar canned and packaged foods together, turning labels forward and rotating older items to use first. This enables at-a-glance inventory-taking and quick location of needed items.

♦ Search for expanded pantry space in an underutilized closet or other area of the home. This way you can stock up on frequently used items on bargain days.

♦ Here's a handy list of staple items for a well-stocked pantry:

Bottled or packaged salad dressings
Bread crumbs
Canned and dry soups
Canned chicken and beef broth; bottled clam juice
Canned fruits and vegetables
Canned or jarred tomato sauces and paste
Canned tuna, shrimp, crabmeat and clams
Cereals
Cooking sherry and wine
Extracts
Flour
Herbs and spices (basil, cloves, cinnamon, dill, parsley, oregano, garlic powder, nutmeg, paprika, tarragon, to name a few, plus any special ones for your favorite ethnic cookery)
Jams, jellies and preserves
Liqueurs (great in desserts, especially when flamed)
Nonfat dry milk
Nuts, raisins and other dried fruits
Oils and vinegars
Packaged cake mixes, frostings
Packaged noodles, rice and sauce products
Pastas, rice and instant potatoes
Peanut butter
Prepared baking mixes, baking powder and baking soda
Salt, pepper
Syrup
Worcestershire, hot-pepper and soy sauces ♦

PREPARATION POINTERS

Once your kitchen is organized, the next step is learning the techniques and tips that can maximize your time, minimize cleanup and help with any problems you may encounter when preparing recipes.

There may be times when you're not sure how much of an ingredient to use, or what to do if you run out of an ingredient when you're preparing a recipe. For those events, use our handy chart "How Much Is Enough?" And for those occasional mishaps when you lose count and use twice the amount of an ingredient by mistake, you'll find advice on how to avoid disaster in the kitchen.

♦ Before starting to cook, read recipes through. Make sure you understand the method. Assemble all ingredients and equipment to save time looking for things once cooking begins.

♦ Attach a clamp inside a cabinet door to hold recipe cards or clippings at eye level. Or cut a slot through a piece of cork glued to the top of a recipe file box. Or use a clear, sturdy plastic holder to keep your cookbook open to the page you need—and to keep the page clean.

♦ Do all the required chopping, slicing and measuring before you turn on the stove or oven.

♦ Preheat the oven or grease baking pans before assembling a recipe. Better to have the pans ready than to waste time waiting for the oven to reach the appropriate temperature.

♦ For mincing and chopping, use the professional chef's technique for faster food preparation: Keeping the point of the knife stationary, lift the handle up and down and pivot it from side to side.

♦ When slicing or trimming vegetables such as carrots, celery or beans, do three or four pieces at once.

♦ When a recipe calls for several ingredients to be measured, there's no need to keep washing and drying measuring cups and spoons. Just plan to measure your dry ingredients first, simply wiping out with a paper towel, if necessary, for the next measure.

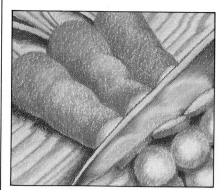

♦ Rinse your glass measuring cup in cold water before adding corn syrup or any other sticky substances. The syrup will pour out quickly and the cup will be easier to wash.

♦ If you're using eggs in a recipe, break them into your measuring cup before measuring the shortening. The shortening won't stick.

♦ If you're measuring 6 cups of flour or sugar for a recipe, count out as many raisins or chocolate pieces as the number of cups. Eat one after adding each cup to help keep track of your count—and reward yourself for being such a great cook!

MEASURING BASICS

Know the measuring basics to speed up your preparation:

3 teaspoons = 1 tablespoon
2 tablespoons = 1 fluid ounce
4 tablespoons = ¼ cup
5⅓ tablespoons = ⅓ cup
8 tablespoons = ½ cup
1 cup = 8 fluid ounces
2 cups = 1 pint or 16 fluid ounces
2 pints = 1 quart or 32 fluid ounces
4 cups = 1 quart
16 ounces = 1 pound

PREPARATION POINTERS

1 gram = .035 ounces
1 kilogram = 2.21 pounds
1 ounce = 28.35 grams
1 teaspoon = 4.9 milliliters
1 cup = 236.6 milliliters
1 liter = 1.06 quarts

HOW MUCH IS ENOUGH?

When a recipe calls for 1 cup of sliced apples or ½ cup fresh lemon juice, how do you know if you have enough? Here's a handy chart that will help:

1 medium apple = 1 cup sliced
8 slices cooked bacon = ½ cup crumbled
3 medium bananas = 2 cups mashed or 2½ cups sliced
1½ slices bread = 1 cup soft crumbs
4 slices bread = 1 cup dry crumbs
½ cup butter or margarine = 1 stick or ¼ pound
1 large carrot = 1 cup grated
1 pound hard cheese = 4 cups shredded (Cheddar, Swiss)

1 pound soft cheese = 5 cups shredded (American, Monterey Jack)
14 graham cracker squares = 1 cup crumbs
22 vanilla wafers = 1 cup finely crushed
19 chocolate wafers = 1 cup crumbs
1 cup heavy cream = 2 cups whipped
1 medium head lettuce = 6 cups torn
1 medium lemon = 2 to 3 tablespoons juice and 2 teaspoons grated peel
3 cups raw mushrooms = 1 cup sliced cooked
1 pound walnuts = 4 cups chopped
1 pound almonds = 3¼ cups chopped
1 medium onion = ½ cup chopped
3 medium potatoes = 1¾ cups mashed
1 pound raw shrimp = 1½ cups (½ pound) cleaned and cooked

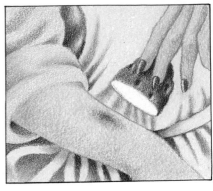

TO THE RESCUE

Don't throw it out, rescue it!

♦ Too much salt in a soup or stew? Add cut raw potatoes and discard them once they've cooked and absorbed the salt.

♦ Too much garlic in a soup or stew? Place parsley flakes in a tea ball or cheesecloth bag and add it to the pot until it soaks up the excess garlic.

♦ Too sweet? Add salt or 1 teaspoon of cider vinegar.

♦ Too much fat? For gravies, pour pan drippings into a tall glass. The grease rises to the top where it can be removed with a spoon or baster. A gravy separator also works well. For a soup or stew, drop ice cubes into the pot; as you stir, the fat clings to the cubes. Discard the cubes before they melt.

KITCHEN SAFETY

An ounce of prevention goes a long way in the kitchen. Here are some "hot" tips for minimizing and coping with fire and burns:

♦ Keep cold water running in the sink while you pour hot water from a pot of vegetables or pasta. It prevents the steam from scalding your hands.

♦ Don't let oil heat to the smoking point. It might ignite.

♦ Place a few pieces of dry bread in the broiler pan when broiling meats to soak up dripping fat. This can eliminate smoking fat as well as reduce the chance that the fat will catch fire.

♦ Sprinkle grease flare-ups or broiler fires with baking soda. If the fire is extinguished quickly, you can still eat a partially burned steak after rinsing off the soda.

♦ If the fire is in the oven, immediately turn off the heat and shut the door. This cuts off the air supply and smothers the fire.

♦ Keep clean, damp sponges in the freezer to relieve pain from minor burns.

♦ Soothe a minor kitchen burn by rubbing gently with the cut side of a raw potato or a paste made from baking soda and water.   ♦

EMERGENCY SUBSTITUTIONS

Just because you don't have a particular recipe ingredient doesn't mean you have to waste time running out to the store or give up attempting a recipe. Learn how to substitute!

WHEN YOU NEED	SUBSTITUTE
1 teaspoon apple or pumpkin spice	½ teaspoon cinnamon, ¼ teaspoon nutmeg, ⅛ teaspoon allspice and ⅛ teaspoon cardamom
1 teaspoon baking powder	¼ teaspoon baking soda plus ½ teaspoon cream of tartar
1 cup buttermilk	1 cup plain yogurt or 1 tablespoon vinegar or lemon juice plus milk to equal 1 cup
1 cup cake flour	1 cup minus 2 tablespoons sifted all-purpose flour
1 ounce unsweetened chocolate	3 tablespoons unsweetened cocoa plus 1 tablespoon butter or margarine
1 tablespoon cornstarch	2 tablespoons all-purpose flour
2 egg yolks	1 whole egg (for thickening)
1 tablespoon fresh herbs	1 teaspoon dry herbs
1 cup skim milk	⅓ cup nonfat dry milk plus ¾ cup water
1 cup whole milk	½ cup evaporated milk plus ½ cup water
1 teaspoon dry mustard	1 tablespoon prepared mustard
1 cup sour cream	3 tablespoons butter plus ⅞ cup buttermilk or yogurt
1 cup sugar	1¾ cups confectioners' sugar (Do not substitute in baking.)
3 cups tomato juice	1½ cups tomato sauce plus 1½ cups water or 1 can (6 ounces) tomato paste plus 3 cans water, dash salt and sugar
1 cup tomato sauce	1 can tomato paste, 1½ cans water plus seasonings

WORK-SAVING SHORTCUTS

With more and more demands on your time, it's important to get the most out of every minute spent in the kitchen. And that means using shortcuts and work-saving tricks such as these:

BREADS AND DESSERTS

♦ Yeast doughs will rise quickly in an unheated oven if the bowl is placed over a smaller pan of hot water. Or put the dough in a container placed on a heating pad set at medium. If the television is being used, let the dough rise on top of the set: It's hard to forget about it that way!

♦ When making cake from a mix, save a little dry mix to dust the cake pans and avoid that floury look.

♦ Before rolling pastry dough, chill it in the refrigerator or freezer to avoid its sticking to a rolling pin. This cuts down on using additional flour that toughens pastry, and lets you roll dough more quickly.

♦ When icing a many-layered cake, insert thin wooden skewers vertically through the layers to prevent the layers from sliding before the icing sets.

♦ To avoid spending time trying to get crumbs out of the frosting of a cake, first spread on a thin layer of frosting. Once this sets, you can apply the rest of the frosting easily and smoothly without cake crumbs getting into it.

♦ For a fast cake topping, place a paper doily with a large design on top of the cake, then dust with confectioners' sugar. Lift the doily off carefully, and you have instant decoration!

♦ For faster, easy-to-whip cream, first chill the bowl and beaters well.

♦ For no-wilt whipped cream, sprinkle ½ teaspoon unflavored gelatine into 1 tablespoon cold water and stir over low heat to dissolve. Let cool. Then add to 1 cup heavy cream in a chilled bowl and whip until stiff.

♦ If you've forgotten to soften butter for baking, or you need it in a hurry, grate it to bring it to room temperature quickly. Or pop it in the microwave at low power for about 30 seconds.

MAIN DISHES

♦ Keep stuffed green peppers, onions and tomatoes from collapsing by baking them in greased muffin tins.

♦ Cut down on cooking time for meat loaf by baking the mixture in individual loaf pans or by baking individual portions in muffin cups.

♦ To shape meatballs in a jiffy—and keep hands clean—use an ice-cream scoop.

♦ Use instant soup mixes to make quick and creamy gravies and sauces. Serve over noodles, rice, vegetables, fish or poultry.

♦ Forget to defrost something for dinner? You can cook frozen meats, poultry and fish without thawing. Just allow more cooking time—about 1½ times that normally required. Microwave ovens are wonderful for defrosting too!

♦ Steaks, chicken, chops and seafood marinated for a few hours in salad dressing have a wonderful broiled or grilled taste—and take less time to cook.

♦ Keep a ready supply of fresh chopped onion, green pepper and parsley in the freezer, in reclosable plastic bags or freezer containers, to pull out quickly any time a recipe calls for them. Grated cheese, bread crumbs and chopped nuts also freeze well and are handy when you need small amounts.

♦ Garlic cloves peel easily and more quickly when placed on a cutting board and hit firmly with the flat side of a French chef's knife.

FRUITS AND VEGETABLES

♦ To peel tomatoes in a jiffy, spear them with a fork and hold over a gas flame until the skin cracks. Or place tomatoes in a bowl, cover with boiling water and let sit for 1 minute. Then peel with a paring knife.

♦ Fresh corn on the cob is a real American favorite, but removing the corn silk can be a tedious task. Here's a handy timesaving trick: Dampen a paper towel or terry cloth and brush downward to

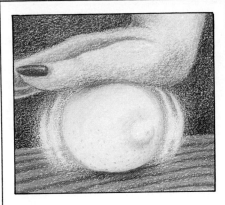

remove every strand in one stroke.

♦ Potatoes bake in about half the usual time when boiled first for 10 minutes.

♦ Cut up canned tomatoes easily and quickly, right in the can, with kitchen shears.

♦ To peel small white onions speedily and easily, plunge into boiling water for a few seconds. Drain immediately and cool in cold water. The skins will slip off easily when you remove the root and stem ends.

♦ When a recipe calls for browning eggplant or other foods in oil, let your broiler save you time and calories. Brush the slices lightly with oil and let brown in the broiler. You'll use less fat then if you pan-broiled.

♦ To squeeze the most juice from a lemon, lime or orange, first roll the fruit on a hard surface, pressing with your hand, or submerge the fruit in hot water for 10 to 15 minutes. You can also heat the fruit in the microwave on HIGH (100%) for 30 seconds.

♦ Turn to frozen fruits for quick-to-fix desserts. Let fruits thaw in the refrigerator during the day to create nighttime treats. Try sliced peaches and strawberries sprinkled with grated orange peel. Or serve mixed fruits topped with lemon or orange sherbet. For instant sundaes, spoon assorted fruits over ice cream or layer in parfait glasses. Dress up plain cake squares by spooning on fruit and heaping on whipped topping.

♦ Fresh fruit and unflavored gelatine can be combined in recipes for an unlimited array of quick-to-prepare, refreshing salads and desserts. There are, however, a few fresh fruits—pineapple, papaya, kiwi fruit, fig and prickly pear—that contain an enzyme that prevents gelatine from gelling. To use these fruits in gelatine recipes, simply boil the cut-up fruit in water for 5 minutes to destroy the enzyme. Drain and let cool for ready use.

CLEANUP

♦ When broiling, put foil in the bottom of the broiler pan and grease the broiler grid to prevent sticking and to make cleanup a snap. Or, after broiling, sprinkle the grid with dry laundry detergent, cover with a dampened paper towel and let sit for a while.

♦ For barbecues, coat the bottoms of pots and pans with bar soap before cooking. Coat the grill top with vegetable oil or cooking spray for speedy cleanups.

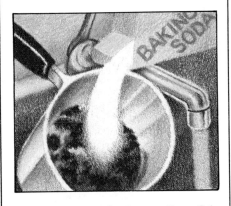

♦ To get rid of onion, garlic or fish odor on a cutting board, rub the board with a cut lemon or lime half. Then wash in soapy water.

♦ To make a grater easier to clean after use, rub it with salad oil before using.

♦ Burned and scorched pans are torture to clean. Here's an easy way out: Sprinkle the burned area liberally with baking soda, then add just enough water to moisten. Let this stand for several hours and you'll usually be able to lift the burned portion right out of the pan.

♦ To restore sparkle to a stained white ceramic sink, place a paper towel across the bottom and saturate with household bleach. Let stand for 30 minutes and the stains should disappear.

♦ For stainless steel sinks, use rubbing alcohol or white vinegar to remove water spots; use club soda to give the sink a nice shine.

♦ Wipe greasy knives with a paper towel before washing for quicker cleaning. ♦

SECRETS OF A SMART SHOPPER

Whether you consider food shopping an exciting adventure, a weekly necessity or a dreaded drudgery…you can save time and money at the supermarket by first spending a few minutes at home planning and organizing and then using some shopping savvy in the aisles. Here are some tips worth checking out:

AT HOME

Plan a Week's Menus. It's not as difficult as it sounds. Take a look in your freezer, refrigerator and pantry. Chances are you have a few packages of meat, fruits and vegetables, breads, some leftovers and assorted canned goods that can join forces to become the components of a week's worth of tasty dinners. But how do you know which main dish to pair with what accompaniment?

Delicious meals depend on a complementary blend of flavors (balance a bland flavor with a zesty or tart one); textures (serve crisp or crunchy foods with soft or mashed foods); colors (colorful vegetables, salads or garnishes can really spark eye appeal); and nutritional values (serve a variety of foods to maximize nutrient intake). Working with your existing inventory of foods as a base, start slotting in main dishes, accompaniments, salads and desserts for each day of the week. Look through cookbooks and magazines for new and exciting recipes that fit into your budget and menu plan and also expand your family's food tastes. Once you have written your menus, you can post them (with any new recipes) for all to see. This way, family members can help get the meal started if you're running late.

Make a List. Use the week's menus to draw up your shopping list, checking all foods and recipe ingredients against supplies on hand. Don't forget to check for herbs and spices and condiments. Add to the list your everyday necessities and family favorites. Arrange the list according to the layout of your store to help ensure that you don't miss any items or waste time running back and forth from aisle to aisle. Make a notation next to the items on your list that are on special or for which you have coupons. Now, more about coupons:

Use Coupons. Clipping, swapping and using cents-off coupons can cut your grocery bill by 5, 10—even up to 50 percent. Note any expiration dates and use these coupons as soon as possible. Arrange a simple filing system so you can easily find coupons to match your shopping list. Take advantage of double or triple values offered by some supermarkets. This can mean even bigger savings.

AT THE STORE

Use a List. Let your list be your guide when shopping. Try to stick to it to avoid temptation and reduce impulse buying.

Don't Shop When You're Hungry. Try to eat something before shopping. If you're hungry, you'll buy more.

Shop Alone. Get a neighbor to watch the children, if possible, while you shop. You'll save time and money.

Check Up and Down. Most of the more expensive foods are displayed at eye level. Check the shelves above and below for better priced goods.

Check Unit Pricing. Look at the shelf tags for unit prices for each item. By knowing the price per ounce or pound, you can easily determine which size jar or package gives the better value for the dollar.

Shop Off-Hours. Avoid the crowds and save time. Early in the morning, at dinnertime or late at night are the typical off-peak hours when crowds are at a minimum in the aisles and at the checkout.

Read Labels. Look for nutritional information and expiration dates.

Buying Meat. When you buy meat, compare prices on the basis of cost per serving rather than cost per pound. Usually, you can plan on two or three servings per pound of roast beef, pork, lamb, chicken or turkey. Rib chops, spare ribs or chicken wings may yield only one or two servings per pound because of the amount of bone and fat they contain.

Compare Prices. Check prices on different forms of the same food. For example, if juice oranges are expensive, look to refrigerated or frozen juice for a possible better buy.

Buy in Bulk. Set aside a little extra money for unadvertised specials. During a sale, stock up on nonperishable items you use regularly or perishable items that you can freeze. If you buy in bulk at least once a month, you'll save time by not having to shop again for things you run out of.

Seasonal Specials. Buy seasonal fruits and vegetables to freeze or can for year-round enjoyment.

Frozen Foods Last. Pick up frozen foods right before checking out. Buy only foods frozen solid, with no dribbles on the package, no odor or other signs of having thawed. Put all frozen foods together in one bag so they'll stay frozen for the trip home. If you have errands after shopping, take along a large insulated cooler in which to place the frozen items.

FAST 'N' FROSTY
· SOUPS ·

Hot, hearty and hours of preparation—that's what most people associate with home-made soups. But to define our collection, you'd have to use words such as cold, refreshing and quick. That's because each of our frosty fruit and vegetable soups can be made in a matter of minutes with the help of a food processor or blender. With the press of a button or switch, you can create sensational soups that require only a fast chill in a bowl of ice or in the refrigerator before serving. Pictured, at left, Cold Curry-Carrot Soup which uses the food processor to slice and purée carrots, onion, broth and yogurt into a tangy tempter. At top, frozen raspberries and yogurt whirl in the blender or processor in seconds for a soup that's sweet and superb. The Lettuce-And-Green-Pea Soup, at right, is a rich blend of lettuce, green peas, onion, broth and cream spiced with nutmeg.

(continued)

Pictured above, a tureen of Strawberry Soup made in seconds by puréeing strawberries and yogurt. Below, a blend of cantaloupe, sherry and orange juice served in a chilled hollowed-out melon half. See opposite page for recipes.

COLD CURRY-CARROT SOUP

(pictured)

1 lb carrots, pared
2½ cans (13¾-oz size) chicken broth
¼ teaspoon salt
Dash pepper
1 medium onion, halved
2 tablespoons butter or margarine
1½ teaspoons curry powder
1½ cups yogurt
3 thin unpared cucumber slices
Coarsely grated pared carrot

DO AHEAD

1. In food processor, using slicing disk, slice carrots.

2. In large saucepan, combine carrots, chicken broth, salt and pepper; bring to boiling; reduce heat and simmer 10 minutes, or until carrots are fork-tender.

3. Slice onion in food processor. In hot butter in skillet, sauté onion and curry powder, stirring occasionally, until onion is tender—5 minutes.

4. In food processor, fitted with the steel blade, purée half of carrot mixture at a time until smooth. Add onion mixture and yogurt; mix until smooth. Turn into serving bowl; refrigerate until well chilled.

TO SERVE

5. Mix well; garnish with sliced cucumber and grated carrot. *Makes 6½ cups; 8 servings.*

RASPBERRY-YOGURT SOUP

(pictured)

2 pkg (10-oz size) frozen red raspberries
2 containers (8-oz size) red-raspberry yogurt
Fresh mint

DO AHEAD

1. Mix berries and yogurt together in blender or food processor. Blend until smooth. Chill well.

TO SERVE

2. Garnish with mint. *Makes about 1 quart; 8 servings.*

STRAWBERRY SOUP

(pictured)

1 quart fresh strawberries
2 containers (8-oz size) strawberry yogurt
2 tablespoons lemon juice

DO AHEAD

1. Gently wash and hull berries. Set aside a few large berries for garnish.

2. In blender or food processor, combine rest of strawberries, the yogurt and lemon juice. Blend to make a purée. Refrigerate until very well chilled.

TO SERVE

3. Serve in chilled serving bowl. Slice reserved berries; float several slices on top of each serving. *Makes 8 servings.*

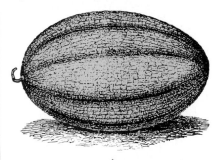

CHILLED CANTALOUPE SOUP

(pictured)

1 (3-lb) ripe cantaloupe
½ cup dry sherry
¼ cup sugar
¼ cup orange juice

DO AHEAD

1. Cut melon in half; scoop out and discard seeds. Scoop out cantaloupe meat.

2. In blender or food processor, fitted with the steel blade, combine cantaloupe and rest of ingredients. Blend until smooth—several times, if necessary. Turn into bowl; chill over ice cubes or refrigerate, covered, until very cold.

TO SERVE

3. Serve in chilled serving bowls. *Makes 4 cups; 5 servings.*

LETTUCE-AND-GREEN-PEA SOUP

(pictured)

1 large head iceberg, romaine or leaf lettuce, shredded (about 8 cups)
1 pkg (10 oz) frozen green peas
½ cup sliced green onion
1 can (13¾ oz) chicken broth
1½ cups light cream
1 teaspoon sugar
1 teaspoon salt
⅛ teaspoon nutmeg
Dash pepper
Thin lemon slices

DO AHEAD

1. In 4-quart kettle, combine shredded lettuce, peas, green onion and chicken broth; bring to boiling over medium heat. Reduce heat and simmer, covered, 10 minutes, or just until lettuce is soft.

2. In blender container or food processor, fitted with the steel blade, place half of lettuce mixture and liquid; cover and blend at high speed 1 minute. Pour into bowl. Repeat with remaining lettuce mixture and liquid. Pour all lettuce mixture back into kettle.

3. Add cream, sugar, salt, nutmeg and pepper to mixture in kettle. Cook over medium heat, stirring, until well blended.

TO SERVE

4. Serve soup hot; or refrigerate until well-chilled—several hours. Serve garnished with lemon slices. *Makes 8 servings.*

GAZPACHO

2 large tomatoes, peeled (1¾ lb)
1 large cucumber, pared and halved
1 medium onion, peeled and halved
1 medium green pepper, quartered and seeded
1 pimiento, drained
2 cans (12-oz size) tomato juice
⅓ cup olive or salad oil
⅓ cup red-wine vinegar
¼ teaspoon hot red-pepper sauce
1½ teaspoon salt
⅛ teaspoon coarsely-ground pepper
2 garlic cloves, split
½ cup packaged croutons
¼ cup chopped chives

DO AHEAD

1. In blender, combine one tomato, half the cucumber, half the onion, a green-pepper quarter, the pimiento and ½ cup tomato juice. Blend, covered, at high speed 30 seconds, to purée the vegetables.

2. In a large bowl, mix the puréed vegetables with remaining tomato juice, ¼ cup olive oil, the vinegar, red-pepper sauce, salt and pepper.

3. Refrigerate mixture, covered, until well chilled—about 2 hours. At the same time, refrigerate 6 serving bowls.

4. Meanwhile, rub inside of small skillet with garlic; reserve garlic. Add rest of oil; heat. Sauté croutons in oil until browned. Set aside until serving time.

5. Chop separately remaining tomato, cucumber, onion and green pepper. Place each of these, and the croutons, in separate bowls. Pass as accompaniments.

TO SERVE

6. Just before serving time, crush reserved garlic. Add to chilled soup, mixing well. Sprinkle with chopped chives. Serve the gazpacho in chilled bowls. Pass the accompaniments. *Makes 6 servings.* ◆

Food-Processor Magic

A food processor is one of the most versatile, timesaving appliances that today's busy cook can own. It can be used in almost any recipe to minimize work and maximize time. A food processor can help put the fun back into meal preparation, and give you the freedom to experiment and go a step beyond everyday foods to create new and exciting dishes you never thought you had the time for. Pictured here, our collection of fancy fare food processor recipes: below, a carrot custard pie. Clockwise: chilly bowls of Curry-Carrot Soup; light-as-air Almond Lace Wafers; an artichoke with garlicky Aioli Sauce; Double-Cheese-And-Ham Quiche; robust Salami Pâté. Recipes begin on page 22.

continued from page 20

ALMOND LACE WAFERS
(pictured)

½ cup blanched almonds
½ cup (1 stick) butter or margarine
½ cup sugar
1 tablespoon all-purpose flour
2 tablespoons milk

1. Preheat oven to 375F. Grease generously and flour well two cookie sheets. Grind almonds in food processor until fine.
2. Combine all ingredients in a small saucepan. Cook over low heat, stirring, until butter melts.
3. Drop by teaspoonfuls, 4 inches apart, on prepared cookie sheets. (Bake only four or five at a time.)
4. Bake 6 minutes, or until cookies are light brown and centers are bubbling. Let stand 1 minute.
5. Working quickly, roll each wafer around the handle of a wooden spoon.
6. Gently slide cookie off handle. Place, seam side down, on wire rack; cool. (If cookies become too crisp to roll, return to oven for a minute or two.) Regrease and reflour cookie sheets before baking each batch. *Makes about 2 dozen.*

COLD SALAMI PATE
(pictured)

2 lb salami, cut into ½-inch cubes (see Note)
1 bunch green onions, washed and cut into 1-inch pieces
4 large sprigs parsley
1½ env unflavored gelatine
1 can (6 oz) mixed-vegetable juice
1 (9-inch long) cucumber, peeled
¼ cup milk
1 pkg (8 oz) cream cheese, softened
5 thin slices of cucumber, cut in half
Rye-bread or pumpernickel rounds

DO AHEAD

1. Place half of the salami, green onion and parsley in food processor, fitted with a steel blade, and blend until smooth. Repeat with remaining half.
2. Turn into large bowl. Lightly oil a 9-by-5-by-3-inch loaf pan.
3. Sprinkle 1 envelope of gelatine over vegetable juice in small saucepan, to soften. Place over low heat, stirring constantly, until gelatine is dissolved. Remove from heat; stir into meat mixture; mix until smooth.
4. Spread half in bottom of prepared pan. Place whole cucumber on center of meat mixture. Spoon remaining meat mixture around cucumber, pressing

lightly, and then spreading evenly on top.
5. In small saucepan, sprinkle remaining gelatine over milk, to soften. Place over low heat, stirring until dissolved. Remove from heat.
6. Add cream cheese, beating with wooden spoon until smooth.
7. Pour on top of pâté. Refrigerate 4 hours, or overnight.

TO SERVE

8. Run a small spatula around edge of mold; place a hot damp dishcloth over bottom; shake gently to release. Remove to serving platter. Garnish with cucumber slices, as pictured. Cut into ¼-inch-thick slices. Serve with rye-bread or pumpernickel rounds. *Makes 16 to 20 servings.*

Note: Use salami that is not too salty.

DOUBLE-CHEESE-AND-HAM QUICHE
(pictured)

Cheese Pastry, recipe follows

FILLING

6 oz ham
½ lb Swiss cheese
1½ cups light cream
½ teaspoon salt
3 eggs

TO BAKE AND SERVE

1. Preheat oven to 375F. Bake pie shell 5 minutes; remove to rack.
2. Meanwhile, chop ham, using shredding disk, in food processor, to measure 1 cup.
3. Spread ham on bottom of cooled pastry shell. Chop cheese in processor; sprinkle over ham.
4. In processor, fitted with the steel blade, combine cream, salt and eggs. Blend just until mixture is smooth, not frothy—3 seconds.
5. Pour egg mixture into pie shell. Bake 40 to 45 minutes, or until top is golden and center is firm when pressed with fingertip.
6. Cool on wire rack 10 minutes. Remove side of pan; keep quiche on bottom of pan; place on serving plate. *Makes 10 servings.*

CHEESE PASTRY

¼ lb Swiss cheese, cut into ½-inch cubes
1⅔ cups sifted all-purpose flour
½ teaspoon salt
⅓ (⅔ stick) cup cold butter, cut into ½-inch cubes
3 to 4 tablespoons ice water

DO AHEAD

1. With shredding disk on food processor, chop cheese.
2. Add flour, salt and butter to processor, fitted with the steel blade. Chop until butter is in fine lumps.
3. Add ice water, and mix until well combined. Form into a ball.
4. Roll pastry on lightly floured pastry cloth to form a 12-inch circle. Lift into a fluted 9-inch pan with removable bottom in place.
5. Press evenly to bottom and side. Refrigerate.

ARTICHOKES WITH AIOLI SAUCE
(pictured)

¼ cup olive or salad oil
6 slices lemon
2 bay leaves
1 garlic clove, split
1 teaspoon salt
⅛ teaspoon pepper
4 large artichokes (about 3 lb)
Aioli Sauce, recipe follows

DO AHEAD

1. In large kettle, combine 3 cups water with olive oil, lemon slices, bay leaves, garlic, salt and pepper; bring to boiling.
2. Meanwhile, trim stalks from bases of artichokes; cut a 1-inch slice from tops. Remove discolored leaves; snip off spike ends.
3. Wash artichokes in cold water; drain.
4. Place artichokes in bottom of kettle, standing on base. Bring back to boiling; reduce heat and simmer, covered, 40 to 50 minutes, or until artichoke bases feel soft. Drain artichokes well. Let cool slightly.
5. Using fingers, pull out leaves in center. With teaspoon, remove hair choke from cavity.

TO SERVE

6. Serve artichokes, warm or cold, with Aioli Sauce in cavity in center. *Makes 4 servings.*

AIOLI SAUCE

1 slice white bread, crust removed
2 tablespoons milk
3 garlic cloves, minced
2 egg yolks
1 cup olive or salad oil
2 tablespoons lemon juice
¼ teaspoon salt
Dash white pepper

DO AHEAD

1. Soak bread in milk for 10 minutes; squeeze hard to remove all milk.

2. Place bread and garlic in food processor; blend 10 seconds, or until mixture forms a paste.

3. Add egg yolks; blend until egg mixture is thick—10 seconds.

4. Add olive oil, 1 tablespoon at a time, blending constantly after each addition until thick.

5. Continue until all oil has been used. Mixture should be thick.

6. Add lemon juice, salt and pepper; blend a few seconds more to mix well. Refrigerate, tightly covered. *Makes 1¼ cups.*

CARROT CUSTARD PIE
(pictured)

CRUST
½ cup whole blanched almonds
½ cup pecans
10 gingersnaps, halved
4 graham crackers, halved
¼ cup (½ stick) butter or margarine, melted

FILLING
1 lb carrots, pared, halved
1 pkg (3 oz) cream cheese, softened
2 tablespoons light-brown sugar
3 eggs
1 teaspoon ground cinnamon
1 teaspoon ground nutmeg
½ teaspoon salt
1 can (8 oz) crushed pineapple, undrained
1 can (14 oz) sweetened condensed milk
1 teaspoon vanilla extract
½ cup heavy cream, whipped
8 thin slices raw carrot

DO AHEAD

1. Prepare Crust: Preheat oven to 375F. In food processor, grind almonds and pecans; then add gingersnaps and graham crackers.

2. Continue running processor; add melted butter, and blend just until combined (a few seconds).

3. With fingers, press mixture evenly on bottom and side of 10-inch pie plate, not on rim.

4. Bake 8 to 10 minutes, or until golden-brown. Cool on wire rack before filling.

5. Make Filling: In medium saucepan, cook carrots, covered, in 1 inch boiling water just until tender—20 minutes. Drain; cool.

6. Purée carrots and cream cheese in processor. Turn into a large bowl.

7. Place brown sugar, eggs, cinnamon, nutmeg, salt and crushed pineapple in processor; process a few seconds to combine.

8. Add condensed milk and vanilla, blending until smooth.

9. Pour into carrot-cream-cheese mixture; mix with wooden spoon until smooth.

10. Turn into prepared crust. Bake 35 to 40 minutes. Remove to rack; cool completely; refrigerate.

TO SERVE

11. Decorate with rosettes of whipped cream and very thinly sliced raw carrots, as pictured. *Makes 8 servings.*

COLD CURRY-CARROT SOUP
(pictured)

For recipe, please see page 19.

CREAMY COLESLAW

3 lb green cabbage
½ lb carrots
1 cup radishes

DRESSING
2 cups mayonnaise
¼ cup prepared horseradish
1 tablespoon sugar
1 tablespoon lemon juice
1 tablespoon grated onion
2 teaspoons salt
½ teaspoon paprika
Chopped parsley (optional)

DO AHEAD

1. Wash cabbage; cut into small wedges; remove core. Wash and pare carrots; cut in half crosswise. Wash radishes; remove stems.

2. In food processor, shred cabbage with slicing or shredding disk, a few wedges at a time. Remove.

3. Shred carrots with shredding disk; add to cabbage.

4. Slice radishes with slicing blade; add to cabbage and carrots; toss to mix well. Refrigerate.

5. Make Dressing: In large bowl, combine mayonnaise and rest of dressing ingredients; mix well. Add vegetables; toss with dressing to coat well.

6. Refrigerate, covered, until well chilled—several hours or overnight.

TO SERVE

7. Garnish with chopped parsley, if desired. *Makes 12 servings.*

HERBED SMOKED SALMON

¼ cup (½ stick) butter or margarine
1 tablespoon snipped dill
1 tablespoon chopped parsley
1 tablespoon chopped chives
Dash dried oregano leaves
4 slices white, rye or pumpernickel bread
8 slices smoked salmon
4 thin slices lemon
Fresh dill or parsley sprigs

DO AHEAD

1. In food processor, mix butter with snipped dill, parsley, chives and oregano. Use to spread on bread slices.

2. Fold salmon slices; place 2 on each slice of bread. Arrange sandwiches on serving platter. Cover tightly with plastic wrap.

TO SERVE

3. Decorate sandwiches with lemon slices and dill sprigs. *Makes 4 sandwiches.*

APPETIZER CHEESE BALL

½ lb Swiss cheese
½ lb Cheddar cheese
1 cup walnuts
2 parsley sprigs
1 pkg (8 oz) cream cheese, softened
1 tablespoon Dijon-style mustard
Assorted crackers

DO AHEAD

1. In food processor, using shredding disk, shred Swiss and Cheddar cheeses. Remove.

2. Using steel blade, chop nuts and parsley together. Remove and set aside. Add cheeses and mustard to processor bowl; mix until smooth and well combined. Refrigerate until firm enough to form into a ball.

3. Form chilled cheese mixture into a ball; roll ball in nut mixture. Refrigerate until serving.

TO SERVE

4. Place on tray; surround with crackers; let stand until cheese is at room temperature. *Makes about 20 servings.* ◆

THE FREEZER:
A Busy Cook's Best Friend

The freezer isn't a place just for ice cubes. You'll be amazed at how many foods can be successfully frozen to retain their optimum freshness and save time when there's no time to cook. Here are the cold facts to show that a freezer can be a busy cook's best friend.

FIRST, THE BASICS

♦ Use good packaging and wrapping materials to freeze food. Freezer wraps and containers should be airtight, moistureproof and vaporproof.

♦ Freezing expands foods and liquids, so allow at least a half-inch of space at the top of the container before putting it in the freezer.

♦ Most foods stick together when frozen, so flash-freeze them to eliminate this problem. Spread food on a cookie sheet, freeze it, then remove and wrap in airtight containers and return to the freezer.

♦ Always scald or steam fresh vegetables before freezing to prevent loss of color, flavor and texture.

♦ The temperature for freezing foods is 0°F or lower. At this temperature, foods freeze faster, with less breakdown in their cellular structure, and they are more likely to retain true flavor and firm texture.

♦ Never place hot foods in the freezer; cool them first in the refrigerator. Or, for large quantities of hot food, cool in a big bowl or sink filled with cold water and ice.

♦ When you want to freeze a large quantity of food all at once, reduce your freezer temperature to −10°F or lower about 24 hours beforehand. This way, your food will be frozen solid in 10 to 12 hours.

♦ When buying fresh meats that are wrapped in plastic, check for holes. If there are no holes, freeze in this wrap up to 2 weeks. For longer storage, cover plastic tightly with freezer wrap.

♦ Thawing and then refreezing is not recommended, so divide large amounts of food into meal-size containers.

♦ If food is completely thawed to room temperature, cook it first, then refreeze.

LOOK AT WHAT YOU CAN FREEZE!

Economize on time, leftovers and bulk purchases by knowing what (and how) to freeze.

Bacon. Crumble extra slices of cooked bacon and freeze to use later as a topping for baked potatoes or salads.

Bananas. Mash overripe bananas, add a little lemon juice and freeze. Perfect for cakes and breads.

Blueberries. Freeze them in the basket they come in, unwashed. Wrap the

container in aluminum foil or plastic wrap.

Bread. Cut stale bread into tiny cubes, toast them for later use as croutons, then pop into the freezer. Bread crumbs freeze well too.

Brown Sugar. Wrap the box well, and the sugar won't harden.

Butter. Store in the original wrapping up to 9 months.

Cheese. Processed cheese, Swiss, Cheddar and even cream-cheese dips can be frozen successfully. Pop soft cheeses such as Monterey Jack and Muenster into the freezer for 15 minutes to make them easier to grate. Parmesan and Romano cheese also are easier to grate when frozen.

Coffee. Coffee beans and ground coffee stay fresh longer when refrigerated or frozen.

Cream. Freeze in original carton if there is a half-inch head space at the top. For leftover whipped cream, drop dollops on a cookie sheet and flash-freeze before storing in plastic bags.

Eggs. Freeze egg whites in a container up to a year. Mix egg yolks with a pinch of sugar or salt before freezing to prevent coagulation.

Flour. Freeze in original bag.

Green Peppers. Wash, halve and remove seeds and ribs from firm peppers. Place in an airtight freezer bag to pull out for later use. This is a great way to make use of an overabundance of peppers from the garden.

Honey. Flash-freeze in ice-cube trays. If it becomes granular, place cubes in a jar.

Ice Cream. To prevent a waxlike film from forming on top of an opened container, press a piece of wax paper against the surface of the remaining ice cream and reseal the container.

Marshmallows. Flash-freeze—no more stale marshmallows!

Pancakes, French Toast, Waffles. Too many? Flash-freeze and toast or heat in the oven to serve.

Pickles, Pimientos, Olives. Condiments in partially filled jars freeze well in their own liquid.

Popcorn. Place cooled popped popcorn in airtight freezer bags; unpopped corn can also be kept in the freezer. (Freezing helps eliminate "old maids" when you pop the corn.)

Potato Chips. Wrap the bag or box and store in the freezer for fresh, crisp chips.

Potatoes. Make patties from leftover mashed potatoes, coat with flour, flash-freeze, then store in plastic bags. Fry in oil for potato pancakes.

MAKE-AHEADS TO FREEZE

◆ Set aside a special evening or part of the weekend for a family "cook-in." Let everyone join in cooking up double and triple batches of favorite meals to freeze.

◆ Remember to slightly undercook meats, pasta and vegetables before freezing to prevent overcooking when reheating. Add crumbs and cheese toppings to frozen dishes just before reheating. (They tend to get soggy if frozen all together.)

◆ If you cater to someone on a special diet, prepare those dishes in quantity. Just freeze separately as individual servings.

◆ Keep a running inventory of your freezer's contents for fast and efficient meal planning and restocking.

◆ Use your freezer to keep shopping trips to a minimum. Bread and other

baked goods can be stored in the freezer up to 3 months. Day-old bread and cake, frequently a bargain, can actually be freshened by 24 hours in the freezer.

◆ Keep a supply of crêpes in the freezer, stacked between waxed-paper separators and tightly wrapped. Just thaw, fill with saucy meats, seafood, vegetables or fruits, heat and serve. Easy, yet elegant!

◆ Brown-bag lunches can be made ahead and frozen to save precious time on hectic mornings. Some fillings that freeze well are meat loaf, sliced meats, cheese and peanut butter. But avoid freezing sandwiches with lettuce, mayonnaise, jellies, fresh vegetables or hard-cooked egg whites. Either slip these latter foods into the sandwich once it has thawed, or pack them separately from the frozen sandwich and let the brown bagger combine them at lunchtime.

◆ Prepare ahead for parties, holiday meals and general entertaining by using the freezer. Fancy desserts, decorative canapés, garnishes, dips for tidbits or a novelty ice ring for a party punch can be made days ahead of the event when more time is available.

◆ It's quite economical to freeze leftover odds and ends: Unused whipped cream can be frozen as rosettes for future garnishes; sliced meats and gravy become a future supper; cubes of cooked chicken turn into a cold salad for lunch or the basis of a casserole dinner.

MAKING THE MOST OF YOUR MICROWAVE

T he next time you have "no time to cook," use your microwave oven to turn out creative, delicious and quick-and-easy meals in a matter of minutes! Just follow our cooking hints, techniques and recipes and you too will be serving spectacular dishes such as Lemon-Orange Coconut Cake, Sliced Beef With Vegetables and Hot German Potato Salad. For tips on using your microwave, and recipes, see page 28.

◆

DAVID VIENS

continued from page 27

A microwave oven offers both convenience and speed and is the most versatile means of cooking yet developed. You can use it for roasting, simmering and baking, as well as for defrosting and re-heating. Good results depend mainly on three factors: the utensils you use, proper timing and your understanding of the various microwave-cooking techniques. Here is what you need to know about all three.

UTENSILS

Both the design and shape of the utensil and the material it is made of can affect the cooking results in a microwave oven.

Shape: The ring or doughnut shape utensil is the most efficient since it will allow the microwave energy to enter the food from several angles. You can devise a ring-shape utensil by placing an empty custard cup, upright, in the center of a round utensil. Leave the empty cup in place throughout the cooking process.

Round and oval shapes are also acceptable for microwave cooking and the sides should be as vertical as possible to keep the depth of the food uniform. Avoid using square- or rectangular-shaped dishes since the corners overcook before the center is done.

The depth of the utensil is important too—generally it is better to have the food spread out in a larger, shallower pan than concentrated in a smaller, deeper one. There is one exception—foods that contain a great deal of liquid (sauces, puddings, etc.) and cakes, cupcakes and quick breads require larger deeper utensils. As a rule of thumb, use a container large enough to hold double the amount actually being cooked.

A trivet or roasting rack should be used with meats and for steaming fresh vegetables. Cakes and other batters will generally cook more evenly when the utensil is elevated on a trivet or rack set in the oven itself.

Material: Metal utensils are generally not recommended for use in microwave ovens though they can be used in certain models. Instead, use ceramic, heat-tempered oven glass and glass-ceramic and plastics marked "for microwave cooking" or "microwave-safe". Paper can be used for defrosting foods, heating snacks, cooking bacon or as a cover for other utensils. Wood should only be used for short-term heating (warming a basket of rolls for example).

TIMING

Several factors affect microwave cooking time. Dense, compact foods, such as potatoes, carrots and roasts take longer to cook than light, porous foods such as cakes or breads. Small pieces cook faster than larger pieces of food. Irregular-shaped items (chicken pieces for example) will cook unevenly, so place the thicker parts toward the outside of the dish for more even cooking. Small amounts of food usually take less time than large amounts. Food that is cold will take longer to microwave than those at room temperature. Foods naturally high in moisture (vegetables, fruits, fish) cook faster than foods low in moisture (dried peas, beans or rice). Fat and sugar attract microwaves and food high in these ingredients cook more quickly than other foods.

IMPORTANT TECHNIQUES

Arrangement: The placement of food within the utensil or the oven is critical. Arrange foods of more or less equal size in a circle, leaving the center empty.

Stirring: Stir foods during the cooking time to combine the heated and unheated portions and to shorten the overall cooking time.

Rearranging: Foods that cannot be stirred (cupcakes, roasts, whole vegetables) need to be rearranged or turned over during the cooking process.

Rotating: Foods such as cakes and pies should be given a half- or quarter-turn during microwaving to permit even cooking.

Shielding: Use small pieces or strips of aluminum foil to cover pieces or parts of foods that tend to get done first.

Piercing: Foods that have thick skins or membranes (potatoes, acorn squash, egg yolks, chicken livers, frankfurters, etc.) must be pierced before microwaving to allow steam to escape and prevent bursting.

Covering: The reason for covering some foods while they cook is to retain the steam for tenderizing, to keep the food moist, to shorten cooking time or to help prevent spattering. When you want to keep foods really moist, use plastic wrap as a covering.

Standing time: Many foods need to stand once they're out of the oven, so that the heat within them can complete the cooking process and the temperature can be equalized. Large dense foods such as meats may need 10 to 15 minutes standing time after you remove them from the oven. Quick-cooking foods, such as vegetables, need only 2 or 3 minutes.

All of the following recipes were tested in a 650-watt microwave oven. For 400- to 500-watt ovens, add 30 seconds to each minute of cooking time; for 500- to 600-watt ovens, add 15 seconds to each minute of cooking time.

SLICED BEEF WITH VEGETABLES
(pictured)

1 lb top-round beef steak, cut 1 inch thick
1 can (16 oz) tomatoes
1 cup thinly sliced carrot
½ cup chopped onion
½ teaspoon dried basil leaves
¼ teaspoon dried oregano leaves
2 tablespoons all-purpose flour
1 teaspoon salt
⅛ teaspoon ground cumin
⅛ teaspoon pepper
1 tablespoon salad oil
1 cup thinly sliced zucchini

8 oz wide egg noodles, cooked according to package directions

1. Slice steak in strips ⅛-inch thick or less and 2 to 2½ inches in length. (See Note.)
2. Drain juice from tomatoes into 1½-quart microwave-safe utensil; break up and reserve tomatoes. Add carrot, onion, basil and oregano to tomato juice; cover with plastic wrap, and microwave at HIGH (100 percent power), 5 minutes, stirring after 2 minutes.
3. Combine flour, salt, cumin and pepper; dredge steak strips. Measure oil into microwave-safe 12-by-7½-by-2-inch utensil or 2½-quart casserole; spread steak strips in layer over bottom of casserole. Cover with waxed paper, and microwave at MEDIUM (50 percent power), 6 minutes, stirring after 4 minutes.
4. Stir in carrot mixture, reserved tomatoes and zucchini. Re-cover with plastic wrap, and microwave at MEDIUM (50 percent power), 20 minutes, or until tender, stirring every 3 minutes. Remove from oven; let stand, covered, 3 minutes. Serve over cooked noodles. *Makes 4 servings.*
Note: Partially freeze steak to facilitate cutting into thin slices.

HOT GERMAN POTATO SALAD
(pictured)

3 baking potatoes (1½ lb)
2 slices bacon, diced
½ cup chopped onion
½ cup chopped celery

DRESSING
⅓ cup cider vinegar
¼ cup water
1 teaspoon sugar
¼ teaspoon ground celery seed

¼ teaspoon caraway seed
¼ teaspoon dried parsley or fresh parsley, finely chopped
¾ teaspoon salt
Dash hot red-pepper sauce

2 to 3 knockwurst, thinly sliced and skin removed

1. Wash and dry potatoes; prick with fork. Arrange potatoes in ring on paper towel. Microwave at HIGH (100% power), 15 minutes, or until almost tender, turning once. Cool potatoes; peel, and slice ¼ inch thick; set aside.

2. In microwave-safe utensil, combine bacon, onion and celery. Cover with waxed paper; microwave at HIGH (100% power), 5 minutes. Stir.

3. In 2-cup glass measure, make Dressing: Mix vinegar, water, sugar, celery seed, caraway seed, parsley, salt and red-pepper sauce. Microwave at HIGH (100% power), 2 minutes.

4. In microwave-safe 2½-quart casserole, arrange half of potatoes, onion and bacon. Pour in half of dressing. Repeat. Arrange knockwurst over potatoes in a circle around edge of casserole. Cover with plastic wrap; microwave at HIGH (100% power), 3 minutes; turn dish. Uncover; microwave at HIGH (100% power), 2 minutes longer, or until heated through. Remove from oven; let stand, covered, 3 to 5 minutes before serving. *Makes 4 servings.*

LEMON-ORANGE COCONUT CAKE
(pictured)

Solid shortening
2 tablespoons graham-cracker crumbs
¼ cup (½ stick) butter or margarine
¾ cup orange marmalade
½ cup flaked coconut
1 pkg (18¾ oz) pudding-style lemon-cake mix
1 cup water
⅓ cup oil
3 eggs

1. Grease microwave-safe 12-cup tube utensil with solid shortening; coat with graham-cracker crumbs.

2. In microwave-safe 2-cup glass measure, place butter; microwave at HIGH (100% power), 45 seconds, or until melted. Add marmalade and coconut; mix well. Spread evenly on bottom of prepared utensil.

3. In large bowl, blend cake mix, water, oil and eggs until moistened. With portable electric mixer, beat 2 minutes at highest speed. Pour batter over marmalade mixture.

4. Microwave at MEDIUM LOW (30% power), 11 minutes, rotating utensil one

quarter-turn every 3 minutes. Microwave at HIGH (100% power), 5½ minutes longer.

5. Cool upright in utensil on flat surface, 10 minutes; turn out onto serving dish. Spoon any remaining marmalade in utensil over cake. Cool completely. *Makes 16 servings.*

APRICOT BRAN MUFFINS

12 paper liners for muffin-pan cups
3 cups whole-bran cereal
1 cup all-purpose flour
2 teaspoons baking powder
½ teaspoon baking soda
¼ teaspoon salt
4 medium-size fresh apricots, halved, pitted and diced (1 cup)
¼ cup (½ stick) butter or margarine, softened
¼ cup lightly packed light-brown sugar, packed to measure
1 large egg
1 cup low-fat buttermilk

1. Line 6 microwave-safe muffin-pan cups with paper liners; set aside.

2. In a large bowl, combine cereal, flour, baking powder, baking soda and salt; mix well. Add apricots; toss lightly, making sure apricot pieces are evenly coated with flour mixture.

3. In small bowl, using wooden spoon, blend butter or margarine with brown sugar until well mixed. Beat in egg and buttermilk.

4. Make a well in center of flour mixture; with fork, stir in butter mixture only until dry ingredients are moistened. Do not beat. Batter will be lumpy.

5. Divide half of the batter evenly among 6 paper-lined muffin-pan cups; microwave at HIGH, 3 to 4 minutes, turning pan one-quarter turn after each minute. Check for doneness at minimum time—wooden pick inserted in center of muffin will come out clean. (Moist spots will disappear upon standing; if muffins are doughy underneath moist spots, additional baking is required.) Immediately remove muffins from cups; let stand on wire rack 2 minutes before serving. Repeat with remaining batter. *Makes 12 muffins.*

TOFU CHILI

2 tablespoons safflower or vegetable oil
1 large onion, chopped
1 medium green pepper, seeded and chopped
1 garlic clove, minced
1½ tablespoons chili powder
1 teaspoon ground cumin seed

½ teaspoon dried oregano leaves
½ teaspoon salt (optional)
¼ teaspoon ground red pepper
1 can (1 lb, 12 oz) whole tomatoes, undrained (use no-salt-added type, if desired)
2 cans (1 lb, 3 oz) red kidney beans, drained
½ lb firm-style tofu, cut into ½-inch cubes
1 cup (4 oz) shredded low-sodium, reduced-calorie Cheddar cheese

1. In a 3-quart microwave-safe casserole, place oil, onion and green pepper. Microwave at HIGH, 6 minutes, stirring after 3 minutes. Stir in garlic, chili powder, cumin seed, oregano leaves, salt and red pepper; microwave at HIGH for a few seconds.

2. Stir in tomatoes. Cover with plastic wrap; fold back one section to vent. Microwave at HIGH, 5 minutes, stirring after 2½ minutes.

3. Stir in beans and tofu; cover again and microwave at HIGH, 5 minutes longer. Remove casserole from microwave; stir in half the cheese; let stand, covered, 10 minutes, before serving with remaining cheese. *Makes 7 (1-cup) servings.*

PORK CHOPS A LA SUISSE

STUFFING
1 cup soft bread crumbs
2 tart apples, peeled and diced
2 tablespoons butter or margarine, melted
½ teaspoon liquid gravy seasoning
⅛ teaspoon crushed caraway seed
⅛ teaspoon salt
Dash pepper

6 pork chops (2 lb), ¾ inch thick
1 tablespoon water
¼ teaspoon liquid gravy seasoning

1. Make Stuffing: Combine all stuffing ingredients in microwave-safe medium-size utensil; mix well. Microwave at HIGH (100% power), 2 minutes, stirring several times.

2. Cut deep slit in side of each chop. Fill with stuffing. Secure with wooden picks.

3. Place prepared chops in single layer in microwave-safe 12-by-7½-by-2-inch utensil, with thickest meaty areas toward edge and end piece toward center of utensil. Combine water and ¼ teaspoon gravy seasoning; brush chops with half of mixture. Cover with waxed paper.

4. Microwave at MEDIUM (50% power), 20 minutes. Turn chops over. Brush with remaining seasoning mixture. Re-cover with waxed paper; microwave at MEDIUM (50% power), 15 minutes, or until tender. Remove from oven; let stand, covered, 5 minutes before serving. *Makes 6 servings.*

continued on page 30

continued from page 29

CRANBERRY-AND-PEAR CRISP

1 pkg (12 oz) cranberries
2 unpeeled pears (1 lb), cored and sliced
2 tablespoons plus ½ cup all-purpose flour
1 cup granulated sugar
1 teaspoon ground cinnamon
½ cup brown sugar, packed
⅓ cup (⅔ stick) butter or margarine
¾ cup regular oats
¾ cup chopped pecans or walnuts
Vanilla ice cream (optional)

1. In microwave-safe 2 quart utensil, thoroughly mix cranberries, pears, 2 tablespoons flour, the granulated sugar and cinnamon.

2. In bowl, combine ½ cup flour and brown sugar; cut in butter until mixture resembles coarse crumbs. Add oats and nuts; sprinkle evenly over fruit mixture.

3. Microwave at HIGH (100% power), 12 minutes, rotating utensil one quarter-turn every 3 minutes. Remove from oven; let stand 5 minutes. Serve topped with ice cream, if desired. *Makes 6 servings.*

CARROT AND POTATO SOUP

2 large baking potatoes (1 lb), peeled
3 carrots (½ lb), pared
1 small onion
1 can (13¾ oz) chicken broth
1 cup milk or light cream
½ teaspoon dried dillweed or
    1½ teaspoons snipped fresh dill
¼ teaspoon salt

1. Cut potatoes, carrots and onion into small pieces or chop in food processor, using chopping blade.

2. Place chopped vegetables in microwave-safe 3-quart utensil; pour ½ of chicken broth over vegetables.

3. Cover with utensil lid or plastic wrap; microwave at HIGH (100% power), 10 minutes.

4. Transfer vegetables and liquid to food processor or blender; process to purée.

5. Return puréed vegetables to utensil; add remaining chicken broth, milk, dill and salt. Cover; microwave at MEDIUM (50% power) for 10 minutes. *Makes 4 to 6 servings.*

POTATOES ROMANOFF

2 patties or 2 cups frozen shredded hash
    brown potatoes
1 cup cottage cheese
1 cup sour cream
2 tablespoons chopped green onion
2 tablespoons chopped parsley
1 garlic clove, minced
½ teaspoon salt
1 tablespoon butter or margarine

1. Place frozen hash brown potatoes in microwave-safe 1-quart casserole. Cover with plastic wrap; microwave at HIGH (100% power), 3 minutes. Stir; microwave at HIGH (100% power), 3 minutes longer.

2. Add cottage cheese, sour cream, green onion, parsley, garlic and salt. Mix well; dot with butter. Cover with plastic wrap; microwave at HIGH (100% power), 4 minutes. Stir.

3. Cover with paper towel; microwave at HIGH (100% power), 2 minutes. Remove from oven; let stand 5 minutes, covered with paper towel, before serving. *Makes 4 servings.*

TOMATOES PRIMAVERA

4 large fresh tomatoes
Salt
Pepper
1 pkg (10 oz) frozen green peas
½ small onion, chopped

¼ cup heavy cream
¼ teaspoon dried marjoram leaves
4 tablespoons packaged herb-flavored
    croutons

1. Cut a ¼-inch slice from stem end of each tomato. Remove pulp and seeds. Season inside of shells lightly with salt and pepper. Turn tomatoes upside down on a paper towel.

2. In microwave-safe 1½-quart utensil, combine peas and onion. Cover lightly with plastic wrap; microwave at HIGH (100 percent power), 5 to 6 minutes, or until just tender; drain.

3. In blender or food processor, place cooked peas and onion, cream, marjoram, ¼ teaspoon salt and dash of pepper. Process until smooth.

4. Spoon 1 tablespoon croutons into each tomato; fill with pea purée.

5. Arrange tomatoes in a circle in a microwave-safe utensil. Microwave at MEDIUM HIGH (70 percent power), 4 to 5 minutes, or just until tomatoes are heated. Garnish with additional croutons, if desired. *Makes 4 servings.*

SPEEDY SPAGHETTI MEAT SAUCE

1 lb ground beef
½ cup chopped onion
¼ teaspoon salt
Dash pepper
1 can (14 oz) Italian tomatoes
¼ cup water
2 tablespoons Parmesan cheese
1 garlic clove, minced
½ teaspoon dried marjoram leaves
½ teaspoon crushed dried rosemary

12 oz pasta, cooked according to package
    directions

1. Combine ground beef with onion; arrange in ring in all-plastic colander or sieve set over microwave-safe 2½-quart utensil. Cover with waxed paper; microwave at HIGH (100% power), 5 minutes, stirring and breaking up beef after 2½ minutes and again after removing from oven.

2. Place colander containing beef on absorbent paper; sprinkle with salt and pepper. Re-cover with waxed paper, and let stand 2 to 3 minutes.

3. Discard fat from 2½-quart utensil, and in it combine tomatoes, water, cheese, garlic, marjoram and rosemary. Cover with waxed paper; microwave at HIGH (100% power), 2 minutes.

4. Stir in beef. Re-cover with waxed paper; microwave at HIGH (100% power), 8 to 10 minutes. Let stand 3 minutes. Serve over cooked pasta. *Makes 6 servings.*

CORN-STUFFED ZUCCHINI
(pictured)

2 medium zucchini (1½ lb), halved
    lengthwise
Salt
3 tablespoons butter or margarine
⅓ cup chopped onion
⅓ cup chopped green pepper
1 pkg (10 oz) frozen corn, thawed
1 teaspoon dried tarragon leaves
¼ teaspoon pepper

1. With spoon, scoop pulp from zucchini halves, leaving ¼-inch shell intact; sprinkle with ⅛ teaspoon salt. Chop zucchini pulp.

2. Place butter in 1-quart microwave-safe utensil; microwave at HIGH (100 percent power), 1 minute, or until melted.

3. Stir in zucchini pulp, onion and green pepper; microwave at HIGH (100 percent power), 3 minutes.

4. Combine corn, tarragon, ⅛ teaspoon salt and the pepper with onion mixture; microwave at HIGH (100 percent power), 2 minutes. Spoon vegetable mixture into zucchini halves, mounding.

5. Place filled zucchini shells in a shallow microwave-safe utensil. Cover with waxed paper; microwave at HIGH (100 percent power), 6 to 8 minutes, or until zucchini is just tender. Remove from oven; let stand, covered, 3 to 5 minutes before serving. *Makes 6 servings.*

JIFFY CRABMEAT

1 tablespoon butter or margarine
½ cup sliced fresh mushrooms
1 small green pepper, cut into ¼-inch
    strips
2 tablespoons toasted slivered almonds
½ teaspoon lemon rind
1 teaspoon lemon juice
1 can (10½ oz) condensed cream of celery
    soup, undiluted
2 tablespoons chopped pimiento
1 tablespoon chopped parsley

Dash hot red-pepper sauce
Dash pepper
1 can (6½ oz) crabmeat, drained, or 1 pkg
    (6 oz) frozen crabmeat, thawed and
    well drained
2 cups hot cooked rice

1. Place butter, mushrooms and green pepper in microwave-safe 2-quart casserole. Cover with plastic wrap, and microwave at HIGH (100% power), 2 minutes.

2. Add all remaining ingredients except rice. Stir to mix.

3. Cover with waxed paper, and microwave at HIGH (100% power), 6 minutes, stirring after 3 minutes. Let stand, covered with waxed paper, 3 minutes. Serve crabmeat mixture over rice. *Makes 4 servings.*

CHICKEN BREASTS VERONIQUE
(pictured)

¼ teaspoon shredded orange peel
½ cup orange juice
1 tablespoon sliced green onion
½ teaspoon instant-chicken-bouillon
    granules
2 medium chicken breasts (1½ to 2 lb),
    skinned and split
Salt
Pepper
Paprika
1 tablespoon cornstarch
1 tablespoon cold water
½ cup seedless green grapes, halved
Parsley (optional)
Orange slices (optional)
Green-grape clusters (optional)

1. In a microwave-safe, 12-by-7½-by-2-inch utensil, combine orange peel, orange juice, green onion and bouillon granules. Add chicken; sprinkle lightly with salt, pepper and paprika. Cover with waxed paper; microwave at HIGH (100 percent power), 10 minutes, rearranging chicken once. Remove chicken to warm platter; cover to keep warm.

2. Measure pan juices. Add water, if necessary, to measure ¾ cup liquid. Blend cornstarch with cold water; stir into pan juices. Microwave at HIGH (100 percent power), 2 minutes, or until thickened and bubbly, stirring after 1 minute. Add grapes; microwave at HIGH (100 percent power), 30 seconds. Spoon some sauce over chicken; pass remainder. Garnish with parsley, orange slices and grape clusters. *Makes 4 servings.*

FISH FILLETS FLORENTINE
(pictured)

1 lb fresh or frozen fish fillets
2 pkg (10-oz size) frozen chopped spinach
½ cup diced onion
1 teaspoon dried dillweed or 1 tablespoon
    snipped fresh dill
Salt
Pepper
4 teaspoons lemon juice
Paprika
¾ cup grated sharp Cheddar cheese

1. To thaw frozen fish, place package on MEDIUM LOW (30 percent power), 6 minutes; halfway through, turn package over. Gently separate fillets under cold running water; pat dry with paper towels.

2. Pierce spinach package on top several times with fork; microwave at HIGH (100 percent power), 5 minutes, to defrost. Press spinach package to remove moisture.

3. Place spinach in a bowl; add onion, dillweed, 1 teaspoon salt and ¼ teaspoon pepper. Spread mixture over microwave-safe, 12-by-7½-by-2-inch utensil. Top with fish fillets; place thicker edges toward outside of dish. Sprinkle fillets with lemon juice, and season lightly with salt, pepper and paprika.

4. Cover with waxed paper; microwave at HIGH (100 percent power), 6 to 8 minutes. After 4 minutes, sprinkle grated cheese over fish, and rotate dish. Remove from oven; let stand 5 minutes before serving. *Makes 4 servings.* ♦

THE WORK-SAVING
·WOK·

Follow the ancient Chinese art of stir-fry cooking and learn a quick-and-easy way to prepare a good meal in a hurry: You just have to be organized and follow our directions! Before you begin cooking, be sure to gather all the utensils and ingredients you'll need to complete the dish from start to finish. Select a very large, heavy skillet, a stainless-steel or aluminum wok or an electric wok. You'll also need two large wooden spoons for tossing the food in the pan. Up to several hours ahead you can slice, dice and mince all the ingredients as directed. Then, just a few minutes before serving, you can start stir-frying. The vegetable and/or meat ingredients are simply tossed vigorously, at a very high temperature, in a small amount of oil until they are tender crisp. Then a small amount of liquid is sometimes added (chicken broth, soy sauce, water or beef bouillon) and the dish is cooked to perfection. The result is a delicious stir-fried dish that not only looks great but tastes great too! Pictured here is one of our favorites: Chicken with Toasted Almonds.

CHICKEN WITH TOASTED ALMONDS

(pictured)

3 (12-oz size) boneless, skinless chicken breasts
5 tablespoons salad oil
2 tablespoons soy sauce
2 teaspoons salt
1½ teaspoons sugar
Dash pepper
1 can (5 oz) water chestnuts, drained and chopped
½ lb fresh snow pea pods, strings removed, or 1 pkg (6 oz) frozen pea pods
1 cup thinly sliced celery
2 cups (8 oz) sliced fresh mushrooms
2 tablespoons cornstarch
⅓ cup water
1 can (14½ oz) clear chicken broth
½ cup toasted slivered almonds

1. Have butcher bone and skin chicken breasts. To make them easier to slice, store in freezing compartment until partially frozen. Then slice into long, thin slivers. Let thaw completely at room temperature.

2. Heat oil in a wok or large skillet. Add chicken slivers, soy sauce, salt, sugar and pepper. Cook, stirring, a few minutes, or just until chicken is no longer pink. With a slotted spoon, remove chicken to a colander set over a bowl.

3. Add chestnuts and vegetables to wok; stir and cook until vegetables are tender-crisp. Return chicken to wok.

4. In small bowl, make a smooth paste of cornstarch, water and ⅓ cup chicken broth. Slowly stir into chicken mixture, with remaining chicken broth. Cook, stirring, until slightly thickened and translucent. Sprinkle top with almonds. *Makes 6 servings.*

SCALLOPS WITH SNOW PEAS

1 lb sea scallops, cut in half
2 leeks
½ lb snow peas
1 tablespoon cornstarch
2 teaspoons soy sauce
¼ teaspoon salt (optional)
⅓ cup water
2 tablespoons salad or peanut oil
1 teaspoon grated fresh ginger
Cooked white rice (optional)

1. Wash scallops; drain well. Prepare leeks: Cut off root ends and green stems. Wash thoroughly. Cut on diagonal into slices ¼ inch thick. Trim ends of snow peas, and remove strings.

2. In small cup, mix cornstarch, soy sauce, salt (if desired) and water; stir until smooth.

3. Heat salad oil in large heavy skillet or wok over high heat. Add scallops; stir-fry 1 minute. Add leeks, snow peas and ginger; stir-fry 1 minute longer.

4. Pour cornstarch mixture over scallops and vegetables. Stir until sauce is thickened. Serve with rice and more soy sauce, if desired. *Makes 4 servings.*

STIR-FRIED "HOT SALAD"

2 tablespoons salad oil
1 medium onion, thinly sliced
1 tablespoon shredded fresh ginger
3 garlic cloves, crushed
1 teaspoon salt
2 stalks celery, cut on diagonal into ½-inch pieces
½ large green pepper, cut into ¼-inch strips
½ large red pepper, cut into ¼-inch strips
2 cups bean sprouts
1½ teaspoons sugar
2 tablespoons soy sauce
½ medium cucumber, peeled and cut into strips
6 lettuce leaves, coarsely chopped
1 tablespoon lemon juice
1 tablespoon sesame oil
Cooked white rice (optional)

1. In wok or large heavy skillet, heat oil over medium heat. Add onion, ginger, garlic and salt; stir-fry ½ minute.

2. Add celery, green and red peppers and bean sprouts. Stir-fry over high heat 2 minutes.

3. Add sugar, soy sauce, cucumber and lettuce. Stir-fry 1½ minutes. Sprinkle with lemon juice and sesame oil; mix well. Turn out into warm serving dish. Serve with rice, if desired. *Makes 6 servings.*

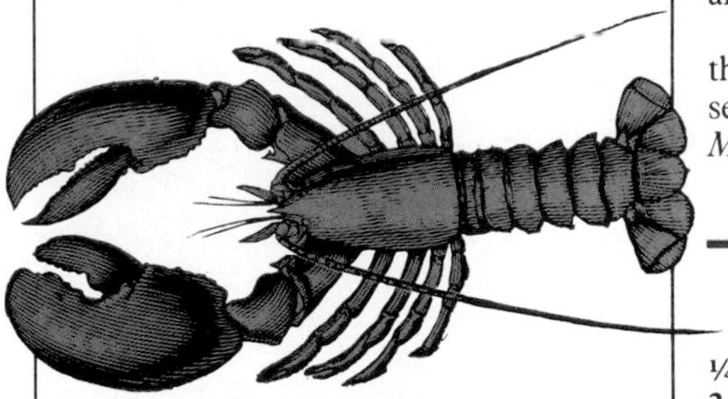

LOBSTER CANTONESE

6 (6- to 8-oz size) frozen rock-lobster tails, thawed
¼ cup salad oil
1 garlic clove, very finely chopped
½ lb ground pork shoulder
2 tablespoons cornstarch
⅓ cup water
¼ cup soy sauce
1 teaspoon sugar
1 teaspoon salt
½ teaspoon pepper

2¼ cups boiling water
2 eggs
½ cup thinly sliced green onions

1. With kitchen shears, cut shell away from lobster meat. Remove meat in one piece, and cut it crosswise in 2-inch sections.

2. Heat oil in wok or large skillet with cover. Add garlic and pork; sauté, stirring, until pork is no longer pink—takes about 10 minutes.

3. Meanwhile, in small bowl, make a smooth mixture of cornstarch and ⅓ cup water.

4. Stir into pork the soy sauce, sugar, salt, pepper, boiling water and cornstarch mixture: bring to a boil. Reduce heat; simmer, stirring, until thickened and translucent—about 10 minutes.

5. Add lobster pieces; cook, covered, over low heat, until lobster is tender—takes about 8 to 10 minutes (do not overcook).

6. In small bowl, beat eggs slightly with fork. Stir, all at once, into lobster mixture (eggs will form shreds). Add green onion. Serve at once. *Makes 6 servings.*

BEAN SPROUTS WITH GREEN ONIONS

¼ cup (½ stick) butter or margarine
8 green onions, with tops, finely chopped
2 cans (1-lb size) bean sprouts, drained
1 tablespoon soy sauce
1 tablespoon finely chopped parsley

1. In hot butter, in wok or large skillet, sauté chopped green onion over low heat, stirring occasionally, until golden and tender—about 3 minutes.

2. Stir in bean sprouts. When heated thoroughly, add soy sauce. Just before serving, sprinkle with chopped parsley. *Makes 6 to 8 servings.*

SNOW PEAS

¼ cup salad oil
3 tablespoons finely chopped onion
2 pkg (8-oz size) frozen, or 1 lb fresh snow pea pods
1 teaspoon salt
⅛ teaspoon pepper

1. Heat oil in wok or large skillet. Add onion and sauté until golden.

2. If using fresh pea pods, snip ends and remove strings. Add pea pods; cook, over high heat, stirring frequently, until tender-crisp—about 5 minutes for frozen, 8 minutes for fresh.

3. Stir in salt and pepper. Serve at once. *Makes 6 to 8 servings.* ◆

TWO

FAST FIXINGS

How often do hours of preparation in the kitchen culminate in meals that are consumed—and enjoyed—in a mere matter of minutes? To help narrow this time gap, we can do one of two things: insist that everyone eat much more slowly, or, better yet, develop a repertoire of recipes that offer simple, short preparation with results worth lingering over. The following pages are packed with quick-to-fix recipes for breakfast, lunch, dinner and beyond. Many make imaginative use of convenience-food products; others employ shortcut-cooking techniques; and still others are streamlined versions of traditional, more time-consuming favorites. But they all measure up to the high standards of today's cooks who insist on recipes that are not only quick and convenient to fit into their busy schedules but also provide the same wholesome goodness and delicious taste of yesterday's scratch cooking.

Good Breakfasts on the Go

I f breakfast at your house is hurried and unappetizing, it's time to wake up to some new, exciting and healthful dishes that put fun into breakfast on the run. We've selected 14 delightfully easy recipes—you can enjoy a different one each day for two whole weeks. And there is something for every taste and every time schedule, from speedy blender breakfast drinks to sophisticated egg dishes to deluxe waffles to creative coffeecakes. When breakfast can be as exciting and interesting as all this, the whole family will get up and go—right to the breakfast table, that is. Recipes begin on page 38.

Say good morning to Oatmeal-Banana Waffles, a warm and wonderful breakfast that's chock-full of great foods and great taste. These waffles combine healthful toasted oats with crunchy pecans, mashed banana, heavy cream and a touch of brown sugar for waffles extraordinaire. From start to finish, you can have a platter of these piping hot waffles ready in about 15 minutes.

There's nothing boring about this breakfast foursome. Clockwise starting at top: Fruit-Topped Waffles are topped with a sauce of sautéed apples, raisins and cinnamon (great with pancakes too). Bananas, yogurt, strawberries and pancake syrup go for a whirl in Eye-Opener Nog. Dilly Smoked-Salmon Frittata combines eggs, Fontina cheese, sour cream, fresh dill and salmon strips in an easy-bake dish. Layers of Brie, ham and onion cradle eggs and cream in Brie Shirred Eggs.

Some creative breakfast sweets: Cranberry Crumble Bread partners cranberry quick-bread mix with canned pumpkin for a double-taste treat. In Caramel Bubble Loaf, balls of cinnamon-and-sugar-coated dough rise to light and luscious heights beneath a caramelized crown studded with chopped pecans.

continued from page 36

OATMEAL-BANANA WAFFLES
(pictured)

¾ cup rolled oats
½ cup chopped pecans
1 cup unsifted all-purpose flour
2 teaspoons baking powder
½ teaspoon salt
1 very ripe banana, mashed
3 eggs, lightly beaten
¾ cup heavy cream
3 tablespoons light-brown sugar

1. Preheat oven to 350F. On baking sheet, toast oats and pecans 8 to 10 minutes. Place in bowl; add flour, baking powder and salt; mix well. In large bowl, combine banana, eggs, heavy cream and light-brown sugar; mix well. Stir in oat mixture just until moistened.

2. Preheat Belgian waffle iron. Using heaping ⅓ cup batter for each waffle, make waffles as waffle-iron manufacturer directs. Keep waffles warm until all batter is used. Serve warm with bananas, pecans and syrup. *Makes 8 waffles.*

FRUIT-TOPPED WAFFLES
(pictured)

1 pkg (10 oz) frozen whole-grain
    waffles (8)
2 tablespoons cornstarch
1½ cups cranberry-apple juice
1 tablespoon butter or margarine
2 small Granny Smith apples, cored and
    sliced
⅓ cup raisins
3 tablespoons sugar
¼ teaspoon ground cinnamon
¼ teaspoon vanilla extract
Cooked bacon

1. Heat waffles as package label directs. Meanwhile, in small cup, blend cornstarch with ¼ cup cranberry-apple juice; set aside.

2. In 10-inch skillet, melt butter. Add apple slices; sauté 3 minutes. Add raisins, sugar, cinnamon, remaining juice and the vanilla. Bring to boiling; stir in cornstarch mixture. Cook until thickened. Spoon over waffles; serve with bacon. *Makes 4 servings.*

EYE-OPENER NOG
(pictured)

1 large ripe banana, sliced
1½ cups milk
1 container (8 oz) vanilla-flavored
    yogurt
2 tablespoons light pancake syrup
1 cup frozen whole hulled strawberries

In blender container, blend banana, milk, yogurt and syrup until smooth. With blender running, add the frozen berries, one at a time; blend until smooth. Pour into 4 tall glasses, dividing evenly. *Makes 4 servings.*

DILLY SMOKED-SALMON FRITTATA
(pictured)

6 eggs
1 cup sour cream
¼ cup unsifted all-purpose flour
¼ lb smoked salmon, cut into
    ¼-inch-wide strips
1 cup (4 oz) shredded Fontina cheese
3 green onions, chopped
2 tablespoons snipped fresh dill
1 tablespoon butter or margarine
Additional sour cream
Dill sprig

1. Preheat oven to 375F. In medium bowl, whisk eggs, sour cream and flour until well blended. Stir in salmon, shredded cheese, green onion and dill.

2. In 10-inch skillet with ovenproof handle, over medium heat, melt butter. When butter sizzles, add egg mixture. Bake 20 minutes, or until set. Garnish with additional sour cream and dill sprig. *Makes 6 to 8 servings.*

BRIE SHIRRED EGGS
(pictured)

¼ lb Brie cheese, diced
¼ lb boiled ham, diced
2 green onions, minced
4 eggs
¼ cup heavy cream
Ground black pepper

1. Preheat oven to 400F. Grease four (6-ounce) custard cups with nonstick cooking spray; place cheese, ham and onion in cups, dividing evenly. Break 1 egg into each cup; drizzle 1 tablespoon heavy cream into each; sprinkle with pepper.

2. Place custard cups in large roasting pan; place pan on oven rack. Fill pan with enough hot water to come up 1 inch on side of custard cups. Bake 18 minutes, or until eggs are set to the desired degree of doneness. Serve eggs from cups. *Makes 4 servings.*

CRANBERRY CRUMBLE BREAD
(pictured)

TOPPING
½ cup unsifted all-purpose flour
¼ cup brown sugar, firmly packed
¼ cup butter, cut in pieces
2 tablespoons chopped walnuts

1 pkg (15.63 oz) cranberry quick-bread
    mix
1 cup canned pumpkin
½ cup water
2 tablespoons salad oil
1 egg

Preheat oven to 350F. Grease and flour bottom of 9-by-5-inch loaf pan. In bowl, with fork, stir topping ingredients until crumbly. In large bowl, combine remaining ingredients. Pour into prepared loaf pan; sprinkle with topping. Bake 45 minutes. Cool in pan 15 minutes; remove to rack. *Makes 12 servings.*

CARAMEL BUBBLE LOAF
(pictured)

1 cup light-brown sugar
½ cup butter or margarine
1 tablespoon light corn syrup
¾ cup chopped pecans
1 pkg (16 oz) hot-roll mix
¼ cup granulated sugar
1½ teaspoons ground cinnamon

1. Grease and flour Bundt pan. In saucepan, bring ½ cup brown sugar, 2 tablespoons butter and the corn syrup to boiling; stir to dissolve sugar. Pour into the prepared Bundt pan. Sprinkle with chopped pecans.

2. Prepare roll mix as package label directs. Shape into 32 equal dough balls.

3. Melt remaining butter. On waxed paper, combine all remaining sugars with the cinnamon. Dip dough balls in butter; roll in sugar. Stack dough balls over pecan mixture in pan; spoon any remaining butter on top. Cover pan with towel; let dough rise in warm (85F), draft-free place, 45 minutes or until double in bulk.

4. Preheat oven to 350F. Bake 35 minutes, or until golden-brown. Invert onto wire rack; serve warm. *Makes 12 servings.*

CHOCOLATE-CREAM CROISSANTS

1 cup heavy cream
1 cup confectioners' sugar
½ teaspoon vanilla extract
¼ teaspoon almond extract
2 squares (1-oz size) semisweet
    chocolate, melted and cooled
¼ cup toasted slivered almonds
6 large croissants, split
1 tablespoon butter, melted
About 2 tablespoons lemon juice
Chocolate curls (optional)

1. With electric mixer, on high, beat heavy cream with ¼ cup confectioners' sugar and the extracts to soft peaks; beat in chocolate. Fold in almonds. With pastry bag fitted with large star tip, pipe mixture over croissant bottoms. Replace croissant tops.

2. In bowl, blend remaining sugar with butter and enough lemon juice to make spoonable; drizzle over croissants. If desired, garnish with chocolate curls. *Makes 4 servings.*

QUICK BACON-AND-EGG SANDWICH

4 slices bacon
2 eggs
¹⁄₁₆ teaspoon seasoned pepper
4 slices processed American cheese
2 kaiser rolls
2 tablespoons softened butter or
    margarine
2 small tomatoes, sliced

1. In 10-inch skillet, over medium heat, cook bacon until almost crisp. Arrange two slices of bacon side by side on each half of skillet. Break one egg over each pair of bacon slices; sprinkle each egg with seasoned pepper. Cover skillet; cook eggs 1 to 2 minutes, or until set. Top each egg with 2 slices of cheese. Cover skillet; cook 1 more minute, or until cheese melts.

2. Cut rolls in half horizontally; spread each half with butter. Arrange tomato slices on bottom halves of rolls, dividing evenly. Place an egg on top of tomatoes; cover with top halves of rolls. *Makes 2 servings.*

BRIE-TOPPED BELGIAN WAFFLES

1 tablespoon sugar
2 teaspoons cornstarch
1 pkg (10 oz) frozen strawberries in
    syrup, thawed

2 tablespoons orange juice
4 frozen prepared Belgian waffles
4 oz Brie cheese
Thin slices of orange (optional)
Parsley sprigs (optional)

1. In saucepan, combine sugar and cornstarch. Stir in frozen strawberries; add orange juice; bring to boiling. Cook, stirring until thickened. Keep warm.

2. Prepare waffles as package label directs; keep warm. Cut the Brie into 4 wedges, dividing evenly. Place 1 wedge on top of each waffle; spoon strawberry sauce on top. If desired, garnish each waffle with orange slices and a parsley sprig. *Makes 4 servings.*

COUNTRY-STYLE FRENCH TOAST

4 slices frozen prepared French toast
¼ cup apricot preserves
1 teaspoon lemon juice
½ cup ricotta cheese
1 large banana, cut crosswise into
    ¼-inch-thick slices
½ teaspoon ground cinnamon

1. Prepare French toast as package label directs; keep warm. In small saucepan, heat apricot preserves with lemon juice, stirring frequently, until warm and smooth.

2. Spread ricotta over French toast; arrange banana slices on top. Spoon warm apricot sauce over ricotta; sprinkle with cinnamon. *Makes 2 servings.*

CALIFORNIA-STYLE HUEVOS RANCHEROS

2 tablespoons butter or margarine
4 eggs
¼ cup prepared salsa
¼ cup shredded extra sharp Cheddar
    cheese
4 slices ripe avocado
2 tablespoons sour cream
Parsley sprigs (optional)

1. In large skillet, over medium heat, melt butter. Break eggs into skillet; cook 3 minutes, or until set.

2. On each of 2 broiler-proof plates, spread salsa, dividing evenly. Top each with 2 eggs. Sprinkle eggs with cheese, dividing evenly. Broil, 4 inches from heat, 1 minute, or until cheese melts.

3. Place avocado and sour cream on plates next to eggs, dividing evenly. Garnish each plate with parsley sprig, if desired. *Makes 2 servings.* ◆

Blender Drinks For Busy Days

APRICOT NOG

1 can (12 oz) chilled apricot nectar
¾ cup chilled buttermilk
2 eggs
¼ teaspoon vanilla extract
2 fresh mint sprigs

In blender, combine the apricot nectar, buttermilk, eggs and vanilla. With blender at high speed, blend 1 minute. Pour into two (16-oz) glasses. Garnish each drink with a mint sprig. Serve immediately. *Makes 2 servings.*

TROPICAL SMOOTHIE

1 cup low-fat strawberry yogurt
1 can (8 oz) crushed pineapple,
    drained
1 small orange, peeled, seeded and
    chopped
1 cup ice cubes
Ground cinnamon
2 strawberries with hulls

In blender, combine yogurt, pineapple, orange and ice cubes. With blender at high speed, blend 1 minute. Pour into two (16-oz) glasses. Sprinkle each drink with cinnamon; garnish each drink with a strawberry. Serve immediately. *Makes 2 servings.*

Sunday Brunch

Here are two no-fuss brunches you'll love a bunch. The Low-Cal Southwestern Brunch is a fiesta of delectable flavors and colors: a western-omelet soufflé roll served with salsa, nonalcoholic daiquiris and fruit-filled cantaloupes. The only thing missing is the calories! The Easy Sunday Brunch is designed around the concept that less time in the kitchen means more time spent enjoying the company of friends. This inviting brunch requires very little preparation; it can be whipped up in a matter of minutes.

LOW-CAL
SOUTHWESTERN BRUNCH

SPARKLING
FRUIT DAIQUIRIS*
SOUTHWEST SOUFFLE ROLL*
WARM BUTTERED
TORTILLAS
SPICED FRESH-FRUIT BOWLS*

Recipes given for starred dishes.

SOUTHWEST SOUFFLE ROLL

(pictured)

4 tablespoons butter or margarine
2 tablespoons all-purpose flour
¾ teaspoon salt
1 cup milk
12 eggs, separated
2 medium green peppers, diced
1 medium onion, diced
½ lb potatoes, diced
¼ teaspoon freshly ground black pepper
2 oz sliced turkey ham, diced
½ cup (2 oz) shredded Monterey Jack
** cheese**
1 jar (12 oz) salsa

1. In saucepan, melt 2 tablespoons butter. Blend in flour and ¼ teaspoon salt; cook until bubbly. Blend in milk; stir until boiling. In bowl, mix egg yolks with some of the hot butter mixture; stir into sauce in pan. Cook, stirring, until hot. Cool.

2. Preheat oven to 400F. Line a 15½-by-10½-by-1-inch jelly-roll pan with parchment paper; grease paper. With electric mixer, at high speed, beat egg whites until stiff peaks form when beaters are raised. Fold in cooled egg-yolk mixture; spread in pan. Bake 20 minutes.

3. Meanwhile, in skillet, over medium-high heat, melt remaining butter. Add vegetables, ground pepper and remaining salt; sauté 12 minutes, or until tender. Stir in ham.

4. Invert soufflé onto clean kitchen towel; remove paper. Top with vegetable mixture and cheese. Beginning at narrow end, roll up, jelly-roll fashion. Place, seam side down, on serving plate. Serve with salsa. *Makes 8 servings.*

SPARKLING FRUIT DAIQUIRIS

(pictured)

1 pkg (10 oz) frozen raspberries in light
** syrup, thawed, pureed and sieved**
1 can (10 oz) frozen banana daiquiri
** fruit mixer**

2 cups ice cubes
1 bottle (28 oz) lemon- or lime-flavored
** sparkling water**
Fresh mint sprigs (optional)

In blender, blend raspberry puree, daiquiri fruit mixer and 2 cups ice cubes; add sparkling water. Pour into glasses filled with ice. If desired, top with mint sprigs. *Makes 8 servings.*

SPICED FRESH-FRUIT BOWLS

(pictured)

SYRUP
⅓ cup sugar
¼ cup fresh lime juice
¼ cup water
½ teaspoon ground cinnamon
½ teaspoon grated lime peel

4 small cantaloupes
6 cups cut-up mixed fruit
1 container (8 oz) nonfat vanilla-
** flavored yogurt**

1. Make Syrup: In saucepan, heat all ingredients to boiling; simmer 6 minutes. Chill.

2. Halve and seed the cantaloupes; scoop out flesh, leaving ¾-inch-thick shell. Dice cantaloupe; chill in bowl with cut-up fruit and Syrup. Fill cantaloupe shells with fruit; top with yogurt. *Makes 8 servings.*

AN EASY SUNDAY BRUNCH

ASSORTED
FRESH FRUIT JUICES
ARTICHOKE FRITTATA*
TOASTED
COUNTRY BREAD
PRUNE-PECAN COFFEECAKE*
MELON WEDGES WITH
FRESH LIME

Recipes given for starred dishes.

PRUNE-PECAN COFFEECAKE

FILLING
¾ cup (about 24) pitted prunes
2 tablespoons unsalted butter or
** margarine**
1 tablespoon granulated sugar
1 teaspoon ground cinnamon
¼ cup pecan halves

1 pkg (10 oz) refrigerated pizza dough

GLAZE
⅓ cup confectioners' sugar
1½ teaspoons fresh lemon juice

1. Preheat oven to 400F. Grease 9-inch round cake pan. Set aside.

2. Make Filling: In food processor, combine prunes, butter, granulated sugar and cinnamon; process until prunes are finely chopped. Add pecans; process until coarsely chopped.

3. On work surface, unroll pizza dough as package label directs; spread with filling. Roll up, jelly-roll fashion; cut crosswise into 15 slices about ¾ inch thick. Arrange slices flat, cut side up, in prepared pan with edges touching. Bake 15 to 18 minutes, or until golden-brown. Remove from oven; let cool on wire rack while making glaze.

4. Make Glaze: In small bowl, combine confectioners' sugar and lemon juice. Mix until well blended. Drizzle over coffeecake. Separate cake into pieces and serve warm. *Makes 6 servings.*

ARTICHOKE FRITTATA

3 tablespoons unsalted butter
1 large onion, halved lengthwise and
** thinly sliced crosswise**
1 pkg (9 oz) frozen artichoke hearts,
** thawed and squeezed dry**
1 jar (7½ oz) roasted red peppers,
** drained, squeezed dry and diced**
1 teaspoon dried oregano leaves,
** crumbled**
¾ teaspoon freshly ground black pepper
¾ teaspoon salt
1 cup frozen peas, unthawed
8 eggs
4 oz whole-milk mozzarella cheese,
** diced**
3 tablespoons grated Parmesan cheese

1. In 12-inch nonstick skillet, melt butter over medium-high heat; add onion. Sauté 4 to 5 minutes, or until soft. Add artichoke hearts, roasted red peppers, oregano and ¼ teaspoon each pepper and salt; sauté 3 to 4 minutes, stirring in peas the last minute of cooking time.

2. In medium bowl, combine eggs and remaining pepper and salt; whisk until blended. Stir in mozzarella cheese. Pour egg mixture over vegetables; over medium heat, cook 5 to 6 minutes, or until edges are set, lifting the egg mixture with spatula and tilting skillet so the uncooked portion runs under the cooked portion, shaking the skillet frequently. Sprinkle with Parmesan cheese; broil 4 inches from heat source 4 minutes or until cheese browns slightly and eggs are set. Slide Frittata onto serving platter. Cut into wedges. *Makes 6 servings.* ◆

Easy Summer Lunches

N o matter what your summertime
schedule, these easy-to-make sandwiches keep pace with sensational taste.
Each has a flair for fresh summer vegetables and herbs in exciting combination
with lean meats, cheeses and seafood
and with breads in all shapes and sizes—
from pita pockets to sourdough rounds.
Our recipes run the gamut from delicious
updated classics, such as a BLT on Italian
bread with creamy avocado slices and a
hearty hero sandwich, to more traditional
summer favorites, such as a soft-shell crab
sandwich topped with tartar sauce and
mixed greens and a lobster roll accented
with herb mayonnaise. Recipes begin on
page 44.

*Clockwise from top left: Tomato-Basil
Chicken Hero, Lamb Souvlaki with Tzatziki
Sauce, Lobster Roll with Herb Mayonnaise.*

continued from page 43

TOMATO-BASIL CHICKEN HERO
(pictured)

2 whole chicken breasts, skinned, boned and split (1½ lb)
3 tablespoons olive oil
¼ teaspoon salt
⅛ teaspoon freshly ground black pepper
4 French bread rolls
1 cup Sun-Dried Tomato Mayonnaise (see box) or plain mayonnaise
12 thin slices prosciutto
3 tomatoes, thinly sliced
12 thin slices smoked fresh mozzarella cheese
12 large fresh basil leaves
12 arugula leaves

1. Brush chicken with 2 tablespoons olive oil; with remaining oil, grease cast-iron ridged grill pan. Heat pan over medium heat; add chicken. Sprinkle with the salt and pepper. Cook 4 minutes on each side, or until golden-brown.

2. Split each roll in half lengthwise without cutting all the way through. Remove some soft bread from center of each roll; spread cut sides of rolls with the mayonnaise.

3. Arrange 3 slices prosciutto on one side of each roll; top with tomato, mozzarella cheese, basil and arugula. Slice chicken diagonally; arrange over arugula. *Makes 8 servings.*

LAMB SOUVLAKI
(pictured)

¾ lb trimmed lamb, cut into 2-by-¾-inch pieces
1 tablespoon olive oil
¼ teaspoon dried oregano leaves
⅛ teaspoon freshly ground black pepper
⅛ teaspoon salt
4 cups shredded romaine lettuce
2 tomatoes, cut into wedges
½ cup sliced red onion
4 large Mediterranean-style pita breads
Tzatziki Sauce (recipe follows)

DO AHEAD
1. In medium bowl, combine lamb, olive oil, oregano, pepper and salt; toss gently until coated. Marinate lamb, covered, in refrigerator or in a cool place 1 hour, stirring occasionally to mix. Drain yogurt for Tzatziki Sauce.

TO SERVE
2. In another bowl, combine lettuce, tomatoes and onion; toss gently. Finish making Tzatziki Sauce.

3. Arrange lamb on four metal skewers; grill or broil 3 inches from heat source 4 to 5 minutes, or until medium-rare. Remove from skewers.

4. Place lettuce mixture on pitas; top with lamb and Tzatziki Sauce. Roll up each pita over filling, making a loose cone. Wrap smaller end of each cone in aluminum foil. *Makes 4 servings.*

TZATZIKI SAUCE

2 cups plain low-fat yogurt
½ cucumber, pared, seeded and finely diced
2 scallions, minced
2 tablespoons minced fresh parsley
2 tablespoons minced fresh mint leaves
2 tablespoons minced fresh dill
⅛ teaspoon freshly ground black pepper
⅛ teaspoon salt

1. Line sieve with cheesecloth; place over bowl. Add yogurt; drain 1 hour. Discard liquid.

2. Place drained yogurt in bowl; add remaining ingredients. Mix well. *Makes 1½ cups.*

LOBSTER ROLL
(pictured)

1 lb cooked lobster meat, shredded (3 cups)
⅓ cup Herb Mayonnaise (see box) or plain mayonnaise
¼ teaspoon freshly ground black pepper
¼ cup melted butter
4 hot-dog buns
Lemon wedges (optional)
Potato chips (optional)

1. In large bowl, combine lobster, mayonnaise and pepper; mix lightly until blended. Brush inside of buns with butter; broil until toasted.

2. Place lobster mixture in buns; serve immediately. Garnish with lemon wedges and serve with potato chips, if desired. *Makes 4 servings.*

AVOCADO BLT

8 slices country Italian bread from an 8-inch round (1-lb) loaf
½ cup Jalapeño-Lime Mayonnaise (see box) or plain mayonnaise
8 Boston lettuce leaves
12 slices tomato
¾ lb bacon, cooked crisp (12 slices)
2 avocados, pared, pitted and quartered lengthwise
¼ teaspoon freshly ground black pepper
⅛ teaspoon salt

1. Spread one side of each bread slice with the mayonnaise. Top spread side of 4 slices with lettuce, tomato, bacon and avocado.

2. Sprinkle with the pepper and salt; top with remaining bread slices. *Makes 4 servings.*

APPLE AND CHICKEN SALAD SANDWICH

DRESSING
¼ cup mayonnaise
¼ cup plain low-fat yogurt
1 tablespoon fresh lemon juice
¼ teaspoon freshly ground black pepper
½ cup chopped watercress

APPLE AND CHICKEN SALAD
¾ lb cooked chicken, shredded
½ lb cooked smoked chicken, shredded
1 cup diced and peeled Granny Smith apple
1 cup diced celery
½ cup toasted pecans, chopped
½ cup golden raisins or dried cherries

16 slices toasted whole-grain or white bread or 8 slices of each
Watercress sprigs

1. Make Dressing: In large bowl, combine ingredients; mix well.

2. Make Apple and Chicken Salad: To dressing, add salad ingredients; toss to coat.

3. Assemble sandwiches: Spread salad over 8 bread slices; top with watercress sprigs and remaining bread slices. *Makes 8 servings.*

MUFFALETA

DRESSING
½ cup olive oil
6 tablespoons red-wine vinegar
2 cloves garlic, crushed
2 tablespoons chopped fresh oregano or 1 teaspoon dried oregano, crushed

OLIVE SALAD
1 jar (7 oz) marinated artichokes, drained and chopped
½ cup pitted black olives, sliced
½ cup pitted Calamata olives, sliced
½ cup roasted red pepper, diced
2 celery stalks, diced
¼ cup Spanish olives, sliced
¼ cup cocktail onions, halved
4 oz mozzarella cheese, diced

8-inch round sourdough bread
4 oz sliced Genoa salami
4 oz sliced soppressata salami
4 oz sliced provolone cheese

DO AHEAD
1. Make Dressing: In small bowl, combine ingredients; whisk until ingredients are blended.

2. Make Olive Salad: In medium bowl, combine ingredients; mix well.

3. Slice off top third of bread in one piece; remove soft bread from inside

bottom piece, leaving a crust shell. Brush cut side of bread top and inside of shell with half the dressing. Add remaining dressing to Olive Salad; mix well; spoon into bread shell. Layer salamis and provolone over salad; place bread top over all. Wrap tightly in plastic wrap and then in aluminum foil. Refrigerate up to 4 hours.

TO SERVE

4. Cut into wedges. Serve at room temperature. *Makes 8 servings.*

Note: If soppressata salami is not available, use all Genoa salami. The taste will not be the same, but the Muffaleta will still be delicious.

MEDITERRANEAN GRILL

¼ cup mayonnaise
¼ cup grated Parmesan cheese
8 slices Italian bread (½-inch-thick)
6 oz Fontina cheese, thinly sliced
1 medium tomato, thinly sliced
4 large arugula leaves
½ red onion, thinly sliced
¼ cup pesto
3 tablespoons butter, melted

1. In bowl, blend mayonnaise with Parmesan cheese; spread over one side of each bread slice, dividing evenly. On prepared side of each of 4 bread slices, arrange in layers, in order, dividing evenly: half the Fontina cheese, all the tomato slices, the arugula, onion, pesto and remaining Fontina cheese. Top with remaining bread slices, prepared side down. Using only half the butter, brush top of each with butter.

2. In large skillet, over medium-low heat, grill sandwiches, buttered side down, until golden-brown. Brush top of each sandwich with remaining butter; turn sandwiches over. Grill until bread is golden-brown and cheese melts. *Makes 4 servings.*

CHICKEN-AND-BRIE ROUND

DRESSING
½ cup whole-grain Dijon-style mustard
½ cup sour cream
3 tablespoons honey

2 pkg (9 oz each) breaded chicken-breast fillets
2 tablespoons salad oil
2 large onions, sliced
1 (12-inch) loaf sourdough bread, sliced in thirds horizontally, warmed
½ bunch watercress
½ lb Brie cheese, cut into ¼-inch-wide slices

1. Preheat oven to 450F. Make Dressing: In bowl, blend ingredients; set

---

THREE FLAVORED MAYOS

Add a few ingredients to bottled mayonnaise to create a special sauce.

JALAPENO-LIME MAYONNAISE

1 cup mayonnaise
3 jalapeños, seeded and minced
2 scallions, minced
2 tablespoons minced fresh cilantro
1 teaspoon grated lime peel
¼ teaspoon chili powder
1 teaspoon fresh lime juice

SUN-DRIED TOMATO MAYONNAISE

1 cup mayonnaise
½ cup (16 halves) sun-dried tomatoes in oil, diced
1 tablespoon minced fresh basil
1½ teaspoons drained capers
¼ teaspoon crushed red-pepper flakes

HERB MAYONNAISE

1 cup mayonnaise
¼ cup minced fresh herbs
1 teaspoon grated lemon peel
1 teaspoon fresh lemon juice
¼ teaspoon coarsely ground black pepper

---

aside. Place chicken on baking sheet; bake 10 minutes, turning once. Heat 2 tablespoons salad oil in large skillet over medium heat. Add onions; sauté until golden-brown.

2. On bottom 2 pieces of bread, layer, in order, dividing evenly, watercress, Brie cheese, chicken, onions and ¼ cup dressing. Stack prepared layers, placing top third of bread over all. Pass remaining dressing. *Makes 4 to 6 servings.*

SOFT-SHELL CRAB SANDWICHES

BATTER
2 cups unsifted self-rising flour
½ teaspoon salt
¼ teaspoon cayenne pepper
1 egg, at room temperature, separated
1 can (12 oz) beer

Vegetable oil for frying
6 medium soft-shell crabs, cleaned, rinsed and patted dry
1 large red onion, cut into ¼-inch-thick slices and separated into rings
2 tablespoons olive oil
1 tablespoon fresh lemon juice
1 teaspoon Dijon-style mustard
⅛ teaspoon freshly ground black pepper
⅛ teaspoon salt
4 large romaine lettuce leaves, julienned
6 large radicchio leaves, julienned
1 cup frisée, torn into pieces
6 onion rolls, split and toasted
1 cup Tartar Sauce (recipe follows)
6 slices tomato

1. Make Batter: In large bowl, combine flour, salt and cayenne pepper; mix. Add egg yolk; gradually stir in beer just until blended. In small bowl of electric mixer, at high speed, beat egg white until stiff; with rubber spatula, fold into batter until no streaks remain. (Batter will be lumpy.)

2. In skillet, heat ¾ inch vegetable oil to 375F on deep-fat thermometer. Preheat oven to 300F. Line 2 baking sheets with paper towels. Set aside.

3. Working with 1 or 2 crabs at a time, dip in batter; fry 2 at a time in the hot oil 2 to 3 minutes on each side, until golden and crisp. Drain on paper towel–lined baking sheets. Keep warm in oven while frying remaining crabs.

4. Toss onion rings in batter; fry in batches in the hot oil 1 to 2 minutes on each side. Drain on paper towel–lined baking sheets; keep warm in oven.

5. To serve: In bowl, mix olive oil with seasonings; add greens; toss. On bottom half of each roll, arrange greens, tomato, crab and 2 tablespoons Tartar Sauce; top with other half of roll. Serve with onion rings; pass remaining sauce. *Makes 6 servings.*

TARTAR SAUCE

1 cup mayonnaise
¼ cup chopped dill pickle
2 tablespoons finely chopped Italian parsley
2 tablespoons fresh lemon juice
1 tablespoon capers, drained
¼ teaspoon cayenne pepper

In bowl, combine ingredients; mix. Chill until ready to serve. *Makes about 1¼ cups.*   ◆

The zesty taste of citrus gives a lift to this tempting trio. From left to right: Fettuccini and Broccoli With Lemon-Garlic Crumb Topping is a delightful meatless entrée that goes from stove top to table in less than 25 minutes. Baked Salmon Steaks With Orange-Onion Confit features salmon steaks marinated in orange juice, garlic and thyme, then baked with roasted onion and orange peel. Pork-Lime Fajitas With Pear-Orange Salsa is a fruity fiesta of flavors served with spiced avocado topping.

Citrus-Splashed Sensations

Oh, what terrific things you can do to food with a splash of freshly squeezed citrus juice and a pinch of citrus peel. It's a wonderful way to wake up the natural goodness and flavors of meats, fish, salads, vegetables and desserts. In these eight tantalizing recipes, the emphasis is on light, healthful, fresh ingredients with a sparkle of sunshine from lemons, limes and oranges. Recipes begin on page 49.

Chicken With Oranges, above, is a speedy sauté with a peel of orange accented with cumin. Arugula-Orange Salad, right, is a "sweet-tart" of a selection, with a tangy lemon-garlic dressing and curls of Parmesan cheese on top—a perfect accompaniment for plain meats.

continued from page 47

FETTUCCINI AND BROCCOLI WITH LEMON-GARLIC CRUMB TOPPING

(pictured)

When grating citrus peel, it's important not to dig too deeply into the peel; the bitter white pith will come off with the peel.

½ cup plus 2 tablespoons butter
1 cup coarse dry bread crumbs
1 garlic clove, crushed
1 tablespoon plus 1 teaspoon grated lemon peel
1 tablespoon finely chopped Italian parsley
¼ teaspoon salt
Freshly ground black pepper
2 garlic cloves, minced or crushed
1 lb fettuccini or linguine
1 bunch broccoli, stems peeled; flowerets and stems chopped
⅓ cup fresh lemon juice

1. In nonstick skillet, over medium-low heat, melt 2 tablespoons butter; add bread crumbs. Sauté 8 minutes, or until golden. Add 1 garlic clove and 1 teaspoon grated lemon peel; cook 1 minute. Add parsley, salt and pepper; mix well. Place in bowl. Clean skillet.

2. Make sauce: In same skillet, over low heat, sauté remaining lemon peel and 2 garlic cloves in ½ cup butter 5 minutes, or until garlic is tender.

3. Meanwhile, in large pan of boiling salted water, cook fettuccini 8 minutes; add broccoli. Cook, stirring, 1 to 2 minutes, or until broccoli is tender-crisp. Drain; return to pan. Add sauce and lemon juice; toss. Transfer to shallow serving bowl; sprinkle with sautéed bread crumbs. Serve immediately. *Makes 6 servings.*

BAKED SALMON STEAKS WITH ORANGE-ONION CONFIT

(pictured)

MARINADE
2 tablespoons fresh orange juice
1 teaspoon grated orange peel
1 garlic clove, crushed
1 teaspoon fresh thyme leaves or a pinch of dried thyme leaves
⅛ teaspoon freshly ground black pepper

2 (1-inch-thick) salmon steaks (1 to 1¼ lb total weight)

ORANGE-ONION CONFIT
2 tablespoons olive oil
1 large Spanish onion, cut lengthwise into ¼-inch-thick slices
4 (3-by-½-inch) strips orange peel, slivered

1 teaspoon fresh thyme leaves or a pinch of dried thyme leaves
½ teaspoon salt
Freshly ground black pepper
Thyme sprigs (optional)
Orange wedges (optional)

1. Make Marinade: In pie plate or shallow glass dish, combine ingredients; mix well. Add salmon steaks; rub all sides with marinade. Marinate at room temperature 30 minutes, or refrigerate and marinate up to 1 hour.

2. Preheat oven to 425F. Make Orange-Onion Confit: In 13-by-9-inch heavy baking dish, combine olive oil, onion, orange peel and thyme; toss to coat. Roast onion 20 minutes or until edges begin to brown, stirring once after 10 minutes. Remove baking dish from oven; add ½ teaspoon salt and the pepper to taste. Toss to coat.

3. Push confit to one side of baking dish, arrange salmon steaks on other side of baking dish. Pour marinade on top of salmon steaks; top with some of the confit. Bake 10 minutes; remove baking dish from oven. Let salmon steaks stand 5 minutes before serving.

4. To serve: Spoon confit onto a serving platter. Carefully remove skin from salmon steaks. Split salmon steaks in half along center bone; lift out bone and discard. Place salmon steaks on platter with confit. If desired, garnish with thyme sprigs and orange wedges. *Makes 4 servings.*

MICROWAVE DIRECTIONS

1. Make Marinade and marinate salmon steaks as directed in Step 1.

2. Make Orange-Onion Confit: In 10-inch microwave-safe glass pie plate, mix olive oil, onion, orange peel and thyme. Cover with plastic wrap; turn back one corner to vent. Cook on HIGH (100% power) 5 minutes. Uncover; mix well. Cook, uncovered, 5 minutes; stir. Cook 2 to 3 minutes longer, or until onions are very tender.

3. Push confit to one side of pie plate; arrange salmon steaks on other side of pie plate. Pour marinade over salmon steaks. Cover with plastic wrap; vent. Cook on HIGH (100% power) 2 minutes. Turn pie plate ½ turn; cook 1 to 2 minutes longer, checking doneness after each minute. Let stand, covered, 2 minutes before final testing for doneness.

PORK-LIME FAJITAS WITH PEAR-ORANGE SALSA

(pictured)

In each element of the fajitas—pork, salsa and topping—use fresh juice for the best taste. And section the orange with a chef's knife—it won't tear up the fruit.

MARINADE
2 tablespoons fresh lime juice
2 garlic cloves, crushed
1 tablespoon vegetable oil
½ teaspoon crushed red-pepper flakes
½ teaspoon salt

¾-lb pork tenderloin

PEAR-ORANGE SALSA
2 firm ripe pears, peeled and diced
1 orange, peeled, sectioned and diced
½ cup thinly sliced scallions
½ cup diced, peeled and seeded cucumber
½ cup diced red pepper
3 tablespoons fresh lime juice
1 tablespoon vegetable oil
1 tablespoon chopped cilantro
1 teaspoon finely chopped fresh jalapeño
1 teaspoon grated orange peel
½ garlic clove, crushed
¼ teaspoon salt
⅛ teaspoon freshly ground black pepper

AVOCADO TOPPING
2 ripe avocados
2 tablespoons fresh lime juice
2 tablespoons chopped cilantro
2 teaspoons finely chopped jalapeño
¼ teaspoon salt

8 (7-inch) flour tortillas
Cilantro sprigs

1. Make Marinade: In glass pie plate, mix ingredients. Add pork; turn to coat. Cover and chill 2 hours, turning often.

2. Preheat oven to 375F. Pour marinade into saucepan. Roast pork on rack in broiler pan 20 minutes, or until just cooked through. Place pork on cutting board; let stand 5 minutes. Turn off oven. Wrap tortillas in aluminum foil; place in hot oven.

3. While pork cooks, make Pear-Orange Salsa: In serving bowl, combine ingredients; mix gently.

4. Make Avocado Topping: In a medium bowl, with fork, mash avocado with remaining topping ingredients just

continued on page 50

continued from page 49

until chunky and blended. Place in bowl; place plastic wrap on surface.

5. Boil marinade until thickened. Thinly slice pork diagonally and then into strips; arrange on platter with warm tortillas and cilantro. Drizzle with marinade. To serve: Arrange pork across each tortilla; top with Avocado Topping, Pear-Orange Salsa, cilantro and, if desired, sour cream. Roll tortilla around filling. *Makes 4 servings (8 fajitas).*

CHICKEN WITH ORANGES
(pictured)

2 tablespoons all-purpose flour
3 teaspoons grated orange peel
1 teaspoon salt
2 boneless chicken breast halves, skinned
2 tablespoons olive oil
4 leeks, sliced and rinsed well (about 2 cups)
1 teaspoon ground cumin
¼ teaspoon crushed red-pepper flakes
2 medium tomatoes, chopped
½ cup chicken broth
2 medium oranges, peeled, white pith removed, sliced
⅓ cup Niçoise olives, pitted

1. In dish, mix flour, 2 teaspoons orange peel and ½ teaspoon salt; coat chicken with mixture. In skillet, over medium-high heat, heat olive oil; sauté chicken until cooked. Remove to platter; keep warm.

2. In drippings, sauté leeks with cumin, red-pepper flakes and remaining salt 4 minutes. Add tomatoes, chicken broth and remaining orange peel; simmer 5 minutes. Add orange slices and olives; pour over warm chicken. *Makes 4 servings.*

ARUGULA-ORANGE SALAD
(pictured)

The secret to this salad's success: Use fresh lemon juice in the dressing, slice the onion very thin, and use imported Parmesan cheese.

1 bulb fennel, quartered lengthwise
2 bunches arugula, stems trimmed
2 medium oranges, peeled, white pith removed, halved lengthwise and sliced
1 red onion, cut into thin rings
3 radishes, thinly sliced

DRESSING

3 tablespoons olive oil
2 tablespoons fresh lemon juice
1 garlic clove, crushed
¼ teaspoon salt

Freshly ground black pepper, to taste
2-oz hard Parmesan cheese

1. Soak fennel in ice water 20 minutes. Drain; pat dry. Thinly slice; place in bowl with arugula, orange slices, onion and radishes.

2. Make Dressing: In small bowl, whisk ingredients until blended. Pour over salad. Toss; place on plates. With vegetable parer, shave curls of Parmesan over each salad. *Makes 4 servings.*

TANGERINE AND GINGER MOUSSE

¼ cup sugar
1 teaspoon grated tangerine peel
1 pkg unflavored gelatin
1 cup fresh tangerine juice
1 tablespoon fresh lemon juice
1 container (8 oz) vanilla-flavored low-fat yogurt
1 tablespoon syrup from bottled stem ginger
½ cup heavy cream, whipped
1 tablespoon minced bottled stem ginger

1. In saucepan, combine sugar, tangerine peel, gelatin and tangerine and lemon juices; mix well. Let stand 10 minutes, or until gelatin softens. Over low heat, cook mixture, stirring, until gelatin dissolves. Transfer to bowl; add yogurt and ginger syrup. Whisk until blended.

2. Stand bowl in larger bowl of ice water, stirring occasionally, 20 minutes, or until thickened. With rubber spatula, fold in whipped cream and minced ginger until blended. Spoon into goblets; chill at least 1 hour before serving. If desired, top with additional grated tangerine peel. *Makes 4 servings.*

KEY LIME PIE

Our pie filling calls for the incomparable flavor of Key lime juice. Use the grated peel of a regular lime since the fragile Key lime is hard to find.

1¼ cups graham cracker crumbs
¼ cup unsalted butter, melted
1¼ cups plus 6 tablespoons sugar
¼ cup cornstarch
¼ cup fresh or bottled Key lime juice
1 teaspoon grated lime peel
3 eggs, separated
1½ cups boiling water

1. Preheat oven to 350F. In bowl, combine graham cracker crumbs and butter. Mix well; press over bottom and on side of 9-inch pie plate. Bake 8 minutes; cool.

2. Make filling: In saucepan, combine 1¼ cups sugar, the cornstarch, Key lime juice and lime peel; mix well. Whisk in egg yolks. Gradually stir in the boiling water until blended. Over medium-high heat, bring to boiling, whisking; cook, whisking, 4 minutes, or until thick. Pour into bowl; stand bowl in larger bowl of ice water to cool mixture. Pour filling into piecrust.

3. Raise oven temperature to 425F. In bowl of electric mixer, at high speed, beat egg whites, adding remaining sugar 1 tablespoon at a time, until stiff; spread over filling to cover completely. Bake 4 minutes, or until golden. Chill at least 8 hours. *Makes 8 servings.*

FOUR-CITRUS COMPOTE WITH MINT SYRUP

1 cup sugar
½ cup water
3 tablespoons julienne fresh mint leaves
2 teaspoons grated lime peel
4 seedless oranges
2 pink grapefruit
2 lemons
2 limes

1. At least 1½ hours before serving: In small saucepan, combine sugar and water. Bring to boiling, stirring until sugar dissolves. Add mint leaves and lime peel; cool.

2. Over large bowl, peel and section fruits, cutting away white pith. Add syrup to fruit mixture; toss gently. Chill at least 1 hour before serving. If desired, garnish with julienne lime peel. *Makes 6 servings.*

MICROWAVE DIRECTIONS

In 1-quart microwave-safe glass bowl, combine sugar and water. Cook, uncovered, on HIGH (100% power) 4 minutes, stirring once, or until sugar dissolves and mixture boils. Stir in mint leaves and lime peel. Continue with recipe as directed in Step 1. ◆

Ten Minutes to Tex-Mex

*W*ant an easy, exciting way to add spice to your meals? Borrow some zest from the Old Southwest with a simple salsa that takes only minutes to make. There are as many salsa recipes as there are ways to enjoy them. The chart below suggests five quick combinations, each with its unique character and degree of spiciness. Pictured here are two typical grilled meats that are "salsified": cilantro-lime Cornish hens and pork chops topped with pineapple-and-red-pepper salsa.

The tastiest summer suppers:
marinated Cornish hens (top) and salsa-topped pork chops.

PIQUANT PORK AND PINEAPPLE
(pictured)

2 cups finely chopped fresh pineapple, with juice
½ cup coarsely chopped red pepper
1 green onion, thinly sliced
1 tablespoon chopped cilantro
2 teaspoons minced fresh ginger
1½ teaspoons sugar
½ teaspoon salt
¼ teaspoon pepper
6 pork loin chops (¾-inch thick)

1. Make salsa: In medium bowl, mix pineapple and its juice, red pepper, green onion, cilantro, ginger, sugar, ¼ teaspoon salt and ⅛ teaspoon pepper. Cover; set aside until ready to serve.

2. Prepare outdoor grill for barbecue. Place pork chops on grill rack to one side of prepared coals, or place on rack in broiler pan; sprinkle with remaining salt and pepper. Grill or broil chops 4 inches from heat 8 minutes. Turn chops; grill or broil 8 minutes longer, or just until cooked. Place on serving platter. Spoon salsa over chops. If desired, garnish with cilantro. *Makes 6 servings.*

GRILLED HENS OLE
(pictured)

⅓ cup loosely packed cilantro, chopped
½ cup mayonnaise
2 tablespoons fresh lime juice
1 large clove garlic, crushed
½ teaspoon salt
2 (1¾ lb each) Cornish hens, split lengthwise in half
1 avocado, peeled, pitted and sliced
8 radishes, sliced

1. Prepare outdoor grill for barbecue. In bowl, mix cilantro, mayonnaise, lime juice, garlic and salt. Brush hens with mixture; place skin side down on grill rack to one side of prepared coals.

2. Grill hens, covered, 4 inches from heat 20 minutes. Turn hens; grill 15 minutes longer. Transfer hens to warm serving platter. Garnish with avocado and radish slices. *Makes 4 servings.* ♦

SALSA IN SECONDS

For five fabulous salsas: Combine ingredients down each column (cucumber, onion, cilantro) or on each diagonal (cucumber, green onions, jalapeño).

1 cup chopped	cucumber	papaya	tomato
⅓ cup chopped	onion	green onions	green pepper
2 tbsp minced	cilantro	parsley	jalapeño

To each combination, add ½ teaspoon chili powder, ¼ teaspoon dried garlic, ¼ teaspoon salt and ⅛ teaspoon black pepper. *Makes 1⅓ cups.*

This meal says "Come to dinner" with a Southern accent. Clockwise, Praline Ice-Cream Pie is a swirl of pecans, maple syrup and ice cream in a prepared graham-cracker crust. Cucumber, celery and roasted red peppers mingle with bottled Italian dressing in Crunchy Cucumber Salad. A spicy seasoning mix coats tuna steaks for a quick-broil Cajun Tuna With Broiled Tomatoes. And don't forget some down-home Cornmeal-Fried Okra. Add crackers, cheeses and wine to complete the Southern hospitality.

RITA MAAS

Dinner in 29 Minutes

The next time you're faced with the challenge of preparing a rush-hour meal, try one of our 29-minute dinners. Each exciting menu offers an appetizer, an entrée, a vegetable and a dessert, carefully selected for timeliness and taste appeal. Some recipes make imaginative use of shortcut ingredients, others are simply quick and easy by nature. You'll want to keep them handy for any day of the week when you want time—and taste—on your side. Recipes begin on page 54.

*Here's an exotic menu with a **Middle Eastern** influence. Clockwise starting at top, **Spiced Shrimp Kebabs** sautés tender shrimp with garlic, ginger, tomato and pineapple. **Pears With Mascarpone** is a spirited delight with a topping of cheese, cream and honey and a sprinkling of miniature cookies. Cinnamon-spiced cutlets simmer with garlic, tomatoes and honey to create fabulous **Turkey Cutlets Marrakesh.** The accompanying **Cilantro Rice and Beans** is a shortcut mix of prepared rice pilaf, black beans and chopped cilantro. Serve with broccoli, crisp pitas and iced tea to make this tasteful journey complete.*

RITA MAAS

continued from page 53

ASSORTED CRACKERS AND CHEESES
CRUNCHY CUCUMBER SALAD★
CAJUN TUNA WITH BROILED TOMATOES★
CORNMEAL-FRIED OKRA★
PRALINE ICE-CREAM PIE★
DRY WHITE WINE

★Recipes given for starred dishes.

GAME PLAN

Prepare dessert; freeze. Prepare salad; preheat broiler. Dredge fish; halve tomatoes. Assemble appetizer. Broil fish and tomatoes; prepare okra.

CRUNCHY CUCUMBER SALAD
(pictured)

1 European-style cucumber, scored
2 celery stalks
1 jar (7 oz) roasted red peppers, drained and chopped
⅔ cup bottled Italian dressing
Lettuce leaves

1. Thinly slice cucumber crosswise. Thinly slice celery on the diagonal. In medium bowl, combine cucumber, celery and peppers. Add dressing; toss until coated. Cover with plastic wrap; refrigerate to chill slightly.

2. To serve: Line platter with lettuce leaves; top with salad. *Makes 4 servings.*

CAJUN TUNA WITH BROILED TOMATOES
(pictured)

4 tuna steaks (½-inch thick)
¼ cup Cajun-Creole seasoning mix (see Note)
4 tomatoes, cut crosswise in half
½ teaspoon salt
¼ teaspoon pepper
Lemon wedges

1. On sheet of waxed paper, coat tuna steaks on both sides with Cajun-Creole seasoning mix; place on broiler pan with tomato halves, cut side up. Sprinkle tomatoes with salt and pepper, dividing evenly.

2. Broil tuna steaks and tomatoes 4 inches from heat 5 minutes. Turn tuna steaks; broil tuna steaks and tomatoes 5 minutes longer. Serve with lemon wedges. *Makes 4 servings.*

Note: Available in specialty food stores, or mix 2 teaspoons each garlic powder, onion powder, Hungarian paprika, freshly ground black pepper, ground red pepper and salt.

CORNMEAL-FRIED OKRA
(pictured)

2 eggs
1 lb small okra, trimmed
⅔ cup yellow cornmeal
1 teaspoon salt
½ teaspoon pepper
1 cup salad oil

1. In medium bowl, beat eggs lightly. Add okra; toss to coat.

2. In plastic bag, mix cornmeal, salt and pepper; add okra, a few at a time, shaking each batch until coated.

3. In large skillet, heat oil over medium-high heat. Fry okra in two batches, turning once, 3 minutes each batch. With slotted spoon, remove okra from skillet; drain on paper towels. *Makes 4 servings.*

PRALINE ICE-CREAM PIE
(pictured)

1 cup toasted pecans
½ cup maple syrup
1 quart vanilla ice cream, slightly softened
9-inch graham cracker pie shell

In small bowl, mix pecans and maple syrup. Spoon softened ice cream and pecan mixture into pie shell, swirling to mix pecan mixture throughout ice cream. Freeze until ready to serve. *Makes 8 servings.*

SPICED SHRIMP KEBABS★
PITA CRISPS
TURKEY CUTLETS MARRAKESH★
CILANTRO RICE AND BEANS★
STEAMED BROCCOLI CROWNS
PEARS WITH MASCARPONE★
ICED TEA

GAME PLAN

Prepare dessert; refrigerate. Prepare appetizers; keep warm. Toast pitas. Make turkey cutlets and rice and beans. Steam broccoli.

SPICED SHRIMP KEBABS
(pictured)

1 can (8¼ oz) pineapple chunks in heavy syrup
1 tablespoon salad oil
3 medium cloves garlic, crushed
⅛ teaspoon ground ginger
⅛ teaspoon ground turmeric
1 tablespoon tomato paste
½ lb shrimp, peeled and deveined
½ teaspoon salt
1 tablespoon lime juice
Dash hot red-pepper sauce

Drain the pineapple; reserve ¼ cup syrup. In skillet, heat oil over medium-high heat. Sauté garlic with spices and tomato paste 2 minutes. Add shrimp; sauté 2 minutes. Stir in pineapple syrup and remaining ingredients; bring to boiling. Add pineapple chunks; place in bowl. Accompany with wooden picks to make kebabs. *Makes 4 servings.*

TURKEY CUTLETS MARRAKESH
(pictured)

1½ teaspoons Maryland-style seafood seasoning
¼ teaspoon ground cinnamon
4 turkey cutlets (1 lb)
2 tablespoons salad oil
1 clove garlic, crushed
1 can (16 oz) whole peeled tomatoes
2 tablespoons honey

Mix seafood seasoning with cinnamon; sprinkle over the turkey cutlets. In skillet, heat oil over medium-high heat; sauté garlic 1 minute. Brown cutlets on both sides. Stir in tomatoes, breaking up with spoon, and honey. Bring to boiling; simmer, covered, 10 minutes. Serve with Cilantro Rice and Beans. *Makes 4 servings.*

The trick to this elegant 29-minute dinner is in the recipes: Each uses seven or fewer ingredients. Broccoli-Corn Chowder begins with condensed soup and becomes a seasoned vegetable surprise in minutes. English Cream Custard in Chocolate Shells starts with prepared vanilla pudding and ends up as an almond-flavored filling in chocolate shells. A simple four-ingredient glaze elevates plain broiled lamb chops to a glorious entrée. German Potato Salad blends bottled vinaigrette dressing with bacon, onion and honey for a timesaving dish with a tang.

CILANTRO RICE AND BEANS
(pictured)

1 package (4 oz) boil-in-bag rice pilaf
  with vegetables, cooked
1 can (16 oz) black beans, drained
2 tablespoons chopped cilantro

In saucepan, combine rice pilaf, beans and cilantro; heat through. *Makes 4 servings.*

PEARS WITH MASCARPONE
(pictured)

3 ripe pears, cored and coarsely
  chopped
2 tablespoons almond-flavored
  liqueur
2 teaspoons lemon juice
3 oz mascarpone cheese
¼ cup heavy cream
1 tablespoon honey

½ cup mini bittersweet almond-flavored
  Italian cookies

1. In bowl, toss pears with liqueur and lemon juice. In small bowl of electric mixer, at high speed, beat mascarpone with heavy cream and honey until stiff. Place bowls in refrigerator until ready to serve.
2. To serve: Spoon the pear mixture into each of four dessert dishes; top each with the mascarpone mixture and Italian cookies. *Makes 4 servings.*

BROCCOLI-CORN CHOWDER★
CHEESE STRAWS
MINT-BROILED LAMB CHOPS★
GERMAN POTATO SALAD★
STEAMED SUGAR SNAP PEAS
**ENGLISH CREAM CUSTARD IN
CHOCOLATE SHELLS★**

★Recipes given for starred dishes.

GAME PLAN

Prepare dessert; refrigerate. Prepare chowder; keep warm. Make potato salad and mint glaze. Broil chops and steam sugar snap peas.

BROCCOLI-CORN CHOWDER
(pictured)

1 can (10¾ oz) cream-of-broccoli soup
½ cup half-and-half
1 can (16 oz) whole-kernel corn
2 tablespoons onion flakes
¼ teaspoon celery seeds
¼ teaspoon seasoned pepper

In saucepan, blend undiluted soup with half-and-half. Whisk in corn and its liquid and remaining ingredients. Bring mixture to boiling. Serve with cheese straws. *Makes 4 servings.*

GERMAN POTATO SALAD
(pictured)

3 slices bacon, cut into ½-inch pieces
1 small onion, sliced
1 tablespoon all-purpose flour
½ cup bottled honey-mustard
  vinaigrette dressing
¼ cup water
2 tablespoons honey
2 cups sliced cooked red new potatoes,
  or canned potatoes

continued on page 79

RITA MAAS

Quick
Money-Saving Meals

Flank-Steak Roulade With Lyonnaise Potatoes

*I*t's possible to serve a quick meal and still save a pretty penny. Too often, quick means costly—steaks and chops can be served up fast, but rarely without straining the family budget. Yet the delicious dishes shown here take little more than a half hour to prepare, are relatively low in cost, and taste like a million dollars. Starting on the next page are recipes for these main courses, as well as for many other hearty entrées.

Steak-And-Vegetable Skillet Dinner

Sausage Continental

STEAK-AND-VEGETABLE SKILLET DINNER
(pictured)

Salt
3 carrots, pared and thinly sliced on diagonal
½ lb chuck steak, partially frozen
Butter or margarine
1 garlic clove, split
1 pkg (10 oz) frozen cut green beans
1 onion, thinly sliced
Instant mashed potato, for 4 servings
Water, milk, butter, salt

1. In about 1 inch lightly salted boiling water, cook carrots, covered, 5 minutes; drain.
2. Slice partially frozen steak very thinly on diagonal.
3. In large skillet, heat 2 tablespoons butter with the garlic; add steak slices; cook quickly until well browned on both sides; remove to warm platter.
4. To drippings in skillet, add carrots, green beans and onion; cook covered, until vegetables are tender—5 minutes, adding more butter if needed and stirring once or twice.
5. Discard garlic. Toss vegetables and meat in skillet with ½ teaspoon salt; add a little butter if mixture seems dry. Serve with instant mashed potato, prepared as package label directs, using amount of liquid specified on package and butter and salt for 4 servings. *Makes 4 servings.*

BAKED TUNA-STUFFED POTATOES

8 large baking potatoes
2 tablespoons butter or margarine
2 cans (7-oz size) tuna, drained and flaked
1 tablespoon grated onion
1 tablespoon chopped parsley or
    1 teaspoon dried parsley flakes
1 can (11 oz) condensed Cheddar cheese soup, undiluted
¼ teaspoon paprika
2 drops hot red-pepper sauce
¼ teaspoon salt
4 slices American cheese, halved

1. Preheat oven to 400F. Wash potatoes; rub with butter and prick with a fork. Bake 45 minutes to 1 hour or until tender (see Note).
2. Meanwhile, in medium bowl, combine remaining ingredients except cheese.
3. Remove a 1-inch slice from top of each potato. Scoop out pulp, leaving a shell. Add pulp to tuna mixture; toss well.
4. Spoon lightly into potato shells, mounding high. Top each with ½ slice cheese. Place in shallow baking pan; bake 15 minutes or until filling is hot and

cheese is melted. *Makes 8 servings.*

Note: To bake potatoes faster: Wash potatoes; rub with butter and prick well with a fork. Insert a large, clean nail through top of potato, about halfway through. Bake 30 to 45 minutes or until tender. Carefully remove nails when done. Or: Wash potatoes; rub with butter and prick well with a fork. Arrange in a circular pattern on a paper towel at least 1 inch apart. Microwave at HIGH (Full Power) 20 minutes or until tender, turning and rearranging after 10 minutes. Let stand 5 minutes.

FETTUCCINI AND BROCCOLI

1 pkg (8 oz) medium noodles
¼ cup salad oil
1 garlic clove, crushed
1 pkg (10 oz) frozen chopped broccoli, thawed and drained
½ cup canned condensed chicken or beef broth, undiluted
½ teaspoon dried basil leaves
¼ cup chopped parsley
¼ cup grated Parmesan cheese
1 cup (8 oz) cottage cheese
½ teaspoon salt
Dash pepper

1. Cook noodles according to package directions; drain.
2. Meanwhile, in hot oil in medium skillet, sauté garlic and thawed drained broccoli, stirring, 5 minutes.
3. Add chicken broth, basil, parsley, Parmesan, cottage cheese, salt and pepper. Stir over low heat until blended—about 2 minutes.
4. Toss broccoli mixture with noodles. Turn into a heated serving dish. *Makes 4 servings.*

SAUSAGE CONTINENTAL
(pictured)

6 sweet Italian sausages (1 lb)
2 tablespoons water
1 pkg (8 oz) wide noodles

1 large unpared red apple, cut into 8 wedges
2 jars (1-lb size) red cabbage, undrained
1 tablespoon caraway seed
¼ cup (½ stick) butter or margarine

1. In 5-quart Dutch oven, over medium heat, cook sausage with 2 tablespoons water, covered, about 15 minutes.
2. Remove cover; turn sausage; continue cooking 10 minutes longer, or until well browned. Remove.
3. Meanwhile, cook noodles as package label directs.
4. In remaining fat in Dutch oven, sauté apple wedges 5 minutes.
5. Add cabbage and sausage; simmer, uncovered, until cabbage is hot and apples are tender but not mushy.
6. Drain noodles; toss with caraway seed and butter.
7. Turn cabbage into center of warm serving platter. Arrange apples and sausage on top, noodles around edge. *Makes 6 servings.*

FLANK-STEAK ROULADE WITH LYONNAISE POTATOES
(pictured)

FLANK-STEAK ROLLS
1 lb flank steak
6 slices bacon

LYONNAISE POTATOES
¼ cup salad oil
2 tablespoons butter or margarine
4 medium potatoes, pared and thinly sliced (about 1¼ lb)
1 cup sliced onion
½ teaspoon salt
Dash pepper
¼ teaspoon dried tarragon leaves

Chopped parsley

1. Make Flank-Steak Rolls: Wipe steak with damp paper towels. Pound steak thin with wooden mallet or edge of saucer. Slice crosswise, on diagonal, into six equal strips.
2. In medium skillet, over medium heat, sauté bacon until partially cooked, not crisp; drain on paper towels.
3. Place one strip of beef on each slice of bacon; roll up jelly-roll style. Secure with a toothpick.
4. Make Lyonnaise Potatoes: In hot oil and butter in large heavy skillet, sauté potatoes, turning frequently, until golden brown and tender—10 to 15 minutes. Add onion; toss with salt, pepper and tarragon; sauté 5 minutes longer.
5. Meanwhile, place roulades on rack in broiler pan; broil, 4 inches from heat, 5 to 7 minutes on each side. Serve with potatoes. Sprinkle with parsley. *Makes 6 servings.* *continued on page 79*

GEORGE RATKAI

A Quick Italian-Style Dinner

*T*hese Baked Stuffed Shells With Meatballs can be made quickly because we use prepared frozen stuffed shells and a jar of spaghetti sauce. While the shells bake, the sauce simmers with the homemade meatballs and you'll have plenty of time left over to make our delicious Gorgonzola Cheese Salad. Add some red wine and Italian bread to complete the meal. See opposite page for our simple directions.

BAKED STUFFED SHELLS
WITH MEATBALLS

1 pkg (18 to 21 oz) frozen cheese-stuffed shells
2 tablespoons (¼ stick) butter or margarine, melted

MEATBALLS
1 lb ground beef chuck
¼ cup packaged dried Italian-style bread crumbs
2 tablespoons minced onion
½ teaspoon salt
Water
1 jar (15 oz) meatless spaghetti sauce
1 teaspoon dried oregano leaves
1 teaspoon dried thyme leaves
Parsley (optional)

1. Preheat oven to 450F. Remove plastic wrap from pan of frozen shells; spoon melted butter over shells and cover pan with aluminum foil. Place in oven and bake as directed. The shells will bake while you prepare the Meatballs and the Gorgonzola Cheese Salad.

2. Make Meatballs: Put ground beef chuck, bread crumbs, onion, salt and ¼ cup water into a large mixing bowl. Using a large wooden spoon or your hands, mix the meat mixture thoroughly. Shape into 24 balls, using about 1 tablespoon meat mixture for each.

3. Put a large skillet over moderately high heat and add meatballs. Cook, turning until browned on all sides—about 10 minutes. Add spaghetti sauce, oregano, thyme and 2 tablespoons water. Simmer, covered, 20 to 25 minutes. Serve over shells. Garnish with parsley, if desired. *Makes 6 to 8 servings.*

GORGONZOLA CHEESE SALAD

2 garlic cloves
1 teaspoon salt
½ cup olive or vegetable oil
3 tablespoons freshly squeezed lemon juice and 1 tablespoon red wine vinegar or ¼ cup red wine vinegar
1 teaspoon dried basil leaves
½ teaspoon ground pepper
2 heads iceberg lettuce
1 cup thinly sliced onion
½ lb Gorgonzola cheese, crumbled

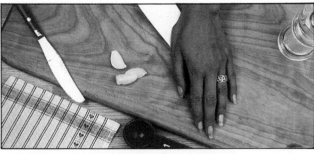

1. Peel garlic and cut each clove in half. Using the flat side of a French chef's knife, smash each piece of garlic and then chop finely. Add salt to garlic and mash together, using the flat side of a small knife or metal spatula to form a smooth paste.

2. Put garlic mixture into a screw-top jar or cruet with top; add olive oil, a mixture of lemon juice and vinegar or all vinegar, basil and pepper. Shake vigorously to combine and place in the refrigerator. Wash lettuce thoroughly under cold running water.

3. Break lettuce into bite-sized pieces and place in a large salad bowl. Add sliced onion and crumbled cheese. Cover and chill until ready to serve. Just before serving, shake salad dressing; pour over salad and toss. *Makes 6 to 8 servings.*

DAVID VIENS

Chicken Parmigiana In 35 Minutes

*C*hicken thighs are always a bargain at the meat counter and,
if you watch for sales, you can make the savings even greater
by stocking your freezer! Then, when you want to make a quick
dinner, try our Chicken Thighs Parmigiana—you'll be amazed at
how quickly they can be prepared. If you have some extra time
early in the day you might want to complete Step 1 of this recipe—
slice the onion, rinse and dry the chicken and press the garlic.
Then, before dinner, just brown the chicken, cook it with spinach
and seasonings and arrange on a bed of hot pasta. See opposite
page for our step-by-step directions—it's as easy as that!

CHICKEN THIGHS PARMIGIANA

8 chicken thighs (about 2 lb)
1 medium onion
2 garlic cloves

¼ cup (½ stick) butter or margarine
1 pkg (10 oz) frozen chopped spinach
Salt

1 teaspoon dried basil leaves
1 pkg (8 oz) spaghetti
¼ cup grated Parmesan cheese

1. Rinse chicken thighs under cold running water and then pat them dry with paper towels; set aside. Peel onion. Using a large sharp knife, cut onion into thin slices; set aside. Peel garlic. Using a garlic press, crush garlic and set aside.

2. In a large skillet, melt butter over moderately high heat. Cook chicken a few pieces at a time, skin side down, for 5 minutes or until golden brown. Return all chicken to skillet, add onion and garlic; cover skillet and cook 5 minutes.

3. Uncover skillet and push chicken to one side. Add frozen block of spinach to skillet; sprinkle with ½ teaspoon salt and the basil. Cover skillet and simmer 15 minutes longer, separating the spinach with a fork as it cooks.

4. Meanwhile cook spaghetti. Bring 4 quarts water and 1½ teaspoons of the salt to a boil in a large saucepot. Add spaghetti, all at once; stir to separate strands and return to a boil. Cook for 7 minutes or until tender but firm to the bite. Drain thoroughly.

5. Uncover skillet and stir spinach together with onion and butter to mix thoroughly. Turn chicken skin side up and sprinkle with ¼ cup Parmesan cheese. Cover skillet and simmer 10 minutes longer or until chicken is tender and thoroughly cooked.

6. Remove skillet from heat. Arrange drained spaghetti on a large platter and top with cooked spinach mixture. Arrange cheese-topped chicken thighs on top and serve immediately. *Makes 4 to 6 servings.*

DAVID VIENS

SHORTCUT
·COOKING·

T hese recipes fit right in with the needs of today's cooks—they're short on preparation time, but go a long way in delivering marvelous taste with exciting good looks. From salads to main dishes to desserts, we've assembled about two dozen favorites using all the shortcuts we know. Many of these dishes can be cooked and served all in one pot. Most of the desserts are easily made with fruit, sherbet or ice cream. And all of them will help you make the most of every minute spent in the kitchen. Recipes start on page 68.

Top: Barbecued Chicken With Cornbread Stuffing. Barbecue sauce provides the glaze and packaged stuffing mix the base for stuffing balls in this uniquely easy meal that's as appropriate on the holiday table as it is for a backyard get-together.

Left: Peaches in Marsala. Canned peach halves, marinated in a spiced wine syrup and dressed with dabs of jelly, are elegant enough to be served in the best crystal stemware.

Right: Chicken Breasts in White Wine. Boneless chicken breasts, simmered in white wine, become a wonderfully light and refreshing one-skillet meal that's especially attractive when garnished with lemon and parsley. Below: Scampi. Large succulent shrimp baked to tender perfection in a matter of minutes in a parslied lemon-butter sauce generously sparked with—what else? —garlic.

Above: Chili-Stuffed Red Peppers. Fill tender red pepper cups with a hot, fast-fix mixture of chili, beans and corn, then top with tortilla chips for a great taste of olé—the easy way! Left: Escalloped Eggplant. For this easy-bake meatless dish, sliced eggplant, tomatoes, onion and cheese are layered on a heatproof serving platter then topped with buttered bread crumbs for oven-to-table convenience.

Right: White-Wine Sherbet. The ultimate in simplicity, this elegant mold is a combination of softened lemon sherbet and dry white wine frozen into a flavor fantasy for the eyes as well as the palate.

Above: Chocolate-Mousse Pie. Four simple ingredients—semi-sweet chocolate chips, sweet butter, eggs and brandy—combine to create a delight-fully sinful dessert that's extra easy when served in a pre-pared pie shell. Right: Fresh Pineapple Melba. Set sail for a tropical taste sensation with these colorful pineapple boats filled with fresh pineapple chunks and mini-scoops of fruited ice and drizzled with a thawed package of frozen raspberries.

*Left: Salad **Mediterranée**. Plain tuna and vegetables are easily transformed into an artistic display when alternately arranged on a serving platter and drizzled with a bottled vinaigrette dressing.*

Above: Oven-"Boiled" Dinner. Chock-full of goodness is one way to describe this hearty combination of knockwurst and vegetables oven-"boiled" in an apple-caraway broth and served with baked apples and a spicy mustard sauce.
Left: Roast Cornish Hens With Fresh Vegetables. Split Cornish hens, basted with a tangy lemon-soy mixture, nestle in a colorful medley of fresh cooked vegetables and giblets laced with a hint of garlic.

A Make-Ahead
Ambrosia Pie

*A*mbrosia *means "immortal," which is why the Greeks and the Romans gave this name to the food of the gods. One taste of this pie and you'll know why it is worthy of its name: It is the richest, most delicious pie you've ever tasted. The crunchy pecan-and-coconut crust is filled with mounds of sliced fresh oranges and a delicious apricot-orange glaze. It's a truly heavenly dessert and it's easy to make, too; all done up to one day before you plan to serve it! See opposite page for easy step-by-step directions.*

AMBROSIA PIE

CRUST
1 cup finely chopped pecans
1 cup canned sweetened flaked coconut
¼ cup sugar
⅓ cup butter or margarine (softened)

FILLING
4 large navel oranges
½ cup sugar
2 tablespoons cornstarch
1¼ cups orange juice

⅔ cup apricot preserves
1 teaspoon vanilla extract

Canned sweetened flaked coconut
(optional for garnish)

1. Prepare this pie up to one day before serving. Make Crust: Preheat oven to 375F. Put pecans, 1 cup coconut, ¼ cup sugar and the butter in a small bowl. Toss with two forks until ingredients are thoroughly combined and all dry ingredients are well moistened with butter.

2. Transfer all but ½ cup pecan-coconut mixture to a 9-inch pie plate; press evenly over the bottom and up the sides of the plate, forming a rim. Place pie plate in oven and bake for 20 minutes or until crust is lightly toasted.

3. Remove pie plate from oven and place on wire rack to cool. Make Filling: Remove peel and white membrane from each orange, using a very sharp knife. Cut oranges crosswise into ¼-inch-thick slices, and then in half. (Oranges should measure 4 cups.)

4. Put sugar and cornstarch in a 2-quart saucepan; mix well with a wooden spoon. Add orange juice, apricot preserves and vanilla extract. Place over moderately high heat and bring to a boil, stirring constantly. Cook for a few minutes until thickened.

5. Filling is done when it becomes translucent. Remove from heat and set aside to cool. Layer oranges in pie shell; pour filling mixture over top. Sprinkle reserved crust mixture evenly around edge of pie.

6. Place pie in the refrigerator to chill overnight or for at least 4 hours. To serve: Decorate edges of pie with more coconut, if desired. Cut into wedges and serve on individual serving plates. *Makes 6 to 8 servings.*

DAVID VIENS

continued from page 62

PEACHES IN MARSALA
(pictured)

1 can (1 lb, 14 oz) peach halves
½ cup cream marsala
1-inch cinnamon stick
Currant jelly

1. Drain peach halves, reserving 1 tablespoon of peach syrup.
2. In medium bowl, combine peaches, marsala, cinnamon stick and reserved syrup.
3. Refrigerate, covered, till peaches are well chilled—at least 2 hours.
4. To serve: Turn peaches and liquid into dessert dish. Dot center of each peach half with a little currant jelly. *Makes 4 to 6 servings.*

CHILI-STUFFED RED PEPPERS
(pictured)

4 small red peppers
1 can (12 oz) corn with red and green peppers
1 can (15 oz) chili with beans
Tortilla chips

1. Slice tops from red peppers; remove ribs and seeds. Cook in gently boiling water to cover 15 minutes, or until just tender; drain; place on small serving platter.
2. Meanwhile, combine corn and chili; heat just to boiling. Use to fill peppers. Garnish with tortilla chips. *Makes 4 servings.*

CHOCOLATE-MOUSSE PIE
(pictured)

1 pkg (6 oz) semisweet chocolate pieces
5 tablespoons sweet butter
4 egg yolks
2 tablespoons brandy
4 egg whites
Graham cracker pie shell, purchased
Whipped cream
Candied violets or chocolate curls
    (optional)

1. In top of double boiler, over hot, not boiling, water, melt chocolate and butter; stir to blend. Remove from hot water.
2. Using wooden spoon, beat in egg yolks, one at a time, beating well after each addition. Set aside to cool. Stir in brandy.
3. When the chocolate mixture has cooled, beat egg whites with rotary beater just until stiff peaks form when beater is slowly raised.

4. With rubber spatula or wire whisk, gently fold chocolate mixture into egg whites, using an under-and-over motion. Fold only enough to combine—there should be no white streaks.
5. Turn into pieshell. Refrigerate overnight.
6. To serve, decorate with whipped cream and, if desired, candied violets or chocolate curls. *Makes 6 to 8 servings.*

OVEN-"BOILED" DINNER
(pictured)

2 large baking potatoes
4 medium carrots
1 head cabbage (1 lb)
4 knockwurst (1 lb)
1¼ cups apple juice
½ teaspoon caraway seed
2 Granny Smith apples
1 tablespoon all-purpose flour
2 teaspoons brown mustard
½ teaspoon prepared horseradish

1. Preheat oven to 375F. Scrub and quarter potatoes. Pare carrots. Wash and quarter cabbage. Prick skin of knockwurst, or slash several times.
2. Arrange potatoes, carrots, cabbage and knockwurst in a large shallow casserole or roasting pan. Pour 1 cup apple juice over all. Sprinkle with caraway. Cover tightly with foil or roasting-pan lid.
3. Bake 35 to 40 minutes, or until potatoes are almost tender. Meanwhile, wash and quarter apples; remove cores. Place in casserole; bake 15 minutes longer or until apples are just tender.
4. Remove vegetables, knockwurst and apple to a serving platter. Pour liquid from pan into a small saucepan. Stir flour into the remaining ¼ cup juice. Stir into pan liquid. Bring to boiling, stirring until thickened. Stir in mustard and horseradish. Pour sauce over "boiled" dinner. *Makes 4 servings.*

BARBECUED CHICKEN WITH CORNBREAD STUFFING
(pictured)

5-lb ready-to-cook roasting chicken
1 cup bottled barbecue sauce
1 pkg (8 oz) cornbread-stuffing mix
1 can (15 or 16 oz) cream-style corn
¼ cup chopped onion
½ teaspoon dried sage leaves
Parsley (optional)

1. Preheat oven to 350F.
2. Wash chicken under cold running water; dry well with paper towels. Place on rack in large roasting pan. Tie legs together; twist wing tips under body.
3. Brush with ⅓ cup barbecue sauce. Roast, uncovered, 1½ hours. (If chicken starts to become too brown after 1 hour, place sheet of foil lightly over top.)
4. Meanwhile, make stuffing balls. Prepare cornbread stuffing as package label directs, substituting corn for water called for and adding onion and sage. Form into 10 balls; place on rack around chicken. Bake with chicken 30 minutes longer.
5. Place chicken on platter; brush with rest of barbecue sauce. Arrange stuffing balls around chicken. Garnish with parsley sprigs, if desired. *Makes 6 servings.*

CHICKEN BREASTS IN WHITE WINE
(pictured)

¼ cup butter or margarine
4 chicken breast halves, skinned and boned (about 1 lb)
⅔ cup dry white wine
¾ teaspoon salt
¼ teaspoon white pepper
4 parsley sprigs
4 lemon wedges

1. Rinse chicken breast halves under cold running water and pat dry with paper towels. In hot butter in skillet, sauté chicken until golden-brown—3 to 4 minutes on a side.
2. Add ⅓ cup wine, ½ teaspoon salt and the pepper. Bring just to boiling; reduce heat and simmer, covered, 20 minutes, or until tender.
3. Remove chicken to heated serving platter. To pan drippings, stir in ⅓ cup wine and ¼ teaspoon salt. Bring just to boiling, stirring to dissolve browned bits in pan; simmer about 5 minutes, or until slightly thickened.
4. Pour sauce over chicken. Garnish with parsley and lemon wedges. *Makes 4 servings.*

SCAMPI
(pictured)

¼ cup (½ stick) butter or margarine
¼ cup salad or olive oil
2 tablespoons chopped parsley
1 tablespoon garlic powder
½ teaspoon salt
Dash ground red pepper
2 tablespoons lemon juice
1 lb large fresh shrimp, shelled and
   deveined, leaving tails on
Lemon wedges (optional)

1. Preheat oven to 400F.
2. In large skillet with metal handle, or heatproof serving dish, melt butter; add oil, half the parsley, the garlic powder, salt, pepper and lemon juice; mix well.
3. Add shrimp, tossing gently with butter mixture; arrange in skillet in single layer.
4. Bake 8 to 10 minutes, or just until tender. Sprinkle with rest of chopped parsley. Bring skillet to the table, garnished with lemon wedges, if desired. *Makes 4 servings.*

ESCALLOPED EGGPLANT
(pictured)

1 medium eggplant (1¼ lb), sliced
   crosswise in ½-inch thick slices
1 large or 2 medium tomatoes (1 lb), sliced
1 large onion, thinly sliced
¾ cup (1½ sticks) butter or margarine,
   melted
½ teaspoon salt
½ teaspoon dried basil leaves
½ pkg mozzarella cheese (about 4 oz),
   sliced
½ cup packaged dried bread crumbs
2 tablespoons grated Parmesan cheese

1. Preheat oven to 450F.
2. On medium-size ovenproof platter, arrange eggplant slices, then tomato and onion slices. Drizzle with ¼ cup melted butter. Sprinkle with salt and basil. Bake, covered, 20 minutes.
3. Cut mozzarella slices in thirds; arrange over top. Stir crumbs into rest of melted butter; sprinkle over top; then sprinkle with Parmesan cheese.
4. Bake, uncovered, 10 minutes, or until cheese is bubbly. *Makes 4 servings.*

PEACHES WITH YOGURT

1 can (1 lb) diet peaches, drained
½ container (8-oz size) plain low-fat yogurt
Dash almond extract

1. Arrange peaches in small glass serving bowl.
2. Combine yogurt and almond ex-
tract; blend well with rubber spatula. Pour over peaches.
3. Refrigerate at least 2 hours, or until well chilled. *Makes 4 servings.*

WHITE-WINE SHERBET
(pictured)

2 pints lemon sherbet
1½ cups dry white wine
Strawberries, hulls left on (optional)
Seedless green grapes (optional)

1. Turn sherbet into large bowl; beat just until smooth, not melted. Quickly stir in the white wine to combine well.
2. Turn into a 6-cup decorative mold (line with plastic wrap first, for easier unmolding.) Freeze until firm—overnight.
3. To serve: Unmold on serving plate. Garnish edge with strawberries and grapes if desired. *Makes 6 to 8 servings.*

BROILED SWORDFISH WITH BARBECUE SAUCE

6 (8-oz size) swordfish steaks, ¾ inch thick
2 teaspoons salt
½ teaspoon pepper
½ teaspoon seasoned salt
5 tablespoons butter or margarine
¼ cup finely chopped onion
¼ cup finely chopped green pepper
½ cup chili sauce
½ cup catsup
⅓ cup lemon juice
2 tablespoons light-brown sugar
1 teaspoon dry mustard
1 tablespoon Worcestershire sauce
½ cup water

1. Wipe steaks with damp paper towels.
2. Combine 1 teaspoon salt, ¼ teaspoon pepper, and the seasoned salt; use to sprinkle both sides of fish.
3. Arrange on greased rack in broiler pan. Dot lightly with 1 tablespoon butter: broil, 4 inches from heat, 5 minutes.
4. Turn fish; dot with 1 tablespoon butter, and broil 7 minutes longer.
5. Meanwhile, make barbecue sauce: In 3 tablespoons hot butter in medium skillet, sauté onion and green pepper until tender—about 5 minutes.
6. Add rest of ingredients, ½ cup water and remaining salt and pepper.
7. Simmer, uncovered, 10 minutes. Serve over swordfish. *Makes 6 servings.*

FRESH PINEAPPLE MELBA
(pictured)

1 small ripe pineapple
¼ cup confectioners' sugar
1 pint lemon or pineapple ice or sherbet
1 pkg (10 oz) frozen raspberries, thawed
Fresh mint leaves

1. With a long-bladed sharp knife, cut pineapple into quarters, right through frond.
2. Remove pineapple from shells. Refrigerate shells.
3. Cut core from pineapple and discard. Cut pineapple into small chunks. Place chunks in medium bowl; stir in confectioners' sugar. Refrigerate until well chilled—at least 3 hours.
4. To serve: Fill shells with chilled pineapple. Top with small scoops of lemon ice (these may be prepared ahead and stored in freezer until ready to use). Spoon raspberries over ice in each shell. Garnish with mint leaves. Serve at once. *Makes 4 servings.*

SALAD MEDITERRANEE
(pictured)

1 lb new potatoes, unpeeled (see Note)
2 pkg (9-oz size) frozen whole green beans
1 cup (8 oz) bottled vinaigrette dressing
Lettuce
3 hard-cooked eggs, quartered
1 medium red onion, thinly sliced
2 medium tomatoes, cut in wedges
1 green pepper, cut into ¼-inch strips
2 cans (7-oz size) solid-pack tuna, drained
   and flaked
½ cup pitted ripe olives

1. In medium saucepan, boil potatoes, covered, 20 minutes or until tender; drain and let cool. Peel and cut into ¼-inch slices.
2. Cook beans according to package directions; drain. In shallow baking dish, place potatoes and beans. Toss with ½ cup dressing, cover and marinate in refrigerator, turning occasionally, at least 2 hours.
3. Chill remaining ingredients.
4. On large serving dish, arrange ingredients as pictured on page 65. Drizzle with remaining dressing. *Makes 6 servings.*

Note: To save time you may use 2 cans (16-oz size) sliced potatoes, drained. Omit Step 1. *continued on page 70*

continued from page 69

EGGS BAKED IN TOMATOES

1 can (1 lb) whole tomatoes
1 tablespoon all-purpose flour
½ green pepper, very thinly sliced
¼ teaspoon dried chervil leaves
4 eggs
½ teaspoon salt
1 tablespoon grated Parmesan cheese
Buttered toast

1. Preheat oven to 400F.
2. Pour tomatoes into an 8- or 9-inch au-gratin dish (or 8-inch pie plate). Stir flour into juice; mix well. Break up large pieces of tomato with a fork.
3. Add green peppers; sprinkle with chervil; mix well.
4. Carefully break eggs, one at a time, into tomato mixture. Sprinkle with salt and Parmesan cheese.
5. Bake 20 minutes, or until eggs are of desired doneness. Serve with buttered toast. *Makes 4 servings.*

PEARS DE MENTHE

2 quarts vanilla ice cream
¼ cup green crème de menthe
1 can (1 lb, 14 oz) pear halves, very well chilled
1 can (8 oz) chocolate syrup

1. Let ice cream stand at room temperature to soften. Turn into a large bowl.
2. With rubber spatula, swirl crème de menthe into soft ice cream just enough to make streaks; do not overmix. Turn ice cream into three or four ice-cube trays or a loaf pan; refreeze until firm—about 4 hours.
3. To serve: Drain pear halves; arrange on glass serving dish. Mound a scoop of ice cream in center of each pear. Pour the chocolate syrup over ice cream. *Makes 8 servings.*

TUNA (OR CHICKEN) MACARONI SUPPER SALAD

1 pkg (8 oz) elbow macaroni
1 cup mayonnaise or cooked salad dressing
½ cup Italian-style dressing
1 tablespoon prepared mustard
2 cups thinly sliced, pared cucumber
1½ cups diced tomato
½ cup diced green pepper
¼ cup coarsely chopped green onion
1 teaspoon salt
⅛ teaspoon pepper
2 cans (7 oz size) solid-pack tuna, drained; or 2 cups diced, cooked chicken
1 hard-cooked egg, chopped
Chicory
Chopped parsley

1. Cook elbow macaroni as package label directs. Drain; rinse with cold water.
2. In large bowl, combine mayonnaise, Italian-style dressing and mustard; mix-well.
3. Add cucumber, tomato, green pepper, green onion, salt, pepper, tuna (in large pieces) and macaroni; toss to mix well. Turn the mixture into a salad bowl.
4. Refrigerate, covered, until well chilled—about 4 hours.
5. Just before serving, garnish with egg, chicory and parsley. *Makes 8 to 10 servings.*

FRUIT IN PORT

2 pkg (12 oz size) frozen mixed fruit, partially thawed
½ cup white port

In medium bowl, combine fruit and port. Refrigerate until serving—at least 1 hour. *Makes 6 servings.*

SAUTEED SCALLOPS

2 lb sea scallops
6 tablespoons (¾ stick) butter or margarine
2 tablespoons chopped shallot
3 tablespoons dry vermouth or dry white wine
2 tablespoons chopped parsley
Lemon wedges (optional)
Parsley (optional)

1. Rinse scallops gently under cold water; drain. If large, cut in half.
2. In hot butter in large, heavy skillet, sauté shallot 2 minutes. Add scallops in a single layer (do half at a time, if necessary). Sauté over medium heat, stirring occasionally, until browned and cooked through—5 to 8 minutes.
3. With slotted spoon, remove to heated platter; keep warm.
4. Add vermouth and parsley to skillet; cook over low heat, stirring to dissolve browned bits, until bubbling—about 1 minute. Pour sauce over the scallops.
5. Garnish scallops with lemon wedges and additional parsley, if desired. *Makes 6 servings.*

PINEAPPLE WITH SOUR CREAM

2 cans (14-oz size) pineapple chunks, drained
¾ cup dairy sour cream
¼ cup maple or maple-flavored syrup
Light-brown sugar

1. Divide pineapple evenly into 6 dessert dishes.
2. In small bowl, combine sour cream with maple syrup until well blended. Spoon over fruit.
3. Refrigerate until well chilled—at least 1 hour.
4. Just before serving, sprinkle brown sugar over each. *Makes 6 servings.*

SPAGHETTI WITH CLAM SAUCE

2 cans (7½-oz size) minced clams
¼ cup olive or salad oil
¼ cup (½ stick) butter or margarine
2 or 3 garlic cloves, crushed
2 tablespoons chopped parsley
1½ teaspoons salt
1 pkg (8 oz) spaghetti, cooked
Grated Parmesan cheese

1. Drain clams, reserving ¾ cup liquid. Set aside.
2. In skillet, slowly heat oil and butter. Add garlic and sauté until golden. Remove from heat.
3. Stir in clam liquid, parsley and salt; bring to boiling. Reduce heat; simmer, uncovered, 10 minutes.
4. Add clams; simmer 3 minutes.
5. Serve hot over spaghetti, with Parmesan cheese. *Makes 4 to 6 servings.*

MELON A LA MODE

1 ripe honeydew melon or cantaloupe, chilled
1 pint vanilla ice cream
1 pkg (10 oz) frozen strawberries, thawed

1. Cut honeydew into quarters; remove and discard seeds.
2. To serve, spoon ice cream into each melon quarter. Spoon strawberries over ice cream. *Makes 4 servings.*

ROAST CORNISH HENS WITH FRESH VEGETABLES
(pictured)

2 fresh Cornish hens or 2 frozen
  Cornish hens, thawed
1½ teaspoons soy sauce
3 tablespoons lemon juice
½ lb broccoli (about ½ bunch)
¼ lb medium mushrooms, halved
½ lb green beans, trimmed
2 large carrots, pared and thinly sliced
1 garlic clove, minced
1 cup water
Lemon wedges

1. Preheat oven to 400F. Split and rinse hens and giblets. Pat dry with paper towels. In 3-quart oblong baking dish, place hens, cut side down, with giblets underneath.

2. Combine soy sauce and lemon juice; brush half of mixture on hens and bake 25 minutes. Brush with remaining mixture; bake an additional 10 to 15 minutes or just until tender.

3. Meanwhile, cut broccoli into flowerets; peel and slice stems.

4. Remove hens to serving platter and keep warm. Coarsely chop giblets. Reserve 1 teaspoon drippings in pan. Add mushrooms to drippings; sauté until golden, about 3 minutes. Add remaining vegetables, garlic and water; simmer, covered, 8 to 10 minutes, or until vegetables are just tender. Toss with giblets.

5. To serve, arrange vegetables and liquid around hens. Garnish with lemon wedges. *Makes 4 servings.*

CHICKEN FAJITAS

12 flour tortillas
1 can (16 oz) refried beans
Salad oil
2 medium onions, cut into ½-inch
  wedges
2 large jalapeño peppers, finely chopped
1 large green pepper, cut into ½-inch-
  wide strips
1 large red pepper, cut into ½-inch-wide
  strips
2 large garlic cloves, crushed
Salt
2 whole boneless chicken breasts,
  skinned and cut into ½-inch-wide
  strips (1¼ lb)
1 teaspoon chili powder
2 tablespoons chopped cilantro (fresh
  coriander) leaves
¼ cup (1 oz) shredded Monterey Jack
  cheese
Prepared picante sauce

1. Steam tortillas as package label directs. In small saucepan, heat refried beans; keep warm.

2. In 5-quart saucepan, heat 2 tablespoons salad oil over high heat. Add onions, peppers, garlic and ½ teaspoon salt; sauté 3 minutes, or until vegetables are tender-crisp. Remove to bowl. Add 2 tablespoons salad oil to drippings in pan. Add chicken, chili powder and ¾ teaspoon salt; sauté 5 minutes, or until chicken is tender. Return vegetable mixture to pan; heat through.

3. Place chicken mixture in bowl on large, warm serving platter; sprinkle with cilantro. Arrange tortillas around bowl. Spoon beans into small bowl; sprinkle with cheese. Spoon picante sauce into another small bowl. Pass tortillas and fillings. *Makes 6 servings.*

CHICKEN STIR-FRY WITH PILAF

1 egg white
2 boneless chicken breasts, skinned, cut
  into ¾-inch-wide strips (1¼ lb)
1 tablespoon rice vinegar
¼ cup soy sauce
1½ teaspoons brown sugar
1 pkg (7 oz) rice-pilaf mix
1 pkg (10 oz) frozen peas, thawed
2 tablespoons salad oil
1 large carrot, pared, cut crosswise and
  diagonally into ¼-inch-thick slices
2 green onions, chopped
1 can (6 oz) mushroom caps in butter,
  drained
2 teaspoons grated gingerroot
1 tablespoon cornstarch
1 cup chicken broth
¼ cup dry roasted peanuts

1. In small bowl, whisk egg white until frothy. Add chicken; toss to coat. Set aside. In another small bowl, combine rice vinegar, soy sauce and brown sugar; set aside.

2. Prepare rice-pilaf mix as package label directs; place in large bowl. Stir in peas. Keep warm.

3. In large skillet, heat 2 tablespoons salad oil over medium-high heat. Add chicken; sauté 1 minute, stirring. Add carrot, green onions, mushroom caps and ginger; cook, stirring 2 minutes, or until onions are tender-crisp.

4. In small bowl, mix cornstarch with ¼ cup chicken broth until blended. Stir in remaining broth; add to chicken mixture. Bring to boiling, stirring; boil 2 minutes. Stir in rice mixture; sprinkle with nuts. *Makes 6 servings.*

CRISPY SALMON STEAKS

½ cup (1 stick) butter or margarine,
  melted
⅛ teaspoon paprika
1 cup crushed saltines
1 cup crushed potato chips
6 (6- to 8-oz size) salmon steaks,
  ¾ inch thick
6 lemon wedges
6 parsley sprigs

1. Combine butter and paprika. Combine saltines and potato chips.

2. Wipe steaks with damp paper towels. Dip each steak into butter mixture, then roll in saltine mixture.

3. Arrange steaks on lightly greased broiler rack in broiler pan. Broil, 6 inches from heat, 5 to 8 minutes.

4. Turn; broil 5 to 8 minutes longer, or until fish flakes easily with fork. Serve each steak with a lemon wedge and parsley sprig. *Makes 6 servings.*

BAKED LOBSTER TAILS

Thawed frozen lobster tails (about
  6 oz each)
Butter or margarine
Round butter crackers
Worcestershire sauce
Lemon juice
Lemon wedges

1. Preheat oven to 400F.

2. With sharp knife, split each lobster tail down center but not all the way through. Arrange lobster tails in baking pan.

3. In split of each one, place 1 teaspoon butter; 2 crackers, crushed; 1 teaspoon Worcestershire; and 1 teaspoon lemon juice.

4. Bake 30 minutes, or until lobster is cooked through. Serve with lemon wedges. Serve 1 lobster tail per person.

GLAZED BROCCOLI MELANGE

¼ cup butter or margarine
1 tablespoon sugar
1 teaspoon salt
¼ cup beef broth
1 pkg (12 oz) baby carrots, pared
¾ lb rutabagas, pared and diced
1½ lb broccoli, cut into flowerets, stems
  pared and sliced crosswise into
  ½-inch pieces
1 can (10 oz) whole peeled chestnuts,
  drained and rinsed
1 red pepper, cut into 1-inch cubes

1. In a large skillet, melt the butter. Add the sugar and salt; stir to dissolve sugar. Add the beef broth, carrots and rutabagas; bring the mixture to boiling. Simmer 4 minutes.

2. Add the broccoli, chestnuts and red pepper; bring to boiling. Simmer, covered, 7 minutes, or until vegetables are tender-crisp. Remove lid; boil 2 minutes to reduce liquid. *Makes 6 servings.*♦

• DISHES •
To Serve When You Have No Time at All

Not having time to cook doesn't have to bring on panic at mealtime. This collection of tantalizing main dishes and desserts proves that a few simple ingredients and a little imagination are all that you need to serve up fabulous creations that really beat the clock. For instance, at lower right, there's a speedy "homemade" tomato sauce teamed with cooked frozen ravioli to make a fast family pleaser. Or for an Oriental flair, simmer beef strips, mushrooms, canned bean sprouts and frozen pea pods in a sweetened soy sauce. And when it's time for dessert, wow 'em with old-fashioned Peach Crumble served warm with vanilla ice cream. Or for culinary simplicity at its best, top a frozen cheesecake with pecan-sundae topping for a sinfully sweet finale...in no time at all! Recipes begin on page 74.

continued from page 73

RAVIOLI WITH TOMATO SAUCE
(Takes 25 minutes; pictured)

2 pkg (12-oz size) frozen ravioli with cheese
2 cans (1-lb size) stewed tomatoes
2 cans (8-oz size) tomato sauce or tomato
sauce with cheese
½ teaspoon dried oregano leaves
½ teaspoon salt
¼ teaspoon garlic powder
Grated Parmesan cheese

1. Cook ravioli, following package-label directions.
2. Meanwhile, in medium saucepan, combine tomatoes, tomato sauce, oregano, salt, and garlic powder.
3. Bring to boiling, stirring occasionally. Reduce heat, and let simmer, uncovered, until ravioli is done.
4. To serve: Arrange drained ravioli in center of serving dish. Spoon sauce around edge, drizzling a little over the ravioli. Sprinkle with Parmesan. *Makes 8 servings.*

CHICKEN IN PATTY SHELLS
(Takes ½ hour)

1 pkg (10 oz) frozen patty shells
3 whole chicken breasts, boned and
skinned (1½ lb)
2 tablespoons butter
1 can (10¾ oz) condensed cream-of-chicken soup
¼ cup dry sherry
¼ cup heavy cream
½ cup salted peanuts or almonds
2 tablespoons frozen chopped chives

1. Bake patty shells as package label directs.
2. Meanwhile, cut chicken breasts into 2-inch pieces.
3. Heat 2 tablespoons butter in Dutch oven. Add chicken; cook over medium heat, covered and stirring occasionally, 10 minutes.
4. Add undiluted cream-of-chicken soup, sherry, cream, salted peanuts and chives; bring to boiling, stirring. Lower heat, and simmer, uncovered, 5 minutes.
5. Serve in patty shells. *Makes 6 servings.*

ORANGE-CHOCOLATE CREAM CAKE
(Takes 10 minutes)

2 cups heavy cream
2 tablespoons confectioners' sugar
4 tablespoons grated orange peel
1 pkg (13½ oz) frozen frosted orange cake
1 pkg (14 oz) frozen frosted chocolate cake

1. Whip cream. Stir in 2 tablespoons sugar and 3 tablespoons grated orange peel.
2. Split orange cake in half lengthwise, to make 2 layers. Repeat with chocolate cake.
3. Place frosted orange layer, frosting up, on serving plate; place frosted chocolate layer, frosting up, on top. Next, add unfrosted orange layer.
4. Spread ⅔ cup whipped-cream mixture over orange layer; then add remaining chocolate layer. Frost top and sides of cake with remaining whipped-cream mixture. Sprinkle 1 tablespoon grated orange peel over top. Refrigerate until dessert time. *Makes 8 to 10 servings.*

CHINESE BEEF WITH PEA PODS
(Takes ½ hour; pictured)

2 lb rib steak, without bone
⅓ cup all-purpose flour
¼ teaspoon ground ginger
3 tablespoons salad oil
2 pkg (6-oz size) frozen whole mushrooms
or 2 cans (6-oz size) whole mushrooms,
drained
½ cup soy sauce
2 tablespoons light-brown sugar
1 can (1 lb) bean sprouts, drained
2 pkg (7-oz size) frozen Chinese pea pods
1 tablespoon cornstarch
2 tablespoons water

1. Wipe steak with damp paper towels. Trim excess fat. Cut meat into strips, ½ inch wide.
2. Mix ⅓ cup flour with ginger. Use to coat meat strips.
3. In 3 tablespoons hot oil in large skillet, sauté meat until browned on all sides — 8 to 10 minutes. Arrange mushrooms on top of meat; simmer, covered, 5 minutes.
4. Meanwhile, in small saucepan, combine soy sauce and brown sugar; bring to boiling. Reduce heat, and simmer, uncovered, 5 minutes.
5. Drain bean sprouts, and add, with pea pods, to meat mixture. Pour soy-sauce mixture over all; return to boiling. Reduce heat, and simmer, covered, 5 minutes longer.
6. Dissolve cornstarch in cold water.

Stir into meat mixture. Cook, stirring, until mixture is thickened and translucent — about 5 minutes. Serve immediately. *Makes 6 to 8 servings.*

JEWEL FRUIT TORTES
(Takes 15 minutes)

1 cup apricot preserves
1 can (1 lb, 1 oz) pear halves
1 can (1 lb, 1 oz) peach halves
1 can (9 oz) mandarin oranges
2 canned pineapple slices
1 pkg (11 oz) sponge-cake layers
6 tablespoons orange juice
2 maraschino cherries
1 can (4½ oz) toasted diced almonds
Whipped cream or frozen whipped topping
Grapes (optional)

1. Place 1 cup apricot preserves in small saucepan; cook over low heat until melted.
2. Meanwhile, drain pears, peaches, oranges and pineapple.
3. Place each sponge-cake layer on a serving plate. Prick surface gently with fork. Sprinkle each with 3 tablespoons orange juice; then brush top and side with some of melted preserves.
4. On each layer, arrange 3 peach halves alternately with 3 pear halves.
In center, place a pineapple ring, cut into 4 sections; decorate with cherry, as pictured. Fill spaces between peaches and pears with orange sections. Press ½ cup toasted almonds around edge of each layer. Glaze fruit with remaining preserves. Serve with whipped cream. Garnish with grapes, if desired. *Makes 2 tortes; serves 10.*

PEACH CRUMBLE
(Takes 15 minutes; pictured)

1 can (1 lb, 14 oz) cling-peach slices
½ lb pecan shortbread cookies
1 tablespoon light-brown sugar
1 teaspoon ground cinnamon
¼ cup (½ stick) butter
¼ cup chopped pecans
1 pint vanilla ice cream

1. Preheat oven to 400F. Drain peach

slices, and arrange in 8-inch round baking dish.

2. Place shortbread cookies in plastic bag; crush to fine crumbs with rolling pin. Add 1 tablespoon brown sugar and 1 teaspoon cinnamon. Sprinkle over peaches. Dot with butter. Sprinkle with chopped pecans.

3. Bake 8 to 10 minutes, or until topping is bubbling. Serve warm, with vanilla ice cream. *Makes 4 servings.*

SUNDAE PIE

(Takes 10 minutes)

1 quart strawberry ice cream
1 prepared 9-inch chocolate crumb pie
    shell
1 env (1 oz) no-melt unsweetened
    chocolate
½ cup corn syrup
1 pkg (7.2 oz) fluffy-white-frosting mix

1. Scoop ice cream into balls, and place in crumb crust (no need to bake). Place in freezer.

2. Make chocolate sauce: In small bowl, mix no-melt unsweetened chocolate with corn syrup until smooth. Set aside.

3. Prepare frosting mix, as package label directs.

4. Remove pie from freezer. Reserve 2 tablespoons chocolate sauce; pour rest over pie. Spread frosting over pie, swirling it on top. Drizzle with reserved chocolate sauce.

5. Return to freezer until serving time. It's best if not frozen more than 1 hour. *Makes 6 to 8 servings.*

BARBECUED
FLANK-STEAK PLATTER

(Takes ½ hour)

3 pkg (9-oz size) frozen French-fried
    potatoes
3 pkg (4-oz size) frozen fried onion rings
2 lb flank steak
1 bottle (1 lb, 2 oz) hickory-smoke
    barbecue sauce

1. In shallow roasting pan, mix potatoes with onion rings. Broil, 5 inches from heat, 10 minutes.

2. Meanwhile, wipe flank steak with damp paper towels.

3. Stir and turn potatoes and onions; drizzle with half the barbecue sauce. Top with flank steak. Cover with foil any potatoes and onions not covered by steak.

4. Broil 8 minutes, brushing steak once with barbecue sauce. Turn steak over; brush with sauce; broil 8 minutes longer, brushing once with remaining sauce. *Makes 6 to 8 servings.*

PECAN CHEESECAKE

(Takes ½ hour, pictured)

1 (1 lb, 2 oz) frozen cheesecake
1 jar (6½ oz) pecan-sundae topping

1. Place frozen cheesecake on serving platter. Top with pecan-sundae topping, carefully arranging pecans in circular platter.

2. Let stand at room temperature 30 minutes. Serve while still partially frozen. *Makes 6 servings.*

SAUTEED CHICKEN LIVERS

(Takes ½ hour)

1 lb chicken livers or 2 pkg (8-oz size)
    frozen chicken livers
½ cup cornmeal
Instant mashed potato for 8 servings
Water, milk, butter, salt
6 slices bacon
2 pkg (4-oz size) frozen fried onion rings
¼ teaspoon salt
3 tablespoons all-purpose flour
1 can (10½ oz) condensed beef bouillon
½ cup milk
Watercress or parsley

1. If using frozen livers, thaw just enough to separate. Coat livers with ½ cup cornmeal.

2. Prepare mashed potato, as package label directs; keep warm.

3. In large skillet, fry bacon until crisp. Drain on paper towels; set aside.

4. Sauté chicken livers in hot bacon drippings 5 minutes per side, or until golden-brown. Drain on paper towels.

5. Meanwhile, heat onion rings in oven or under broiler, as package label directs. Sprinkle with ¼ teaspoon salt.

6. Mound potato in center of serving platter. Toss chicken livers with onions, and arrange around potato. Keep warm.

7. Pour drippings from skillet; return 3 tablespoons. Stir in 3 tablespoons flour, undiluted beef bouillon, and ½ cup milk. Bring to boiling, stirring constantly. Reduce heat, and simmer, uncovered, 3 minutes.

8. Garnish platter with watercress or parsley. Pass gravy. *Makes 6 servings.*

PORK-AND-POTATO PIE

(Takes 25 minutes)

1½-lb piece cooked fresh-ham roll
1 can (1 lb, 4 oz) apple slices
¼ cup cracker meal
¼ teaspoon dried sage leaves
1½ teaspoons salt
¼ teaspoon pepper
4 tablespoons (½ stick) butter
1 can (13¾ oz) chicken broth, undiluted

Instant mashed potato for 8 servings
Milk, butter, salt

1. Preheat oven to 400F.

2. Cut ham roll into ½-inch cubes. Place in 8-inch round baking dish. Stir in undrained apples, cracker meal, sage, salt and pepper.

3. Dot top with 3 tablespoons butter. Add ¾ cup chicken broth. Cover baking dish with foil; bake 15 minutes.

4. Meanwhile, prepare mashed potato, as package label directs, substituting remaining 1 cup chicken broth for 1 cup water.

5. Remove foil from baking dish. Spoon potato over meat mixture, swirling top. Dot with 1 tablespoon butter.

6. Broil, 3 inches from heat, just until potato is golden-brown—5 to 7 minutes. *Makes 6 servings.*

CHERRY PIE DELUXE

(Takes 15 minutes)

1 cup dairy sour cream
2 teaspoons sugar
¼ teaspoon almond extract
1 (8-inch) baked cherry pie
2 tablespoons canned toasted slivered
    almonds

1. Preheat oven to 325F.

2. In small bowl, mix sour cream with sugar and almond extract.

3. Spread cream mixture over top of pie. Sprinkle with 2 tablespoons slivered almonds.

4. Bake 10 minutes. *Makes 4 or 5 servings.*

QUICK TORTE

(Takes 10 minutes)

12-oz frozen pound cake
3 tablespoons light or golden rum
¼ cup red-raspberry or strawberry
    preserves
¼ cup apricot or peach preserves
1 can (1 lb) ready-to-spread chocolate
    frosting

1. Split pound cake lengthwise into 3 even layers. Sprinkle each layer with 1 tablespoon rum.

2. Spread bottom layer with ¼ cup raspberry preserves. Set second layer on top; spread with ¼ cup apricot preserves. Add top layer. Frost top and sides with 1 cup chocolate frosting (see Note).

3. At serving time, cut into slices. *Makes 8 servings.*

Note: You will have about ½ cup chocolate frosting left over. It may be refrigerated, covered, for two weeks. Use it to sandwich vanilla wafers to have with ice cream for dessert.

◆

Quick, Delicious Dinners For Two

Most recipes are designed with at least four people in mind, and adapting them for two isn't always as simple as cutting the amounts in half. Large cuts of meat mean leftovers, and a diet of steaks and chops can be monotonous—not to mention expensive. And if you both work, time can be a problem. We asked our editors how they solved this problem, and have used their suggestions—and several of their recipes—to create delectable dishes that can be cooked in an hour or less. Left, festive Cornish Hens roasted with tarragon and wine and served with Wild-And-White-Rice Pilaf. Other alternatives (see page 78) include Pork Chops With Red Cabbage, Cheese-Stuffed Peppers and Chicken Cacciatore with new potatoes prepared in a pressure cooker.

continued from page 77

ROAST CORNISH HENS★
WILD-AND-WHITE-RICE PILAF★
GREEN SALAD
CANTALOUPE
WITH STRAWBERRIES
WHITE WINE

★Recipes given for starred dishes.

ROAST CORNISH HENS
(pictured)

2 Cornish hens (see Note), about 1¼ lb
   each
¼ cup (½ stick) butter or margarine
¾ cup dry white wine
Dried tarragon leaves
Salt
Pepper
2 garlic cloves, peeled
Garlic salt
1 tablespoon all-purpose flour
½ cup water
Wild-And-White-Rice Pilaf, below

1. Wash hens under cold running water; drain. Dry with paper towels.
2. Make basting sauce: Melt butter in saucepan; stir in ¼ cup wine and 1 teaspoon tarragon.
3. Sprinkle inside of each hen with ¼ teaspoon salt, ⅛ teaspoon pepper and 1 tablespoon tarragon. Place one garlic clove inside each. Sprinkle outside of each liberally with garlic salt. Refrigerate.
4. About 1 hour before serving, preheat oven to 400F. Place hens in a shallow roasting pan without a rack. Roast, basting often with sauce, 1 hour, or until hens are browned and tender.
5. Place hens on platter; keep warm.
6. Make gravy: Dissolve flour in remaining wine; stir into drippings in pan with ½ cup water. Bring to boiling; stirring until thickened.
7. To serve: Turn Wild-and-White-Rice Pilaf into center of platter; arrange hens on top. Serve with gravy. *Makes 2 servings.*
Note: If hens are frozen, let thaw overnight in refrigerator.

WILD-AND-WHITE-RICE PILAF

1¼ cups water
½ tablespoon butter or margarine
½ cup (about ½ pkg; 6-oz size)
   long-grain-and-wild-rice mix
1½ tablespoons seasoning from packet

1. Measure 1¼ cups water and the butter in medium saucepan.

2. Stir in rice mix and seasoning mix. Bring to boil.
3. Cover tightly, and cook over low heat until all water is absorbed—about 25 minutes

ANNA MARIE'S CHICKEN
CACCIATORE★
BUTTERED SPAGHETTI
ITALIAN BREAD
ANTIPASTO SALAD
CHIANTI

★Recipes given for starred dishes.

ANNA MARIE'S
CHICKEN CACCIATORE

½ chicken, cut into 2 serving pieces (about
   1¼ lb)
2 tablespoons oil
1 onion, sliced
1 can (16 oz) whole tomatoes, chopped
   (reserve ½ liquid)
1 garlic clove, minced
½ cup white wine
½ teaspoon salt
½ teaspoon dried oregano leaves
½ teaspoon dried basil leaves
¼ teaspoon pepper
2 tablespoons chopped parsley or
   2 teaspoons dried parsley flakes
6 small new potatoes, scrubbed
Chopped parsley

PRESSURE COOKER:

1. Wash chicken under cold running water and pat dry with paper towels. In pressure cooker, heat oil and brown chicken about 10 minutes.
2. Add remaining ingredients except parsley for garnish. Cook as manufacturer directs, approximately 12 minutes.
3. Turn into serving dish and sprinkle with chopped parsley. *Makes 2 servings.*

SKILLET METHOD:

1. Wash chicken under cold running

water and pat dry with paper towels. In medium skillet, heat oil and brown chicken; drain.
2. In medium bowl, blend remaining ingredients except parsley for garnish; add to skillet. Simmer, covered, stirring occasionally, 40 minutes or until chicken and potatoes are tender.
3. Turn into serving dish and sprinkle with chopped parsley. *Makes 2 servings.*

MICROWAVE METHOD:

1. Omit oil. Wash chicken under cold running water and pat dry with paper towels. In 2-quart casserole, heat chicken, covered, at HIGH (Full Power) 10 minutes, rearranging once; drain.
2. In medium bowl, blend remaining ingredients except parsley for garnish; add to chicken. Heat, covered, 8 minutes longer or until chicken and potatoes are tender, rearranging chicken once. Let stand, covered, 5 minutes.
3. Turn into serving dish and sprinkle with chopped parsley. *Makes 2 servings.*

PAM'S CHEESE-STUFFED
PEPPERS★
BAKED POTATOES
FRENCH BREAD
ORANGE SHERBET WITH
FRESH FRUIT
RED WINE

★Recipes given for starred dishes.

PAM'S CHEESE-STUFFED
PEPPERS

4 small green peppers, washed
¼ lb sharp Cheddar cheese, in ¼-inch
   cubes
¼ lb Swiss cheese, in ¼-inch cubes
¼ lb Gruyère cheese, in ¼-inch cubes
1 small tomato, in 4 slices
1 tablespoon packaged dry bread crumbs
1 teaspoon melted butter
½ teaspoon dried basil leaves

1. Preheat oven to 375F.
2. In boiling water (2 inches deep) in a 3-quart saucepan, parboil peppers until tender—10 minutes.
3. Drain peppers; cut off tops; remove seeds. Place, standing upright, on lightly greased baking dish.
4. Stuff peppers with the three kinds of cheese cubes, dividing evenly. Top each pepper with a tomato slice; then sprinkle with bread crumbs tossed with melted butter and basil, dividing evenly. Bake 20 minutes, or until hot and cheese is melted. *Makes 2 servings.*

PORK CHOPS WITH RED CABBAGE*
GREEN SALAD
CORNBREAD
PEARS IN PORT
COFFEE

*Recipes given for starred dishes.

PORK CHOPS WITH RED CABBAGE

2 loin or rib pork chops (1-inch thick)
2 tablespoons packaged dry bread
   crumbs
¾ teaspoon salt
¼ teaspoon pepper
3 tablespoons butter or margarine
1 jar (1 lb) sweet-and-sour red cabbage,
   drained
½ tart red apple, sliced
¼ cup red wine
2 tablespoons currant jelly
Salt

1. Wipe pork chops with damp paper towels. Pound chops on both sides with edge of saucer to flatten.
2. Mix the bread crumbs with ¾ teaspoon salt and the pepper. Use to coat chops evenly on each side.
3. In hot butter in medium skillet,

brown pork chops, turning on each side, until golden-brown—15 to 20 minutes. Remove pork chops. Drain off fat, leaving 1 tablespoon in skillet.
4. To drippings remaining in skillet, add red cabbage, apple, wine, currant jelly and salt to taste; mix well. Bring just to boiling; place pork chops on top of red-cabbage mixture; simmer, covered, 20 minutes. *Makes 2 servings.* ♦

continued from page 55

In large skillet, sauté bacon 2 minutes; drain on paper towels. In drippings in pan, sauté onion 1 minute. Blend in flour. Remove from heat; blend in dressing, water and honey. Bring to boiling, stirring; boil 1 minute, or until thickened. Stir in potatoes and reserved bacon until coated and hot. *Makes 4 servings.*

ENGLISH CREAM CUSTARD IN CHOCOLATE SHELLS
(pictured)

1 container (4.5 oz) prepared vanilla-
   flavored pudding
¾ cup heavy cream, whipped
½ teaspoon almond extract
8 (1-oz size) purchased chocolate shells
½ pint strawberries, hulled and sliced
½ pint blueberries, rinsed and drained

In bowl, blend the pudding with whipped cream and almond extract; spoon into 4 chocolate shells and top with berries, dividing evenly. Top each with a chocolate shell. *Makes 4 servings.*

MINT-BROILED LAMB CHOPS
(pictured)

GLAZE
¼ cup mint-flavored apple jelly
1 large clove garlic, crushed
¼ teaspoon dried rosemary leaves,
   crushed
1 tablespoon Dijon-style mustard

8 rib lamb chops (½-inch thick)

In saucepan, bring glaze ingredients to boiling, stirring. Broil chops on rack over broiler pan 2 inches from heat 3 minutes. Brush grilled side of chops with half the glaze; broil 3 minutes. Repeat for other side of chops. Serve on warm platter. *Makes 4 servings.* ♦

continued from page 57

FLOUNDER MARINARA

2 tablespoons butter or margarine
1 cup sliced onion
2 tablespoons all-purpose flour
1 can (1 lb) stewed tomatoes
½ teaspoon dried basil leaves
1 pkg (16 oz) frozen flounder fillets
¼ cup grated Parmesan cheese

1. Preheat oven to 375F.
2. In hot butter in skillet with heatproof handle, over medium heat, sauté sliced onion, stirring, about 5 minutes. Remove from heat; stir in flour, stewed tomatoes and basil. Mix until smooth.
3. Slice frozen fillets in 6 pieces (thaw slightly, if necessary). Place in sauce. Sprinkle with Parmesan cheese.
4. Bake, covered, 10 minutes. Remove cover; bake 5 to 7 minutes longer, or until golden. *Makes 6 servings.*
Note: If desired, remove cover; broil 6 inches from heat until golden—5 to 7 minutes.

QUICK SCALLOP PAELLA

2¼ cups cold water
1 cup long-grain white rice
Salt
¼ teaspoon dried thyme leaves
Butter or margarine
1 lb sea scallops, washed and drained
1 medium green pepper, cut into strips
1 medium red pepper, cut into strips
4 (3-inch) slices salami, cut into eighths

1. In heavy, medium-size saucepan with tight-fitting cover, combine 2¼ cups cold water with the rice, 1 teaspoon salt, the thyme and 1 tablespoon butter. Bring to boiling, uncovered.
2. Reduce heat; simmer, covered, 15 to 20 minutes, or until rice is tender and liquid is absorbed.
3. In 2 tablespoons butter in large skillet, sauté scallops 5 minutes, turning.
4. Add green and red pepper; sauté, stirring, until pepper and scallops are tender—about 5 minutes.
5. Add cooked rice and the salami to scallop mixture. Simmer, covered, 5 minutes. *Makes 4 to 6 servings.* ♦

Like Mother Used to Make, But Quicker

*H*omemade snacks are the best kind—and the most economical. We used all the easy shortcuts we knew for these after-school treats. Remember the little pastries your mother made from leftover dough? Ours were made from piecrust mix. We used buttermilk refrigerator biscuits for Doughnuts and Cinnamon Twists, bread for the Toasted-Coconut Jelly Rolls. And we've revived icebox cookies, the kind you can keep in the fridge, ready to slice and bake as the kids walk in the door. Recipes for all these and more begin on page 82.

continued from page 81

Photograph on pages 80 and 81: 1. Vanilla-Nut and Butterscotch Icebox Cookies. 2. Pinwheel Icebox Cookies. 3. Scotch Oatmeal Shortbread. 4. Popcorn Balls. 5. Dutch Nut Strips. 6. Toasted-Coconut Jelly Rolls. 7. Quick Glazed Doughnuts and "Holes." 8. Cinnamon Twists. 9. Turnovers. 10. Jelly Tarts.

VANILLA-NUT ICEBOX COOKIES

2 cups sifted all-purpose flour
1½ teaspoons baking powder
⅔ cup (1 stick plus 2⅔ tablespoons) butter or margarine, softened
1 cup sugar
1 egg
1 teaspoon vanilla extract
1 cup finely chopped salted peanuts

1. On sheet of waxed paper, sift flour with baking powder. In large bowl, with wooden spoon or portable electric mixer at medium speed, beat butter until light. Gradually beat in sugar. Add egg and the vanilla extract; continue beating until very light and fluffy.

2. At low speed, beat in half of flour mixture; mix in rest with a wooden spoon to form a stiff dough. Add chopped nuts, mixing to combine well.

3. Turn out dough onto a lightly floured surface. Divide in half. Shape each half into a roll 7 inches long. Wrap each roll in plastic wrap or foil. Refrigerate until firm—about 8 hours or overnight. Or place in freezer 1 hour, or until firm. (Rolls of cookie dough may be stored in the refrigerator for a week to ten days, longer in freezer. Slice and bake as desired.)

4. Preheat oven to 375F. With sharp knife, cut as many ¼-inch slices as desired for baking at one time. Rewrap rest of roll and refrigerate. Place slices, 2 inches apart, on ungreased cookie sheets. Bake 8 to 10 minutes, or until lightly browned. With spatula, lift cookies to wire rack. Let cool completely. *Makes about 5 dozen.*

BUTTERSCOTCH ICEBOX COOKIES

3½ cups sifted all-purpose flour
1 teaspoon baking soda
1 cup (2 sticks) butter or margarine, softened
2 cups light-brown sugar, packed
2 eggs
1 teaspoon vanilla extract
1 cup chopped salted peanuts

1. Sift the flour with the baking soda.

2. In large bowl of electric mixer, at medium speed, beat butter until light. Gradually beat in sugar. Add eggs and vanilla; continue beating until very light and fluffy.

3. At low speed, beat in half of flour mixture until smooth. Mix in rest with a wooden spoon to form a stiff dough. Add peanuts; mix well.

4. Turn out dough onto lightly floured surface. Divide the dough in thirds. Shape each third into a roll 8 inches long.

5. Wrap each in plastic wrap or foil; refrigerate until firm—about 8 hours or overnight. Or place rolls in freezer for 1 hour, or until firm. (Rolls may be stored in refrigerator a week to ten days, longer in freezer.)

6. Preheat oven to 375F. With sharp knife, cut as many ¼-inch slices as desired for baking at one time. Rewrap rest of roll; refrigerate.

7. Place slices, 2 inches apart, on ungreased cookie sheets. Bake 8 to 10 minutes, or until lightly browned. Remove to wire rack; cool. *Makes about 8 dozen.*

PINWHEEL ICEBOX COOKIES

FILLING

1½ cups raisins, chopped
¼ cup granulated sugar
2 tablespoons lemon juice
⅓ cup water
¼ cup chopped walnuts

COOKIE DOUGH

2 cups unsifted all-purpose flour
½ teaspoon salt
½ teaspoon baking soda
¾ cup (1½ sticks) butter or margarine, softened
½ cup granulated sugar
½ cup dark-brown sugar, packed
1 egg, beaten
½ teaspoon vanilla extract

1. Make Filling: In small saucepan, combine raisins, ¼ cup granulated sugar, the lemon juice and ⅓ cup water. Cook, stirring constantly, 5 minutes, or until thickened and liquid has been absorbed. Remove from heat; stir in nuts; cool completely.

2. Make Cookie Dough: Sift flour with salt and baking soda.

3. In small bowl of electric mixer, at medium speed, cream butter with both kinds of sugar until light and fluffy. Beat in the egg and vanilla extract.

4. At low speed, beat in flour mixture just until combined. Divide dough in half.

5. Roll out dough, one half at a time, between two sheets of waxed paper, to form 11-by-7-inch rectangle. Spread each rectangle with half of filling.

6. From wide end, roll up rectangles tightly. Wrap each in waxed paper; refrigerate 2 hours or overnight. Or place in freezer for 1 hour, or until firm. (Rolls may be stored in refrigerator a week to ten days, longer in freezer. Bake fresh as desired.)

7. Preheat oven to 375F. With sharp knife, slice cookies ¼ inch thick. Arrange, 1 inch apart, on lightly greased cookie sheets. Bake 8 to 10 minutes, or until golden. *Makes 6 dozen.*

SCOTCH OATMEAL SHORTBREAD

3 cups quick-cooking oats
⅔ cup sugar
½ cup sifted all-purpose flour
½ teaspoon salt
¾ cup (1½ sticks) butter or margarine
1 teaspoon vanilla extract

1. Preheat oven to 350F. Lightly grease a 13-by-9-by-2-inch pan.

2. In large bowl, combine oats, sugar, flour and salt.

3. With pastry blender or 2 knives, cut in butter until texture of coarse cornmeal. Stir in vanilla extract; mix well.

4. With hands, press mixture evenly into prepared pan.

5. Bake 20 to 25 minutes, or until golden. Cool slightly.

6. Cut into bars 2" × 1½" while still warm. Let cool completely in pan. *Makes 32 bars.*

RAISIN-PEANUT POPCORN BALLS

5 cups freshly popped popcorn
1 cup raisins
1 cup salted peanuts
¾ cup light-brown sugar, packed
⅔ cup granulated sugar
½ cup water
⅓ cup light corn syrup
½ teaspoon vanilla extract

1. In large bowl, combine popcorn, raisins and peanuts; toss to mix well.

2. In heavy saucepan, combine both

kinds of sugar, ½ cup water and the corn syrup. Stir to mix well. Bring to boiling; boil, without stirring, to 250F on candy thermometer, or until a small amount in cold water forms a hard ball. Remove from heat; add vanilla extract.

3. Pour syrup over popcorn mixture. Mix well with wooden spoon. With buttered hands, quickly form into balls. *Makes 10 popcorn balls.*

CEREAL POPCORN BALLS:

Make recipe above, substituting 2 cups favorite prepared cereal, such as puffed wheat, puffed rice or wheat flakes, for peanuts and raisins.

PEANUT-BUTTER POPCORN BALLS

3 cups miniature marshmallows
2 tablespoons butter or margarine
½ cup chunk-style peanut butter
5 cups freshly popped popcorn

In large, heavy kettle over low heat, cook marshmallows, butter and peanut butter, stirring, until marshmallows are melted. Add the popcorn; stir to mix well. With buttered hands, form into balls. *Makes 6 large popcorn balls.*

TOASTED-COCONUT JELLY ROLLS

12 slices white bread, crust removed (do not use thin-sliced bread)
¼ cup light-brown sugar, packed
¼ cup margarine, softened
¾ cup flaked coconut
Jelly, jam or peanut butter

1. Preheat oven to 425F. Roll each slice of bread slightly with rolling pin.
2. Cream sugar with margarine; use to spread on bread slices. Sprinkle coconut in a layer on a sheet of waxed paper.
3. Place bread slices, sugar side down, on coconut, pressing into coconut. Spread top of bread with jelly. Roll up from short side, to form small jelly rolls.
4. Place, seam side down, on cookie sheet. (Secure rolls with wooden pick, if necessary.) Bake 4 to 5 minutes or until golden. Serve warm. *Makes 12.*

DUTCH NUT STRIPS

½ cup (1 stick) butter or margarine, softened
½ cup light-brown sugar, packed
1 teaspoon vanilla extract

1 cup sifted all-purpose flour
½ cup finely chopped salted peanuts

1. Preheat oven to 375F.
2. In large bowl, using wooden spoon, beat butter, brown sugar and the vanilla extract until smooth and fluffy.
3. Add flour, mixing until well combined. Stir in nuts.
4. With palms of hands (lightly floured), pat dough evenly onto an ungreased cookie sheet, to form a rectangle 10 inches wide and 15 inches long.
5. Bake 10 to 12 minutes, or until golden-brown.
6. With sharp knife, immediately cut hot cookies into strips 1 inch wide and 2½ inches long.
7. Remove to wire rack; cool completely. Store in cookie jar. *Makes 5 dozen.*

LITTLE PASTRIES — TURNOVERS, JELLY TARTS, ROUNDS

1 cup piecrust mix
Water
Applesauce, or drained canned crushed pineapple, or preserves
Sugar
Jelly or jam
Confectioners' sugar

1. Preheat oven to 400F or 425F (see variations below).
2. Mix piecrust mix with 2 tablespoons cold water as package label directs. Roll out to form a 12-inch circle, about ⅛ inch thick. Cut as desired.
3. For Turnovers, cut into circles (2, 3 or 4 inches in diameter). Cover half of pastry with applesauce or crushed pineapple or preserves; use 1 tablespoon filling for 4-inch; ½ tablespoon for 3-inch; 1 teaspoon for 2-inch. Moisten edges of turnovers with water; fold other half of pastry over; pinch edge together to seal. Brush tops with water. Prick with fork. Place on cookie sheet and bake at 400F 20 minutes or until pastries are golden-brown. For Rounds: Cut 2-inch circles.

Brush with water; prick with fork. Bake pastries, at 425F, 8 minutes.

4. For Jelly Tarts, cut 2-inch circles; cut ½-inch rounds from centers of half the circles. Brush with water, prick with fork and bake at 425F, 8 minutes. Cool. Spread half of 2-inch rounds with jelly or preserves; top with rounds with hole in center.

5. Sift confectioners' sugar lightly over tops of all pastries. *Makes 9 to 12 assorted pastries.*

QUICK GLAZED DOUGHNUTS AND "HOLES"

1 pkg (8 oz) buttermilk refrigerator biscuits
Honey or orange marmalade
Water (optional)
⅓ cup (5⅓ tablespoons) butter or margarine, melted
Cinnamon-sugar (see Note)

1. Preheat oven to 450F.
2. Flatten biscuits; cut out center from each (about ½ inch). Stretch each biscuit to form a 4-inch ring. Place on cookie sheet.
3. Bake 6 to 8 minutes, or until golden-brown.
4. Bake centers 4 to 6 minutes or until golden-brown.
5. While still warm, brush doughnuts and "holes" with honey or marmalade thinned with a little water, or dip in melted butter; then roll in cinnamon-sugar. *Makes 10 doughnuts and "holes."*

Note: Mix ⅓ cup granulated sugar with 1 teaspoon ground cinnamon.

CINNAMON TWISTS

1 pkg (8 oz) buttermilk refrigerator biscuits
Butter or margarine
¼ cup sugar
1 teaspoon ground cinnamon

VANILLA GLAZE
¼ cup confectioners' sugar
¼ teaspoon vanilla extract
Water

1. Preheat oven to 400F. Lightly grease a cookie sheet.
2. Flatten each biscuit into a 4-inch round. Spread each with ½ teaspoon butter. Combine sugar and cinnamon and sprinkle on buttered rounds. Cut in half. Place one half on top of other and twist together. Press ends on cookie sheet to secure.
3. Bake 8 to 10 minutes; cool slightly.
4. For Vanilla Glaze, combine confectioners' sugar, vanilla extract and a little water. Drizzle glaze over warm twists. *Makes 10 twists.* ◆

THREE

DO-AHEAD COOKING: TIME WELL SPENT

◆

Spending spare time now to save time later when it's in short supply is the basis of do-ahead cooking. It means thinking ahead to those times and occasions when you know you'll be the busiest: the day of a big party, for example, or certain week nights when it seems there's never enough time to prepare a good meal for the family. With hectic schedules demanding more and more of your spare time, do-ahead meals have become the cornerstone in the busy cook's repertoire. The challenge, of course, is to find recipes that offer quick preparation, use of simple ingredients and exciting, appetizing results. We've met that challenge with this section full of delicious do-aheads—ranging from appetizers to desserts (and almost everything in between)— guaranteed to help turn otherwise frantic situations into relaxed and enjoyable occasions to savor with family and friends.

DAZZLING
Cook-Ahead Meals

Some dishes are especially good when made in advance. The ones that follow can easily be cooked ahead and refrigerated (in fact, they're at their best when left to chill overnight). At dinnertime, just serve them cold or at room temperature. Above, a beautiful Fresh Cold Beet Soup, ruby-red and sparked with the flavor of onion and lemon, topped with dollops of sour cream and bits of lacy dill. A mere half-pound of shrimp goes a long way when the shrimp are split and served with spaghetti (below), in a rich tomato sauce spiked with herbs and garlic.

GEORGE RATKAI

A salad of tender new potatoes and crisp zucchini tossed in a zesty, wine-flavored vinaigrette dressing.

A Rosedale Pasta Salad: spirals of tender macaroni tossed with broccoli flowerets, crisp pea pods, red peppers and plump cherry tomatoes—glistening in a dressing of lemon, garlic and herbs.

Above, an ah-so-good combination of chicken chunks, broccoli, scallions and rice is attractively arranged on a fan of crisp pea pods and topped with an oriental-style sauce. Below left, Vegetable Salad Provencale: The freshest and most colorful garden vegetables—green peppers, yellow squash, rosy tomatoes—are cut in large, luscious chunks and marinated in a dressing lively with basil and coriander. Top off the warmest evening with the most glorious Grasshopper Pie (below right)—a cool green cloud of chiffon flavored with crème de menthe and crème de cacao, in a chocolate-cookie crust. Recipes for all these and more begin on page 89.

VEGETABLE SALAD PROVENCALE
(pictured)

2 large green peppers (¾ lb)
2 medium summer squash (¾ lb)
6 tablespoons olive or salad oil
3 medium onions (¾ lb), sliced
2 garlic cloves, crushed
1 teaspoon dried basil leaves
½ teaspoon ground coriander
1 bay leaf, crumbled
1 teaspoon salt
Dash pepper
3 tablespoons lemon juice
½ cup dry white wine
3 medium tomatoes (1 lb), sliced ¼ inch thick
Chopped parsley

DO AHEAD

1. Wash peppers; halve. Remove ribs and seeds. Cut lengthwise into ½-inch-wide strips; cut strips into 1-inch-long pieces.

2. Scrub summer squash; cut into round slices, ¼ inch thick.

3. In 2 tablespoons hot oil in large skillet, sauté onion and garlic 5 minutes, or until onion is transparent. With slotted spoon, remove to medium bowl.

4. Add 2 tablespoons oil to skillet. In hot oil, sauté green pepper, turning frequently, 5 minutes. With slotted spoon, remove to bowl.

5. Add 2 tablespoons oil to skillet. In hot oil, sauté squash, turning frequently, 5 minutes.

6. Return onion and green pepper to same skillet. Stir in basil, coriander, bay leaf, salt, pepper, lemon juice and white wine; mix well; bring mixture to boiling. Layer tomato slices on top; simmer, covered, 5 minutes.

7. Turn into a shallow serving dish; refrigerate, covered, until well chilled—overnight.

TO SERVE

8. Before serving, sprinkle with chopped parsley. *Makes 8 servings.*

SHRIMP SPAGHETTI
(pictured)

1 pkg (8 oz) spaghetti
½ lb unshelled raw shrimp
¼ cup salad or olive oil
½ cup chopped onion
2 garlic cloves, crushed
3 medium tomatoes (1 lb), peeled and coarsely chopped; or 1 can (1 lb) tomatoes, undrained
⅛ teaspoon pepper
1 teaspoon dried basil leaves
½ teaspoon salt
¼ cup chopped parsley
½ cup pitted black olives
Grated Parmesan cheese

DO AHEAD

1. Cook spaghetti according to package directions; drain well; return to kettle.

2. Rinse shrimp; remove shells, and devein. Using a small sharp knife, split each shrimp in half down the back.

3. In hot oil in medium skillet, over medium heat, sauté onion, garlic and shrimp, stirring, until onion is golden and shrimp turn pink—about 5 minutes. Remove shrimp; set aside.

4. Add tomatoes, pepper, basil and salt; bring to boiling; simmer, uncovered, 5 minutes. Return shrimp to skillet.

5. Pour shrimp mixture over spaghetti; toss until well coated.

6. Turn onto a platter; garnish with parsley and olives. Cover with plastic wrap and refrigerate.

TO SERVE

7. Remove from refrigerator 1 hour before serving time. Serve, with grated Parmesan cheese, at room temperature. *Makes 4 servings.*

BAKED CHICKEN BREASTS SUPREME

6 (12-oz size) chicken breasts
2 cups sour cream
¼ cup lemon juice
4 teaspoons Worcestershire sauce
4 teaspoons celery salt
2 teaspoons paprika
1 garlic clove, finely chopped
4 teaspoons salt
½ teaspoon pepper
1¾ cups packaged dry bread crumbs
½ cup (1 stick) butter or margarine
½ cup shortening

DO AHEAD

1. Cut chicken breasts in half; wash under cold running water and pat dry with paper towels.

2. In large bowl, combine sour cream with lemon juice, Worcestershire, celery salt, paprika, garlic, salt and pepper.

3. Add chicken to sour-cream mixture, coating each piece well.

4. Refrigerate, covered, overnight.

NEXT DAY

5. Preheat oven to 350F.

6. Remove chicken from sour-cream mixture. Roll in crumbs, coating evenly. Arrange in single layer in large, shallow baking pan.

7. Melt butter and shortening in small saucepan. Spoon half over chicken.

8. Bake chicken, uncovered, 45 minutes. Spoon rest of butter mixture over chicken.

9. Bake 10 to 15 minutes longer, or until chicken is tender and nicely browned. *Makes 12 servings.*

FRESH COLD BEET SOUP
(pictured)

2 bunches baby beets, with beet greens (1 lb each with leaves)
Water
1 large onion
3 tablespoons snipped fresh dill
1 teaspoon salt
¼ cup lemon juice
3 tablespoons light-brown sugar
Sour cream
Snipped fresh dill

DO AHEAD

1. Gently wash beets, leaving skins intact. Remove leaves, and store for another use.

2. Place beets in large saucepan. Cover with 4 cups cold water; bring to boiling. Reduce heat; simmer, covered, 40 to 45 minutes, or until beets are tender.

3. With slotted utensil, remove beets; cool, then slip off skins. Reserve beet juice.

4. Coarsely grate beets and onion on coarse grater; or use food processor.

5. Add water to beet juice to make 4 cups. Return to saucepan; return to boiling. Add grated beets, onion and 3 tablespoons dill. Simmer, uncovered, 10 minutes.

6. Add salt, lemon juice and brown sugar; stir until sugar is dissolved. Remove from heat. Turn into a bowl.

7. Refrigerate, covered, until well chilled—several hours or overnight.

TO SERVE

8. Top each serving with a spoonful of sour cream and a little snipped dill. *Makes 6 cups, 8 (¾-cup) servings.*

CHICKEN ORIENTALE
(pictured)

2 whole chickens, each cut into 8 pieces (about 2½ lb each)
¼ cup salad oil
1 large carrot, pared and sliced diagonally
1 teaspoon salt
¼ teaspoon pepper

SAUCE

1 can (15¼ oz) unsweetened pineapple chunks
Water
½ cup sugar
2 tablespoons cornstarch

continued on page 90

continued from page 89

¾ cup cider vinegar
1 tablespoon soy sauce
¼ teaspoon ginger
1 chicken-bouillon cube

½ small green pepper, cut in ¼-inch-wide
    strips, then into diagonal slices
1 medium red pepper, cut in ¼-inch-wide
    strips
1 pkg (7 oz) precooked rice
1 tablespoon salad oil
1 cup broccoli flowerets
1 pkg (6 oz) frozen Chinese pea pods

1. Wash chicken under cold running water and pat dry with paper towels.

2. Heat oil in large skillet. Add chicken, a few pieces at a time, and brown on all sides. Remove as browned to shallow roasting pan, arranging pieces skin side up. Strew carrot slices over and around chicken. Sprinkle with salt and pepper.

3. Meanwhile, preheat oven to 350F.

4. Make Sauce: Drain the pineapple chunks, pouring syrup into 2-cup measure. Add water to make 1¼ cups.

5. In medium saucepan, combine sugar, cornstarch, pineapple syrup, vinegar, soy sauce, ginger and bouillon cube; bring to boiling, stirring constantly. Boil 2 minutes. Pour over chicken.

6. Bake, uncovered, 30 minutes. Add pineapple chunks and green and red pepper; bake 30 minutes longer, or until chicken is tender.

7. Meanwhile, prepare rice as package directs.

8. About 5 minutes before chicken is done, heat 1 tablespoon salad oil in a medium skillet. Stir-fry broccoli in hot oil, tossing to coat, about 1 minute. Cover, and cook 2 minutes longer.

9. With a slotted spoon lift broccoli to a small bowl; keep warm.

10. In same skillet, toss frozen pea pods just to heat through, about 2 minutes.

11. To serve, turn prepared rice onto a large serving platter; spoon baked chicken and vegetables over rice. Garnish chicken with broccoli flowerets and edge the platter with pea pods, as pictured. *Makes 8 servings.*

GRASSHOPPER PIE
(pictured)

Chocolate-Cookie-Crumb Pie Shell,
    purchased or homemade, recipe
    follows

FILLING
4 eggs, separated
2 env unflavored gelatine
¾ cup milk

¾ cup sugar
⅛ teaspoon salt
⅓ cup green crème de menthe
⅓ cup white crème de cacao
1½ cups heavy cream
Green food color (optional)

Grated chocolate

DO AHEAD

1. Make or purchase pie shell; refrigerate homemade shell.

2. Make Filling: Let egg whites warm to room temperature in large bowl of electric mixer—about 1 hour.

3. Sprinkle gelatine over milk in top of double boiler; let soften 3 minutes.

4. Add egg yolks, ½ cup of the sugar and the salt; beat with rotary beater or fork until well blended. Cook over boiling water, stirring constantly, about 5 minutes, or until gelatine dissolves and custard coats a metal spoon.

5. Remove double-boiler top from bottom. Stir crème de menthe and crème de cacao into custard mixture.

6. Set double-boiler top in bowl of ice cubes and water. Cool, stirring occasionally, 10 to 15 minutes, or until custard mixture is the consistency of unbeaten egg white.

7. Meanwhile, in medium bowl, whip heavy cream; refrigerate. Also, beat egg whites until soft peaks form when beater is slowly raised. Gradually beat in remaining ¼ cup sugar. Continue beating until stiff peaks form.

8. With rubber spatula or wire whisk, fold custard mixture into egg whites. Then fold in whipped cream and 1 or 2 drops food color, if desired, until mixture is just combined.

9. Mound high in prepared pie shell. Sprinkle grated chocolate around edge. Refrigerate 3 hours, or until filling is firm.

TO SERVE

10. Serve chilled. *Makes 10 servings.*

CHOCOLATE-COOKIE-CRUMB
PIE SHELL

25 crisp chocolate wafers (about 2-inch
    diameter), broken
¼ cup (½ stick) butter or margarine,
    melted

1. In blender or processor, place cookies and melted butter; blend just until cookies become crumbs.

2. Turn into 9-inch pie plate. With back of spoon, press evenly on bottom and side and on rim.

ROSEDALE PASTA SALAD BOWL
(pictured)

DRESSING
½ cup olive or salad oil
¼ cup lemon juice
1 teaspoon salt
¼ teaspoon freshly ground pepper
⅛ teaspoon crushed red pepper
2 garlic cloves, crushed
2 tablespoons snipped fresh chives
1 tablespoon snipped fresh basil or
    1 teaspoon dried basil leaves
2 teaspoons snipped fresh dill or
    ½ teaspoon dried dillweed

1 pkg (8 oz) spirelle pasta (or other pasta)

VEGETABLES
2 tablespoons olive or salad oil
½ lb broccoli, cut into 1½-inch flowerets
½ red pepper, cut into ¼-inch-wide strips
¼ lb whole fresh snow pea pods, ends
    trimmed
½ pint cherry tomatoes, washed, stems
    removed
¼ cup chopped parsley

DO AHEAD

1. Make Dressing: In jar with tight-fitting lid, combine oil, lemon juice, salt, pepper, red pepper, garlic, chives, basil and dill; shake until well combined.

2. Cook spirelle as package label directs; drain; turn into large salad bowl; add dressing; toss to combine.

3. Prepare Vegetables: In the oil in a large skillet, toss broccoli flowerets and red-pepper strips; stir-fry 5 minutes, or until vegetables are just crisp. Add pea pods; cook 1 minute. Cook vegetables, covered, 1 to 2 minutes. Do not overcook. Cool completely.

4. In a glass or pottery salad bowl, lightly toss spirelle, vegetables, cherry tomatoes and parsley until well coated with dressing. Refrigerate several hours, to chill well.

TO SERVE

5. Toss well before serving. *Makes 6 servings.*

NEW-POTATO-
AND-ZUCCHINI SALAD
(pictured)

DRESSING
¼ cup tarragon vinegar
1½ teaspoons salt
1 teaspoon freshly ground pepper
¼ cup canned condensed consommé,
     undiluted
⅓ cup dry white wine
1½ tablespoons chopped fresh tarragon or
     1½ teaspoons dried tarragon leaves
2 tablespoons chopped fresh chives or dill
¾ cup salad or olive oil

2 lb very small new potatoes
Boiling water
1 teaspoon salt
1 lb (3 medium) zucchini
2 tablespoons salad or olive oil

DO AHEAD
1. Make Dressing: In bowl or jar with
tight-fitting lid, combine vinegar and rest
of dressing ingredients; mix very well.
2. Scrub potatoes. Place in medium
saucepan; add boiling water to cover,
along with salt. Bring to boiling; boil
gently, covered, 30 minutes, or just until
fork-tender.
3. Drain, then peel potatoes; while
still warm, toss with dressing in large
bowl until very well coated.
4. Wash zucchini; cut into ⅓-inch-
thick slices.
5. In oil in medium skillet, sauté
zucchini, turning occasionally, until just
tender—about 3 minutes; cool slightly.
Add to potato mixture; toss gently. Salad
can be served warm. Or let cool; cover
and refrigerate until thoroughly chilled.
Toss several times in marinade.

TO SERVE
6. Before serving, toss gently again
to coat with dressing. *Makes 8 servings.*

CUCUMBER-BUTTERMILK
SOUP

2 medium cucumbers (1 lb)
2 cups buttermilk
1 can (13¾ oz) chicken broth
Water
1 teaspoon salt
Dash pepper
1 tablespoon lemon juice
2 tablespoons chopped fresh chives
Lemon slices
Cucumber slices for garnish (optional)

DO AHEAD
1. Pare cucumbers; cut in half
lengthwise. With teaspoon, scoop out and
discard seeds. Shred cucumber on a
coarse grater; or use food processor.

2. In a large bowl, combine cucumber, buttermilk, chicken broth plus water
to make 2 cups, salt, pepper, lemon juice
and chives; mix well.
3. Refrigerate mixture, covered, until it is well chilled—several hours or
overnight.

TO SERVE
4. Stir very well just before serving.
Garnish each serving with a lemon slice
and, if desired, a slice of cucumber.
Makes 6 cups; 8 (¾-cup) servings.

BAKED ZITI CASSEROLE

SAUCE
¼ cup olive or salad oil
1 cup finely chopped onion
1 garlic clove, crushed
1 can (2 lb, 3 oz) Italian tomatoes
1 can (6 oz) tomato paste
1½ cups water
2 tablespoons chopped parsley
1 tablespoon salt
1 tablespoon sugar
1 teaspoon dried oregano leaves
½ teaspoon dried basil leaves
¼ teaspoon pepper

1 pkg (1 lb) ziti macaroni

CHEESE LAYER
2 cartons (15-oz size) ricotta cheese
1 pkg (8 oz) mozzerella cheese, diced
⅓ cup grated Parmesan cheese
2 eggs
1 tablespoon chopped parsley
1 teaspoon salt
¼ teaspoon pepper

3 tablespoons grated Parmesan cheese

DO AHEAD
1. Make Sauce: In hot oil in 6-quart
kettle, sauté onion and garlic until
golden-brown—about 10 minutes. Add
undrained tomatoes, tomato paste, water,
2 tablespoons parsley, 1 tablespoon salt,
the sugar, oregano, basil and ¼ teaspoon
pepper; mix well, mashing tomatoes with
fork.
2. Bring to boiling; reduce heat;

simmer, covered and stirring occasionally, 1 hour.
3. Cook ziti as package label directs.
4. Make Cheese Layer: In large bowl,
combine ricotta, mozzarella, ⅓ cup Parmesan, the eggs, parsley, salt and pepper. Beat with wooden spoon until
blended.
5. Spoon a little sauce into a 5-quart
casserole. Layer a third of ziti, cheese
mixture and sauce. Sprinkle sauce with
1 tablespoon Parmesan. Repeat twice.
Cover and refrigerate.

TO SERVE
6. Preheat oven to 350F. Remove
casserole from refrigerator while pre-
heating oven. Bake 60 minutes or until
heated through. *Makes 8 to 10 servings.*

MUSSELS WITH SPINACH
SAUCE

1½ dozen mussels

SPINACH SAUCE
1 cup mayonnaise
½ cup chopped spinach
⅓ cup chopped parsley
⅓ cup chopped watercress
1 tablespoon snipped fresh chives
1 tablespoon snipped fresh dill
2 teaspoons dried tarragon leaves
1 tablespoon lemon juice
Dash salt

½ cup white wine
½ garlic clove, crushed

DO AHEAD
1. Check mussels, discarding any
that are not tightly closed. Scrub well
under cold running water to remove sand
and seaweed. With a sharp knife, trim
off the "beard" around edges. Let soak
1 to 2 hours in cold water.
2. Meanwhile, make Spinach Sauce.
Combine all ingredients in blender or
food processor, and beat until smooth.
Turn into a small bowl; refrigerate, covered. Makes 1¼ cups.
3. Lift mussels from water, and place
in a colander. Rinse with cold water; let
drain.
4. Place mussels in large skillet; add
wine and garlic.
5. Cook, covered, over high heat, 5
to 8 minutes, or until shells open. Shake
skillet frequently, so mussels will cook
uniformly.
6. With slotted utensil, remove mussels to serving dish; refrigerate, covered,
at least 1 hour.

TO SERVE
7. Spoon 1 tablespoon Spinach Sauce
on top of each mussel in shell. *Makes 6
appetizer servings.* ◆

A
Cook-Ahead
✦ Plan ✦
To Save Time
And Money

Doing the bulk of your cooking on the weekend has a double advantage. It saves time, obviously, but it also saves money because it automatically involves planned use of leftovers. Take the plump roasting chicken on the top shelf at right: It takes less than an hour to cook on top of the stove, during which time it yields a jar of chicken stock for future soups and stews. Breast meat can then be cut off and frozen to make Chicken-And-Macaroni Salad (bottom right). Later on, the leg meat is used for Chicken Kebabs (bottom left), and the wings, back and odd bits of meat for the Chicken and Cabbage Orientale on the middle shelf. Of course, nobody wants to have chicken three times a week. So, while the roaster is stewing in the pot, a Pot Roast of Lamb or Beef can be simmering on another burner. From either you get one Sunday dinner, plus a variety of lamb or beef dishes to freeze for quick weekday meals.

For recipes, please turn to page 94.

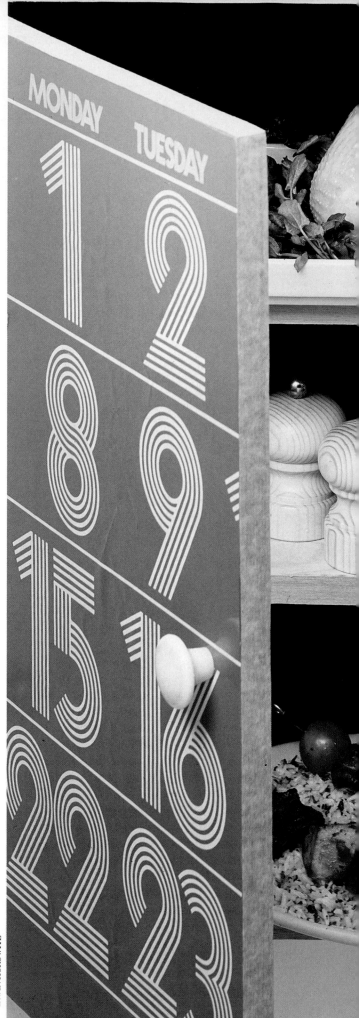

IRWIN HOROWITZ

continued from page 92

CHICKEN IN THE POT
(pictured)

5-lb whole roasting chicken, cut up
6 cups water
1 stalk celery
1 large onion, quartered
1 tablespoon salt
½ teaspoon pepper

1. Wash chicken well under cold, running water and pat dry with paper towels.

2. In large kettle, place chicken and giblets, 6 cups water, the celery and onion. Bring to boiling; reduce heat and simmer, covered, 20 minutes. Remove chicken legs and thighs; set aside. Continue cooking chicken about 30 minutes longer. Add salt and pepper during last 5 minutes of cooking.

3. Lift out chicken; use as directed in recipes that follow.

Makes 6 cups chicken stock. Use in recipes calling for chicken stock, or freeze in plastic containers for future use.

CHICKEN KEBABS
(pictured)

MARINADE
⅔ cup chili sauce
½ cup applesauce
1 tablespoon sugar
1 small onion, chopped
1 tablespoon soy sauce
Dash salt
Dash pepper

8 chunks cooked chicken (1-inch cubes),
    from legs and thighs
½ green pepper, parboiled and quartered

1 pared, cooked medium potato, quartered
8 cherry tomatoes
1 tablespoon salad oil
4 cups hot cooked rice

1. Make Marinade: In shallow glass dish, combine chili sauce, applesauce, sugar, onion, soy sauce, the salt and pepper; mix well. Use to marinate chicken, covered, 3 to 4 hours or overnight.

2. On four metal skewers, arrange pieces of chicken, green pepper, potato and tomatoes, as pictured. Place skewers in shallow baking pan, with ends of skewers resting on edge of pan.

3. Combine 1 tablespoon salad oil with remaining marinade. Use to brush chicken and vegetables.

4. Broil 4 minutes per side, 4 inches from heat, brushing with marinade once or twice. Serve skewers on rice. Heat and pass remaining marinade. *Makes 4 servings.*

CHICKEN AND CABBAGE ORIENTALE
(pictured)

3 tablespoons salad oil
Meat from chicken wings and back, sliced
    (1½ cups)
2 pared carrots, thinly sliced on diagonal
2 teaspoons salt
4 cups coarsely sliced green cabbage
½ cup water chestnuts, thinly sliced
1 tablespoon cornstarch
⅓ cup water
Soy sauce

1. In hot oil in large skillet, sauté chicken and carrot over high heat, stirring, about 5 minutes.

2. Sprinkle with salt; add cabbage and water chestnuts; cook 15 to 20 minutes, or until vegetables are tender.

3. Meanwhile, dissolve cornstarch in water; stir into vegetable mixure. Cook, stirring, until liquid is thickened and translucent. Serve at once, with soy sauce. *Makes 4 or 5 servings.*

CHICKEN-AND-MACARONI SALAD
(pictured)

1½ cups elbow macaroni
Salt
2 cooked chicken breast halves, in large
    pieces
1 can (8 oz) sliced beets, drained
1 can (8 oz) peas, drained
1 can (8¼ oz) sliced pineapple, drained
    and quartered
½ cup mayonnaise or cooked salad
    dressing
3 tablespoons sugar

1 teaspoon salt
⅛ teaspoon pepper
Iceberg lettuce

1. In 6 cups boiling water in large saucepan, cook macaroni with 1½ teaspoons salt 15 minutes, or just until tender; drain. Refrigerate to chill well.

2. Set aside several pieces of chicken, ¼ cup sliced beets, ½ cup peas and 8 pineapple quarters.

3. In large bowl, combine macaroni, rest of chicken, beets, peas, pineapple and the remaining ingredients, except lettuce. Toss lightly to mix well. Refrigerate, covered, to chill well.

4. To serve, toss again. Arrange lettuce around edge of salad bowl. Fill center with salad. Garnish top with reserved chicken, beets, peas and pineapple. *Makes 6 to 8 servings.*

POT ROAST OF LAMB

5½-lb boned shoulder of lamb (see Note)
¼ cup chopped parsley
1 garlic clove, crushed
1 teaspoon salt
½ teaspoon dried basil leaves
½ teaspoon dried marjoram leaves
¼ teaspoon pepper
2 tablespoons butter or margarine
½ cup chopped onion
½ cup chopped celery
½ cup chopped carrot
1 can (10½ oz) condensed beef broth,
    undiluted
½ cup red wine
1 bay leaf
2 lb medium potatoes, peeled and halved
2 tablespoons all-purpose flour
¼ cup cold water

1. Wipe lamb with damp paper towels. Trim off fat; spread meat flat.

2. In small bowl, combine parsley, garlic, salt, basil, marjoram and pepper.

3. Spread parsley mixture evenly over lamb. Roll up, jelly-roll fashion, as tightly as possible. Tie with twine.

4. In hot butter in Dutch oven, brown roast well on all sides—about 20 minutes. Remove roast.

5. In same pan, sauté onion, celery and carrot until soft. Drain off fat.

6. Return roast to pan. Add beef broth, wine and bay leaf; bring to boiling. Reduce heat and simmer, covered, turning meat once, 1½ hours.

7. Add potato; simmer, covered, 40 minutes longer, or until lamb and potato are tender.

8. Remove lamb and potato to heated serving platter. Remove string from lamb. Keep warm. Skim fat from pan liquid. Remove bay leaf.

9. Mix flour with ¼ cup cold water

until smooth. Stir into pan liquid; bring to boiling, stirring. Reduce heat and simmer 3 minutes. Spoon some of gravy over meat. Pass the rest.

Makes 6 to 8 servings, with leftovers for other dishes. (If desired, remove enough cooked lamb for one or two of the dishes that follow; wrap and freeze, or refrigerate if using within a few days.)

Note: Weight after lamb shoulder is boned. Use bones for making Scotch Broth, recipe follows.

SCOTCH BROTH

LAMB STOCK
Bones from Pot Roast of Lamb, page 94
Water
1 large onion, quartered
1½ teaspoons salt
4 black peppercorns
½ bay leaf

SCOTCH BROTH
4 cups lamb stock
½ cup chopped onion
½ cup finely diced celery
1 cup finely diced carrot
½ cup diced turnip
2 tablespoons butter or margarine
1 cup cooked lamb pieces
¼ cup uncooked pearl barley
2 tablespoons chopped parsley

DO AHEAD
1. Day before, make Lamb Stock: In 5-quart Dutch oven, combine lamb bones, 6 cups water, the quartered onion, salt, peppercorns and bay leaf; bring to boiling. Reduce heat; cover and simmer 2 hours.

2. Strain broth; add water if necessary to make 4 cups. Get as much meat from bones as possible; add leftover lamb, if necessary, to make 1 cup in all. Discard bones. Let stock cool; refrigerate overnight.

NEXT DAY
3. Make Scotch Broth: Skim fat from surface of lamb stock. In Dutch oven, sauté onion, celery, carrot and turnip in hot butter until golden—2 minutes. Add stock, meat and barley; bring to boiling. Reduce heat; simmer, covered, 1 hour, or until barley is tender.

4. Just before serving, sprinkle with chopped parsley. Season with salt and pepper, if necessary. *Makes 4 cups.*

LAMB-AND-WHITE-BEAN CASSEROLE

2 tablespoons butter or margarine
1 large onion, sliced

1 garlic clove, crushed
½ teaspoon salt
½ teaspoon dried basil leaves
¼ teaspoon dried rosemary leaves
1 can (16 oz) tomatoes, undrained
1 tablespoon chopped parsley
2 cups cooked lamb, cut into 1-inch pieces (from Pot Roast of Lamb, page 94)
2 cans (1-lb, 4-oz size) white kidney beans, drained
1 bay leaf

1. In 2 tablespoons hot butter in 3-quart saucepan, sauté onion and garlic until golden—3 minutes. Stir in salt, basil and rosemary.

2. Add tomatoes (break up whole tomatoes with fork). Simmer, uncovered, 20 minutes. Heat oven to 350F.

3. Stir in parsley, lamb and kidney beans. Turn into 2-quart casserole. Top with bay leaf. Bake, uncovered, 30 minutes. *Makes 4 to 6 servings.*

SAVORY POT ROAST

5-lb boneless lean chuck pot roast
6 tablespoons (¾ stick) butter or margarine
1½ cups chopped onion
2 garlic cloves, crushed
⅓ cup all-purpose flour
¼ cup wine vinegar
1 tablespoon anchovy paste
2 tablespoons honey or corn syrup
2 cans (10½-oz size) condensed beef broth, undiluted
2 bay leaves
4 sprigs parsley
1 teaspoon black peppercorns

1. Wipe pot roast with damp paper towels.

2. In hot butter in 6-quart Dutch oven, brown roast well over medium heat, turning on all sides with wooden spoons, about 20 minutes. Remove roast; set aside. Preheat oven to 325F.

3. Add onion and garlic to drippings in Dutch oven; cook over low heat about 5 minutes, or until tender.

4. Remove from heat; stir in flour until smooth. Add vinegar, anchovy paste, honey and broth; stir to mix.

5. Tie bay leaves, parsley and peppercorns in cheesecloth bag; add to Dutch oven. Bring to boiling, covered.

6. Place in oven; roast 3 to 3½ hours, or until meat is fork-tender. Remove and discard cheesecloth bag.

7. Remove pot roast to platter. Serve with sauce from Dutch oven. *Makes 6 servings,* with leftovers for other dishes.

BEEF CURRY

2 tablespoons butter or margarine
1½ cups sliced onion
1 garlic clove, crushed
3 teaspoons curry powder
1½ teaspoons salt
1 teaspoon ground ginger
2 cups cubed (1-inch cubes) cooked beef (from Savory Pot Roast, above)
Water
1 can (10½ oz) condensed beef broth, undiluted
1 cup diced, pared tart apple
½ cup canned pineapple chunks, with ½ cup juice from pineapple
2 tablespoons all-purpose flour
4 cups hot cooked rice

1. In hot butter in medium skillet, sauté onion, garlic, curry powder, salt and ginger, stirring, 5 minutes.

2. Add beef, mixing well.

3. Add water to beef broth to make 2 cups. Stir into beef mixture. Bring to boiling. Reduce heat; simmer, covered, 20 minutes; add apple and pineapple with ½ cup juice; simmer, uncovered, 10 minutes, to reduce liquid.

4. Dissolve flour in ½ cup water. Add to beef mixture. Bring to boiling, stirring, until thickened.

5. Serve hot over rice. *Makes 4 or 5 servings.*

TOMATO-MEAT SAUCE

4 lb ground chuck
Salad or olive oil
4 medium onions, chopped
1 large carrot, chopped
1 stalk celery, chopped
3 garlic cloves, crushed
1 lb Italian sweet sausage, cut up
2 cans (16-oz size) whole tomatoes
1 can (16 oz) tomato purée
1 can (6 oz) tomato paste
1 teaspoon dried oregano leaves
1½ tablespoons salt
½ teaspoon pepper
½ cup dry red wine
⅓ cup all-purpose flour
1 cup water

1. Spread ground chuck evenly in bottom of 15½-by-10½-by-1-inch pan, lined with waxed paper. Freeze until firm—1 hour.

2. Cut chuck lengthwise into strips ¾ inch wide; cut strips into ¾-inch cubes.

3. In ¼ cup hot oil in 6-quart Dutch oven, sauté onion, carrot, celery and garlic, stirring, 5 minutes. Remove from heat.

4. In 2 tablespoons hot oil in large
continued on page 101

DO-AHEAD
◆ SUPER ◆ SUPPERS
FOR A CROWD

Ask friends to drop by for a delicious meal on a Sunday evening or on the day of the telecast of a special concert or game. Each of the dishes shown here can be prepared ahead, so you won't miss any fun. At right is a luscious offering to tempt a group gathered to watch the Super Bowl (but appropriate for any other occasion as well): a hearty Linebacker's Lasagna made with a combination of ground meat, two kinds of sausage and savory tomato sauce; a crisp salad of mixed greens; and a basket of whole-wheat Italian bread. We've included more surefire suggestions for another easy feast: a fabulous Glazed Corned Beef, a creamy Potato Salad, a selection of relishes, and some mouth-watering desserts. Menus and recipes begin on page 98.

SUPER BOWL PA...

Date:
Place:

continued from page 96

SUPER-BOWL-SUNDAY BUFFET
CROCK OF HERRING★
CAPONATA★
ROASTED RED PEPPERS★
LINEBACKER'S LASAGNA★
VEGETABLE SALAD BOWL★
TOSSED GREEN SALAD BOWL
WHOLE WHEAT ITALIAN BREAD
BUTTER
SUPER-BOWL-SUNDAY CAKE★
HOT COFFEE   BEER
SODAS ON ICE

★Recipes given for starred dishes.

CROCK OF HERRING

1 large carrot, pared
1 large onion, peeled
3 jars (12-oz size) herring in wine sauce,
**   undrained**
12 pitted black olives
¼ teaspoon black peppercorns

DO AHEAD

1. Cut carrot on diagonal into ⅛-inch-thick slices. Slice onion paper-thin.

2. In large glass container or bowl, combine carrot and onion slices, herring in wine sauce, black olives and peppercorns.

3. Refrigerate, covered, at least 24 hours. *Makes 12 servings.*

CAPONATA
(EGGPLANT RELISH)

1 large eggplant
½ cup plus 2 tablespoons olive or salad oil
2½ cups sliced onion
1 cup diced celery
2 cans (8-oz size) tomato sauce
¼ cup red-wine vinegar
2 tablespoons sugar
2 tablespoons drained capers
½ teaspoon salt
Dash pepper
12 pitted black olives, cut in slivers

DO AHEAD

1. Wash eggplant; cut into ½-inch cubes.

2. In ½ cup hot oil in large skillet, sauté eggplant until tender and golden-brown. Remove eggplant, and set aside.

3. In 2 tablespoons hot oil in same skillet, sauté onion and celery until tender—about 5 minutes.

4. Return eggplant to skillet. Stir in tomato sauce; bring to boiling. Lower heat, and simmer, covered, 15 minutes.

5. Add vinegar, sugar, capers, salt, pepper and olives. Simmer, covered and stirring occasionally, 20 minutes longer.

6. Refrigerate, covered, overnight. *Makes 12 servings.*

ROASTED RED PEPPERS

8 medium-size sweet red peppers (2½ lb)
1 cup olive or salad oil
¼ cup lemon juice
2 teaspoons salt
3 small garlic cloves
3 anchovy fillets

DO AHEAD

1. Preheat oven to 450F.
2. Wash red peppers; drain well.
3. Place peppers on cookie sheet; bake about 20 minutes, or until skin of peppers becomes blistered and charred. With tongs, turn peppers every 5 minutes.
4. Place hot peppers in a large kettle; cover kettle, and let stand 15 minutes.
5. Peel off charred skin with sharp knife. Cut each pepper into fourths. Remove ribs and seeds, and cut out any dark spots.
6. In large bowl, combine olive oil, lemon juice, salt and garlic. Add peppers and toss lightly to coat with oil mixture.
7. Pack pepper mixture and anchovy fillets into a 1-quart jar; cap. Refrigerate several hours or overnight.

TO SERVE

8. Serve as an appetizer or in a tossed salad. *Makes 12 servings.*

LINEBACKER'S LASAGNA
(pictured)

MEAT SAUCE

1 lb sweet Italian sausage
1 lb hot Italian sausage
1 lb ground beef
1 cup finely chopped onion
4 garlic cloves, crushed
¼ cup sugar
Salt
1 tablespoon dried basil leaves
1½ teaspoons fennel seed
½ teaspoon pepper
½ cup chopped parsley
2 cans (2-lb, 3-oz size) Italian-style
**   tomatoes**
4 cans (6-oz size) tomato paste
1 cup water

Ricotta Filling, recipe follows
1 pkg (1 lb) curly lasagna noodles (23)
½ lb mozzarella cheese, shredded
½ cup grated Parmesan cheese
Parsley sprigs

DO AHEAD

1. Make Meat Sauce: Remove sausage meat from outer casing. Chop meat coarsely.

2. In 5-quart Dutch oven, over medium heat, sauté sausage, beef (break up beef with wooden spoon), onion and garlic, stirring frequently, until well browned—20 minutes.

3. Add sugar, 1 tablespoon salt, the basil, fennel, pepper and chopped parsley; mix well. Add undrained tomatoes, tomato paste and 1 cup water, mashing tomatoes with wooden spoon.

4. Bring to boiling; reduce heat; simmer, covered and stirring occasionally, until thick—1½ hours.

5. Meanwhile, make Ricotta Filling.

6. Cook lasagna: In 8-quart kettle, bring 5 quarts water and 1 tablespoon salt to boiling. Add lasagna, 2 or 3 at a time. Return to boiling; boil, uncovered and stirring occasionally, 10 minutes, or until just tender. Drain in colander; rinse under cold water; drain well. Dry on paper towels.

7. In bottom of a casserole (see Note) dish (about 12 by 15 inches, 7-quart capacity), spoon 4 cups sauce. Set aside 16 lasagna. Place remaining lasagna in sauce covering bottom. Spread 2 cups Ricotta Filling evenly over lasagna. Top with 4 cups sauce.

8. Fill 16 reserved lasagna with Ricotta Filling, using ⅓ cup for each. Roll up; arrange, sealed side down, in sauce to form a single layer.

9. Spoon more sauce over each rolled lasagna. (For very saucy lasagna, use all the remaining sauce.) To make, as pictured, use a little sauce, cover and refrigerate.

TO SERVE

10. Remove from refrigerator and let stand at room temperature about 1 hour. Preheat oven to 375F.

11. Sprinkle each roll with mozzarella and Parmesan. Cover with foil; bake 40 minutes. Remove foil; bake 10 minutes longer, or until bubbling.

12. Let cool slightly before serving. Heat remaining sauce, if any, to serve with lasagna. Garnish edge of dish with parsley sprigs. Serve one filled lasagna with some of lasagna and sauce underneath to each person. *Makes 16 servings.*

Note: If necessary, use two (12-by-8-inch) dishes, dividing ingredients in half.

RICOTTA FILLING

3 containers (15-oz size) ricotta or cottage
**   cheese, drained**
2 eggs
½ lb mozzarella cheese, grated

1 teaspoon salt
¼ cup chopped parsley

In large bowl, combine ricotta, eggs, mozzarella, salt and parsley; mix well.

VEGETABLE SALAD BOWL

DRESSING

½ cup white vinegar
1 cup olive or salad oil
1½ teaspoons salt
¼ teaspoon pepper
½ teaspoon dry mustard
1 garlic clove, crushed

2 cups carrot, thinly sliced on diagonal
2 cups celery, sliced diagonally
2 cups cucumber, pared, quartered lengthwise, seeded and sliced diagonally
2 cups thinly sliced cauliflower
1 large sweet onion, thinly sliced
1 pint cherry tomatoes, washed and stems removed
¼ cup chopped parsley

DO AHEAD

1. Make Dressing: Combine all ingredients in jar with tight-fitting lid; shake vigorously. Chill until ready to use. Shake again before using.

2. Make salad: In large bowl, layer all vegetables; refrigerate, covered, until well chilled—several hours.

TO SERVE

3. Add dressing to vegetables. Toss gently to mix well; turn into chilled bowl; sprinkle with parsley. *Makes 12 servings.*

SUPER-BOWL-SUNDAY CAKE

Orange-Chiffon-Cake Layers, recipe follows

CREAM FILLING

½ cup granulated sugar
3 tablespoons cornstarch
2¾ cups milk
2 tablespoons butter or margarine
6 egg yolks, lightly beaten
½ teaspoon vanilla extract
1 cup (8 oz) chopped mixed candied fruit
½ cup miniature semisweet chocolate pieces
3 tablespoons light rum

APRICOT COATING

⅔ cup apricot preserves
2 teaspoons lemon juice

GLAZE

1¼ cups sifted confectioners' sugar
3 tablespoons milk

5 pieces of citron, 3 to 4 inches long
1 red candied cherry

DO AHEAD

1. Make Orange-Chiffon-Cake Layers as directed (recipe follows). Cool completely.

2. Make Cream Filling: In medium saucepan, combine granulated sugar and cornstarch; mix well. Gradually add 2¾ cups milk, stirring until smooth. Add butter.

3. Bring to boiling, stirring constantly; boil 1 minute. Stir a little of hot mixture into egg yolks; return to saucepan, stirring. Bring to boiling; then remove from heat. Stir in vanilla.

4. Turn into medium bowl. Place in larger bowl filled with ice cubes to cool completely—about 40 minutes. Stir occasionally.

5. Stir in candied fruit, chocolate and rum. Refrigerate until needed. Makes about 3 cups.

6. To assemble cake: Slice layers in half horizontally to make four layers.

7. Place a layer, cut side up, on cake plate. Spread with a third of the cream filling. Repeat with remaining layers and filling, ending with top layer, cut side down.

8. Make Apricot Coating: Melt preserves in small saucepan; strain. Add lemon juice. Brush over entire surface of cake. Refrigerate.

9. Make Glaze: In small bowl, combine confectioners' sugar with milk; beat until smooth.

10. Brush glaze over top of cake. Decorate, as pictured, with citron and candied cherry. Refrigerate. *Makes 16 servings.*

ORANGE-CHIFFON-CAKE LAYERS

1 cup egg whites (7 to 8 egg whites, depending upon size)
2¼ cups sifted cake flour
1½ cups sugar
3 teaspoons baking powder
1 teaspoon salt
½ cup salad oil
4 egg yolks
¾ cup orange juice

3 tablespoons grated orange peel
½ teaspoon cream of tartar

1. In large bowl of electric mixer, let egg whites warm to room temperature—about 1 hour. Meanwhile, preheat oven to 350F.

2. Sift flour with sugar, baking powder and salt into another bowl; make well in center. Add, in order, oil, egg yolks, orange juice and orange peel; beat with spoon until smooth.

3. With electric mixer at high speed, beat egg whites with cream of tartar until very stiff peaks form.

4. With wire whisk or rubber spatula, using an under-and-over motion, gradually fold batter gently into egg whites just until blended. Do not stir.

5. Pour into two ungreased 9-by-1½-inch round layer-cake pans; bake 30 to 35 minutes, or until cake tester inserted in center comes out clean.

6. Invert cakes by hanging pan between two other pans; let cool completely—about 1 hour.

7. With spatula, carefully loosen cake from pan; hit pan sharply on table; remove cake. Wrap loosely in foil until ready to assemble.

EASY SUPER-BOWL-SUNDAY CAKE

1 pkg (16 oz) angel food cake mix
3 tablespoons grated orange peel

FILLING

2 pkg (3⅛-oz size) vanilla pudding and pie filling mix
3 cups milk
3 tablespoons light rum
½ cup miniature semisweet chocolate pieces
1 cup (8 oz) chopped mixed candied fruit

DO AHEAD

1. Preheat oven to 375F. Prepare cake as package label directs, folding orange peel into batter. Pour into two ungreased 9-inch cake pans. Bake 25 minutes, or until cake springs back when gently pressed with fingertips. To cool, hang pan inverted between two other pans to cool completely.

2. Make Filling: In medium saucepan, combine pudding mix and milk; mix well. Cook, stirring, over medium heat, until mixture comes to a full rolling boil. Turn into medium bowl; place waxed paper directly on surface.

3. Place in large bowl of ice to cool quickly. Add rum, chocolate and candied fruit. Refrigerate until needed.

4. Assemble cake as directed above; refrigerate until serving. *Makes 16 servings.*

continued on page 100

continued from page 99

SUPER-BOWL DELICATESSEN BUFFET
FIRST-STRING
HAM-AND-OLIVE LOAF★
GLAZED CORNED BEEF★
PUMPERNICKEL AND RYE BREAD
TOUCHDOWN POTATO SALAD★
HAM-DEVILED EGGS★
PICKLED BEETS AND ONIONS★
GREEN PEPPERS STUFFED WITH
COLESLAW★
WEDGE OF CHEDDAR CHEESE
OVERTIME APPLE CAKE★ OR
GLAZED BAKED APPLES★
VANILLA ICE CREAM
HOT COFFEE   BEER
SODAS ON ICE

★Recipes given for starred dishes.

FIRST-STRING HAM-AND-OLIVE LOAF

2 eggs
3 cups soft bread crumbs
1¼ cups milk
1 cup finely chopped onion
1 cup finely chopped green pepper
3 tablespoons catsup
3 tablespoons prepared mustard
½ teaspoon salt
¼ teaspoon pepper
2½ lb ground cooked ham
½ lb ground pork
½ lb ground veal
18 stuffed olives
½ cup apple jelly, melted

DO AHEAD

1. In large bowl, combine eggs, bread crumbs, milk, onion, green pepper, catsup, mustard, salt and pepper; beat with a fork until well combined. Let stand 5 minutes.
2. Add meats; mix well with fork.
3. On foil-lined large baking pan, form half of ham mixture into a loaf about 14 inches long and 6 inches wide.
4. Press stuffed olives, three to a row, over entire surface, ½ inch apart. Spoon rest of ham mixture over top; press lightly. Freeze 1 hour.

TO SERVE

5. Preheat oven to 350F.
6. Bake 30 minutes; remove from oven. Brush entire loaf with half of melted apple jelly.
7. Bake 40 more minutes.
8. Remove loaf to platter. Brush with rest of jelly. Serve hot or cold. *Makes 16 servings.*

GLAZED CORNED BEEF

8-lb corned-beef brisket
2 medium onions, peeled and quartered
2 bay leaves
1 teaspoon salt
10 black peppercorns
1 garlic clove
4 whole cloves

GLAZE
½ cup dark corn syrup
1 tablespoon prepared mustard

DO AHEAD

1. Put brisket in large kettle; cover with cold water.
2. Add onions, bay leaves, salt, peppercorns, garlic and cloves. Bring to boiling.
3. Reduce heat, and simmer, covered, about 4 hours, or just until corned beef is fork-tender.
4. Remove corned beef from cooking liquid. Cool completely. Refrigerate, covered, overnight.
5. Next day, make Glaze: In small saucepan, combine corn syrup and mustard.
6. Bring to boiling over medium heat, stirring constantly. Reduce heat, and simmer, uncovered, 10 minutes, stirring occasionally. Remove from heat and let cool.
7. Trim any excess fat from corned beef. Place meat on rack in broiler pan. Brush top and sides with some of the glaze.
8. Run under broiler, 5 or 6 inches from heat, 10 minutes; brush several times with remaining glaze.
9. Let corned beef cool. Refrigerate until ready to serve. *Makes 12 servings.*

TOUCHDOWN POTATO SALAD

5 lb medium potatoes
½ cup Italian-style dressing

DRESSING
3 cups mayonnaise or cooked salad
    dressing
1½ cups finely chopped onion
1½ cups cubed pared cucumber
1 cup coarsely chopped green pepper
1 can (4 oz) pimientos, drained and diced
⅔ cup sliced sweet gherkins
⅓ cup pickle juice

4 hard-cooked eggs, sliced
2 hard-cooked eggs, shelled
½ cup chopped green pepper

DO AHEAD

1. In boiling salted water to cover, cook unpared potatoes, covered, just until tender—about 30 minutes. Drain.

2. Peel warm potatoes; cut into 1-inch cubes. Toss with Italian dressing.
3. Make Dressing: In large bowl, combine mayonnaise, onion, cucumber, 1 cup chopped green pepper, the pimientos, gherkins and pickle juice; mix well.
4. Drain potatoes; add to dressing, along with sliced eggs; toss until potatoes are well coated. Refrigerate, covered, until well chilled—several hours or overnight.

TO SERVE

5. Turn into salad bowl; cut eggs in half; chop whites; put yolks through sieve. Garnish around edge with chopped green pepper, chopped egg whites and yolk. *Makes 12 servings.*
Note: For 6 servings, cut recipe in half; follow directions above.

HAM-DEVILED EGGS

6 hard-cooked eggs, shelled
1 can (2¼ oz) deviled ham
¼ cup mayonnaise or cooked salad
    dressing
Dash hot red-pepper sauce
1 tablespoon prepared mustard
¼ teaspoon Worcestershire sauce
⅛ teaspoon onion powder
1 tablespoon chopped parsley

DO AHEAD

1. Halve eggs lengthwise. Remove yolks to a medium bowl. Reserve whites.
2. Using fork, mash yolks. Add rest of ingredients, except chopped parsley, to the mashed yolks; mix until smooth.
3. Fill each white with yolk mixture, mounding high.
4. Sprinkle tops of deviled eggs with parsley. Refrigerate. *Makes 12 halves.*

PICKLED BEETS AND ONIONS

2 cans (1-lb size) whole beets
1 cup white-wine vinegar
½ cup sugar
1 teaspoon salt
3 whole cloves
4 black peppercorns
1 small bay leaf
2 medium onions, peeled and thinly sliced

DO AHEAD

1. Drain beets, reserving 1¼ cups liquid. Place beets in 1½- to 2-quart jar.
2. In medium saucepan, combine vinegar, sugar, salt, cloves, peppercorns, bay leaf and reserved liquid; bring to boiling. Reduce heat, and simmer, uncovered, 5 minutes.
3. Add onion slices to jar. Pour beet liquid over beets and onions. Refriger-

ate, covered, several hours or overnight. *Makes 12 servings.*

GREEN PEPPERS STUFFED WITH COLESLAW

6 large green peppers
1 green cabbage (2 lb)
1 large red pepper
1 cup cider vinegar
⅓ cup sugar
1 teaspoon salt
¼ teaspoon pepper

DO AHEAD

1. Bring 2 quarts of water to boiling in a large kettle.

2. Wash green peppers, and cut in half crosswise. Carefully remove ribs and seeds. Cut off stem even with end of pepper. Place peppers in water; return to boiling. Cover, turn off heat and let stand 5 minutes. Drain peppers immediately, and rinse in cold water.

3. Wash and shred cabbage. Wash red pepper; remove ribs and seeds, and cut into thin slices. Combine cabbage, red pepper, vinegar, sugar, salt and pepper in a large bowl. Toss until well combined.

4. Drain pepper halves well. Place on cookie sheet or large baking pan. Turn slaw into peppers, dividing evenly. (Be sure to divide dressing remaining in bowl evenly.) Cover tightly. Refrigerate at least 2 hours. *Makes 12 servings.*

OVERTIME APPLE CAKE

2 cups all-purpose flour
2 cups granulated sugar
2 teaspoons baking soda
1 teaspoon ground cinnamon
½ teaspoon ground nutmeg
½ teaspoon salt
4 cups finely diced pared raw apple (about 1½ lb)
½ cup chopped walnuts
½ cup (1 stick) butter or margarine, softened
2 eggs

CREAM-CHEESE FROSTING
1 pkg (8 oz) cream cheese, softened
1 tablespoon butter or margarine
1 teaspoon vanilla extract
2½ to 3 cups confectioners' sugar

½ cup chopped walnuts

DO AHEAD

1. Preheat oven to 325F. Grease a 13-by-9-by-2-inch baking pan.

2. Into large bowl, sift flour with granulated sugar, soda, cinnamon, nutmeg and salt.

3. Add apple, nuts, ½ cup butter and the eggs. Beat until just combined—it will be thick. Turn into pan.

4. Bake 1 hour, or until top springs back when lightly pressed with fingertip. Cool in pan on wire rack.

5. Meanwhile, make Cream-Cheese Frosting: In medium bowl, with electric mixer, at medium speed, beat cream cheese with butter and vanilla until creamy.

6. Add confectioners' sugar; beat until light and fluffy.

7. Spread over top of cake, swirling decoratively. Sprinkle with nuts. *Makes 12 servings.*

GLAZED BAKED APPLES

½ cup sugar
¼ cup light corn syrup
¼ cup water
½ cup apricot preserves
2 tablespoons butter or margarine
6 large baking apples (about 3 lb)
Ice cream, softened
Light cream (optional)

DO AHEAD

1. Preheat oven to 375F.

2. In small saucepan, combine sugar, corn syrup and ¼ cup water. Bring to boiling, stirring; reduce heat; cook, covered, 5 minutes. Remove from heat. Stir in preserves and butter.

3. Wash apples. Remove cores, but do not cut through blossom ends. Peel about 1 inch around stem ends.

4. Place, peeled ends down, in a 12-by-8-by-2-inch baking dish. Pour syrup mixture over apples. Cover dish with foil.

5. Bake, covered, 30 minutes. Remove foil; turn apples peeled end up; baste with syrup in pan. Bake, uncovered and basting occasionally, 20 to 30 minutes, or until tender.

6. Let cool in dish on wire rack, basting with syrup once or twice. Refrigerate.

TO SERVE

7. Serve chilled or at room temperature with soft ice cream or, if desired, light cream. *Makes 6 servings.*

Note: You will need to double recipe to serve 12. ◆

A COOK-AHEAD PLAN

continued from page 95

skillet, sauté half of frozen chuck and half of Italian sausage until well browned. Remove from skillet to Dutch oven. Repeat with rest.

5. Add tomatoes, tomato purée, tomato paste, oregano, salt, pepper and wine. Bring to boiling; reduce heat; simmer, covered, 30 minutes.

6. In small bowl, combine flour with 1 cup water, stirring until smooth. Gradually add to sauce, stirring constantly. Return to boiling, stirring constantly. Reduce heat; simmer, uncovered, 30 minutes. Cool; turn into four (1-quart) or eight (1-pint) jars or plastic containers. Refrigerate if using within a week; freeze if storing for a longer period. *Makes 4 quarts or 8 pints.* Use as suggested in recipes that follow.

DO-AHEAD CHILI

2 tablespoons salad oil
½ cup chopped green pepper
¼ cup chopped onion
1 garlic clove, crushed
1 to 1½ tablespoons chili powder
2 cups Tomato-Meat Sauce, page 95
1 can (17 oz) tomatoes, undrained
2 cans (1-lb size) red kidney beans, undrained
½ teaspoon salt

3 cups hot cooked rice (optional)

1. In hot oil in 5-quart Dutch oven, sauté green pepper, onion, garlic and chili powder, stirring, until vegetables are tender—about 5 minutes.

2. Add all remaining ingredients; simmer, uncovered, 25 minutes, or until very thick. Serve with rice, if desired. *Makes 4 or 5 servings.*

EASY MANICOTTI

4 cups (1 quart or 2 pints) Tomato-Meat Sauce, page 95
2 pkg (18-oz size) frozen manicotti, partially thawed
2 tablespoons grated Parmesan cheese

1. Preheat oven to 350F.

2. Into bottom of 2-quart, shallow baking dish or 13-by-9-by-1¾-inch baking pan, spoon 2 cups Tomato-Meat Sauce.

3. Separate manicotti, and place on top of sauce in a single layer.

4. Spoon remaining 2 cups sauce over manicotti. Bake, covered, 45 minutes. Remove from oven.

5. Sprinkle with Parmesan cheese. Bake, uncovered, 10 to 15 minutes longer, or until hot and bubbly. *Makes 6 to 8 servings.* ◆

"LET'S EAT OUT!"

◆

E ating out does not have to be at a restaurant, but can be on the terrace or patio, in the backyard or even farther afield. This splendid meal is as elegant as any you'd select in the best of restaurants, and it also offers the same relaxed enjoyment because each of these dishes can be done ahead and easily toted to the outside dining area of your choice. To begin: Country Pâté, far right, made of ground pork and a thick layer of herb-seasoned spinach, baked to full flavor. It's refrigerated overnight, then glazed with a wine gelatine—great by itself or with dark bread. Below it: a velvety Cream-Of-Carrot Soup garnished with zesty fresh mint and served ice cold. Center, bottom: moist, tender chicken breasts bathed in a do-ahead tonnato cream sauce of tuna and anchovy fillets. Near right, bottom: Glazed Ham-And-Spinach Roulade—a delicious mixture of ground ham, pork and veal rolled, then sliced to reveal a pinwheel of sharp cheese-and-onion-laced spinach. Above, two very grand finales: a colorful open-face pie brimming with fresh strawberries and golden pears; and a wonderfully rich walnut cake dripping with butterscotch frosting. Recipes for all these and more begin on page 120.

GEORGE RATKAI

◆ S A L A D S ◆
TURN OVER A NEW LEAF!

*T*he way to give greens a fresh taste: Toss greens with pasta, meat or fish to make a hearty and healthful supper or use greens to update an old classic, such as potato salad, to make a sumptuous side dish. These salads all look and taste sensational—great for Saturday-night entertaining or for Sunday family suppers. Recipes begin on page 107.

Nosegay Salad

Walnut Garden Slaw

Gnocchi and Chicory Salad

How to rev up your old salad recipes? Instead of using mayonnaise, substitute sour cream, low-fat yogurt or full-flavored balsamic vinegar. Experiment with new greens—add radicchio, romaine or arugula. Provide a surprise—a touch of fruit, such as Asian pears or raisins, lends unexpected sweetness.

Italian Grilled Chicken Salad

Marinated Seafood Salad

NOSEGAY SALAD
(pictured)

This festive-looking salad is a perfectly cool main course for celebratory lunches or dinners.

DRESSING
2 medium cloves garlic
½ cup mango chutney
¼ cup red-wine vinegar
⅓ cup olive oil

½ pkg (17¼-oz size) frozen puff pastry, thawed (1 sheet)
12 green onions, trimmed
3 large thick carrots, pared
½ lb sugar snap peas
2 tablespoons lemon juice
6 baby artichokes
1 bunch green leaf lettuce, washed
1 bunch red leaf lettuce, washed
2 Belgian endives, leaves separated
4 navel oranges, peeled and sectioned
1 lb cooked and skinned fresh beets or
    1 lb canned and drained beets, julienne
½ lb smoked turkey, julienne
1 bunch radish sprouts
1 bunch enoki mushrooms

DO AHEAD
1. Make dressing: In food processor, puree garlic, chutney and vinegar. With motor running, pour in oil in a steady stream; process until blended. Pour into serving bowl; refrigerate.

2. Preheat oven to 425F. On work surface, roll puff pastry to 13½-by-12-inch rectangle; with fork, prick all over. Cut into six (6-by-4½-inch) rectangles. Working with one rectangle at a time, moisten one short side with water, press moistened side onto one long side. Roll folded pastry into a cone shape, pressing lightly to seal; fill center with crumpled aluminum foil. Place cones, seam side down, on baking sheet. Bake 11 minutes, or until golden. Cool slightly on baking sheet; remove foil. Remove cones to wire rack; cool completely.

3. Make green-onion flowers and carrot curls: Using white part only, slit each green onion lengthwise several times up to but not through root end. Place in bowl of ice water. With vegetable parer, make long wide strips of carrot. Roll up each strip; insert a wooden pick into each to hold curl. Place in ice water with green-onion flowers; set aside.

4. In 2 inches of boiling water in a medium saucepan, cook sugar snap peas 3 minutes. With slotted spoon, remove to colander; rinse with cold water to stop cooking. Add lemon juice and artichokes to boiling water in pan; cook 12 minutes. Drain; rinse with cold water to stop cooking.

TO SERVE
5. Arrange individual salads: Drain green-onion flowers and carrot curls.

Using photograph as a guide, extend small end of a pastry cone over edge of each of six large plates. Arrange lettuces and endive leaves over wide end of cone and the plate; top with remaining ingredients. Pass dressing. *Makes 6 servings.*

WALNUT GARDEN SLAW
(pictured)

DRESSING
½ cup salad oil
½ cup walnut pieces
1½ teaspoons salt
¼ teaspoon freshly ground black pepper
⅓ cup red-wine vinegar
2 tablespoons Dijon-style mustard

1 small head savoy cabbage, cored and shredded (4 cups)
4 medium cucumbers, scored and thinly sliced
1 lb fresh peas, shelled, or 1 cup frozen peas
2 medium carrots, shredded

DO AHEAD
1. Make dressing: In large skillet, heat oil over medium-high heat. Add walnuts; sauté 3 minutes, or until lightly browned. Line plate with paper towels; with slotted spoon, remove walnuts to prepared plate to drain. Remove skillet from heat; cool oil. Pour oil into jar with tight-fitting lid. Add remaining dressing ingredients; shake to blend.

2. In large bowl, combine remaining ingredients. Add dressing; toss to coat. Cover with plastic wrap; refrigerate at least 2 hours to blend flavors, stirring occasionally.

TO SERVE
3. Spoon into serving dish or, if desired, into a hollowed-out savoy cabbage. Sprinkle with reserved walnuts. *Makes 7 servings.*

continued on page 108

The Meal-in-a-Salad Guide

To make a salad that serves four a complete meal, mix 4 cups greens, 1½ cups protein, 1 cup vegetable, 1½ cups starch and ¾ cup dressing.

MAIN-DISH MEALS

GREENS	+	PROTEIN	+	VEGETABLE	+	STARCH	+	DRESSING
Romaine	+	Shrimp	+	Broccoli	+	Elbow Twists	+	Buttermilk
Iceberg	+	Chicken	+	Artichoke Hearts	+	Chick-Peas	+	Caesar Salad
Green Leaf	+	Roast Beef	+	Zucchini	+	New Potatoes	+	Blue Cheese
Boston	+	Ham	+	Green Beans	+	Brown Rice	+	Thousand Island
Escarole	+	Turkey	+	Peas & Carrots	+	Rotelle	+	Vinaigrette
Spinach	+	Swiss Cheese	+	Tomato	+	Cheese Croutons	+	Creamy Herb

continued from page 107

GNOCCHI AND CHICORY SALAD
(pictured)

1 pkg (16 oz) frozen gnocchi
2 yellow peppers, cut in rings
½ head chicory, broken in bite-size pieces
½ pint cherry tomatoes, halved
½ cup bottled Dijon-vinaigrette dressing
¼ cup crumbled Gorgonzola or other blue cheese
¼ cup chopped Italian parsley
¼ teaspoon freshly ground black pepper
¼ teaspoon salt

DO AHEAD

1. In large saucepan of boiling, salted water, cook gnocchi as package label directs. Drain in colander; place in large bowl. Add yellow peppers, chicory and tomatoes.

TO SERVE

2. In small bowl, whisk remaining ingredients until blended; pour over gnocchi mixture. Toss to coat; place on serving platter. Serve at room temperature. Garnish with toasted pine nuts, if desired. *Makes 8 servings.*

ITALIAN GRILLED CHICKEN SALAD
(pictured)

DRESSING
¼ cup sun-dried tomatoes in oil, drained and minced
2 large cloves garlic, crushed
2 tablespoons finely chopped fresh basil leaves
½ teaspoon salt
⅛ teaspoon freshly ground black pepper
1 cup olive oil
½ cup lemon juice

6 chicken breast halves, boned and skinned (2 lb)
1 medium eggplant, cut in 1½-inch pieces
1 medium zucchini, cut crosswise in ½-inch-thick slices
½ orange pepper, cut in 1½-inch pieces
½ red pepper, cut in 1½-inch pieces
½ yellow pepper, cut in 1½-inch pieces
1 medium head green leaf lettuce, washed
1 pkg (9 oz) small mozzarella balls, drained

DO AHEAD

1. Make dressing: In medium bowl, whisk dressing ingredients until blended.

2. In shallow glass baking dish, coat chicken with ½ cup dressing. Cover; marinate in refrigerator 1 hour, turning chicken occasionally. In medium bowl,

---

toss eggplant, zucchini and peppers with ⅔ cup dressing until coated. Drain, reserving dressing; arrange vegetables on skewers.

TO SERVE

3. Prepare outdoor grill for barbecue. Drain chicken. Over low coals, cook chicken and vegetables, with grill covered, 10 minutes, turning chicken once and skewers occasionally, brushing chicken with dressing.

4. Arrange lettuce on serving plate. In small bowl, toss mozzarella balls with remaining dressing. Slice chicken crosswise; arrange mozzarella balls, chicken and skewers on prepared plate. *Makes 6 servings.*

MARINATED SEAFOOD SALAD
(pictured)

This chilled main-dish salad can be made the day before you plan to serve it.

COOKING LIQUID
1½ cups dry vermouth
1½ cups water
¼ cup white vinegar
1 small onion, halved
1 lemon, quartered
1 bay leaf
¼ teaspoon whole allspice

DRESSING
¼ cup chopped parsley
1 large clove garlic, crushed
¾ teaspoon salt
½ teaspoon dried basil leaves
½ teaspoon dried oregano leaves
¾ cup olive or salad oil
2 tablespoons balsamic vinegar
2 tablespoons red-wine vinegar
1 tablespoon lemon juice
⅛ teaspoon hot red-pepper sauce

½ lb shrimp, shelled and deveined, tails intact
1 lb cleaned fresh or frozen squid, sliced crosswise in ½-inch-wide rings (cut tentacles, if large)
2 dozen mussels, scrubbed
½ lb fresh spinach, washed
4 large plum tomatoes, sliced lengthwise

DO AHEAD

1. Prepare cooking liquid: In large

---

saucepan, bring ingredients to boiling; simmer, covered, 5 minutes.

2. Meanwhile, make dressing: In jar with tight-fitting lid, shake ingredients until blended. Set aside.

3. In simmering cooking liquid, cook shrimp 1 minute. Add squid; cook 1 to 2 minutes longer, or until shrimp and squid are tender and opaque. With slotted spoon, remove shrimp and squid to large bowl. Bring liquid in pan to boiling; add mussels; cook, covered, 6 to 8 minutes, or until shells open. (Discard any mussels that do not open.) Remove cooked mussels from shells; add mussels and dressing to shrimp and squid. Toss to coat. Cover; refrigerate at least 2 hours, stirring occasionally.

TO SERVE

4. Remove and discard stems from spinach. Arrange several spinach leaves on one side of platter; shred remaining leaves and arrange on other side of platter. Using photograph as a guide, arrange tomatoes on top of whole leaves; spoon seafood mixture on top of the shredded leaves. Drizzle dressing over tomatoes. *Makes 4 servings.*

FRESH CORN SALAD

4 to 6 large ears fresh corn
3 tablespoons chopped parsley
2 teaspoons salt
1 teaspoon sugar
1½ teaspoons minced fresh basil or ½ teaspoon dried basil leaves
¼ teaspoon ground red pepper
½ cup salad oil
¼ cup cider vinegar
2 teaspoons lemon juice
1 medium green pepper, coarsely chopped
1 medium red pepper, coarsely chopped
½ cup chopped green onions
Lettuce leaves

DO AHEAD

1. In a 6- to 8-quart kettle, bring 4 quarts water to boiling. Meanwhile, remove husks from corn. When water is boiling, add corn; cover and return to boiling—about 2 minutes. Immediately remove kettle from heat; let stand, cov-

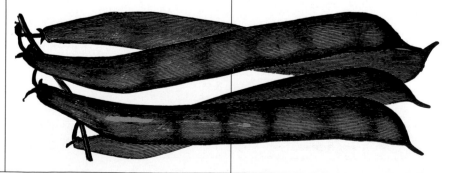

ered, 5 minutes. Drain; plunge corn immediately into a large bowl of ice water to stop further cooking.

2. In large bowl, combine parsley, salt, sugar, basil, ground red pepper, salad oil, cider vinegar and lemon juice; whisk vigorously to combine.

3. With sharp knife, cut corn off cobs to get 3 cups kernels. Add to bowl along with green and red peppers and green onions; mix well. Cover and chill several hours or overnight.

TO SERVE

4. Line a 1½-quart salad bowl or 8 individual salad plates with lettuce leaves. Spoon corn mixture into bowl or onto salad plates. *Makes 8 servings.*

GREEK BREAD SALAD

DRESSING
1 small clove garlic
1 teaspoon dried oregano leaves
⅛ teaspoon pepper
3 tablespoons red-wine vinegar
½ cup olive oil

SALAD
½ head romaine lettuce, washed and coarsely chopped
2 large tomatoes, diced
1 bunch radishes, sliced
1 large seedless cucumber, thinly sliced
8 oz feta cheese, crumbled
½ cup Greek olives, pitted and chopped

12-inch ring Italian bread

DO AHEAD

1. Make dressing: In food processor, mince garlic; add oregano, pepper and vinegar. With motor running, pour in oil in a steady stream; process until the mixture is blended.

2. Pour dressing into large salad bowl. Add salad ingredients; toss to coat.

3. Slice bread horizontally in half; remove inside, leaving ½-inch-thick shell (reserve bread from inside for another use); fill bottom half with salad. Cover with top half of bread; refrigerate up to 2 hours.

TO SERVE

4. Slice bread ring crosswise into sandwiches. *Makes 10 servings.*

WALNUT-FRUIT SALAD WITH BRIE AND MUSTARD CROUTONS

CROUTONS
4 cups stale ½-inch bread cubes
¼ cup butter or margarine, melted
3 tablespoons whole-grain Dijon-style mustard

DRESSING
½ teaspoon salt
⅛ teaspoon pepper
¼ cup raspberry vinegar
½ cup walnut oil

½ medium head iceberg lettuce (1 lb)
1 small head radicchio
¼ lb curly endive
1 bunch watercress, tough stems removed
1 medium green or red Bartlett pear, cored and sliced
1 lb seedless green or red grapes
6 oz Brie cheese, cubed
½ cup walnut pieces

DO AHEAD

1. Make croutons: Preheat oven to 350F. Place bread cubes in large roasting pan. In small bowl, blend butter with mustard; pour over bread cubes; toss to coat. Bake 15 minutes, tossing occasionally. Set aside to cool.

2. Meanwhile, make dressing: In small bowl, whisk salt, pepper and vinegar until blended. Gradually whisk in oil until blended.

TO SERVE

3. Break lettuce, radicchio, endive and watercress into bite-size pieces. Place in large bowl. In small bowl, combine pear, grapes, cheese and walnuts; toss with ¼ cup dressing until coated. Add remaining dressing to lettuce mixture; toss until coated.

4. Place lettuce mixture on each of six large plates and top each with pear mixture, dividing evenly. Sprinkle croutons over each salad. *Makes 6 servings.*

HAM AND RICE SALAD

SALAD
6 cups water
1½ cups brown rice
1 teaspoon salt
¼ cup thinly sliced prosciutto
1 large celery stalk, thinly sliced
½ cantaloupe, cubed
½ medium red pepper, diced
½ cup chopped pecans, toasted
⅓ cup pitted dates, chopped

DRESSING
¼ teaspoon pepper
3 tablespoons lemon juice
2 tablespoons prepared mustard
⅓ cup salad oil

1 bunch arugula, rinsed and patted dry
½ head curly endive, rinsed and patted dry

DO AHEAD

1. In large saucepan, bring water to boiling. Add rice and salt; return water to boiling; cover; simmer until rice is tender, about 30 minutes. Drain well.

2. Meanwhile, julienne prosciutto;

place in large bowl with remaining salad ingredients. With large fork, stir in rice until mixed.

3. Make dressing: In small bowl, whisk pepper, lemon juice and mustard until blended. Gradually whisk in oil until blended. Pour dressing over rice mixture, toss to coat. Cover with plastic wrap; refrigerate.

TO SERVE

4. Line large platter with arugula and endive. Spoon salad on top. *Makes 6 servings.*

BUFFET POTATO SALAD

Instead of adding mayonnaise to this salad, we added vinaigrette for a fresh taste.

2 lb small red new potatoes, scrubbed
½ teaspoon salt
3 ears corn on the cob, husked, each cut in 6 pieces
2 large carrots, pared, scored and cut crosswise in thin slices
2 cups broccoli flowerets

DRESSING
2 green onions, sliced
2 tablespoons chopped parsley
1 cup bottled vinaigrette dressing

Crisp lettuce leaves
4 oz aged provolone cheese

DO AHEAD

1. In 5-quart saucepan, cover potatoes with water. Add salt; cover saucepan. Bring to boiling; simmer 15 minutes, or until potatoes are tender. With slotted spoon, remove potatoes to colander; rinse with cold water to stop cooking. Quarter or halve potatoes, depending on size; place in large bowl.

2. In boiling water in which potatoes were cooked, cook corn, covered, 4 minutes; add carrots the last minute of cooking time. When vegetables are tender, with slotted spoon, remove to colander. Rinse with cold water to stop cooking. Drain; place in bowl with potatoes.

3. In boiling water in which vegetables were cooked, cook the broccoli 30 seconds. Drain; rinse with cold water to stop cooking. Drain; place in bowl with potatoes.

4. Make dressing: In small bowl, whisk ingredients until blended; add to vegetables in bowl. Toss mixture to combine. Cover with plastic wrap; refrigerate 2 hours to blend flavors, stirring occasionally.

TO SERVE

5. Line platter with lettuce leaves; spoon potato salad on top. With vegetable parer, shave cheese into curls over salad. *Makes 6 servings.* ♦

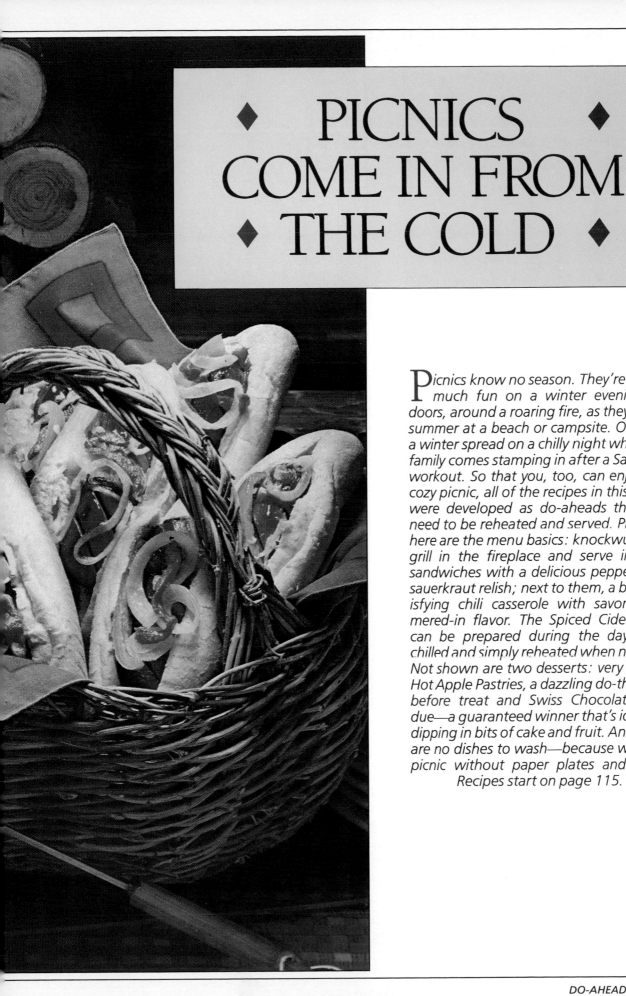

PICNICS ◆ COME IN FROM ◆ ◆ THE COLD ◆

Picnics know no season. They're just as much fun on a winter evening indoors, around a roaring fire, as they are in summer at a beach or campsite. Or serve a winter spread on a chilly night when the family comes stamping in after a Saturday workout. So that you, too, can enjoy the cozy picnic, all of the recipes in this menu were developed as do-aheads that just need to be reheated and served. Pictured here are the menu basics: knockwursts to grill in the fireplace and serve in hero sandwiches with a delicious pepper-and-sauerkraut relish; next to them, a big, satisfying chili casserole with savory simmered-in flavor. The Spiced Cider Bowl can be prepared during the day, then chilled and simply reheated when needed. Not shown are two desserts: very special Hot Apple Pastries, a dazzling do-the-day-before treat and Swiss Chocolate Fondue—a guaranteed winner that's ideal for dipping in bits of cake and fruit. And there are no dishes to wash—because what's a picnic without paper plates and cups? Recipes start on page 115.

SHAPE-UP VEGETABLE SALADS

◆

*T*hink there's nothing new with vegetables? Think again! People everywhere are discovering (and rediscovering) the great taste and wonderful do-ahead convenience of molded vegetable salads like the ones pictured here. Made with gelatine, fresh vegetables and assorted simple ingredients, these appetizing beauties add sparkle to any meal. Below and directly to the right: coleslaw and potato salad. Other delicious possibilities (from top to bottom) are a tangy gazpacho mold, rimmed by avocado slices; a lemony circle of pineapple and cucumber, crowned with watercress; a ruby-red ring of beets in aspic; and a mold of creamy avocado. Recipes for these and more start on page 114.

◆

GEORGE RATKAI

continued from page 112

AVOCADO SALAD MOLD
(pictured)

1 cup boiling water
1 pkg (3 oz) lime gelatine
2 tablespoons lemon juice
3 tablespoons chopped parsley
2 cups puréed avocado
¼ cup heavy cream, whipped
¾ cup mayonnaise

DO AHEAD

1. Pour boiling water over gelatine in large bowl, stirring to dissolve. Add lemon juice.

2. Set in bowl of ice, stirring occasionally, until mixture is consistency of unbeaten egg white—25 to 35 minutes.

3. Add parsley, avocado, whipped cream and mayonnaise to gelatine mixture; mix well.

4. Turn into 5-cup decorative mold or ring mold; refrigerate until firm—2 to 3 hours.

TO SERVE

5. Unmold by loosening edge of mold with small spatula. Invert over serving platter; place a hot, damp dishcloth over mold; shake to release; lift off mold. *Makes 8 servings.*

MOLDED COLESLAW
(pictured)

1 head green cabbage, shredded (10 cups)
1 cup coarsely grated carrot
1 large green pepper, cut in rings
1 medium-size sweet onion, cut in rings
1 cup sugar
1 teaspoon dry mustard
1 teaspoon celery seed
1 tablespoon salt
1 cup white vinegar
¾ cup salad oil
2 env unflavored gelatine

DO AHEAD

1. In large bowl, make layers of cabbage, carrot, green pepper and onion. Sprinkle sugar over top.

2. In small saucepan, combine mustard, celery seed, salt, vinegar and oil; mix well. Bring to a full boil, stirring; pour over slaw. Refrigerate, covered, at least 4 hours.

3. Drain coleslaw; measure liquid. You should have 1½ cups. Refrigerate coleslaw.

4. In small saucepan, sprinkle the gelatine over coleslaw liquid; let stand to soften.

5. Place over low heat; stir until gelatine is dissolved. Remove from heat.

6. Set in bowl of ice, stirring occa-

sionally, until mixture is consistency of unbeaten egg white—25 to 30 minutes.

7. Stir chilled gelatine mixture into coleslaw; mix well.

8. Carefully pack into 3-quart Bundt pan or ring mold. Refrigerate until firm—2 to 3 hours.

TO SERVE

9. Unmold by running a small spatula around edge of mold. Invert over serving plate; hold a hot, damp dishcloth over inverted mold; shake to release. If necessary, dampen cloth again with hot water. *Makes 12 to 16 servings.*

CUCUMBER-PINEAPPLE ASPIC
(pictured)

1 can (1 lb, 4 oz) pineapple chunks
1 cup boiling water
2 pkg (3-oz size) lemon-flavored gelatine
¼ cup white-wine vinegar
¼ teaspoon salt
2 medium cucumbers, pared and grated (2 cups)
½ cup finely chopped celery
¼ cup prepared horseradish
1 tablespoon grated onion
About 20 paper-thin slices cucumber
Watercress

DO AHEAD

1. Drain pineapple, reserve liquid.

2. In medium bowl, pour boiling water over gelatine; stir until dissolved. Stir in reserved pineapple liquid, vinegar and salt.

3. Set in bowl of ice, stirring occasionally, until mixture is consistency of unbeaten egg white—about 35 minutes.

4. Fold in grated cucumber, celery, horseradish, onion and pineapple chunks until well blended.

5. Line a 5½-cup ring mold with thin cucumber slices. Turn gelatine mixture into mold.

6. Refrigerate until firm—at least 3 hours.

TO SERVE

7. Unmold by running a small spatula around edge of mold. Invert over platter; place a hot, damp dishcloth over inverted mold, and shake gently to release. Fill center with watercress. *Makes 8 to 10 servings.*

MOLDED POTATO SALAD
(pictured)

3 lb (8 medium) potatoes, cooked and diced, about ½ inch (6¾ cups)
¾ cup finely chopped onion
¾ cup bottled herb-garlic salad dressing
2 env unflavored gelatine
1½ cups water

1½ cups mayonnaise or cooked salad dressing
⅓ cup pickle juice
3 tablespoons lemon juice or cider vinegar
2 teaspoons salt
1 cup cubed pared cucumber
½ cup chopped green pepper
1 can (4 oz) pimientos, drained and diced
⅓ cup sliced sweet gherkins
2 hard-cooked eggs, shelled (optional)
Radishes (optional)

DO AHEAD

1. In large bowl, combine warm potato and the onion with salad dressing; toss lightly to combine; let stand 1 hour.

2. Sprinkle gelatine over 1½ cups water in saucepan to soften. Place over low heat; stir until gelatine is dissolved. Remove from heat.

3. In medium bowl, combine mayonnaise, pickle juice, lemon juice and salt; stir until smooth. Gradually stir in gelatine.

4. Set in bowl of ice, stirring occasionally, until mixture is consistency of unbeaten egg white—25 to 30 minutes.

5. To potato mixture, add cucumber, green pepper, pimientos and sweet gherkins; toss lightly to combine. Stir in chilled gelatine mixture.

6. Carefully pack into a 2½-quart bowl. Refrigerate until firm—3 to 4 hours or overnight.

TO SERVE

7. Unmold by running a small spatula around edge of bowl. Invert over serving plate; hold a hot, damp dishcloth over inverted bowl, and shake to release. If necessary, dampen cloth again with hot water. Refrigerate.

8. If desired, decorate with whites from hard-cooked eggs, radishes and sieved egg yolks, as pictured. *Makes 12 servings.*

JULIENNE BEETS IN ASPIC
(pictured)

1 cup boiling water
1 pkg (3 oz) lemon-flavored gelatine
¾ cup cold water
2 tablespoons lemon juice
1 can (1 lb) julienne beets, drained
1 tablespoon grated onion
2 tablespoons prepared horseradish
1¼ teaspoons salt
Dash pepper

DO AHEAD

1. Pour boiling water over gelatine in medium bowl; stir until gelatine is dissolved; add ¾ cup cold water and lemon juice.

2. Set in bowl of ice, stirring occasionally, until mixture is consistency of unbeaten egg white—25 to 30 minutes.

continued on page 135

continued from page 111

A WINTER PICNIC

(Planned for 8 to 10)

SPICED CIDER BOWL*
**KNOCKWURST HEROES* WITH
SAUERKRAUT AND SAUTEED
PEPPERS
OR MEXICALI CHILI***
**BASKET OF HOT FRENCH FRIES
PICKLES AND OLIVES
WARM CHOCOLATE FONDUE***
**WITH CAKE AND FRUIT
FOR DIPPING
OR HOT APPLE PASTRIES***
WITH VANILLA ICE CREAM

*Recipes given for starred dishes.

SPICED CIDER BOWL

(pictured)

1 gallon cider (see Note)
½ cup light-brown sugar, packed (optional)
8 to 10 (3-inch) cinnamon sticks, broken into pieces
10 to 15 whole allspice
20 to 25 whole cloves
10 small red apples, washed

DO AHEAD

1. In 6-quart kettle, bring all ingredients except apples to boiling; simmer, uncovered, about 30 minutes. Strain through a double layer of cheesecloth.
2. Refrigerate the cider until needed.

TO SERVE

3. Reheat in a large kettle. Float small apples on top. Place a cinnamon-stick stirrer in each mug, if desired. *Makes 8 to 10 servings.*
Note: Use unpasteurized cider, if possible.

KNOCKWURST HEROES

(pictured)

4 green peppers (about 1½ lb)
4 large yellow onions (about 2 lb)
4 tablespoons olive or salad oil
1 jar (7½ oz) roasted sweet red peppers, cut into strips
1 can (8 oz) sauerkraut, drained
8 to 10 knockwursts
1 cup prepared barbecue sauce, heated
8 to 10 hero rolls (6 inches long), heated
Crushed red pepper (optional)

DO AHEAD

1. Cut peppers in half lengthwise; remove ribs and seeds. Cut lengthwise into ½-inch strips.
2. Peel onions; slice into ¼-inch-thick slices.

3. Heat oil in large skillet. Add green pepper and onion; cook over medium heat, stirring frequently, until tender-crisp—about 10 minutes. Stir in red pepper and sauerkraut. Cool, cover and refrigerate.

4. About 15 minutes before serving time, reheat pepper-and-onion relish. Make 4 or 5 diagonal slashes, ½ inch deep, in each knockwurst. Broil knockwursts, basting with some of barbecue sauce, 4 to 6 inches from heat, turning often to brown evenly, 10 minutes, or until done. (See Note.)

TO SERVE

5. Split rolls almost through. Place a knockwurst in each roll. Top with pepper-and-onion relish amd more barbecue sauce. Season with crushed red pepper, if desired. Serve at once. *Makes 8 to 10 sandwiches.*
Note: Or put knockwursts on long-handled forks or sticks, and cook in fireplace.

MEXICALI CHILI

(pictured)

¼ cup salad oil
1 cup chopped onion
1 cup chopped green pepper
1 garlic clove, crushed
2 lb ground beef chuck
2 cans (1-lb size) tomatoes, undrained
1 can (6 oz) tomato paste
2 tablespoons chili powder
1 tablespoon sugar
3 teaspoons salt
¼ teaspoon pepper
⅛ teaspoon paprika
2 bay leaves
1 teaspoon ground cumin
1 teaspoon dried basil leaves
Dash ground red pepper
2 cans (1-lb size) kidney beans, drained
½ cup grated Cheddar cheese

DO AHEAD

1. In hot oil in large skillet, sauté onion, green pepper and garlic, stirring, until tender—about 5 minutes. Drain.
2. In a 5-quart Dutch oven, brown

the beef. Drain fat from beef; add drained vegetable mixture.

3. Add all remaining ingredients except beans and cheese; simmer ½ hour, or until very thick. Cool, cover and refrigerate.

TO SERVE

4. Reheat meat mixture slowly—about 20 minutes. Add beans; heat gently several minutes. Sprinkle with Cheddar cheese. Run under broiler a few seconds, just to melt cheese. *Makes 8 servings.*

CHOCOLATE FONDUE

2 pkg (6-oz size) semisweet chocolate pieces
1 can (13 oz) evaporated milk, undiluted
½ cup orange juice, kirsch or rum
1 tablespoon grated orange peel

For dipping in fondue: Pineapple chunks, marshmallows, squares of poundcake or angel-food cake, banana slices, dates, maraschino cherries, pitted dried prunes, dried apricots

DO AHEAD

1. In a heavy saucepan, combine chocolate and evaporated milk. Cook, stirring constantly, over low heat until chocolate is melted. Stir in orange juice and peel; remove from heat. Cool, cover and refrigerate.

TO SERVE

2. Reheat, stirring, in top of double boiler, just before serving.
3. Serve warm in fondue pot; surround with cake and fruit for dipping on fondue forks or other long-handled forks. *Makes 8 to 10 servings.* ◆

HOT APPLE PASTRIES

PASTRY

2½ cups all-purpose flour
1 tablespoon sugar
1 teaspoon salt
1 cup shortening
1 egg
⅔ cup milk

FILLING

⅔ cup cornflake crumbs
5 cups sliced, pared tart apples
1½ cups sugar
1½ teaspoons ground cinnamon

GLAZE

1 egg white, slightly beaten
1 cup sifted confectioners' sugar
2 tablespoons lemon juice

DO AHEAD

1. Make Pastry: In medium bowl,
continued on page 135

MEALS
IN A
HURRY
WITH
MAKE-AHEAD
SAUCES

Aflavorful homemade sauce can turn an otherwise plain meal into something special. But the catch is that making a rich, thick sauce takes time. The solution? Cook a large potful and freeze it in convenient servings. Then you can prepare any of these delicious dishes—and more—at a moment's notice. Clockwise from the center: Chicken-Broccoli Divan, with a zesty Cheese Sauce; Chili With Polenta; Chicken Cacciatore, simmered in Marinara Sauce; scallops in curry sauce; and Eggplant Parmigiana in a savory meat sauce. For these recipes and others, plus freezing tips, turn to page 118.

continued from page 117

NOTES ON FREEZING AND USING BASIC SAUCES

1. Assemble necessary packaging materials before preparing sauces. Sauces should be packed in sturdy, leakproof containers (plastic freezing containers) with straight sides and wide mouths for easy removal. They may be frozen overnight in rigid containers, removed frozen from the containers and repackaged in plastic bags or other moisture-vapor-resistant material made especially for freezing. Or they may be frozen directly in plastic bags in rigid containers and removed when completely frozen. This permits reuse of the containers while giving the sauces a form that allows for easy freezer packing. Be sure to seal tightly.

2. Before freezing sauces, cool slightly at room temperature; refrigerate until completely cooled; package immediately.

3. Freeze sauces in amounts specified in individual recipes—cups, pints, quarts. Leave ½- to ¾-inch head space in containers. Label containers clearly with sauce, amount and date.

4. To use, thaw sauces overnight in refrigerator or several hours at room temperature. They do not have to be completely thawed for use.

5. One larger container takes longer to thaw than several smaller ones.

MARINARA SAUCE

3 cans (2-lb, 3-oz size) Italian-style tomatoes, undrained
2¾ cups chopped onion
6 garlic cloves, crushed

1½ teaspoons dried basil leaves
1½ teaspoons dried oregano leaves
1½ teaspoons fennel seed
1½ teaspoons sugar
6 teaspoons salt
¼ teaspoon pepper (optional)

1. In a large 8-quart kettle, mix all ingredients. Bring to boiling over medium heat, stirring until tomatoes are slightly broken up.

2. Reduce heat; simmer, covered and stirring occasionally, 2 hours, or until thickened and flavors blend. Cool. *Makes 3 quarts*. (One quart is enough for ½ pound of spaghetti.)

CHILI SAUCE

1 lb ground chuck (in chunks)
2 medium onions, chopped
1½ to 2 tablespoons chili powder
2 cans (1-lb size) dark-red kidney beans
1 can (1 lb, 12 oz) whole tomatoes, undrained
1 teaspoon salt
⅛ teaspoon pepper
¼ teaspoon garlic powder
½ teaspoon sugar
¼ cup catsup

1. In large kettle, over medium heat, sauté ground chuck, stirring, until red color disappears. Pour off fat.

2. Add chopped onion and chili powder; cook, stirring, about 5 minutes, or until onion is tender.

3. Drain one can of beans; use one can undrained. Add with rest of ingredients to meat, breaking up tomatoes with fork; stir to mix well. Simmer slowly, covered and stirring occasionally, until thickened and flavors are blended—about 1 hour. *Makes 2 quarts*. (Use one quart with 2 or 3 cups cooked rice for 4 servings.)

CHEESE SAUCE

¾ cup (1½ sticks) butter or margarine
¾ cup all-purpose flour
3 teaspoons salt
⅛ teaspoon ground nutmeg
1 quart milk
2 cups canned condensed chicken broth, undiluted
4 egg yolks
1 cup light cream or half and half
2 cups grated sharp Cheddar cheese

1. Melt butter in large saucepan. Remove from heat; stir in flour, salt and the nutmeg until smooth. Gradually add milk and chicken broth; bring to boiling, stirring constantly; boil 2 minutes, or until mixture is slightly thickened.

2. In small bowl, with wire whisk or wooden spoon, beat egg yolks with cream. Beat in a little of the hot mixture. Pour back into saucepan; cook over low heat, stirring constantly, until sauce is hot—do not boil. Remove from heat. Stir in cheese. *Makes 2 quarts*.

CURRY SAUCE

½ cup (1 stick) butter or margarine
2 garlic cloves, crushed
2 cups chopped onion
4 to 6 teaspoons curry powder
2 cups chopped pared tart apple
¾ cup all-purpose flour
½ teaspoon ground cardamom
2 teaspoons ground ginger
½ teaspoon pepper
5 cans (10¾-oz size) condensed chicken broth, undiluted
4 teaspoons grated lemon peel
4 tablespoons lemon juice
2 tablespoons chutney

1. In hot butter in large skillet, sauté garlic, onion, curry powder and apple until onion is tender—about 5 minutes. Remove from heat. Stir in flour, cardamom, ginger and pepper; mix well. Cook over low heat, stirring, several minutes.

2. Gradually stir in chicken broth, lemon peel and juice. Bring to boiling, stirring. Reduce heat; simmer, uncovered and stirring occasionally, 50 minutes; add chutney. *Makes 7 cups*.

SPAGHETTI MEAT SAUCE

1½ lb ground chuck
2 cups finely chopped onion
2 garlic cloves, crushed
2 tablespoons sugar
2 tablespoons salt
2 teaspoons dried basil leaves
1 teaspoon dried oregano leaves
⅛ teaspoon crushed red pepper
2 cans (2-lb, 3-oz size) Italian-style tomatoes, undrained
1 can (6-oz) tomato paste
1 can (1 lb) tomato purée

1. In 5-quart Dutch oven, over medium heat, sauté ground chuck (break into chunks with wooden spoon) 10 minutes. Add onion and garlic, stirring frequently, until meat is browned and vegetables are tender—about 10 minutes longer.

2. Add sugar, salt, basil, oregano and crushed red pepper; mix well. Add tomatoes, tomato paste and tomato purée; mash tomatoes with wooden spoon. Bring to boiling; reduce heat; simmer, covered and stirring occasionally, until thickened—1½ to 2 hours. *Makes 3 quarts*. (One quart is enough for ½ pound of spaghetti.)

CURRIED SCALLOPS
(pictured)

1 lb sea scallops
2 tablespoons butter or margarine
1 pint (2 cups) Curry Sauce, page 118
1 lime, cut into 8 wedges.

1. Rinse scallops gently under cold water; drain. If large, cut in half.
2. In hot butter in large, heavy skillet, sauté scallops over medium heat, stirring occasionally, until golden-brown and cooked through —5 to 8 minutes.
3. Add curry sauce to skillet; simmer over low heat, stirring until heated through—8 to 10 minutes.
4. To serve: Turn into four scallop shells or 1-quart casserole. Garnish with lime wedges. *Makes 4 servings.*

CHICKEN CACCIATORE
(pictured)

4-lb roasting chicken, cut into 8 pieces
3 tablespoons olive or salad oil
4 tablespoons (½ stick) butter or margarine
1½ pints (3 cups) Marinara Sauce, page 118
2 tablespoons chopped parsley
½ teaspoon salt
¼ teaspoon pepper
¼ lb mushrooms, washed and sliced
1 tablespoon all-purpose flour
2 tablespoons water

1. Wash chicken under cold running water and pat dry with paper towels.
2. Heat oil and 3 tablespoons butter in 6-quart Dutch oven. Add chicken, a few pieces at a time, and brown well on all sides. Remove as browned.
3. Return chicken to Dutch oven; add Marinara Sauce, parsley, salt and pepper. Simmer, covered, 45 to 50 minutes, or until chicken is tender.
4. Meanwhile, sauté mushrooms in 1 tablespoon butter about 3 minutes.
5. Combine flour with water; stir into sauce. Add mushrooms; cook 10 minutes longer, or until sauce is thickened. *Makes 8 servings.*

CHILI WITH POLENTA
(pictured)

2½ cups cold water
½ teaspoon salt
¾ cup yellow cornmeal
1 egg, beaten
1 quart (4 cups) Chili Sauce, page 118
2 tablespoons butter or margarine, melted
¾ cup grated sharp Cheddar cheese

1. In 3½-quart heavy saucepan, bring cold water and the salt to boiling. Add cornmeal slowly, stirring constantly with wooden spoon.
2. Reduce heat; simmer, uncovered and stirring occasionally, until mixture is thick and leaves side of pan. Continue cooking, covered, 10 minutes.
3. Remove from heat; stir in egg, mixing well.
4. Pour into lightly greased 8½-by-4½-by-2½-inch loaf pan; refrigerate until stiff enough to cut—3 hours.
5. Just before serving, cut 10 to 12 slices. In medium saucepan, over medium heat, bring sauce to boiling. Spread in bottom of 2-quart casserole. Arrange polenta slices, overlapping, over top. Brush polenta with butter; then sprinkle with Cheddar cheese.
6. Run under broiler until heated through and top is golden-brown. *Makes 8 servings.*
Note: Polenta may be made the day before and refrigerated overnight. Just before serving, proceed as above.

EGGPLANT PARMIGIANA
(pictured)

1 quart (4 cups) Spaghetti Meat Sauce, page 118
1 large eggplant (1½ lb)
2 eggs, slightly beaten
1 tablespoon water
½ cup packaged dry bread crumbs
1¼ cups grated Parmesan cheese
⅓ cup salad oil
1 pkg (8 oz) mozzarella cheese, sliced

1. Preheat oven to 350F. Lightly grease a 13-by-9-by-2-inch baking dish.
2. Over medium heat, bring sauce to boiling. Keep warm.
3. Wash eggplant; do not peel. Cut crosswise into slices ½ inch thick.
4. In pie plate, combine eggs and water; mix well.
5. On a sheet of waxed paper, combine bread crumbs with ½ cup Parmesan cheese; mix well.
6. Dip eggplant slices into egg mixture, coating well. Then dip into crumb mixture, coating evenly.
7. Sauté eggplant slices, a few at a time, in 1 tablespoon hot oil until golden-brown and crisp on both sides. Add more oil as needed.
8. Arrange half of eggplant slices in bottom of prepared baking dish. Sprinkle with half of remaining Parmesan cheese. Top with half of mozzarella. Cover with half of meat sauce.
9. Arrange remaining eggplant slices over meat sauce. Cover with rest of meat sauce, mozzarella and Parmesan.

10. Bake, uncovered, 25 minutes or until cheese is melted and slightly browned. *Makes 6 servings.*

CHICKEN-BROCCOLI DIVAN
(pictured)

2 (12-oz size) whole chicken breasts, split
Butter or margarine
½ cup chicken broth
1½ cups Cheese Sauce, page 118
¼ cup dry white wine
1 pkg (10 oz) frozen broccoli spears
¼ cup grated Parmesan cheese

1. Wash chicken breasts under cold running water and pat dry with paper towels. With a sharp knife, carefully remove skin and bone, keeping breasts intact.
2. In 4 tablespoons hot butter in medium skillet, over medium heat, sauté chicken 10 minutes on each side. Add broth; simmer, covered, 10 minutes.
3. Preheat oven to 350F. Grease a 12-by-8-by-2-inch shallow baking dish.
4. In a small saucepan, combine Cheese Sauce and white wine.
5. Bring to boiling over medium heat, stirring constantly. Reduce heat; simmer 3 minutes. Remove from heat.
6. Meanwhile, cook broccoli as package label directs; drain well.
7. Arrange in prepared dish. Place chicken on top. Spoon sauce over chicken; sprinkle with Parmesan.
8. Bake 15 minutes, or until sauce is bubbly and top is lightly browned. *Makes 4 servings.*

CURRIED CHICKEN BREASTS EN CASSEROLE

3 whole chicken breasts (about 2½ lb), split
¼ cup (½ stick) butter or margarine
1 quart (4 cups) Curry Sauce, page 118
1 large banana, peeled and sliced
Fluffy cooked rice

1. Skin chicken; wash under cold running water and pat dry with paper towels. Brown chicken, a few pieces at at time, in hot butter in large skillet, 5 minutes per side. Preheat oven to 375F.
2. Return all chicken to skillet. Add Curry Sauce; bring to boiling. Reduce heat; simmer, covered, 20 minutes. Remove cover and cook 10 minutes longer or until chicken is tender. Add banana; simmer 5 minutes.
3. Arrange chicken breasts, overlapping slightly, in 2-quart shallow casserole or serving platter.

continued on page 120

continued from page 102

CHICKEN BREASTS TONNATO
(pictured)

4 (1-lb size) chicken breasts, split in half
1 large onion, sliced
1 celery stalk, sliced
1 carrot, pared and sliced
2 parsley sprigs
1 teaspoon salt
½ teaspoon dried thyme leaves
1 can (10¾ oz) condensed chicken broth, undiluted
1 cup water
Tonnato Sauce, recipe follows
1 head iceberg lettuce, shredded
Capers
2 tomatoes, each cut into 4 wedges
Watercress sprigs

DO AHEAD

1. Wash chicken under cold running water and pat dry with paper towels. In large skillet, combine chicken, onion, celery, carrot, parsley, salt, thyme, chicken broth and water; bring to boiling.

2. Reduce heat; simmer, covered, 30 minutes, until chicken is fork-tender.

3. Remove skillet from heat; let chicken cool in the broth. Meanwhile, make Tonnato Sauce, reserving 16 anchovies.

4. Remove chicken from broth; strain and reserve broth for future use. Remove and discard skin and bone. Cover and refrigerate.

TO SERVE

5. On large round platter lined with shredded lettuce, arrange chicken breasts in a circle.

6. Spoon Tonnato Sauce over each breast. Garnish each breast with 2 anchovy fillets and 2 capers, as pictured.

7. Place tomato wedges between chicken breasts. Garnish center with watercress. *Makes 8 servings.*

TONNATO SAUCE

1 can (2 oz) anchovy fillets
1 cup mayonnaise
1 can (7 oz) tuna, drained
½ cup finely chopped celery
½ teaspoon salt
Dash black pepper
1 tablespoon lemon juice

1. Drain anchovy fillets; chop two fillets; use rest for garnish.

2. In blender or food processor, combine chopped anchovies with all remaining ingredients; blend until smooth.

3. Turn into 2-cup container with tight-fitting lid; refrigerate, covered, until ready to use. *Makes 1¼ cups.*

MEALS IN A HURRY—WITH MAKE-AHEAD SAUCES

continued from page 119

4. Spoon sauce over chicken breasts. Serve with rice. Nice served with chutney. *Makes 6 servings.*

GOLDEN BUCK

1½ cups Cheese Sauce, page 118
¼ teaspoon prepared mustard
Dash ground red pepper
6 eggs
6 slices white bread or 3 English muffins, split
Tomato slices (optional)

1. In small saucepan, over medium heat, combine Cheese Sauce, mustard and pepper. Stir constantly until sauce is smooth and hot. Remove from heat; keep over hot water.

2. Poach eggs. In shallow pan or skillet, bring water (about 1 inch deep) to boiling point. Reduce heat to simmer. Break each egg into a saucer; quickly slip egg into water. Cook, covered, 3 to 5 minutes. Lift out of water with slotted pancake turner. Drain well on paper towels. Toast bread.

3. To serve: Spoon about 2 tablespoons sauce on each slice of toast; top with a poached egg. Spoon any remaining sauce over eggs. Garnish with a tomato slice, if desired. *Makes 6 servings.*

CONEY ISLAND HOT DOGS

6 frankfurter rolls
6 frankfurters
1½ cups Chili Sauce, page 118
Chopped onion
Pickle relish or hot sauerkraut
Catsup
Mustard

1. Sprinkle rolls lightly with water; wrap tightly in foil. Heat in 350F oven while heating frankfurters.

2. In large saucepan, bring 1 quart water to boiling. Add frankfurters. Cover, and turn heat very low; heat 5 to 8 minutes. Meanwhile, in small saucepan, heat Chili Sauce.

3. To serve: Fill each warm roll with a frankfurter; top with chili. Pass onion, pickle relish, catsup and mustard. *Makes 6 servings.* ◆

COUNTRY PATE
(pictured)

½ lb sliced bacon

SPINACH LAYER
2 pkg (10-oz size) frozen chopped spinach, thawed and drained
½ cup chopped onion
¼ cup chopped parsley
1 garlic clove, crushed
½ teaspoon dried marjoram leaves
1 teaspoon dried thyme leaves
1 teaspoon salt
Dash ground nutmeg
Dash pepper

PORK LAYER
1½ lb ground pork (2½ cups)
½ lb ground ham
½ cup coarsely chopped black olives
½ cup chopped onion
1 garlic clove, crushed
½ teaspoon dried marjoram leaves
1 teaspoon dried thyme leaves
½ teaspoon salt
Dash hot red-pepper sauce
2 eggs, slightly beaten
¼ cup brandy

GLAZE
1 tablespoon unflavored gelatine
¼ cup water
1 cup dry white wine
3 pitted black olives, halved
1 carrot slice

DO AHEAD

1. Line 2-quart soufflé dish with bacon. Preheat oven to 400F.

2. Make Spinach Layer: In large bowl, combine spinach, ½ cup onion, parsley, 1 garlic clove, ½ teaspoon each, marjoram and thyme, 1 teaspoon salt, nutmeg and pepper; mix well.

3. Prepare Pork Layer: In medium bowl, combine pork, ham, olives, onion, garlic, marjoram, thyme, salt, pepper sauce, eggs and brandy; mix well.

4. Divide pork mixture into thirds, spinach mixture in half.

5. Press each layer in prepared mold as follows: a third of pork and half of spinach. Repeat, finishing with remaining third of pork. Cover with foil.

6. Place in pan of boiling water (1 inch deep). Bake 1½ hours.

7. Remove pâté from hot water; cool completely on rack. Refrigerate overnight.

NEXT DAY

8. Unmold: Loosen edge with spatula; turn out on wire rack on a tray. Discard bacon; smooth pâté. Refrigerate.

9. Prepare Glaze: Sprinkle gelatine over water in small saucepan. Add wine; stir over low heat until gelatine is dissolved. Set pan in ice water; stir until slightly thickened (starts to jell)—15 minutes.

10. Use half of glaze to cover pâté. Refrigerate to set glaze 30 minutes.

11. Decorate, as pictured, with ring of black olives and carrot slice in center.

12. Reheat remaining glaze; rechill. Spoon over pâté. Refrigerate. Nice with crackers or small slices of rye bread. *Makes 40 servings.*

CREAM-OF-CARROT SOUP WITH FRESH MINT
(pictured)

For recipe, turn to page 19.

GLAZED HAM-AND-SPINACH ROULADE
(pictured)

1 cup milk
1 egg
2 tablespoons catsup
2 tablespoons prepared brown mustard
1 teaspoon salt
⅛ teaspoon pepper
2 cups soft fine white-bread crumbs
1½ lb ground cooked ham (5 cups)
½ lb ground raw pork
½ lb ground raw veal
2 tablespoons finely chopped onion
2 tablespoons chopped parsley

SPINACH FILLING

2 pkg (10-oz size) frozen chopped spinach, thawed and drained
2 tablespoons butter or margarine
¼ cup finely chopped onion
¼ cup grated sharp Cheddar cheese
½ cup sour cream

½ cup apple jelly

DO AHEAD

1. In large bowl, combine milk, egg, catsup, mustard, salt and pepper; mix well. Stir in crumbs; let stand 5 minutes. Add meats, 2 tablespoons onion and parsley; mix well.

2. Make Spinach Filling: In hot butter in medium skillet, sauté onion until golden—about 5 minutes, stirring constantly. Add spinach, cheese and sour cream; mix well. Remove from heat.

3. Preheat oven to 350F. Roll out ham mixture between two sheets of waxed

paper placed on damp surface. Roll to form a rectangle 14 by 10 inches.

4. Remove top sheet of waxed paper. Spread meat evenly with spinach filling; roll up as for jelly roll, starting with narrow edge. Place the roulade, seam side down, in shallow roasting pan lined with foil.

5. Bake, uncovered, 1 hour. Meanwhile, melt apple jelly.

6. Remove from oven; brush surface with apple jelly. Let stand 10 minutes before removing to a serving platter. Refrigerate until ready to serve.

TO SERVE

7. Serve at room temperature. *Makes 10 servings.*

BUTTERSCOTCH WALNUT CAKE
(pictured)

3 cups all-purpose flour
½ teaspoon baking powder
1 cup (2 sticks) butter or margarine
½ cup shortening
2 cups (1 lb) light-brown sugar
1 cup granulated sugar
5 eggs
1 teaspoon vanilla extract
1 cup milk
1 cup coarsely chopped walnuts

BUTTERSCOTCH FROSTING

½ cup (1 stick) butter or margarine
1 cup light-brown sugar, firmly packed
⅓ cup half-and-half or evaporated milk, undiluted
1¼ cups confectioners' sugar
1 teaspoon vanilla extract

1 cup walnuts

DO AHEAD

1. Preheat oven to 350F. Lightly grease a 10-by-4-inch tube pan.

2. Sift together flour and baking powder; set aside.

3. In large bowl of electric mixer, at medium speed, beat 1 cup butter and the shortening until creamy. Gradually beat in 2 cups brown sugar and the granulated sugar, beating until light and fluffy. Beat in eggs, one at a time, beating well after each addition. Add 1 teaspoon vanilla.

4. At low speed, beat in flour mixture (in fourths), alternately with milk (in thirds), beginning and ending with flour mixture. Stir in chopped walnuts.

5. Pour batter into prepared pan; bake 65 to 75 minutes, or until cake tester inserted in center comes out clean.

6. Cool in pan on wire rack 20 minutes. Remove from pan; cool thoroughly.

7. Make Butterscotch Frosting: In small saucepan, melt butter over low heat. Remove from heat. Add brown

sugar, stirring until smooth. Over low heat, bring to boiling, stirring; boil, stirring, 1 minute. Remove from heat.

8. Add half-and-half. Over low heat, return just to boiling. Remove from heat. Let cool to 110F on candy thermometer or until bottom of saucepan feels lukewarm.

9. With wooden spoon, beat in confectioners' sugar until smooth. Add vanilla. (If frosting is too thin, add a little more sugar.) Spread over cake, letting it run down sides. Sprinkle top with walnuts. *Makes 16 servings.*

FRESH STRAWBERRY-PEAR PIE
(pictured)

PASTRY

1½ cups all-purpose flour
3 tablespoons sugar
⅛ teaspoon salt
⅔ cup (1⅓ sticks) butter or margarine
2 tablespoons white vinegar

FILLING

2 pints fresh strawberries, washed and drained
3 ripe fresh pears
⅔ cup sugar
⅛ teaspoon salt
¼ teaspoon ground cinnamon
½ cup all-purpose flour
½ cup strawberry preserves, melted

DO AHEAD

1. Sift 1½ cups flour with 3 tablespoons sugar and ⅛ teaspoon salt into medium bowl. Cut in butter with pastry blender or 2 knives (used scissors-fashion) until mixture resembles coarse cornmeal.

2. Add vinegar, stirring until mixture is moistened. With hands, shape into a ball. Refrigerate 1 hour.

3. Meanwhile, prepare Filling. Hull and slice berries. Set aside ½ pint. Pare, core and thinly slice 2 pears. Preheat oven to 375F.

4. In small bowl, combine sugar, salt, cinnamon and flour; mix well.

5. Add to strawberries and pears in large bowl, tossing lightly to combine.

6. Press pastry evenly onto bottom and side of a 9-inch pie plate, ½ inch above side to form edge. Crimp decoratively.

7. Turn filling into pastry-lined pie plate, mounding in center. Bake 55 to 60 minutes, until filling is hot and bubbly.

8. Pare and slice remaining pear. Remove baked pie to rack; cool ½ hour. Top with remaining strawberries and sliced pear. Brush with melted preserves. Refrigerate about 2 hours.

TO SERVE

9. Serve cold. *Makes 8 servings.* ◆

MAKE-AHEAD
B·U·F·F·E·T

Prepare most of this savory feast for eight a day ahead, and then enjoy your own party. From right to left, glorious Brie, festooned with grapes, apples and pears; Tapenade—toast triangles served with blended olives, garlic, anchovies and tuna; cheese-and-mustard cream-puff dumplings (Gnocchi); salad with roasted green peppers; Beef Balls Provençale (herbs, vegetables and sauce)…and French bread. Recipes for these delectables are on page 140.

Do-Ahead
Entertaining

A re excuses like "I don't know what to serve"; "It's too much work"; and "There's no room in the house" preventing you from entertaining as much as you'd like? If so, get ready to say good-bye to excuses. We've eliminated the guess-work...and the last-minute work...from enter-taining with the delightful do-ahead menus in this offering. And you can forget about not having room in the house because these menus lend themselves to outdoor settings. Our seven mar-velous menus take care of everything from a fam-ily dinner on the porch to an elegant picnic supper for eight or ten (perfect to take to an outdoor concert). There's a lunch on the terrace (serves eight), a Sunday brunch in the garden (for twelve), an afternoon tea, a collection of delectable party hors d'oeuvres and a glorious chocolate cake to feed a dozen hungry teenagers. All the food can be prepared ahead of time and eaten cold—at home or elsewhere. For the family—coleslaw and tomatoes with a tangy boiled dressing, above left. The antipasto platter (above right) has three dif-ferent relishes: fresh mushrooms and black olives with cherry tomatoes, mixed marinated vegeta-bles, and marinated artichoke hearts. It's a won-derful do-ahead hors d'oeuvre. Pictured below, delicate Salmon Mousse to serve at luncheon with fresh cucumbers and watercress. (continued)

For an afternoon tea party (opposite page) a trio of fresh fruits creates a simple but succulent display, while packaged cake mix and a sweetened lemon cream bake together for a Lemon-Swirl Marble Cake that's glazed or dusted with confectioners' sugar. Dine in style on the veal-and-ham loaf, top right. It's baked with wine and shallots, then chilled overnight in a parsley glaze. The Individual Rhubarb-And-Strawberry Pies, middle right, are the perfect finish for a family feast. Make them ahead to serve cold, or reheat and top with ice cream. If you're inviting guests over for cocktails, go all out with our Ham Pâté en Croûte, below right. It's not nearly as hard to make as it looks: Our shortcut crust is a loaf of French bread hollowed out, filled with pâté and then chilled until ready to slice. Above, a special totable fruit dish. The make-ahead cookie shells and strawberries in sauce can be packed separately and assembled just before serving. Menus and recipes start on page 130.

Fabulous Party Hors d'Oeuvre

A cocktail party is nothing more than a gathering of friends, a few drinks and some delicious nibbles. The next time you are entertaining, serve this impressive and easy-to-make hors d'oeuvre: a warm creamy wheel of Brie nestled in a crust of pastry and topped with fresh fruit. Complement the Brie with a glass of Alsace Riesling wine or Bordeaux wine.

WARM FRUITED BRIE

1 pkg (15 oz) refrigerated all-ready piecrust	1 cup seedless green grapes
2-lb wheel Brie cheese, about 8 inches in diameter	½ pint raspberries
2 apples, cored and sliced	1 cup apple juice
	1 tablespoon cornstarch

1. Do ahead: Preheat oven to 400F. On a large baking sheet, unfold one piecrust. Place Brie in center of piecrust. Turn under edge of piecrust to within ½ inch of cheese and decoratively flute edge. Remove Brie and set aside.

2. Prick piecrust with a fork to prevent pastry from puffing while it is baking. Place baking sheet on center rack in oven and bake piecrust 10 minutes. Remove from oven; transfer to a wire rack to cool.

3. Unfold second piecrust and place on lightly floured board or work surface. With tip of a paring knife, cut out four (2-inch-long) oval-shaped leaves; mark veins on leaves with back of knife. Place leaves on a baking sheet; bake 5 minutes, or until golden brown. Remove from oven; cool on wire rack.

4. To serve: Preheat oven to 350F. Place baked fluted piecrust on baking sheet; place Brie on piecrust. Arrange apple slices around top edge of cheese; place grapes and raspberries in the center. Place fruit-topped Brie in oven and bake 10 minutes.

5. Meanwhile, in a small saucepan, blend apple juice and cornstarch. Bring mixture to boiling over medium-high heat and cook, stirring constantly, 1 minute, or until mixture is clear and thick. Remove saucepan from heat.

6. Remove Brie from oven and arrange pastry leaves on top. Brush leaves and fruit with apple-juice glaze. Allow to stand 15 minutes, or until cheese softens. Carefully transfer to a serving board or plate. Cut into wedges. *Makes 24 wedges.*

continued from page 126

A FAMILY SUPPER ON THE PORCH
(Planned for 6)

**FLANK STEAK PROVENCAL★
IN ONION ROLLS
BEAN SALAD VINAIGRETTE★
COLESLAW WITH TOMATOES★
INDIVIDUAL RHUBARB-AND-
STRAWBERRY PIES★
ICED TEA**

★Recipe given for starred dishes.

FLANK STEAK PROVENCAL

1 flank steak (about 2 lb)
1 tablespoon salad oil
2 teaspoons chopped parsley
1 garlic clove, crushed
1 teaspoon salt
1 teaspoon lemon juice
⅛ teaspoon pepper
Parsley sprigs
Green onions
Onion rolls
Mustard Butter, recipe follows

DO AHEAD

1. With sharp knife, trim excess fat from steak. Wipe with damp paper towels. Lay steak on cutting board.

2. Combine salad oil, parsley, garlic, salt, lemon juice and pepper. Brush half of mixture over steak; let stand about 45 minutes.

3. Place steak, oil side up, on lightly greased broiler pan. Broil, about 4 inches from heat, 5 minutes. Turn steak; brush with remaining oil mixture; broil 4 to 5 minutes longer. The steak will be rare. Cook longer for medium rare.

TO SERVE

4. Cut steak into thin slices, on the diagonal. Arrange on serving board or platter. Garnish with parsley sprigs and green onions. Place basket of onion rolls and the Mustard Butter nearby. *Makes about 6 sandwich servings.*

MUSTARD BUTTER

½ cup (1 stick) butter or margarine, softened
½ teaspoon dried thyme leaves
2 tablespoons strong prepared mustard
2 tablespoons chopped parsley

In small bowl, combine all ingredients until well blended. Use to spread on onion rolls.

BEAN SALAD VINAIGRETTE

VINAIGRETTE DRESSING
1 cup olive or salad oil
⅓ cup red-wine vinegar
1 teaspoon salt
⅛ teaspoon pepper
2 tablespoons chopped capers
2 tablespoons chopped green onion

1 can (1 lb, 4 oz) chick peas, drained
1 can (1 lb) whole baby carrots, drained and sliced
1 can (1 lb) red kidney beans, drained
1 can (1 lb, 4 oz) white kidney beans, drained
Romaine-lettuce leaves, washed and crisped
¼ cup chopped green onion

DO AHEAD

1. Make Vinaigrette Dressing: Combine all ingredients in jar with tight-fitting lid. Shake vigorously.

2. Refrigerate dressing until ready to use. Shake it again just before using.

3. In large bowl, combine vinaigrette dressing with chick peas, carrot and red and white kidney beans; toss lightly to combine; refrigerate.

TO SERVE

4. Just before serving, line salad bowl with romaine leaves. Turn bean mixture into bowl. Sprinkle with ¼ cup chopped green onion. *Makes 8 to 10 servings.*

COLESLAW WITH TOMATOES
(pictured)

1 head green cabbage, slivered (10 cups)
1 large green pepper, cut in rings
2 medium-size sweet onions, cut in rings
1 cup sugar
1 teaspoon dry mustard
2 teaspoons sugar
1 teaspoon celery seed
1 tablespoon salt
1 cup white vinegar
¾ cup salad oil
1 cup cherry tomatoes, halved

DO AHEAD

1. In large bowl, make layers of cabbage, green pepper and onion; sprinkle 1 cup sugar over top.

2. In saucepan, combine mustard, 2 teaspoons sugar, the celery seed, salt, vinegar and oil; mix well. Bring to a full boil, stirring; pour over slaw. Refrigerate, covered, at least 4 hours.

TO SERVE

3. To serve, add tomatoes; toss salad to mix well. *Makes 8 servings.*

INDIVIDUAL RHUBARB-AND-STRAWBERRY PIES
(pictured)

Sugar
⅓ cup all-purpose flour
1 pkg (1 lb) frozen rhubarb without sugar, thawed
1 pint strawberries, washed, hulled and cut into thick slices
1 pkg (11 oz) piecrust mix
2 tablespoons (¼ stick) butter or margarine
1 egg yolk
1 tablespoon water

DO AHEAD

1. In large bowl, combine ⅔ cup sugar and the flour. Add rhubarb and strawberries, tossing lightly to combine; let stand 30 minutes.

2. Prepare piecrust mix as package label directs. Shape into a ball; divide into thirds.

3. On lightly floured surface, divide two-thirds of pastry into six pieces. Roll out each into a 7-inch circle. Use to line six (4½-inch size) pie plates. Refrigerate, along with remaining pastry, until ready to use.

4. Preheat oven to 400F.

5. Roll out remaining pastry into a rectangle 12 by 4½ inches. Cut into 24 (4½-inch) strips ½ inch wide.

6. Into each pie shell, turn ½ cup rhubarb mixture, mounding in center. Dot top of each with 1 teaspoon butter.

7. Moisten rim of pastry shell slightly with warm water. Press 4 pastry strips to edge of each pie, as pictured. Turn crust under, all around, and crimp edge with fork.

8. Combine egg yolk with water; mix well. Use to brush over pastry. Sprinkle lightly with sugar. Place on a cookie sheet with edges, as juice may run over. Bake 30 minutes, or until golden-brown and bubbly. Cool on wire rack.

TO SERVE

9. Gently loosen edge of pastry; remove pie from pie plate. Nice served slightly warm with ice cream. *Makes 6 servings.*

LUNCH ON THE TERRACE
(Planned for 8)

**CHILLED TOMATO CONSOMME
SALMON MOUSSE WITH SLICED
CUCUMBERS***
**HOT BUTTERED ROLLS
LIME SHERBET WITH
STRAWBERRIES
ICED TEA**

*Recipes given for starred dishes.

SALMON MOUSSE
WITH SLICED CUCUMBERS
(pictured)

1 env unflavored gelatine
¼ cup white wine
½ cup boiling water
½ cup mayonnaise
1 tablespoon lemon juice
1 tablespoon grated onion
½ teaspoon hot red-pepper sauce
½ teaspoon paprika
1 teaspoon salt
3 cans (7¾-oz size) salmon, drained
1 cup heavy cream
2 tablespoons snipped fresh dill
2 medium unpared cucumbers, washed
Bottled herb salad dressing
Watercress
Snipped fresh dill

DO AHEAD

1. In medium bowl, sprinkle gelatine over wine; let stand 5 minutes to soften. Add boiling water; stir until gelatine is dissolved. Let cool.

2. Add mayonnaise, lemon juice, onion, red-pepper sauce, paprika and salt; stir to mix well.

3. Set bowl in large bowl of ice cubes; let stand, stirring occasionally, until consistency of unbeaten egg white— about 10 minutes.

4. Lightly grease a 4-cup mold. Remove any skin and bones from salmon. Place salmon and ½ cup heavy cream in blender; blend to make a purée. Beat remaining ½ cup cream until stiff.

5. Using a wire whisk, fold salmon purée, whipped cream and 2 tablespoons dill into slightly thickened gelatine mixture, using an under-and-over motion to combine thoroughly. Turn into prepared mold. Refrigerate until well chilled and firm enough to unmold—at least 2 hours.

6. Slice cucumbers thin; turn them into a shallow baking dish. Toss with enough salad dressing to coat well. Refrigerate the cucumbers, covered.

TO SERVE

7. To unmold: Loosen around edge of mold with sharp knife; invert on serving platter. Place a hot damp cloth over mold; shake to release. Repeat if necessary.

8. Garnish platter with sliced cucumbers and watercress. Sprinkle cucumbers with snipped dill. *Makes 8 servings.*

COCKTAILS ON THE PATIO
(Planned for 12)

WARM FRUITED BRIE*
ASSORTED CRACKERS
HAM PATE EN CROUTE*
ANTIPASTO-STYLE
VEGETABLE PLATTER*
HERRING IN SOUR CREAM
WITH CHIVES
ASSORTED NUTS   COCKTAILS

*Recipes given for starred dishes.

WARM FRUITED BRIE
*(pictured, page 128;
step-by-step recipe, pictured, page 129)*

HAM PATE EN CROUTE
(pictured)

¼ lb (1 stick) butter or margarine, softened
2 cups ground cooked ham
1 tablespoon grated onion
1 teaspoon crushed garlic
3 tablespoons heavy cream
2 teaspoons strong mustard
1 teaspoon dry mustard
2 tablespoons chopped parsley
2 tablespoons chopped chives
¼ teaspoon black pepper
2 teaspoons Worcestershire sauce
1 loaf French bread (about 8 inches long
    and 3 inches wide)

DO AHEAD

1. In large bowl of electric mixer at high speed, cream butter until light and fluffy. Then beat in ham, a little at a time. Then add remaining ingredients, except bread, beating to combine well. Refrigerate until the mixture is firm enough to spread.

2. Slice ends off bread. Remove inside of bread, leaving a crust about ¼ inch thick. (Reserve inside of bread to make bread crumbs).

3. Stand bread on one end; with a spoon, gently push ham mixture into hollow, to fill completely. Refrigerate, wrapped in foil, several hours, or until cool enough to slice.

TO SERVE

4. Cut into slices about ¼ inch thick.

Makes about 30 (¼-inch) slices.
Note: You will need to double this recipe for 12 people.

ANTIPASTO-STYLE VEGETABLE
PLATTER
(pictured)

**Marinated Artichoke Hearts, recipe
    follows
Mushroom-And-Olive Relish, recipe
    follows
Mixed-Vegetable Relish, recipe follows**

DO AHEAD

1. Day before, prepare Mushroom-and-Olive Relish, Mixed-Vegetable Relish and Marinated Artichoke Hearts.

TO SERVE

2. On large chilled platter, arrange vegetables in rows, as pictured. *Makes 10 servings.*

MARINATED ARTICHOKE
HEARTS

2 pkg (9-oz size) frozen artichoke hearts
1 cup bottled herb-garlic salad dressing,
    well chilled

1. Cook artichoke hearts as package label directs. Drain well. Cool completely in large shallow dish.

2. Pour salad dressing over artichokes; toss to combine; refrigerate overnight to chill well, stirring several times.

MUSHROOM-AND-OLIVE
RELISH

1 lb medium-size fresh mushrooms
2 teaspoons chopped parsley
¼ teaspoon salt
⅛ teaspoon pepper
½ teaspoon dried oregano leaves
¼ teaspoon dried basil leaves
2 tablespoons grated onion and juice
1 garlic clove, pressed
⅓ cup chopped pimiento-stuffed olives
1 teaspoon sugar
¼ cup salad oil
¼ cup white-wine vinegar
1 cup black pitted olives, drained
1 cup cherry tomatoes, washed

DO AHEAD

1. Wash and dry mushrooms; trim stems; leave whole.

2. In large saucepan, combine mushrooms with 2 cups water. Bring to boiling; reduce heat and simmer 5 minutes, or until almost tender. Drain. Arrange in large, shallow baking dish.

continued on page 132

continued from page 131

3. Combine rest of ingredients except black olives and tomatoes; mix very well; pour over mushrooms. Refrigerate, covered, and stirring gently occasionally, at least 12 hours.

TO SERVE

4. Add black olives and cherry tomatoes before serving. *Makes about 10 servings.*

MIXED-VEGETABLE RELISH

½ small head cauliflower, cut in flowerets
  and sliced
2 carrots, pared, cut in 2-inch strips
2 stalks celery, cut in 1-inch pieces (1 cup)
1 green pepper, cut in 2-inch strips
1 jar (4 oz) pimientos, drained, cut in strips
1 jar (3 oz) pitted green olives, drained
¾ cup wine vinegar
½ cup olive or salad oil
2 tablespoons sugar
1 teaspoon salt
½ teaspoon dried oregano leaves
¼ teaspoon pepper
¼ cup water

DO AHEAD

1. In large skillet, combine all ingredients. Bring to boil; stir occasionally. Reduce heat; simmer, covered, 5 minutes.

2. Cool; then refrigerate at least 24 hours. Drain well. *Makes 8 to 10 antipasto servings.*

AN AFTERNOON PARTY
(Planned for 10 to 12)

**FRESH FRUIT PLATTER★
LEMON-SWIRL MARBLE CAKE★
PITCHER OF ICED TEA**

★Recipes given for starred dishes.

FRESH FRUIT PLATTER
(pictured)

1 pint strawberries, washed (leave hulls
  on)
1 lb small seedless green grapes, washed
  and cut in clusters
3 cups fresh pineapple wedges

DO AHEAD

1. Prepare fruits and chill well.

TO SERVE

2. Arrange on large round glass platter, as pictured, alternating pineapple with green grapes. Place strawberries in center. *Makes 10 to 12 servings.*

LEMON-SWIRL MARBLE CAKE
(pictured)

LEMON FILLING
8 egg yolks
1 cup granulated sugar
½ cup lemon juice
¼ cup (½ stick) butter or margarine
2 tablespoons grated lemon peel

CAKE
2 pkg (16-oz size) pound-cake mix
1 cup milk
½ cup orange juice
1 tablespoon grated orange peel
8 egg whites
½ teaspoon cream of tartar

LEMON GLAZE (see Note)
2 cups confectioners' sugar
2 tablespoons light cream
2 tablespoons lemon juice
Coarsely grated lemon peel

DO AHEAD

1. Make Lemon Filling: In top of double boiler, using a wooden spoon, beat egg yolks; stir in granulated sugar, ½ cup lemon juice, the butter and 2 tablespoons lemon peel. Cook, stirring occasionally, over simmering water until thick and smooth. Remove from hot water. Cover; set aside to cool completely.

2. Make Cake: Heavily grease and flour a 9-inch bundt pan. Turn both packages of cake mix into large electric mixer bowl. Add milk; blend just until dry ingredients are moistened. Add orange juice; beat 4 minutes; stir in orange peel.

3. Preheat oven to 325F. In another large bowl, using clean beaters, beat egg whites and cream of tartar until stiff peaks form when beaters are slowly raised. With wire whisk, using an under-and-over motion, gently fold whites into cake batter just until combined. Remove 1 cup batter, which can be used to bake as cupcakes, if desired.

4. Pour one-fourth remaining batter into pan. Spoon one-third lemon filling over center of batter (not touching pan). Repeat, layering twice with batter and filling; end with batter.

5. With knife, cut through batter and filling, making a zigzag around pan,

being careful not to let knife touch bottom and side of pan. Bake 1 hour and 20 minutes, or until surface springs back when gently pressed with fingertip. Let cool in pan on wire rack 10 minutes. Turn out of pan; cool completely.

6. Make Lemon Glaze: In small bowl, combine confectioners' sugar, cream and lemon juice; stir to dissolve any lumps and until mixture is smooth. Use to frost top of cooled cake and let run down side. *Makes 16 servings.*

Note: If desired, omit glaze; sift confectioners' sugar over top before serving.

AN ELEGANT PICNIC
(Planned for 8 to 10)

**COLD SENEGALESE SOUP★
GLAZED VEAL-AND-HAM LOAF★
THREE-BEAN SALAD BOWL★
HERB-BUTTERED FRENCH BREAD★
FRESH STRAWBERRIES WITH
STRAWBERRY SAUCE IN
COOKIE SHELLS★
CHILLED WHITE WINE**

★Recipes given for starred dishes.

COLD SENEGALESE SOUP

3 tablespoons butter or margarine
1 medium onion, chopped
1 medium carrot, pared and diced
1 stalk celery, sliced
2 tablespoons curry powder
1½ tablespoons all-purpose flour
1 tablespoon tomato paste
2 cans (10¾-oz size) condensed chicken
  broth, undiluted
2 cups water
1 tablespoon almond paste
1 tablespoon currant jelly
10 whole cloves
1 cinnamon stick
1½ cups heavy cream
2 tablespoons shredded coconut or 1
  cooked carrot, thinly sliced, for garnish
Chopped parsley

DO AHEAD

1. In hot butter in large saucepan, sauté onion, carrot, celery and curry powder until golden—about 5 minutes. Remove from heat.

2. Stir in flour until well blended. Add tomato paste; cook, stirring, 1 minute.

3. Gradually stir in the undiluted chicken broth and water; bring to boiling, stirring constantly. Stir in almond paste and jelly; add cloves and cinnamon stick; simmer, uncovered and stirring occasionally, ½ hour.

4. Strain; cool. Then refrigerate until very well chilled—several hours or overnight.

TO SERVE

5. When ready to serve, skim off any fat from surface. Blend in cream. Serve in bouillon cups. Top each serving with coconut or carrot slices and the parsley. *Makes 8 to 10 servings.*

GLAZED VEAL-AND-HAM LOAF
(pictured)

5 slices bacon
2 lb veal for scaloppini, pounded thin
2 lb thinly sliced ham
1 tablespoon salt
½ teaspoon pepper
½ cup chopped parsley
⅓ cup finely chopped shallots
1 teaspoon dried thyme leaves
1 bay leaf
⅔ cup dry white wine
Parsley Glaze, recipe follows
Parsley sprigs and sweet gherkins
   (optional)

DO AHEAD

1. Line a 9-by-5-by-3-inch loaf pan with bacon. Preheat oven to 325F.

2. Then, in loaf pan, layer veal and ham alternately, beginning and ending with veal and sprinkling each layer with a little salt, pepper, parsley, shallot and thyme. Place bay leaf on top; pour white wine over all.

3. Cover top with foil. Bake 2 hours. Cool on wire rack several hours (while loaf cools, place a heavy casserole on top to weight it down).

4. Unmold loaf on serving platter. Remove and discard bacon slices. Refrigerate loaf.

5. Several hours before serving, make Parsley Glaze. Brush slightly thickened glaze over top of loaf several times, to coat well. (If glaze becomes too thick, reheat slightly.) Refrigerate at least 1 hour before serving.

TO SERVE

6. Garnish platter with parsley sprigs and tiny sweet gherkins, if desired. Cut loaf crosswise into thin slices. *Makes 10 to 12 servings.*

PARSLEY GLAZE

1 env unflavored gelatine
1 cup water
¼ cup white wine
¼ cup lemon juice
½ cup chopped parsley

1. Sprinkle gelatine over ½ cup of the water in small saucepan; let stand 5 minutes to soften. Heat gently, stirring, to dissolve gelatine.

2. Stir in ½ cup cold water, the wine, lemon juice and parsley. Place in a large bowl of ice; stir occasionally until slightly thickened—about 15 minutes.

THREE-BEAN SALAD BOWL

½ bottle (8-oz size) Italian-style salad
   dressing
1 tablespoon Worcestershire sauce
¾ cup sweet-pickle relish, drained
1 can (1 lb) cut wax beans, drained
1 can (1 lb) cut green beans, drained
1 can (15 oz) kidney beans, drained
½ cup sliced red onions
1 quart torn salad greens (optional)

DO AHEAD

1. In large bowl, combine salad dressing, Worcestershire, pickle relish and all the beans; toss lightly to combine.

2. Refrigerate, covered, until well chilled—about 4 hours.

TO SERVE

3. Just before serving, add onion and salad greens; toss to combine.

4. Turn into salad bowl. *Makes 8 servings.*

HERB-BUTTERED FRENCH BREAD

½ cup (1 stick) butter or margarine,
   softened
½ teaspoon paprika
½ teaspoon dried rosemary leaves
¼ teaspoon dried marjoram leaves
2 tablespoons finely chopped parsley
1 loaf French bread, cut on diagonal at
   1-inch intervals

In small bowl, combine butter, paprika, rosemary, marjoram and parsley, mixing until well blended. Spread mixture on French-bread slices. Wrap in foil. Heat. *Makes 8 to 10 servings.*

FRESH STRAWBERRIES WITH STRAWBERRY SAUCE IN COOKIE SHELLS
(pictured)

1 quart fresh strawberries

STRAWBERRY SAUCE
2 pkg (10-oz size) frozen strawberries,
   partially thawed

Cookie Shells, recipe follows

DO AHEAD

1. Wash berries; drain. Remove hulls. Refrigerate until serving.

2. Make Sauce: Press frozen strawberries through sieve, or blend in electric blender, covered, about 1 minute. Refrigerate until serving.

TO SERVE

3. At serving time, place strawberries in Cookie Shells, dividing evenly. Pour strawberry sauce over berries, dividing evenly. Serve at once. *Makes 10 to 12 servings.*

COOKIE SHELLS

1 pkg (12 oz) sugar-cookie mix
1 teaspoon butter or margarine
1 egg

DO AHEAD

1. Preheat oven to 375F. Prepare cookie mix as package label directs, using butter and egg. Divide dough into 12 balls.

2. On ungreased cookie sheets, pat each ball to make a 4-inch circle, leaving space between cookies. Bake four at a time (no more) about 7 minutes, or until golden and center is firm. Do not underbake.

3. Meanwhile, grease bottom of four (6-ounce) custard cups.

4. Let cookies cool on cookie sheet 1 minute. Then, with broad spatula, remove one at a time and mold over bottom of custard cup, to form a shell, as pictured. Cookie shells may be made several days ahead, unless weather is very humid, and stored at room temperature in a closed tin container to keep crisp. *Makes 12 cookie shells.*

A TREAT FOR TEENAGERS
(Planned for 12)

PICNIC CHOCOLATE CAKE★
CHILLED WATERMELON
LEMONADE

★Recipes given for starred dishes.

PICNIC CHOCOLATE CAKE

CAKE
1 cup unsweetened cocoa
2 cups boiling water
2¾ cups sifted all-purpose flour
2 teaspoons baking soda
½ teaspoon salt
½ teaspoon baking powder
1 cup (2 sticks) butter or margarine,
   softened
2½ cups granulated sugar
4 eggs

continued on page 134

continued from page 133

1½ teaspoons vanilla extract

FROSTING
1 pkg (6 oz) semisweet chocolate pieces
½ cup light cream
1 cup (2 sticks) butter or margarine
2½ cups confectioners' sugar

DO AHEAD

1. In medium bowl, combine cocoa with boiling water; mix with wire whisk until smooth. Cool completely. Sift flour with soda, salt and baking powder.

2. Preheat oven to 350F. Grease well and lightly flour a 13-by-9-by-2-inch pan.

3. In large bowl of electric mixer, at high speed, beat butter, granulated sugar, eggs and vanilla, scraping bowl occasionally, until light—about 5 minutes. At low speed, beat in flour mixture (in fourths), alternately with cocoa mixture (in thirds), beginning and ending with flour mixture. Do not overbeat.

4. Turn into pan; smooth top. Bake 45 minutes, or until surface springs back when gently pressed with finger.

5. Cool in pan 10 minutes. Carefully loosen side with spatula; remove from pan. Cool on rack.

6. Make Frosting: In medium saucepan, combine chocolate pieces, cream and butter; stir over medium heat until smooth. Remove from heat. With whisk, blend in confectioners' sugar. In bowl set over ice, beat until it holds shape.

7. Frost top of cake; refrigerate until serving time or time to take to picnic, so that icing will be firm. *Makes 12 servings.*

SUNDAY BRUNCH IN THE GARDEN
(Planned for 10 to 12)

SPRITZERS
BRIOCHE FILLED WITH CHICKEN SALAD★
DEVILED EGGS WITH RED CAVIAR★
FRESH PINEAPPLE IN SHELL★
COFFEE

★Recipes given for starred dishes.

CHICKEN SALAD IN BRIOCHE

4- to 4½-lb ready-to-cook roasting chicken
2 large carrots, pared and cut into 1-inch pieces
2 stalks celery, cut in 1-inch pieces
1 large onion, sliced
4 whole cloves
10 black peppercorns
2 teaspoons salt
1 bay leaf

2 cups water
1 can (13¾ oz) chicken broth
1 cup mayonnaise or cooked salad dressing
½ cup sour cream
2 teaspoons lemon juice
2 tablespoons milk or light cream
1 teaspoon salt
Dash pepper
1 to 1½ teaspoons curry powder
2 cups coarsely chopped celery
1 cup seedless green grapes, washed and halved

Individual Brioches, recipe follows (or buy 12 brioches from a bakery)
Watercress
⅓ cup toasted blanched whole almonds (see Note)

DO AHEAD

1. Remove giblets and neck from chicken. Rinse chicken well under cold water. Place, breast side down, in an 8-quart kettle.

2. Add carrot, cut-up celery, onion, cloves, whole peppercorns, 2 teaspoons salt, the bay leaf, water and the chicken broth.

3. Bring to boiling over high heat. Reduce heat and simmer, covered, about 2 hours, or until chicken is tender. Remove kettle from heat.

4. Let stand, uncovered and frequently spooning broth in kettle over chicken, 1 hour, or until cool enough to handle. Lift out chicken. Strain broth, and refrigerate, covered, to use as desired.

5. Cut legs, thighs and wings from chicken. Remove skin. Then remove meat from bones in as large pieces as possible. Set aside.

6. Pull skin from remaining chicken. With sharp knife, cut between the breastbone and meat, removing breast meat in large piece. Then check carefully, and remove any additional meat. Refrigerate, covered, to chill—about 1½ hours.

7. Make salad: In large bowl, com-

bine mayonnaise, sour cream, lemon juice, milk, salt, pepper and curry powder; stir to mix well. Add chopped celery and grapes to dressing.

8. Cut pieces of chicken meat into small pieces; there should be almost 4 cups. Add all meat to dressing. Toss lightly, to coat well.

9. Refrigerate, covered, until serving time—at least 1 hour.

TO SERVE

10. Cut caps from 12 brioches. Spoon out a ½-inch-deep hollow. Fill each with chicken salad, mounding high. Replace caps, tucking a watercress sprig in each. Garnish each with several almonds. *Makes 12 servings.*

Note: To toast almonds: Preheat oven to 350F. Place almonds in shallow pan, and bake just until toasted—8 to 10 minutes. Cool.

INDIVIDUAL BRIOCHES

½ cup warm water (105 to 115F)
1 pkg active dry yeast
¼ cup sugar
1 teaspoon salt
1 teaspoon grated lemon peel
1 cup (2 sticks) butter or margarine, softened
6 eggs
4 cups sifted all-purpose flour
1 egg yolk
1 tablespoon water

DO AHEAD

1. If possible, check temperature of warm water with thermometer. Sprinkle yeast over water in large bowl of electric mixer; stir until dissolved.

2. Add sugar, salt, lemon peel, butter, 6 eggs and 3 cups flour; at medium speed, beat 4 minutes. Add remaining flour; at low speed, beat until smooth—about 2 minutes.

3. Cover bowl with waxed paper and

damp towel; let rise in warm place (85F), free from drafts, until double in bulk—about 1 hour. Refrigerate, covered, overnight.

NEXT DAY

4. Grease 16 (3-inch) muffin-pan cups.

5. Stir down dough with wooden spoon. Dough will be soft. Turn out onto lightly floured pastry cloth or board; divide in half. Return half to bowl; refrigerate until ready to use.

6. Working quickly, shape three-fourths of dough on board into an 8-inch roll. With floured knife, cut into eight pieces. Shape each into ball; place in prepared muffin cup.

7. Divide remaining fourth of dough into eight parts; shape into balls. With finger, press indentation in center of each large ball; fill with small ball.

8. Cover with towel; let rise in warm place (85F), free from drafts, until double in bulk—about 1 hour.

9. Meanwhile, shape refrigerated half of dough, and let rise, as directed.

10. Preheat oven to 375F.

11. Combine egg yolk with 1 table-spoon water; brush on brioches. Bake 15 to 20 minutes, or until golden. *Makes 16.*

Note: Freeze extra brioches, wrapped in foil. Reheat to serve.

DEVILED EGGS WITH RED CAVIAR

12 eggs
¾ cup mayonnaise or cooked salad dressing
1 tablespoon white vinegar
1 teaspoon dry mustard
1½ teaspoons Worcestershire sauce
¾ teaspoon salt
⅛ teaspoon pepper
⅛ teaspoon paprika
Parsley sprigs
2 tablespoons red caviar

1. Hard-cook eggs: Cover eggs with water to an inch above them; bring rapidly to a boil. Take pan off heat and let stand 20 minutes. Cool immediately, in cold water, to prevent dark surface on yolks and so shells can be removed easily. Remove shells. Cool eggs completely.

2. Halve eggs lengthwise. Take out yolks, being careful not to break whites.

3. Press yolks through a sieve into medium bowl. Add remaining ingredients, except parsley and caviar; mix with fork until smooth and fluffy.

4. Lightly mound yolk mixture in egg whites. Garnish each with a parsley sprig and ¼ teaspoon red caviar. *Makes 12 servings.*

FRESH PINEAPPLE IN SHELL

DO AHEAD

1. With long knife, cut each chilled pineapple into quarters, right through frond. Remove core. Then, with knife, cut between shell and fruit, separating fruit from shell in one piece. Leaving fruit in place, slice in half; then cut crosswise eight times to make wedges. Refrigerate.

TO SERVE

2. Serve fruit right in shell. *Each pineapple makes 4 servings. (For 12 servings, you will need 3 pineapples.)* ◆

PICNICS COME IN FROM THE COLD

continued from page 115

combine flour, sugar, salt, shortening, egg and milk; mix well with fork to form a soft dough. Form into ball. Refrigerate, wrapped in waxed paper, about 30 minutes.

2. Preheat oven to 400F.

3. On lightly floured pastry cloth or waxed paper, roll half of dough to form a 12-by-10-inch rectangle. Place on a 17-by-14-inch cookie sheet.

4. To make Filling: Sprinkle pastry evenly with cornflake crumbs; then layer with apples. Combine sugar and cinnamon; mix well. Sprinkle evenly over apples.

5. Roll out other half of pastry to a 12-by-10-inch rectangle. Fit over apples; pinch edges to seal tightly.

6. Brush with egg white. Bake about 40 minutes until top is golden-brown.

7. Meanwhile, combine confectioners' sugar and lemon juice; mix until smooth. Drizzle glaze evenly over pastry while hot from oven.

TO SERVE

8. Wrap pastry loosely in foil; reheat 8 to 10 minutes. Serve warm, cut into squares, with ice cream. *Makes 12 servings.* ◆

SHAPE-UP VEGETABLE SALADS

continued from page 114

3. Stir beets, onion, horseradish, salt and pepper into gelatine mixture; pour into 5-cup decorative or plain ring mold.

4. Refrigerate until firm—2 to 3 hours.

TO SERVE

5. Unmold by running a small spatula around edge of mold. Invert over serving plate; hold a hot, damp dish-cloth over inverted mold, and shake to release. Refrigerate until ready to serve. *Makes 6 servings.*

GAZPACHO SALAD MOLD WITH SLICED AVOCADOS
(pictured)

3 env unflavored gelatine
2 cans (1-pt, 2-oz size) tomato juice
⅓ cup red-wine vinegar
⅓ cup olive or salad oil
1½ teaspoons salt
¼ teaspoon hot red-pepper sauce
1 garlic clove, pressed
2 large tomatoes, peeled and finely diced (1½ cups)
1 large cucumber, pared and finely diced (1½ cups)
1 medium-size green pepper, finely diced (¾ cup)
½ cup finely chopped onion
1 canned pimiento, drained and chopped
¼ cup chopped chives
3 large ripe avocados (about 2¼ lb)
Lemon juice
⅓ cup bottled oil-and-vinegar dressing

DO AHEAD

1. In medium saucepan, sprinkle gelatine over 1 can tomato juice to soften. Place over low heat, stirring constantly, until gelatine is dissolved. Remove from heat.

2. Stir in remaining tomato juice, the vinegar, oil, salt, red-pepper sauce and garlic. Set in bowl of ice, stirring occasionally, until mixture is consistency of unbeaten egg white—30 minutes.

3. Fold in diced tomato, cucumber, green pepper, onion, pimiento and chives until well combined. Pour into 2½-quart mold that has been rinsed in cold water.

4. Refrigerate until firm—at least 6 hours.

5. Unmold by running a small spatula around edge of mold. Invert over serving platter; place a hot, damp dish-cloth over inverted mold, and shake gently to release. Refrigerate.

TO SERVE

6. Just before serving, peel and slice avocados. Brush with lemon juice. Arrange the avocado slices around the molded salad and pour salad dressing over them. *Makes 12 to 14 servings.* ◆

DELICIOUS DO-AHEAD DESSERTS

W hen you want a tempting dessert that's a little bit special, have one of these on hand. They look spectacular, taste divine and yet are surprisingly simple to make. All can be prepared ahead of time; most can be frozen. Pictured above: A giant cream puff provides the edible bowl for this sensational cherries jubilee dessert. The puff can be baked ahead, and just before serving, filled with ice cream and drenched with a flaming cherry-brandy sauce. Two layers of orange-nut glazed shortcake (easily made from packaged biscuit mix) are stacked between fresh sliced strawberries then topped with a ring of whipped-cream dollops in a dramatic Strawberry Upside-Down Shortcake. At right, an icy mountain of Watermelon Ice, shaped by your favorite dessert mold. Continuing clockwise, a Chocolate Candy-Bar Pie topped with rosettes of whipped cream and grated chocolate; elegant Poached Pears Rosé; Fresh-Peach Yogurt Pie crowned with peach slices; a sensational gâteau, gaily striped with apricots, blueberries, strawberries and whipped cream. Recipes for these and other do-ahead desserts begin on page 138.

GEORGE RATKAI

continued from page 136

WATERMELON ICE
(pictured)

¼ large ripe watermelon (5 lb)
⅓ cup white rum
1 pint vanilla ice cream

DO AHEAD

1. Peel melon; remove seeds, and cut into cubes. Purée in blender or processor. Add rum. Pour into a 13-by-9-inch pan, and freeze until just firm.

2. Allow ice cream to soften slightly. Cut frozen melon purée into cubes, and whip in electric mixer.

3. Beat ice cream into melon. Freeze in ice-cube trays (see Note); or pack in a 7-cup mold or air-tight container. Store in freezer.

TO SERVE

4. Invert on serving platter to unmold. Cover with warm damp cloth. Shake to release. Let stand to soften slightly. *Makes 7 cups, 8 to 10 servings.*

Note: To make dessert less icy, freeze, beat again until creamy, not melted. Do not mold. Serve at once.

FRESH-PEACH YOGURT PIE
(pictured)

2 env unflavored gelatine
½ cup water
1 pkg (10 oz) frozen sliced peaches, slightly thawed
2 containers (8-oz size) peach yogurt
8-inch graham-cracker pie shell (homemade or store-bought)
2 or 3 large fresh peaches
1 tablespoon lemon juice
¼ cup apricot preserves

DO AHEAD

1. Sprinkle gelatine over ½ cup water in top of double boiler; let stand 5 minutes to soften.

2. Turn peaches and juice into blender or processor.

3. Place softened gelatine over boiling water in double boiler. Stir to dissolve gelatine. Add to peaches in blender. Blend until peaches are finely chopped and mixture thickens.

4. Turn into medium bowl. Using wire whisk, fold in yogurt until well combined. Turn into pie shell.

5. Refrigerate until well chilled and firm enough to cut—about 8 hours or overnight.

TO SERVE

6. Peel peaches; slice; dip in lemon juice. Arrange slices over top of pie. Melt preserves; brush over peach slices. *Makes 6 servings.*

FRESH BERRY GATEAU
(pictured)

2 pkg (13¾-oz size) frozen orange cake
1 to 1½ cups fresh blueberries, washed and drained
1 can (1 lb) unpeeled apricot halves, drained
½ pint fresh raspberries or strawberries, washed and drained
¼ cup apricot preserves, melted
1 cup heavy cream
2 tablespoons confectioners' sugar

DO AHEAD

1. Remove frozen orange cakes from foil pans; place on serving plate, side by side, to make a rectangle 8 by 12 inches.

2. Arrange fruit in diagonal strips, as pictured, starting with one-third of the blueberries in center. On each side, arrange apricot halves, overlapping.

Then continue with remaining blueberries on each side of apricot halves. Place raspberries in each corner. Brush fruit with melted preserves.

3. In medium bowl, combine heavy cream and confectioners' sugar. With electric mixer, beat until stiff.

4. Using spatula, frost sides of cake with some of whipped cream. Turn rest of cream into pastry bag with number-4 tip. Make ruching between fruits. Refrigerate until serving.

TO SERVE

5. Cut into serving-size squares. *Makes 10 to 12 servings.*

CHOCOLATE-CANDY PIE
(pictured)

20 regular-size marshmallows
½ cup milk
1 bar (8 oz) milk chocolate with almonds
1½ cups heavy cream
Chocolate-Cookie-Crumb Pie Shell, purchased or homemade, recipe on page 90

DO AHEAD

1. In medium saucepan, combine marshmallows and milk. Cook over low heat, stirring occasionally, until marshmallows are melted.

2. Add chocolate bar, broken in several pieces; remove from heat; stir to melt chocolate. Refrigerate 10 minutes.

3. Whip 1 cup cream; fold into chocolate mixture. Pour into pie shell.

4. Refrigerate pie at least 3 hours.

TO SERVE

5. Whip rest of cream. Turn into pastry bag with a number-4 star tip; make rosettes around pie, as pictured. If desired, sprinkle with grated chocolate. *Makes 6 to 8 servings.*

POACHED PEARS ROSE
(pictured)

1 cup sugar
6 lemon slices
1 cup water
2 cups rosé wine
6 fresh pears, pared (with stems)
8 small clusters of green grapes

DO AHEAD

1. In 4-quart Dutch oven, combine sugar, lemon and water; bring to boiling, stirring, until sugar dissolves.

2. Add wine and pears; simmer, covered, until tender—about 30 minutes. (Turn pears once while cooking.)

3. Remove from heat. Place pears and syrup in large bowl; refrigerate, cov-

ered, until well chilled—several hours. Turn pears once while they are refrigerated so that color is evenly distributed.

TO SERVE

4. Serve pears with syrup spooned over them; garnish with green grapes. *Makes 6 servings.*

CREAM-PUFF SHORTCAKE WITH CHERRIES JUBILEE

(pictured)

GIANT CREAM PUFF
1 cup water
½ cup (1 stick) butter or margarine
¼ teaspoon salt
1 cup sifted all-purpose flour
4 eggs

CHERRIES JUBILEE
1 can (1 lb, 14 oz) pitted Bing cherries
⅓ cup granulated sugar
2 teaspoons cornstarch
¼ cup brandy

1½ quarts cherry-vanilla ice cream
Confectioners' sugar

DO AHEAD

1. Make Giant Cream Puff: Preheat oven to 400F. In medium saucepan, over medium heat, bring water, the butter and salt to boiling. Remove the saucepan from heat.

2. With wooden spoon, beat in flour all at once. Return to low heat; continue beating until mixture forms ball and leaves side of pan. Remove from heat.

3. Beat in eggs, one at a time, beating hard after each addition until mixture is smooth. Continue beating until dough is shiny and satiny and breaks in strands. Turn onto ungreased cookie sheet, and spread dough to make 8-inch round about 1 inch thick.

4. Bake 60 minutes, or until puffed and deep golden-brown. Turn off oven heat; leave cream puff in oven 10 minutes; then remove to wire rack. Split in half, to let steam escape. Cool completely.

5. Meanwhile, make Cherries Jubilee: Drain cherries, reserving liquid. In small saucepan, combine granulated sugar and cornstarch; stir in cherry liquid.

6. Bring to boiling, stirring; boil gently 2 minutes, or until thickened and translucent. Remove from heat; let cool.

TO SERVE

7. Just before serving, spoon ice cream into bottom half of cream puff, mounding slightly. Add top, and sprinkle with confectioners' sugar.

8. Add the cherries to cherry sauce; reheat gently. Then pour into a metal serving bowl.

9. Cut giant puff in wedges at table.

10. Heat brandy, over very low heat, just until vapor rises. Pour over cherries, and ignite. Spoon, flaming, over cream-puff wedges. *Makes 10 servings.*

SHORTCAKE IN A BOWL

2 pints strawberries, washed and drained
Confectioners' sugar
1 cup heavy cream
½ teaspoon vanilla extract
1 pkg (3 oz) ladyfingers

DO AHEAD

1. Select 10 to 12 pretty berries for top. Remove hulls from rest. Slice into bowl; toss with 2 tablespoons confectioners' sugar.

2. Using rotary beater, beat cream with 2 tablespoons confectioners' sugar and the vanilla.

3. Arrange one-third of ladyfingers in bottom of a 1½-quart glass serving bowl. Top with one-third sliced berries and one-third whipped cream. Repeat layering, ending with whipped cream.

4. Garnish top with reserved whole berries. Refrigerate several hours, or until well chilled and blended. *Makes 8 servings.*

STRAWBERRY UPSIDE-DOWN SHORTCAKE

(pictured)

3 pints strawberries,* washed, hulled and sliced
¾ cup granulated sugar
1 cup heavy cream
2 tablespoons confectioners' sugar

UPSIDE-DOWN CAKE
½ cup (1 stick) butter or margarine
1 cup light-brown sugar, firmly packed
6 tablespoons orange juice
1 cup walnut or pecan halves
2½ cups packaged biscuit mix
⅓ cup granulated sugar
¼ cup (½ stick) butter or margarine, melted
1 egg
1 cup milk

DO AHEAD

1. In large bowl, combine sliced strawberries and ¾ cup granulated sugar. Refrigerate until needed.

2. In small bowl, whip cream with confectioners' sugar until stiff. Refrigerate until needed.

3. Make Upside-Down Cake: Preheat oven to 425F. Divide ½ cup butter between two 9-by-1½-inch round layer-cake pans; melt over low heat. Remove from heat. Add half the brown sugar and orange juice to each pan; mix well, and spread evenly over bottom of pans. Ar-

range walnuts in center of each pan, dividing evenly.

4. In large bowl, combine biscuit mix and the ⅓ cup sugar; make a well in center. Add melted butter, egg and milk. Beat with fork just until smooth and well blended. Spoon batter over nuts and sugar mixture in each pan, dividing evenly.

5. Bake 20 minutes, or until tops are a deep golden-brown. With spatula, loosen edge of cake from pans; invert each onto wire rack set on waxed paper. Let cool.

TO SERVE

6. If layers have been allowed to cool completely, preheat oven to 425F. Wrap each layer, glazed side up, loosely in foil; reheat 10 to 12 minutes. Remove from oven. Place one layer, glazed side up, on serving plate. Cover with half of strawberries. Top with second layer, glazed side up. Spoon on remaining strawberries, mounding in center. Surround with some of whipped cream. Pass remaining cream. Serve immediately, while still warm. *Makes 8 servings.*

*Or use 3 packages (10-oz size) frozen strawberry slices, thawed slightly and drained; omit sugar. Or substitute one 1¼-lb bag of frozen whole berries, thawed, for the fresh fruit.

STRAWBERRY SHORTCAKE DELUXE

1 pkg (1 lb, 2.5 oz) lemon-chiffon cake mix
1 tablespoon grated lemon peel
2 eggs
3 pints large strawberries
3 cups heavy cream
1½ cups confectioners' sugar
2 teaspoons vanilla extract
⅓ cup red-currant jelly

DO AHEAD

1. Preheat oven to 350F.

2. Prepare lemon-chiffon cake mix as package label directs, adding lemon peel with 2 eggs called for. Turn into 2 ungreased 9-by-9-by-2-inch baking pans.

3. Bake 30 to 35 minutes, or until surface springs back when gently pressed with fingertip. Invert pans immediately by hanging each between 2 other pans. Let the cakes cool completely—will take about 1½ hours.

4. Meanwhile, wash and hull strawberries. Refrigerate until needed.

5. In large bowl, combine cream, sugar and vanilla. Refrigerate until well chilled—at least 1 hour. Then beat with electric mixer, at medium speed, until stiff. Return to refrigerator until needed.

6. To assemble cake: Set aside in re-
continued on page 140

continued from page 139

frigerator 1 cup of whipped cream, for decorating the cake. Select 16 of the largest strawberries, and set them aside in refrigerator, for decorating the cake.

7. Split one cake into 2 even layers. (Wrap and freeze second cake, to serve another day.) Place bottom layer, cut side up, on serving tray. Spread with about 1 cup whipped cream. Top with remaining strawberries, standing each berry, hulled side down, in cream. Spread whipped cream around berries to make layer even. Top with other cake layer, cut side down, pressing gently.

8. Spread top and sides with thin layer of whipped cream. Refrigerate cake at least 2 hours.

TO SERVE

9. Shortly before serving, melt currant jelly over low heat. Brush jelly on reserved strawberries. Arrange berries in 4 rows on cake. With reserved whipped cream, in pastry bag with number-6 star tip, decorate cake. Serve at once, or refrigerate until needed. *Makes 16 servings.*

FRESH LEMON SHERBET

1 env unflavored gelatine
Water
1½ cups sugar
1½ teaspoons grated lemon peel
½ cup lemon juice
⅛ teaspoon salt
1 teaspoon vanilla extract
1 egg white

DO AHEAD

1. In small bowl, sprinkle gelatine over ¼ cup cold water. Let stand 5 minutes, to soften.

2. In individual saucepan, combine sugar and 1 cup cold water; bring to boiling, stirring to dissolve sugar. Boil, uncovered, 3 minutes. Remove from heat. Add gelatine, stirring to dissolve.

3. Add 1 cup water, the lemon peel, lemon juice, salt and vanilla. Turn into ice-cube freezing tray; freeze until almost firm about 1 inch from edge all around.

4. Turn into a large bowl; add egg white; beat until smooth and fluffy. Return to ice-cube tray. Refreeze until firm. *Makes 6 servings.*

Note: If storing more than one day, freezer-wrap with foil.

Accessories in photographs on pages 136 and 137 from Meiselman Imports, Inc., New York City. ◆

---

continued from page 122
All recipes pictured on pages 122 and 123.

MENU
TAPENADE★   TOAST POINTS
BEEF BALLS PROVENCALE★
GNOCCHI★
ROASTED-GREEN-PEPPER SALAD
WITH BASIL VINAIGRETTE★
DELLA-ROBBIA BRIE★   PECANS
FRENCH BREAD (SEE NOTE)
ASSORTED HOLIDAY COOKIES
DEMITASSE   DRY RED WINE

★Recipes given for starred dishes.
Note: See page 293 for recipe.

TAPENADE

1 can (2 oz) anchovy fillets, drained
1½ cups pitted ripe olives
1 can (7 oz) tuna, drained
1 teaspoon Dijon mustard
2 garlic cloves, crushed
¼ cup olive oil
4 hard-cooked eggs, shelled
2 tablespoons cognac
Toast points
2 pitted ripe olives, halved

DO AHEAD

1. In blender or food processor, combine anchovy fillets (reserve 3 for garnish), olives, tuna, mustard, garlic, olive oil, 3 of the eggs, halved, and cognac. Blend until smooth. Turn into medium bowl. Refrigerate, tightly covered.

TO SERVE

2. Turn tapenade into a serving dish, mounding. Garnish top with remaining egg yolk pressed through a strainer; sprinkle the chopped white around edge. Arrange 3 anchovy fillets and black olives as pictured. Surround with toast points. *Makes 20 appetizer servings.*

BEEF BALLS PROVENCALE

SAUCE

1 large leek, washed
¼ cup (½ stick) butter or margarine
2 tablespoons olive or salad oil
1 cup chopped onion
12 small white onions, peeled
2 garlic cloves, crushed
1 can (1 lb, 12 oz) tomatoes, undrained, crushed
1 can (10½ oz) beef broth, undiluted
1½ cups dry red wine
1 tablespoon dried thyme leaves
1 pkg (12 oz) small whole carrots, pared

MEATBALLS

2 lb ground beef

1 teaspoon salt
¼ teaspoon pepper
1 cup fresh bread crumbs
¼ cup water
3 tablespoons grated onion

2 tablespoons butter or margarine
3 zucchini (1 lb) washed, sliced ¼ inch
    thick
12 pitted ripe olives
Peel of 1 navel orange
1 tablespoon cornstarch
¼ cup cold water

DAY AHEAD

1. Make Sauce: Trim leek. Cut off root end and most of green; cut in ¼-inch slices.

2. In ¼ cup hot butter and the oil, in 6-quart Dutch oven, sauté chopped onion, leek, whole onions and garlic, stirring, until golden—5 minutes. Remove whole onions and set aside.

3. To drippings in Dutch oven, add tomatoes, broth, wine and thyme. Bring to boiling; reduce heat, and simmer, covered and stirring occasionally, 1 hour.

4. Add whole onions and carrots; cook, covered, 15 minutes.

5. Make Meatballs: In large bowl, lightly mix beef with salt and pepper. Combine with bread crumbs, water and grated onion; mix well. Shape into meatballs, 1½ inches in diameter (*makes 25*).

6. In hot butter in large skillet, sauté meatballs (half at a time) until browned all over. Remove from skillet as they brown.

7. Add meatballs to sauce; simmer, covered, 30 minutes longer.

8. Add zucchini, olives and orange peel to Dutch oven; cook 10 minutes longer.

9. In small bowl, combine cornstarch and water; mix until smooth; stir into meat mixture. Simmer, uncovered, stirring occasionally, 5 minutes or till thickened.

10. Remove from heat; cool completely. Refrigerate, covered, overnight.

NEXT DAY

11. Remove beef balls from refrigerator 1½ hours before serving.

12. Simmer, covered, stirring occasionally, until hot—about 40 to 50 minutes.

13. Turn into serving dish. Garnish with the orange peel. *Makes 8 servings.*

GNOCCHI

1½ cups water
¾ cup (1½ sticks) butter or margarine
1 teaspoon salt
1½ cups all-purpose flour
6 eggs
⅓ cup grated Parmesan cheese

1½ teaspoons dry mustard
6 tablespoons (¾ stick) butter or
    margarine, melted
6 tablespoons grated Parmesan cheese

DAY AHEAD

1. In large saucepan, combine water, ¾ cup butter and salt; bring to boiling. Remove from heat.

2. With wooden spoon, beat in flour. Over low heat, beat mixture until it leaves the side of pan and forms a ball—1 to 2 minutes. Remove from heat.

3. Add eggs, one at a time, beating with portable electric mixer after each addition until well blended; continue beating until dough is shiny and satiny and breaks into strands. Stir in ⅓ cup cheese and mustard.

4. In a 6-quart kettle, bring 3 quarts lightly salted water to boiling. Reduce heat so that water is below boiling point.

5. Turn gnocchi dough into pastry bag with number-6 rosette tip. Pipe in a stream into simmering water, cutting with scissors into 1-inch lengths. Cook a fourth of dough at a time. Simmer, uncovered, 4 to 5 minutes, or until gnocchi rise to surface. Remove with slotted spoon; drain on paper towels. Repeat until all dough is used.

6. Arrange in a shallow baking dish (12 by 8 inches). Cool, cover, refrigerate.

NEXT DAY

7. Remove gnocchi from refrigerator 30 minutes before serving.

8. Pour melted butter over the top. Sprinkle with cheese. Broil, 4 inches from heat, about 5 minutes until top is golden. *Makes 12 servings.*

ROASTED-GREEN-PEPPER SALAD

6 medium-size green peppers (about 2 lb)

BASIL VINAIGRETTE
1 cup olive or salad oil
⅓ cup red-wine vinegar
1 teaspoon salt
⅛ teaspoon pepper
1 teaspoon dried basil leaves

4 Belgian endives, washed and drained
Escarole, washed and drained
1 red onion, peeled and sliced
2 large tomatoes, each cut into 8 wedges

DAY AHEAD

1. Roast peppers: Place on baking sheet. Broil, 6 inches from heat, turning every 5 minutes with tongs, until skin of peppers is blistered and charred.

2. Place hot peppers in a Dutch oven; cover. Let stand 15 minutes.

3. With sharp knife, peel off charred skin. Cut each pepper into fourths. Remove ribs and seeds. Wash and drain peppers well. Cut into 1-inch strips.

4. Make Basil Vinaigrette: In large bowl, combine oil, vinegar, salt, pepper and basil. Add green-pepper strips; toss to coat. Pack into a jar; cap. Refrigerate overnight.

5. Separate endive leaves. Store in plastic bag in refrigerator with escarole.

NEXT DAY

6. Arrange endive and escarole around edge of chilled serving dish. Drain roasted peppers; reserve dressing. Curl peppers in center of dish. Encircle peppers with onion slices and tomato wedges, as pictured. Pass remaining dressing. *Makes 8 servings.*

DELLA-ROBBIA BRIE

2-lb Brie cheese
1 lb seedless green grapes, washed
¼ cup lemon juice
¼ cup water
2 Red Delicious apples
2 Anjou or Bartlett pears
Whole pecans
French bread

DO AHEAD

1. Remove paper from Brie, but leave outer coating intact. Place cheese in center of large, round serving platter.

2. Separate grapes into small clusters.

3. In large bowl, combine lemon juice and water. Cut apples and pears in half; remove cores. Slice each half into 4 pieces. Place in lemon water.

4. Drain apples and pears; arrange in groups, along with grapes. Refrigerate.

TO SERVE

5. About an hour before serving, remove platter from refrigerator.

6. Serve cheese with 2 to 4 slices of apple and pear, grapes, a few pecans and thin slices of French bread. *Makes 24 servings.* ◆

FOUR

FREEZE-AHEAD FAVORITES

If you're like most people, your freezer is probably confined to storing juice concentrates, ice cream, vegetables, meats, perhaps some convenience foods and, of course, ice cubes. But your freezer can also become the most valuable time-saver in the kitchen when you use it to take advantage of great tasting freeze-ahead recipes such as those we've assembled in this section. Make room for home-baked breads such as Cranberry-Filled Lattice Coffeecake. Keep packages of leftover turkey ready to create sensational suppers such as Turkey Breast Marsala that will be gobbled up with delight. Bet you can't keep the freezer stocked with enough of our scrumptious homemade ice cream-and-cookie sandwiches—Marbled-Brownie Bars, anyone? Freezing captures the fresh taste of fruits at their seasonal peak in our luscious pies to enjoy year 'round. And with our selection of delectable, freezable scratch cakes (how does Walnut-Spice Cake sound?), it might just be worth investing in a bigger freezer.

Quick-And-Easy Home-Baked
BREADS

The enticing aroma of home-baked breads filling the air brings back fond and delicious memories of grandma's kitchen. She knew that baking every day was the only way to provide her family with freshness at its flavorful best. But today's cooks who want to indulge in that same fresh-baked goodness have a time-saving advantage—easy bake-and-freeze breads like those pictured here. All it takes is a few hours to whip up as many batches as needed, then simply bake, wrap and freeze. Freezing locks in that same-day freshness and moistness while preserving the texture perfectly. Then, whenever you yearn for that fresh-baked flavor, just unwrap and let thaw or warm in the oven. Now that's convenience that even grandma would approve of! Recipes begin on page 146.

1. Easy Holiday Loaf, 2. Oatmeal Batter Bread, 3. Whole-Wheat-Currant Soda Bread, 4. Fig Pinwheels, 5. Cereal-Yeast Bread, 6. Raisin Black Rye Bread, 7. California Braided Ring, 8. Pumpkin Muffins, 9. Swedish Cardamom Cake, 10. Honey-Prune Bread, 11. Cranberry-Filled Lattice Coffeecake

RUDY MULLER

continued from page 145

EASY HOLIDAY LOAF

(pictured)

2 cups prepared biscuit mix
⅔ cup quick-cooking oats
⅔ cup sugar
1 cup unsweetened applesauce
¼ cup milk
2 eggs
½ cup chopped red and green candied
    cherries
¼ cup chopped walnuts

1. Preheat oven to 350F. Grease well a 9-by-5-by-3-inch loaf pan.
2. In large bowl, combine all ingredients. With wooden spoon, beat vigorously 30 seconds.
3. Turn into prepared pan. Bake 55 to 60 minutes, or until cake tester inserted in center comes out clean. If bread gets too brown, cover lightly with foil.
4. Let cool in pan on wire rack 10 minutes. To remove, loosen sides with spatula; remove loaf from pan. Cool completely.

TO FREEZE
5. Wrap in heavy-duty foil or plastic wrap; label, seal and place in freezer.

TO THAW AND SERVE
6. Remove from freezer; let stand, wrapped, at room temperature, 1½ to 2 hours. Unwrap; cut in thin slices to serve. *Makes 1 loaf (16 slices).*

WHOLE-WHEAT-CURRANT SODA BREAD

(pictured)

1½ cups all-purpose flour
1 teaspoon baking powder
1 teaspoon baking soda
½ teaspoon salt
1½ cups whole wheat flour
½ cup currants
1½ cups buttermilk

1. Preheat oven to 375F. Grease well a small cookie sheet.
2. Into large mixing bowl, sift all-purpose flour, baking powder, soda and salt. Add whole wheat flour and currants; with fork, mix well.
3. Add buttermilk; mix with fork just until dry ingredients are moistened.
4. Turn out onto lightly floured pastry cloth or board, and knead gently until smooth—about 1 minute.
5. With floured hands, shape into an 8-inch oval on prepared cookie sheet. Press a large, floured knife on top of loaf to make five slashes 1 inch deep.
6. Bake 35 to 40 minutes, or until

top is golden and loaf sounds hollow when tapped with knuckle.
7. Remove to wire rack. Cool completely.

TO FREEZE
8. Wrap in heavy-duty foil or plastic wrap; label, seal and place in freezer.

TO THAW AND SERVE
9. Remove from freezer; let stand, wrapped, at room temperature, 1 to 1½ hours. Unwrap; slice to serve. *Makes 1 loaf (14 slices).*

OATMEAL BATTER BREAD

(pictured)

5¼ to 5¾ cups all-purpose flour
2 pkg fast-rising yeast
⅓ cup sugar
1½ teaspoons salt
1½ cups water
½ cup (1 stick) butter or margarine,
    softened
2 cups quick-cooking oats
2 whole eggs
1 egg white, beaten
2 tablespoons quick-cooking oats

1. In large bowl of electric mixer, combine 2¼ cups of the flour, the yeast, sugar and salt; mix well.
2. In small saucepan, heat water and butter until warm (120 to 130F); butter does not need to melt.
3. Add to flour mixture along with 2 cups oats and the whole eggs; beat at low speed just until ingredients are moistened. Beat at medium speed 3 minutes, occasionally scraping side of bowl with rubber spatula.
4. Using wooden spoon, gradually beat in remaining 3 to 3½ cups flour, to make a soft dough.
5. Place in greased bowl, turning dough over to bring up greased side. Cover with towel; let rise in warm place, free from drafts (85F), or until double in bulk—about 35 to 40 minutes.
6. Turn batter into two greased 1½-quart soufflé dishes. Let rise, uncovered, in warm place 30 to 35 minutes, or until double in bulk. Preheat oven to 375F.
7. Bake 30 to 35 minutes, or until golden-brown.
8. Immediately remove from soufflé dishes to wire rack; brush tops with egg white; sprinkle with oats. Cool completely.

TO FREEZE
9. Wrap each loaf in heavy-duty foil or plastic wrap; label, seal and place in freezer.

TO THAW AND SERVE
10. Remove 1 loaf from freezer. Let

stand, wrapped, at room temperature, 1½ to 2 hours. Unwrap; cut in slices to serve. *Makes 2 loaves (14 slices each).*

FIG PINWHEELS

(pictured)

2½ cups prepared biscuit mix
⅔ cup milk
2 tablespoons unsalted butter or
    margarine, softened
¼ cup granulated sugar
½ teaspoon ground cinnamon
½ cup finely chopped dried figs
¼ cup (½ stick) unsalted butter or
    margarine, melted
½ cup confectioners' sugar
3 to 4 teaspoons milk

1. Preheat oven to 425F. Grease a large cookie sheet.
2. In medium bowl, combine biscuit mix and ⅔ cup milk. With wooden spoon, beat vigorously for 1 minute.
3. On lightly floured pastry cloth or board, turn dough over to coat with flour. Roll dough into a 16-by-7-inch rectangle, ¼ inch thick.
4. Spread with softened butter. Sprinkle with mixture of granulated sugar and cinnamon, then with figs.
5. Starting from a long edge, roll up, jelly-roll fashion. Pinch edges to seal.
6. Cut crosswise into 1-inch slices; place, cut side up, 1½ inches apart on prepared cookie sheet.
7. Bake about 15 minutes, or until golden-brown. Brush with melted butter.
8. Remove to wire rack; cool slightly. Meanwhile, combine confectioners' sugar and enough milk to make mixture thick and spreadable. With teaspoon, spoon over rolls in thin spiral, as pictured.

TO FREEZE
9. Place rolls, unwrapped, in freezer, 15 to 20 minutes or until icing is hard. Remove from freezer and wrap rolls individually in plastic wrap. Place in a shallow freezer container; label and store in freezer.

TO THAW AND SERVE
10. Remove from freezer. Let stand, wrapped, at room temperature, 45 minutes to 1 hour. Unwrap and serve. *Makes 16 rolls.*

PUMPKIN MUFFINS

(pictured)

2¼ cups all-purpose flour
2 teaspoons baking powder
½ teaspoon baking soda
1 teaspoon ground cinnamon
½ teaspoon ground nutmeg

½ teaspoon salt
1 cup canned pumpkin
1 cup sugar
½ cup milk
2 eggs
¼ cup salad oil
¼ cup sunflower seed

1. Preheat oven to 400F. Lightly grease 12 (3-inch) muffin-pan cups.

2. On sheet of waxed paper, sift together flour, baking powder, soda, cinnamon, nutmeg and salt; set aside.

3. In large bowl, combine pumpkin, sugar, milk, eggs and oil; beat with wooden spoon until well blended.

4. Add flour mixture, beating just until smooth; stir in sunflower seed.

5. Spoon batter into prepared muffin-pan cups. If desired, sprinkle tops with additional sunflower seed. Bake 20 to 25 minutes, or until golden-brown.

6. Remove muffin-pan cups to wire rack; loosen edge of each muffin with spatula; turn out.

TO FREEZE

7. Let muffins cool completely on wire rack. Wrap muffins individually in foil; place in a shallow freezer container. Label and store in freezer.

TO THAW AND SERVE

8. Preheat oven to 400F. Remove from freezer. Place muffins, wrapped, on a cookie sheet; heat in oven 15 minutes. Or remove foil wrapping and heat, on waxed paper, in microwave oven 1½ minutes. Serve hot. *Makes 12 muffins.*

SWEDISH CARDAMOM CAKE
(pictured)

4 to 4¼ cups all-purpose flour
2 pkg fast-rising yeast
½ cup sugar
2 teaspoons ground cardamom
1 teaspoon salt
½ teaspoon ground cinnamon
¼ teaspoon ground cloves
¼ teaspoon ground ginger
½ cup water
½ cup milk
½ cup (1 stick) butter or margarine,
    softened
4 eggs
¼ cup chopped candied orange peel
Whole blanched almonds (optional)

1. Grease well two shallow, 1-quart, decorative tube pans. In large bowl of electric mixer, combine 1½ cups of the flour, the yeast, sugar, cardamom, salt, cinnamon, cloves and ginger; mix well.

2. In small saucepan, heat water, milk and butter until warm (120 to 130F); butter does not need to melt.

3. Add to flour mixture along with the eggs; beat, at low speed, just until ingredients are moistened. Beat, at me-

dium speed, 3 minutes, occasionally scraping side of bowl with rubber spatula.

4. Using wooden spoon, gradually stir in remaining 2½ to 2¾ cups flour to make a soft batter. Stir in orange peel.

5. Place almonds in bottom of pans, around side, if desired. Turn batter into pans, dividing evenly. Cover with towel; let rise in warm place (85F), free from drafts, until cakes are light and double in bulk—about 40 to 50 minutes. Preheat the oven to 375F.

6. Bake 25 to 30 minutes, or until golden-brown. Remove from pans; cool completely on wire rack.

TO FREEZE

7. Wrap cakes separately in heavy-duty foil or plastic wrap; label, seal and place in freezer.

TO THAW AND SERVE

8. Remove 1 cake from freezer; let stand, wrapped, at room temperature, 1 to 1½ hours. Unwrap; slice in wedges to serve. *Makes 2 cakes (8 slices each).*

RAISIN BLACK RYE BREAD
(pictured)

2½ to 3 cups all-purpose flour
2 cups rye flour
2 pkg fast-rising yeast
2 cups whole-bran cereal
2 teaspoons salt
1½ cups milk
½ cup water
½ cup dark molasses
¼ cup salad oil
1 sq (1 oz) unsweetened chocolate,
    chopped
½ cup seedless raisins
¼ cup water
½ teaspoon cornstarch

1. In large bowl of electric mixer, combine 1 cup of the all-purpose flour, 1 cup rye flour, the yeast, bran cereal and salt; mix well.

2. In small saucepan, heat milk, ½ cup water, molasses, oil and chocolate over low heat just until warm (120 to 130F); chocolate does not need to melt.

3. Add to flour mixture; beat at low speed just until blended; beat at medium speed 3 minutes, occasionally scraping side of bowl with rubber spatula.

4. With wooden spoon, stir in raisins and remaining rye flour; add enough of the remaining all-purpose flour (1½ to 2 cups) to make a stiff dough.

5. Turn out onto lightly floured pastry cloth or board. Knead until smooth and elastic—about 5 minutes.

6. Place in greased bowl; turn dough to bring up greased side. Cover with towel; let rise in warm place (85F), free from drafts, until almost double in

bulk—about 40 minutes.

7. Turn dough out onto lightly floured pastry cloth or board. Divide in half. Shape each half into a round, 8-inch loaf. Place on large greased cookie sheet. Cover; let rise in warm place (85F), free from drafts, until almost double in bulk—about 30 minutes. Preheat oven to 375F.

8. Bake 40 to 45 minutes. Five minutes before end of baking time, remove loaves from oven; brush surface of each loaf with ¼ cup water mixed with the cornstarch. Return loaves to oven; bake until glaze is shiny and loaves sound hollow when tapped with knuckle.

9. Remove to wire rack; cool completely.

TO FREEZE

10. Wrap loaves separately in heavy-duty foil or plastic wrap; label, seal and place in freezer.

TO THAW AND SERVE

11. Remove 1 loaf from freezer. Let stand, wrapped, at room temperature, 1 to 1½ hours. Unwrap; slice to serve. *Makes 2 round loaves (14 slices each).*

CEREAL-YEAST BREAD
(pictured)

1¾ cups crushed flaked whole-grain cereal
    with raisins
5½ to 6¼ cups all-purpose flour
2 pkg fast-rising yeast
2 teaspoons salt
1 cup water
1 cup milk
⅓ cup (⅔ stick) butter or margarine,
    softened
½ cup honey
2 whole eggs
1 egg white, mixed with 1 teaspoon water

1. In large bowl of electric mixer, combine 1½ cups cereal, 2½ cups of the flour, the yeast and salt; mix well.

2. In small saucepan, heat water, milk and butter over low heat just until warm (120-130F); butter does not need to melt.

3. Add milk mixture, honey and 2 whole eggs to flour mixture; beat at low speed just until ingredients are moistened. Beat at medium speed 3 minutes, occasionally scraping the bowl with rubber spatula.

4. With wooden spoon, stir enough of the remaining flour (3 to 3¾ cups) to make a soft dough.

5. Turn out onto lightly floured pastry cloth or board. Knead until smooth—about 5 minutes; add rest of flour as needed.

6. Place in greased bowl, turning dough over to bring up greased side.
continued on page 160

A Freezerful of
TURKEY DINNERS

The poor turkey! No one gives it a second thought until Thanksgiving rolls around. But turkey's economy and ease of cooking make it perfect for year 'round enjoyment. And by freezing the leftovers, you have the makings for a bonanza of wonderfully exciting leftover meals: Turkey Chowder; Turkey-Clam-And-Corn Pie; Turkey à la King and Turkey Tetrazzini, of course, and also Turkey Salad Oriental, Turkey Paella, Turkey Ragout and Turkey Breast Marsala.

Here's what to do: As soon as possible after serving the turkey, scoop out all the extra stuffing, place it in a covered container or in a moisture-proof wrapping and refrigerate. Remove the meat that's left on the bones. Store whatever you plan to use in the next two days in the refrigerator. To freeze the rest, separate the large slices from the smaller pieces and freeze in individual packets the types and amounts of meat you'll need for each of the recipes you plan to make. To package for freezing, wrap meat securely in heavy-duty foil, making several double folds over each opening. Seal with freezer tape, and mark the contents with a freezer pencil. Don't forget to date the packages. In order for the cooked turkey to retain its good quality, you'll need to use it within six months. Leftover gravy can be frozen or stored in the refrigerator for up to two days. And don't throw out the carcass—it makes delicious Turkey Broth (see recipe, page 150) to use for soup now or to freeze for later. Be sure to reheat broth or gravy to the boiling point before serving. Recipes begin on page 150.

continued from page 149

TURKEY PAELLA
(pictured)

½ cup salad oil
1½ cups chopped onion
1 garlic clove, crushed
1 can (10¾ oz) condensed chicken broth, undiluted
1 bottle (8 oz) clam juice
1 can (1 lb) tomatoes
1 teaspoon salt
¼ teaspoon pepper
¼ teaspoon saffron
1½ cups long-grain white rice
1 cup frozen peas
1 pkg (9 oz) frozen artichoke hearts
3 cups cooked turkey, cubed
Chopped parsley

1. Preheat oven to 350F.
2. In hot oil in large skillet, sauté onion and garlic until onion is golden—about 5 minutes.
3. Stir in undiluted chicken broth, clam juice, tomatoes, salt, pepper and saffron; bring to boiling, stirring. Stir in rice, peas and artichoke hearts; return to boiling.
4. Pour into a 2-quart shallow baking dish. Arrange pieces of turkey over the rice mixture.
5. Bake, uncovered, 55 to 60 minutes, or until rice is tender and all liquid is absorbed.
6. To serve: Fluff rice with a fork. Arrange some of the artichoke hearts in center of paella. Sprinkle with chopped parsley. *Makes 6 servings.*

TURKEY TETRAZZINI

SAUCE
½ cup (1 stick) butter or margarine
½ cup all-purpose flour
1½ teaspoons salt
Dash ground nutmeg
Dash ground red pepper
2 cups milk
1 can (10¾ oz) condensed chicken broth, undiluted
2 egg yolks
½ cup light cream
¼ cup dry sherry

1 pkg (8 oz) thin spaghetti
4 cups cooked turkey, in large pieces
1 can (6 oz) sliced mushrooms
1 cup grated sharp Cheddar cheese

1. Make Sauce: Melt butter in medium saucepan. Remove from heat; stir in flour, salt, nutmeg and red pepper until smooth. Gradually stir in milk and undiluted chicken broth; bring to boiling, stirring constantly. Boil gently, stirring constantly, 2 minutes, or until mixture is slightly thickened.
2. In small bowl, beat egg yolks with cream. Gently beat in a little of hot mixture. Return to saucepan; cook over low heat, stirring constantly, until sauce is hot—do not let it boil. Remove from heat; add sherry.
3. Preheat oven to 300F.
4. Cook spaghetti in kettle as package label directs; drain. Return spaghetti to kettle. Add 2 cups sauce and toss until well blended.
5. Add turkey and mushrooms to the remaining sauce.
6. Turn spaghetti into a 12-by-8-by-2-inch baking dish. Spoon turkey mixture over top. Sprinkle with the grated cheese.
7. Bake, covered, 25 minutes; uncover and bake 10 minutes more, or until piping hot. *Makes 8 servings.*

TURKEY RAGOUT

Butter or margarine
1 large onion, sliced
2 medium zucchini, sliced (about 3 cups)
½ cup sliced celery
4 cups cooked turkey, in large chunks (about 1½-inch)
½ lb small fresh mushrooms
1 can (1 lb) whole carrots, drained
⅔ cup dry white wine
⅔ cup canned condensed chicken broth
1 can (10¾ oz) condensed cream-of-celery soup
1 can (10¾ oz) condensed cream-of-chicken soup
¼ teaspoon dried thyme leaves
¼ teaspoon dried marjoram leaves
Chopped parsley

1. Preheat oven to 350F.
2. In 4 tablespoons hot butter in large, heavy skillet, sauté onion, zucchini and celery until almost tender and lightly browned—about 10 to 15 minutes. Combine with turkey in a 3-quart casserole.
3. In same skillet, brown mushrooms, adding more butter if needed. Add to turkey mixture in casserole. Add carrots.
4. Stir wine into drippings in skillet, then add undiluted chicken broth, celery soup, chicken soup, thyme and marjoram. Bring to boiling, stirring to loosen browned bits in pan. Pour wine mixture over turkey and vegetables in casserole, and mix lightly with a fork.
5. Bake, covered, 1 hour, or until bubbling in center. Sprinkle with chopped parsley. *Makes 6 servings.*

TURKEY CHOWDER
(pictured)

4 slices bacon, cut up
1 cup chopped onion
4 cups (1¾ lb) cubed, pared potato
2 cups Turkey Broth, recipe follows
2 pkg (10-oz size) frozen whole-kernel corn, thawed
¼ cup (½ stick) butter or margarine
2½ teaspoons salt
¼ teaspoon pepper
2 cups cooked turkey, cubed
2 cups milk
1 cup heavy cream
2 tablespoons chopped parsley
Chowder crackers

1. In 5-quart Dutch oven or heavy kettle, sauté bacon until crisp; remove and reserve.
2. In bacon fat, sauté onion, stirring, until golden—about 5 minutes. Add potato and Turkey Broth. Bring to boiling; simmer, covered, about 30 minutes, or just until potato is tender but not mushy.
3. Meanwhile, in medium saucepan, combine corn, butter, salt, pepper, turkey and milk. Simmer, covered and stirring occasionally, 5 minutes.
4. Add to potato mixture, along with the heavy cream. Cook, stirring occasionally, until hot—do not boil.
5. Turn into warm soup tureen; sprinkle with reserved crisp bacon and the chopped parsley. Serve with chowder crackers. *Makes 8 to 10 servings.*

TURKEY BROTH

Carcass from turkey
5 cups water
2 carrots, pared and halved
3 parsley sprigs
3 celery tops
2 onions, halved
2 teaspoons salt
10 black peppercorns
1 bay leaf

1. Break up carcass. Place in 6-quart kettle with water, the carrots, parsley, celery tops, onions, salt, peppercorns and bay leaf.
2. Bring to boiling; reduce heat; simmer, covered, 2 hours. Strain.
3. Return to kettle; bring back to boiling; boil gently, uncovered, to reduce to 3 cups. Refrigerate. *Makes 3 cups.*

TURKEY BREAST MARSALA

4 to 6 tablespoons (½ to ¾ stick) butter or margarine
8 slices (about ¼ inch thick) cooked turkey breast
Dash pepper
4 thin slices prosciutto, cut in half
1 pkg (8 oz) mozzarella cheese, cut in 8 slices
½ cup Marsala
Chopped parsley

1. Heat 4 tablespoons butter in large, attractive skillet. Sauté turkey slices, in single layer, until golden on both sides—1 minute on each side. Add more butter as needed. Remove turkey slices as browned and keep warm.

2. Return all slices to skillet, overlapping. Sprinkle with pepper. Place a slice of prosciutto and one of cheese on each slice of turkey. Pour Marsala over all.

3. Cook, covered, 3 to 5 minutes, or until heated through and cheese is melted. Remove from heat. Sprinkle with parsley. Serve from skillet. *Makes 6 servings.*

TURKEY SALAD ORIENTAL

(pictured)

1 can (8 oz) water chestnuts, drained
1 cup cubed cooked turkey
½ cup pitted black olives

DRESSING
¼ cup salad oil
3 tablespoons wine or cider vinegar
½ teaspoon ground ginger
½ teaspoon salt
⅛ teaspoon pepper
¼ teaspoon soy sauce

2 tablespoons chopped green onion
1 quart mixed salad greens, in 1½-inch pieces
3 hard-cooked eggs, quartered

1. Slice each water chestnut, lengthwise, into thirds. In medium bowl, combine chestnuts with turkey and olives.

2. Prepare Dressing: In jar with tight-fitting lid, combine all ingredients for dressing; shake vigorously to combine.

3. Pour dressing over turkey mixture; toss lightly to mix well. Refrigerate, covered, at least 3 hours.

4. To serve: Toss onion and salad greens with turkey mixture. Garnish with hard-cooked eggs. *Makes 4 to 6 servings.*

TURKEY A LA KING

SAUCE
¼ cup (½ stick) butter or margarine
2 tablespoons grated green pepper
½ lb fresh mushrooms, thickly sliced
¼ cup all-purpose flour
1 teaspoon salt
2 cups Turkey Broth, recipe page 150, or chicken broth
1 cup light cream or half-and-half
1 egg yolk

3 cups cooked turkey, cut into 1½-inch pieces
1 canned pimiento, cut into strips
4 slices white toast, halved diagonally

1. Make Sauce: In hot butter in large skillet, sauté green pepper and mushrooms, stirring, over low heat 5 minutes.

2. Remove from heat; stir in flour and salt; then gradually stir in Turkey Broth and light cream until smooth. Bring to boiling, stirring; simmer, stirring, 5 minutes, or until thickened.

3. Stir small amount of hot mixture into egg yolk, mixing well. Pour back into hot sauce; cook a few minutes. Add turkey and pimiento strips; cook gently 5 minutes, or until hot.

4. Turn into serving dish. Arrange toast points around edge. *Makes 4 servings.*

MANHATTAN TURKEY CHOWDER

2 tablespoons salad oil
1 cup sliced onion
3 cups Turkey Broth, recipe page 150, or chicken broth
2 cups water
½ garlic clove, crushed
½ cup coarsely chopped celery
4 parsley sprigs, chopped
1 teaspoon dried thyme leaves
Dash sugar
1 teaspoon salt
1 can (1 lb, 12 oz) whole tomatoes, undrained
2 cups cut-up, pared potato
2 cups cooked turkey, cut into ½-inch pieces

1. In hot oil in 5-quart Dutch oven, sauté onion, stirring, until golden—about 5 minutes.

2. Add Turkey Broth, water, the garlic, celery, parsley, thyme, sugar and salt. Add undrained tomatoes, breaking up with fork. Add potato.

3. Over medium heat, cook, covered, 35 minutes, or until potato is tender but not mushy.

4. Add turkey; simmer 5 minutes. Taste for seasoning; add salt if needed. *Makes 1¾ quarts; 6 servings.*

TURKEY AND FRUIT CURRY

3 tablespoons butter or margarine
1 cup chopped onion
2 to 3 teaspoons curry powder
1 large tart apple, pared, sliced
¼ cup all-purpose flour
½ teaspoon ground ginger
1 teaspoon salt
¼ teaspoon pepper
2½ cups Turkey Broth, recipe page 150, or chicken broth

2 teaspoons grated lime peel
2 tablespoons lime juice
3 cups cooked turkey, cut into 1-inch pieces
2 bananas, peeled, cut into ½-inch chunks
1 can (8 oz) pineapple chunks, in their own juice, undrained
Hot white rice
Chutney (optional)

1. In 3 tablespoons hot butter in large skillet, sauté onion, curry powder and apple until onion is tender—about 5 minutes.

2. Remove from heat. Stir in flour, ginger, salt and pepper; mix well.

3. Gradually stir in Turkey Broth; add lime peel and juice.

4. Bring to boiling, stirring. Reduce heat; simmer, covered, 20 minutes, stirring occasionally.

5. Stir in turkey, banana and pineapple. Heat gently just to boiling.

6. Serve over white rice. Nice with chutney. *Makes 8 servings.*

TURKEY-CLAM-AND-CORN PIE

2 tablespoons butter or margarine
½ lb small white onions, peeled
½ cup chopped celery
6 tablespoons all-purpose flour
1 teaspoon salt
¼ teaspoon pepper
¼ teaspoon dried thyme leaves
1 can (8 oz) minced clams, undrained
1 cup Turkey Broth, recipe page 150, or chicken broth
1 cup light cream
1 can (12 oz) whole-kernel corn
3 cups cooked turkey, in large pieces
2 hard-cooked eggs, coarsely chopped
Pastry for 1-crust pie
1 egg yolk
1 teaspoon water

1. Heat butter in large skillet or Dutch oven. Add onions and celery; cook, covered, 10 minutes; remove from heat.

2. Stir in flour, salt, pepper and thyme until well combined. Gradually stir in clams, Turkey Broth and cream. Add corn and turkey.

3. Bring to boiling, stirring constantly. Reduce heat; simmer, stirring occasionally, 10 minutes. Turn into a 2-quart shallow baking dish. Stir in eggs.

4. Preheat oven to 400F. Make pastry.

5. Roll pastry to fit top of baking dish with a ½-inch overhang. Place over turkey mixture; turn edge under; seal to rim of dish and crimp. Make several slits in top for steam vents. Beat egg yolk with water; brush over pastry.

6. Bake 30 minutes, or until crust is deep golden. *Makes 6 servings.*

Note: You may use canned chicken broth.

♦

COLD 'N' CRUNCHY SANDWICH TREATS

Ice cream and cookies know no season—and neither do these soul-satisfying homemade ice-cream-and-cookie sandwiches. Whether it's to beat the heat of the July sun or to re-energize after a day of winter activities, these frozen goodies do the trick deliciously. Pictured below, we've developed eight unique 'n' crunchy cookie recipes (what fun that was!) to sandwich around your favorite ice cream. Creations such as crunchy Peanut-Butter Bars, spicy Ginger Crinkles and rich Chocolate-Heart Cookies you just can't buy in any store. They stay fresh in the freezer for weeks—if they last—to enjoy snack-time, party-time, anytime. Recipes begin on page 154.

continued from page 153

All ice-cream sandwiches are pictured on pages 152 and 153.

OATMEAL-COOKIE ICE-CREAM SANDWICHES

½ gallon (brick) coffee or vanilla ice cream
12 round Oatmeal Cookies, recipe follows
12 doughnut-shape Oatmeal Cookies, recipe follows
12 chocolate kisses

1. Remove ice cream from freezer; discard carton. With long sharp knife, cut lengthwise into six even pieces.
2. With 3-inch round, plain cutter, cut two rounds from each piece.
3. Sandwich each ice-cream round between a round and a doughnut-shape Oatmeal Cookie; press chocolate kiss into hole.

TO FREEZE

4. Place in freezer; freeze until firm—about 2 hours.
5. Store in individual plastic bags, or wrap in foil. Label and return to freezer. *Makes 12 sandwiches.*
Note: Pack remaining ice cream into a plastic container; freeze for later use.

OATMEAL COOKIES

1¾ cups all-purpose flour
1 teaspoon baking soda
1 teaspoon salt
1 cup (2 sticks) butter or margarine, softened
1 cup light-brown sugar, packed
1 egg
1 teaspoon vanilla extract
¼ cup milk
3 cups quick-cooking rolled oats

1. Sift together flour, baking soda and salt; set aside.
2. In large bowl of electric mixer, beat butter, sugar, egg and vanilla until mixture is smooth and blended.
3. At low speed, beat in flour mixture until smooth. Stir in milk.
4. With wooden spoon, stir in oats until well blended. Refrigerate, covered, about 3 hours.
5. Preheat oven to 400°. Lightly grease cookie sheet.
6. On lightly floured surface, roll out half of dough to ⅛-inch thickness.
7. Cut out with 3-inch round cookie cutter.
8. Place 1 inch apart on prepared cookie sheet. Bake 10 to 12 minutes, or until golden-brown. Remove to wire rack

to cool completely.
9. Roll out remaining half of dough, and cut out with 3-inch doughnut cutter. Bake as in Step 8. *Makes 42 cookies.*

BROWNIE ICE-CREAM SANDWICHES

½ gallon (brick) vanilla or Neapolitan ice cream
30 Brownie Bars, recipe follows
Multicolor nonpareils (optional)

1. Remove ice cream from freezer; discard carton. With long sharp knife, cut ice cream crosswise into three even pieces; cut each piece into five (1-inch) slices.
2. Place each ice-cream slice between two Brownie Bars. If necessary, trim off ends of ice cream. If desired, dip edges in nonpareils.

TO FREEZE

3. Freeze until firm—about 2 hours.
4. Store in individual plasic bags, or wrap in foil. Label and return to freezer. *Makes 15 sandwiches.*

BROWNIE BARS

1 pkg (1 lb, 7 oz) brownie mix
½ cup water
1 egg

1. Preheat oven to 350F. Lightly grease and flour 15½-by-10½-by-1-inch jelly-roll pan.
2. Bake brownies, as directed on package, using the water and egg, 25 to 30 minutes. Remove to rack; cool completely.
3. With sharp knife, cut lengthwise into three equal pieces; cut crosswise into ten rows. *Makes 30 bars.*

PEANUT-BUTTER ICE-CREAM SANDWICHES

½ gallon (brick) coffee ice cream
40 Peanut-Butter Bars, recipe follows

1. Remove ice cream from freezer; discard carton. With long sharp knife, cut ice cream crosswise into five even slices; cut each slice into four quarters.
2. Place each ice-cream piece between two Peanut-Butter Bars.

TO FREEZE

3. Freeze until firm—about 2 hours.
4. Store in individual plastic bags, or wrap in foil. Label and return to freezer. *Makes 20 sandwiches.*

PEANUT-BUTTER BARS

1¼ cups sifted all-purpose flour
½ teaspoon baking powder
¾ teaspoon baking soda
¼ teaspoon salt
½ cup (1 stick) butter or margarine, softened
½ cup chunk-style peanut butter
½ cup granulated sugar
½ cup light-brown sugar, packed
1 egg
½ cup chopped peanuts

1. Preheat oven to 350F. Lightly grease bottom of 15½-by-10½-by-1-inch jelly-roll pan.
2. Sift flour with baking powder, soda and salt. Set aside.
3. In large bowl, with portable electric mixer at medium speed, beat butter with peanut butter. Add the sugars gradually; beat until light and fluffy. Beat in egg.
4. Add flour mixture; beat at low speed until well combined.
5. Turn into prepared pan, spreading evenly. Sprinkle with chopped peanuts.
6. Bake 15 minutes, or until lightly browned. Remove to rack to cool 5 minutes.
7. With sharp knife, cut lengthwise into five parts; cut crosswise into eight pieces. *Makes 40 bars.*

CHOCOLATE-HEART ICE-CREAM SANDWICHES

½ gallon (brick) strawberry ice cream
20 Chocolate-Heart Cookies, recipe follows

1. Remove ice cream from freezer; discard carton. With long sharp knife, cut lengthwise into five even pieces.
2. With 3¼-inch heart-shape cookie cutter, cut two ice-cream hearts from each piece. Place each ice-cream heart between two Chocolate- Heart Cookies.

TO FREEZE

3. Place in freezer; freeze until firm—about 2 hours.
4. Store in individual plastic bags or wrap in foil. Label and return to freezer. *Makes 10 sandwiches.*
Note: Pack the remaining ice cream into a plastic container, to be frozen for later use.

CHOCOLATE-HEART COOKIES

2 cups all-purpose flour
⅔ cup unsweetened cocoa

½ teaspoon salt
½ teaspoon baking soda
1 cup (2 sticks) butter or margarine, softened
1½ cups sugar
2 eggs
1 teaspoon vanilla extract
1 egg white, slightly beaten (optional)
¾ cup chopped nuts (optional)

1. Sift flour with cocoa, salt and baking soda; set aside.

2. In large bowl of electric mixer, combine butter, sugar, eggs and vanilla. Beat at medium speed until smooth and well blended.

3. Add flour mixture, a small amount at a time, beating at low speed after each addition. Refrigerate, covered, 1 hour.

4. Preheat oven to 350F. Lightly grease baking sheet.

5. Remove dough from refrigerator; divide in half. On lightly floured surface or pastry cloth, roll dough, half at a time, ⅛ inch thick.

6. With 3¼-inch heart-shape cookie cutter, cut out cookies. If desired, brush edge of half the cookies with egg white; sprinkle with nuts.

7. Place 2 inches apart on prepared cookie sheet. Bake 8 to 10 minutes, or just until cookies are set. Remove to rack; cool completely. *Makes 40 hearts.*

CARROT-RAISIN ICE-CREAM SANDWICHES

½ gallon (brick) vanilla or Neapolitan ice cream
20 Carrot-Raisin Cookies, recipe follows

1. Remove ice cream from freezer; discard carton. With a long sharp knife, cut the ice cream lengthwise into five even pieces.

2. With 3-inch round cookie cutter, cut two rounds from each piece.

3. Sandwich each ice-cream round between two Carrot-Raisin Cookies.

TO FREEZE

4. Freeze until firm—about 2 hours.

5. Store in individual plastic bags or wrap in foil. Label and return to freezer. *Makes 10 sandwiches.*

Note: Pack remaining ice cream into a plastic container; freeze for later use.

CARROT-RAISIN COOKIES

2 cups all-purpose flour
2 teaspoons baking powder
½ teaspoon salt
¼ cup shortening
½ cup (1 stick) butter or margarine, softened
Sugar

1 egg
1 teaspoon vanilla extract
2 cups grated raw carrot
½ cup chopped raisins
Salad oil

1. Sift flour with baking powder and salt; set aside.

2. In large bowl of electric mixer, at medium speed, beat shortening, butter, ½ cup sugar, the egg and vanilla until light and fluffy. At low speed, beat in flour mixture; then beat in grated carrot, beating just until combined. With a wooden spoon, stir in the chopped raisins. Refrigerate, covered, 1 hour.

3. Preheat oven to 350F. Lightly grease several cookie sheets.

4. Drop by rounded tablespoonfuls, 2 inches apart, on prepared cookie sheets. Flatten each cookie with bottom of glass brushed with oil, then dipped in sugar.

5. Bake 15 to 20 minutes, or until golden-brown. Cool completely. *Makes 28 Cookies.*

GINGER-CRINKLE ICE-CREAM SANDWICHES

½ gallon (brick) coffee or vanilla ice cream
20 Ginger Crinkles, recipe follows

1. Remove ice cream from freezer; discard carton. With long sharp knife, cut ice cream lengthwise into five even pieces.

2. With 3-inch round cookie cutter, cut two rounds from each piece.

3. Place each ice-cream round between two Ginger Crinkles (sugared side outside).

TO FREEZE

4. Freeze until firm—about 2 hours.

5. Store in individual plastic bags, or wrap in foil. Label and return to freezer. *Makes 10 sandwiches.*

Note: Pack remaining ice cream into a plastic container; freeze for later use.

GINGER CRINKLES

2¼ cups all-purpose flour
2 teaspoons baking soda
¼ teaspoon salt
1 teaspoon ground cinnamon
1 teaspoon ground ginger
1 teaspoon ground cloves
¾ cup soft shortening
1 cup light-brown sugar, packed
1 egg
¼ cup light or dark molasses
Granulated sugar
Water

1. Sift flour with baking soda, salt and spices; set aside.

2. In large bowl of electric mixer, at medium speed, beat shortening, brown sugar and egg until light and fluffy.

3. Beat in molasses until smooth.

4. At low speed, beat in flour mixture until well combined. Refrigerate 1 hour.

5. Meanwhile, preheat oven to 375F. Lightly grease cookie sheets.

6. With hands, roll 2 tablespoons slightly rounded-off dough into balls, 2 inches in diameter. Dip tops in granulated sugar. Place, sugar side up, 4 inches apart, on prepared cookie sheets.

7. Sprinkle each with 3 to 4 drops water.

8. Bake 10 to 12 minutes, or until golden. Remove to wire racks; cool. *Makes 20 cookies.*

MARBLED-BROWNIE ICE-CREAM SANDWICHES

½ gallon (brick) vanilla, pistachio or coffee ice cream
30 Marbled-Brownie Bars, recipe follows

1. Remove ice cream from freezer; discard carton. With long sharp knife, cut ice cream crosswise into three even pieces; cut each piece into five 1-inch slices.

2. Place each ice-cream slice between two Marbled-Brownie Bars. If necessary, trim off ends of ice cream.

TO FREEZE:

3. Freeze until firm—about 2 hours.

4. Store in individual plastic bags, or wrap in foil. Label and return to freezer. *Makes 15 sandwiches.*

MARBLED-BROWNIE BARS

1½ cups sifted all-purpose flour
⅓ teaspoon baking powder
¼ teaspoon salt
¾ cup (1½ sticks) butter or margarine, softened
1½ cups sugar
3 eggs
1 teaspoon vanilla extract
3 squares (1-oz size) unsweetened chocolate, melted

1. Preheat oven to 350F. Lightly grease and flour a 15½-by-10½-by-1-inch jelly-roll pan.

2. Sift flour with baking powder and salt; set aside.

3. In large bowl, with electric mixer at medium speed, beat butter, sugar, eggs and vanilla until light.

4. Stir in flour mixture until well combined.

5. Divide batter in half. Stir choco-

continued on page 161

Freeze in Freshness

S pring's succulent strawberries, summer's juicy peaches and tomatoes, autumn's crisp apples— each season brings its own bouquet of fresh produce at its juicy and flavorful peak—but, alas, for a brief time only. Wouldn't it be wonderful to capture all of that freshness to enjoy months later? With our collection of easy freeze-ahead desserts and main dishes you can do just that. Our fruit pies, such as the Deep-Dish Apple Pie pictured above, take fresh-from-the-tree fruit and mix it with other ingredients into a scrumptious filling which is then frozen in a foil-lined pie plate. Once frozen, simply remove

from the plate and freeze up to six months. When ready to bake, unwrap and slip the filling into the same plate along with a quick pastry crust for a warm and wonderful taste of freshness. There are also flaky pastry recipes such as these Cherry Pinwheels, plus an elegant Chocolate Soufflé that freezes beautifully—whenever the urge strikes, all you need to do is pop them into the oven to bake, and enjoy. And to make the rest of the meal as fresh-tasting and fuss-free as the dessert, you'll find a selection of fabulous freeze-ahead main-dish recipes. Recipes begin on opposite page.

DEEP-DISH PIES
(pictured)

**Frozen Apple-Pie Filling, recipe follows,
or frozen Cranberry-Apple Filling,
recipe follows**
Butter or margarine
Frozen Pastry Rounds, recipe follows
**Granulated sugar or 1 egg yolk mixed with
2 teaspoons water**

1. Remove one package of frozen filling from freezer; unwrap; place in lightly greased 1½-quart casserole. Dot top with 2 tablespoons butter. Let stand at room temperature 1 hour.

2. Also remove one pastry round; let stand at room temperature, along with filling. Preheat oven to 400F.

3. With sharp knife, make several slits in center of pastry. Place pastry round on top of filling; with fingers, crimp edge of pastry to edge of dish. Sprinkle top with 1 teaspoon sugar; or brush with egg yolk mixed with water. Bake 50 to 60 minutes, or until top is nicely browned and apples are tender. Nice served warm with ice cream. *Makes 6 servings.*

APPLE-PIE FILLING
(for freezer)

2 lb tart cooking apples
1 tablespoon lemon juice
1 cup sugar
3 tablespoons all-purpose flour
½ teaspoon ground nutmeg
⅛ teaspoon ground cloves

1. Wash apples; pare; core; slice thinly into large bowl. Sprinkle with lemon juice.

2. Combine sugar, flour, nutmeg and cloves; gently toss with apple, mixing well.

3. Turn into a foil-lined (use a large sheet of foil) round foil pan, about 8½ inches in diameter.

TO FREEZE

4. Freeze; lift out filling; bring foil over apples to wrap securely; label and freeze. *Makes filling for one deep-dish apple pie.*

CRANBERRY-APPLE FILLING
(for freezer)

2 cups cranberries (see Note)
1½ cups sugar
¼ cup all-purpose flour
**2 tablespoons maple or maple-flavored
syrup**
**6 large tart apples (3 lb), pared, cored and
sliced**

1. In a large bowl, mix cranberries with sugar, flour and maple syrup.

2. Add apple slices; toss lightly to mix well.

TO FREEZE

3. Turn into two foil-lined (use a large sheet of foil) round foil pans, about 8½ inches in diameter. Freeze; lift out filling; bring foil over filling to wrap securely; label and freeze. *Makes filling for two deep-dish cranberry-apple pies.*

Note: You may use frozen cranberries; if not frozen, cut cranberries in half with sharp knife.

FROZEN PASTRY ROUNDS

**2 pkg (11-oz size) piecrust mix; or
Homemade Pastry:**
4 cups sifted all-purpose flour
2 teaspoons salt
1½ cups shortening
½ cup ice water

1. Prepare piecrust mix as package label directs. Divide dough into fourths, and roll into four (11-inch size) rounds.

2. Or make Homemade Pastry: Sift the all-purpose flour with salt into a very large bowl.

3. With pastry blender, or two knives, using a short, cutting motion, cut in shortening until mixture resembles coarse cornmeal.

4. Quickly sprinkle the ice water, 1 tablespoon at a time, over all of the pastry mixture, tossing lightly with fork after each addition and pushing dampened portion to side of bowl; sprinkle only dry portion remaining. (Pastry should be just moist enough to hold together, not sticky.)

5. Shape pastry into a ball; wrap in waxed paper, and refrigerate until ready to use. Divide in fourths; flatten each fourth with palm of hand.

6. On lightly floured pastry cloth, using a covered rolling pin, roll out each fourth of pastry to an 11-inch circle.

7. Cut waxed paper into 12-inch circles. Stack pastry rounds with waxed paper in between.

TO FREEZE

8. Freezer-wrap, seal and label. Store in box, if desired, in freezer. These store well at 0°F about 6 months. *Makes 4 pastry rounds.*

FREEZER DANISH PASTRY

1½ cups (3 sticks) sweet butter, softened
¼ cup all-purpose flour
¾ cup milk
⅓ cup sugar
1 teaspoon salt

½ cup very warm water (105-115F)
2 pkg active yeast
1 egg
3¾ cups all-purpose flour

1. In bowl, with wooden spoon, beat butter and ¼ cup flour until smooth. Spread on waxed paper (on wet surface) to 12-by-8-inch rectangle. Refrigerate on cookie sheet.

2. Heat milk slightly. Add sugar and salt; stir to dissolve. Cool to lukewarm.

3. Check temperature of water with thermometer. Pour into large bowl; sprinkle with yeast; stir to dissolve. Stir in milk mixture, egg and 3 cups flour; beat with wooden spoon until smooth. Mix in rest of flour with hand until dough leaves side of bowl.

4. Refrigerate, covered, ½ hour. Turn out onto lightly floured pastry cloth; with covered rolling pin, roll into 16-by-12-inch rectangle. Place chilled butter mixture on half of dough; remove paper. Fold other half of dough over butter; pinch the edges to seal.

5. With fold at right, roll out from center to a 16-by-8-inch rectangle. From short side, fold dough into thirds, making three layers; seal edges, chill, wrapped in foil, 1 hour. Repeat rolling and folding (if butter breaks through, brush with flour); seal edges; chill ½ hour.

6. Roll; fold again; seal edges; chill, wrapped in foil, 3 hours or overnight.

TO FREEZE

7. Divide cold pastry into thirds. Wrap each third in foil; seal, label and freeze. Or, if desired, make up ⅓ into Cherry Pinwheels and ⅓ into Cinnamon Bear Claws. Freeze as recipes direct. (Unbaked Danish pastry may be stored in freezer at 0°F for several months, if desired.) *Makes enough dough for about 18.*

TO BAKE

8. Bake as directed in recipes that follow.

CHERRY PINWHEELS
(pictured)

⅓ recipe Danish Pastry Dough, above
Cherry or apricot preserves
Sugar Glaze, recipe follows

1. Pinch off a small piece of dough and reserve for centers. On lightly floured pastry cloth or board, roll rest of dough into rectangle, 12 by 8 inches. With sharp knife, cut into six 4-inch squares.

2. Arrange squares, 1½ inches apart on tray or in shallow box. In each corner of each square, make a cut, at 45-degree angle, 1½ inches long.

continued on page 158

continued from page 157

3. In center of each square, place 1 tablespoon preserves.

4. To make pinwheels: Bring every other point of dough to center of square; then press in center, to fasten.

5. Roll out the small piece of reserved dough ⅛ inch thick. Using a 1¼-inch round cutter, cut 6 rounds. Moisten bottom of rounds slightly with water; place in center of each pinwheel, to cover points.

TO FREEZE

6. Wrap tray with foil; seal, label and freeze.

TO BAKE

7. Line a cookie sheet with brown paper. Arrange pinwheels, 2 inches apart, on ungreased brown paper.

8. Let rise in warm place (85F), free from drafts, until double in bulk—1 to 1¼ hours. Meanwhile, preheat oven to 375F. Make Sugar Glaze.

9. Bake 15 minutes, or until golden-brown. Let cool slightly on wire rack. Drizzle glaze over rolls. *Makes 6.*

Note: To serve pinwheels for breakfast, remove frozen pastries from freezer and place on brown-paper-lined sheet; keep in refrigerator overnight.

CINNAMON BEAR CLAWS

⅓ recipe Danish Pastry Dough, page 157
4 tablespoons (½ stick) sweet butter, melted
½ teaspoon ground cinnamon mixed with 2 tablespoons granulated sugar
½ cup chopped walnuts or pecans
¼ cup chopped raisins
1 teaspoon grated lemon peel
Sugar Glaze, recipe follows

1. On lightly floured pastry cloth or floured board, roll dough to an 18-by-9-inch rectangle. Brush with half of butter; then sprinkle generously with cinnamon-sugar mixture, leaving a ¼-inch edge all around.

2. Combine walnuts, raisins and peel. Sprinkle evenly over sugared surface.

3. From longer side, fold one-third of dough over. Then bring opposite side over this, to make a three-layer strip 18 by 3 inches. Pinch together, to seal.

4. With sharp knife, cut strip crosswise into six sections. On folded side of each, make three 1-inch cuts, evenly spaced.

TO FREEZE

5. Arrange on tray. Separate "claws" slightly. Brush tops with rest of butter. Wrap tray with foil; seal, label and freeze.

TO BAKE

6. Line a cookie sheet with brown

paper. Arrange "claws," 2 inches apart, on ungreased brown paper. Let rise in warm place (85F), free from drafts, until double in bulk—1 to 1¼ hours.

7. Meanwhile, preheat oven to 375F. Also, make Sugar Glaze.

8. Bake 15 to 20 minutes, or until golden-brown. Let cool slightly on wire rack. Drizzle glaze over warm rolls. *Makes 6.*

Note: To serve claws for breakfast, remove pastries from freezer and place on brown-paper-lined sheet; keep in refrigerator overnight.

SUGAR GLAZE

½ cup confectioners' sugar
¼ teaspoon vanilla extract
1 tablespoon milk

In small bowl, combine confectioners' sugar, vanilla and milk; mix well. Drizzle over warm rolls to glaze thinly.

CHOCOLATE SOUFFLE WITH CHOCOLATE SAUCE AND CHANTILLY CREAM
(pictured)

8 egg whites
6 egg yolks
½ cup all-purpose flour
¾ cup unsweetened cocoa
1 cup granulated sugar
¼ teaspoon salt
2 cups milk
4 tablespoons (½ stick) butter or margarine, softened
1 teaspoon vanilla extract
¼ teaspoon cream of tartar
Granulated sugar
Chocolate Sauce, recipe follows
Chantilly Cream, recipe follows

1. Place egg whites in large bowl of electric mixer, yolks in a small bowl. Let whites warm to room temperature—about 1 hour.

2. Line a 2-quart straight-side soufflé dish or 8 (6-ounce size) soufflé dishes with foil or plastic wrap (be sure it extends 2 inches above the edge).

3. In medium-size, heavy saucepan, with wire whisk, mix flour, cocoa, ¾ cup granulated sugar and the salt. Gradually blend in milk. Cook, stirring, over medium heat until mixture comes to a boil.

4. Beat egg yolks with a wire whisk. Beat in some of cocoa mixture. Gradually stir yolk mixture into rest of mixture in saucepan. Add 2 tablespoons butter and the vanilla, stirring, until combined. Set aside to cool slightly.

5. Add cream of tartar to egg whites. With electric mixer at high speed, beat just until soft peaks form when beaters

are slowly raised; scrape side of bowl several times with rubber spatula so that egg whites are beaten throughout.

6. Add ¼ cup granulated sugar, 2 tablespoons at a time, beating well after each addition. Beat just until stiff peaks form when beaters are slowly raised.

7. Turn a third of cocoa mixture over top of egg whites. Using a wire whisk or rubber spatula, gently fold mixture into whites, using under-and-over motion, just until combined. Fold in rest of cocoa mixture, half at a time.

TO FREEZE

8. Turn into prepared dish (use 1 cup filling for each 6-ounce size). Freeze until firm—several hours or overnight. Grasping foil, remove frozen soufflé from dish; wrap securely; place in plastic bag; label and freeze—no longer than one month.

TO BAKE

9. Butter inside of 2-quart soufflé dish or eight 6-ounce dishes. Sprinkle evenly with granulated sugar.

10. Fold a 26-inch-long piece of waxed paper lengthwise into thirds. Lightly butter one side, and sprinkle with 2 tablespoons granulated sugar. Wrap around soufflé dish, sugared side against dish, to form a collar extending 2 inches above top (collar is not needed for 6-ounce size). Remove soufflé from freezer; unwrap; place in dish. Let stand at room temperature for 1 hour for large soufflé, ½ hour for small soufflés.

11. Preheat oven to 350F. Make Chocolate Sauce and Chantilly Cream.

12. Bake about 80 minutes for large soufflé, 25 minutes for 6-ounce size, or until puffed and center is not quite firm when gently shaken.

13. Remove waxed paper. Serve at once, with Chantilly Cream and Chocolate Sauce. *Makes 8 servings.*

CHANTILLY CREAM

1 cup heavy cream
2 tablespoons confectioners' sugar

1. In small bowl, mix cream and sugar. Refrigerate until well chilled.

2. Beat just until stiff with rotary beater. Refrigerate until serving. *Makes 2 cups.*

CHOCOLATE SAUCE

¼ cup sugar
½ cup light cream
1 pkg (4 oz) sweet cooking chocolate
1 square (1 oz) unsweetened chocolate

1. In top of double boiler, combine

sugar, 2 tablespoons cream; cook over boiling water until sugar is dissolved.

2. Cut up both kinds of chocolate. Remove double boiler from heat, but leave top over bottom. Add chocolate to cream mixture, stirring until melted.

3. With spoon, beat in remaining cream. Serve warm. *Makes about 1 cup.*

FROZEN PEACH-BLUEBERRY PIE

2 tablespoons lemon juice
3 cups sliced, pitted, peeled peaches
(about 2¼ lb)
1 cup blueberries
1 cup sugar
2 tablespoons quick-cooking tapioca
½ teaspoon salt

1 pkg (11 oz) piecrust mix
2 tablespoons butter or margarine

1. Sprinkle lemon juice over fruit in large bowl.

2. Combine sugar with tapioca and salt. Add to fruit, tossing lightly to combine. Let stand 15 minutes.

TO FREEZE

3. Line a 9-inch pie plate with heavy-duty foil, making sure foil extends at least 6 inches beyond rim.

4. Turn filling into pie plate; bring foil over top, to cover loosely. Freeze several hours, or until filling is firm.

5. Remove frozen, foil-wrapped filling from pie plate; cover top tightly with foil. Label and return to freezer until ready to bake. Filling may be stored as long as 6 months.

TO BAKE

6. Make piecrust mix as package label directs. Preheat oven to 400F.

7. On lightly floured surface, roll out half of pastry into an 11-inch circle. Use to line 9-inch pie plate; trim.

8. Remove filling from freezer; discard foil. Place filling in pastry-lined pie plate. Dot with butter.

9. Roll out remaining pastry into an 11-inch circle. Make several slits near center, for steam vents. Adjust over filling; trim. Fold edge of top crust under bottom crust; crimp edge.

10. Bake 45 to 50 minutes, or until crust is golden.

11. Cool partially on wire rack; serve slightly warm. *Makes 6 servings.*

HOMEMADE RAVIOLI WITH ITALIAN TOMATO SAUCE

Italian Tomato Sauce, recipe follows

RAVIOLI FILLING
1 carton (15 oz) ricotta cheese
1 pkg (8 oz) mozzarella cheese, finely diced
¼ cup grated Parmesan cheese

1 egg
1 tablespoon chopped parsley
½ teaspoon dried basil leaves or
¼ teaspoon crushed fennel seed
½ teaspoon salt
⅛ teaspoon pepper

NOODLE DOUGH
3 cups all-purpose flour
4 eggs
3 to 4 tablespoons water
2 tablespoons salt
2 tablespoons salad oil

Grated Parmesan cheese

1. Make Italian Tomato Sauce (recipe follows).

2. Meanwhile, make Ravioli Filling: In medium bowl, combine all filling ingredients. Beat with wooden spoon until well blended. Set aside.

3. Make Noodle Dough: Measure flour into medium bowl; make well in center. Add eggs and water. Beat with wooden spoon until dough forms ball and leaves side of bowl.

4. Turn out onto lightly floured pastry cloth or floured surface. Knead until smooth and elastic—6 to 8 minutes. Cover with a large bowl; let the dough rest for 30 minutes. Divide dough in quarters.

5. On lightly floured surface, roll one quarter (keep remaining dough covered with plastic wrap) into 17-by-13-inch rectangle. Cover with plastic wrap.

6. Roll a second quarter into a 17-by-13-inch rectangle. Drop half of filling by teaspoonfuls in 24 evenly spaced mounds on this dough rectangle (six lengthwise and four across). Set remaining filling aside. Place first dough rectangle on top; trim edges with pastry wheel. Run pastry wheel between mounds of filling, to make 24 ravioli; press edges with tines of fork, to seal.

7. Place on flour-covered sheet of waxed paper to dry—about 15 minutes. Turn once. Repeat with remaining dough and filling.

TO FREEZE

8. Freeze on waxed paper on cookie sheets. When frozen, remove from cookie sheets; wrap in foil; label, date, freeze.

TO COOK

9. In large kettle, bring 6 quarts water to boiling. Add salt, oil and ravioli. Boil gently, covered, 20 to 25 minutes. Turn half of ravioli into colander at a time; drain very well.

10. Turn ravioli into large heated serving dish. Top with some Italian Tomato Sauce; pass remaining sauce. Sprinkle ravioli with Parmesan. *Makes 8 to 10 servings.*

Note: Store ravioli in freezer at 0°F up to six months.

ITALIAN TOMATO SAUCE

1 can (2 lb, 3 oz) Italian tomatoes
¼ cup salad oil
1 cup finely chopped onion
1 garlic clove, crushed
1 can (6 oz) tomato paste
1½ cups cold water
2 sprigs parsley
1 tablespoon salt
2 teaspoons sugar
1 teaspoon dried oregano leaves
½ teaspoon dried basil leaves
¼ teaspoon pepper

1. Purée undrained Italian tomatoes in electric blender.

2. In hot oil in large saucepan, sauté onion and garlic until golden-brown—about 5 minutes.

3. Add puréed tomato, tomato paste, water, the parsley sprigs, salt, sugar, oregano, basil and pepper; mix well.

4. Bring to boiling; reduce heat; simmer, covered and stirring occasionally, 1 hour.

5. Cool slightly at room temperature; refrigerate until completely cooled.

TO FREEZE

6. Pour sauce into sturdy leakproof containers, leaving ½- to ¾-inch head space. Label and freeze.

TO USE

7. Reheat sauce over very low heat until thawed, stirring occasionally. Bring to boiling; remove from heat. *Makes 6 cups, 8 servings.*

MEAT LOAF EN CROUTE

2 eggs
½ cup packaged dry bread crumbs
½ cup milk
½ cup finely chopped onion
½ cup finely chopped green pepper
1½ teaspoons salt
½ teaspoon dried marjoram leaves
¼ teaspoon pepper
1½ lb lean ground pork (see Note)
½ lb ground chuck

1 pkg (11 oz) piecrust mix
1 egg yolk mixed with 2 teaspoons water

1. In large bowl, combine eggs, bread crumbs, milk, onion, green pepper, salt, marjoram and pepper; beat with fork until well combined. Let stand 5 minutes.

2. Add ground pork and ground chuck; mix well with fork.

3. Line a 9-by-5-by-2¾-inch loaf pan with foil, leaving a 6-inch overlap of foil. Pack in meat-loaf mixture. Freeze 1 hour. Fold over foil to form package; remove from loaf pan. Seal, label and return foil

continued on page 160

continued from page 159

package to freezer.

4. For Meat Loaf en Croûte: Do not freeze meat loaf, but refrigerate in loaf pan 1 hour, to chill well.

5. Prepare piecrust mix according to package directions. Form into a ball. On a lightly floured pastry cloth or floured board, roll pastry to an 18-by-14-inch rectangle. Cut a 4-inch strip from one end; reserve for decoration.

6. Turn out chilled meat loaf in center of pastry. Bring all four sides of pastry over meat loaf; moisten edges lightly with water; press edges to seal.

7. Place loaf, sealed-pastry side down, on foil 12 inches wide, 16 inches long.

8. Cut strips from remaining piece of pastry, about ⅓ inch wide for stem. Cut flower patterns, ¾ inch wide, with cutters; with sharp knife, cut out leaf patterns; moisten slightly with water. Press decoratively into pastry top.

TO FREEZE

9. Wrap in foil; seal, label and freeze.

TO BAKE

10. Preheat oven to 350F. Remove meat loaf from freezer; unwrap. With small cutter or knife, cut two or three holes, about ½ inch in diameter, for steam vents. Place on rack in shallow roasting pan. Brush pastry with egg yolk-water mixture.

11. Bake 2 hours (brush again with egg-yolk mixture), or until golden-brown and meat loaf is thoroughly cooked. Remove to warm serving platter. Let stand 15 minutes before slicing. Nice served with Mushroom Sauce (recipe follows). Frozen meat loaf may be stored in freezer several months at 0°F. *Makes 8 servings.*

Note: Fresh pork can be ground in a food processor, or ask butcher to grind.

MUSHROOM SAUCE

3 tablespoons butter or margarine
1 cup sliced fresh mushrooms
3 tablespoons all-purpose flour
Dash ground red pepper
1 can (10¾ oz) condensed chicken broth, undiluted
¼ cup half-and-half

1. Make Mushroom Sauce: Melt butter in medium saucepan. Add mushrooms; sauté, stirring occasionally, about 5 minutes. Remove from heat; stir in flour and pepper until smooth.

2. Add chicken broth and half-and-half. Cook over medium heat, stirring constantly, until boiling. Reduce heat; simmer 3 minutes. Serve with Meat Loaf en Croûte. *Makes 8 servings.* ◆

continued from page 147

Cover with towel. Let rise in warm place (85F), free from drafts, until double in bulk—30 to 40 minutes.

7. Turn dough out onto lightly floured pastry cloth or board. Divide in half. Let rest, covered, 10 minutes. Roll out one half into a 16-by-8-inch rectangle; roll up, starting from short end. Press ends even; pinch to seal; tuck under loaf.

8. Place, seam side down, in greased 9-by-5-by-3-inch loaf pan. Repeat with other half of dough. With scissors, cut five V-shaped notches on top of each loaf.

9. Cover with towel; let loaves rise in warm place, free from drafts, until sides come up to top of pans and tops are rounded—30 minutes. Preheat oven to 375F.

10. Bake 35 to 40 minutes, or until golden-brown. If crust seems too brown after 25 minutes of baking, cover with foil.

11. Turn out of pans onto wire rack; brush tops with beaten egg-white mixture; sprinkle with ¼ cup cereal (omitting raisins). Serve warm, or cool completely.

TO FREEZE

12. When loaves are thoroughly cool, wrap them separately in heavy-duty foil or plastic wrap; label, seal and place in freezer.

TO THAW AND SERVE

13. Remove 1 loaf from freezer; let stand, wrapped, at room temperature, 1 to 1½ hours. Meanwhile, if serving hot, preheat oven to 375F. Heat loaf, wrapped in foil, 20 to 25 minutes. Unwrap and slice to serve. *Makes 2 loaves (16 slices each).*

CRANBERRY-FILLED LATTICE COFFEECAKE
(pictured)

CRANBERRY-ORANGE FILLING
½ cup granulated sugar
2 tablespoons cornstarch
⅔ cup orange juice
2 cups cranberries, chopped
½ cup chopped walnuts

1 pkg (14 oz or 1 lb) white-yeast-bread mix
1 egg white, mixed with 1 teaspoon water
Coarse sugar or sugar cubes, crushed (optional)

1. Make Cranberry-Orange Filling: In medium saucepan, combine sugar and cornstarch; mix well. Stir in the orange juice.

2. Add cranberries; cook over medium heat, stirring constantly, until

thickened—about 5 minutes. Remove from heat. Add nuts. Set aside to cool.

3. Prepare bread mix as package label directs.

4. Turn dough out onto a lightly floured pastry cloth or surface. With greased or floured hands, shape dough into a ball; knead for 5 minutes.

5. Cover dough with mixing bowl; let rest for 5 minutes. Grease a cookie sheet. Preheat oven to 350F.

6. On lightly floured surface, roll dough into a 12-by-8-inch rectangle. Transfer to prepared cookie sheet. Spread filling over the center third of the dough. On each long side, cut six 1-inch-wide strips, 2 inches deep. Starting at one end, bring strips at an angle over filling, alternating from one side to the other.

7. Cover coffeecake with towel; place cookie sheet over a large roasting pan half-filled with hot tap water; let rise 15 minutes.

8. Uncover dough and brush with the egg-white mixture. Sprinkle with the coarse sugar.

9. Bake 30 to 35 minutes, or until golden-brown. Remove from cookie sheet to wire rack; cool completely.

TO FREEZE

10. Wrap coffeecake in heavy-duty foil or plastic wrap; label, seal and place in freezer.

TO THAW AND SERVE

11. Remove from freezer; let stand, wrapped, at room temperature, 1½ to 2 hours. Unwrap and slice to serve. *Makes 1 loaf (20 slices).*

HONEY-PRUNE BREAD
(pictured)

1½ cups (9 oz) chopped pitted prunes
⅓ cup apple juice
2¼ cups all-purpose flour
2 teaspoons baking powder
1 teaspoon baking soda
1 teaspoon salt
⅓ cup wheat germ
2 eggs
½ cup honey
½ cup salad oil
¼ cup plain yogurt
3 pitted prunes, halved

1. Preheat oven to 300F. Lightly grease three 5¾-by-3¼-by-2¼-inch loaf pans.

2. In small bowl, combine chopped prunes and apple juice; mix well.

3. Onto sheet of waxed paper, sift flour, baking powder, soda and salt; stir in wheat germ.

4. In large bowl, with wooden spoon, beat together eggs, honey, oil and yogurt. Stir in prune mixture; mix well.

5. Add flour mixture; beat just until combined. Turn into prepared pans, dividing evenly. Place 2 prune halves, cut side down, on top of each loaf.

6. Bake 50 to 60 minutes, or until cake tester inserted in center comes out clean.

7. Cool in pans 10 minutes. Remove from pans; cool completely on wire rack.

TO FREEZE

8. Wrap loaves separately in heavy-duty foil or plastic wrap; label, seal and place in freezer.

TO THAW AND SERVE

9. Remove 1 or more loaves from freezer; let stand, wrapped, at room temperature, 1 to 1½ hours. Unwrap; cut in thin slices to serve. *Makes 3 small loaves (10 slices each).*

CALIFORNIA BRAIDED RING
(pictured)

7 to 7½ cups all-purpose flour
2 pkg fast-rising yeast
2 teaspoons salt
1 cup milk
½ cup water
¼ cup (½ stick) butter or margarine
⅓ cup honey
3 eggs
1½ cups coarsely shredded carrots

1 cup golden raisins
1½ tablespoons grated orange peel
1 egg, beaten with 1 teaspoon water

1. In large bowl of electric mixer, combine 2½ cups of the flour, the yeast and salt; mix well.

2. In small saucepan, heat milk, ½ cup water and the butter over low heat just until warm (120-130F); butter does not need to melt.

3. Add milk mixture, honey and 3 eggs to flour mixture; beat at low speed just until ingredients are moistened. Beat at medium speed 3 minutes, occasionally scraping side of bowl with rubber spatula.

4. With spoon, stir in carrots, raisins, orange peel and enough of the remaining flour (4½ to 5 cups) to make a soft dough.

5. Turn out onto lightly floured pastry cloth or board. Knead until smooth and elastic—about 5 minutes.

6. Place in greased bowl, turning dough over to bring up greased side. Cover with towel. Let rise in warm place (85F), free from drafts, until double in bulk—30 to 40 minutes.

7. Turn dough out onto lightly floured pastry cloth or board. Divide in half; divide each half into 3 equal parts. Using palms of hands, roll each part into an 18-inch-long rope. Braid together 3 ropes on a greased cookie sheet; pinch ends together to make a 9-inch ring, stretching dough if necessary. Repeat with remaining ropes. Cover with towel.

8. Let rise in warm place, free from drafts, until double in bulk—about 30 minutes. Preheat oven to 375F.

9. Brush surface of each ring with beaten egg mixture.

10. Bake 35 to 40 minutes, or until golden-brown. If crust seems too brown after 25 minutes of baking, cover with foil. Remove to wire rack; cool completely.

TO FREEZE

11. Wrap rings separately in heavy-duty foil or plastic wrap; label, seal and place in freezer.

TO THAW AND SERVE

12. Remove 1 ring from freezer; let stand, wrapped, at room temperature, 1½ to 2 hours. Unwrap; slice in wedges to serve. *Makes 2 rings (18 slices each).* ◆

---

continued from page 155
late into one half, mixing well.

6. Spoon plain and chocolate batters, alternating, into prepared pan. With spatula or knife, cut through batter with knife in opposite directions, to give marbled effect.

7. Bake 25 to 30 minutes, or until lightly browned. Remove to rack; cool completely.

8. With sharp knife, cut lengthwise into three equal pieces; cut crosswise into ten rows. *Makes 30 bars.*

SUGAR-COOKIE ICE-CREAM SANDWICHES

½ gallon (brick) strawberry or pistachio ice cream
20 heart, diamond or serrated-edge Sugar Cookies, recipe follows

1. Remove ice cream from freezer; discard carton. With long sharp knife, cut ice cream lengthwise into five even pieces.

2. With 3¼-inch heart-shape cookie cutter (or diamond or round), cut two ice-cream hearts from each piece.

3. Place each ice-cream heart between two Sugar-Cookie hearts.

TO FREEZE

4. Freeze until firm—about 2 hours.

5. Store in individual plastic bags, or wrap in foil. Label and return to freezer. *Makes 10 sandwiches.*

Note: Pack remaining ice cream into a plastic container; freeze for later use.

SUGAR COOKIES

2 cups sifted all-purpose flour
½ teaspoon baking powder
¼ teaspoon salt
½ teaspoon ground nutmeg
½ cup (1 stick) butter or margarine, softened
⅔ cup sugar
1 egg
1 teaspoon vanilla extract
1 egg white, slightly beaten (optional)
Multicolor nonpareils or mini semisweet chocolate pieces or chopped nuts (optional)

1. On sheet of waxed paper, sift flour with baking powder, salt and nutmeg; set aside.

2. In large bowl of electric mixer, at high speed, beat butter, sugar, egg and vanilla until smooth and fluffy.

3. With wooden spoon, stir in half of flour mixture, mixing with hands, if necessary.

4. Refrigerate dough, covered, several hours or overnight.

5. Preheat oven to 375F. Lightly grease cookies sheets. Divide dough into two parts; refrigerate until ready to roll out.

6. On lightly floured pastry cloth or board, roll out dough, one part at a time, ⅛-inch thick.

7. With floured 3¼-inch heart-shape cookie cutter—or diamond-shape (3 inches wide, 4 inches long)—cut out cookies. Place 2 inches apart on prepared cookie sheets. For round serrated-edge cookies, use a 3-inch scalloped cookie cutter. If desired, brush half of the cookies with egg white; sprinkle with nonpareils; or brush edge only, and sprinkle with mini chocolate pieces or chopped nuts.

8. Bake 8 minutes, or just until set and lightly browned around edges. Remove to wire rack; cool completely. *Makes 20 cookies.* ◆

HOME-BAKED CAKES
A SLICE OF THE PAST

Some things are worth the effort—and home-baked cake is one of them. These cakes have the old-time richness that comes from the best natural ingredients—apples, carrots, bananas, buttermilk and eggs, nuts and spices. They're moist and satisfying and perfect to serve with coffee after a movie or a tough game of cards. Best of all, you can freeze them—one advantage our great-grandmothers did not have. Clockwise from right: Carrot Whipped-Cream Cake; Banana-Date Cake; Walnut-Spice Cake with Caramel Frosting; and Fresh-Apple Cake with Cream-Cheese Frosting and chopped walnuts. Recipes for these and more, page 164.

♥   ♥

GEORGE RATKAI

continued from page 163

FRESH-APPLE CAKE
(pictured)

3 cups sifted all-purpose flour
1½ teaspoons baking soda
½ teaspoon salt
3 cups finely chopped, pared tart apple
½ cup chopped walnuts or pecans
1 teaspoon grated lemon peel
2 cups sugar
1½ cups salad oil
2 eggs
Cream-Cheese Frosting, recipe follows
1 cup chopped walnuts

1. Preheat oven to 350F. Grease well and flour three 9-by-1½-inch round layer-cake pans. Sift flour with baking soda and salt. In small bowl, combine chopped apple, ½ cup chopped nuts and the lemon peel.

2. In large mixing bowl, combine sugar, salad oil and eggs; beat well with wooden spoon. Add sifted dry ingredients, mixing until smooth.

3. Add apple mixture; stir until well combined. Spread evenly into prepared pans. Bake 30 to 40 minutes, or until surface springs back when pressed lightly with fingertip.

4. Cool in pans 10 minutes. Remove from pans; cool thoroughly on wire rack.

TO FREEZE

5. Wrap layers separately in foil or plastic wrap; seal, label and place in freezer. Or, if desired, you may fill and frost this cake as directed. Freeze completed cake, unwrapped, about 1 hour until frosting is hard. Remove from freezer; wrap cake in foil or plastic wrap. Seal, label and store in freezer.

TO THAW

6. Remove layers from freezer. Let stand, wrapped, at room temperature, 1 hour. Or remove frosted cake from freezer. Let stand, wrapped, at room temperature, 2 hours.

TO FROST

7. Unwrap cake layers, if frozen separately. Make Cream-Cheese Frosting.

8. Fill and frost cake as pictured. Press remaining 1 cup nuts on side. Refrigerate until serving time. *Makes 10 to 12 servings.*

CREAM-CHEESE FROSTING

1 pkg (8 oz) cream cheese, softened
1 tablespoon butter or margarine, softened
1 teaspoon vanilla extract
2½ to 3 cups confectioners' sugar

1. In medium bowl, with portable electric mixer at medium speed, beat cream cheese, butter and vanilla until light and creamy.

2. Add confectioners' sugar; beat until of spreading consistency. *Makes 2½ cups.*

CARROT WHIPPED-CREAM CAKE
(pictured)

3 cups sifted all-purpose flour
2 teaspoons baking powder
1 teaspoon baking soda
2 teaspoons ground cinnamon
1 teaspoon salt
2 cups granulated sugar
1½ cups salad oil
4 eggs
3 cups grated carrot (1 lb)

WHIPPED-CREAM FROSTING
2 cups heavy cream, chilled
½ cup confectioners' sugar
1 teaspoon vanilla extract

Pecan or walnut halves

[handwritten: 1 TBS ORANGE { ZEST LEMON }]

1. Preheat oven to 350F. Sift flour with baking powder, soda, cinnamon and salt. Grease well and flour three 9-by-1½-inch round layer-cake pans.

2. In large mixing bowl, with electric mixer at medium speed, beat granulated sugar, salad oil and eggs until well blended—about 2 minutes. Add carrot; mix well.

3. At low speed, gradually add flour mixture, beating just until well combined. Batter will be thin. Pour batter into prepared pans, dividing evenly. Bake 30 to 35 minutes, or until surface springs back when gently pressed with fingertip.

4. Cool in pans 10 minutes. Carefully loosen sides with spatula; remove from pan. Cool completely on racks.

TO FREEZE

5. Wrap layers separately in foil or plastic wrap; seal, label and store in freezer.

TO THAW

6. Remove layers from freezer; let stand, wrapped, at room temperature, 1 hour.

TO FROST

7. Make Whipped-Cream Frosting: In medium bowl, whip cream with confectioners' sugar and vanilla until stiff. Refrigerate if not using at once.

8. Put layers together with frosting, ¾ cup for each layer. Frost side and top. (If desired, decorate edge and bottom as pictured, using a pastry bag with number-6 star tip.) Arrange pecan halves on top. Refrigerate 1 hour before serving. *Makes 10 to 12 servings.*

BANANA-DATE CAKE
(pictured)

2¾ cups sifted all-purpose flour
2 teaspoons baking powder
½ teaspoon baking soda
¼ teaspoon salt
½ cup (1 stick) butter or margarine, softened
1½ cups granulated sugar
2 eggs
2 teaspoons vanilla extract
1 cup mashed ripe banana
½ cup buttermilk
½ cup finely chopped dates
¼ cup chopped walnuts or pecans
Confectioners' sugar

1. Preheat oven to 350F. Grease well a 9-by-5-by-3-inch loaf pan. Sift flour with baking powder, soda and salt.

2. In large bowl, with electric mixer at high speed, beat butter, granulated sugar, eggs and vanilla, occasionally scraping side of bowl with rubber spatula, until light and fluffy—about 3 minutes.

3. In small bowl, combine banana and buttermilk. At low speed, beat in flour mixture (in fourths) alternately with banana mixture (in thirds), beginning and ending with flour mixture; beat until smooth—about 1 minute.

4. Stir in dates and walnuts. Pour batter into prepared pan; bake 1 hour and 10 to 15 minutes, or until cake tester inserted in center comes out clean. Cool in pan, on wire rack, 15 minutes. Then turn out on rack; cool completely.

TO FREEZE

5. Wrap loaf in foil or plastic wrap; seal, label and freeze.

TO THAW AND SERVE

6. Remove cake from freezer. Let stand, wrapped, at room temperature, 1 to 1½ hours.

7. Remove wrapping. Dust top with confectioners' sugar. Slice to serve. *Makes 1 loaf, 10 servings.*

WALNUT-SPICE CAKE
(pictured)

1 cup seedless raisins
1 cup walnuts
1 teaspoon baking soda
1 cup boiling water
1½ cups sifted all-purpose flour
1 teaspoon ground cinnamon
¼ teaspoon salt
½ cup (1 stick) butter or margarine
1 cup sugar
1 whole egg
2 egg yolks
1 teaspoon lemon juice
1 teaspoon vanilla extract
Caramel Frosting, recipe follows

1. Preheat oven to 325F. Grease lightly with butter two 8-by-1½-inch layer-cake pans.

2. Coarsely chop raisins and walnuts; place in medium bowl. Add baking soda; then stir in boiling water. Set aside to cool.

3. Sift flour with cinnamon and salt.

4. In large bowl, with electric mixer at medium speed, beat butter until creamy. Add sugar, a little at a time, beating until light and fluffy. Stop mixer once or twice, and scrape down side of bowl with rubber spatula.

5. Add whole egg and the egg yolks, one at a time, beating after each addition and scraping down side of bowl with spatula. Beat until light and fluffy. Add lemon juice and vanilla.

6. With wooden spoon, beat in flour mixture, in fourths, alternately with raisin mixture, in thirds, beginning and ending with flour mixture. Pour batter into prepared pans.

7. Bake 45 minutes, or until top springs back when lightly pressed with fingertip and cake has pulled away from pan at edge.

8. Cool in pans on wire rack 5 minutes. With small spatula, loosen around edge. Turn out on wire rack; turn top up; let cool completely.

TO FREEZE

9. Wrap layers separately in foil or plastic wrap; seal, label and place in freezer. Or, if desired, you may fill and frost this cake as directed. Freeze completed cake, unwrapped, about 1 hour, until frosting is hard. Remove from freezer; wrap cake in foil or plastic wrap. Seal, label and store in freezer.

TO THAW

10. Remove layers from freezer. Let stand, wrapped, at room temperature, 1 hour. Or remove frosted cake from freezer. Let stand, wrapped, at room temperature, 2 hours.

TO FROST

11. Make Caramel Frosting. Unwrap cake layers, if frozen separately.

12. Put layers together with some of Caramel Frosting. Frost top and side with remaining frosting, making swirls with tip of spatula, as pictured. *Makes 10 to 12 servings.*

CARAMEL FROSTING

¾ cup (1½ sticks) butter or margarine
1½ cups light-brown sugar, packed
½ cup light cream or evaporated milk, undiluted
3 cups confectioners' sugar
1½ teaspoons vanilla extract

1. Melt butter in small saucepan over low heat. Remove from heat.

2. Add brown sugar, stirring until smooth. Over low heat, bring to boiling, stirring; boil, stirring, 1 minute. Remove from heat.

3. Add cream; over low heat, return just to boiling. Remove from heat; let cool to 110F on candy thermometer, or until bottom of pan feels lukewarm.

4. With portable electric mixer at medium speed, or with wooden spoon, beat in confectioners' sugar until frosting is thick. (If it seems too thin to spread, gradually beat in a little more confectioners' sugar.) Add vanilla.

5. Set in bowl of ice water; beat until frosting is thick enough to spread. *Makes enough to fill and frost top and side of an 8-inch or 9-inch two-layer cake.*

MARBLE LOAF CAKE

1½ squares (1-oz size) unsweetened chocolate
2½ cups sifted cake flour
¾ teaspoon salt
3 teaspoons baking powder
½ cup (1 stick) butter or margarine, softened
1½ cups sugar
3 eggs
¾ teaspoon vanilla extract
¾ cup milk

1. Melt chocolate over hot, not boiling, water. Let cool.

2. Preheat oven to 350F. Grease and flour a 9-by-5-by-3-inch loaf pan.

3. Sift flour with salt and baking powder.

4. With electric mixer at medium speed, beat butter and sugar until light.

5. Add eggs and vanilla, beating until very light and fluffy.

6. At low speed, beat in flour mixture (in fourths), alternately with milk (in thirds), beginning and ending with flour mixture.

7. In medium bowl, combine about one-third of the batter with chocolate.

8. Spoon plain and chocolate batters

alternately into prepared pan. With knife, cut through batter, forming a Z.

9. Bake 65 minutes, or until cake tester comes out clean.

10. Cool in pan 15 minutes. Remove from pan; cool thoroughly on wire rack.

TO FREEZE

11. Wrap loaf in foil or plastic wrap; seal, label and place in freezer.

TO THAW AND SERVE

12. Remove cake from freezer. Let stand, wrapped, at room temperature, 1 to 1½ hours. To serve, cut in thin slices. *Makes 1 loaf, 10 servings.*

COCONUT CHIFFON CAKE

1 cup egg whites (6 or 7)
2 cups sifted cake flour
1⅓ cups sugar
2½ teaspoons baking powder
1 teaspoon salt
½ cup salad oil
6 egg yolks
⅔ cup water
2 tablespoons coconut extract
1 teaspoon vanilla extract
½ teaspoon cream of tartar
1 can (3½ oz) flaked coconut
Confectioners' sugar (optional)

1. Let egg whites warm to room temperature in large bowl of electric mixer—about 1 hour. Meanwhile, preheat oven to 325F.

2. Sift flour with sugar, baking powder and salt into another large bowl. Make well in center.

3. Add, in order, oil, egg yolks, water and the coconut and vanilla extracts; beat with spoon until smooth.

4. Beat egg whites at high speed with cream of tartar until stiff peaks form when beaters are slowly raised.

5. With whisk or rubber spatula, using an under-and-over motion, gently fold egg-yolk mixture and flaked coconut into egg whites just to blend.

6. Pour into an ungreased 10-inch tube pan; bake 50 to 60 minutes, or until cake springs back when gently pressed with fingertip.

7. Invert cake over neck of bottle; let cool completely—about 1½ hours.

8. Carefully loosen cake from pan; remove.

TO FREEZE

9. Wrap in foil or plastic wrap; seal, label and place in freezer.

TO THAW AND SERVE

10. Remove cake from freezer. Let stand, wrapped, at room temperature, 1 to 1½ hours. Serve plain or sprinkle lightly with confectioners' sugar. Slice to serve. *Makes 8 to 10 servings.* ◆

FIVE

NO-FUSS COOKING

◆

What first comes to mind when you hear "No-Fuss Cooking"? Opening a few cans of something, heating up a frozen pizza, perhaps gathering the family around take-out food? That's fine…but we'd like to expand your definition of no-fuss cooking with the exciting recipes and timesaving ideas on the pages that follow. No-fuss cooking can mean marvelous no-cook menus that build on prepared convenience foods from the deli or bakery. Or no-fuss cooking can mean that when a few simple ingredients are combined and attractively presented, you have a simply scrumptious meal fit for any occasion. Easy cleanup is another important aspect of no-fuss cooking…and our array of sensational "disposable" meals (baked and served in throwaway pans, foil or cooking bags) puts an end to messy pots and pans! No-fuss cooking also means convenient, quick-to-fix, go-anywhere meals that fit perfectly into travel and vacation plans. And when it comes to desserts, no-fuss cooking can be described as absolutely delectable when all it takes is a few short-cut ingredients and less than 30 minutes to create any of our elegant sweet treats.

Tex-Mex Poolside Supper

Good-Looking, No-Cooking Meals

The best thing about these attractive, appetizing meals is that you don't have to cook them. The deli, bakery or grocery store does the hard (and hot) part. All you do is mix and chill, arrange and eat. For menus and "recipes," see page 172.

Country French Picnic, opposite page

MICHAEL WEISS

Summertime Patio Party

Scandinavian Smorgasbord

No-Fuss Children's Party

Italian Alfresco

continued from page 169

COUNTRY FRENCH PICNIC
(Planned for 8)

TUNA NICOISE PATE EN CROUTE*
RADISHES, GREEN ONIONS AND OLIVES
SAUSAGE-VEGETABLE SALAD*
CAMEMBERT OR WEDGE OF BRIE
GRANNY SMITH APPLES AND GRAPES
WINE AND CHAMPAGNE

*Recipes given for starred dishes.

TUNA NICOISE PATE EN CROUTE
(pictured)

2 cans (6½-oz size) solid white tuna, drained
¼ cup bottled oil-and-vinegar dressing
½ can (2-oz size) flat anchovies, drained
1 small red onion, chopped
¼ cup pitted Niçoise or other black olives, chopped
1 loaf French baguette or bread (20 inches long and 3 inches wide)
1 bunch small radishes with leaves
1 bunch small green onions, trimmed

1. In electric blender or food processor, combine tuna, ¼ cup dressing and the anchovies; blend at high speed, or process until smooth, occasionally scraping down side of container. Stir in the chopped onion and olives.
2. Cut off ends of French bread; cut bread crosswise into 4 pieces. With small, sharp knife, remove inside of each bread piece, leaving a ½-inch thick crust. (Save inside bread pieces and bread ends for bread crumbs.) Spoon ½ cup tuna niçoise pâté into each hollowed-out piece. Wrap each in plastic wrap; refrigerate. To serve: Cut each piece into ½-inch slices; arrange on platter. Garnish platter with radishes and green onions. *Makes 8 servings.*

SAUSAGE-VEGETABLE SALAD
(pictured)

¾ cup olive or salad oil
¼ cup red-wine vinegar
2 tablespoons chopped parsley
1 small garlic clove, minced
1 teaspoon sugar
½ teaspoon salt
¼ teaspoon cracked black pepper
1 lb fully-cooked garlic sausage or kielbasa
1 pkg (10 oz) frozen small whole green beans

Lettuce leaves
1 can (1 lb) whole new potatoes, drained
1 pint cherry tomatoes, stems removed

1. In large bowl, with wire whisk, combine oil, vinegar, parsley, garlic, sugar, salt and pepper until well mixed. Slice sausage into ¼-inch diagonal slices.
2. Place frozen green beans in strainer; run under cold water until they separate; pat dry on paper towels. Line a serving platter with lettuce, and mound sausage slices in center.
3. Toss green beans, potatoes and tomatoes separately in dressing; with slotted spoon, remove each to platter. Drizzle vegetables and sausage with remaining dressing. *Makes 8 servings.*

SUMMERTIME PATIO PARTY
(Planned for 8)

COLD TOMATO BISQUE*
FESTIVE HAM*
COLESLAW-VEGETABLE SALAD*
BAKERY CORN MUFFINS
BERRY PIE*
ICED TEA OR LEMONADE

*Recipes given for starred dishes.

COLD TOMATO BISQUE
(pictured)

2½ cups cold milk
1 can (10¾ oz) condensed tomato soup, undiluted
1 can (10¾ oz) condensed cream-of-potato soup, undiluted
1 container (8 oz) sour cream
1 tablespoon chopped chives
Crushed ice (optional)

In electric blender, combine 1½ cups milk, the soups and sour cream; blend at medium speed until smooth. Pour soup into a serving bowl; stir in remaining milk. Cover with plastic wrap; refrigerate 2 hours, or until well chilled. Before serving, garnish with chopped chives. Place soup bowl over a large bowl of crushed ice, if desired. *Makes 8 (¾ cup) servings.*

FESTIVE HAM
(pictured)

½ cup mayonnaise
1 tablespoon prepared yellow mustard
½ teaspoon ground turmeric
Dash ground white pepper
3-lb canned or plastic-wrapped ham
16 capers
Watercress (optional)

1. In small bowl, combine mayonnaise, mustard, turmeric and pepper; mix well. Cover, and refrigerate 2 hours, or until well chilled.
2. Spoon mayonnaise mixture into a pastry bag fitted with number-30 open-star tip. Place ham on platter. With sharp knife, score 1½-inch diamonds into top of ham. Using the scoring as a guide, decoratively pipe mayonnaise mixture onto ham. Pipe scallops around edge of ham. At points where lines meet, place a caper. Garnish platter with watercress, if desired. *Makes 12 servings.*

COLESLAW-VEGETABLE SALAD
(pictured)

3 large carrots, pared and coarsely shredded
3 lb delicatessen coleslaw
2 large (8-oz size) red peppers, halved, seeded and cut into ½-inch squares
½ head romaine, shredded
2 diagonal cucumber slices, halved (optional)

Set aside ½ cup shredded carrots for garnish. In a 2½-quart, straight-sided glass bowl, layer one-fourth of the coleslaw, the red pepper, one-fourth of the coleslaw, the lettuce, another one-fourth of the coleslaw, remaining carrots and remaining coleslaw. Top with reserved shredded carrots and the cucumber slices. Cover with plastic wrap; refrigerate 3 hours, or until well chilled. *Makes about 12 servings.*

BERRY PIE
(pictured)

1 env unflavored gelatine
¼ cup cold water
¼ cup very hot tap water
1 pkg (8 oz) cream cheese, softened
¼ cup sugar
1 container (8 oz) sour cream (see Note)
1 (9-inch) graham cracker pie shell
3 tablespoons currant jelly
½ teaspoon hot tap water
½ cup fresh raspberries
½ pint fresh blueberries or blackberries
Whipped cream or dessert topping in aerosol can

1. In small bowl, sprinkle gelatine over ¼ cup cold water; let stand 5 minutes to soften. Add ¼ cup hot water, stirring until gelatine is dissolved.
2. In small bowl, with electric mixer at medium speed, beat cream cheese and sugar until fluffy. Reduce speed to low; gradually beat in gelatine mixture and sour cream until well blended. Pour into pie shell. Refrigerate at least 45 minutes, or several hours.

3. Meanwhile, in small bowl, combine 3 tablespoons currant jelly and the hot water; mix until jelly is smooth. Just before serving, mound raspberries in center of pie; arrange blueberries around edge; brush or drizzle berries with currant jelly. Garnish edge with whipped topping. *Makes 8 servings.*

Note: One 8-ounce container plain low-fat yogurt may be substituted for sour cream, if desired.

TEX-MEX POOLSIDE SUPPER

(Planned for 6)

**CRAB "SEVICHE" WITH AVOCADO★
ROAST-BEEF TACOS★
MEXICAN MOCHA MOUSSE★
WHITE-GRAPE-JUICE SANGRIA**

★Recipes given for starred dishes.

CRAB "SEVICHE" WITH AVOCADO

(pictured)

**¼ cup lime juice (about 2 small limes)
2 tablespoons olive or salad oil
2 green onions, trimmed and chopped
1 can (4 oz) whole green chilies, drained
1 lb imitation crabmeat sticks, cut into
    1-inch lengths
10 pitted ripe olives, sliced
Dash pepper
1 small (8 oz) ripe avocado**

1. In large bowl, with wire whisk, combine lime juice, oil and green onions. Cut green chilies crosswise in half; remove and discard any seeds; cut chilies lengthwise into ¼-inch strips. Add chilies, crabmeat, olives and pepper to lime-juice mixture; toss to mix well. Cover with plastic wrap, and refrigerate at least 2 hours or overnight, tossing occasionally.

2. Just before serving, cut avocado lengthwise in half; remove pit; peel. Cut each half into 6 slices. For each serving, top 2 slices with ⅓ cup seviche. *Makes 6 appetizer servings.*

ROAST-BEEF TACOS

(pictured)

**4 slices (¼ inch thick) delicatessen roast
    beef (about 1 lb)
1 jar (12 oz) medium-hot picante salsa or
    taco sauce
½ teaspoon dried oregano leaves
1 pkg (4½ oz) taco shells (12 to pkg)
¼ head green leaf lettuce, cut into thin
    strips**

**1 pkg (4 oz) shredded Cheddar cheese
    (1 cup)
1 medium tomato, halved, seeded and
    chopped**

Cut roast-beef slices into 2-by-¼-inch strips. In small bowl, toss beef with ½ cup salsa and the oregano. Divide roast-beef strips evenly among taco shells. Top each with some lettuce, cheese, and tomato. Spoon 1 teaspoon salsa over each. Serve with additional remaining salsa. *Makes 6 servings.*

MEXICAN MOCHA MOUSSE

**2 cups milk
2 teaspoons instant coffee
2 pkg (3½- or 4⅛-oz size) instant chocolate
    pudding and pie filling mix
½ cup coffee-flavored liqueur
2 cups frozen whipped topping with real
    cream, thawed
Whipped topping (optional)
Fresh-strawberry slices (optional)**

In 2-cup measuring cup, measure milk; stir in instant coffee until dissolved. In large bowl, combine pudding mix, milk mixture and liqueur. With wire whisk, beat mixture until slightly thickened; fold in 2 cups whipped topping. Spoon into stemmed glasses. Garnish with additional whipped topping and strawberry slices, if desired. *Makes 8 servings.*

SCANDINAVIAN SMORGASBORD

(Planned for 8)

**MARINATED SARDINES
WITH CAVIAR-CUCUMBER
CANAPES★
SMOKED-SALMON SANDWICHES★
BEET, HERRING AND POTATO
SALAD★
ASSORTED FLATBREADS
PEAR WITH DANISH BLUE CHEESE
ICE-COLD BEER OR AQUAVIT**

★Recipes given for starred dishes.

MARINATED SARDINES WITH CAVIAR-CUCUMBER CANAPES

(pictured)

**3 tablespoons lemon juice
3 tablespoons olive or salad oil
1 teaspoon sugar
2 teaspoons prepared yellow mustard
2 teaspoons chopped parsley
Dash hot red-pepper sauce**

**3 cans (3¾-oz size) Norway sardines
    packed in water, drained
Caviar-Cucumber Canapés, recipe follows
Lettuce leaves
Lemon wedges**

1. In small bowl, with wire whisk, combine lemon juice, oil, sugar, mustard, parsley and red-pepper sauce until well mixed. Place drained sardines in a 9-by-9-by-2-inch glass dish; drizzle lemon mixture over sardines. Cover with plastic wrap; refrigerate 3 hours or overnight.

2. Just before serving, prepare Caviar-Cucumber Canapés. Line serving platter with lettuce. Using small pancake turner, carefully transfer or lift marinated sardines to center of platter, keeping them intact. Arrange lemon wedges and some of the canapés around sardines. *Makes 8 servings.*

CAVIAR-CUCUMBER CANAPES

**1 small cucumber, unpared
⅓ cup sour cream
1 tablespoon red lumpfish caviar**

Thinly slice cucumber on the diagonal into about 24 slices; place on small tray. Spoon a scant teaspoon sour cream onto each slice; top with ⅛ teaspoon caviar. *Makes 2 dozen.*

SMOKED-SALMON SANDWICHES

(pictured)

**1 container (8 oz) soft cream cheese
1 tablespoon chopped fresh dill or
    1 teaspoon dried dillweed
8 slices pumpernickel
½ lb sliced smoked salmon (⅛-inch-thick
    slices)
1 small red onion
Dill sprigs (optional)**

1. In small bowl, combine cream cheese and chopped dill. Cut each slice of pumpernickel crosswise in half. Cut salmon slices on the diagonal into 1-inch-wide strips. Cut onion lengthwise in half, then crosswise into thin slices.

2. Place bread halves on work surface with rounded sides facing in same direction. Spread each with cream-cheese mixture; top with 2 or 3 salmon strips and an onion slice.

3. On 12-inch round platter, arrange some of the sandwiches, pinwheel fashion, around edge. Place remaining sandwiches in center, overlapping to fit. Garnish center with dill, if desired. *Makes 8 servings.*

continued on page 179

Oven-Steamed Seafood With Spanish Rice:
*This elegant medley is made by combining a frozen rice mixture with succulent shrimp,
squid and mussels in a special oven-cooking bag. It's sealed, then baked (or microwaved)
on a disposable, heat-resistant paper pan.*

Chili-Tortilla Casserole:
*Corn tortillas, in a throwaway foil pan, form the crust of this colorful south-of-the-border
quiche. Then fill it with layers of chili con carne, pinto beans, green chilies, cheese and
quiche mixture, and bake it.*

Quick & Easy
HOT DINNERS

We've taken the heat out of cooking with these luscious meals. They're a cinch to prepare and a snap when cleanup time comes. The secret: disposable cookware (foil, parchment paper, paper pans, oven-cooking bags). Recipes begin on page 176.

Foil-Baked Cabbage With Corned Beef:
Large green cabbage leaves in a foil package hold a hearty mixture of shredded cabbage,
cream-of-celery sauce, potatoes, carrots and corned beef.

continued from page 175

Why quick and easy? Disposable foil and paper pans, parchment paper and oven-cooking bags double up as both cooking and serving dishes, so there are no pots, pans, bowls or platters to clean. And, if you mix ingredients in a plastic food-storage bag or paper bowl or cup, you'll be out of the kitchen even sooner. (All you'll have to wash up is a knife, cutting board, mixing bowl, spoon and measuring utensils.) A bonus: Because our no-cleanup recipes are baked (in a regular or microwave oven) using oven-cooking bags and pans or grilled in foil packages, the foods retain their natural moisture, flavor and nutrients.

TYPES OF DISPOSABLE COOKWARE AND WRAPPING MATERIAL

Aluminum-foil baking pans are available in a wide range of shapes and sizes. Use them only in a regular oven (*not* a microwave) or on a barbecue grill. Although they are disposable, they *can* be washed and used again.

Paper pans are made from polyester-coated paper shaped into a variety of baking pans primarily for microwave-oven use, although they can tolerate a regular oven up to 400F.

Oven-cooking bags, made of nylon film, are available in three sizes. Food sealed in oven-cooking bags may be baked in a regular or microwave oven.

Aluminum foil comes in three widths (12, 14 and 18 inches) and three thicknesses (regular, heavy-duty and extra-heavy). Use regular foil to cover baking pans, heavy-duty for foil packages and extra-heavy for outdoor cooking.

Parchment paper is a silicone-coated paper used to line cookie sheets and baking pans or to make food packages. The term "en papillote" in a recipe means that foods are cooked in coated parchment paper (also called cooking or kitchen parchment). Uncoated parchment paper is used to make pastry bags—not for cooking or baking.

CHILI-TORTILLA CASSEROLE

(pictured)

Salad oil
1 (11-by-9-by-1½-inch) disposable aluminum foil baking pan
1 pkg (12, 6-inch diameter) fresh corn tortillas
1 can (15 oz) chili con carne
1 pkg (8 oz) shredded Cheddar cheese (2 cups)
1 can (15 oz) pinto or red kidney beans, drained
1 can (4 oz) chopped green chilies

1 container (1 lb, 10 oz) frozen 3-cheese-flavor premixed quiche filling, thawed
2 green onions, root ends trimmed
1 large tomato, stem end removed, cut into 9 wedges

1. With pastry brush, oil foil baking pan; place tortillas in pan, and lightly oil both sides of each tortilla. Place 2 tortillas, overlapping, on each long side of pan. Remove and cut remaining 8 tortillas in half; place 2 halves, rounded sides up, on each short side of pan; arrange 4 halves on bottom of pan so that entire inner surface of pan is lined with tortillas.

2. Spread chili con carne evenly over tortillas on bottom of pan. Sprinkle half of shredded Cheddar over chili-con-carne layer. Spread pinto beans evenly over cheese. Arrange remaining 8 tortilla halves to cover bean layer.

3. Preheat oven to 375F. Sprinkle green chilies over tortilla layer. Pour quiche mixture over chilies. Bake 45 to 50 minutes, or until tortillas are lightly browned and mixture is set. Remove from oven; let stand 10 minutes before cutting.

4. Meanwhile, cut white ends from green onions (refrigerate white ends to use in another recipe). Cut green part of onions crosswise into ¼-inch pieces. Garnish casserole with remaining cheese, the green onions and tomato wedges. *Makes 9 servings.*

FOIL-BAKED CABBAGE WITH CORNED BEEF

(pictured)

1 can (10¾ oz) condensed cream-of-celery soup, undiluted
½ cup water
1 tablespoon prepared spicy brown mustard
1 teaspoon caraway seed
¼ teaspoon pepper
18-inch-wide heavy-duty foil
Nonstick cooking spray
1 head (2½ lb) green cabbage with nice outer leaves
1 can (12 oz) corned beef, cut into 2-by-1-by-½-inch slices
1 can (1 lb) whole baby carrots, drained
1 can (1 lb) whole new potatoes, drained
1 (12¼-by 8¼-inch-by-1¼ inch) disposable aluminum-foil baking pan

1. In small bowl, stir together celery soup, water, mustard, caraway seed and pepper; set aside. Preheat oven to 450F.

2. Tear off two 24-inch-long sheets of foil; place one sheet crisscross over the other; spray surface with nonstick cooking spray. Remove eight large outer leaves from cabbage. In center of foil, place six leaves, rounded side down, to form a shallow bowl about 10 inches in

diameter; set aside remaining two leaves.

3. From remaining head of cabbage, shred enough to measure 4 cups (refrigerate leftover cabbage to use in another recipe). Into cabbage-leaf bowl, place 2 cups shredded cabbage. Over cabbage, place half of corned beef, carrots and potatoes. Spoon half of soup mixture over meat and vegetables. Repeat layering with other half of ingredients. Place remaining two cabbage leaves, rounded side up, on top of meat and vegetables. Lift up sides of foil so that cabbage completely encloses layered meat and vegetables. Fold edges of foil together several times so that package is tightly sealed.

4. Place foil package in foil baking pan. Bake 30 to 40 minutes, or until heated through. (To check contents, after 30 minutes, remove from oven, and carefully unfold foil; if shredded cabbage is still crisp and contents not hot enough, reseal, and return to oven.) To serve, carefully unfold and roll back foil edges of package to form its own serving bowl. *Makes 4 servings.*

CHICKEN-AND-BROCCOLI TERIYAKI

2½-to-3-lb broiler-fryer, cut in eighths or tenths
1-quart plastic sandwich storage bag
1 pkg (8¾ oz) main-dish mix for chicken teriyaki
Water
1 (11-by-9-by-1½-inch) disposable aluminum-foil baking pan
1 small bunch (about 1 lb) broccoli, cut into flowerets

1. Remove and discard any excess fat from chicken. Preheat oven to 400F. In plastic bag, combine glaze-mix packet from chicken teriyaki and ¼ cup water; twist to close, and shake to mix well; set aside.

2. In foil pan, combine teriyaki sauce-mix and rice packets with 3¼ cups water; mix well. Place chicken pieces, skin side up, in pan. Bake, uncovered, 45 minutes.

3. Remove pan from oven. Arrange broccoli over chicken and rice. Spoon glaze evenly over chicken pieces; bake 15 minutes longer. Remove pan from oven; let stand 5 minutes before serving. *Makes 6 servings.*

Note: To cook in a microwave oven, prepare glaze as directed in Step 1. Place 16-by-10-inch oven-cooking bag in a 10⅝-by-8¹/₁₆-by-1-inch disposable paper pan for microwave and regular ovens. In bag, place *sauce mix, rice packets* and *1 tablespoon all-purpose flour;* add 2½ cups *water.* With spoon, stir gently to mix. Add *chicken,* skin side up, thickest parts at outer edge. Close bag, and fasten with nylon tie. Make six ½-inch slits in top of bag. Microwave at HIGH 20 minutes. Remove bag and pan from oven; cut open top of bag, avoiding steam. Add *broccoli*, and spoon *glaze* over chicken pieces. Return to microwave oven; microwave at HIGH 5 to 10 minutes longer, or until chicken and broccoli are done. Let stand 5 minutes before serving.

OVEN-STEAMED SEAFOOD WITH SPANISH RICE
(pictured)

1 (16-by-10-inch) oven-cooking bag
1 (10⅝-by-8¹⁄₁₆-by-1-inch) disposable paper pan for microwave and regular ovens
2 pkg (11-oz size) frozen Spanish-style rice, thawed
1 tablespoon all-purpose flour
16 medium shrimp (about ¾ lb), shelled and deveined (leave tail segment attached, if desired)
12 medium mussels, cleaned
2 squid, cleaned, bodies cut into ½-inch rings and tentacles cut in half (see Note)

1. Preheat oven to 400F. Place cooking bag in paper pan. Place rice in cooking bag; sprinkle contents of both Spanish-rice seasoning packets and the flour evenly over rice. With spoon, stir gently to mix.

2. Pat shrimp, mussels and squid dry with paper towels; place seafood on rice. Close bag, and fasten with nylon tie; make six ½-inch slits in top of bag. Bake 20 minutes, or until mussels open. (To cook in microwave oven, cook at HIGH 10 minutes, rotating pan once after 5 minutes.) To serve, carefully cut a cross on top of bag; fold points of bag back. Serve directly from cooking bag. *Makes 4 servings.*

Note: If squid is unavailable, increase shrimp to 1 pound.

BAKED-POTATO SUPPER

4 large (8-oz size) baking potatoes
4 (6-by-4½-by-1¼-inch) disposable paper pans for microwave and regular ovens
¼ teaspoon dried thyme leaves
⅛ teaspoon pepper
1 can (15 oz) brown gravy with beef chunks
1 can (1 lb) mixed vegetables, drained
12-inch-wide foil or waxed paper

1. Preheat oven to 400F. Under cold water, scrub potatoes well. Dry thoroughly with paper towels. With fork, prick each potato over entire surface. Bake 50 to 60 minutes. (To cook in a microwave oven, cook at HIGH 12 to 16

minutes, or until potatoes are fork-tender.)

2. Remove potatoes from oven; cool slightly. Slash an X in top of each potato; then gently squeeze to fluff up potato. Place each potato in paper pan; sprinkle each with some thyme and pepper; top with one-fourth of gravy and one-fourth of vegetables.

3. Cover with foil, and bake 10 minutes more. (Or cover loosely with waxed paper; microwave at HIGH 5 minutes more, or until potatoes are heated through.) *Makes 4 servings.*

LOW-SODIUM FISH AND VEGETABLES EN PAPILLOTE

1 medium carrot, scraped
¼ lb fresh snow pea pods, stem ends and strings removed
8 green onions, root ends trimmed
18-inch-wide heavy-duty foil or 15-inch-wide cooking parchment paper
4 small (3-oz size, ½ inch thick) fresh fillets of sole or flounder, or 1 pkg (12 oz) individually wrapped frozen fillets of sole or flounder
1 lemon, cut into eight ⅛-inch slices
2 tablespoons unsalted butter, margarine or olive oil
1 teaspoon salt-free herb-and-spice blend
1 (15-by-10½-by-1-inch) disposable aluminum-foil cookie sheet or (13-inch square) paper oven liner/cookie sheet for microwave and regular ovens

1. Cut carrot crosswise in half; cut carrot and pea pods lengthwise into ⅛-inch julienne strips. Cut green onions crosswise in half, then lengthwise into julienne strips.

2. Preheat oven to 450F. Tear off four 12-inch-long sheets of foil or parchment paper. Place 1 fresh or unthawed frozen fish fillet in center of each piece of foil or paper. (If the number of frozen fish fillets is uneven, divide into four equal portions.) On each fish fillet, place 2 lemon slices and one-fourth of the carrot, pea pods and green onions; dot with butter, and sprinkle with herb-and-spice blend.

3. For each packet, bring long sides of foil or paper together over fish. Fold together 1 inch of foil or paper, and crease; repeat folding until foil or paper fits loosely around food. Repeat folding technique at each short end until packet is tightly sealed. Place packets on disposable foil or paper cooking sheet.

4. Bake fish 10 minutes. (To cook in a microwave oven, place paper packets—do not use foil—on paper cookie sheet; microwave at HIGH 5 minutes.) Transfer to serving plates. Serve directly from packets. *Makes 4 servings.*

YOGURT-MARINATED CHICKEN BREASTS

4 whole chicken breasts, skinned and boned, or 8 boneless skinned chicken-breast halves
2 (1-gallon size) plastic food-storage bags

MARINADE
1 container (8 oz) plain low-fat yogurt
1 tablespoon instant minced onion
2 tablespoons lemon juice
2 tablespoons olive or salad oil
1 teaspoon ground coriander
1 garlic clove, minced
½ teaspoon ground cumin
½ teaspoon ground turmeric
¼ teaspoon salt
⅛ teaspoon ground red pepper

2 (12-by-9 inch) disposable aluminum-foil broiler pans (optional)
Fresh cilantro or coriander leaves (optional)

1. Cut each whole chicken breast in half; set aside.

2. Make Marinade: Into a double thickness of food-storage bags, spoon half of yogurt. Stir remaining marinade ingredients into yogurt in container; mix well. Spoon seasoned yogurt into food-storage bag; gently stir to combine with unseasoned yogurt. Place chicken pieces in bag; close tightly with tie provided. Gently turn bag upside down to coat chicken pieces evenly with yogurt marinade. Refrigerate at least 1 hour or overnight.

3. Prepare outdoor grill for barbecuing, or preheat indoor grill or broiler. Grill chicken, 4 inches above low coals, 10 minutes, turning once after 5 minutes. Or place chicken pieces in disposable broiler pans. Broil, 6 inches from heat, 8 minutes, or until chicken pieces are lightly browned. (If necessary, broil one pan of chicken at a time; cover, and keep warm while broiling second pan of chicken.) Garnish with fresh cilantro leaves. *Makes 8 servings.*

MACARONI AND CHEESE "DIVAN"

1 pkg (1 lb, 4 oz) frozen macaroni and cheese
1 (12¼-by-8¼-by-1¼-inch) disposable aluminum-foil pan
12-inch-wide foil
1 pkg (10 oz) frozen broccoli cuts, partially thawed and separated into pieces
1 can (7 oz) luncheon meat, cut into ½-inch cubes

1. Preheat oven to 450F. Remove block of frozen macaroni and cheese from *continued on page 178*

continued from page 177

its pan to cutting board. With large, sharp knife, cut crisscross into quarters; place in foil pan, spacing them as far apart as possible. Place broccoli and luncheon meat around macaroni and cheese.

2. Cover pan tightly with foil; bake 30 minutes. Stir well before serving to combine ingredients. *Makes 4 servings.*

Note: To cook in a microwave oven, place ingredients in 8-by-8-by-1⁹⁄₁₆-inch disposable paper pan. Cover pan with plastic wrap; fold back one corner to vent. Microwave at HIGH 5 minutes; rotate pan a quarter turn; stir, and microwave 5 minutes longer; rotate pan a quarter turn; stir, and microwave 5 minutes longer; rotate pan a quarter turn, and microwave 3 minutes longer. Let stand, covered, 5 minutes before serving.

BACON-CORN MUFFINS WITH FRIED CHICKEN

1 disposable aluminum-foil muffin pan (six 3-inch cups)
Nonstick cooking spray
1 pkg (8 or 8½ oz) corn-muffin mix
1 large egg
⅓ or ½ cup milk
1 can (8 oz) whole-kernel corn, drained
2 tablespoons cooked bacon bits (from a 3-oz jar)
1 pkg (2 lb) frozen batter-coated fully cooked fried chicken

1. Preheat oven to 400F. Spray muffin-pan cups with nonstick cooking spray. Prepare corn-muffin mix as package label directs, adding egg and amount of milk called for on package. Stir in corn and bacon bits. Pour batter into muffin cups, dividing evenly.

2. Bake chicken and muffins as package labels direct. Remove muffins from cups; serve immediately with chicken. *Makes 4 servings.*

Note: A 10-ounce package of cornbread mix with its own foil pan may be substituted for the corn-muffin mix. Prepare as package label directs, stirring in corn and bacon. Bake in foil pan as directed on package.

EASY CURRIED-CHICKEN PIE

FILLING

2 cans (6¾-oz size) or 3 cans (5-oz size) chunk white and dark chicken with broth
1 Granny Smith apple, cored and cut into ½-inch cubes
¼ cup chopped almonds
¼ cup dried currants
¼ cup sour cream
1 tablespoon curry powder

1 teaspoon instant minced onion
½ teaspoon ground cinnamon
Dash ground red pepper

1 pkg (15 oz) refrigerated all-ready piecrusts
1 (13-inch) disposable aluminum-foil pizza pan

1. Make Filling: In medium bowl, mix chicken with its broth and remaining filling ingredients until well mixed. Remove piecrusts from package. Unfold crusts; remove plastic cover. Preheat oven to 425F.

2. On foil pizza pan or parchment-paper-lined, nondisposable pizza pan or 15½-by-12-inch baking sheet, place one piecrust. Spoon filling onto center of crust, and spread to within 1 inch of edge; moisten the edge with water. Place remaining piecrust over filling mixture. With fork, gently press edges to seal. With knife, cut eight 1-inch slits on top crust to vent. Bake 30 minutes, or until golden-brown. Using slits as a guide, cut pie into 8 wedges. *Makes 8 servings.*

HERBED GOAT CHEESE BAKED IN GRAPE LEAVES

1 jar (1 lb) grape leaves in brine
1 (11 oz) log-shape, uncoated, rindless goat cheese (chèvre)
1 (10⅝-by-8¹⁄₁₆-by-1-inch) disposable paper pan for microwave and regular ovens
2 tablespoons olive oil
1 tablespoon fresh thyme leaves or 1 teaspoon dried thyme leaves
Freshly ground pepper
Unsalted crackers or water biscuits

1. Remove grape leaves from jar; select 12 large leaves; return others to brine in jar. (Refrigerate leftover grape leaves to use in another recipe.) Rinse leaves with cold water; place flat on paper towels to dry. Preheat oven to 350F.

2. Cut cheese log crosswise into 12 slices. Lightly oil paper pan. Place leaves, four at a time, in pan. Put a cheese slice in center of each grape leaf. Drizzle ½ teaspoon oil over each; sprinkle with some thyme and pepper. Fold pointed ends of grape leaf over cheese to meet in center; turn packet upside down to seal. Repeat with remaining leaves and cheese slices. Place packets evenly, in one layer, in pan.

3. Bake 4 to 5 minutes, or until cheese packets are warm and soft when lightly touched. (To cook in a microwave oven, cook at MEDIUM 2 minutes, turning after 1 minute.) To serve: Transfer cheese packets to small serving plate; let each person unwrap packets and spread cheese on crackers or biscuits; the grape leaf can be eaten as well. *Makes 12 appetizers.*

STUFFED ACORN SQUASH

2 large (1½-lb size) acorn squash, halved lengthwise and seeded
4 (6-by-4½-by-1¼-inch) disposable paper pans for microwave and regular ovens
12-inch-wide foil or plastic wrap
¾ cup dry herb-seasoned- or chicken-flavor-stuffing mix
1 can (15 oz) gravy with chunky chicken or turkey
½ pkg (6-oz size) frozen snow pea pods, each halved crosswise
½ cup frozen pearl onions or drained canned small whole onions

1. Preheat oven to 375F. Place each squash half, cut side down, in a paper pan. Add 2 tablespoons water to each pan; cover with foil. Bake 30 minutes; turn squash, cut side up; drain pan. (To cook squash in a microwave oven, add 1 tablespoon water to each pan; cover with plastic wrap; fold back one corner to vent. Microwave at HIGH 9 minutes, or until fork-tender; turn, and drain.)

2. Spoon 3 tablespoons dry stuffing mix into cavity of each squash; top with one-fourth of the gravy. Divide pea pods and onions among squash. Gently stir into gravy mixture; re-cover with foil or plastic wrap. Bake 15 minutes longer (or microwave at HIGH 5 minutes longer), or until squash and filling are heated through. *Makes 4 servings.*

ITALIAN VEGETABLES WITH GRILLED STEAK

1 medium (¾ to 1 lb) eggplant, cut into 1-inch cubes
1 large (6 to 8 oz) green pepper, seeded and cut into ¼-inch strips
½ lb fresh mushrooms
1 small (4 oz) yellow squash, cut in ¼-inch slices
1 medium red onion, thinly sliced
1 (8-inch square) disposable aluminum-foil pan or 18-inch-wide heavy-duty foil
1 large garlic clove
1 jar (14 oz) or 1 can (14¾ oz) pizza sauce
1½-lb top-round steak, cut 1 inch thick
1 (12-by-9-inch) disposable aluminum-foil broiler pan

1. Prepare outdoor grill for barbecuing, or preheat oven to 450F. Combine all vegetables except garlic in foil pan. Or place the vegetables in the center of a 24-inch-long sheet of foil.

2. Using garlic press, press garlic into jar of pizza sauce; stir to blend; pour over vegetables. Cover pan tightly with foil. If using a 24-inch-long sheet of foil, bring the two short (18-inch) sides of the foil together so that they meet at one side
continued on page 193

continued from page 173

BEET, HERRING AND POTATO SALAD
(pictured)

3 lb delicatessen potato salad
Lettuce leaves
1 jar (1 lb) herring in white-wine sauce, chilled and drained
1 jar (1 lb) sliced pickled beets, chilled and drained
Parsley sprig (optional)

1. With plastic wrap, line an 8½-by-4½-by-2½-inch loaf pan, leaving a 3-inch overhang. Fill pan with potato salad, lightly tapping pan on counter to settle mixture. Smooth top with spatula. Cover top of potato salad with plastic-wrap overhang; refrigerate at least 2 hours, or overnight.

2. To unmold salad: Uncover salad. Invert large, rectangular serving platter over loaf pan; holding pan against platter, turn loaf pan upside down. Lift off pan and plastic wrap. Line outer edges of platter with lettuce leaves. Arrange half of the herring at each end of platter. Arrange half of the beets on each side of platter. Garnish with parsley, if desired. *Makes 12 servings.*

NO-FUSS CHILDREN'S PARTY
(Planned for 12)

"ZEBRA" PEANUT SANDWICH LOAF★
CHOCOLATE-FROSTED ANGEL CAKE WITH ICE-CREAM BALLS★
FRUITY PARTY FAVORS★
BERRY-FRUIT PUNCH★

★Recipes given for starred dishes.

"ZEBRA" PEANUT SANDWICH LOAF
(pictured)

1 loaf (1 lb) unsliced white bread
½ cup low-sugar apricot preserves
½ cup creamy peanut butter or almond butter
½ cup dark seedless raisins
1 container (8 oz) soft strawberry cream cheese
1 pkg (8 oz) cream cheese, softened
3 tablespoons milk
1 cup unsalted peanuts or natural almonds, chopped

1. Trim crust from bread, leaving a long block of white bread. Cut bread lengthwise into four slices. With rolling pin, slightly flatten each slice.

2. Place one slice of bread on waxed paper; spread with apricot preserves. Top with second slice of bread; spread with peanut butter. Pat ¼ cup raisins into peanut butter. Top with third slice of bread; spread with soft strawberry cream cheese; top with remaining bread slice.

3. Turn loaf on its side so that the layers are vertical; place on serving platter. In small bowl, with electric mixer, beat cream cheese and milk until light and fluffy. Spread top and sides of loaf with cream cheese mixture. Pat some peanuts onto sides of loaf; decorate top with remaining peanuts and raisins. Refrigerate until firm—about 2 hours. To serve: With serrated knife, using a gentle sawing motion, cut loaf into ½-inch-thick slices. *Makes 16 servings.*

CHOCOLATE-FROSTED ANGEL CAKE WITH ICE-CREAM BALLS
(pictured)

9 cream-filled chocolate-sandwich cookies
1 container (1 lb) ready-to-spread milk-chocolate frosting
⅓ container (9-oz size) chocolate-covered vanilla-ice-cream nuggets
½ gallon vanilla ice cream
1 roll chewy strawberry, grape or cherry fruit-leather snack
1 cup wheat-bran cereal shreds or wheat-and-barley cereal nuggets
36 mini semisweet-chocolate pieces
1 pkg (1 lb, 4 oz) ready-to-serve angel-food cake

1. Line small tray or cookie sheet with waxed paper. Separate cookies through cream centers. To make six boy's hats, place six cookie halves, cream side down, on tray. Spread a small amount of frosting on top center of each cookie half; set an ice-cream nugget on frosting.

2. On same tray, place remaining 12 cookie halves, cream side up. With small ice-cream scoop (2-inch diameter), scoop ice cream into 12 balls, placing each on a cookie half as it is scooped. Freeze ice-cream balls and hats. (Freeze leftover ice cream for another use.)

3. Unwrap and unroll fruit-leather snack, and remove plastic backing; cut into 15 ¼-inch-wide strips. Set aside eight of the longest strips. Cut one of the remaining short strips into 12 tiny triangles to use for noses or mouths. Tie each of the remaining six strips into a bow. Set aside all fruit-leather pieces. Place the cereal on waxed paper.

4. Make six "girl" Ice-Cream Balls: Remove ice-cream balls, one at a time, from freezer. Insert 2 mini chocolate pieces for the eyes, 1 chocolate piece for the nose and one fruit-leather triangle for the mouth. Pat or stick cereal onto the top, side and back for hair. Put a dab of frosting on top; press a bow onto frosting. Refreeze decorated ice-cream balls.

5. Make six "boy" Ice-Cream Balls: Remove ice-cream balls, one at a time, from freezer. Insert 2 chocolate pieces for the eyes, 1 piece for the mouth and 1 fruit-leather triangle for the nose. Pat or stick cereal onto the top, side and back for the hair. Put a dab of frosting on top; press a hat onto frosting. Refreeze decorated ice-cream balls. (The ice-cream balls can be made a day ahead.)

6. Place cake on plate; frost top and side with remaining frosting. With reserved fruit-leather strips, make a zigzag pattern around side of cake. Place two girl and two boy ice-cream balls on top of cake where the ends of the strips form a point. Serve remaining ice-cream balls along with the cake. *Makes 12 servings.*

FRUITY PARTY FAVORS
(pictured)

¼ pkg (4-oz size) chewy grape, cherry or strawberry fruit-leather snacks
¼ pkg (4-oz size) chewy apricot or orange fruit-leather snacks
2 pkg (4.8-oz size) chewy strawberry fruit bars
2 pkg (4.8-oz size) chewy apricot fruit bars
12 fluted cupcake paper liners

Unwrap and unroll two grape and two apricot fruit-leather snacks, and remove plastic backing. Cut each into ¼-inch wide strips. Unwrap fruit bars; stack them in groups of two bars, using the same flavor or one of each flavor; press together. To decorate stacks as gift packages, using contrasting-color fruit-leather strips, place one strip lengthwise over stack and another strip around the center, crosswise; press ends of strips onto bottom of stack. Or wrap two fruit-leather strips around the fruit-bar stack in a spiral, if desired. Form remaining strips into bows; use to finish off packages. Place each package in a paper liner. *Makes 12 party favors.*

BERRY-FRUIT PUNCH
(pictured)

2 bottles (1½ qt) cranberry-raspberry juice, chilled
4 cups orange juice, chilled

continued on page 189

ALLAN NEWMAN/THE NEWMAN-O'NEILL GROUP, INC.

Quick and Crunchy Fish Fillets

*T*his tasty fish dish is prepared in a nontraditional way: The fillet of sole is dipped in a Romano-cheese mixture, sprinkled with crunchy chopped cashew nuts, then cooked by a technique called oven frying. Serve with tartar sauce, steamed rice and a tossed green salad—dinner will be ready in a flash.

A STEP-BY-STEP RECIPE

CASHEW FISH FILLETS

3 tablespoons butter or margarine
1 egg
¾ cup grated Romano cheese
2 tablespoons all-purpose flour
6 (4-oz size) sole or turbot fillets
3 tablespoons vegetable oil
½ cup chopped unsalted dry-roasted
    cashew nuts

TARTAR SAUCE
½ cup mayonnaise
1 tablespoon freshly squeezed lemon
    juice
½ teaspoon Worcestershire sauce
2 tablespoons sweet pickle relish,
    drained
1 tablespoon finely chopped shallot

1 tablespoon tiny capers, drained
⅛ teaspoon salt
⅛ teaspoon freshly ground black pepper

Lemon wedges and parsley sprigs

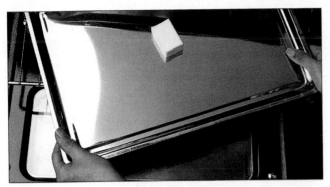

1. Preheat oven to 425F. Place 3 tablespoons butter in a 15-by-10½-by-1½-inch jelly-roll pan or large shallow rimmed baking pan. Place pan on center rack of oven for 3 to 4 minutes, or until butter melts. Begin to prepare fish fillets while butter melts.

2. Place egg in a pie plate and beat slightly with a wire whisk. On a piece of waxed paper, combine Romano cheese and flour; mix thoroughly. Dip a fish fillet in the beaten egg, coating thoroughly and letting excess drip into pie plate.

3. Transfer egg-coated fish to cheese mixture and coat both sides. Set aside. Repeat until all fish fillets are coated with egg and cheese mixture. Remove jelly-roll pan with melted butter from oven. Add vegetable oil and swirl to blend.

4. Arrange coated fish fillets in jelly-roll pan, turning once to coat with the butter-oil mixture. Sprinkle the fillets with chopped cashews, pressing lightly so nuts stick to fish. Bake on top rack of oven for 10 minutes, or until fish flakes easily when separated with a fork.

5. Make Tartar Sauce: In a small bowl, combine Tartar Sauce ingredients. Stir with a wooden spoon until thoroughly blended. If desired, add a few drops of hot red-pepper sauce to Tartar Sauce for a sharper flavor. Refrigerate until ready to use.

6. Remove fish fillets from oven. Using a slotted spatula, transfer fish fillets to a warm serving platter. If desired, garnish with lemon wedges and parsley sprigs. Serve the fish fillets with chilled Tartar Sauce. *Makes 6 servings.*

ALLAN NEWMAN/THE NEWMAN-O'NEILL GROUP, INC.

Summertime Dessert Magic

*Y*ou *don't need a magic wand to turn an ordinary angel-food cake into a light, luscious, refreshing summertime dessert in minutes! Savor this angel-food cake filled with layers of ice cream and topped with swirls of whipped cream. Perfect on a hot summer day. Or make this dessert and freeze it for a special occasion.*

ICE-CREAM ANGEL CAKE

10-inch angel-food cake
1 quart strawberry ice cream, softened
2 cups peach ice cream, softened
2 cups heavy cream

½ cup confectioners' sugar
½ teaspoon almond extract
2 kiwifruit, sliced
6 whole strawberries

1. Freeze store-wrapped cake until firm—2 hours or overnight. Remove from freezer and unwrap. Insert wooden picks into cake to mark horizontal lines to use as guides for cutting cake into four equal layers. Using a large serrated knife, slice cake horizontally into four layers.

2. On a large flat plate or a small wooden board, place bottom layer of cake. Using a rubber spatula, spread with 2 cups strawberry ice cream, just to the edge of the cake. Top with second cake layer; spread with peach ice cream.

3. Top with third cake layer; spread with remaining strawberry ice cream and top with fourth cake layer, aligning cake layers. Wrap in plastic wrap or freezer wrap. Freeze several hours or overnight, or until cake is very firm.

4. About 1 hour before serving the cake: In the chilled bowl of an electric mixer, combine heavy cream, confectioners' sugar and almond extract. At high speed, beat until stiff peaks form when beaters are raised.

5. Unwrap frozen cake and transfer to a serving plate. Spread about three-fourths of the whipped cream on top and side of cake. Fill pastry bag fitted with a ½-inch star tip with remaining whipped cream. Pipe rosettes of whipped cream decoratively on top of cake.

6. Garnish with fruit and serve immediately. Or cover ungarnished cake with a cake cover and freeze. To serve: Remove cake from freezer and let stand 1 hour in the refrigerator. Garnish with fruit just before cutting into wedges to serve. *Makes 12 servings.*

MOVABLE FEASTS

Vacation cooking—in a rented cottage, chalet or condo; on a boat; or at a campsite—often means relying on transportable, easily stored packaged foods. Vacation cooking involves planning meals you can cook in minimum space with a minimum amount of equipment—and in a minimum amount of time. After all, you have other things to do on vacation! But you can do all those other things and still serve delicious meals. Take this elegant fish, for example. It's red snapper, but the recipe works for any fish of comparable size that you've bought or caught. Wrap the fish in foil with wine and mushrooms and cook it over coals or bake it in the oven while you do quick and wonderful things with peas, salad greens, fresh fruit and packaged cake to complete one of your vacation meals. Recipes start on page 186.

continued from page 185

BAKED FISH IN FOIL*
PETIT POIS*
JULIENNE POTATOES
WARM FRENCH BREAD
AVOCADO SALAD PLATTER
FRESH STRAWBERRIES AND
RASPBERRIES
SPONGE CAKE
COFFEE   CHILLED WHITE WINE

*Recipes given for starred dishes.

BAKED FISH IN FOIL
(pictured)

**3-lb whole fish, cleaned and ready to cook
   (see Note)**
1 garlic clove, peeled and crushed
**¼ cup (½ stick) butter or margarine,
   softened**
1 teaspoon salt
⅛ teaspoon pepper
½ teaspoon dried thyme leaves
1 teaspoon all-purpose flour
**½ lb deveined, shelled large shrimp (leave
   shell on tail)**
½ lb fresh mushrooms, sliced
3 tablespoons lemon juice
½ cup dry white wine
¼ cup chopped parsley
1 teaspoon grated lemon peel

1. Preheat oven to 375F. Wash fish, inside and out, under cold running water. Dry well on paper towels.
2. In small bowl, combine garlic, butter, salt, pepper, thyme and flour; mix well.
3. Place fish on double thickness of 24-by-18-inch heavy-duty foil.
4. In cavity of fish, place 1 tablespoon garlic mixture, 4 shrimp and ½ cup mushrooms. Sprinkle with 1 tablespoon lemon juice and 2 tablespoons wine.
5. Dot top of fish with remaining garlic mixture. Arrange remaining shrimp and mushrooms over top; sprinkle with remaining lemon juice and white wine, the parsley and lemon peel.
6. Bring long sides of foil together over fish, and secure with a double fold. Fold both ends of foil upward several times. Place on cookie sheet.
7. Bake 40 minutes (allow 10 to 12 minutes per pound), or until fish flakes easily when tested with a fork. Serve with juices in foil spooned over top. *Makes 4 to 6 servings.*
   Note: Red snapper, bluefish, mackerel, bass, shad or similar whole fish.

PETIT POIS IN FOIL

6 lettuce leaves
1 pkg (10 oz) frozen peas
1 teaspoon sugar
½ teaspoon salt
Dash pepper
2 tablespoons butter or margarine

1. Preheat oven to 375F.
2. On double thickness of 20-by-18-inch heavy-duty foil, arrange lettuce leaves, overlapping, to form a circle. Break peas into small chunks; place on lettuce; sprinkle with sugar, salt and pepper; dot with butter.
3. Bring ends of foil together; fold over, to make secure.
4. Bake in oven, along with fish, 30 to 40 minutes, or until tender. Serve with juices in foil. *Makes 4 servings.*

HOT BOUILLON
HAM-AND-CABBAGE CASSEROLE*
MARINATED SLICED TOMATOES
PUMPERNICKEL   BUTTER
JELLY-ROLL TRIFLE*
MILK   COFFEE

*Recipes given for starred dishes.

HAM-AND-CABBAGE CASSEROLE

Water
2 teaspoons instant minced onion
1½ teaspoons salt
8 small whole unpared new potatoes
**½ small head cabbage, cut into 4 wedges
   and cored**
**6 large carrots, pared and cut into 4-inch
   sticks**
1-lb canned ham or corned beef
**4 tablespoons (½ stick) butter or
   margarine**
Hot-dog relish

1. Set electric skillet at 300F. In the skillet, bring 3 cups water to boiling; add onion and salt.
2. Add potatoes; cook, covered, 25 minutes, or until tender. (Add another ½ cup water during cooking, if necessary.)

3. Add cabbage and carrot; cook 10 minutes longer.
4. Place ham in center of skillet; dot vegetables with butter. Cover, and cook 5 minutes longer.
5. Serve right from skillet, along with relish. *Makes 4 servings.*

JELLY-ROLL TRIFLE

**1 pkg (3½ or 4 oz) instant vanilla pudding
   mix**
2 cups milk (see Note)
2 medium-size ripe bananas
1 pkg (7 oz) individual jelly rolls
Sherry (optional)

1. Prepare pudding mix with the milk, as package label directs.
2. Slice bananas, on the diagonal, ¼ inch thick; stir into the prepared vanilla pudding.
3. Cut each jelly roll into 6 slices. Sprinkle with a little sherry. In bottom of 1-quart glass serving bowl, make a layer of jelly-roll slices; line side of bowl with more slices.
4. Pour pudding into prepared dish. Top with rest of jelly-roll slices. *Makes 4 to 6 servings.*
   Note: Use reconstituted nonfat dry milk, if you like, or if fresh milk is not available.

HIBACHI HORS D'OEUVRES:
BEEF BALLS EN BROCHETTE*
TERIYAKI*
AVOCADO-AND-BANANA KEBABS*
SCAMPI ON SKEWERS*

*Recipes given for starred dishes.

BEEF BALLS EN BROCHETTE

25 (8- or 10-inch) bamboo skewers
1 lb ground chuck
1 can (4½ oz) deviled ham
3 oz Roquefort or blue cheese
3 large peppers
25 cherry tomatoes
Salt
Pepper

1. In a pan of cold water, soak bamboo skewers at least 15 minutes to prevent charring. Meanwhile, in medium bowl, combine chuck and deviled ham; mix lightly with fork.
2. Cut cheese into 25 cubes. Cut green peppers into 2-by-1-inch pieces.
3. Shape the meat mixture around

cheese cubes, to form 25 meatballs.

4. On each skewer, thread a meatball, a green-pepper piece, and a cherry tomato at end. Sprinkle lightly with salt and pepper. Refrigerate.

5. At serving time, broil, on hibachi or in broiler, about 5 minutes on each side, or until nicely browned. Cheese will be melted on inside. *Makes 25.*

TERIYAKI

20 (8- or 10-inch) bamboo skewers
1¼ cups cream sherry
1 cup soy sauce
¼ cup condensed chicken broth, undiluted
1¼ lb flank steak
1 can (15¼ oz) pineapple chunks, drained
20 preserved kumquats, drained

1. In a pan of cold water, soak bamboo skewers at least 15 minutes to prevent charring. Meanwhile, in small saucepan, combine sherry, soy sauce and chicken broth. Bring just to boiling; remove from heat. Pour into a shallow, 2-quart baking dish; let cool.

2. Wipe flank steak with damp paper towels. Trim off excess fat. Slice steak across the grain on the diagonal to make about 24 slices ¼ inch thick.

3. Arrange steak slices in marinade; refrigerate, covered, 2 hours or longer.

4. Just before cooking, cut steak slices into 1½-inch squares. Thread on skewers, as pictured, alternating steak with pineapple and kumquats.

5. Broil, on hibachi or in broiler, about 2 minutes per side. Serve at once. *Makes about 20.*

AVOCADO-AND-BANANA KEBABS

12 (8- to 10-inch) bamboo skewers
12 slices bacon
1 large, not-too-ripe avocado
2 medium-size ripe bananas
1 large, not-too-ripe papaya
Lemon juice
Honey

1. In a pan of cold water, soak bamboo skewers at least 15 minutes to prevent charring. Meanwhile, cook bacon until almost done: It should still be limp.

2. Peel avocado, bananas and papaya; cut into ¾-inch chunks. Brush with lemon juice, then with honey.

3. Thread bacon and fruit on 12 skewers, weaving bacon between pieces of fruit.

4. At serving time, broil, on hibachi

or in broiler, 2 minutes on each side, or until bacon is crisp. *Makes 12.*

SCAMPI ON SKEWERS

16 (8- to 10-inch) bamboo skewers
1 lb (16) large shelled, deveined shrimp (leave shells on tails)
½ cup (1 stick) butter or margarine
¼ cup chopped parsley
6 garlic cloves, crushed, or 1 teaspoon garlic salt
2 to 4 drops hot-pepper sauce
¼ cup lemon juice

1. In pan of cold water, soak bamboo skewers at least 15 minutes to prevent charring. Meanwhile, with sharp knife, slit shrimp down back, almost in half. Thread each lengthwise on a skewer.

2. In small saucepan, melt butter. Add rest of ingredients; slowly bring to boiling; then remove from heat.

3. Brush shrimp on all sides with butter mixture. Refrigerate, covered, at least ½ hour.

4. At serving time, broil, on hibachi or in broiler, 4 to 5 minutes; turn, and broil shrimp on other side 4 to 5 minutes. *Makes 16.*

CASSEROLE MEXICANA★
COLESLAW WITH ONION DRESSING★
CINNAMON BAKED APPLES★
CHEESE AND CRACKERS
BEER   ICED TEA

★Recipes given for starred dishes.

CASSEROLE MEXICANA

1 lb ground chuck
1 pkg (12.3 oz) Mexican-style dinner (see Note)
Water
1 can (8¾ oz) whole-kernel corn, undrained
½ pkg (12-oz size) corn-muffin mix
1 egg
⅓ cup milk

1. Preheat oven to 400F.

2. In 10-inch skillet with a heat-resistant handle, brown chuck; drain off fat.

3. Stir in sauce and seasoning from skillet dinner, along with 1½ cups water. Bring to boiling; stir in noodles from dinner and the corn. Reduce heat, and simmer, covered and stirring occasionally, 5 minutes.

4. Meanwhile, prepare ½ package of

corn-muffin mix, as package label directs, using egg and milk.

5. Remove skillet from heat. Spread batter over meat mixture. Bake 15 minutes or until golden-brown. *Makes 4 servings.*

Note: Use corn chips another time.

COLESLAW WITH ONION DRESSING

¼ cup bottled creamy onion salad dressing
¼ teaspoon dry mustard
¼ teaspoon sugar
½ pkg (1-lb size) prepared coleslaw

1. In large bowl, mix bottled salad dressing, mustard and sugar.

2. Add coleslaw; toss lightly until combined. Refrigerate until serving. *Makes 4 servings.*

CINNAMON BAKED APPLES

1 can (1 lb, 5 oz) baked apples
1 cup applesauce
¼ teaspoon ground cinnamon
1 tablespoon butter or margarine
Milk, light cream or ice cream

1. Drain apples, reserving syrup. Slice apples crosswise into thirds.

2. In medium skillet, combine reserved syrup, applesauce, cinnamon and butter. Bring to boiling; reduce heat; add apple slices; simmer, uncovered, 10 minutes, basting with sauce in skillet several times.

3. Serve warm with milk, cream or ice cream. *Makes 4 servings.*

HAMBURGERS ON THE GRILL
CARAVAN PIZZAS★
SLICED CUCUMBER SALAD
BUTTERSCOTCH BREAD PUDDING★
MILK   COFFEE

★Recipes given for starred dishes.

CARAVAN PIZZAS

3 pkg (8-oz size) refrigerator crescent dinner rolls
1 can (15 oz) tomato-herb sauce
½ lb mozzarella cheese, sliced
1 tablespoon bottled herb-and-garlic dressing
1 tablespoon grated Parmesan cheese

1. Preheat oven to 375F. Lightly grease two cookie sheets or a 15-by-10-

continued on page 188

continued from page 187

by-1-inch jelly-roll pan.

2. Spread out roll of dough. Cut large rectangles apart. Press dough together at perforations to make 12 rectangles in all.

3. Arrange rectangles on cookie sheets. Roll up two opposite ends of each rectangle about 1 inch, to form a rim.

4. Spoon about 1½ tablespoons tomato sauce over each rectangle. Cut each cheese slice into 4 strips. Arrange 4 strips on each rectangle. Sprinkle each with salad dressing and cheese.

5. Bake 15 minutes, or until cheese is melted and crust is slightly browned. Serve hot. *Makes 12.*

BUTTERSCOTCH BREAD PUDDING

1 cup dark-brown sugar, packed
5 slices buttered fresh white or raisin bread, cut into ½-inch squares
4 eggs
1⅓ cups milk
Dash salt

1. Generously butter inside of double-boiler top; pour in brown sugar; then add bread squares.

2. Beat eggs with milk and salt; pour over bread; don't stir. Cook over boiling water, covered, 1 hour.

3. Serve warm, with its own sauce. Very good with ice cream. *Makes 4 servings.*

QUICK SALADE NICOISE★
CRACKED-PEPPER BREADSTICKS★
MANDARIN-ORANGE CREAM★
ASSORTED COOKIES
ICED TEA

★Recipes given for starred dishes.

QUICK SALADE NICOISE

2 cans (7-oz size) tuna, drained
2 tablespoons sliced stuffed green olives
½ cup bottled herb-and-garlic salad dressing
1 can (1 lb) whole new potatoes, drained and sliced
1 can (8 oz) French-style green beans, drained
1 teaspoon instant minced onion
1 can (8¼ oz) small whole beets
¾ cup thinly sliced cucumber
⅛ teaspoon salt
⅛ teaspoon sugar
Crisp lettuce

½ cup grated, pared carrots
1 tomato, quartered
1 can (2 oz) anchovy fillets, drained
2 hard-cooked eggs, halved

1. In small bowl, break up tuna with fork; gently toss with olives and 2 tablespoons salad dressing; refrigerate, covered.

2. In bowl, toss sliced potato and green beans with ¼ cup dressing and the instant minced onion; refrigerate until ready for serving.

3. Toss beets with remaining dressing; refrigerate.

4. Sprinkle sliced cucumber with salt and sugar; refrigerate.

5. To serve: Arrange lettuce in large salad bowl. Mound tuna mixture in center. Arrange mounds of potato and beans, beets, carrot and cucumber around tuna. Garnish with tomato, anchovies and eggs. Bring to table, and toss gently. Pass more dressing, if desired. *Makes 4 to 6 servings.*

CRACKED-PEPPER BREADSTICKS

1 pkg (8 oz) refrigerator crescent dinner rolls
1 teaspoon coarsely cracked black pepper

1. Preheat oven to 375F.

2. Spread out roll dough. Press the dough together at perforations, making 4 large rectangles. Cut each rectangle in half lengthwise, to make 8 strips.

3. Sprinkle evenly with ½ teaspoon pepper.

4. Roll each strip lengthwise; then roll them in the remaining pepper. Place, 1 inch apart, on an ungreased cookie sheet.

5. Bake 10 to 12 minutes, or until golden-brown. Serve hot. *Makes 8.*

MANDARIN-ORANGE CREAM

1 container (16 oz) low-fat vanilla yogurt
2 tablespoons orange-flavor instant breakfast drink
1 can (11 oz) mandarin-orange sections, drained

1. Put vanilla yogurt into a small bowl. Sprinkle orange-flavor instant breakfast drink over yogurt.

2. Stir gently with a serving spoon, just until drink powder is dissolved and thoroughly blended with yogurt.

3. Set aside 12 orange sections for garnish; fold remaining orange sections into orange-yogurt mixture. Spoon into 4 dessert dishes; top each with reserved fruit. Refrigerate until very cold—about 2 hours. *Makes 4 servings.*

NEAPOLITAN CASSEROLE★
BUTTERED CANNED GREEN BEANS
GARLIC BREAD
CHILLED CANNED PEARS OR APRICOTS
PEANUT-DATE BARS
MILK   RED WINE OR ICED COFFEE

★Recipes given for starred dishes.

NEAPOLITAN CASSEROLE

¼ cup salad oil
6 Italian sweet sausages (about 1¼ lb)
2 cups uncooked elbow macaroni
1 lb ground chuck
1 can (6 oz) tomato paste
2 cans (1-lb size) stewed tomatoes
1 can (8 oz) tomato sauce with onion
1 tablespoon garlic salt
½ teaspoon pepper
2 tablespoons Italian seasoning (see Note)
2½ cups water
½ lb sliced Muenster cheese (optional)

1. In hot oil in electric skillet, set at 275F, brown the sweet sausage well on all sides.

2. Add macaroni and ground chuck; sauté, stirring, 5 minutes, or until beef loses its pink color.

3. Stir in tomato paste, stewed tomatoes, tomato sauce, seasonings and the water. Bring to boiling, stirring; reduce heat, and simmer, covered, 45 minutes.

4. Arrange cheese slices over top; heat just until cheese melts slightly. *Makes 6 servings.*

Note: Or use 1 tablespoon each of dried basil leaves and dried oregano leaves.

CHICKEN BREASTS BAKED IN FOIL★
GREEN RICE★
ASPARAGUS VINAIGRETTE★
FRESH FRUIT BOWL
CHEESE AND CRACKERS
WHITE WINE   COFFEE

★Recipes given for starred dishes.

CHICKEN BREASTS BAKED IN FOIL

2 pkg (1½-oz size) sour-cream-sauce mix
1¼ cups milk or reconstituted nonfat dry milk
2 tablespoons lemon juice
2 teaspoons instant minced onion
¼ teaspoon dried thyme leaves

¼ teaspoon salt
2 cans (4½-oz size) small shrimp, rinsed
    and drained (optional)
¼ cup (½ stick) butter or margarine
¾ cup packaged dry bread crumbs
3 (1-lb size) chicken breasts, split in half

1. In medium bowl, combine sour-cream-sauce mix, milk, lemon juice, onion, thyme, salt and shrimp; mix well.

2. Preheat oven to 375F. In small skillet, melt butter; mix in bread crumbs.

3. Wash chicken breasts; dry on paper towels. Lightly butter one side of 6 sheets of heavy-duty foil. Place about 1 tablespoon sour-cream sauce in center of each sheet of foil; place a half chicken breast on top. Spread rest of sour-cream sauce over chicken breasts to coat, dividing the sauce evenly; sprinkle the chicken with buttered bread crumbs.

4. Fold foil, to close each packet completely. Arrange in single layer on shallow baking pan. Bake 1 hour, or until tender. *Makes 6 servings.*

GREEN RICE

2 cups water
2 packets (.19-oz size) or 2 teaspoons
    instant chicken broth
¼ teaspoon pepper
2 tablespoons butter or margarine
2 cups packaged precooked white rice
⅓ cup bottled herb-and-garlic salad
    dressing
½ cup chopped green onions or parsley

1. In medium saucepan, bring 2 cups water, the instant chicken broth, pepper and butter to boiling, uncovered.

2. Stir in rice. Remove from heat; let stand covered, 5 minutes, or until the rice is tender and the water is absorbed.

3. Fluff up with fork; add salad dressing and onion, mixing gently with fork. Green Rice may be served hot or cold. *Makes 4 or 5 servings.*

ASPARAGUS VINAIGRETTE

1 can (1 lb) white asparagus, drained
1 can (1 lb) green asparagus, drained
⅓ cup bottled herb-and-garlic dressing
2 tablespoons chopped stuffed green
    olives
1 hard-cooked egg, chopped

1. Arrange asparagus on serving platter, alternating white and green asparagus in small bunches.

2. In measuring cup, combine salad dressing, olives and egg; mix well. Pour over asparagus. Refrigerate, covered, until well chilled—at least 30 minutes. *Makes 4 or 5 servings.*

---

continued from page 179

2 bottles (1 liter) lemon-lime-flavored soft
    drink, chilled
1 large navel orange, sliced
Ice cubes

In 6-quart punch bowl, combine cranberry-raspberry juice, orange juice and lemon-lime-flavored soft drink. Stir in orange slices and ice cubes. Serve immediately. *Makes 24 (1 cup) servings.*

ITALIAN ALFRESCO
(Planned for 8)

**HONEYDEW WEDGES WITH LIME
ANTIPASTO SALAD***
TURKEY TONNATO OVER PASTA*
BREADSTICKS
QUICK ZUPPA INGLESE*
CHIANTI

*Recipes given for starred dishes.

ANTIPASTO SALAD
(pictured)

3 jars (6-oz size) marinated artichoke
    hearts, chilled
4 jars (3¾- or 4-oz size) marinated
    mushrooms, chilled
1 can (1 lb, 3 oz) chick-peas or garbanzos,
    drained
1 small onion, chopped
¼ cup chopped parsley
½ lb thinly sliced Genoa salami or 1 pkg
    (8 oz) sliced hard salami
2 slices (¼-inch thick) provolone
    (about 1 lb)
3 cans (2-oz size) flat anchovies, drained
3 jars (9¾-oz size) giardiniera or mixed
    garden salad, chilled and drained
Lettuce leaves
1 jar (1 quart) red and green pickled
    peppers, chilled and drained
2 medium tomatoes, stem ends removed,
    sliced

1. Into a 2-cup measuring cup, drain and reserve the marinade from artichoke hearts and mushrooms. In a small bowl, combine chick-peas, onion, 2 tablespoons chopped parsley and ½ cup reserved marinade; mix well. Cover with plastic wrap; refrigerate till ready to arrange antipasto.

2. Fold each slice of salami in half; roll into a cone shape; cover and refrigerate. Cut provolone into ¼-inch strips; pat anchovies dry on paper towels. Wrap an anchovy around each provolone strip.

3. To arrange antipasto: Place small bowl in center of an 18-inch round serving platter. Spoon giardiniera salad into bowl. Line platter around bowl with lettuce; arrange artichoke hearts, pickled

---

peppers, mushrooms, provolone strips, tomatoes, chick-pea salad and salami cones on leaves. Drizzle tomatoes with some marinade. (Refrigerate leftover marinade to use in other recipes.) Sprinkle remaining parsley on tomatoes and mushrooms. *Makes 8 servings.*

TURKEY TONNATO
OVER PASTA

TONNATO SAUCE
½ can (2-oz size) rolled anchovies with
    capers, drained
½ cup mayonnaise
1 can (3½ oz) tuna, drained
¼ cup finely chopped celery
1½ teaspoons lemon juice
Dash pepper

2 lb delicatessen pasta-and-vegetable salad
    in vinaigrette
1 pkg (about 1½ lb) oven-roasted breast of
    turkey, skin removed

1. Make Tonnato Sauce: Unroll anchovies; reserve capers. Pat anchovies dry on paper towels. In electric blender or food processor, fitted with the steel blade, combine 2 anchovy fillets with remaining sauce ingredients; blend until smooth. Turn into small container with tight-fitting lid; refrigerate, covered, until well chilled—about 2 hours.

2. On large serving platter, mound pasta-vegetable salad. Slice turkey into ¼-inch-thick slices; arrange on top of salad. Spoon Tonnato Sauce over turkey; garnish with remaining anchovy fillets and capers. *Makes 8 servings.*

QUICK ZUPPA INGLESE
(pictured)

1 pkg (3 oz) ladyfingers
¼ cup Amaretto or almond-flavored
    liqueur
¼ cup chopped natural almonds
2 pkg (1-lb size) refrigerated ready-to-serve
    vanilla pudding (4 individual cups each)
Frozen whipped topping with real cream,
    thawed
10 whole natural almonds

1. Separate ladyfingers. Line bottom and side of 1½-quart bowl with ladyfingers, cut side up; brush with liqueur. Sprinkle bottom with 2 tablespoons chopped almonds. Top with contents of one package (4 individual cups) of pudding; sprinkle remaining chopped almonds over pudding. Top with remaining pudding. Cover; refrigerate several hours, or till chilled.

2. Before serving, spoon dollops of whipped topping onto pudding; garnish with whole almonds. *Makes 8 servings.*◆

ELEGANT DESSERTS

In Practically No Time

No, they weren't created by the local pastry chef, nor did they take hours of painstaking work. The four delectable desserts pictured here can all be prepared in 30 minutes or less (we tested them!) with the help of such ingredients as prepared cakes, canned fruit, preserves and ice cream. Party Fruit Kuchen starts with a cake layer that's topped with canned fruits, cherries and a sugar glaze, then studded with nuts. Molded Rice Custard uses precooked rice, pudding mix and peaches to concoct a quick-freeze delight. Chocolate-Raspberry Torte is four layers high and fabulously fast to prepare. Melted marshmallows and candy bars, whipped topping and a prepared graham cracker crust become a whimsical Candy-Bar Pie in minutes. For recipes, see page 192.

continued from page 191

PARTY FRUIT KUCHEN
(pictured)

1 can (17 oz) apricot halves
1 (9-inch) baker's sponge or yellow-cake layer (see Note)
6 large canned pear halves (16-oz size), drained
6 maraschino cherries
¼ cup (½ stick) butter or margarine
½ cup light-brown sugar, packed
½ cup walnuts or pecans, chopped
Whipped cream or whipped dessert topping in an aerosol can

1. Drain apricots, reserving liquid.
2. Place cake layer on serving plate. Prick surface with fork. Spoon ¼ cup reserved apricot liquid over cake.
3. Make pattern of fruit over top of cake, as pictured, alternating 1 pear half with 2 apricot halves in circle on cake. In center, place pear half. Reserve remaining fruit for another use. Decorate with cherries, as shown in photograph.
4. In small saucepan, melt butter; remove from heat; stir in the light-brown sugar.
5. Spread side of cake with ½ cup butter mixture; also fill in spaces between fruit around edge. Press nuts on side and edge.
6. To remaining butter mixture, add 2 tablespoons reserved liquid from apricots. Heat, stirring; pour evenly over cake. Serve with whipped cream. *Makes 8 to 10 servings.*

Note: Or use layer made from a cake mix.

MOLDED RICE CUSTARD
(pictured)

4 cups milk
¼ cup sugar
2 cups packaged precooked white rice
2 pkg (10-oz size) frozen sliced peaches (see Note)
1 pkg (3¼ oz) vanilla pudding and pie filling mix
⅓ cup orange juice or light rum
¼ cup apricot preserves
Crystallized violets or blueberries or slivered almonds

1. In large saucepan, combine 3 cups milk and the sugar. Bring to boiling; add rice. Mix with fork. Over low heat, cook rice, stirring occasionally with a fork, 8 minutes—no longer. Rice will absorb liquid if it stands.
2. Meanwhile, drain peaches, reserving liquid. In medium saucepan, combine pudding mix, ¾ cup reserved peach liquid and 1 cup milk; bring to boiling, stirring. Remove from heat and add ¼ cup orange juice.
3. Add ¾ cup vanilla pudding to rice along with 1 package peaches; mix well with fork. Turn into a mold or bowl about 5 inches in diameter and 4½ inches deep; do not pack. Place in freezer to chill quickly. Also, place rest of pudding in freezer to chill quickly—about 15 minutes.
4. Meanwhile, in small saucepan, melt apricot preserves with remaining orange juice. Add remaining peaches.
5. To serve: Turn rice out on serving platter. Pour chilled pudding over top and around bottom. Arrange peaches in preserves around edge. Decorate top with peaches and crystallized violets or blueberries or slivered almonds, as desired. *Makes 8 servings.*

Note: Use quick-thaw peaches; thaw as label directs while rice cooks.

CHOCOLATE-RASPBERRY TORTE
(pictured)

2 pkg (13¼-oz size) frozen frosted chocolate cake
Kirsch (optional)
¾ cup raspberry preserves
1 cup heavy cream, well chilled
2 tablespoons confectioners' sugar

1. Split each frozen cake in half to make 2 layers. (There will be 4 layers in all.)
2. On serving plate, place one layer, frosting side up. Next, top with unfrosted layer. Sprinkle with 2 tablespoons kirsch; then spread with half of raspberry preserves.
3. Top with another layer, frosting side up; then add unfrosted layer. Again, sprinkle with 2 tablespoons kirsch. Spread with rest of preserves.
4. With rotary beater, beat cream with sugar until stiff. Use to frost sides of cake all around; make a ½-inch border around top of cake. Serve at once or refrigerate until serving.
5. To serve: Cut cake in half lengthwise. Then cut each half into 1-inch slices. *Makes 12 to 14 servings.*

CANDY-BAR PIE
(pictured)

¾ cup milk
3 bars (3¾-oz size) milk chocolate with almonds, broken into pieces
30 regular-size marshmallows
2 cups nondairy frozen whipped topping
1 (9-inch) prepared graham cracker pie shell
Chocolate curls, optional

1. In medium saucepan, combine milk, milk chocolate and marshmallows. Cook, stirring, over low heat until chocolate and marshmallows are melted. Pour into a shallow pan; place in freezer to cool quickly—5 to 10 minutes.
2. Fold 1½ cups whipped topping into chocolate mixture until thoroughly combined. Turn into pie shell. Return pie to freezer 10 minutes to chill.
3. Spread remaining whipped topping over pie. Decorate with chocolate curls, if desired. Refrigerate if not serving at once. *Makes 8 servings.*

STRAWBERRY FANCY SHORTCAKE

2 pints fresh strawberries, washed and hulled
3 tablespoons currant jelly, melted
2 tablespoons confectioners' sugar
1 (1 lb, 1 oz) frozen, frosted 3-layer vanilla cake
½ cup heavy cream, whipped

1. Select 16 of the largest berries. Brush each with melted jelly; place them upright on a flat plate. Refrigerate. Slice rest of berries into bowl; toss lightly with sugar.
2. With sharp knife, cut through filling of frozen cake to separate into layers. Carefully lift off layers, placing bottom layer on serving plate.
3. Spread with half of whipped cream. Layer with half of sliced berries; repeat with second layer and remaining whipped cream and sliced berries.
4. Place top layer on top. Arrange whole berries on top in rows of four. Refrigerate until serving. *Makes 8 servings.*

CHOCOLATE-SUNDAE PIE

1 (8-inch size) frozen prepared pie shell
2 pints peppermint ice cream
1 cup canned chocolate syrup
Whipped cream in an aerosol can
Maraschino cherries with stems
1 cup broken walnuts

1. Preheat oven to 450F. Bake pie shell as package label directs. Cool on wire rack.
2. Meanwhile, make scoops of ice cream; freeze.
3. To serve: Fill shell with ice cream, mounding in center. Pour half of syrup over top.
4. Decorate with rosettes of whipped cream; place a cherry on each rosette. Sprinkle all over with nuts. Serve; pass rest of syrup. *Makes 6 servings.*

NEAPOLITAN ICE-CREAM CAKE

2 pkg (3-oz size) ladyfingers (about 24)
⅓ cup light rum
½ pint pistachio ice cream, slightly
    softened
1 pint strawberry ice cream, slightly
    softened
½ cup canned chocolate syrup

1. Sprinkle ladyfingers lightly with the rum. Line a mold about 6 inches in diameter and 5 inches deep with some of the ladyfingers.

2. Fill bottom with pistachio ice cream; cover with a layer of ladyfingers; add strawberry ice cream; top with remaining ladyfingers.

3. Place in freezer 20 minutes or until serving.

4. To serve: Unmold cake on platter; pour syrup over top. *Makes 6 to 8 servings.*

PINEAPPLE TIER CAKE

1 (9-inch) and 1 (8-inch) baker's sponge or
    yellow-cake layers (see Note)
1 can (1 lb, 4 oz) sliced pineapple
    (10 slices)
1 jar (12 oz) apricot preserves
1 cup heavy cream, whipped stiff, or 1 can
    (6¾ oz) whipped dessert topping in an
    aerosol can
10 whole strawberries, washed,
    hulls left on

1. Using sharp knife, trim 8-inch layer to measure 6½ inches across.

2. Drain pineapple, reserving liquid. Cut each slice in half crosswise.

3. In small saucepan, combine 2 tablespoons reserved pineapple juice with apricot preserves. Heat, stirring, until melted. Strain through small strainer.

4. On serving plate, place 9-inch cake layer; drizzle with 2 tablespoons pineapple liquid. Brush entire surface with apricot glaze.

5. Spread the center with ½ cup whipped cream, covering a 6½-inch round only. Place small cake layer on top; drizzle with 1 tablespoon pineapple liquid.

6. Brush entire cake with apricot glaze. Decorate with halved pineapple slices and strawberries.

7. With rest of whipped cream in a pastry bag with number-6 decorating tip or can of topping, make rosettes on cake. Refrigerate. *Makes 10 servings.*

Note: Or use layers made from a cake mix.

1-2-3 SOUFFLE

1 tablespoon butter
Granulated sugar
4 egg whites
Dash salt
1 jar (12-oz) apricot or cherry preserves
¼ cup slivered almonds
Confectioners' sugar
Whipped cream (optional)

1. Preheat oven to 400F. Lightly butter inside of a 1-quart soufflé dish; then sprinkle dish evenly with granulated sugar.

2. In medium bowl, with portable electric mixer at high speed, beat the egg whites with a dash of salt until foamy. Add 1 tablespoon granulated sugar; continue beating until stiff peaks form when the beaters are slowly raised.

3. With rubber spatula or wire whisk, gently fold preserves into egg whites just until combined. Turn into soufflé dish. Sprinkle top with slivered almonds. Bake 20 minutes, or until golden.

4. To serve: Sift a little confectioners' sugar over the top of the soufflé. Serve soufflé with whipped cream, if desired. *Makes 6 servings.*

EASY PEAR TRIFLE

1 pkg (3 oz) egg-custard mix
1¾ cups milk
2 cups vanilla wafers, quartered
⅓ cup orange juice or sherry
1 can (1 lb, 1 oz) pear halves, drained
½ cup frozen dessert topping

1. Make egg custard, following package directions, with 1¾ cups milk. Remove from heat; refrigerate.

2. In small bowl, toss vanilla wafers with orange juice. Remove ½ cup of the mixture.

3. With remaining cookie mixture, line bottom of 1½-quart serving dish.

4. Arrange pear halves over crumbs; spoon custard over pears. Sprinkle surface with reserved ½ cup crumbs.

5. Place in freezer to chill quickly—10 to 15 minutes. Before serving, decorate with topping. *Makes 6 servings.* ◆

continued from page 178

of packet; fold down loosely in two or three ½-inch folds, allowing for heat circulation and expansion. Roll ends up and over again; crimp to seal.

3. Grill foil pan, 6 inches above medium-low coals, 20 minutes, or bake 20 to 25 minutes in oven, till vegetables are tender, stirring once. If grilling foil packet, grill, 4 inches above medium-hot coals, 10 minutes; turn packet; cook 10 to 15 minutes more, or until vegetables are tender.

4. To cook steak: Grill, 4 inches above medium-low coals, 10 minutes, turning once. Or turn oven to broil; place steak on broiler pan. Broil, 4 inches from heat, 10 minutes, turning once. To serve: Remove steak to board. Slice very thinly across the grain, if possible. Serve with vegetables. *Makes 4 servings.*

Note: To cook vegetables in microwave oven, place with pizza sauce in 8 by-8-by-1⁹⁄₁₆-inch disposable paper pan. Cover tightly with plastic wrap; turn back one corner to vent. Microwave at HIGH 5 minutes; turn pan a quarter turn; microwave at HIGH 5 minutes more; turn pan a quarter turn; microwave at HIGH 4 minutes longer, or until peppers are done.

BARBECUED CHEESE-FRANK KEBABS

10 (8- or 10-inch) bamboo skewers
1 pkg (1 lb) cheese frankfurters
1 small (4 oz) zucchini
1 small (4 oz) yellow squash
1 jar (14 oz) whole onions, drained
½ cup bottled barbecue sauce
2 (12-by-9-inch) disposable aluminum-foil
    broiler pans (optional)

1. In a pan of cold water, soak bamboo skewers at least 15 minutes to keep them from charring. Meanwhile, cut frankfurters crosswise in thirds; cut zucchini and yellow squash into ¼-inch slices.

2. Drain skewers; alternately thread frankfurters with zucchini, yellow squash and onions on each skewer.

3. Prepare outdoor grill for barbecuing, or preheat indoor grill or broiler. Brush kebabs with barbecue sauce. Grill kebabs, 4 inches above medium coals, 12 to 15 minutes, turning once or twice and brushing generously with barbecue sauce. Or place 5 kebabs on each disposable broiler pan. Broil, 6 inches from heat, 8 minutes. Turn kebabs, and brush with remaining barbecue sauce; broil 5 minutes longer, or until vegetables are fork-tender. (If necessary, broil one pan of kebabs at a time; cover, and keep warm while broiling second pan.) *Makes 10 kebabs.* ◆

SIX

30-MINUTE MEALS

What can you accomplish in a mere 30 minutes? Well, you can read a section of the newspaper, watch a television program or, would you believe it, create a scrumptious home-cooked meal from start to finish! No, you don't have to prepare anything ahead of time, nor do you have to tear around the kitchen at a frantic, fast-forward pace. All you need do is turn the pages to uncover the secret of more than 30 "half-hour menus." There are marvelous meals to enjoy year round, including tempting international favorites, bountiful brunches, elegant dinners for company or just for two and festive holiday fare. From appetizer through dessert, each menu includes a list of all necessary ingredients plus a simple step-by-step preparation schedule that allows you to squeeze every minute out of that precious half hour. Plan to include at least one of these timesaving meals in your busy week—because you never know when 30 minutes is all you can spare!

MENU

A Sunday Dinner

(Planned for Four to Six)

**CHICKEN SAUTE WITH
FRESH-TOMATO SAUCE**

PARMESAN POLENTA

**ROMAINE AND CUCUMBER
SALAD**

**CRUSTY HARD ROLLS
BUTTER**

**PEACH SHORTCAKE
IN A BOWL**

ICED COFFEE OR TEA

YOU WILL NEED:
1 tablespoon butter for cooking, plus ¼ lb
 (1 stick) for serving
3 skinless, boneless chicken breasts,
 halved
1 large onion
1½ lb fresh plum tomatoes
4 or 5 fresh ripe peaches
2 tablespoons granulated sugar
1 tablespoon lemon juice
½ teaspoon dried basil leaves
¼ teaspoon dried oregano leaves
1½ teaspoons salt
2¼ cups water
½ pint heavy cream
2 tablespoons confectioners' sugar
½ teaspoon vanilla extract
1 pkg (3 oz) ladyfingers
1 tablespoon chopped walnuts or pecans
1 cup yellow cornmeal
1 head romaine, washed and crisped
1 large cucumber
Prepared salad dressing
6 tablespoons (1½ oz) grated Parmesan
 cheese
1 tablespoon all-purpose flour
4 to 6 hard rolls
Coffee, instant or brewed
Tea (optional)
Cream, sugar, lemon (optional)

6:00 to 6:10 P.M.

1. Melt 1 tablespoon butter in a very large skillet. Brown chicken breast halves 5 minutes on each side.

2. Peel and thinly slice onion. Wash tomatoes, and cut into eighths.

3. Peel and slice peaches into small bowl. Add granulated sugar and lemon juice. Toss. Set aside.

6:10 to 6:20 P.M.

1. Add onion, tomatoes, basil, oregano and 1 teaspoon of the salt to chicken. Simmer, covered, until chicken is tender—about 15 minutes.

2. Bring 2 cups of water to boiling in medium saucepan.

3. Whip heavy cream with confectioners' sugar and vanilla. Drain juice from the peaches; drizzle some over ladyfingers. Set aside several peach slices for garnish.

4. In 1-quart serving bowl, layer half of peaches, then half of ladyfingers; top with half of cream. Repeat layering remaining peaches, ladyfingers and cream. Garnish with reserved peach slices. Sprinkle with chopped nuts; place in freezer until serving.

5. Add ½ teaspoon salt to the boiling water. Very slowly add the cornmeal, stirring constantly. Cook over low heat,

stirring until thick—5 minutes. Lightly oil a 1-quart mold for the polenta.

6:20 to 6:30 P.M.

1. Break the romaine into large pieces; arrange around edge of salad bowl. Wash and slice cucumber; place in center of salad. Serve with prepared dressing.

2. Stir ¼ cup of the Parmesan cheese into polenta; turn into prepared mold. Let stand 1 minute; unmold onto platter. Sprinkle with remaining Parmesan.

3. Arrange the chicken around polenta. Stir the flour in ¼ cup water to dissolve. Stir into simmering tomato mixture; cook until thick. Spoon over chicken.

MENU

A Company Brunch
(Planned for Six)

ASPARAGUS FRITTATA

WINTER FRUIT SALAD

WARM CROISSANTS

MILK   CINNAMON CAFE

YOU WILL NEED:
1 medium-size red pepper
¼ lb fresh mushrooms
1 pkg (10 oz) frozen asparagus spears,
   thawed
2 tablespoons butter or margarine for
   cooking, plus ¼ lb (1 stick) for serving
½ cup frozen chopped onion
8 eggs
1 cup milk
1 pkg (4 oz) shredded mozzarella cheese
½ teaspoon dried basil leaves
½ teaspoon salt
Dash pepper
1 head romaine, washed and crisped
2 oranges
1 can (1 lb, 13 oz) pear halves, drained
2 pkg (5½-oz size) frozen croissants
12 tablespoons (¾ cup) Benedictine
   liqueur
6 long cinnamon sticks
6 cups freshly brewed coffee
Cream and sugar (optional)
Milk (optional)
Prepared salad dressing

12:00 to 12:10 P.M.

1. Preheat oven to 375F. Wash red pepper; remove stem, seeds and ribs. Slice red pepper and mushrooms into ¼-inch-thick slices. Keep four asparagus spears whole; cut remaining spears crosswise into thirds.

2. Melt butter in 12-inch ovenproof skillet. Over medium heat, sauté red pepper, mushrooms, asparagus and onion 3 minutes, or until vegetables are tender.

3. In medium bowl, combine eggs, milk, cheese, basil, salt and pepper; mix well. Remove the four whole asparagus spears and five of the red-pepper strips from skillet; keep warm.

12:10 to 12:20 P.M.

1. Pour egg mixture into hot skillet; bake frittata about 20 minutes, or until mixture is set.

2. Line salad bowl with large romaine leaves; tear remaining romaine into bite-size pieces in bowl. Cut rind from oranges; cut oranges into ¼-inch-thick slices. Arrange oranges and pears over lettuce, as pictured; refrigerate.

12:20 to 12:30 P.M.

1. Place croissants on a cookie sheet; warm on bottom shelf of oven, along with frittata, 10 minutes. Spoon 2 table-

spoons liqueur into each of six mugs; add a cinnamon stick to each.

2. Remove frittata from oven; garnish with reserved vegetables, as pictured; place on trivet on table. Remove croissants from oven, and arrange in basket. Fill mugs with hot coffee; stir with cinnamon stick. Serve with cream and sugar, if desired. Pass dressing with fruit salad.

MENU

A Minute-Steak Dinner
(Planned for Four)

SHRIMP-AND-TOMATO SOUP

STEAK DIANE

FRENCH-FRIED POTATOES

LEMON-BUTTERED BRUSSELS SPROUTS

HOT ROLLS

MOCHA CAKE

BEER   COFFEE

YOU WILL NEED:
1 (13¼ oz) frozen frosted chocolate cake
1 teaspoon unseasoned meat tenderizer
1 tablespoon dry mustard
½ teaspoon pepper
4 cube or minute steaks, ½ inch thick (1½ lbs)
1 pkg (16 oz) or 2 pkg (7-oz size) frozen crinkle-cut French-fried potatoes
1 cup heavy cream
¼ cup confectioners' sugar
1 tablespoon instant coffee
½ teaspoon vanilla extract
1 can (10¾ oz) condensed cream of shrimp soup
1 can (8¼ oz) tomatoes, undrained
¼ cup dry sherry
½ cup evaporated milk
2 pkg (10-oz size) frozen brussels sprouts
1 pkg (7½ oz) rolls
6 tablespoons butter for cooking, plus ¼ lb (1 stick) for serving
3 tablespoons Worcestershire sauce
Salt
2 tablespoons lemon juice
Beer (optional)
Coffee, instant or brewed
Cream, sugar (optional)
Chopped parsley

6:00 to 6:10 P.M.

1. Preheat oven to 450F.

2. Remove frozen cake from package to thaw.

3. Combine meat tenderizer, dry mustard and pepper; mix well. Sprinkle evenly over both sides of steaks (placed on waxed paper), patting mixture gently into meat.

4. Spread frozen French fries in single layer on cookie sheet or shallow pan. Place in 450F oven 18 to 20 minutes, or until crisp.

6:10 to 6:20 P.M.

1. In a medium bowl, combine heavy cream, confectioners' sugar, instant coffee and vanilla extract. With rotary beater, beat until cream is stiff enough to hold its shape. Spread on top of cake, making swirls. Cut into 8 squares.

2. In a medium saucepan, combine shrimp soup, tomatoes, sherry and evaporated milk. Place over low heat; stir occasionally.

6:20 to 6:30 P.M.

1. Cook brussels sprouts as package label directs.

2. Heat rolls, wrapped in foil, in oven with potatoes.

3. In large skillet, in ¼ cup (½ stick) hot butter, sauté steaks until browned, about 2 minutes. Turn steaks; sauté un-

til browned; sprinkle with Worcestershire sauce; cook 1 or 2 minutes longer, or until done. Arrange at one end of platter.

4. Place potatoes on same platter; sprinkle with salt.

5. Drain brussels sprouts; squeeze lemon juice over top; dot with remaining 2 tablespoons butter. Keep platter warm.

6. Make coffee. Sprinkle soup with chopped parsley.

MENU

Sweet-And-Sour Shrimp
(Planned for Four)

**SWEET-AND-SOUR
SHRIMP IN
PINEAPPLE SHELLS**

CURRIED RICE

**CHINESE-STYLE
PEA PODS**

AVOCADO SALAD BOWL

HOT BUTTERED ROLLS

**CHOCOLATE-CHIP
PARFAITS**

ICED COFFEE OR TEA

YOU WILL NEED:
1 pint chocolate-chip ice cream
1 pkg (6 oz) curried-rice mix
Water
4 tablespoons butter for cooking, plus
⅟₄ lb (1 stick) for serving
4 cups salad greens, washed and crisped
1 large ripe avocado
¼ cup green crème de menthe
1 medium-size (3½ lb) ripe pineapple
1 medium green pepper
1 medium onion
1 pkg (7½ oz) poppy-seed rolls
1 lb shrimp, shelled and deveined
2 pkg (10-oz size) Chinese pea pods
½ cup apricot preserves
1 tablespoon cider vinegar
1 tablespoon soy sauce
½ teaspoon ground ginger
Prepared Italian-style salad dressing
Iced coffee or tea
Cream, sugar, lemon (optional)

6:00 to 6:10 P.M.

1. Remove ice cream from freezer to soften slightly.

2. In medium saucepan with tight-fitting cover, cook rice with water and butter as label directs.

3. Tear salad greens into salad bowl. Peel and slice avocado ½ inch thick; cut slices in half. Add to salad greens; refrigerate, tightly covered.

4. Swirl crème de menthe into ice cream. Spoon into serving dishes. Return to freezer.

6:10 to 6:20 P.M.

1. Preheat oven to 300F. With sharp knife, cut pineapple in half lengthwise, right through frond. Cut pineapple from shells in one piece, leaving ½-inch-thick shells. Remove and discard core; cut pineapple into bite-size chunks. Thinly slice green pepper and onion.

2. Arrange the pineapple shells on heatproof platter; place in oven to heat.

3. Wrap rolls in foil; place in oven to heat.

6:20 to 6:30 P.M.

1. In 2 tablespoons hot butter in large skillet, sauté shrimp and onion together about 5 minutes, stirring. Add pineapple and green pepper; cook, stirring occasionally, several minutes until pepper is crisp-tender.

2. In medium saucepan, cook pea pods as label directs.

3. In measuring cup, combine apricot preserves, vinegar, soy sauce and ginger; mix well. Pour over shrimp mixture; cook, stirring, several minutes; green pepper should be tender. Spoon into pineapple shells.

4. Drain pea pods; add 1 tablespoon butter. Toss salad with ⅓ cup salad dressing. Place warm rolls in a basket.

MENU

Greek-Style Dinner
(Planned for Four)

DILL CHICKEN ROLLS

AVGOLEMONO SAUCE

PARSLEYED RICE

GREEK SALAD

YOGURT 'N' HONEY PARFAITS

CHILLED WHITE WINE

COFFEE

GEORGE RATKAI

YOU WILL NEED:
1 can (10¾ oz) condensed chicken broth
3 cups water
1½ cups long-grain white rice
2 tablespoons lemon juice
½ teaspoon salt
½ teaspoon dried dillweed
White pepper
4 skinless, boneless, chicken breast halves
½ cup crumbled shredded-wheat biscuits
¼ cup honey
2 cups vanilla yogurt
1 medium tomato
1 small red onion
½ head romaine, washed and crisped
½ cup feta cheese, crumbled
½ cup black olives
Prepared oil-and-vinegar dressing
¼ cup chopped parsley
1 egg
1 tablespoon all-purpose flour
Lemon slice (optional)
Fresh dill (optional)
Coffee, instant or brewed
Cream and sugar (optional)
Chilled white wine

6:00 to 6:10 P.M.

1. Bring chicken broth and 2 cups of the water to boiling in medium saucepan; stir in rice. Reduce heat; simmer, covered, 20 minutes.

2. In medium skillet, bring 1 cup water, the lemon juice and salt to boiling. Sprinkle dillweed and a dash of pepper over each chicken cutlet. Roll each cutlet from narrow end; secure with toothpicks. Place chicken rolls in boiling water; reduce heat; simmer, covered, 15 minutes, just until chicken is firm and tender.

6:10 to 6:20 P.M.

1. Place 2 tablespoons each crumbled shredded-wheat biscuits into four parfait glasses; drizzle each with 1 tablespoon honey; top each with ½ cup yogurt. Refrigerate parfaits until dessert time.

2. Wash and slice tomato; cut slices in half. Peel and slice red onion; set aside. Break romaine into salad bowl; top with crumbled feta cheese, black olives and sliced red onion; refrigerate. At serving time, toss with prepared dressing.

6:20 to 6:30 P.M.

1. Fluff up rice with fork; stir in chopped parsley. Spoon onto serving platter. Remove chicken rolls from liquid; reserve broth. Arrange chicken rolls on the parsleyed rice.

2. Beat egg with flour in small saucepan. Slowly pour in ¾ cup reserved broth. Stir over medium heat until the mixture is slightly thickened.

3. Arrange the tomato slices around rice. Spoon some sauce over chicken rolls; pass remaining sauce. Garnish with lemon slice and dill, if desired.

A Taste of Tuscany
(Planned for Four)

TUSCAN SUMMER SALAD
WARM ITALIAN ROLLS
STRAWBERRY SHORTCAKE
ICED ESPRESSO
WHITE WINE

YOU WILL NEED:
1 cup packaged biscuit mix
Granulated sugar
1 teaspoon vanilla extract
⅓ cup milk
1 lb green beans
¼ cup tarragon wine vinegar
¼ cup lemon juice
½ cup olive oil
¼ teaspoon dried tarragon leaves
½ teaspoon salt
1 garlic clove, pressed
¼ lb medium mushrooms
¼ cup black olives
1 lemon
¼ lb Brie
½ lb Swiss cheese
1 pint fresh strawberries
1 pkg already-baked Italian rolls
¼ lb (1 stick) butter for serving (optional)
1 head Boston lettuce, washed and crisped
1 head radicchio (if unavailable, use more
   lettuce)
½ pint heavy cream (optional)
Espresso coffee, instant or brewed
Cream and sugar (optional)
Chilled white wine

6:00 to 6:10 P.M.
1. Preheat oven to 375F. Grease and flour 4 sculptured or regular muffin cups.
2. In a medium bowl, combine biscuit mix, ¼ cup sugar, vanilla and milk. Stir together until just combined. Spoon into muffin cups. Bake 15 to 20 minutes, or until the centers spring back when gently pressed.
3. Bring 1 cup water to boiling in a medium saucepan. Remove stem ends of beans; wash thoroughly. Simmer, covered, 8 to 10 minutes.

6:10 to 6:20 P.M.
1. In a large bowl, combine tarragon wine vinegar, lemon juice, olive oil, tarragon, salt, ½ teaspoon sugar and garlic.
2. Wash and slice mushrooms. Add to the dressing along with ¼ cup black olives. Make four thin slices of lemon. Cut into quarters. Add to dressing.
3. Drain beans thoroughly; cut cheeses into ½-inch cubes. Add both to dressing. Toss until well coated.

6:20 to 6:30 P.M.
1. Wash and set aside four unhulled strawberries. Wash remaining strawberries; remove hulls. Slice into a medium bowl, and toss with 2 tablespoons sugar. Turn off oven; remove cakes. Set rolls in oven to warm.
2. Line sides of a large salad bowl

with Boston lettuce and radicchio. Break remaining lettuce and radicchio into bottom of bowl. Toss vegetables in dressing again; then turn into center of salad greens.
3. Remove shortcakes from pans. Split ¾ of the way through the centers. Place on serving plates. Spoon strawberries in center and over top of cakes. Garnish each with a whole strawberry. Serve with whipped cream, if desired.

MENU

A Family Favorite

(Planned for Four)

PORK CHOPS WITH APPLE-CRANBERRY SAUCE

CARROT-CUCUMBER SALAD

CARAWAY-RYE BREAD

CHOCOLATE-ALMOND CREAM

CHILLED BEER

SPICY APPLE CIDER
(for the children)

The falling leaves of autumn bring thoughts of picking apples, brisk walks in the woods and cozy evenings by the fireplace. You certainly won't want to spend hours in the kitchen, so we've planned this dinner just for you — all to be prepared in just 30 minutes!

YOU WILL NEED:
2 env unflavored gelatine
1½ cups milk
¾ cup heavy cream
½ cup semisweet chocolate pieces
¼ cup granulated sugar
½ teaspoon almond extract
1½ cups ice cubes (10 to 12)
1 pkg (3 oz) ladyfingers
8 romaine lettuce leaves, washed and crisped
2 cucumbers
2 carrots
4 rib pork chops, cut ½-inch thick (1 lb)
½ teaspoon powdered sage
½ teaspoon salt
Dash ground pepper
1 teaspoon vegetable oil
1 cup apple cider or juice
½ cup whole-berry cranberry sauce
2 tablespoons light-brown sugar, packed to measure, mixed with 1 tablespoon cornstarch

1 red cooking apple, cored and cut into 16 wedges
Parsley sprig (optional)
Bottled salad dressing of your choice
Caraway-rye bread, bought at the market
¼ lb (1 stick) butter for serving
Cold beer
2 cups apple cider or juice
2 cinnamon sticks
2 whole allspice
2 whole cloves

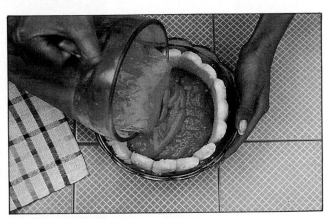

1. Prepare Chocolate-Almond Cream: In blender container, sprinkle gelatine over ½ cup cold milk. Bring 1 cup milk to a boil; add to softened gelatine and process at low speed 1 minute. Add heavy cream, chocolate, sugar and almond extract; process at high speed 1 minute.

2. Add ice cubes to chocolate mixture, 1 at a time; process at high speed until dissolved. Line a 1½-quart glass serving bowl with ladyfingers; pour in chocolate mixture; cover and refrigerate. (Before serving, garnish with more chocolate pieces, if desired.)

3. Make Salad: Arrange romaine lettuce on a salad plate. Wash cucumbers; score lengthwise with the tines of a fork; slice thinly. Arrange cucumbers in a circular pattern on lettuce. Pare and coarsely shred carrots; mound in center of cucumbers; cover and refrigerate.

4. Sprinkle pork chops with sage, salt and pepper. Heat oil in a medium-sized skillet over medium-high heat; sauté chops 5 to 7 minutes on each side. While chops cook, make Sauce: In a small saucepan, gradually stir 1 cup apple cider and cranberry sauce into sugar-cornstarch mixture.

5. Bring to a boil over moderately high heat; add apple wedges and simmer, uncovered, 2 to 3 minutes or until apples are tender. Arrange pork chops on a serving platter and spoon Apple-Cranberry Sauce over the chops. Garnish with a sprig of parsley, if desired.

6. Pour salad dressing over cucumber salad. Serve with chops, sauce, caraway-rye bread and frosty mugs of cold beer. For the children, heat 2 cups apple cider with cinnamon, allspice and cloves; serve in mugs. For dessert, serve the Chocolate-Almond Cream.

DAVID VIENS

MENU

A Salad Supper On the Terrace
(Planned for Four)

GARDEN PASTA SALAD
PARMESAN-CHEESE BREAD
POUNDCAKE A LA MODE
RED WINE   COFFEE

GEORGE RATKAI

YOU WILL NEED:
Salt
1 head broccoli
1 large carrot
1 medium zucchini
1 medium yellow squash
1 large red pepper
1 medium red onion
2 pkg (8-oz size) cavatelli
Salad oil
1 cup prepared Italian salad dressing
1 loaf Italian bread
½ cup grated Parmesan cheese
1 pkg (12¾ oz) chocolate-chip poundcake
¼ cup prepared fudge topping
1 pint vanilla ice cream
Red wine
Coffee, instant or brewed
Cream and sugar (optional)

6:00 to 6:10 P.M.

1. In large kettle, bring 6 quarts salted water to boiling. Wash broccoli; cut into flowerets. Wash and pare carrot; wash zucchini, yellow squash and red pepper. Cut these vegetables into julienne strips. Peel and thinly slice red onion.

2. Place cavatelli in boiling water. Cook as package label directs. Preheat broiler.

6:10 to 6:20 P.M.

1. Heat 2 tablespoons oil in a large skillet. Add broccoli and carrot; stir-fry 3 minutes. Add zucchini, yellow squash and red pepper to skillet; stir-fry 2 minutes. Remove to medium bowl; add sliced red onion and ½ cup salad dressing. Place in freezer.

2. Drain cavatelli; toss with remaining salad dressing. Turn onto platter; place in freezer. Split bread; brush with ¼ cup oil. Sprinkle with Parmesan cheese.

6:20 to 6:30 P.M.

1. Cut poundcake into ½-inch-thick slices. Place on individual dessert plates; set aside until dessert time.

2. Place bread in broiler, 6 inches from heat, about 3 to 5 minutes, or until cheese is golden. In small saucepan, over medium heat, warm fudge topping. Place

bread in basket. Remove cavatelli and vegetables from freezer. Top cavatelli with vegetables; toss before serving. Make coffee.

3. At dessert time, place 1 scoop ice cream on each slice of poundcake; top with 1 tablespoon hot fudge topping.

MENU

Microwave Dinner
(Planned for Two)

GLAZED CORNISH HENS

CORNBREAD STUFFING

HONEYED BABY CARROTS

LETTUCE WEDGES

PEARS AND STRAWBERRY SAUCE

WHITE WINE   COFFEE

YOU WILL NEED:

2 (1-lb size) Cornish hens, thawed if frozen
1 pkg (10 oz) frozen cornbread stuffing in a
   pouch
1 pkg (10 oz) frozen baby carrots
½ small head iceberg lettuce
2 large radishes
1 medium pear
½ cup water
1 tablespoon lemon juice
1 pkg (10 oz) frozen quick-thaw
   strawberries in syrup, thawed
2 tablespoons cornstarch
2 tablespoons teriyaki sauce
¼ cup water
1 tablespoon butter
1 tablespoon honey
Prepared creamy salad dressing
Parsley
Mint (optional)
White wine
Coffee, instant or brewed
Cream and sugar (optional)

6:00 to 6:10 P.M.

1. Before starting, see Note. Place Cornish hens, breast sides down, in a small baking dish; cover with waxed-paper tent. Microwave 6 minutes. Slit stuffing pouch open. Place carrots in bowl; cover with waxed paper.

2. Cut the lettuce into two wedges, and refrigerate on small plates. Cut each radish into eight wedges without cutting through; place in ice water.

6:10 to 6:20 P.M.

1. Turn hens breast sides up; microwave 6 minutes more. Halve pear lengthwise; core; place in pie plate, cut sides up. Combine ¼ cup of the water and lemon juice; pour over halves. Cover with waxed paper.

2. In bowl, mix strawberries, their syrup and 1 tablespoon cornstarch. Remove hens from oven; place on serving platter; cover. Microwave stuffing and carrots 3 minutes.

3. Strain pan juices from hens into saucepan; blend in remaining tablespoon cornstarch, the teriyaki sauce and ¼ cup water. Cook over medium heat, stirring, until thickened. Keep warm.

6:20 to 6:30 P.M.

1. Drain carrots of all liquid; stir in butter and honey. Return to oven; microwave carrots and stuffing 2 minutes more. Remove; keep warm. Microwave the pear halves and strawberry sauce 5 minutes, stirring strawberry sauce once. Let stand, covered.

2. Garnish lettuce with radishes; top with creamy dressing. Spoon stuffing into a dish. Arrange carrots around hens; garnish with parsley. Pour some teriyaki glaze over hens; pass remainder. At dessert time, serve pear halves with some sauce over each; if desired, garnish with mint. Refrigerate leftover strawberry sauce to use on ice cream or cake another time.

Note: With this microwave menu, cook foods in microwave cookware on HIGH power.

MENU

An Old-Fashioned Meal
(Planned for Four or Five)

QUICK BEEF STEW WITH BISCUITS

GREEN SALAD WITH CHERRY TOMATOES

LEMON-FILLED POUNDCAKE

CIDER

COFFEE   TEA

YOU WILL NEED:
1 pkg (10¾ oz) frozen poundcake
1 lb lean ground beef
½ teaspoon salt
¼ teaspoon ground allspice
½ teaspoon dried thyme leaves
⅛ teaspoon pepper
1 bag (24 oz) frozen vegetables for stew
1 tablespoon salad oil
½ pint cherry tomatoes
4 to 5 cups mixed salad greens, washed and crisped
1 medium-size red pepper
1 can (10¾ oz) condensed cream of mushroom soup
1 can (10½ oz) condensed beef broth
1 pkg (10 oz) refrigerated biscuits
½ cup heavy cream
1 tablespoon confectioners' sugar
1 can (1 lb, 5 oz) lemon pudding and pie filling
2 teaspoons freshly grated lemon peel (optional)
1 tablespoon chopped chives or parsley
Prepared salad dressing
Cider
Coffee, instant or brewed
Tea (optional)
Cream, sugar, lemon (optional)

6:00 to 6:10 P.M.

1. Remove frozen cake from package to thaw.

2. Bring 2 cups water to boiling in a medium saucepan.

3. Toss together ground beef, salt, allspice, ¼ teaspoon of the thyme and the pepper. Shape into a 5-inch square, and cut into 16 cubes. Preheat oven to 400F.

4. Add vegetables to boiling water. Bring back to boiling; boil, uncovered, 18 minutes, or until tender.

5. Heat the oil in large skillet; add beef cubes; sauté on all sides.

6. Wash and halve cherry tomatoes. Add to greens in bowl; refrigerate.

6:10 to 6:20 P.M.

1. Wash and slice red pepper. Add pepper strips to ground-beef cubes; sauté 5 minutes. Add mushroom soup, beef broth and remaining ¼ teaspoon thyme. Mix well. Bring to boiling; then reduce heat, and simmer, uncovered, 10 minutes.

2. Separate biscuits; cut each in half crosswise. Arrange on ungreased baking sheet. Bake until they are golden—10 minutes.

3. Beat cream with confectioners' sugar. Fold ¼ cup of sweetened whipped cream into half of lemon filling. (Refrig-

erate other half of filling for use another time.)

6:20 to 6:30 P.M.

1. Split poundcake into three layers. Place bottom on serving plate; spread with ¼ cup lemon mixture. Add the middle cake layer; spread with ¼ cup lemon mixture, and top with remaining cake layer. Frost sides of cake with remaining lemon mixture. Swirl remaining whipped cream on top. If desired, sprinkle top with lemon peel. Refrigerate until serving.

2. Drain vegetables, and fold into beef mixture; turn into a casserole. Arrange biscuits around edge, as pictured; sprinkle with chives.

3. At serving time, pass bottled dressing with salad.

MENU

A Pretty Patio Supper
(Planned for Four or Five)

SPINACH-AND-CHEESE-FILLED CREPES

BROILED TOMATOES

LEAF LETTUCE SALAD WITH BLACK OLIVES

BREADSTICKS

STRAWBERRY SORBET

VANILLA COOKIES

COFFEE　　TEA

CHILLED WHITE WINE

YOU WILL NEED:
1 pint lemon sherbet
1 pkg (10 oz) frozen chopped spinach
1 pint fresh strawberries
1 cup milk
⅔ cup all-purpose flour
2 eggs
1 teaspoon salt
3 teaspoons butter
4 tablespoons grated Parmesan cheese
1 pkg (16 oz) small-curd cottage cheese
¾ teaspoon dried basil leaves
1 pkg (8 oz) sliced Swiss cheese
3 large tomatoes
¼ teaspoon dried thyme leaves
1 lb leaf lettuce, washed and crisped
1 can (8 oz) pitted black olives
Prepared salad dressing
1 pkg (5½ oz) breadsticks
1 pkg (9½ oz) brown-edge cookies
Coffee, instant or brewed
Tea (optional)
Cream, sugar, lemon (optional)
Chilled white wine

6:00 to 6:10 P.M.

1. Soften sherbet. Bring ½ cup water to boiling in medium saucepan. Add spinach; cook as label directs.

2. Wash, hull strawberries; reserve one berry for each serving. Blend rest of berries in blender with sherbet until crushed. Pour into an 8- or 9-inch square pan; freeze.

3. Preheat oven to 450F. Place a 15½-by-10½-by-½-inch baking pan in oven to heat. Blend milk, flour, 2 eggs and ¼ teaspoon of the salt in blender until smooth.

4. Remove the pan from oven; brush with 2 teaspoons of the butter. Add half the batter; tip pan to cover evenly. Bake until crêpe is golden at edges and firm—5 to 7 minutes.

6:10 to 6:20 P.M.

1. Sprinkle 17-inch sheet of waxed paper with 2 tablespoons of the Parmesan cheese. Drain spinach. In a small saucepan, heat cottage cheese over very low heat.

2. Remove crêpe from oven; loosen edge and turn out onto Parmesan cheese. Butter hot pan with remaining teaspoon butter. Pour on remaining batter, tipping to cover pan. Bake as above.

3. Stir ½ teaspoon of the basil and ¼ teaspoon salt into very well drained spinach. Spread evenly over crêpe. Top with Swiss cheese.

6:20 to 6:30 P.M.

1. Wash and quarter tomatoes; remove stem ends. Sprinkle with remaining ½ teaspoon salt and thyme.

2. Drain cottage cheese. Turn second crêpe out onto spinach-cheese layer. Reset oven to broil. Spread cottage cheese on crêpe, sprinkle with remaining ¼ teaspoon basil and 2 tablespoons Parmesan. Roll from short end, and place on heatproof platter. Arrange tomatoes around it. Broil, 6 inches from heat, until golden and tomatoes are just hot—about 5 minutes.

3. Break lettuce into salad bowl. Drain olives; place on lettuce. Pass dressing.

4. Scoop sorbet into dishes. Top with berry.

MENU

A Turkey Surprise
(Planned for Two)

CRANBERRY COCKTAIL

TURKEY-DIVAN-AND-
HOT-HERBED-BISCUIT
CASSEROLE

SALAD BOWL FOR TWO

FRESH-ORANGE SUNDAES

COFFEE   TEA
CHILLED WHITE WINE

YOU WILL NEED:
¾ cup biscuit mix
½ teaspoon dried basil leaves
½ teaspoon dried thyme leaves
1 tablespoon salad oil
About ¾ cup half-and-half
1 egg yolk
½ head Boston lettuce, washed and
    crisped
1 medium tomato
Cracked pepper
Prepared salad dressing
1 pint vanilla ice cream
¼ bunch broccoli (6 oz)
⅛ lb medium mushrooms
2 tablespoons butter
2 tablespoons all-purpose flour
½ cup turkey or chicken broth
¼ cup white wine
1 cup leftover cut-up turkey
2 medium navel oranges
½ cup orange marmalade
1 tablespoon orange juice
Cranberry cocktail, chilled
Coffee, instant or brewed
Tea (optional)
Cream, sugar, lemon (optional)
Chilled white wine

6:00 to 6:10 P.M.

1. Preheat oven to 450F. Butter a 3-cup round casserole. In small bowl, combine biscuit mix, ¼ teaspoon basil and ¼ teaspoon thyme; mix well. Add 1 tablespoon oil and 3 tablespoons half-and-half; stir just until moistened. Spoon onto ungreased cookie sheet, to make a 5-inch biscuit with a 1-inch hole in center.

2. Beat egg yolk slightly; brush over biscuit. Bake 8 to 10 minutes.

3. Break lettuce into small salad bowl. Wash tomato; cut into wedges. Sprinkle with cracked pepper; add to lettuce. Toss with dressing at serving time.

6:10 to 6:20 P.M.

1. Set ice cream out to soften. In a small saucepan, bring 1 cup water to boiling. Wash broccoli; divide into flowerets. Pare and slice stem (you should have ¾ cup). Cook broccoli until just tender—5 minutes. Drain well.

2. Wash and quarter mushrooms. Sauté in butter in a heavy saucepan; stir in flour until lightly browned. Remove from heat. Gradually stir in turkey broth, white wine, ½ cup half-and-half, ¼ teaspoon each of basil and thyme.

3. Cook mushroom mixture until thickened. Fold in turkey, and simmer 5 minutes.

6:20 to 6:30 P.M.

1. Wash oranges; cut into wedges, leaving them attached at bottom. Carefully peel skin from oranges almost to bottom. Place oranges on dessert plates.

2. Push the wedges apart slightly, and place a 2¼-inch ball of ice cream in the center of each. Place in freezer until dessert time—not more than ½ hour.

3. Fold broccoli into turkey mixture. Turn into casserole; top with biscuit ring.

4. Combine ½ cup orange marmalade and 1 tablespoon orange juice. Pour over dessert before serving.

Dinner
En Brochette
(Dinner for Two)

**LAMB AND ZUCCHINI
EN BROCHETTE**

HERB-BUTTERED RICE

**GREEN SALAD WITH
BLACK OLIVES**

FRESH BREAD

FRESH PEACH ORIENTALE

COFFEE   **TEA**

YOU WILL NEED:
1 small zucchini
2 shoulder lamb chops (¾ lb in all)
1 garlic clove, pressed
¼ teaspoon salt
¼ teaspoon dried rosemary leaves
⅛ teaspoon cracked pepper
8 cherry tomatoes
Prepared herb salad dressing
1 small onion
½ teaspoon dried chervil leaves
4 tablespoons (½ stick) butter for cooking,
    plus ⅛ lb (½ stick) for serving
Packaged precooked rice for 2 servings
½ small head Bibb lettuce, washed and
    crisped
8 pitted ripe olives
Bread
2 fresh ripe peaches or nectarines
1 shredded-wheat biscuit
2 tablespoons honey
3 tablespoons apricot preserves
Light cream or vanilla ice cream
Coffee, instant or brewed
Tea (optional)
Cream, sugar, lemon (optional)

6:00 to 6:10 P.M.

1. Wash zucchini. Trim ends. Cut in 8 pieces. Add to ½ cup boiling water. Bring to boil; simmer, covered, 3 minutes.

2. Remove bones from chops. On wooden board, pound lamb flat with mallet or edge of saucer Spread garlic over surface of lamb. Mix salt, rosemary and cracked pepper. Sprinkle over lamb; pound into surface. Slice into strips 1 inch wide. Overlap several strips to make four long ones. Weave on four skewers, alternating with zucchini and cherry tomatoes. Place in a baking pan; drizzle each with 1 teaspoon dressing.

6:10 to 6:20 P.M.

1. Chop onion. In small saucepan, sauté onion and chervil in 2 tablespoons butter. Add to boiling water for rice; prepare as label directs for 2 servings.

2. Break greens into a bowl. Top with 8 olives. Refrigerate. At serving time, toss with dressing.

3. Preheat broiler. Place skewers under broiler, 4 inches from heat. Broil until browned—about 5 minutes. Turn; spoon some of the marinade over meat; broil 3 to 5 minutes more, or until meat is of desired doneness.

6:20 to 6:30 P.M.

1. Wash peaches. Cut in half; re-move pits. Place fruit in two heatproof serving dishes. Break the shredded-wheat biscuit in half. Crumble one half over each serving of peaches.

2. In small skillet, combine honey, apricot preserves and remaining 2 tablespoons butter. Bring to boiling. Pour over shredded wheat; toss to mix.

3. Remove skewers to serving platter with rice. At dessert time, tilt dishes slightly, and spoon syrup over peaches again. Serve with cream or ice cream.

A Special Seafood Dinner
(Planned for Four)

POACHED FILLETS OF SOLE

POTATO PUFFS

BUTTERED PEAS WITH ONIONS

GREEN SALAD AND CHERRY TOMATOES

HOT CROISSANTS

LEMON ICE

**COFFEE   TEA
WHITE WINE**

GEORGE RATKAI

YOU WILL NEED:
1 pint lemon sherbet
Salad greens, washed and crisped
1 pint cherry tomatoes
3 lemons
1 pkg (10 or 16 oz) frozen potato puffs
1 pkg (5½ oz) croissants
1 small onion
2 tablespoons butter for cooking, plus ¼ lb (1 stick) for serving
1 pkg (12 or 16 oz) frozen fillets of sole or halibut
½ pint fresh oysters (optional)
1 teaspoon salt
Dash white pepper
1 bay leaf
½ cup white wine
1 pkg (10 oz) frozen peas and onions
1 tablespoon all-purpose flour
¼ cup milk
Prepared Italian-style salad dressing
Coffee, instant or brewed
Tea (optional)
Cream, sugar, lemon (optional)
Chilled white wine

6:00 to 6:10 P.M.

1. Remove lemon sherbet from freezer to soften slightly.

2. Break greens into salad bowl. Wash cherry tomatoes; cut in half; add to greens. Refrigerate until serving.

3. Grate 1 tablespoon lemon peel. Squeeze 2 lemons to make 5 tablespoons juice. Slice remaining lemon; halve slices; set aside.

4. Turn sherbet into medium bowl. With portable electric mixer, beat in 4 tablespoons of the lemon juice and the grated peel. Spoon into four parfait glasses. Freeze.

6:10 to 6:20 P.M.

1. Preheat oven to 425F. Arrange the potato puffs on cookie sheet. Wrap croissants loosely in foil.

2. Chop 1 small onion; sauté in 1 tablespoon hot butter in medium skillet, stirring, 3 minutes, or until tender. Meanwhile, cut frozen fish into fourths; arrange on top of onion in skillet. (If using oysters, pour with juice over fish.) Sprinkle with salt and white pepper, 1 tablespoon of the lemon juice and 3 pieces lemon. Add a bay leaf and ½ cup white wine. Cook, covered, over low heat until fish flakes easily with fork—8 to 10 minutes.

3. Heat potato puffs as package label

directs. Heat croissants in bottom of oven.

6:20 to 6:30 P.M.

1. Cook peas and onions as package label directs.

2. In small bowl, combine flour and milk, stirring until smooth.

3. With slotted spatula, lift out fish, draining well. Arrange on shallow, heat-proof serving dish. Remove lemon and bay leaf.

4. Remove potatoes and croissants from oven. Keep warm.

5. Into fish stock in skillet, stir flour mixture. Cook, stirring, until thickened. Spoon over fish. If desired, place under broiler until golden. Garnish with remaining lemon slices.

6. Toss salad with dressing. Drain vegetables; add remaining tablespoon butter.

MENU

A Hearty Ham Supper
(Planned for Six)

GLAZED HAM STEAK

CORN GRIDDLECAKES

ASPARAGUS WITH LEMON BUTTER

CREAMY COLESLAW

WARM APPLE DUMPLINGS WITH ICE-CREAM SAUCE

COFFEE   CIDER

YOU WILL NEED:
1 can (16 oz) apricot halves
½ cup brown sugar
¼ teaspoon ground cloves
1 2½-lb fully cooked ham steak,
    1 inch thick
2 pkg (12¾-oz size) unbaked frozen
    apple dumplings
1 pint peach or butter pecan ice cream
⅔ cup all-purpose flour
1 teaspoon baking powder
½ teaspoon salt
2 teaspoons sugar
1 teaspoon instant minced onion
1 can (12 oz) whole-kernel corn, drained
2 eggs
6 tablespoons butter for cooking
½ cup milk
2 pkg (10-oz size) frozen asparagus spears
1 lemon
1 lb creamy coleslaw, purchased from
    delicatessen
Chopped parsley
½ teaspoon ground cinnamon
Coffee, instant or brewed
Cream and sugar (optional)
Cider

6:00 to 6:10 P.M.

1. Drain apricots, reserving syrup. In a large skillet, combine brown sugar, cloves and the reserved syrup. Bring to boiling; add ham steak; simmer gently, covered, 25 to 30 minutes.

2. Preheat oven to 475F. Place one oven rack on lowest rung in oven. Lightly grease two cookie sheets; place on lowest rack in oven to heat.

3. Place 6 apple dumplings in a baking pan; bake as package label directs.

6:10 to 6:20 P.M.

1. Let ice cream soften at room temperature in small serving bowl.

2. In medium bowl, combine flour, baking powder, salt, sugar, minced onion, the whole-kernel corn, eggs, ¼ cup melted butter or margarine and milk. With wooden spoon, stir just until combined. Drop by tablespoonfuls onto hot cookie sheets, to make 12 cakes. Bake on lowest rack of oven 5 minutes. Turn with spatula; bake 5 minutes longer. Keep warm until serving.

6:20 to 6:30 P.M.

1. Cook asparagus as package label directs; drain. Drizzle with juice of ½ lemon and 2 tablespoons melted butter. Top with lemon slices.

2. Add apricots to ham. Simmer until just heated.

3. Arrange ham and apricots on a serving platter. Spoon some of pan liquid over top.

4. Turn coleslaw into salad bowl. Sprinkle with chopped parsley.

5. Swirl ½ teaspoon cinnamon into soft ice cream. Serve with dumplings.

A Mexican Fiesta
(Planned for Six)

TOSTADAS DE CARNE
GREEN CHILI SALSA
TROPICAL FRUIT SALAD
CHILLED SANGRIA

Thirty minutes will be just enough time to do all the preparation necessary for this festive Mexican dinner. It's beautiful enough to serve to family or friends and has a truly authentic "South of the Border" flavor. It's a fascinating combination of contrasting flavors, textures, shapes and colors—a spicy salsa topping for the crispy vegetable-and-beef-topped tortilla, a sweet-but-tart fruit salad and a big pitcher of icy-cold Sangria!

YOU WILL NEED:
1 whole navel orange, sliced
1 whole lemon, sliced
1 whole lime, sliced
1 red apple, cored and cut into chunks
1 bottle red Burgundy wine, chilled
1 cup orange juice
¼ cup sugar
¼ cup orange-flavored liqueur (optional)
1 can (1 lb, 4 oz) unsweetened pineapple chunks, undrained
2 whole navel oranges, peeled and cut into ¼-inch-thick slices
2 bananas, peeled and cut into ½-inch pieces
1 tablespoon lime juice
1 can (1 lb) whole peeled tomatoes, undrained
1½ cups chopped onion
1 can (4 oz) chopped green chilies, undrained
1 can (4 oz) taco sauce
6 corn tortillas

1 tablespoon vegetable oil
1 small ripe avocado, pitted and peeled
1 lb ground beef round
1 garlic clove, pressed
2 teaspooons chili powder
½ teaspoon ground cumin
½ teaspoon dried oregano leaves
½ teaspoon salt
Dash cayenne pepper
1 medium fresh ripe tomato, chopped
2 cups shredded iceberg lettuce
1 pkg (4 oz) shredded Cheddar cheese
½ can (4 oz) sweetened flaked coconut
1 lime, cut into wedges
1 bottle (16 oz) club soda, chilled

1. Prepare Sangria and Salad: Put 1 sliced orange, sliced lemon and lime, apple, wine, orange juice, sugar and liqueur into a large pitcher. Stir until sugar dissolves; refrigerate. Put pineapple with juice, 2 sliced oranges, banana and lime juice into bowl. Toss; cover and refrigerate.

2. Make Salsa: Drain canned tomatoes (reserve ¼ cup juice). In a small bowl with knife and fork, break up tomatoes. Add ¾ cup chopped onion, green chilies and taco sauce; mix well. Spoon into bowl; set aside. Brush both sides of tortillas with oil and arrange on baking sheet.

3. Place tortillas under broiler, 6 inches from heat source, and broil for about 5 to 6 minutes or until lightly browned and crisp. Remove from broiler and set aside to let cool. Put avocado into a small bowl; mash slightly, using a fork; cover and set aside.

4. In a medium-sized skillet, over medium-high heat, sauté ground beef with remaining ¾ cup chopped onion and the garlic until the meat is lightly browned. Add reserved ¼ cup tomato juice, chili powder, cumin, oregano, salt and the cayenne pepper.

DAVID VIENS

5. Reduce heat to low and simmer meat mixture for about 3 minutes or until most of the liquid evaporates (do not cover skillet). Spoon meat mixture onto the tortillas; top with layers of chopped tomato, shredded lettuce, cheese and mashed avocado.

6. Garnish each tortilla with a piece of chopped tomato, if desired. Arrange on a decorative platter; serve with Green Chili Salsa. Sprinkle flaked coconut over fruit salad and serve with lime wedges. Add club soda to Sangria and lots of ice; serve with dinner.

MENU

Company Chicken

(Planned for Four)

CHUTNEY ROAST CHICKEN

CURRIED RICE

BUTTERED BROCCOLI
SPEARS

AVOCADO, GREEN ONION
AND LETTUCE SALAD BOWL

BUTTERED HOT ROLLS

PEARS HELENE

CHOCOLATE BROWNIES

COFFEE   TEA

YOU WILL NEED:
1 pkg (13 oz) frozen chocolate brownies
1 pkg (6 oz) curried-rice mix
2 cups water
1 jar (10 oz) chutney-type relish
2 tablespoons lemon juice
2 tablespoons light corn syrup
2 (1- to 1½-lb size) ready-to-eat barbecued
   chickens
1 large ripe avocado
1 bunch green onions
½ cup prepared oil-and-vinegar salad
   dressing
2 pkg (10-oz size) frozen broccoli spears
1 can (1 lb, 14 oz) pear halves, stored in
   refrigerator to chill
1 pint vanilla ice cream
½ cup chocolate syrup
Fresh mint sprigs
Butter
1 pkg dinner rolls
1 head Boston lettuce, washed and crisped
Paprika
Watercress sprigs
Lemon wedges (optional)
Preserved kumquats
Raisins
Coffee, instant or brewed
Tea (optional)
Cream, sugar, lemon (optional)

6:00 to 6:10 P.M.

1. Preheat oven to 350F. Remove frozen brownies from freezer; thaw as directed on package label.

2. Start cooking curried-rice mix as package label directs, decreasing the amount of water called for to 2 cups.

3. Combine ⅔ cup chutney-type relish, lemon juice and corn syrup; mix until well blended.

4. Slash skin in several places over breasts of both chickens. Make a slit in each leg and wing. Cover chickens with chutney mixture. Wrap chickens in foil; bake 15 minutes, or until heated through.

6:10 to 6:20 P.M.

1. Make salad: Cut avocado in half; remove pit; peel. Cut into ½-inch slices. Slice green onion to measure ½ cup. In bowl, combine avocado, green onion and oil-and-vinegar dressing. Refrigerate.

2. Start cooking the frozen broccoli in slightly salted water, as package labels direct.

3. Drain pear halves. For each serving, place a pear half in a sherbet dish, then a scoop of ice cream. Place in freezer until serving time. (To serve, pour chocolate syrup over top. Garnish each with a sprig of mint.)

4. Lightly butter number of rolls desired. Wrap loosely in foil. Heat in oven.

6:20 to 6:30 P.M.

1. Separate Boston lettuce into leaves in salad bowl. Add avocado and onion; toss gently. Sprinkle with paprika. Garnish with sprigs of watercress.

2. Drain broccoli; season with butter. Arrange on serving platter with chicken. Garnish with lemon wedges, if you wish. Serve with preserved kumquats, raisins and additional chutney-type relish as accompaniments.

MENU

An Oriental Feast
(Planned for Two)

HOT-AND-SOUR SOUP

STIR-FRIED SHRIMP AND PEA PODS

CELLOPHANE NOODLES

FRESH PINEAPPLE SOUFFLE

COFFEE   CHINESE BEER

YOU WILL NEED:
1 pkg (3 oz) cellophane noodles
3 eggs
¼ lb medium mushrooms
2 scallions
⅛ lb snow peas
1 small Chinese cabbage
1 small carrot
½ lb shelled raw shrimp
Soy sauce
1 can (13¾ oz) chicken broth
1 cup water
1 fresh pineapple
1 can (8 oz) bamboo shoots
1½ teaspoons white vinegar
4 to 6 drops hot red-pepper sauce
1 tablespoon salad oil
1 teaspoon cornstarch
1 tablespoon sugar
1 tablespoon slivered unblanched almonds
Coffee, instant or brewed
Cream and sugar (optional)
Chinese beer

6:00 to 6:10 P.M.

1. Place noodles in small saucepan. Cover with hot water; set aside. Separate 2 eggs; put whites in small bowl of mixer.

2. Wash the vegetables. Slice the mushrooms; chop scallions; break off stem ends of snow peas; slice enough cabbage to make 2 cups. Peel carrot, and slice very thinly.

3. Wash shrimp; split in half, removing vein. Drain, and toss with 1 tablespoon soy sauce.

6:10 to 6:20 P.M.

1. In medium saucepan, combine chicken broth and 1 cup water. Remove ¼ cup; bring remaining broth to boiling over low heat.

2. Wash pineapple; slice in half through frond. Refrigerate half for later use. Remove inside of remaining half; discard core. Chop the pineapple into ¼-inch chunks.

3. Sliver enough bamboo shoots to make ¼ cup. Add bamboo shoots, ¼ cup mushrooms, 1 tablespoon scallion, carrot, ½ teaspoon soy sauce, the white vinegar and hot-pepper sauce to the simmering broth.

6:20 to 6:30 P.M.

1. Preheat oven to 325F. Separate noodles with a fork. Bring just to boiling. Drain well; toss with 1 teaspoon soy sauce. Beat egg yolks with remaining egg. Pour into boiling soup slowly, while stirring, to make strands.

2. Drain shrimp; add drippings to reserved broth. Heat oil in medium skillet. Stir-fry shrimp 1 minute. Add remaining mushrooms, cabbage and snow peas. Stir-fry 2 minutes longer. Stir cornstarch into reserved broth mixture. Stir into shrimp. Cook until thickened. Arrange on platter with noodles. Top with remaining scallion.

3. Beat egg whites until frothy. Gradually add 1 tablespoon sugar; beat until stiff peaks form. Spoon over pineapple. Sprinkle with almonds. Place the pineapple half on a cookie sheet, and bake until golden—about 15 minutes.

MENU

The Italian Touch

(Planned for Four or Five)

**MEATBALLS,
ITALIAN STYLE,
EN CROUTE**

**SPINACH-AND-ROMAINE
SALAD**

**WARM CHERRY CRISP
WITH SOFT VANILLA
ICE CREAM**

COFFEE **RED WINE**

GEORGE RATKAI

YOU WILL NEED:
2 cups natural-type ready-to-eat oat cereal
1 can (1 lb, 5 oz) cherry-pie filling
¼ teaspoon almond extract
¼ teaspoon ground cinnamon
6 tablespoons melted butter
1 loaf (16 oz) unsliced white bread
¼ cup grated Parmesan cheese
1 lb ground chuck
1 medium green pepper
1 yellow onion
1 can (16 oz) stewed tomatoes
½ teaspoon dried basil leaves
¼ teaspoon dried thyme leaves
1½ pints vanilla ice cream
2 tablespoons all-purpose flour
**½ lb fresh young spinach, washed and
    crisped**
¼ head romaine, washed and crisped
Prepared Italian-style salad dressing
Coffee, instant or brewed
Cream and sugar (optional)
Red wine

6:00 to 6:10 P.M.

1. Preheat oven to 400F. Measure 1 cup cereal into a 1-quart shallow baking dish. Combine cherry-pie filling with almond extract and cinnamon; mix well. Pour onto cereal. Sprinkle 1 cup cereal around edge of baking dish. Drizzle 2 tablespoons of the melted butter over cereal. Bake, uncovered, 15 minutes.

2. Remove a ¾-inch-thick slice from top of bread. With fork, scoop out inside of bread, making a trough 2-by-1½-by-6-inches deep. Place loaf on foil in shallow baking pan. With remaining 4 tablespoons butter, brush top, sides and inside of bread; sprinkle with ¼ cup Parmesan; coat sides evenly. Bake 10 minutes.

6:10 to 6:20 P.M.

Slowly heat a large skillet. Pat ground chuck into a square; divide into 16ths. Carefully shape into 16 balls. Brown lightly in skillet—about 5 minutes—adding a little butter if needed.

2. Wash and slice green pepper, peel and slice onion; add to meatballs; sauté 5 minutes.

3. Reserve ¼ cup liquid from can of tomatoes; add tomatoes and rest of liquid, basil and thyme to skillet; simmer, covered, 5 minutes.

6:20 to 6:30 P.M.

1. Remove cherry crisp from oven; cool slightly. Place ice cream in refrigerator to soften.

2. In measuring cup, combine ¼ cup tomato liquid with 2 tablespoons flour; stir until smooth. Stir into mixture in skillet; cook, covered, 5 minutes longer, or until slightly thickened.

3. Remove stems from spinach; break spinach and romaine into bowl; toss with ¼ cup or more dressing.

4. Place bread on serving platter; spoon meatball mixture into and around bread.

MENU

Festive Canadian Supper
(Planned for Six)

GLAZED CANADIAN BACON WITH APPLES

WHIPPED SWEET POTATOES

ENDIVE WITH WATERCRESS SALAD

HOT CROISSANTS, BUTTER

HOLIDAY LOG

COFFEE

CHILLED ROSE WINE

YOU WILL NEED:
1 (11 oz) jelly roll
2 tablespoons apricot jam or orange marmalade
2 tablespoons orange juice
½ pint heavy cream
3 tablespoons confectioners' sugar
2 tablespoons unsweetened cocoa
¾ teaspoon vanilla
Candied cherries
Angelica or green spearmint leaves
Sliced almonds or pecan halves
2 cans (1-lb, 1-oz-size) water-packed sweet potatoes
2 Belgian endives
2 bunches watercress
2 large or 3 medium apples
4 tablespoons (½ stick) butter for cooking, plus ¼ lb (1 stick) for serving
½ cup plus 2 tablespoons brown sugar
¼ teaspoon ground ginger
1 pkg (5½ oz) croissants
1¼ lb Canadian bacon, sliced ¼ inch thick
½ cup white wine
Prepared oil-and-vinegar dressing
Coffee, instant or brewed
Cream and sugar (optional)
Chilled rosé wine

6:00 to 6:10 P.M.

1. Place jelly roll on cake plate. Combine jam or marmalade and orange juice; mix well. Brush over cake until all is absorbed. Using a rotary beater, beat heavy cream with confectioners' sugar, cocoa and ½ teaspoon vanilla until stiff. Use to frost cake all over. Draw tines of fork lengthwise on cake to simulate bark of tree. Decorate with cherries, angelica and nuts as pictured. Refrigerate until serving.

2. In medium saucepan, combine sweet potatoes with liquid from 1 can; simmer, covered, 10 minutes.

6:10 to 6:20 P.M.

1. Wash and drain endive; separate into leaves. Wash and drain watercress; remove long stems. Break large endive leaves in half; toss endive and watercress in salad bowl; refrigerate.

2. Wash apples and slice crosswise, ½ inch thick; remove cores.

3. In 2 tablespoons butter in large skillet, sauté apple slices on both sides until golden-brown. Lift out as they brown. Return apples to skillet; sprinkle with ½ cup brown sugar and ¼ teaspoon ground ginger. Simmer, covered, 5 minutes.

4. Warm croissants in low oven.

6:20 to 6:30 P.M.

1. With portable electric mixer, beat sweet potatoes with ⅓ cup liquid from potatoes, 2 tablespoons brown sugar, 2 tablespoons butter and ¼ teaspoon vanilla. Turn into a serving dish.

2. Add bacon and white wine to apples; simmer, covered, 5 minutes.

3. Place rolls in basket. Toss salad with dressing.

4. Arrange apples and bacon in serving dish; pour pan drippings over; garnish apples with almonds.

MENU

A Cool International Dinner

(Planned for Two)

DIJON-CHICKEN STUFFED TOMATOES

TABOULI WITH SHREDDED SPINACH

FRENCH BAGUETTE

TRIPLE COFFEE SUNDAES

ICED COFFEE

CHILLED WHITE WINE

GEORGE RATKAI

YOU WILL NEED:
⅓ cup cracked wheat (bulgar)
Salt
1 garlic clove, split
1 whole chicken breast, boned and skinned
1 teaspoon olive oil
1 pint coffee ice cream
½ lb fresh spinach
2 large ripe tomatoes
Prepared Italian-style salad dressing
¼ cup plain yogurt
1 teaspoon Dijon-style mustard
Fresh mint
2 slices cucumber
2 black olives
1 French-bread baguette
¼ lb (1 stick) butter for serving
2 tablespoons coffee-flavored liqueur
¼ teaspoon instant coffee granules
Coffee candies (optional)
Iced coffee, instant or brewed
Cream and sugar (optional)
Chilled white wine

6:00 to 6:10 P.M.

1. Bring 2 cups water to boiling. Stir in ⅓ cup cracked wheat, a dash salt and garlic. Return to boiling; lower heat, and cook, covered, 15 minutes.

2. Cut chicken breast into ¾-inch chunks. Heat olive oil in a medium skillet. Sauté chicken, uncovered and stirring occasionally, until it is cooked through—7 to 10 minutes.

3. Set ice cream out to soften. Rinse and drain spinach.

6:10 to 6:20 P.M.

1. Spread chicken on a metal baking pan. Place in freezer. Chill two serving plates.

2. Wash tomatoes; slice off tops. With a spoon, scoop out center of tomatoes. Shake out and discard seeds. Chop tomato tops and centers. Drain cracked wheat; remove garlic. Spread wheat in pan, and place in freezer.

3. Scoop ice cream into two sherbet dishes. Place in freezer. With a sharp knife, shred drained spinach.

6:20 to 6:30 P.M.

1. Remove chicken from freezer; turn into small bowl. Add chopped tomato and 1 tablespoon prepared dressing to chicken.

2. Stir together yogurt and mustard. Fill tomatoes with half of chicken mix-

ture; spoon on some of mustard sauce. Add remaining chicken; top with remaining sauce. Garnish each tomato with chopped mint and a sprig of fresh mint.

3. Arrange the spinach on chilled plates. Remove wheat to a bowl. Toss with ¼ cup dressing. Spoon onto plates, dividing evenly. Place a stuffed tomato in center of each plate. Garnish each with a cucumber slice and a black olive. Pass more dressing.

4. To serve dessert, spoon liqueur over ice cream. Sprinkle with coffee granules, and top with a coffee candy, if desired.

A Patio Supper
(Planned for Four)

HAM BARBECUE ON ITALIAN BREAD

SARATOGA FRIES

QUICK COLESLAW

PINEAPPLE CHEESECAKE IN A BOWL

COFFEE   ICED TEA

CHILLED BEER

YOU WILL NEED:
Salad oil
3 large baking potatoes
1 can (8 oz) crushed pineapple in pineapple juice
1 env unflavored gelatine
10 (3-inch) chocolate wafers
1 pkg (8 oz) cream cheese
¼ cup confectioners' sugar
2 tablespoons semisweet chocolate pieces
½ cup heavy cream
1 small cabbage (1 lb)
1 jar (8 oz) coleslaw dressing
2 medium tomatoes
1 small bunch watercress
1 loaf Italian bread
1 large onion
1 large green pepper
1 can (15½ oz) barbecue sandwich sauce
½ lb sliced boiled ham
Coffee, instant or brewed
Instant iced tea
Cream, sugar, lemon (optional)
Chilled beer

6:00 to 6:10 P.M.

1. In a small skillet, heat 1 inch of oil to 385F. Wash, dry and thinly slice unpared potatoes. Fry, one-fourth at a time, until golden. Drain well and keep warm.

2. Drain juice from crushed pineapple into cup. Stir gelatine into juice. Set aside to soften. Bring 1 inch water to boiling; remove from heat. Set cup of gelatine mixture in water. Stir until dissolved.

3. Place cookies in a plastic bag; roll to make crumbs. Stir in 1 teaspoon oil. Pat into bottom of an 8-inch pie plate or dish. Combine cream cheese and confectioners' sugar in bowl of electric mixer. Gradually beat in gelatine mixture. Put 2 tablespoons chocolate pieces in a measuring cup; set cup in hot water.

6:10 to 6:20 P.M.

1. Slowly beat ½ cup heavy cream into the cream-cheese mixture. Beat until very light and fluffy. Fold in crushed pineapple. Carefully spoon the mixture onto crumbs. When chocolate is melted, drizzle over cheese mixture. Place in freezer until dessert time—no longer than ½ hour.

2. Meanwhile, wash and quarter the cabbage. Remove core; carefully slice each quarter almost to bottom, leaving slices together. Remove to plate; top with

dressing. Wash tomatoes; cut into sixths. Arrange on platter with cabbage. Garnish with watercress.

3. Split the loaf of Italian bread; cut each piece in half. Arrange on a platter.

6:20 to 6:30 P.M.

1. Peel and slice onion. Wash green pepper; remove seeds, and slice. Sauté in 1 tablespoon oil until lightly browned. Add barbecue sandwich sauce; reduce heat, and simmer, covered, 5 minutes.

2. Cut ham into strips; add to sauce. Return to boiling; spoon onto Italian bread.

MENU

A Russian Delight

(Planned for Four)

CHICKEN LIVERS STROGANOFF

WHITE-AND-WILD RICE

BUTTERED GREEN VEGETABLE

SPINACH-AND-BACON SALAD

ROLLS   BUTTER

PINEAPPLE-AND-STRAWBERRY COUPE

SHORTBREAD COOKIES

COFFEE   ICED TEA

YOU WILL NEED:
4 slices bacon
1 pkg (6 oz) white-and-wild rice mix
1 lb chicken livers
¼ lb medium mushrooms
1¼ cups water
1 pkg frozen green vegetable (asparagus, green beans, peas)
1 fresh pineapple
1 pint strawberries
¼ cup orange juice
Packaged rolls
¼ lb (1 stick) butter for serving
1 lb fresh spinach, washed and crisped
Prepared salad dressing
2 tablespoons all-purpose flour
½ pint sour cream
Fresh dill (optional)
1 pkg shortbread cookies
Coffee, instant or brewed
Instant iced tea
Cream, sugar, lemon (optional)

6:00 to 6:10 P.M.

1. Cut bacon into 1-inch pieces, and, in a large heavy skillet, sauté until crisp.

2. Prepare white-and-wild-rice mix according to package directions, using only ½ of each packet of the seasoning mix. Reserve remaining seasoning mix.

3. Remove bacon pieces to paper towels to drain well. Pour off all but 2 tablespoons of the drippings. Drain livers well. Add to skillet, and sauté until well browned on all sides—8 to 10 minutes.

6:10 to 6:20 P.M.

1. Wash the mushrooms; drain well and slice. Add to chicken livers. Sauté, stirring, 2 minutes longer. Add remaining seasoning mix from the rice, along with 1 cup of the water. Cover, and simmer 10 minutes.

2. Put water on to boil for vegetable. Remove the frond and peel the pineapple. Slice 1 inch thick. Cut into cubes, removing core and eyes.

3. Wash the strawberries. Drain them well, and remove the stems. Arrange pineapple and strawberries in brandy snifter. Drizzle with ¼ cup orange juice. Place in freezer until serving—no more than half an hour.

6:20 to 6:30 P.M.

1. Prepare green vegetable according to directions on the package.

2. Heat rolls, if desired.

3. Remove stems from spinach; break into salad bowl. Top with bacon pieces. Serve with prepared salad dressing.

4. Drain the white-and-wild rice, and spoon onto a serving dish.

5. Stir flour into the remaining ¼ cup of water until smooth. Add to liver mixture; bring just to boiling; reduce heat, and cook, stirring, until thickened. Fold in ¾ cup of the sour cream. Heat gently—do not bring to boiling. Spoon onto rice, and garnish with fresh dill, if desired.

MENU

Italian Chicken Dinner
(Planned for Four)

FONTINA CHICKEN ON FUSILLI

BASIL ITALIAN BEANS

GARLIC KNOTS

LEMON SHERBET

ANISETTE COOKIES

RED WINE   COFFEE

YOU WILL NEED:
1¼ teaspoons salt
1 pkg (11 oz) refrigerated bread sticks
2 garlic cloves, minced
2 tablespoons salad oil
1 pkg (12 oz) frozen, breaded chicken patties
½ teaspoon dried oregano leaves
2 slices fontina cheese
1 jar (15½ oz) spaghetti sauce with mushrooms and chunk tomatoes
Grated Parmesan cheese
1 small onion
1 medium red pepper
1 pkg (1 lb) fusilli or spaghetti
1 pint lemon sherbet
1 pkg (9 oz) frozen Italian green beans
½ teaspoon dried basil leaves
Fresh flat-leaf parsley (optional)
Packaged anisette cookies
Coffee, instant or brewed
Cream and sugar (optional)
Red wine

6:00 to 6:10 P.M.

1. Preheat oven to 400F. In 5-quart kettle, bring 3 quarts water and 1 teaspoon salt, if desired, to boiling. Unroll and separate bread-stick dough into strips; form each into a knot. Place on ungreased cookie sheet. In cup, mix garlic and 1 tablespoon of the oil; brush over knots. Bake 10 to 12 minutes, or until golden-brown.

2. On a small cookie sheet, place chicken patties; sprinkle with oregano. Cut each cheese slice into 2 triangles; set aside. In a small saucepan, over medium-low heat, heat spaghetti sauce.

6:10 to 6:20 P.M.

1. Remove garlic knots from oven; sprinkle with 2 tablespoons Parmesan. Arrange in napkin-lined basket; keep warm. Bake the chicken patties 12 to 15 minutes.

2. Peel and slice onion. Remove and discard stem, ribs and seeds from pepper. Cut pepper into ½-inch strips; cut strips in half crosswise.

3. Add fusilli to the salted boiling water; cook 12 to 15 minutes, or until tender. Scoop lemon sherbet into four dessert dishes; keep in freezer until dessert time.

6:20 to 6:30 P.M.

1. In skillet, over medium-high heat, heat remaining tablespoon oil. Add onion and red pepper; cook 2 minutes; stir in beans, basil and ¼ teaspoon salt. Cook, covered and stirring often, 5 minutes.

2. Drain fusilli; place on platter; top with three-fourths of spaghetti sauce, then the chicken patties. Spoon remaining sauce on patties; top each with cheese. Garnish with flat-leaf parsley, if desired. Spoon bean mixture into serving dish. Pass Parmesan with fusilli. At dessert time, serve sherbet with cookies.

MENU

Tuna-Tomato Favorite
(Planned for Two)

CHILLED TUNA
WITH PINK MAYONNAISE
IN TOMATO SHELLS

CRISP PEPPER SLAW

TOASTED POTATO CHIPS

BUTTERED HOT ROLLS

STRAWBERRIES IN PORT

ROLLED COOKIES

ICED TEA   COFFEE

YOU WILL NEED:
2 large ripe tomatoes
½ stalk celery
1 green onion
1 can (7 oz) solid-pack tuna
3 tablespoons mayonnaise
1 tablespoon chili sauce
½ teaspoon lemon juice
¼ teaspoon Worcestershire sauce
¼ teaspoon salt
¼ teaspoon hoeseradish
1 pkg (8 oz) shredded cabbage
¼ cup pepper relish
¼ cup coleslaw dressing
1 pkg (10 oz) quick-thaw frozen
**   strawberries**
Butter
1 pkg soft rolls
1 pkg waffled potato chips
¼ cup port
1 pkg (5¼ oz) curled or rolled party
**   cookies**
Confectioners' sugar
Lettuce leaves, washed and crisped
Parsley sprigs (optional)
Instant iced tea
Coffee (optional)
Cream and sugar (optional)

6:00 to 6:10 P.M.

1. Cut a ½-inch-thick slice from stem end of tomatoes. With spoon, scoop out centers of tomatoes, leaving a shell. Invert tomatoes to drain; then refrigerate. Cut up center of one tomato coarsely. (Refrigerate center of other tomato, to use another day.)

2. Slice ½ stalk celery and 1 green onion. Drain tuna.

3. Make tuna salad: In medium bowl, combine mayonnaise, chili sauce, lemon juice, Worcestershire sauce, salt and horseradish; mix until smooth. Add cut-up tomato, celery, green onion and tuna; toss until well blended. Cover, and place in freezer to chill quickly.

6:10 to 6:20 P.M.

1. Preheat oven to 300F.

2. For coleslaw: Rinse shredded cabbage under cold running water; drain well on paper towels. Turn into medium bowl. Add pepper relish and coleslaw dressing; toss well. Cover, and place in freezer to chill quickly.

Start thawing frozen strawberries as the package label directs.

6:20 to 6:30 P.M.

1. Lightly butter number of rolls desired; wrap in foil. Spread potato chips on large, shallow pan. Place rolls and

potato chips in oven to heat—8 to 10 minutes.

2. Mix strawberries with ¼ cup port. Refrigerate until serving time.

3. Arrange party cookies in dish. Sift confectioners' sugar over top.

4. Fill tomato shells with tuna salad, mounding high. Place on serving platter, with coleslaw on lettuce, as pictured. Garnish with parsley sprigs, if desired.

5. Place hot rolls and potato chips in serving dishes or baskets just before serving the dinner.

MENU

A Rich Turkey Pie
(Planned for Four or Five)

TURKEY PIE

GREEN SALAD BOWL

HOT CHEDDAR-CHEESE ROLLS

PINEAPPLE UPSIDE-DOWN CAKE WITH WHIPPED CREAM

COFFEE   TEA

RED WINE

YOU WILL NEED:
¼ lb fresh mushrooms
6 tablespoons (½ stick plus 2 tablespoons) butter for cooking
3 cups salad greens, washed and crisped
¼ teaspoon dried dillweed
½ pint heavy cream
1 can (10¾ oz) chunky vegetable soup
½ cup chicken broth or water
2 tablespoons all-purpose flour
⅓ cup red wine
2½ cups leftover cooked turkey, cut in chunks
1 pkg (7 oz) frozen rolls
Instant mashed potatoes for 6 servings
Water, milk, butter, salt
⅔ cup light-brown sugar
1 can (8½ oz) sliced pineapple
5 maraschino cherries
4 pecan or walnut halves
1 pkg (19 oz) spongecake layers
¼ cup (1 oz) grated Cheddar cheese
Prepared oil-and-vinegar salad dressing
Coffee, instant or brewed
Tea (optional)
Cream, sugar, lemon (optional)
Red wine

6:00 to 6:10 P.M.

1. Wash and slice mushrooms. In 1 tablespoon hot butter in medium skillet, sauté mushrooms until tender—about 5 minutes.

2. Break salad greens into bowl. Sprinkle with dillweed. Refrigerate.

3. With rotary beater, whip cream until stiff; turn into serving bowl; refrigerate.

4. Add soup and chicken broth or water to the mushrooms; bring to boiling. Add flour to red wine; stir to dissolve. Stir into boiling soup mixture; cook, stirring, until slightly thickened. Preheat oven to 350F.

6:10 to 6:20 P.M.

1. Add turkey to soup mixture; simmer, covered, 10 minutes.

2. Heat rolls as package directs.

3. Prepare mashed potato as directed for 6 servings.

4. In 8-inch skillet, melt ¼ cup butter over low heat. Stir in light-brown sugar until melted.

6:20 to 6:30 P.M.

1. Drain pineapple; arrange rings in brown sugar in skillet with cherries and nuts, as pictured. Place one spongecake layer on top of pineapple. (Freeze other layer.) Heat, covered, 3 minutes. Invert

on cake plate so that pineapple is on top.

2. Remove rolls from oven. Place on cookie sheet.

3. In each roll, make three (½-inch-deep) diagonal cuts; sprinkle cheese in cuts; run under boiler just to melt.

4. Turn turkey mixture into 1½-quart shallow baking dish. Spoon mashed potato around edge to make a border, or put through pastry bag with large star tip. Drizzle 1 tablespoon melted butter over potato; run under broiler just to brown.

5. Toss salad with dressing.

MENU

All-American Patio Party
(Planned for Four)

BROILED FLANK STEAK WITH LEMON BUTTER SAUCE

BROILED TOMATO HALVES

BUTTERED CORN ON THE COB

GREEN SALAD WITH FRESH MUSHROOMS

HOT GARLIC BREAD

RASPBERRY CREME BRULEE

ICED TEA

GEORGE RATKAI

YOU WILL NEED:
1 pkg (10 oz) quick-thaw frozen raspberries
4 to 6 ears fresh corn
2 large ripe tomatoes
¼ lb fresh mushrooms
8 tablespoons (1 stick) butter
1 garlic clove, pressed
½ teaspoon salt
1 tablespoon lemon juice
1 tablespoon chopped parsley
¼ teaspoon dried tarragon leaves
1 1½-lb flank steak
Instant meat tenderizer (optional)
1 loaf French bread
Prepared oil-and-vinegar salad dressing
Salad greens, washed and crisped
1 container (4 oz) vanilla yogurt
4 tablespoons brown sugar
Instant iced tea
Lemon (optional)

6:00 to 6:10 P.M.

1. Run water over package of raspberries, to thaw slightly.

2. In large kettle, bring 3 quarts water to boil. Husk corn. Wash tomatoes and mushrooms.

3. Place 2 tablespoons butter in small dish. Press garlic into butter; soften. Place 6 tablespoons butter in saucepan. Add salt, lemon juice, chopped parsley and tarragon. Stir over low heat, to melt butter.

6:10 to 6:20 P.M.

1. Wipe steak with damp paper towels. Sprinkle with tenderizer, as label directs. Place on broiler pan. Brush with the melted butter sauce, using about 1½ tablespoons. Place under broiler, 4 inches from heat source, about 7 minutes.

2. Purée raspberries in blender until smooth. Divide into four individual soufflé dishes. Set dishes in shallow pan in freezer.

3. Cook corn in boiling water, covered, 7 minutes. Split bread in half; stir garlic into butter; spread on bread.

6:20 to 6:30 P.M.

1. Slice tomatoes in half; brush generously with butter sauce. Turn steak; brush with butter sauce. Broil tomatoes on broiler pan with steak. Broil steak 7 minutes, not well done.

2. Slice mushrooms; toss with 2 tablespoons salad dressing. Arrange with the crisped greens in serving bowl. At serving time, toss with more dressing.

3. Divide yogurt over top of puréed raspberries. Sprinkle 1 tablespoon brown sugar over each serving. Place under broiler, along with the bread. Watch carefully; remove dessert when sugar is melted and bubbly and bread when it is golden.

4. Drain corn; place in basket. Serve steak with remaining butter sauce. Carve in very thin slices, on the diagonal, against the grain.

MENU

A Supper From The Sea
(Planned for Two or Three)

BOUILLABAISSE

GREEN SALAD WITH SWISS CHEESE

TOASTED HERB-GARLIC BREAD

FROZEN STRAWBERRY CHARLOTTE

CHILLED WHITE WINE

COFFEE

YOU WILL NEED:
1 pkg (10 oz) frozen peas
1 pint strawberry ice cream
1 pkg (3 oz) ladyfingers
1 can (8 oz) pineapple chunks in pineapple juice
¼ cup apricot jam
1 medium onion
1 can (16 oz) stewed tomatoes
1 cup white wine
¼ teaspoon salt
Dried basil leaves
Dash pepper
2 garlic cloves, pressed separately
6 fresh mussels* (optional)
1 8-oz frozen lobster tail
½ lb fresh sole or flounder fillet
6- to 8-inch loaf French bread or hero roll
2 tablespoons butter, softened
3 cups escarole, broken into pieces
⅛ lb Swiss cheese, in one piece
Prepared salad dressing
6 whole strawberries, washed
Coffee, instant or brewed
Cream and sugar (optional)
Chilled white wine

*Mussels should be firmly closed before cooking; discard if open.

6:00 to 6:10 P.M.

1. In small saucepan, bring to boiling ¼ cup water. Add ½ package peas; cook 2 minutes. Drain; chill. (Wrap remaining ½ package and return to freezer.)

2. With paring knife, cut around bottom of ice-cream carton. Run cold water over sides of carton. Remove lid; from bottom, push ice cream, top down, onto a plate. Freeze.

3. Split five ladyfingers; place, cut side up, on waxed paper. Open the pineapple; sprinkle ladyfingers with 3 tablespoons juice from can.

4. In small bowl, combine apricot jam with 1 tablespoon pineapple juice. Drain pineapple.

5. Slice onion. Place in large saucepan with stewed tomatoes, white wine, salt, ¼ teaspoon basil, pepper and 1 of the pressed garlic cloves. Boil.

6. Scrub mussels; slice lobster tail (through shell) into four pieces. Wash fillet; cut into four pieces.

6:10 to 6:20 P.M.

1. Add frozen lobster and mussels to soup. Return to boiling; simmer until lobster is tender and mussels are opened—15 minutes.

2. Place the ladyfingers around ice cream. Arrange pineapple around mold in dish; place three chunks on top. Brush

ladyfingers and pineapple with apricot mixture; freeze.

3. Split French bread; place on cookie sheet. Combine soft butter, remaining pressed garlic clove and ⅛ teaspoon basil; spread on bread.

6:20 to 6:30 P.M.

1. Add fish fillet to soup last 7 minutes of cooking.

2. Broil bread until golden.

3. Break escarole into salad bowl. Cut cheese into cubes; add to salad with peas. Toss with dressing.

4. Garnish dessert with berries.

MENU

Supper, Polish Style
(Planned for Four to Six)

KIELBASA

CARAWAY SAUERKRAUT

BUTTERED MASHED POTATO

CUCUMBER SALAD

BLACK BREAD   BUTTER

CHERRY COBBLER A LA MODE

COFFEE   BEER

YOU WILL NEED:
1 can (1 lb, 5 oz) cherry-pie filling
½ teaspoon almond extract
1 tablespoon butter or margarine for
    cooking, plus ¼ lb (1 stick) for serving
½ cup packaged biscuit mix
2 tablespoons sugar
¼ cup milk
2 medium cucumbers
1 medium onion
Prepared oil-and-vinegar salad dressing
1 tablespoon snipped fresh dill or parsley
Lettuce, washed and crisped
2 cans or 2 pkg (1-lb size) sauerkraut
1½ cups apple juice or cider
2 teaspoons caraway seeds
1 lb kielbasa
Instant mashed potato for 6 servings
Water, milk, butter, salt
½ teaspoon instant minced onion
1 loaf black bread
1 pint vanilla ice cream
Beer (optional)
Coffee, instant or brewed
Cream, sugar (optional)

6:00 to 6:10 P.M.

1. Preheat oven to 400F. Combine the cherry-pie filling and almond extract in a 1-quart shallow baking dish; mix well. Dot with the tablespoon butter or margarine.

2. In a small bowl, combine biscuit mix, 1 tablespoon of the sugar and the milk. Stir with fork just until blended. Spoon over cherry filling around edge of dish by rounded teaspoonfuls about one inch apart, to form a border. Sprinkle this border with remaining tablespoon sugar. Bake 20 to 25 minutes, or until biscuit is baked through and is golden-brown.

3. Wash and thinly slice the cucumbers and onion. Toss with ¼ cup of the dressing and the snipped dill or parsley. Turn into salad bowl lined with lettuce. Refrigerate until ready to serve.

6:10 to 6:20 P.M.

1. Drain sauerkraut in colander; rinse under cold water; drain.

2. In 4-quart Dutch oven, combine the sauerkraut, apple juice or cider and the caraway seed. Cover and bring the sauerkraut to boiling.

3. Wash kielbasa and dry on paper towels. Prick all over with fork; place on top of sauerkraut in Dutch oven; reduce

heat and simmer gently, covered, 20 minutes, or until hot.

6:20 to 6:30 P.M.

1. Prepare instant mashed potato with water, milk, butter and salt as the package label directs, adding the minced onion to liquid. Turn into a heated serving dish.

2. Turn sauerkraut and kielbasa into another heated serving dish.

3. Let cobbler cool slightly before serving with vanilla ice cream.

MENU

An Elegant Dinner Treat
(Planned for Four)

EGGS AND TOMATOES WITH PINK MAYONNAISE

BREAST OF CHICKEN AND HAM EN CROUTE

BUTTERED FRESH ASPARAGUS

FRENCH BREAD   **BUTTER**

STRAWBERRY MACAROON PIE

COFFEE   **TEA**

CHILLED WHITE WINE

YOU WILL NEED:
2 frozen 9-inch pie shells
2 chicken breasts, boned, skinned and split in half
3 tablespoons butter for cooking, plus ¼ lb (1 stick) for serving
¼ teaspoon dried thyme leaves
1½ lb fresh asparagus
1 pkg (4 or 5 oz) Brie, Camembert or Gruyère cheese
4 slices boiled ham (¼ lb)
1 raw egg
1 pkg (9¼ oz) coconut-macaroon bars
1½ pints vanilla ice cream
4 leaves romaine, washed and crisped
1 large ripe tomato
4 hard-cooked eggs, shelled
2 tablespoons catsup
1 teaspoon capers, drained
½ cup mayonnaise
Lemon slices
1 pint strawberries
2 tablespoons sugar
2 tablespoons orange-flavored liqueur
2 tablespoons flaked coconut
1 loaf French bread
Coffee, instant or brewed
Tea (optional)
Cream, sugar, lemon (optional)
Chilled white wine

6:00 to 6:10 P.M.

1. Thaw pie shells. Rinse chicken breasts; drain well. In 1 tablespoon butter, sauté chicken, covered, on both sides until golden. Sprinkle with thyme.

2. Preheat oven to 400F. Cut off tough ends of asparagus. Wash well.

3. Cut cheese into thin slices. Remove pie shells from pans. Cut each in half. Cut a diamond in the center of each half. Place a slice of ham, cheese and a chicken breast half on each. Fold pastry over; pinch together.

4. Place, seam side down, on an ungreased cookie sheet. Beat raw egg slightly. Brush over pastry. Bake 20 minutes, or until golden.

6:10 to 6:20 P.M.

1. Unwrap 4 macaroons. Split, then cut each in half diagonally. Lightly grease an 8-inch pie plate. Arrange some macaroons around the edge. Fit remaining into bottom of plate.

2. Scoop ice cream into pie shell. Place in freezer.

3. Place a romaine leaf on each of 4 salad plates. Wash tomato; trim off ends; slice into 4 rounds. Place one on each lettuce leaf. Slice eggs with slicer; arrange on tomatoes.

4. Stir catsup and capers into mayonnaise. Spoon over eggs. Chill.

6:20 to 6:30 P.M.

1. Bring 1 cup water to boiling in a medium skillet. Add the asparagus. Cover; return to boiling; cook 8 minutes, until just tender. Drain well; dress with 2 tablespoons butter. Serve with lemon slices.

2. Wash and drain strawberries. Set aside three. Hull remaining strawberries; slice; toss with sugar and liqueur. At dessert time, spoon sliced strawberries over pie. Top with whole berries. Spinkle with 2 tablespoons coconut.

MENU

Fresh-Vegetable Dinner
(Planned for Four)

**CABBAGE ROLL
WITH TOMATO SAUCE**

**CUCUMBER-LETTUCE
SALAD**

FALL FRUIT MERINGUE

COFFEE   CIDER

GEORGE RATKAI

YOU WILL NEED:
1⅓ cups water
⅓ cup white rice
¼ teaspoon salt
2 eggs
¼ lb medium mushrooms
1 can (16 oz) stewed tomatoes
1 can (8 oz) tomato sauce
¼ teaspoon dried dillweed
1 medium onion
1 small zucchini
9 large cabbage leaves
2 large apples
2 large pears
1 tablespoon lemon juice
2 tablespoons honey
Apple cider
1 teaspoon salad oil
1 garlic clove, pressed
½ lb ground lamb
2 tablespoons granulated sugar
1 head romaine, washed and crisped
1 cucumber
Prepared salad dressing
Coffee, instant or brewed
Cream and sugar (optional)

6:00 to 6:10 P.M.

1. Bring 1⅓ cups water to boiling; add rice and salt. Simmer, covered, until rice is tender—about 18 minutes. Separate the eggs, and wash the fruit and vegetables.

2. Slice the mushrooms. Combine mushrooms with stewed tomatoes, tomato sauce and dill in a medium saucepan. Bring to boiling; simmer, covered, until serving.

3. Peel and chop onion; shred zucchini. Bring 1 cup water to boiling in a large skillet. Place the cabbage leaves in skillet; cover; simmer 5 minutes.

6:10 to 6:20 P.M.

1. Cut apples and pears into eighths; core. Toss with lemon juice, honey and ¼ cup cider in medium saucepan. Simmer, covered, until just tender—3 to 5 minutes. Preheat oven to 400F.

2. Drain cabbage; keep warm. Heat oil in same pan. Add onion, garlic and lamb. Sauté, stirring, until meat is browned.

3. Turn fruit and liquid into shallow baking dish. Beat egg whites until frothy. Gradually add sugar; beat until stiff peaks form. Spoon onto fruit. Bake until meringue is golden—2 minutes.

6:20 to 6:30 P.M.

1. Drain meat mixture. Stir in zucchini, ¼ cup tomato mixture, rice, and lightly beaten egg yolks. Cover; simmer 1 minute.

2. Break romaine into bowl. Slice cucumber onto salad. Serve with dressings.

3. Place a 16-inch piece of foil on counter. Lay 3 cabbage leaves, sides overlapping, at one long edge of foil. Place two more rows of 3 leaves slightly overlapping row above. Spoon rice mixture onto leaves. Roll up, jelly-roll fashion, and slide onto platter, using foil to handle. Spoon sauce over and around cabbage roll.

MENU

Supper à la Provençale
(Planned for Four)

SCALLOPS PROVENCALE

WHITE RICE WITH HERBS

SPINACH-AND-VEGETABLE SALAD

HOT CRESCENT ROLLS

ORANGE-STRAWBERRY CAKE

CHILLED WHITE WINE OR ICED TEA

YOU WILL NEED:
1 pkg (13¾ oz) frozen orange cake
1 pkg (5½ oz) frozen crescent rolls
2 cups water
Packaged precooked rice
1 teaspoon instant minced onion
Chopped parsley
1 tablespoon butter for cooking plus
 ¼ lb (1 stick) for serving
1½ lb sea scallops
8 large strawberries
1 garlic clove
¼ cup apricot preserves
1 teaspoon water
½ cup chopped walnuts
1 can (8¼ oz) whole tomatoes
¼ teaspoon salt
Dash pepper
¼ teaspoon dried thyme leaves
1 tablespoon lemon juice
½ cup white wine
1 tablespoon all-purpose flour
½ lb fresh young spinach, washed and
 crisped
1 cucumber, chilled
¼ lb large fresh mushrooms
Prepared salad dressing
Chilled white wine (optional)
Iced tea
Sugar, lemon (optional)

6:00 to 6:10 P.M.

1. Remove cake from foil pan to serving plate to thaw. Also, remove the rolls from package to thaw.

2. Bring 2 cups water to boiling. Prepare rice as package label directs for four servings, adding the minced onion and 1 teaspoon chopped parsley.

3. In 1 tablespoon hot butter in a large skillet, sauté scallops until golden all over, turning several times—8 to 10 minutes.

6:10 to 6:20 P.M.

1. Meanwhile, wash eight large strawberries. Press garlic in garlic press.

2. Melt apricot preserves with the teaspoon water over low heat. Use to brush sides of cake; reserve some to glaze tops of berries. Press chopped nuts into sides of cake, making a border around top of cake. Slice strawberries in half; arrange in rows on top, as pictured. Brush with rest of melted preserves.

3. Drain tomatoes, reserving juice. Cut tomatoes into pieces; add to scallops along with salt, the garlic, pepper, thyme, lemon juice and white wine.

6:20 to 6:30 P.M.

1. In small bowl, combine juice reserved from tomatoes with 1 tablespoon flour, stirring to dissolve flour. Stir into

the scallop mixture. Simmer gently, covered, 5 minutes, or until slightly thickened.

2. Meanwhile, heat rolls, if desired.

3. Break the spinach into salad bowl. Wash, peel and slice cucumber. Wash mushrooms, and slice thin. Add cucumber and mushrooms to salad. Toss with salad dressing at serving time.

4. Turn rice into serving bowl; sprinkle rice and scallops with chopped parsley. Serve scallops right from the skillet. Make iced tea.

MENU

Something Special for Last-Minute Guests

(Planned for Four to Six)

SLICED BEEF IN BURGUNDY WITH MUSHROOMS

BUTTERY NOODLES

MARINATED BROCCOLI-AND-RED-PEPPER SALAD

FRENCH ROLLS BUTTER

FRESH-FRUIT-AND-SHERBET TART

COFFEE   TEA BURGUNDY

GEORGE RATKAI

YOU WILL NEED:
1 roll (1 lb, 1 oz) refrigerated sugar-cookie dough
1 bunch fresh broccoli (about 1 lb)
1 large red pepper
Prepared herb-flavored oil-and-vinegar salad dressing
1 small head lettuce, washed and crisped
3 quarts water
1 lb boneless beef chuck, in one piece, partially frozen
½ teaspoon meat tenderizer
2 scallions
½ lb large fresh mushrooms
1 large onion
1 pint fresh strawberries
¼ lb seedless green grapes
2 teaspoons sugar
1 pkg (8 oz) curly noodles
1⅓ tablespoons butter for cooking, plus ¼ lb (1 stick) for serving
1 can (10½ oz) condensed beef broth
¼ teaspoon dried thyme leaves
2 tablespoons all-purpose flour
½ cup Burgundy wine
6 French rolls
1 quart lemon sherbet
Coffee, instant or brewed
Tea (optional)
Cream, sugar, lemon (optional)
Burgundy

6:00 to 6:10 P.M.

1. Preheat oven to 400F. Cut 22 ¼-inch cookie slices from roll. Arrange 12 slices, edges touching, to make a 9-inch circle on ungreased cookie sheet. Fill in center with remaining 10 slices. With fingers, press slices firmly together where they touch. Bake 12 to 15 minutes, until golden and firm. Let cool briefly; loosen cookie tart shell from pan, slide gently onto wire rack.

2. Thinly slice broccoli lengthwise through stem and flower. Cut pepper into strips. In bowl, toss with 1 cup dressing. Place in freezer to chill quickly—no more than 15 minutes. Arrange lettuce in salad bowl; refrigerate.

3. Bring 3 quarts water to boiling in a large saucepan.

4. Slice beef very thinly, on diagonal. Sprinkle with meat tenderizer.

6:10 to 6:20 P.M.

1. Thinly slice 2 scallions. Slice mushrooms and onion. Wash and drain berries and grapes. Reserve 10 strawberries. Thinly slice remainder; toss with sugar.

2. Cook noodles in boiling water as package directs.

3. Cool cookie rounds 5 minutes. Slide onto serving platter, and place in freezer.

6:20 to 6:30 P.M.

1. Heat 1 tablespoon butter in large skillet. Sauté meat slices quickly on each side over high heat. Remove as browned; reserve. Add onion and mushrooms to skillet. Sauté until golden. Add beef broth and thyme; bring to boiling. Stir flour into wine; stir into broth. Cook until thickened.

2. Drain noodles. Toss with 1 teaspoon butter and scallions on platter. Fold beef into Burgundy sauce; reheat; spoon onto noodles.

3. Add marinated vegetables to salad bowl. Put rolls in a basket.

4. Scoop sherbet onto cookie crust; freeze. To serve, add whole berries and grapes. Pass sliced berries.

MENU

An Outdoor Brunch
(Planned for Six)

GRAPEFRUIT-JUICE SPRITZER

BAKED HAM-AND-ZUCCHINI PUFFS

TOSSED-GREEN-SALAD BOWL

RASPBERRY-JAM COFFEECAKE

CANTALOUPE WITH STRAWBERRIES AND BLUEBERRIES

COFFEE   TEA

YOU WILL NEED:
4 eggs
2 cups biscuit mix
¼ cup granulated sugar
⅔ cup milk
4 shortbread cookies
2 tablespoons brown sugar
¼ teaspoon ground cinnamon
¼ cup seedless red-raspberry preserves
1 medium zucchini (½ lb)
1 large head romaine, washed and crisped
½ cup pitted black olives
Prepared salad dressing
6 slices white bread
6 slices Cheddar cheese
6 slices boiled ham
Prepared yellow mustard
½ teaspoon cream of tartar
¼ teaspoon salt
½ cup (2 oz) grated Cheddar cheese
1 cantaloupe
1 pint fresh strawberries
½ cup fresh blueberries
Fresh mint (optional)
3 cups grapefruit juice
3 cups lemon-lime carbonated drink, chilled
1 lime, thinly sliced
Coffee, instant or brewed
Tea (optional)
Cream, sugar, lemon (optional)

12:00 to 12:10 P.M.

1. Separate eggs. Place whites in large bowl of electric mixer. Place yolks in medium bowl. Grease, flour a 9-inch round cake pan.

2. Preheat oven to 400F. Add biscuit mix, granulated sugar and milk to egg yolks. Stir until just combined. Turn into prepared pan.

3. Crumble 4 shortbread cookies; mix with brown sugar and cinnamon. Sprinkle over batter. Place ¼ cup preserves in small bowl; stir until smooth. Spoon over top. Bake 20 minutes, or until firm to touch.

4. Bring ½ cup water to boiling in a small saucepan. Wash and slice zucchini; add to boiling water. Cook, covered, 5 minutes.

12:10 to 12:20 P.M.

1. Break romaine into bowl; top with olives; refrigerate. To serve, toss with dressing.

2. Place 6 slices of bread on a cookie sheet. Top each with 1 slice cheese. Divide ham on cheese. Drain zucchini well. Place on ham. Spread each with ½ teaspoon mustard.

3. Add cream of tartar and salt to egg whites. Beat until stiff, not dry. Fold in grated cheese. Spoon onto zucchini. Bake until puffed—5 minutes.

12:20 to 12:30 P.M.

1. Cut cantaloupe lengthwise into thirds; cut each third in half; remove seeds. Place on individual plates. Wash strawberries and blueberries. Arrange on melon. Garnish with mint; if desired. Refrigerate.

2. In a 2-quart pitcher, combine grapefruit juice and carbonated drink. Add sliced lime. To serve, pour over ice.

3. Remove the coffeecake from oven. Cool slightly; loosen; remove to serving plate, using two spatulas.

MENU

An Elegant Seafood Dinner
(Planned for Two)

POACHED SALMON STEAKS

CUCUMBER SAUCE

TWO-TONE BEAN SALAD

CROISSANTS

STRAWBERRIES AND CREAM

WHITE WINE   COFFEE

GEORGE RATKAI

YOU WILL NEED:
½ lb green beans
½ lb wax beans
½ cup water
½ cup white wine
1 bay leaf
¼ teaspoon salt
Dash pepper
2 salmon steaks, ¾ inch thick, about 1 lb
¼ cup walnut halves
Prepared salad dressing
9 leaves Boston lettuce, washed and crisped
1 pint strawberries
2 tablespoons rum
1 large cucumber
1 pkg (5½ oz) frozen croissants
3 tablespoons butter for cooking, plus ⅛ lb (½ stick) for serving
Fresh dill
Fresh parsley
1 tablespoon all-purpose flour
1 pkg (8 oz) whipped topping, thawed
Coffee, instant or brewed
Cream and sugar (optional)
Chilled white wine

6:00 to 6:10 P.M.

1. In medium saucepan, bring 1 cup water to boiling. Wash green and wax beans; remove stem ends; cut into 2-inch pieces. Place in saucepan; cover; simmer 5 minutes.

2. In medium skillet, combine water, white wine, the bay leaf, salt and pepper; bring to boiling. Place salmon steaks in skillet; cover; simmer 10 to 12 minutes, or until fish flakes easily.

6:10 to 6:20 P.M.

1. Preheat oven to 325F. Drain beans in colander; immerse colander in ice water. Toss cooled beans with walnuts and prepared salad dressing. Line serving bowl with Boston lettuce; spoon beans into center; refrigerate until serving time.

2. Wash and hull strawberries; toss with rum; arrange in serving bowl; refrigerate.

3. Wash cucumber; cut 8 thin slices; reserve for garnish. Pare, seed and chop remainder of the cucumber. Place the croissants in the oven.

6:20 to 6:30 P.M.

1. With spatula, carefully remove salmon steaks to serving platter; cover; keep warm. Strain broth into measuring cup, to measure ¾ cup broth. Melt 1

tablespoon butter in skillet, and sauté the chopped cucumber 2 to 3 minutes.

2. Place the sautéed cucumber, two sprigs each of dill and parsley into blender or food processor; add 2 tablespoons fish broth; blend until smooth. In skillet, melt 2 tablespoons butter; stir in flour. Gradually add remaining fish broth and puréed cucumber mixture; cook, stirring, until sauce is slightly thickened.

3. Spoon some of the sauce around the salmon steaks. Garnish platter with cucumber slices and parsley. Remove croissants from oven; place in basket. At dessert time, spoon whipped topping over strawberries. Pass additional topping, if desired.

MENU

A Family Supper

(Planned for Six)

LINGUINE PRIMAVERA WITH SAUSAGES

TOMATO-AND-AVOCADO SALAD

GARLIC BREAD

RUM CAKE WITH GREEN GRAPES

**COFFEE
CHILLED WHITE WINE**

YOU WILL NEED:
4 sweet or hot Italian sausages
¼ lb mushrooms
1 red pepper
1 onion
¼ lb green beans
Flowerets from 1 large stalk broccoli
1 small zucchini
1 small yellow squash
¼ cup (½ stick) butter, softened
1 garlic clove, pressed
¼ teaspoon dried basil leaves
1 loaf Italian bread
1 baker's angel-food cake
½ cup orange juice
¾ cup apricot preserves
2 tablespoons rum
1 pkg (1 lb) linguine
¼ lb green seedless grapes
1 tablespoon salad oil
½ cup water
1 head romaine, washed and crisped
2 ripe tomatoes
1 ripe avocado
2 tablespoons lemon juice
Prepared salad dressing
3 tablespoons butter
Grated Parmesan cheese
Coffee, instant or brewed
Cream and sugar (optional)
Chilled white wine

6:00 to 6:10 P.M.

1. Bring 6 quarts water to boil in a large kettle. Place sausages and 2 cups water in a large skillet. Cook, covered, 20 minutes.

2. Wash and slice mushrooms and red pepper. Peel and slice onion. Wash green beans; trim ends; cut in half diagonally. Wash broccoli; separate into flowerets. Wash and slice zucchini and squash.

3. Combine softened butter, garlic and basil. Split bread; spread with garlic butter.

6:10 to 6:20 P.M.

1. Place cake on plate with raised edge. Using a cake tester, make holes in top. In a small saucepan, stir together orange juice, ¼ cup of the apricot preserves and rum. Bring to boiling; spoon over cake.

2. Place linguine in boiling water. Cook as package directs. Preheat broiler.

3. Melt the ½ cup apricot preserves in same saucepan. Brush over cake. Wash and drain grapes. Arrange on and around cake; refrigerate.

4. Remove sausages; discard liquid. Add 1 tablespoon oil to skillet along with mushrooms, red pepper and onion. Cook, stirring, 2 minutes. Slice sausages. Add sausages, green beans, broc-coli and ½ cup water to skillet; cover; simmer 5 minutes.

6:20 to 6:30 P.M.

1. Arrange romaine in salad bowl. Slice tomatoes. Peel and slice avocado; toss with lemon juice. Arrange tomatoes and avocado on romaine. Pass dressing.

2. Add zucchini and squash to mixture in skillet. Simmer, covered, 5 minutes.

3. Broil garlic bread 6 inches from heat until golden.

4. Drain linguine; turn onto platter. Toss with 3 tablespoons butter; top with vegetables and some Parmesan. Serve with more cheese.

SEVEN

ONE-DISH MEALS

♦

As the old saying goes, ''Too many cooks spoil the broth.'' To offer a paraphrase, ''Too many pots and pans spoil the fun and creativity that cooking can bring.'' True, every so often it's great to attack the kitchen and whip up a week's supply of meals or some exotic recipe without giving a second thought to the pile of dirty pots, pans and utensils that will surely result. But during the average week, most busy cooks look forward to spending as little time and energy as possible in the kitchen. To them we devote this section and all the time-saving, one-dish recipes it contains. From hearty casseroles to main-dish salads to quaint quiches, you'll find an exciting array of easy-to-prepare, easy-to-serve dishes that offer fantastic flavor and something you may never have had before—time to relax while cooking.

HEARTY CASSEROLES AND STEWS

In any language, a one-dish recipe can be translated to mean "easy," "timesaving" and just plain "terrific." On the following pages we've gathered our favorite international one-dish main meals, all adapted to American tastes and life-styles. Here, a group centered on two hearty staples: pasta and beans. Top, Frankfurters With Brown Beans, a favorite of Dutch farmers. Continuing clockwise: Tuscany Bean Soup, rich as any stew; Mexican Tamale Pie, served with cheesy cornbread squares; Hungarian Beef-Balls Paprikash; and a luscious Scandinavian-inspired Zucchini-Tuna-And-Macaroni Casserole. Recipes start on page 241.

SATISFYING

S·A·L·A·D·S

ONE-DISH MEALS

W hat's colorful, refreshing, deliciously dressed and gaining in popularity among health-conscious Americans? Salad! Easy-to-prepare, main-dish salads offer a bonanza of inviting flavors and textures—and make-ahead convenience too. Shown here, a trio of one-dish salad ideas perfectly suited for lunch, dinner or a late-night supper. Upper left, a hearty Ensalada Mexicana, composed of cold chicken, marinated garbanzo beans, corn chips, cheese and avocado slices atop fresh spinach leaves, all topped with a spicy Guacamole Sauce used as a salad dressing. Lower left, an individual portion of Cold Ratatouille—the classic French mixture of eggplant, zucchini, green pepper and mushrooms sautéed in olive oil and spices, then chilled and served in a hollowed-out eggplant shell. Above, a sumptuous serving of White-Bean-And-Tuna Salad, garnished with tomatoes, cucumbers, watercress and olives and nestled on a bed of crisp romaine.
Recipes begin on page 240.

continued from page 239

WHITE-BEAN-AND-TUNA SALAD
(pictured)

DRESSING
¾ cup salad oil
¼ cup red-wine vinegar
1½ teaspoons dry mustard
1 teaspoon salt
1 teaspoon ground coriander
¼ teaspoon pepper
1 garlic clove, crushed

1 lb dried Great Northern beans
Water
3 carrots, pared
1 bay leaf
1 teaspoon dried thyme leaves
1 tablespoon salt
½ cup chopped green onion
1½ cups sliced celery, cut on the diagonal
¼ cup chopped parsley
½ head romaine, washed and crisped
2 cans (7-oz size) tuna, drained, chilled
1 medium unpeeled cucumber, thinly sliced, chilled
3 medium tomatoes, each cut into 6ths, chilled
12 pitted black olives, halved, chilled

DAY BEFORE

1. Make Dressing: In jar with tight-fitting lid, combine oil, vinegar, mustard, 1 teaspoon salt, the coriander, pepper and garlic; shake vigorously until combined.

2. Wash beans; drain. Turn into a large kettle. Cover with cold water; let stand 4 to 5 hours. Add 1 quart water to cover. Over medium heat, gently simmer beans with carrot, bay leaf, thyme and salt, covered, 1 to 1½ hours, or until tender but not mushy. Drain. Reserve carrot, cut into ¼-inch pieces.

3. In large shallow dish, combine warm (not hot) beans, dressing, green onion, celery, parsley and carrot; toss lightly to combine. Refrigerate, covered, 4 hours or overnight, to blend flavors.

NEXT DAY

4. Before serving: Line a large serving platter with romaine. Mound marinated beans in center. Arrange chilled tuna, cucumber and tomato in mounds around edge of plate. Garnish with black olives. *Makes 8 servings.*

ENSALADA MEXICANA
(pictured)

½ cup salad oil
¼ cup cider vinegar
1 teaspoon salt
⅛ teaspoon pepper

2 cans (1 lb, 4-oz size) garbanzos, drained
½ cup coarsely chopped red pepper
½ cup coarsely chopped green onion
½ lb fresh spinach
½ lb Monterey Jack cheese
3 cups cooked skinless and boneless chicken, cut into large pieces, chilled
1 medium avocado, peeled and sliced
1 small red onion, sliced
1 pkg (6 oz) corn chips, regular size
Guacamole Sauce, recipe follows

DAY BEFORE

1. In large bowl, combine salad oil, vinegar, salt and pepper; mix well. Add garbanzos, red pepper and green onion; toss lightly to combine. Refrigerate, covered, overnight.

2. Wash spinach; remove and discard stems. Place in plastic bag, or wrap in plastic wrap, refrigerate. Cut cheese into pieces ¼ inch wide and 2 inches long, refrigerate. Meanwhile, make Guacamole Sauce; refrigerate, covered.

NEXT DAY

3. Just before serving, assemble salad: Place spinach in large chilled serving dish.

4. Arrange the garbanzos, chicken, cheese, avocado, red onion and corn chips in groups on spinach. Pass Guacamole Sauce to spoon over salad. *Makes 8 servings.*

GUACAMOLE SAUCE

2 medium tomatoes, peeled
2 ripe avocados (about 1½ lb)
¼ cup finely chopped onion
2 tablespoons finely chopped canned mild or hot green chilies
3 tablespoons white vinegar
1 tablespoon salt

1. In medium bowl, crush tomatoes with potato masher, or use food processor.

2. Halve avocados lengthwise; remove pits and peel. Slice avocados into crushed tomatoes; then mash or process until well blended.

3. Add onion, chilies, vinegar and salt; mix well. *Makes about 3 cups.*

Note: Any leftover sauce may be used as a dip with tortilla chips.

COLD RATATOUILLE IN EGGPLANT SHELL
(pictured)

1 medium green pepper (4 oz)
1½ medium zucchini (½ lb)
¼ lb medium mushrooms
½ medium eggplant (½ lb)
6 tablespoons salad or olive oil
½ cup thinly sliced onion
1 garlic clove, crushed
16 cherry tomatoes, washed and halved
1 teaspoon salt
⅛ teaspoon pepper
2 tablespoons chopped parsley
2 small eggplants (optional) or lettuce (optional)

DAY BEFORE

1. Wash pepper; halve. Remove ribs and seeds. Cut lengthwise into ¼-inch-thick slices.

2. Scrub zucchini. Cut on diagonal into ¼-inch-thick slices. Wash mushrooms; slice lengthwise, right through stems, ¼ inch thick.

3. Wash eggplant; do not peel. Cut lengthwise into quarters; then cut crosswise into ½-inch slices.

4. In 2 tablespoons hot oil in medium skillet, sauté green pepper, mushrooms, onion and garlic 5 minutes, or until onion is transparent. With slotted spoon, remove to medium bowl.

5. Add 2 tablespoons oil to skillet. In hot oil, sauté zucchini, turning frequently, until tender—10 minutes. With slotted utensil, remove from skillet to same bowl.

6. Add remaining oil to skillet. In hot oil, sauté eggplant, turning occasionally, until tender—5 minutes.

7. Return vegetables to same skillet. Layer cherry tomatoes on top. Sprinkle with salt, pepper and 1 tablespoon parsley. Stir gently to mix.

8. Simmer mixture, covered, over low heat 10 minutes.

9. Remove cover; cook 5 minutes longer, basting occasionally with pan juices, or until liquid has evaporated.

10. Refrigerate, covered, until very well chilled—overnight.

NEXT DAY

11. If desired, serve Ratatouille in eggplant shell, as pictured: Wash and halve small eggplants; scoop out inner portion, leaving shell. (Reserve eggplant pulp for another use.) Or serve in lettuce cups. Sprinkle with remaining parsley. *Makes 4 servings.*

SALADE FRANCAISE

RAVIGOTE DRESSING
2 tablespoons chopped onion
2 tablespoons chopped parsley
2 tablespoons capers
½ teaspoon dried tarragon leaves
¼ cup white wine
1 cup mayonnaise
1 hard-cooked egg white, finely chopped
1 tablespoon lemon juice

2½ lb fresh asparagus
1½ teaspoons salt
1 pkg (9 oz) frozen artichoke hearts
2 lb mussels
Chicory
Pimiento strips
½ lb mushrooms, washed and sliced
2 tablespoons lemon juice
3 medium tomatoes, washed and sliced

DAY BEFORE

1. Make Ravigote Dressing: In small saucepan, combine onion, parsley, capers, tarragon and white wine. Bring to boiling; simmer, uncovered, to reduce liquid to 2 tablespoons—about 2 minutes. Cool 10 minutes.

2. In small bowl, combine mayonnaise, egg white, lemon juice and wine mixture; mix well. Refrigerate, covered. Makes 1¼ cups.

3. Break or cut off tough ends of asparagus. Wash asparagus well under cold running water. If asparagus is sandy, scrub with brush. With vegetable parer, scrape skin and scales from stalks.

4. Bunch stalks together; tie with string, or use rubber band. Place upright in deep saucepan. Add boiling water (about 1 inch deep) and the salt.

5. Return to boiling; cook, covered, 12 to 15 minutes. Pierce lower part of stalks with fork, to see if they are tender. Drain well; refrigerate.

6. Cook artichoke hearts according to package directions; drain and refrigerate.

NEXT DAY

7. Steam mussels: Check mussels, discarding any that are not tightly closed. Scrub well under cold running water, to remove sand and seaweed.

8. Place mussels in large skillet; pour in ¾ cup boiling water. Cover and steam over medium heat 3 minutes (just until the shells open). Drain. Discard any mussels that do not open. Turn into a serving bowl. Let mussels cool to room temperature or chill slightly, if preferred.

9. To serve: Line large chilled serving dish with chicory. Arrange, in groups, asparagus (garnished with pimiento strips), artichoke hearts, mushrooms sprinkled with lemon juice, sliced tomatoes and mussels. Pass Ravigote Dressing with salad. *Makes 6 servings.* ◆

continued from page 237

TUSCANY BEAN SOUP
(pictured)

1 pkg (1 lb) dried white Great Northern Beans
Water
1 tablespoon salt
1 can (10¾ oz) condensed chicken broth, undiluted
½ teaspoon dried marjoram leaves
1 bay leaf
⅛ teaspoon pepper
2 tablespoons salad oil
1½ cups sliced onion
1 garlic clove, crushed
1 cup carrots, sliced diagonally ½ inch thick
2 large potatoes (¾ lb), pared and cut into julienne strips
1 pkg (10 oz) frozen chopped spinach, thawed
Grated Parmesan cheese

DAY BEFORE

1. Wash beans; drain. Cover beans with 6 cups cold water. Refrigerate, covered, overnight.

NEXT DAY

2. Turn beans and liquid (do not drain) into an 8-quart kettle; add salt, 6 cups water, chicken broth, the marjoram, bay leaf and pepper. Bring to boiling; reduce heat; simmer, covered, about 1 hour.

3. Meanwhile, in hot oil in medium skillet, sauté onion, garlic and carrot, stirring, until onion is golden—about 5 minutes.

4. After bean mixture has cooked 1 hour, add onion mixture, potato and frozen spinach. Cook, covered, until beans and vegetables are tender. Serve sprinkled with Parmesan cheese. *Makes 3 quarts, 1 cup per serving.*

FRANKFURTERS WITH BROWN BEANS
(pictured)

1 lb pinto or red kidney beans
Water
1 tablespoon salt
1 lb carrots, pared, sliced diagonally ½ inch thick
4 onions, peeled and quartered
2 garlic cloves, crushed
2 lb potatoes, peeled and sliced ½ inch thick
2 red apples, washed, cored, cut into 6 wedges
1 lb frankfurters
Hot mustard (optional)

DAY BEFORE

1. Wash beans; drain. Cover beans with 6 cups cold water. Refrigerate, covered, overnight.

NEXT DAY

2. Turn beans and liquid (do not drain) into an 8-quart kettle; add salt, 1 cup water, carrot, onion and garlic. Bring to boiling; reduce heat, and simmer gently, covered, 45 minutes.

3. Add potato slices; cook, covered, 20 minutes.

4. Slash each frankfurter on the diagonal several times. Add apple wedges and frankfurters; cook, covered, 10 more minutes, or until all vegetables are tender but not mushy. Serve with hot mustard, if desired. *Makes 8 servings.*

TAMALE PIE
(pictured)

4 cups water
1 teaspoon salt
1 cup yellow cornmeal
½ cup grated Cheddar cheese

CHILI CON CARNE
1 lb ground chuck (in chunks)
1½ cups sliced onion
1½ to 2 tablespoons chili powder
2 cans (1-lb size) dark-red kidney beans
1 can (1 lb, 12 oz) whole tomatoes, undrained
1 teaspoon salt
⅛ teaspoon pepper
¼ teaspoon garlic powder
½ teaspoon sugar
¼ cup catsup

DAY BEFORE

1. Cook cornmeal: In a heavy, 4-quart saucepan, bring 4 cups water and 1 teaspoon salt to a full, rolling boil. Slowly add cornmeal, stirring constantly with a wire whisk—mixture will get very thick.

2. Turn heat low; cook, uncovered and stirring frequently, 20 minutes. Add ¼ cup cheese. Turn into buttered 13-by-9-by-2-inch baking dish; let stand 20 minutes. Refrigerate, covered, overnight.

NEXT DAY

3. Make Chili con Carne: In large heavy skillet, over medium heat, sauté ground chuck, stirring, until red color disappears.

4. Add onion and chili powder; cook,

continued on page 249

A Collection
Of Dazzling Quiches

*Q*uiche looks spectacular, but the ingredients are simple
as pie (which it is): savory custard and grated cheese
in a pie shell. Give it the extra added pizzazz of
seasonal vegetables or the heartiness of salami and
ham. Above: Ratatouille Quiche, a marvelous vegetable
melange. Recipes begin on page 244.

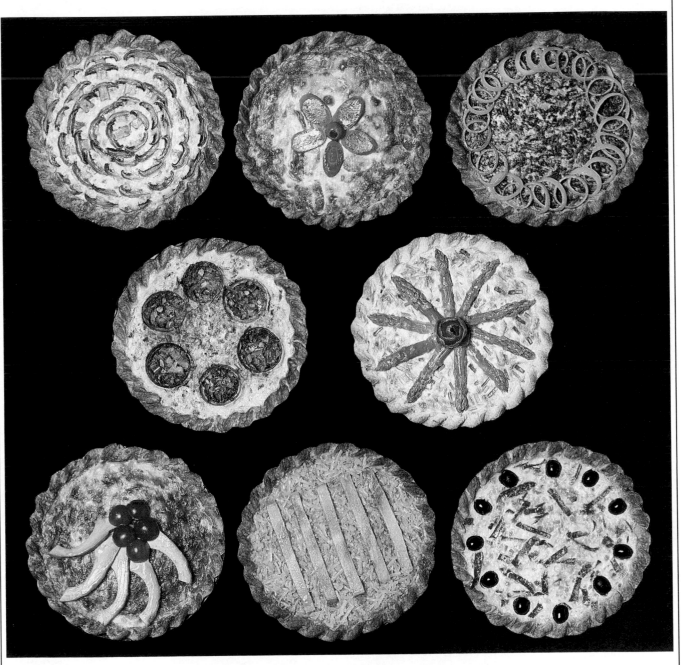

Fresh Mushroom Quiche   Carrot Quiche   Spinach Quiche
Broccoli-Mushroom Quiche   Asparagus Quiche
Avocado Quiche   Ham-And-Cheddar Quiche   Salami-Corn Quiche

continued from page 242

OUR BASIC QUICHE

9-inch unbaked pie shell
1 egg white, slightly beaten

FILLING
4 bacon slices
2 cups natural Swiss cheese, grated (8 oz)
4 eggs
1½ cups half-and-half light cream
¼ teaspoon salt
⅛ teaspoon ground nutmeg
Dash pepper

1. Brush inside of pie shell with egg white; refrigerate.
2. Preheat oven to 375F.
3. Make Filling: Fry bacon until crisp; drain; crumble. Sprinkle over bottom of pie shell. Sprinkle cheese over bacon.
4. In medium bowl, with wire whisk or rotary beater, beat eggs with half-and-half, salt, nutmeg and pepper just until combined but not frothy.
5. Slowly pour into the pie shell.
6. Bake, placed on low rack in oven, 35 to 40 minutes, just until puffy and golden.
7. Remove to wire rack to cool 10 minutes before serving. *Makes 8 servings.*

RATATOUILLE QUICHE

(pictured)

9-inch unbaked pie shell
1 egg white, slightly beaten

FILLING
¼ cup salad oil
½ cup chopped green pepper
½ cup chopped onion
1 garlic clove, crushed
1 small zucchini (¼ lb) scrubbed and cut
**   crosswise into ¼-inch-thick slices**
1 small eggplant (¼ lb), cut into ¼-inch
**   slices, then into quarters**
¾ teaspoon salt
Dash pepper
1 ripe tomato, peeled and cut into
**   8 wedges**
1½ cups natural Swiss cheese, grated
**   (6 oz)**
4 eggs
¾ cup half-and-half or light cream
⅛ teaspoon ground nutmeg
Dash pepper

1 tablespoon chopped parsley

1. Brush inside of pie shell with egg white; refrigerate.
2. Make Filling: In hot oil in large skillet, sauté green pepper, chopped onion, garlic, the zucchini and eggplant, stirring frequently, until tender—5 minutes. Sprinkle with ½ teaspoon salt and pepper.

3. Place tomato wedges on top; simmer, covered, over low heat, 5 minutes. Set aside.
4. Preheat oven to 375F.
5. Sprinkle cheese over bottom of pie shell.
6. In medium bowl, with wire whisk or rotary beater, beat eggs with half-and-half, ¼ teaspoon salt, nutmeg and pepper just until combined but not frothy.
7. Drain ratatouille: arrange attractively over grated cheese in bottom of prepared pie shell, as pictured. Pour egg mixture over the vegetables. Bake, placed on lower rack in oven, 35 minutes, or until custard is puffy and set in center.
8. Cool on wire rack 10 minutes before serving. Serve warm, sprinkled with 1 tablespoon chopped parsley. *Makes 8 servings.*

FRESH MUSHROOM QUICHE

(pictured)

9-inch unbaked pie shell
1 egg white, slightly beaten

FILLING
2 tablespoons butter or margarine
¾ lb mushrooms, thinly sliced (3 cups)
4 bacon slices
2 cups natural Swiss cheese, grated (8 oz)
4 eggs
1½ cups half-and-half or light cream
¼ teaspoon salt
⅛ teaspoon ground nutmeg
Dash pepper

1. Brush inside of pie shell with egg white; refrigerate.
2. Make Filling: In butter in medium skillet, sauté mushrooms, stirring, until golden-brown. Set aside.
3. Preheat oven to 375F.
4. Fry bacon until crisp; drain; crumble. Sprinkle over bottom of pie shell. Sprinkle cheese over bacon.
5. In medium bowl, with wire whisk or rotary beater, beat eggs with half-and-half, salt, nutmeg and pepper just until combined but not frothy.
6. Arrange sautéed mushrooms over cheese in a circular pattern, as pictured; pour egg mixture over top.
7. Bake, placed on low rack in oven,

35 to 40 minutes, just until puffy and golden.
8. Remove to wire rack to cool 10 minutes before serving. *Makes 8 servings.*

CARROT QUICHE

(pictured)

9-inch unbaked pie shell
1 egg white, slightly beaten

FILLING
½ lb carrots (3 medium), pared and cut
**   into ¼-inch diagonal slices**
2 tablespoons butter or margarine
½ cup onion, finely chopped
4 bacon slices
1½ cups natural Swiss cheese, grated
**   (6 oz)**
4 eggs
1 cup half-and-half or light cream
¼ teaspoon salt
⅛ teaspoon ground nutmeg
Dash pepper

Pimiento-stuffed olive half (optional)

1. Brush inside of pie shell with egg white; refrigerate.
2. Make Filling: Place carrots in medium skillet with enough salted water to cover; simmer, covered, 20 minutes, or until tender. Drain well. Reserve 5 slices for garnish.
3. Meanwhile, in medium skillet, melt butter. Sauté onion until golden—about 5 minutes. Add remaining carrot slices; mix well. Set aside.
4. Preheat oven to 375F.
5. Fry bacon until crisp; drain, crumble. Sprinkle over bottom of pie shell. Sprinkle cheese over bacon.
6. In medium bowl, with wire whisk or rotary beater, beat eggs with half-and-half, salt, nutmeg and pepper just until combined but not frothy.
7. Turn carrot-onion mixture into prepared pie shell on top of grated cheese. Pour egg mixture over top.
8. Bake, placed on lower rack in oven, 40 minutes, or until slightly firm in center. Remove to wire rack to cool 10 minutes before serving. Garnish center, as pictured, with carrot slices and pimiento-stuffed olive half, if desired. *Makes 8 servings.*

SPINACH QUICHE
(pictured)

9-inch unbaked pie shell
1 egg white, slightly beaten

FILLING
6 tablespoons (¾ stick) butter or margarine
½ cup chopped onion
1 pkg (10 oz) frozen chopped spinach, thawed and well-drained
2 tablespoons chopped parsley
4 bacon slices
1½ cups natural Swiss cheese, grated (6 oz)
4 eggs
1 cup half-and-half or light cream
¼ teaspoon salt
⅛ teaspoon ground nutmeg
Dash pepper

1 cup sliced onion rings

1. Brush inside of pie shell with egg white; refrigerate.
2. Make Filling: In 4 tablespoons butter in medium skillet, sauté onion until golden—about 5 minutes. Add chopped spinach and parsley; mix well. Remove from heat. Turn into large bowl. Set aside.
3. Preheat oven to 375F.
4. Fry bacon until crisp; drain; crumble. Spinkle over bottom of pie shell. Sprinkle cheese over bacon.
5. In medium bowl, with wire whisk or rotary beater, beat eggs with half-and-half, salt, nutmeg and pepper just until combined but not frothy.
6. Combine spinach and egg mixtures; pour into pie shell over grated cheese.
7. Bake, placed on lower rack in oven, 45 to 50 minutes, or until set in the center. Meanwhile, in remaining 2 tablespoons butter, sauté sliced onion rings until golden. Remove from heat. Arrange onion rings around edge of baked quiche, overlapping slightly. Let cool on wire rack 10 minutes before serving. *Makes 8 servings.*

BROCCOLI-MUSHROOM QUICHE
(pictured)

9-inch unbaked pie shell
1 egg white, slightly beaten

FILLING
6 large mushrooms
1 tablespoon lemon juice
¼ cup (½ stick) butter or margarine
½ cup chopped onion
1 pkg (10 oz) frozen chopped broccoli, thawed and well-drained
2 tablespoons chopped parsley

¾ teaspoon salt
Dash pepper
2 cups natural Swiss cheese, grated (8 oz)
4 eggs
1 cup half-and-half or light cream
⅛ teaspoon ground nutmeg
Dash pepper

1. Brush inside of pie shell with egg white; refrigerate.
2. Make Filling: Wash mushrooms; remove stems and chop coarsely. Toss with lemon juice.
3. In butter in medium skillet, sauté mushroom caps, stirring, until tender—about 5 minutes. Remove from skillet, drain on paper towels.
4. In remaining fat in skillet, sauté onion and the chopped mushroom stems, stirring, about 5 minutes. Add broccoli, parsley, ½ teaspoon salt and dash pepper; mix well. Remove from heat.
5. Preheat oven to 375F.
6. Sprinkle cheese over bottom of pie shell.
7. In medium bowl, with wire whisk or rotary beater, beat eggs with half-and-half, ¼ teaspoon salt, nutmeg and pepper just until combined but not frothy.
8. Spoon 1 rounded tablespoon of broccoli mixture into each mushroom cap. Turn the rest into bottom of prepared pie shell over grated cheese.
9. Pour egg mixture over all. Arrange the 6 stuffed mushrooms on top.
10. Bake, placed on lower rack in oven, 40 to 45 minutes, or until puffy and golden. Remove to wire rack; cool 10 minutes before serving. *Makes 8 servings.*

ASPARAGUS QUICHE
(pictured)

9-inch unbaked pie shell
1 egg white, slightly beaten

FILLING
1½ lb fresh asparagus
4 bacon slices
2 cups natural Swiss cheese, grated (8 oz)
4 eggs
1½ cups half-and-half or light cream
¼ teaspoon salt
⅛ teaspoon ground nutmeg
Dash pepper

1 plum tomato

1. Brush inside of pie shell with egg white; refrigerate
2. Make Filling: Wash asparagus; break off and discard tough white portion. Scrape ends of asparagus with vegetable parer. Set aside ten of the best spears for decoration—they should be 4 inches long. Cut rest of asparagus into ½-inch pieces.
3. In large saucepan, bring 1 quart water to boiling; add 1 teaspoon salt and the asparagus. Bring back to boiling; reduce heat; simmer, covered, 5 minutes. Drain; rinse asparagus under cold water to prevent further cooking. Set aside.
4. Preheat oven to 375F.
5. Fry bacon until crisp; drain; crumble. Sprinkle over bottom of pie shell. Sprinkle cheese over bacon.
6. In medium bowl, with wire whisk or rotary beater, beat eggs with half-and-half, ¼ teaspoon salt, nutmeg and pepper just until combined but not frothy.
7. Sprinkle cut-up asparagus over cheese in bottom of pie shell.
8. Pour egg mixture into pie shell. Arrange reserved asparagus spears, spoke-fashion, on pie, as pictured.
9. Bake, placed on lower rack in oven, 40 minutes until puffy and golden. Remove to wire rack to cool 10 minutes.
10. Before serving, place tomato rose in center: With sharp knife, cut a ½-inch strip of skin around tomato, in a continuous spiral. Wind the strip around until a rose shape is formed. *Makes 8 servings.*

AVOCADO QUICHE
(pictured)

9-inch unbaked pie shell
1 egg white, slightly beaten

FILLING
4 bacon slices
2 cups natural Swiss cheese, grated (8 oz)
4 eggs
1 cup half-and-half or light cream
¼ teaspoon salt
⅛ teaspoon ground nutmeg
Dash pepper
1 medium avocado (¾ lb)
2 tablespoons lemon juice
Salt and pepper

3 cherry tomatoes, halved

1. Brush inside of pie shell with egg white; refrigerate.
2. Preheat oven to 375F.
3. Make Filling: Fry bacon until crisp; drain; crumble. Sprinkle over bottom of pie shell. Sprinkle 1 cup cheese over bacon.
4. In medium bowl, with wire whisk or rotary beater, beat eggs with half-and-half, ¼ teaspoon salt, nutmeg and pepper just until combined but not frothy.
5. Halve avocado lengthwise; remove pit and skin. Slice avocado; reserve five slices (sprinkle with lemon juice; refrigerate, covered). Cube remaining avocado; layer in bottom of prepared pie shell on top of grated cheese. Sprinkle lightly with salt and pepper.

continued on page 257

The End of
Ho-Humburger

◆

Good old faithful hamburger. It's usually a part of everyone's weekly shopping list. But after you've run through your ground beef repertoire once or twice, even the kids can get bored. Fortunately, hamburger is obligingly versatile and can be transformed into any number of one-dish culinary delights. And pasta, grains, cheese and vegetable protein can make a little go a long way. Hamburger tips: Buy chuck—it's as nutritious and tastes as good as more expensive round and sirloin. For maximum flavor and juiciness, it should be ground only once. Here, left to right: Hamburger Steak au Poivre, Mexican Tamale Pie, an unusual curry casserole called Bobotie and our own McCall'sburger made with, of all things, peanut butter. For recipes, turn to page 248.

IRWIN HOROWITZ

continued from page 247

HAMBURGER STEAK AU POIVRE
(pictured)

1½ lb ground chuck (freshly-ground)
3 teaspoons freshly ground coarse black pepper
¼ cup (½ stick) butter or margarine
½ cup Burgundy
1 beef-bouillon cube, crumbled
Ratatouille, see Note
2 tablespoons chopped parsley

1. Shape beef into one large oval patty, about 5 inches wide and 7 inches long. Sprinkle each side with 1½ teaspoons pepper.

2. In 2 tablespoons hot butter, in medium skillet, brown each side over medium heat about 2 minutes.

3. Reduce heat; cook over low heat 15 minutes, turning once, for medium-rare. Remove to warm serving platter.

4. Stir remaining butter into drippings in skillet along with wine and bouillon cube. Stir over medium heat to dissolve bouillon cube and any browned bits in pan. Bring just to boiling; simmer gently 2 minutes; pour over hamburger steak.

5. Spoon warm Ratatouille around hamburger just before serving. Sprinkle with 2 tablespoons chopped parsley. *Serves 6.*

Note: Make Ratatouille (page 240), Steps 1 through 9, substituting 2 medium tomatoes (¾ lb) peeled and cut into wedges, instead of 16 cherry tomatoes.

BOBOTIE
(pictured)

2 tablespoons butter or margarine
2 medium onions, sliced
2 lb ground chuck
1 egg
¼ cup milk
2 slices white bread, cubed
½ cup dried apricots, finely chopped
½ cup dark raisins
12 blanched almonds, chopped
2 tablespoons sugar
1 tablespoon curry powder
2 tablespoons lemon juice
2 teaspoons salt
¼ teaspoon pepper
1 bay leaf, crushed

TOPPING
2 eggs
1½ cups milk
½ teaspoon tumeric
½ teaspoon salt
5 bay leaves

Hot cooked rice
Chutney

1. In hot butter, in large skillet, sauté onion until golden—about 5 minutes. Add chuck; sauté until browned. Remove from heat.

2. Preheat oven to 350F.

3. In large bowl, combine egg, milk and the bread cubes, mashing bread with fork. Add apricots, raisins, almonds, sugar, curry, lemon juice, 2 teaspoons salt, pepper and crushed bay leaf; mix until well blended.

4. Add meat mixture; mix with fork. Turn into 2½-quart (10-inch), shallow casserole, spreading evenly.

5. Bake, uncovered, 30 minutes.

6. Meanwhile, make Topping: In small bowl, beat eggs with milk, tumeric and salt just until blended.

7. Remove casserole from oven. Pour topping over meat mixture. Arrange 5 bay leaves in center as pictured.

8. Bake 10 to 15 minutes longer, or just until topping is set. Garnish, if desired, with whole almonds and black olives. Serve with rice and chutney. *Makes 8 servings.*

McCALL'S BURGER
(pictured)

¼ cup creamy-style peanut butter
1 lb ground chuck
½ teaspoon salt
¼ teaspoon pepper
Butter or margarine
5 hamburger buns

1. In large bowl, with fork, lightly mix peanut butter, ground chuck, salt and pepper just until combined.

2. Divide into 5 burgers, about ½ cup for each one. Flatten gently.

3. Arrange in large skillet, not overlapping. Cook over medium heat about 4 minutes to a side, or until of desired doneness. Serve in buttered buns. *Makes 5 servings.*

GREEK PASTITSIO

2 teaspoons salt
½ lb elbow macaroni
5 tablespoons butter or margarine
2 medium onions, chopped
1 lb ground chuck
2 cans (8-oz size) tomato sauce
1 teaspoon salt
2 garlic cloves, minced
2 teaspoons ground cinnamon
3 tablespoons all-purpose flour
2¼ cups milk
3 eggs
Dash salt
Pepper
Nutmeg

1. In a large saucepan, bring 2 quarts water and 2 teaspoons salt to a boil over high heat. Add macaroni all at once, stirring to prevent pasta from sticking together. Cook as package directs until pasta is tender but still slightly firm to the teeth. Drain.

2. Heat 2 tablespoons butter in a 10-inch skillet; add chopped onion and sauté slowly until just golden-brown. Add meat (break up lumps with the back of a wooden spoon), sautéing until it has lost its red color.

3. Add tomato sauce, 1 teaspoon salt, the garlic and 1 teaspoon ground cinnamon. Simmer 20 minutes. Meanwhile, grease a 13-by-9-by-2-inch baking dish; add half of the macaroni. Top with meat sauce, spreading it evenly over macaroni. Add remaining macaroni.

4. Preheat oven to 350F. In medium saucepan, melt remaining 3 tablespoons butter and stir in flour. Remove from heat; slowly stir in milk. Beat with a wire whisk until smooth; return to heat and simmer about 5 minutes until thickened. Remove from heat and cool slightly.

5. In a medium-size bowl, beat eggs slightly with a wire whisk. Slowly add half of the warm cream sauce, beating constantly. Return mixture to remaining sauce in pan, and beat until smooth. Season to taste with salt, pepper and nutmeg.

6. Sprinkle top of macaroni with remaining cinnamon and pour sauce over all. Tap pan hard on counter so that sauce goes to bottom. Bake 40 minutes, or until the custard is firm. Let stand at room temperature for 10 minutes before serving. *Makes 6 to 8 servings.*

MEXICAN TAMALE PIE
(pictured)

4 cups water
1 teaspoon salt
1 cup yellow cornmeal
½ cup grated Parmesan cheese
1 tablespoon olive or salad oil
1 garlic clove, crushed
1½ lb ground chuck
1 can (8 oz) tomato sauce
1 can (6 oz) tomato paste
½ cup water
2 tablespoons instant minced onion
1 pkg (1.25 oz) chili-seasoning mix
½ teaspoon salt
1 teaspoon sugar
1 can (15¼ oz) red kidney beans, drained
1 can (12 oz) vacuum-packed whole-kernel corn with sweet peppers
¼ cup chopped pitted black olives
½ cup pitted black olives, halved
1 cup grated Cheddar cheese

1. Day before, cook cornmeal: In a heavy, 4-quart saucepan, bring 4 cups water and 1 teaspoon salt to a full, rolling boil. Slowly add cornmeal, stirring con-

stantly with a wire whisk—mixture will get very thick.

2. Turn heat low; cook, uncovered and stirring frequently, 20 minutes. Add Parmesan cheese. Turn into buttered 13-by-9-by-2-inch baking dish; let stand 20 minutes. Refrigerate, covered, overnight.

3. Next day, in hot oil in a large skillet, sauté garlic until soft; do not brown. Remove from skillet; set aside.

4. Add ground chuck; sauté, stirring, until red color is gone. Drain off excess fat.

5. Add tomato sauce, tomato paste and water; mix well.

6. Add reserved garlic, minced onion, chili-seasoning mix, salt, sugar, kidney beans, corn and chopped olives; mix well. Cook over medium heat, un-

covered and stirring, until mixture is heated through.

7. Preheat oven to 375F. Cut cornmeal mixture into 24 squares.

8. Spoon meat mixture into a shallow, 3-quart casserole. Around inside edge of casserole, place 12 cornmeal squares. Overlap remaining cornmeal squares, along with halved black olives, over meat, as pictured. Sprinkle with Cheddar cheese.

9. Bake, uncovered, 25 to 30 minutes, until bubbly and cheese is melted. *Makes 8 servings.*

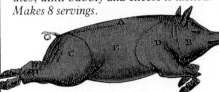

CONEY-ISLAND BURGER

4 oz ground chuck, shaped into a cylinder
¼ cup prepared barbecue sauce
Hot-dog roll
Mustard
Salt
1 tablespoon pickle relish
1 tablespoon chopped onion

1. Sauté hamburger over medium heat, turning on all sides, until nicely browned and of desired doneness—about 5 minutes in all.

2. Add barbecue sauce to skillet; simmer several minutes.

3. Spread roll with mustard. To serve: Place hamburger in roll; sprinkle with salt, top with relish and onion. *Makes 1 serving.* ◆

HEARTY CASSEROLES AND STEWS

continued from page 241

stirring, about 5 minutes, or until onion is tender.

5. Drain one can beans; use one can undrained. Add with rest of ingredients to meat, breaking up tomatoes with fork; stir to mix well. Simmer slowly, covered and stirring occasionally, until thickened and flavors are blended—30 minutes.

6. Preheat oven to 375F.

7. Cut cornmeal mixture into 24 squares. Pour meat mixture into shallow 3-quart casserole. Arrange 12 cornmeal squares, overlapping, around edge; top with second layer. Sprinkle with remaining cheese. Bake, uncovered, 25 to 30 minutes, or until cheese is melted. *Makes 8 servings.*

BEEF-BALLS PAPRIKASH

(pictured)

1 lb ground chuck
½ teaspoon salt
Dash pepper
½ cup packaged dry bread crumbs
1 egg
2 tablespoons margarine
1 lb onions, peeled and sliced (3 cups)
1 tablespoon paprika
½ teaspoon salt
⅛ teaspoon pepper
1 can (10½ oz) beef broth, undiluted
3 tablespoons all-purpose flour
1 cup sour cream
Poppy-Seed Noodles, recipe follows

1. Make Beef Balls: In large bowl, lightly toss ground chuck with ½ teaspoon salt, dash pepper, the bread crumbs and egg until well combined.

2. Using hands, gently shape chuck

mixture into 10 balls, each about 2 inches in diameter.

3. In hot margarine in large skillet, brown beef balls well all over. Reduce heat; cook gently about 10 minutes. Remove beef balls.

4. Add onion to drippings; sauté until tender and golden-brown—about 10 minutes.

5. Add paprika, salt and pepper, stirring until well blended. Stir in ¾ cup beef broth. Bring to boiling.

6. Add meatballs; then reduce heat, and simmer, covered, 30 minutes.

7. In small bowl, combine flour and remaining beef broth, stirring until smooth. Gradually add to beef mixture, stirring constantly. Simmer, uncovered, stirring occasionally, 5 minutes longer.

8. Just before serving, place sour cream in small bowl. Slowly add ½ cup hot gravy. Slowly add to beef mixture, stirring until well blended. Heat, but do not boil. Serve with Poppy-Seed Noodles. *Makes 5 servings.*

POPPY-SEED NOODLES

1 tablespoon salt
1 pkg (7 or 8 oz) wide noodles (3 cups)
¼ cup (½ stick) margarine, melted
1 tablespoon poppy seed

1. In large kettle, bring 3 quarts water and salt to a rapid boil. Add noodles.

2. Bring back to boiling. Cook, uncovered, stirring occasionally with long fork to prevent sticking, just until tender—7 to 10 minutes. Do not overcook.

3. Drain in colander or sieve. Do not rinse. Toss noodles with melted margarine and poppy seed. *Makes 5 servings.*

ZUCCHINI-TUNA-AND-MACARONI CASSEROLE

(pictured)

1 pkg (16-oz size) spiral or elbow macaroni

SAUCE
5 tablespoons margarine
½ lb zucchini, washed and thinly sliced (1½ cups)
1 cup sliced celery, cut on the diagonal
½ cup chopped onion
¼ cup all-purpose flour
1 teaspoon salt
1 teaspoon dried dillweed
2 cups milk
Grated Parmesan cheese

1 can (6½ oz) tuna, drained and flaked
1 cup grated fresh bread crumbs (2 slices)

1. Cook macaroni as package label directs; drain. Preheat oven to 350F.

2. Meanwhile, make Sauce: In 3 tablespoons margarine in 3-quart saucepan, sauté zucchini, celery and onion, stirring, about 5 minutes. Remove from heat.

3. Add flour, salt and dill; stir until smooth. Add milk, a small amount at a time, stirring after each addition. Return to heat.

4. Over medium heat, bring to boiling, stirring constantly. Reduce heat; simmer 3 minutes. Add ¼ cup grated Parmesan cheese; mix well.

5. In large bowl, combine cooked macaroni and the tuna with sauce; toss gently. Turn into 2-quart shallow baking dish. In small bowl, combine crumbs, 2 tablespoons Parmesan and 2 tablespoons melted margarine; toss gently.

6. Sprinkle over casserole. Bake 30 to 35 minutes, or until hot and bubbly. *Makes 8 servings.* ◆

CASSEROLES
◆ FOR EVERY TASTE ◆

A hearty casserole that feeds a crowd is traditional for informal get-togethers. It should be easy to prepare and easy to serve from one dish—but it needn't be ordinary. These casseroles are our time-tested best. They include almost every kind of meat, and range from a sophisticated lamb dish to everyone's favorite, tuna casserole. Below left, Chicken in Wine With Vegetables—a make-ahead version of the classic French coq au vin. The chicken pieces are first flamed in brandy, then cooked in an herbed wine sauce with a mix of colorful vegetables. Next, casserole-style Veal Paprikash and Noodles—veal cooked with small onions and carrots, paprika and sour cream and flavored with fresh dill. Below it, exotic Curried Lamb Casserole—cubes of lamb combined with zucchini, artichoke hearts and potato slices in a curry-scented tomato sauce. These and more recipes begin on page 252.

continued from page 250

CURRIED LAMB CASSEROLE
(pictured)

2 tablespoons salad oil
2 lb lamb shoulder, cut in 1½-inch cubes
2 medium onions, sliced
1 garlic clove, crushed
2 teaspoons curry powder
1 chicken-bouillon cube, crumbled
2 lb potatoes, pared and very thinly sliced
1 tablespoon salt
Dash pepper
½ lb zucchini, sliced
1 pkg (9 oz) frozen artichoke hearts
2 cans (1-lb size) tomatoes
Chopped parsley

1. In hot oil in large skillet, sauté lamb cubes, one-third at a time, until browned well on all sides (takes about 20 minutes in all). Remove lamb as it browns. Preheat oven to 350F.

2. Add onion, garlic, curry powder and bouillon cube to drippings in skillet; sauté until onion slices are golden—about 5 minutes.

3. Return lamb cubes to skillet, mixing well.

4. In a 3-quart casserole, arrange a layer of half of meat mixture and half of potato, salt, pepper, zucchini, artichoke hearts and tomatoes (use 1 can drained and 1 can undrained). Make a second layer with other half of these ingredients.

5. Bake, covered, 1½ hours. Remove cover; continue baking 1 hour longer, or until lamb and potato are tender. To serve, sprinkle top with parsley. *Makes 6 to 8 servings.*

CHICKEN IN WINE WITH VEGETABLES
(pictured)

2 (2-lb size) chickens, cut into quarters
¼ lb bacon, coarsely chopped
20 small onions, peeled
¼ cup Cognac or brandy
4 shallots, chopped
2 teaspoons dried thyme leaves
2 bay leaves, crumbled
2 or 3 parsley sprigs
2 garlic cloves, pressed
½ lb fresh mushrooms, sliced
4 carrots, pared and cut in 1-inch pieces
2¾ cups dry red wine
1 tablespoon salt
½ teaspoon pepper
1 teaspoon sugar
¼ teaspoon ground nutmeg
3 chicken-bouillon cubes, crumbled
½ green pepper, seeds and ribs removed, cut into strips
1 medium tomato, cut into eighths
⅓ cup all-purpose flour
2 tablespoons chopped parsley

DAY BEFORE

1. Wash chicken quarters under cold running water and pat dry with paper towels.

2. In 6-quart Dutch oven or flame-proof casserole, heat bacon; add onions; sauté over medium heat until golden. Lift out onions and bacon with slotted spoon.

3. Add chicken quarters; sauté, turning, until chicken is golden-brown all over.

4. In a metal ladle, heat Cognac slightly; pour over chicken; ignite.

5. Add shallots, thyme, bay leaves, parsley sprigs, garlic, mushrooms, carrot, bacon, onion and 2 cups wine. Add salt, pepper, sugar, nutmeg and bouillon cubes; stir to mix well. Bring to boiling; reduce heat; simmer, covered, 50 minutes (place a sheet of waxed paper over the top of the Dutch oven; place lid over this).

6. Combine ¾ cup wine with flour to make a smooth mixture; stir into liquid in Dutch oven. Bring to boiling, stirring. Sauce will be slightly thickened. Remove from heat and let cool; then refrigerate, covered.

NEXT DAY

7. Preheat oven to 350F. Add green-pepper strips and cut-up tomato. Reheat, covered, 50 to 60 minutes. Sprinkle with the chopped parsley. May be served with boiled new potatoes, if desired. *Makes 8 servings.*

VEAL-PAPRIKASH-AND-NOODLE CASSEROLE
(pictured)

⅓ cup all-purpose flour
2 teaspoons salt
¼ teaspoon pepper
⅓ cup salad oil
3 lb stewing veal, cut in 1½-inch cubes
2½ to 3 tablespoons paprika
1 lb yellow onions, peeled and sliced
12 small white onions, peeled (1½ lb)
2 cans (10½-oz size) condensed beef broth, undiluted
½ teaspoon Worcestershire sauce
6 carrots, pared and halved crosswise
1 pkg (8 oz) wide noodles
1 pint sour cream
Fresh dill sprigs or chopped parsley

1. On waxed paper, combine flour, 1 teaspoon salt and the pepper. Use to coat veal. Reserve remaining flour mixture.

2. In some of hot oil in Dutch oven or 4-quart casserole, brown veal, a third at a time, adding oil as needed. Remove as browned.

3. Preheat oven to 350F.

4. Stir paprika into drippings in Dutch oven. Add sliced onion and small white onions, and sauté, stirring, about 10 minutes. Remove Dutch oven from heat.

5. Stir in reserved flour mixture until well blended. Stir in beef broth, Worcestershire, carrot, browned veal and 1 teaspoon salt. Bake, covered, 1 hour and 50 minutes.

6. Meanwhile, cook noodles as package label directs. Add drained, cooked noodles to Dutch oven; bake 10 minutes longer.

7. Stir a little hot liquid from Dutch oven into 1 cup sour cream. Gradually stir into veal mixture until well blended. Garnish with remaining 1 cup sour cream and fresh dill sprigs, as pictured on page 251. *Makes 6 to 8 servings.*

EGGPLANT-AND-MEAT-PATTIES-PARMIGIANA CASSEROLE

TOMATO SAUCE
2 tablespoons butter or margarine
½ cup chopped onion
1 garlic clove, crushed
1 can (1 lb) tomatoes, undrained
1 can (8 oz) tomato sauce
1 tablespoon sugar
½ teaspoon salt
1 teaspoon dried oregano leaves
½ teaspoon dried basil leaves
¼ teaspoon pepper

1 large eggplant (1½ lb)
¼ cup all-purpose flour
1 teaspoon seasoned salt
⅛ teaspoon pepper
¼ cup salad oil

MEAT PATTIES
1½ lb ground chuck
1 egg, slightly beaten
½ cup soft bread crumbs (1 slice)
¼ teaspoon salt

¼ cup grated Parmesan cheese
½ pkg (8-oz size) mozzarella cheese, sliced

1. Make Tomato Sauce: In hot butter in medium saucepan, sauté onion and garlic until onion is golden-brown—about 5 minutes. Add remaining sauce ingredients; bring to boiling. Reduce heat and simmer, uncovered, 10 minutes.

2. Meanwhile, wash eggplant. Cut crosswise into ½-inch-thick slices. Combine flour, seasoned salt and pepper; use to coat eggplant.

3. In 2 tablespoons hot oil in skillet, sauté eggplant slices, a few at a time. Add more oil as needed. Remove slices as they brown.

4. Preheat oven to 350F.

5. Make Meat Patties: In medium bowl, combine ground chuck, egg, bread crumbs and salt; mix gently. Shape into 8 patties, ½ inch thick. In large skillet,

without fat, over medium heat, brown meat patties on each side.

6. Spoon half of tomato sauce into a shallow, round 10-inch baking dish. Arrange eggplant and meat alternately around side of dish. Spoon remaining sauce in middle and on top. Sprinkle with Parmesan cheese; top with mozzarella.

7. Bake, uncovered, 20 to 25 minutes, or just until mozzarella is melted and golden. *Makes 8 servings.*

QUICK-SOLE CASSEROLE

2 lb fillets of sole
2 tablespoons butter or margarine
½ teaspoon salt
½ cup water
2 pkg (10-oz size) frozen chopped spinach
1 can (10¾ oz) condensed cream-of-shrimp soup, undiluted
3 tablespoons sherry
1 tablespoon butter or margarine, melted
3 tablespoons packaged dry bread crumbs
2 tablespoons grated Parmesan cheese

1. Preheat oven to 375F.
2. Wash sole and pat dry with paper towels. Fold fillets in half crosswise; arrange in a single layer in a 12-by-8-by-2-inch baking dish.
3. Dot fish with 2 tablespoons butter; sprinkle with salt. Pour on ½ cup water.
4. Cover dish with foil; bake 20 minutes
5. Meanwhile, cook spinach as the package label directs. Drain very well.
6. Also, in medium saucepan, heat cream-of-shrimp soup to boiling. Stir in sherry.
7. Remove fish from baking dish; discard liquid. Spread spinach over bottom of dish; top with fillets of sole. Pour shrimp-soup mixture over fish.
8. Combine melted butter with bread

crumbs and cheese; sprinkle over top
9. Bake, uncovered, 20 minutes until bubbly. *Makes 6 servings.*

PORK-CHOP-AND-POTATO BAKE

4 rib or shoulder pork chops (2 lb)
1 teaspoon salt
⅛ teaspoon pepper
1 medium onion, sliced
4 medium potatoes, peeled and sliced (2 lb)
1 can (11 oz) condensed Cheddar-cheese soup, undiluted

1. Preheat oven to 350F. Wipe pork chops with damp paper towels. Trim extra fat from chops. Heat fat in medium skillet. In hot fat, brown chops well on both sides, sprinkling with salt and pepper. Drain well on paper towels.
2. Place pork chops in a 2-quart shallow casserole (about 10 inches in diameter). Arrange onion slices, then potato slices, over top. Spoon cheese soup over all.
3. Bake, covered, 1 hour, or until meat and potato are tender. *Makes 4 servings.*

TUNA-AND-MACARONI DELUXE CASSEROLE

1 pkg (8 oz) elbow macaroni
¼ cup (½ stick) margarine
1 cup day-old white-bread cubes
½ cup chopped onion
½ cup chopped green pepper
1 can (10¾ oz) condensed cream-of-celery soup, undiluted
1 cup milk
1 pkg (4-oz size) sharp Cheddar cheese, grated (1 cup)
1 teaspoon Worcestershire sauce
2 cans (7-oz size) chunk-style tuna, undrained

1. Preheat oven to 375F. Cook macaroni as package label directs. Drain. Turn macaroni into a 2-quart casserole.
2. Melt margarine in skillet. Remove 2 tablespoons, and toss with bread cubes; set aside.
3. Sauté onion and green pepper in remaining margarine until tender—about 5 minutes. Remove from heat.
4. Stir in soup, milk, cheese and Worcestershire; mix until well blended. Add tuna; pour over macaroni, and mix gently. Sprinkle prepared bread cubes over top.
5. Bake, uncovered, 30 minutes, or until bubbly and golden-brown. *Makes 8 servings.*

PORK-CHOP-AND-WHITE-BEAN CASSEROLE

1 lb (2 cups) dried white navy beans
4 teaspoons salt
½ teaspoon pepper
2 garlic cloves, pressed
2 bay leaves, crumbled
¼ cup (½ stick) butter or margarine
2 onions, finely chopped (about 2 cups)
1 green pepper, finely chopped (about 1 cup)
1 can (1 lb) tomatoes, undrained
1 teaspoon dried oregano leaves
1 teaspoon dried thyme leaves
¼ cup finely chopped parsley
6 rib or shoulder pork chops (3 lb)

DAY BEFORE

1. Cover beans with cold water; refrigerate, covered, overnight.

NEXT DAY

2. Drain beans; turn into a 4- or 5-quart Dutch oven; cover with 5 cups cold water. Add 3 teaspoons salt, ¼ teaspoon pepper, garlic and bay leaves. Bring to boiling; reduce heat; simmer gently, covered, 1 hour, or until beans are just tender, stirring several times during cooking. Drain. Turn beans back into Dutch oven. Preheat oven to 350F.
3. Meanwhile, in ¼ cup hot butter, sauté chopped onion until golden—about 5 minutes. Add green pepper, tomatoes, oregano, thyme and parsley; cook 5 more minutes. Stir vegetable mixture into drained beans.
4. Wipe pork chops with damp paper towels. Trim extra fat from chops; heat fat in a large skillet. Brown chops on both sides, sprinkling with 1 teaspoon salt and ¼ teaspoon pepper. Drain on paper towels.
5. Tuck pork chops into bean mixture, covering completely.
6. Bake, covered, 1 hour and 15 minutes; bake, uncovered, 15 minutes longer. If desired, garnish top with more chopped parsley. *Makes 6 servings.* ◆

GREAT
PASTA-BILITIES

A h, pasta—any way you serve it, it's a winner! Once confined to traditional Italian cookery, pasta has burst forth in all shapes, sizes and colors to become an American favorite. It's versatile, economical, healthful and just a quick boil away from being the key ingredient in our collection of delicious one-dish meals. Clockwise starting at top left: Eggplant-Arugula Salad combines a sautéed medley of three kinds of peppers and eggplant with tricolor pasta shells, toasted pine nuts, chopped basil and arugula for a quick-to-fix lunch or brunch; Fettuccini Peking features chicken flavored with honey, ginger and soy sauce, then stir-fried with snow peas and red pepper, tossed with tomato fettuccini and served cold; Seafood Fra Diavolo is an elegant dish sure to impress company—spaghetti is topped with a make-ahead seasoned tomato sauce chock-full of littleneck clams, mussels, lobster and shrimp. Recipes begin on page 256.

continued from page 255

FETTUCCINI PEKING

(pictured)

2 green onions, chopped
1 tablespoon grated gingerroot
1/3 cup soy sauce
1 tablespoon honey
2 teaspoons dark sesame oil
1 lb boneless, skinless chicken, cut into 1/2-inch-wide strips
1 pkg (8 oz) tomato fettuccini
3 tablespoons salad oil
1/2 lb snow peas, trimmed
1 red pepper, seeded and cubed
2 medium cloves garlic, crushed
2 tablespoons toasted sesame seeds

1. In medium bowl, mix green onions, gingerroot, soy sauce, honey and sesame oil. Add chicken strips; toss to coat. Set aside.

2. Cook fettuccini as package label directs; drain. Place in large bowl; toss with 1 tablespoon salad oil. Set aside.

3. In wok or large skillet, heat 2 tablespoons salad oil over medium-high heat until hot. Add chicken and stir-fry about 5 minutes, or until tender. Push chicken to side of wok; add snow peas, red pepper and garlic; stir-fry until vegetables are tender-crisp, about 3 minutes. Add chicken-and-vegetable mixture to fettuccini; toss gently to mix well. Cover; refrigerate until ready to serve (not longer than the day prepared), tossing occasionally. Just before serving, sprinkle with toasted sesame seeds. *Makes 6 servings.*

EGGPLANT-ARUGULA SALAD

(pictured)

4 to 5 small (about 3 oz each) eggplants
1 red pepper
1 yellow pepper
1 Italian frying pepper
1/2 small red onion
5 tablespoons olive oil
1 medium clove garlic, crushed
1/2 cup chopped basil leaves
1/2 teaspoon pepper
1/2 teaspoon salt
1 pkg (8 oz) tricolor rotelle, cooked and drained
3 tablespoons balsamic vinegar
1 jar (1 3/4 oz) pine nuts, toasted
1 bunch (4 oz) arugula, chopped

1. Pare eggplants; cut crosswise into 1/4-inch-thick slices. Set aside. Cut red and yellow peppers into thin strips; set aside. Cut Italian pepper and onion crosswise into thin slices; set aside.

2. In large skillet, heat 2 tablespoons olive oil over medium heat until hot. Cook eggplant in batches until browned on both sides, removing eggplant to large bowl as it cooks and adding 2 tablespoons oil if needed. In same skillet, in 1 tablespoon oil, sauté peppers and onion until softened, about 5 minutes. Stir in garlic, basil, pepper and salt; transfer ingredients to bowl with eggplant. Stir in remaining ingredients. Serve immediately. *Makes 4 to 6 servings.*

SEAFOOD FRA DIAVOLO

(pictured)

Make the sauce up to 2 days before serving and refrigerate. Reheat at serving time and add cooked seafood.

SAUCE
3 tablespoons olive oil
2 small onions, chopped
3 cloves garlic, minced
1 1/2 teaspoons crushed red-pepper flakes
2 cans (28-oz size) tomatoes in puree
1/2 cup dry white wine
2 teaspoons dried basil leaves, crumbled
1 teaspoon salt
1 teaspoon grated orange peel

1 dozen littleneck clams, scrubbed
1 dozen small mussels, scrubbed
1 lb peeled shrimp, tails intact
1/2 lb cooked lobster tails, cut into 1/2-inch slices
2 lb spaghetti, cooked and drained
1 tablespoon chopped fresh parsley

1. Make Sauce: In 3-quart saucepan, heat olive oil over medium heat. Add onions, garlic and red-pepper flakes. Over medium-low heat, sauté 10 minutes, or until soft. Add tomatoes, wine, basil, salt and orange peel; break up tomatoes. Simmer 30 minutes or until thickened; stir occasionally.

2. Meanwhile, in 1/2 inch boiling water in skillet, arrange clams in single layer. Cover; steam 4 to 8 minutes, checking clams every minute. With tongs, remove open ones to bowl; cover. Keep warm. Discard unopened clams. Add mussels to water in pan; steam 1 or 2 minutes, removing open ones to bowl with clams. Discard unopened mussels.

3. Over medium heat, add shrimp to sauce. Cook 3 minutes, or until pink. Add lobster, clams and mussels; heat through.

4. Place hot spaghetti in serving bowl. Top with sauce; sprinkle with parsley. *Makes 8 servings.*

VERMICELLI CHEESE BAKE

1 cup (4 oz) uncooked vermicelli, broken
1/4 cup grated Parmesan cheese
1/4 cup butter or margarine
1/4 cup unsifted all-purpose flour
2 cups milk
2 cups (8 oz) shredded Cheddar cheese
1 teaspoon dry mustard
1/4 teaspoon pepper
6 eggs, separated
6 oz cooked chicken, cubed
1 cup frozen peas, thawed
1 teaspoon salt

1. Cook vermicelli as package label directs; set aside. Preheat oven to 375F. Grease 10-cup soufflé dish. Sprinkle with the Parmesan cheese.

2. In large saucepan, over low heat, melt butter. Whisk in flour until blended; cook 1 minute, or until bubbly. Remove from heat; blend in milk. Bring to boiling, stirring until thickened; boil 1 minute. Stir in Cheddar cheese, mustard and pepper until cheese melts. Remove from heat; whisk in egg yolks, one at a time. Stir in cooked vermicelli, chicken and peas; transfer to large bowl.

3. In large bowl of electric mixer, at medium speed, beat egg whites with salt until foamy. Beat at high speed until stiff peaks form when beaters are raised. With rubber spatula, fold egg whites into pasta mixture until no white streaks remain; pour into prepared soufflé dish. Bake 20 minutes; reduce heat to 350F. Bake 40 minutes, or until center is just set. *Makes 6 to 8 servings.*

HAM-AND-PEPPERS FETTUCCINI

2 tablespoons butter or margarine
1 large onion, cut into 1/4-inch wedges
1 medium red pepper, cut into 2-by-1/4-inch strips
1 medium yellow pepper, cut into 2-by-1/4-inch strips
2 medium cloves garlic, crushed
1/2 teaspoon dried rosemary leaves
3 tablespoons all-purpose flour
2 cups half-and-half
1/4 lb boiled ham, cut into 2-by-1/4-inch strips
1/2 pkg (9-oz size) frozen peas, thawed (1 cup)
1/2 cup grated Parmesan cheese
1/8 teaspoon pepper
1 pkg (12 oz) fettuccini, cooked
Rosemary sprig

1. In large glass bowl, combine butter, onion, pepper strips, garlic and rosemary. Cover with plastic wrap; turn back one corner to vent. Microwave at HIGH (100% power) 5 minutes, stirring once.

2. Stir in flour until blended. Gradually add half-and-half, stirring until smooth. Add ham, peas, Parmesan cheese and 1/8 teaspoon pepper; mix well. Microwave, uncovered, at HIGH (100% power) 8 minutes, stirring occasionally, until boiling and slightly thickened.

3. Add cooked fettuccini; toss to coat with sauce. Microwave at MEDIUM (50% power) 2 minutes, or until heated through. If desired, garnish with rosemary sprig. *Makes 4 to 6 servings.*

THREE-CHEESE LASAGNA

1 tablespoon olive oil
1 large onion, chopped
½ lb mushrooms, sliced
½ lb zucchini or yellow squash, sliced
1 medium clove garlic, crushed
½ teaspoon dried rosemary leaves, crushed
½ teaspoon dried oregano leaves, crushed
½ teaspoon salt
⅛ teaspoon pepper
1 jar (40 oz) spaghetti sauce
½ lb uncooked lasagna noodles
1 container (15 oz) ricotta cheese
2 cups (8 oz) shredded mozzarella cheese
¾ cup grated Parmesan cheese

1. In glass bowl, combine olive oil, onion, mushrooms, zucchini, garlic, rosemary, oregano, ½ teaspoon salt and ⅛ teaspoon pepper. Cover with plastic wrap; turn back one corner to vent. Microwave at HIGH (100% power) 6 minutes, stirring once.

2. In microwave-safe, shallow 2½-quart baking dish, spread 1 cup spaghetti sauce. Cover with 3 uncooked lasagna noodles; spread with half the ricotta cheese. Drain vegetable mixture; arrange half the mixture over the ricotta cheese. Sprinkle with half the mozzarella and ¼ cup Parmesan; spoon 1 cup sauce over cheeses. Repeat with remaining ingredients, ending with 3 uncooked lasagna noodles. Spread with 1 cup sauce; sprinkle with remaining Parmesan.

3. Cover dish; vent. Microwave at MEDIUM (50% power) 35 to 40 minutes, or until noodles are tender, rotating baking dish every 10 minutes. Let stand, covered, 5 minutes. *Makes 8 servings.*

LINGUINE WITH PUTTANESCA SAUCE

2 tablespoons extra-virgin olive oil
3 cloves garlic, minced
1 can (2 oz) anchovy fillets, minced
1 can (28 oz) tomatoes with puree
1 tablespoon capers
¼ cup chopped oil-cured black olives
¼ cup chopped green olives
½ teaspoon pepper
1 lb linguine, cooked and drained
Chopped fresh parsley (optional)
Grated Parmesan cheese (optional)

1. In 2-quart saucepan, heat olive oil over medium-high heat. Add garlic and anchovies; sauté 1 minute. Add tomatoes, capers, black and green olives and pepper. Stir; break up tomatoes. Lower heat; simmer 15 minutes.

2. Place hot linguine in bowl; top with sauce. Sprinkle with parsley; pass the Parmesan cheese, if desired. *Makes 4 servings.*

PESTO WITH POTATOES AND GREEN BEANS

3 new potatoes, quartered
¾ teaspoon salt
½ lb green beans, cut into 1-inch pieces
8 oz linguine, cooked and drained
1 container (7 oz) refrigerated pesto
2 tablespoons grated Parmesan cheese
½ teaspoon pepper

1. In large saucepan, cover potatoes with water; add ¼ teaspoon salt. Heat to boiling; cook 10 minutes, or until tender. With slotted spoon, remove to large bowl; cool. Return potato water to boiling; add green beans. Cook 3 or 4 minutes, or until crisp-tender; drain. Add to potatoes. Add hot linguine.

2. In medium bowl, combine remaining salt and other remaining ingredients. Mix well; add to potato mixture. Toss. *Makes 4 servings.* ◆

continued from page 245

Sprinkle evenly with reserved cup of cheese. Pour egg mixture over cheese.

6. Bake, placed on bottom rack in oven, 35 to 40 minutes, or until quiche is puffy and set in center. Remove to wire rack to cool 10 minutes. Garnish before serving, as pictured, with avocado slices and 3 cherry tomatoes, halved. *Makes 8 servings.*

HAM-AND-CHEDDAR QUICHE
(pictured)

9-inch unbaked pie shell
1 egg white, slightly beaten

FILLING
1 cup (4 oz) ground cooked ham
4 eggs
1½ cups half-and-half or light cream
¼ teaspoon salt
⅛ teaspoon ground nutmeg
Dash pepper

5 cooked ham strips, 6 inches long, ¼ inch wide
1 cup grated Cheddar cheese (4 oz)

1. Brush inside of pie shell with egg white; refrigerate.

2. Preheat oven to 375F.

3. Make Filling: Sprinkle ground cooked ham over bottom of pie shell.

4. In medium bowl, with wire whisk or rotary beater, beat eggs with half-and-half, salt, nutmeg and pepper just until combined but not frothy.

5. Pour egg mixture into pie shell. Bake, placed on lower rack in oven, 35 to 40 minutes, just until puffy and golden.

6. Remove from oven; arrange the ham strips on top of quiche, as pictured. Sprinkle cheese between ham strips.

7. Return quiche to oven; bake 5 minutes, or just until cheese melts. Remove to wire rack to cool 10 minutes before serving. *Makes 8 servings.*

SALAMI-CORN QUICHE
(pictured)

9-inch unbaked pie shell
1 egg white, slightly beaten

FILLING
2 cups natural Swiss cheese, grated (8 oz)

4 eggs
1 cup half-and-half or light cream
⅛ teaspoon ground nutmeg
Dash pepper
2 tablespoons butter or margarine
1 cup chopped onion
1 can (8 oz) cream-style corn
⅛ lb Italian salami, cut into 2-inch-long strips, ¼-inch wide

Pitted ripe olives, halved

1. Brush inside of pie shell with egg white; refrigerate.

2. Preheat oven to 375F.

3. Make Filling: Sprinkle cheese over bottom of pie shell.

4. In medium bowl, with wire whisk or rotary beater, beat eggs with half-and-half, nutmeg and pepper just until combined but not frothy.

5. In butter, sauté chopped onion until golden—about 5 minutes. Remove from heat. Add cream-style corn and Italian salami strips.

6. Spoon corn mixture over grated cheese; pour egg mixture on top. Garnish edge with halved pitted ripe olives. Bake, on lower rack in oven, 40 minutes, or just until quiche is puffy and golden. Remove to wire rack to cool 10 minutes before serving. *Makes 8 servings.* ◆

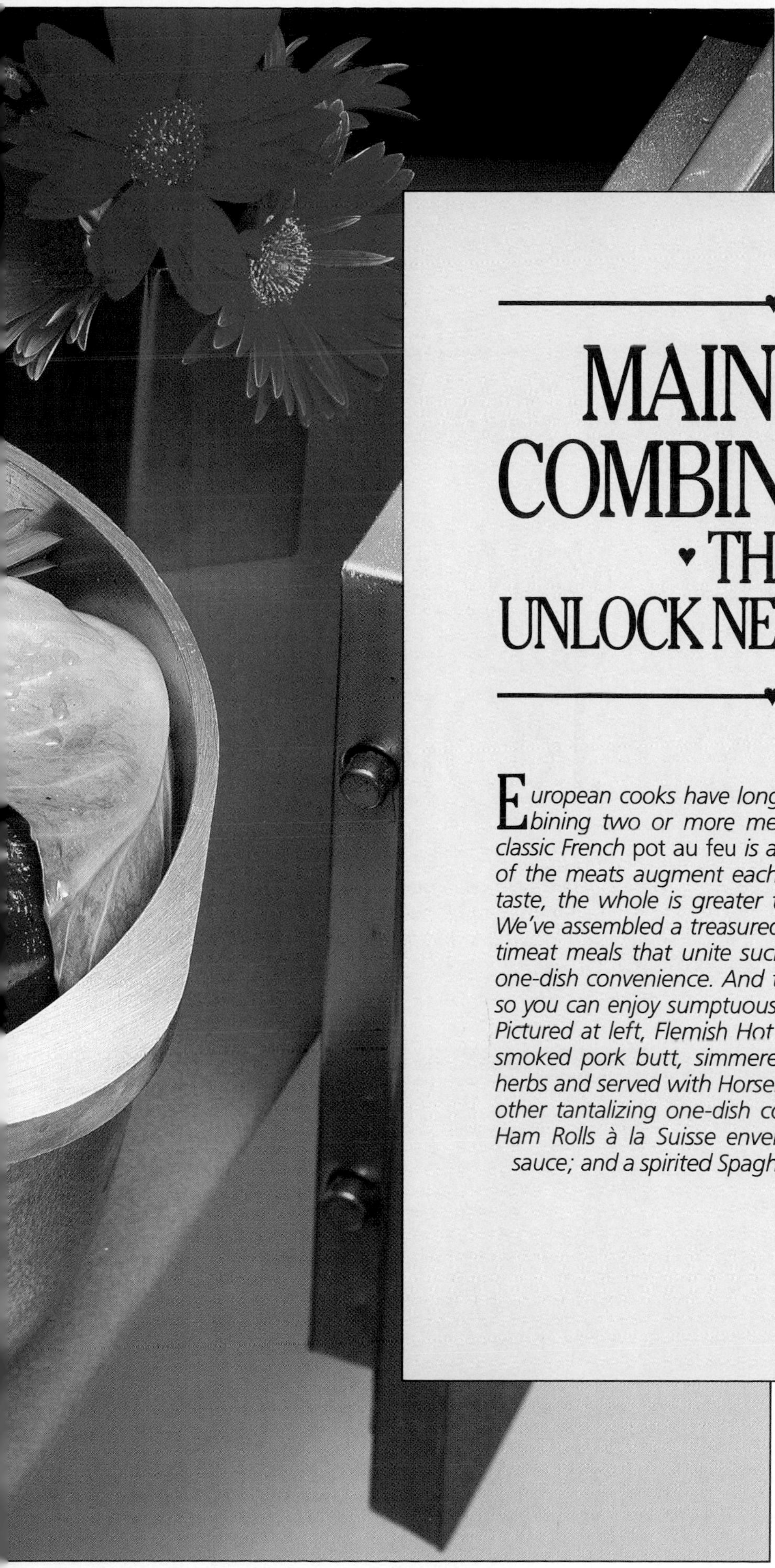

MAIN-DISH COMBINATIONS
♥ THAT ♥
UNLOCK NEW FLAVORS

European cooks have long known the secret of combining two or more meats in the same dish—the classic French pot au feu *is a good example. The flavors of the meats augment each other, so that in terms of taste, the whole is greater than the sum of the parts. We've assembled a treasured collection of no-fuss, multimeat meals that unite such unique tastes with all-in-one-dish convenience. And these recipes make enough so you can enjoy sumptuous leftovers during the week. Pictured at left,* Flemish Hot Pot, *a plump broiler and a smoked pork butt, simmered together with wine and herbs and served with Horseradish Sauce. On page 269, other tantalizing one-dish combinations: Chicken-And-Ham Rolls à la Suisse enveloped in a mustard-cheese sauce; and a spirited Spaghetti and Meatballs Napoli.*

**Tortilla-Tamale Pie: Strips of cheese
arranged over beef and tomatoes**

25 REALLY MARVELOUS
MAIN-DISH
CASSEROLES

S ome with meat, some without; some use leftovers, some
use convenience products. Here's almost a month's worth
of easy-bake one-dish meals—a versatile selection
designed to fit any taste, any occasion, and any busy
schedule. Try them all! For recipes,
see page 262.

**Chicken-And-Ham Casserole: Ham slices alternate with poached chicken breasts,
baked in fresh mushroom sauce and sprinkled with Parmesan cheese**

Creamy Turkey Pie: Shredded turkey with mushrooms and peas, topped with Cheddar-cheese biscuits

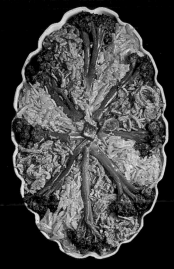

Leftover Ham and Broccoli: Ham and noodles, with cheese, French-fried onions, a broccoli pinwheel

Potato Moussaka: Meat-and-potatoes—a spicy dish!

Sausage Paella: Italian sausages, colorful green peppers and tomatoes— a succulent mix made with chicken broth and rice

Hamburger Basquaise: Zucchini, red peppers and more dazzle sautéed burgers

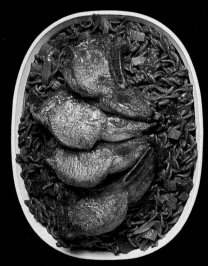

Pork Chops and Pasta: Twists of spinach pasta—a surprise with baked pork

Fanciful fish: Garnish halibut or cod with tomato, onion and green pepper, and bake in savory tomato sauce.

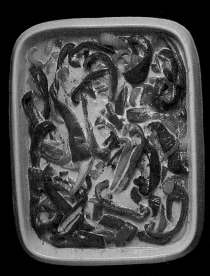

Peppers, Onions and Cheese: Vegetarian's delight

continued from page 260

HAMBURGER BASQUAISE
(pictured)

1½ lb chuck, coarsely ground
1 tablespoon butter or margarine

FILLING
2 red peppers (8 oz each)
2 medium zucchini (1 lb)
2 tablespoons salad or olive oil
½ cup sliced onion
1 teaspoon salt
½ teaspoon dried tarragon leaves
⅛ teaspoon dried crushed red pepper
2 medium tomatoes, peeled and cut in
    thirds

1. Preheat oven to 350F. Gently shape chuck into six thick patties. In hot butter in medium skillet, sauté patties, turning until lightly browned on both sides; set aside.

2. Make Filling: Wash pepper, halve; remove ribs and seeds; cut lengthwise into ¼-inch-thick slices.

3. Scrub zucchini; cut into ¼-inch-thick slices.

4. In hot oil in large skillet, sauté red pepper, zucchini and onion 5 minutes, or until onion is golden. Reserve 7 to 8 slices of red pepper for garnish.

5. Add salt, tarragon and crushed red pepper and mix lightly to combine. Cook over medium heat, covered, 10 minutes.

6. Arrange hamburgers in bottom of shallow, 2-quart baking dish. Cover with filling. Layer tomato wedges and reserved pepper slices on top. Bake, covered with foil, 20 minutes, or until vegetables are tender. *Makes 6 servings.*

TURKEY PIE
WITH CHEESE BISCUITS
(pictured)

¼ cup (½ stick) butter or margarine
½ cup chopped onion
1 cup sliced fresh mushrooms
¼ cup all-purpose flour
1 teaspoon salt
Dash ground red pepper
2 cups milk
1 pkg (10 oz) frozen green peas, thawed
2 cups cooked turkey or chicken, cut into
    ½-inch pieces

CHEESE BISCUITS
2 cups prepared biscuit mix
½ cup grated Cheddar cheese
2 tablespoons chopped pimiento
⅔ cup water

1. Preheat oven to 425F. In hot butter in medium saucepan, sauté onion and mushrooms, stirring, about 5 minutes.

Remove from heat; stir in flour, salt and ground red pepper; mix until smooth. Add milk. Cook over medium heat, stirring constantly, until mixture comes to boiling; simmer 3 minutes.

2. Add peas and turkey to mushroom mixture. Turn into a 1½-quart baking dish.

3. Make Cheese Biscuits: In medium bowl, combine biscuit mix and cheese; mix well with fork.

4. Add pimiento and water; stir until all biscuit mix is absorbed.

5. Turn soft dough out onto a lightly floured pastry cloth or board. Roll over to coat with flour.

6. Roll into a rectangle 8 by 4½ inches. Cut into eight triangles each 4½ by 2 inches. Arrange biscuits on top of turkey mixture in baking dish with flat side against side of dish.

7. Bake 20 to 25 minutes, or until mixture is bubbly and biscuits are golden-brown. *Makes 6 servings.*

LEFTOVER HAM AND
BROCCOLI
(pictured)

1 pkg (8 oz) medium noodles
1½ cups cooked ham, cubed
1 can (10¾ oz) cream-of mushroom soup
1 cup milk
½ cup sour cream
1 pkg (10 oz) broccoli spears, thawed
1 cup (4 oz) grated sharp Cheddar cheese
1 can (2.8 oz) French-fried onions
Pimiento

1. Preheat oven to 350F. Cook noodles according to package directions; drain.

2. In medium bowl, combine noodles and ham. Layer in bottom of greased, 2-quart oval baking dish.

3. In medium saucepan, combine mushroom soup and milk; bring to boiling, stirring constantly. Remove from heat; add sour cream.

4. Pour soup mixture over noodles and ham. Arrange broccoli on top, spoke-fashion, as pictured.

5. Bake, covered with foil, 20 minutes. Remove from oven. Alternate grated cheese and French-fried onions on top, as pictured. Bake 5 minutes, or just until cheese is melted. Garnish center with pimiento. *Makes 6 servings.*

CURRIED RICE AND BEEF

¼ cup (½ stick) butter or margarine
1 cup chopped onion
1 pkg (10 oz) frozen green peas, thawed
4 cups cooked rice

½ cup sliced pitted ripe olives
2 tablespoons diced pimiento
2 to 3 teaspoons curry powder
½ cup light cream
½ teaspoon salt
1 can (10¾ oz) cream-of-mushroom soup
½ cup chicken broth
3 cups cooked beef, cut into 1-inch pieces
Toasted blanched whole almonds

1. Preheat oven to 350F. In hot butter in medium skillet, sauté onion until golden—about 5 minutes. Remove from heat. Add peas, rice, olives, pimiento, curry powder, cream and salt; mix well.

2. Turn half of rice mixture into bottom of 3-quart baking dish.

3. In medium saucepan, combine mushroom soup and chicken broth; bring to boiling, stirring. Remove from heat; add beef; mix well. Add to baking dish.

4. Spoon remaining rice mixture over beef layer, spreading evenly. Garnish edge with toasted almonds.

5. Bake, covered with foil, 30 to 40 minutes, or until hot. *Makes 8 servings.*

CHICKEN-AND-HAM
CASSEROLE
(pictured)

3 chicken breasts, halved (about 3 lb)
1 can (10¾ oz) condensed chicken broth,
    undiluted
¼ cup (½ stick) butter or margarine
½ cup chopped onion
1 cup sliced fresh mushrooms
¼ cup all-purpose flour
½ teaspoon salt
¼ teaspoon ground nutmeg
1 cup milk
3 slices baked ham, ⅛ inch thick, halved
2 tablespoons grated Parmesan cheese
2 tablespoons chopped parsley

1. Wipe chicken breasts with damp cloth. In a large skillet, bring broth to boiling. Add chicken breasts; reduce heat, and simmer, covered, 20 minutes, or until tender. Remove chicken; reserve broth.

2. Meanwhile, in medium skillet, melt butter; sauté onion and mushrooms 2 minutes. Remove from heat; stir in flour, salt and nutmeg. Gradually stir in milk and 1½ cups reserved broth. Bring to boiling; simmer 1 minute; remove from heat.

3. Preheat oven to 400F. Remove skin from chicken breasts. Arrange chicken in a 12-inch oval baking dish. Pour mushroom sauce over chicken breasts.

4. Alternate ham slices with chicken breasts. Sprinkle Parmesan cheese over top. Bake, uncovered, 15 minutes, or until cheese is browned. Garnish with chopped parsley. *Makes 6 servings.*

BAKED PORK CHOPS AND PASTA
(pictured)

4 thin shoulder pork chops (about 1 lb, ¾ inch thick)
2 tablespoons salad oil
1 cup sliced onion
½ cup chopped celery
1 garlic clove, crushed
1 can (1 lb) stewed tomatoes, undrained
1 can (8 oz) tomato sauce
½ teaspoon dried thyme leaves
½ teaspoon salt
⅛ teaspoon pepper
1 pkg (8 oz) spinach twists or other pasta

1. Preheat oven to 350F. Wipe chops with damp paper towels; trim and discard excess fat.

2. In hot oil in medium skillet, sauté chops on both sides until browned; set aside.

3. In drippings in skillet, sauté onion, celery and garlic, stirring occasionally, until tender—about 5 minutes.

4. Add tomatoes, tomato sauce, thyme, salt, pepper and browned pork chops. Bring to boiling; simmer, covered, 20 minutes.

5. Meanwhile, cook spinach twists according to package directions. Drain well.

6. With a slotted spoon, lift pork chops onto a plate. Combine pasta with tomato mixture; mix well. Turn into 2-quart baking dish.

7. Arrange chops on top. Bake, covered, 30 minutes, or until chops are tender. *Makes 4 servings.*

SAVORY HALIBUT CASSEROLE
(pictured)

¼ cup butter or margarine
8 slices onion, cut ¼-inch thick
1 medium green pepper, sliced into 8 thin rings
½ cup chopped celery
1 teaspoon salt
1 teaspoon dried basil leaves
¼ teaspoon pepper
1 can (1 lb) stewed tomatoes
2 pkg (16-oz size) frozen halibut or cod
8 slices plum tomatoes

1. Preheat oven to 375F. Grease a 12-by-8-by-2-inch baking dish.

2. In hot butter in medium skillet, sauté onion, green pepper and celery until tender—about 5 minutes.

3. Add salt, basil, pepper and stewed tomatoes. Bring to boiling, stirring; simmer, uncovered, 15 minutes. Spoon 1 cup sauce into bottom of prepared baking dish.

4. Cut fish in each package into four pieces. Place in baking dish. Spoon remaining sauce over fish.

5. On each piece of fish, arrange, in this order, a green-pepper ring, onion slice and plum tomato slice.

6. Bake, covered with foil, 30 minutes, basting once with pan liquid. Remove foil; bake 10 minutes, or until fish flakes easily. *Makes 8 servings.*

SAUSAGE PAELLA
(pictured)

2 tablespoons salad oil
6 sweet Italian sausages
2 small green peppers (½ lb), chopped
1½ cups chopped onion
1 garlic clove, crushed
½ bay leaf, crushed
2 teaspoons paprika
1 teaspoon salt
2 cups long-grain white rice
1 can (1 lb, 12 oz) tomatoes, undrained
1 can (10¾ oz) condensed chicken broth, undiluted
Water
Parsley (optional)

1. In hot oil in heavy 6-quart Dutch oven, over medium heat, brown sausages; remove, and set aside. Preheat oven to 350F.

2. To drippings in Dutch oven, add green pepper, onion, garlic and bay leaf; sauté, stirring, over medium heat until onion is tender—5 minutes.

3. Add paprika, salt and rice to Dutch oven. Cook, stirring, until rice is lightly browned and coated with paprika—about 10 minutes.

4. Drain tomatoes; turn liquid into 4-cup measuring cup. Add chicken broth and enough water to make 4 cups; mix well. Add with tomatoes to Dutch oven; bring just to boiling; remove from heat.

5. Turn into a 3-quart casserole; arrange sausages, spoke-fashion, on top. Bake, covered, 1 hour, or until rice has absorbed all liquid. Garnish with parsley, if desired. *Makes 8 servings.*

TORTILLA-TAMALE PIE
(pictured)

Salad oil
1½ lb ground beef
1 cup chopped onion
1 garlic clove, crushed
½ teaspoon salt
¼ teaspoon dried marjoram leaves
1 tablespoon all-purpose flour
1 can (8 oz) tomato sauce
1 can (10½ oz) beef broth, undiluted
1 can (16 oz) hominy, drained
½ cup raisins
½ cup pitted black olives, halved
1 pkg 5-inch corn tortillas (12)
½ lb Monterey Jack cheese, cut into 9 strips
Pimiento (optional)

1. Preheat oven to 350F. In 1 tablespoon oil in large skillet, over medium heat, sauté beef, onion, garlic, salt and marjoram, stirring constantly, about 5 minutes. Remove from heat.

2. Stir in flour. Gradually add tomato sauce, beef broth, hominy and raisins. Over medium heat, bring to boiling, stirring; reduce heat; simmer, uncovered, 5 minutes. Add black olives.

3. Meanwhile, with 2 tablespoons oil, brush both sides of tortillas; drain on paper towels. Grease pan lightly with oil. Arrange tortillas, overlapping in bottom of 12-inch round baking dish; ½ inch of tortillas should extend above rim of dish.

4. Turn beef mixture into prepared dish. Bake, uncovered, 25 minutes; remove from oven. Arrange Monterey Jack cheese, spoke-fashion, in center. Return to oven to melt cheese—5 minutes. Decorate, if desired, with pimiento cut into a star shape. *Makes 8 servings.*

POTATO MOUSSAKA
(pictured)

MEAT SAUCE
2 tablespoons butter or margarine
1 cup chopped onion
1 lb ground chuck or lamb
1 garlic clove, crushed
¼ teaspoon ground allspice
¼ teaspoon ground cinnamon
1 teaspoon salt
2 cans (8-oz size) tomato sauce

½ cup (1 stick) butter or margarine
2 tablespoons salad or olive oil
6 medium potatoes (2 lb), peeled and sliced ¼ inch thick

YOGURT CREAM SAUCE
2 tablespoons butter or margarine
2 tablespoons all-purpose flour
½ teaspoon salt
Dash pepper
1 cup milk
1 cup yogurt
2 eggs

3 tablespoons grated Parmesan cheese
2 tablespoons dry bread crumbs
Ground cinnamon (optional)

1. Make Meat Sauce: In 2 tablespoons hot butter in 3½-quart Dutch oven, sauté onion, chuck and garlic, stirring, until brown—10 minutes. Add allspice, ¼ teaspoon cinnamon, 1 teaspoon salt and the tomato sauce; bring to boiling, stirring. Reduce heat; simmer, uncovered, ½ hour.

2. In hot butter and oil in large skil-

continued on page 264

continued from page 263

let, over medium heat, sauté sliced potatoes, turning, until lightly browned on both sides. Layer half, overlapping slices in bottom of 2-quart baking dish (12 by 7½ by 2 inches).

3. Preheat oven to 350F.

4. Make Yogurt Cream Sauce: In medium saucepan, melt butter. Remove from heat; stir in flour, salt and pepper. Add milk gradually. Bring to boiling, stirring, until mixture is thickened. Remove from heat. In small bowl, beat yogurt and eggs with wire whisk. Beat some hot cream-sauce mixture into egg mixture; return to saucepan; mix well. Set aside.

5. To assemble casserole: Sprinkle potatoes with 2 tablespoons Parmesan cheese.

6. Stir bread crumbs into meat sauce; spoon evenly over potatoes; layer rest of potato slices, overlapping as before.

7. Pour cream sauce over all. Sprinkle top with rest of cheese. Bake 35 to 40 minutes, or until golden-brown and top is set. If desired, sprinkle cinnamon in diagonal lines, as pictured. *Makes 12 servings.*

PEPPERS, ONIONS AND CHEESE

(pictured)

3 green peppers (1 lb)
3 red peppers (1 lb)
2 tablespoons butter or margarine
2 tablespoons salad or olive oil
2 cups thinly sliced onion
2 tablespoons all-purpose flour
1 teaspoon salt
½ teaspoon crushed cumin
½ teaspoon crushed coriander
¼ teaspoon pepper
4 large eggs
1 cup yogurt
½ cup sour cream
½ lb sliced Cheddar cheese
Paprika

1. Preheat oven to 375F. Grease a 2½-quart baking dish.

2. Wash green and red peppers; cut in half. Remove seeds and ribs. Slice into thin strips.

3. In hot butter and oil in large skillet, over medium heat, sauté onion, stirring until golden—about 5 minutes. Add peppers; cook over low heat, stirring, about 10 minutes. Stir in flour, salt, cumin, coriander and pepper; mix well. Stir until all liquid is absorbed. Remove from heat.

4. In medium bowl, combine eggs, yogurt and sour cream; beat with electric mixer until smooth.

5. Spread half the pepper mixture on the bottom of prepared casserole. Top with half the sliced cheese. Repeat layering. Pour egg mixture over all. Sprinkle with paprika.

6. Bake, uncovered, 30 to 40 minutes, or until firm. *Makes 6 servings.*

CALIFORNIA CHEESE-AND-RICE CASSEROLE

¼ cup (½ stick) butter or margarine
1 cup chopped onion
4 cups freshly cooked white rice
2 cups sour cream
1 cup cream-style cottage cheese
1 large bay leaf, crumbled
½ teaspoon salt
⅛ teaspoon pepper
2 cans (4-oz size) chopped green chilies, drained
2 cups grated sharp Cheddar cheese (½ lb)
1 tomato, sliced
Chopped parsley

1. Preheat oven to 375F. Lightly grease a 12-by-8-by-2-inch (2-quart) baking dish.

2. In hot butter in large skillet, sauté onion until golden—about 5 minutes.

3. Remove from heat; stir in hot rice, sour cream, cottage cheese, bay leaf, salt and pepper; toss lightly to mix well.

4. Layer half of rice mixture in bottom of baking dish, then half of chilies; sprinkle with half of cheese. Repeat.

5. Bake, uncovered, 25 minutes, or until bubbly and hot. Garnish with sliced tomato. Sprinkle with chopped parsley. *Makes 8 servings.*

CHEESE-SCALLOPED POTATOES AND HAM

2½ lb potatoes, pared and sliced ½ inch thick (about 6 cups)
1½ cups sliced onion
5 medium carrots, pared and diagonally sliced ¼ inch thick (2 cups)
2 teaspoons salt

CHEESE SAUCE
3 tablespoons butter or margarine
2 tablespoons all-purpose flour
1 teaspoon salt
Dash pepper
1½ cups milk
1½ cups grated sharp Cheddar cheese (6 oz)

2 cups cubed cooked ham

1. Preheat oven to 375F. Lightly grease a 2½-quart, shallow baking dish.

2. In 2 cups boiling water in large skillet, cook potato, onion, carrot and 2 teaspoons salt, covered, 10 minutes, or just until partially tender. Drain.

3. Make Cheese Sauce: In small saucepan, melt butter, remove from heat; stir in flour, salt and pepper; then stir in milk, blending well.

4. Over medium heat, bring just to boiling, stirring, until thickened and smooth. Stir in 1 cup cheese; cook, stirring, over low heat until cheese is melted.

5. In prepared casserole, layer half of potato, onion, carrot and 1 cup ham; top with half of cheese sauce; repeat with remaining ham, vegetables and sauce. Sprinkle top with remaining cheese.

6. Bake, covered with foil, 30 minutes, or until vegetables are tender when pierced with fork. If desired, uncover top during last 10 minutes of baking to brown top. *Makes 8 servings.*

ZITI-AND-EGGPLANT CASSEROLE

1 pkg (8 oz) ziti or other pasta

TOMATO SAUCE
2 tablespoons butter or margarine
½ cup chopped onion
1 garlic clove, crushed
1 lb ground chuck
1 can (1 lb, 12 oz) tomatoes, undrained
1 teaspoon dried oregano leaves
½ teaspoon salt
⅛ teaspoon pepper

1 eggplant (1½ lb), washed
½ cup (1 stick) butter or margarine, melted
1 cup shredded mozzarella
¼ cup grated Parmesan cheese

1. Cook ziti as package label directs; drain well.

2. Make Tomato Sauce: In hot butter in medium skillet, sauté onion and garlic, stirring, until golden—about 5 minutes.

3. Add ground chuck; sauté, stirring, until meat is browned. Drain excess fat.

4. Add tomatoes, oregano, salt and pepper; mix well. Bring to boiling; reduce heat; simmer, uncovered, stirring occasionally, 15 minutes, until thick.

5. Meanwhile, prepare eggplant:

Slice unpeeled eggplant lengthwise into ⅓-inch-thick slices.

6. Brush both sides of eggplant slices with melted butter. Arrange in single layer in broiler pan. Broil, about 4 inches from heat, 4 minutes on each side, or until golden-brown.

7. Preheat oven to 350F. To assemble: Layer ziti in bottom of dish. Pour half of sauce over it; sprinkle with mozzarella. Overlap eggplant slices around edges of dish. Add remaining sauce. Sprinkle with Parmesan. Bake 30 minutes, or until bubbly and golden. *Makes 8 servings.*

FAMILY-FAVORITE MACARONI AND CHEESE

1 pkg (8 oz) elbow macaroni
¼ cup (½ stick) butter or margarine
¼ cup all-purpose flour
1 teaspoon salt
⅛ teaspoon pepper
2 cups milk
2 cups grated Cheddar cheese (8 oz)

1. Preheat oven to 375F. Cook macaroni as label directs; drain.

2. Meanwhile, melt butter in a medium saucepan; remove from heat. Stir in the flour, salt and pepper until smooth. Gradually stir in milk. Bring to boiling, stirring. Reduce heat, and simmer 1 minute.

3. Stir in 1½ cups cheese and the macaroni. Pour into a 1½-quart casserole, and sprinkle remaining cheese over top.

4. Bake 15 to 20 minutes, or until cheese is golden-brown. *Makes 6 servings.*

OVERNIGHT CHICKEN CASSEROLE

2 cups milk
2 cans (10¾-oz size) condensed cream-of-mushroom soup, undiluted
1 pkg (8 oz) cavatelli or other pasta
1 pkg (10 oz) frozen green peas, thawed
2 cups diced cooked chicken or turkey
1 cup finely chopped onion
1½ cups grated Cheddar cheese (6 oz)
4 hard-cooked eggs
¼ teaspoon salt
6 pimiento strips
Chopped parsley

DAY BEFORE

1. In large bowl, combine milk, soup, uncooked cavatelli, peas, chicken, onion, cheese, three hard-cooked eggs (sliced) and salt. Mix well. Refrigerate overnight, tightly covered.

NEXT DAY

2. About 1½ hours before serving,

preheat oven to 325F. Lightly grease a 13-by-9-by-2-inch baking dish. Pour cavatelli mixture into casserole.

3. Bake, uncovered, 1 hour and 15 minutes, or until hot and bubbly. Cut remaining hard-cooked egg into six wedges. Arrange egg and pimiento strips in daisy pattern on top of casserole. Sprinkle with parsley. *Makes 8 servings.*

GREEK MACARONI-SPINACH CASSEROLE

1 pkg (8 oz) elbow macaroni
¼ cup (½ stick) melted butter or margarine
2 tablespoons salad or olive oil
1 lb ground beef or lamb
1 cup chopped onion
1 garlic clove, crushed
½ teaspoon salt
Dash ground allspice
Dash pepper
1 can (1 lb) tomatoes, undrained
½ cup water
2 pkg (10-oz size) frozen chopped spinach, thawed, drained
½ cup feta cheese, crumbled
¼ cup milk
2 eggs
½ cup grated Parmesan cheese
¼ cup grated fresh bread crumbs

1. Preheat oven to 350F. Grease 12-by-8-inch baking dish. Cook macaroni according to package directions; drain. Toss with melted butter.

2. In oil, sauté beef, onion and garlic, stirring, over medium heat until meat is browned. Add salt, allspice, pepper, tomatoes (crush tomatoes with fork) and water. Bring to boiling; simmer, uncovered and stirring occasionally, about 20 minutes.

3. Layer half the macaroni on bottom of prepared dish. Spread with spinach; sprinkle feta over spinach. Layer with remaining macaroni; spoon meat sauce over the top.

4. In small bowl, beat together milk, eggs and Parmesan cheese. Pour over meat sauce. Sprinkle with bread crumbs. Bake 30 minutes. Remove to wire rack to cool 10 minutes before cutting into squares. *Makes 8 servings.*

BAKED CAVATELLI CASSEROLE

1 pkg (8 oz) cavatelli macaroni or other pasta

SAUCE

¼ cup (½ stick) butter or margarine
¼ cup all-purpose flour
1 teaspoon salt
¼ teaspoon pepper
2 cups milk
¼ cup grated Parmesan cheese

CHEESE LAYER

1 lb cream-style cottage cheese
1 egg
2 tablespoons chopped parsley
½ teaspoon salt
⅛ teaspoon pepper

¼ lb mozzarella cheese, sliced
Paprika

1. Preheat oven to 350F. Cook cavatelli as package label directs; drain.

2. Make Sauce: Melt butter in medium saucepan; remove from heat. Stir in flour, 1 teaspoon salt and ¼ teaspoon pepper until smooth. Gradually stir in milk. Over medium heat, bring to boiling, stirring. Reduce heat; simmer 1 minute. Remove from heat. Stir in Parmesan cheese. In medium bowl, combine cavatelli and sauce.

3. Make Cheese Layer: In medium bowl, combine cottage cheese, egg, parsley, salt and pepper; mix well.

4. In bottom of 2-quart baking dish, spoon half of cavatelli mixture. Layer with cheese mixture. Spoon on remaining cavatelli mixture.

5. Arrange sliced mozzarella on top; sprinkle with paprika. Bake, uncovered, 30 to 35 minutes, or until hot and bubbly. *Makes 8 servings.*

SMOKED HAM HOCKS WITH LIMA BEANS

6 smoked ham hocks (3 lb)
2 teaspoons celery seed
5 cups water
1 lb dried large lima beans
3 tablespoons butter or margarine
1 cup chopped onion
2 garlic cloves, finely chopped
1 cup chopped celery
1 can (1 lb, 1 oz) whole tomatoes, undrained
¼ teaspoon pepper
1 teaspoon salt

1. Wipe ham hocks with damp paper towels.

2. In 6-quart Dutch oven or kettle, combine ham hocks, celery seed and water. Bring to boiling. Reduce heat, and simmer, covered, 1 hour.

3. Wash lima beans; drain. Add to ham hocks; simmer, covered, 1 hour. Skim off excess fat.

4. Meanwhile, in hot butter in medium skillet, sauté onion and garlic until onion is soft—about 5 minutes.

5. Add celery, tomatoes, pepper and salt; bring to boiling, stirring. Reduce heat; simmer, uncovered, 15 minutes. Remove from heat.

6. Preheat oven to 350F.

7. Add tomato mixture to ham-hock

continued on page 268

Pasta Perfect

*N*orthern Italian cuisine is influenced by the French and Austrian styles of cooking, with their use of subtle flavors and cream and cheese sauces. In contrast, the Southern areas of Italy use highly flavored tomato sauces. Experience the simplicity of Northern Italian foods by making our Fettuccini Verde Alfredo—spinach pasta topped with a creamy Parmesan cheese sauce. We serve it with Garlic Bruschetta—thick slices of toasted Italian bread rubbed with garlic, topped with tomato slices and chopped olives, and broiled until hot.

A STEP-BY-STEP RECIPE

FETTUCCINI VERDE ALFREDO WITH GARLIC BRUSCHETTA

PASTA
1 pkg (9 oz) refrigerated fresh spinach
  fettuccini or linguine
1 tablespoon vegetable oil

ALFREDO SAUCE
½ cup butter or margarine
1 cup heavy cream
1 cup grated Parmesan cheese
1 egg yolk, beaten
1 tablespoon freshly squeezed lemon
  juice
¼ teaspoon ground black pepper
1 tablespoon water

GARLIC BRUSCHETTA
12 thick slices Italian bread
3 cloves garlic, halved
Olive oil
Coarse salt (sea salt)
6 very thin slices ripe tomato, cut in half
Chopped pitted ripe black olives
Freshly ground black pepper or crushed
  red pepper flakes

1 jar (3 oz) pine nuts

1. Prepare Pasta: In a large saucepan over high heat, bring 3 quarts water to a rolling boil. Add fettuccini, stirring with a large fork to separate strands. Cover saucepan and return water to boiling. Uncover and cook 2 or 3 minutes, stirring occasionally until fettuccini is al dente.

2. Place large colander in sink. Pour fettuccini and water into colander; drain thoroughly. Return drained fettuccini to saucepan. Add vegetable oil; toss well. Cover saucepan to keep warm. (If fettuccini needs to be reheated, transfer it to glass bowl; reheat in microwave, stirring occasionally.)

3. Prepare Alfredo Sauce: In a medium saucepan, over medium-high heat, heat butter and cream, stirring constantly, until butter is melted. Using a wire whisk, whisk in Parmesan cheese, beaten egg yolk, lemon juice and ¼ teaspoon black pepper.

4. Bring sauce almost to boiling, whisking constantly. Reduce heat to medium-low and simmer sauce 3 minutes, whisking constantly. Remove from heat; add 1 tablespoon water to sauce, whisking until thoroughly blended. Cover saucepan and set aside to keep sauce warm.

5. Prepare Garlic Bruschetta: Under hot broiler, toast bread slices on both sides until lightly browned. Rub one side of each slice with cut side of garlic. Drizzle or brush with olive oil and sprinkle lightly with coarse salt. Top each slice of Italian bread with a half slice of tomato and some chopped black olives.

6. Sprinkle with freshly ground pepper. Return to broiler and broil until tomato is heated thoroughly. To serve: Transfer hot fettuccini to serving platter, pour Alfredo Sauce over fettuccini and top with pine nuts. Place Garlic Bruschetta in basket; serve immediately. *Makes 6 servings.*

continued from page 265

mixture. Turn out into 3-quart casserole. Bake, covered tightly, until ham hocks and beans are tender and almost all the liquid has been absorbed—30 to 40 minutes. *Makes 6 to 8 servings.*

LAMB-VEGETABLE CASSEROLE

2 tablespoons salad oil
6 lamb patties (1½ lb)
4 large potatoes (2 lb), peeled and sliced
2 cups sliced onion
2 large tomatoes (1 lb), sliced
1 large green pepper (8 oz), seeded and cut into thin rings
1 teaspoon salt
1 teaspoon dried basil leaves
Dash pepper
¼ cup shredded Cheddar cheese

1. Preheat oven to 350F. In large skillet, in hot oil, sauté lamb patties until lightly browned on both sides. Discard excess fat.
2. In bottom of 2½-quart baking dish, layer the sliced potatoes and half the other vegetables. Sprinkle with half the seasonings. Arrange lamb patties on top.
3. Top with remaining onion, tomato and green pepper. Sprinkle with remaining seasonings.
4. Bake, covered, 50 to 60 minutes, or until vegetables are tender. Remove from oven; sprinkle with shredded cheese. Bake 5 minutes longer, or just until cheese is melted. *Makes 6 servings.*

BAKED SWISS FONDUE

⅔ cup butter or margarine, softened
1 garlic clove, crushed
1 teaspoon dry mustard
1 loaf (10 oz) Italian or French bread
3 cups grated natural Swiss cheese (¾ lb)
3 tablespoons grated onion
1 teaspoon salt
1 teaspoon paprika
¼ cup all-purpose flour
3 cups milk
1 cup dry white wine
3 eggs, beaten

DAY BEFORE
1. In small bowl, cream ⅓ cup butter with the garlic and ½ teaspoon dry mustard until well blended.
2. Remove ends of bread; cut loaf into ¼-inch-thick slices. Spread one side of each with butter mixture.
3. Line bottom and side of a heavy, earthenware, 2-quart casserole with some of bread slices, buttered side down.
4. In large bowl, combine cheese, onion, salt, paprika and remaining mus-

tard; toss until well blended.
5. In medium saucepan, melt remaining ⅓ cup butter; remove from heat. Stir in flour. Gradually stir in milk; bring to boiling over medium heat.
6. Stir in wine. Stir a little hot mixture into eggs; pour back into saucepan, stirring.
7. Arrange alternate layers of cheese mixture, remaining bread slices and wine sauce in casserole, ending with bread, buttered side up.
8. Refrigerate, covered, overnight.

NEXT DAY
9. Preheat oven to 350F. Bake casserole 40 minutes, or until puffy and golden-brown on top. *Makes 6 servings.*

BARLEY-VEGETABLE CASSEROLE

½ cup uncooked barley
2 zucchini (¾ lb)
2 summer squash (¾ lb)
Salt
¼ cup (½ stick) butter or margarine
2 tablespoons salad oil
2 cups sliced onion
2 small tomatoes (¾ lb), sliced
2 cups grated Cheddar cheese (8 oz)

1. Grease a 10-inch, shallow, 2-quart round or oval baking dish. Cook barley according to package directions; drain.
2. Turn cooked barley into prepared dish. Preheat oven to 350F.
3. Wash zucchini and summer squash; slice diagonally ½ inch thick.
4. In large skillet, place zucchini and summer squash; add 1 teaspoon salt and 1 cup boiling water. Return to boiling, covered; reduce heat, and simmer, covered, 2 minutes. Drain well in colander, set aside.
5. In same skillet, in hot butter and oil, sauté onion until tender—about 5 minutes.
6. On top of barley, layer tomatoes, half of onion, 1 cup grated cheese, the zucchini and summer squash, then remainder of onion and cheese.
7. Bake, covered tightly with foil, 30 minutes. Uncover; bake 5 minutes more, to evaporate liquid. *Makes 8 servings.*

EGGPLANT-AND-TOMATO CASSEROLE

2 medium eggplants (about 2½ lb)
Salt
¼ cup salad oil
2 garlic cloves, finely chopped
2 tablespoons all-purpose flour
2 cans (1-lb size) stewed tomatoes, undrained

2 teaspoons sugar
1 teaspoon paprika
⅛ teaspoon pepper
⅛ teaspoon dried basil leaves
½ cup grated Parmesan cheese

1. Preheat oven to 375F. Lightly grease 2-quart casserole.
2. Wash and peel eggplants; cut into 2-inch cubes. In 6-quart saucepan, in small amount of boiling salted water, simmer eggplant 10 minutes. Drain.
3. Meanwhile, in hot oil in large skillet, sauté garlic until golden—about 3 minutes. Remove from heat.
4. Stir in flour, tomatoes, sugar, paprika, pepper and basil. Cook, stirring, over medium heat, until mixture boils and is thickened.
5. In prepared casserole, layer eggplant cubes, alternately with tomato mixture, to fill casserole. Top with grated cheese.
6. Bake 30 minutes, or until lightly browned. *Makes 6 to 8 servings.*

PORK-PEAR PIE

2 tablespoons salad oil
2 lb lean boneless pork, cut into 1-inch cubes
1 cup chopped onion
1½ teaspoons rubbed sage
1 teaspoon salt
¼ teaspoon pepper
1 can (10¾ oz) condensed chicken broth, undiluted
3 pears, peeled, each cut into 8 slices
2 tablespoons all-purpose flour

POTATO TOPPING
Instant mashed potato for 8 servings
Water, milk, butter, salt
2 tablespoons grated Parmesan cheese

1. In hot oil in a large skillet, sauté pork cubes until brown on all sides—20 minutes. Remove.
2. Add onion to skillet; sauté until golden—5 minutes. Add sage, salt, pepper and browned pork cubes; mix well. Discard excess fat.
3. Stir in chicken broth. Bring to boiling, stirring; simmer, covered, 60 minutes, or until pork is fork-tender.
4. Preheat oven to 350F. Toss pear slices with flour; add to skillet; stir until combined. Simmer, covered, 10 minutes, or until pears are tender and sauce is thickened. Remove from heat. Turn into 2-quart round baking dish.
5. Make Potato Topping: Prepare instant mashed potato as directed on label. Spoon potato over pork mixture. Sprinkle with Parmesan cheese. Bake, uncovered, 20 to 30 minutes, or until potato is lightly browned on top. *Makes 6 servings.* ◆

continued from page 259

FLEMISH HOT POT
(pictured)

2 cans (10¾-oz size) condensed chicken
  broth, undiluted
1½ cups dry white wine
3 tablespoons lemon juice
2 bay leaves
1 teaspoon dried thyme leaves
7 black peppercorns
2 celery stalks, cut up
6 medium onions, peeled
Whole cloves
4 carrots, pared
4 turnips, pared and quartered
1 smoked pork shoulder butt (2 lb)
1 whole broiler-fryer (4 lb), washed
4 leeks, washed and trimmed
½ medium green cabbage, cut in 4 wedges
Peel of 1 lemon, cut in a spiral

Horseradish Sauce, recipe follows

1. In an 8-quart Dutch oven or kettle, combine chicken broth, wine, lemon juice, bay leaves, thyme, peppercorns, celery, onions (one onion studded with cloves), carrots and turnip.

2. Bring to boiling; reduce heat and simmer, covered, 30 minutes. Add pork butt; simmer, covered, 1 hour.

3. Add chicken; simmer, covered, 30 minutes. Add leeks, cabbage and lemon spiral; simmer, covered, 30 minutes longer, until all are tender. Remove and discard bay leaves. Meanwhile, make Horseradish Sauce.

4. Serve right from kettle with Horseradish Sauce. Nice with boiled potatoes. *Makes 8 to 10 servings.*

HORSERADISH SAUCE

3 tablespoons prepared horseradish,
  undrained
1 tablespoon prepared mustard
3 tablespoons lemon juice
½ teaspoon salt
1 cup sour cream

In medium bowl, combine all ingredients; mix well with rotary beater. Refrigerate, covered, until serving.

SPAGHETTI AND MEATBALLS NAPOLI

MEATBALLS
2 eggs
½ cup milk
3 slices whole-wheat bread, crumbled
¾ lb ground beef
½ lb ground pork
¼ lb ground veal
1 medium onion, finely chopped
⅓ cup finely chopped green pepper
2 tablespoons chopped parsley
1 large garlic clove, crushed
1 teaspoon salt
½ teaspoon pepper
Dash ground cloves
Dash ground nutmeg

SAUCE
½ lb round steak
¼ lb salt pork
1 garlic clove
¼ cup white wine
1 can (1 lb, 12 oz) tomatoes, undrained
1 can (6 oz) tomato paste
½ cup water
2 tablespoons chopped parsley
1 teaspoon salt
¼ teaspoon pepper
¼ teaspoon dried basil leaves

1 pkg (1 lb) spaghetti
½ cup grated Parmesan cheese

1. Make Meatballs: Preheat oven to 450F. In medium bowl, beat eggs slightly. Add milk and bread; mix well. Let stand 5 minutes.

2. Add rest of meatball ingredients; mix until well blended.

3. Shape into 12 balls—about 2½ inches in diameter. Place in a well-greased shallow baking pan.

4. Bake, uncovered, 15 minutes. Brush meatballs with pan drippings; bake 15 minute longer.

5. Meanwhile, make Sauce: Wipe round steak with damp paper towels. Cut into ½-inch chunks. Set aside.

6. Chop salt pork in little pieces. Place in Dutch oven with garlic; sauté until it is well browned. Push garlic and salt pork to one side of pan; add chunks of beef, and brown on all sides.

7. Add wine; simmer, covered, 10 minutes.

8. Stir in tomatoes, tomato paste, ½ cup water, the parsley, salt, pepper and basil; bring to boiling. Reduce heat; simmer, uncovered, ½ hour.

9. Add meatballs; simmer, covered and stirring occasionally, 1 hour longer.

10. Cook spaghetti as package label directs; drain.

11. To serve: Place spaghetti on serving dish; top with meatballs and sauce, and sprinkle with grated Parmesan cheese. *Makes 5 servings.*

CHICKEN-AND-HAM ROLLS A LA SUISSE

3 whole chicken breasts (about 1½ lb in
  all), boned, skinned and halved
6 thin slices baked ham
1 egg
1 tablespoon prepared mustard
2 tablespoons water
¼ cup grated Parmesan cheese
½ teaspoon salt
¼ teaspoon white pepper
½ cup package dry bread crumbs
6 tablespoons (¾ stick) butter or
  margarine, melted

SAUCE
2 tablespoons butter or margarine
2 tablespoons all-purpose flour
½ teaspoon salt
¼ teaspoon white pepper
1 tablespoon prepared mustard
1½ cups milk
½ cup dry white wine
1 cup grated Swiss cheese (4 oz)

1. Preheat oven to 425F. Line 12-by-8-by-2-inch baking dish with foil.

2. Wash chicken breasts; pat dry with paper towels. To flatten chicken, place each half, smooth side down, on sheet of waxed paper; cover with second sheet. Using a mallet, pound chicken to about ¼-inch thickness.

3. Place a slice of ham on each piece of chicken; roll up from short end; secure with a toothpick.

4. Combine egg, 1 tablespoon mustard and 2 tablespoons water; mix well. On a sheet of waxed paper, mix together Parmesan cheese, ½ teaspoon salt, ¼ teaspoon pepper and the bread crumbs.

5. Dip chicken rolls in egg mixture, then in crumb mixture, coating evenly. Arrange in single layer in bottom of foil-lined pan; spoon 1 tablespoon melted butter over each roll.

6. Bake, uncovered, 45 minutes, or until richly browned and fork-tender.

7. Meanwhile, make Sauce: In small, heavy saucepan, melt 2 tablespoons butter. Remove from heat; stir in flour, salt, pepper and mustard. Add milk gradually, stirring constantly. Return to heat. Bring to boiling, stirring. Add wine and all but 2 tablespoons of the Swiss cheese; simmer, stirring, 1 minute.

8. Pour ¾ of sauce into bottom of 12-by-8-by-2-inch baking dish. Place chicken rolls on top. Pour rest of sauce over chicken rolls. Sprinkle with remaining Swiss cheese. Place under broiler 1 minute. *Makes 6 servings.* ◆

EIGHT

EASY, ELEGANT ENTERTAINING

Formal or casual, for a hundred or a handful, whatever the season or reason, entertaining never seems to go out of style. There's a certain excitement in coming together to share some time—and some food—with friends and family. And the gathering is all the more enjoyable (especially for the host or hostess) when the food is quick and simple enough to prepare, yet elegant enough to impress. That's exactly what you'll find in this section: recipes that offer make-ahead convenience and speedy preparation, and an amazing variety of menus to bring out the best of any occasion. Whether it's a progressive dinner party or a buffet dinner, a casual barbecue or a posh cocktail party, we've got new and creative ideas that let you entertain with flair...with time left over to share.

Progressive Dinner

What could be more enjoyable than going out to eat? How about going out to eat in four different places...all in one night? That's what a progressive dinner is: A group of people, usually living in the same neighborhood, start at one house for appetizers and cocktails, then move on to others for the main course, salad and dessert. Each host or hostess is responsible for only one course instead of the whole meal. This joint entertaining leaves everyone with plenty of time to enjoy the fruits of the others' labor. Why not plan a progressive dinner with your neighbors soon? It's a great way to divide the work...and multiply the fun. Recipes begin on page 275.

Our progressive dinner menu starts with the appetizers pictured above. **Warm Pâté Tart** is a uniquely delicious pie that features a layer of liver pâté topped with a spiced mixture of eggs, cream and cheese, all baked in a prepared pie shell. Two great make-ahead ideas—**Pickled Mushrooms** and **Garlic Olives**—are arranged on the tray below.

GEORGE RATKAI/PAUL DOME

On to the next house for the main dish: Beef and Eggplant Provençale, a marvelous medley of beef cubes simmered in a Burgundy-sparked tomato sauce and sautéed eggplant. This hearty casserole is easily prepared in the morning, then reheated just before serving with toasted garlic bread.

At this stop, everyone can sample a delightful assortment of cheeses and crackers while enjoying a refreshing salad made earlier in the day from five different crisp greens, celery and cucumbers. A quick toss with oil and vinegar and it's ready to go.

The evening ends at the "dessert house" with an elegant Apricot-Rum Cake that's soaked with flavor inside and out. An apricot-rum syrup is poured into holes poked in the cake. Then the entire cake is brushed with an apricot-orange glaze and refrigerated. Garnish with grapes and pass with whipped cream, coffee and cordials.

Recipes given for starred dishes.

COCKTAILS
WARM PATE TART★
PICKLED MUSHROOMS,★
GARLIC OLIVES,★
AND CRISP RELISHES

**CASSEROLE OF BEEF AND
EGGPLANT PROVENCALE**★
**TOASTED PARMESAN GARLIC
BREAD**★
DRY RED WINE OR BEER

MIXED GREEN SALAD BOWL★
**ASSORTED-CHEESE BOARD
(EDAM, CHEDDAR, ROQUEFORT,
SWISS, GOURMANDISE,
CAMEMBERT)**
BASKET OF ASSORTED CRACKERS

**APRICOT-RUM CAKE WITH
WHIPPED CREAM**★
COFFEE AND LIQUEURS

★Recipes given for starred dishes.

WARM PATE TART
(pictured)

2 (9-inch size) unbaked pie shells
5 eggs
6 cans (4¾-oz size) liver pâté
¾ cup chopped onion
4 garlic cloves, crushed
½ cup packaged dry bread crumbs
Ground nutmeg
2 tablespoons (¼ stick) butter or
   margarine
2 cups heavy cream
½ teaspoon salt
Dash ground red pepper
⅔ cup grated Parmesan cheese
¼ cup dry sherry

DO AHEAD

1. Prepare pie shells. Refrigerate.
2. Separate 1 egg, placing white in small bowl, yolk in large bowl. Beat egg white. Brush over pie shells.
3. Preheat oven to 375F. In large bowl, combine pâté, ½ cup onion, the garlic, bread crumbs and ½ teaspoon nutmeg; mix well. Spoon into prepared pie shells, spreading evenly.
4. In hot butter in small skillet, sauté remaining ¼ cup onion about 2 minutes, or until lightly golden. Set aside.
5. Add remaining 4 eggs to egg yolk. Beat with cream, salt, red pepper and dash nutmeg until well combined but not frothy. Stir in sautéed onion, cheese and sherry. Pour half over pâté in each pie shell.
6. Bake 35 to 40 minutes, or until a

knife inserted 1 inch from edge comes out clean.
7. Let cool on wire rack about 1 hour.

TO SERVE

8. Serve warm; cut each tart into 12 wedges. *Makes 24 wedges.*

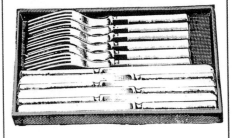

PICKLED MUSHROOMS
(pictured)

Salt
1 lb fresh button mushrooms
¼ cup chopped onion
½ garlic clove, finely chopped
2 tablespoons chopped parsley
2 bay leaves
Dash pepper
¼ teaspoon dried tarragon leaves
½ cup dry white wine
¼ cup white vinegar
2 tablespoons olive or salad oil
2 teaspoons lemon juice

DO AHEAD

1. Add ½ tablespoon salt to 3 cups cold water. Wash mushrooms in this; drain.
2. Combine remaining ingredients and ¼ teaspoon salt in large saucepan. Add the mushrooms; bring to boiling.
3. Then reduce heat, and simmer, covered, 8 to 10 minutes, or until mushrooms are tender. Cool.
4. Refrigerate, covered, in marinade at least 2 hours, or until ready to use.

TO SERVE

5. Drain just before serving. *Makes about 20.*

GARLIC OLIVES
(pictured)

1 can (7 oz) large pitted ripe olives
½ cup red-wine vinegar
¼ cup salad oil
¼ teaspoon crushed red pepper
1 garlic clove, minced
¼ cup finely chopped onion
1 teaspoon dried oregano leaves

DO AHEAD

1. Turn olives and their liquid into a quart jar with tight-fitting lid.

2. Add vinegar and rest of ingredients; cover tightly; shake well.
3. Refrigerate several days, shaking jar occasionally.

TO SERVE

4. Drain just before serving. *Makes about 36.*

BEEF AND EGGPLANT
PROVENCALE
(pictured)

BEEF IN WINE
⅓ cup olive or salad oil
4½ lb beef chuck, cut into 1½-inch cubes
2 lb small white onions, peeled
⅓ cup all-purpose flour
2 tablespoons sugar
1 tablespoon salt
½ teaspoon dried basil leaves
½ teaspoon dried thyme leaves
⅛ teaspoon pepper
Dash ground cloves
1 can (1 lb, 12 oz) Italian tomatoes,
   undrained
1½ cups Burgundy
2 bay leaves

EGGPLANT
2 medium eggplants (2 lb)
3 eggs
¼ cup water
1 cup packaged seasoned dry bread
   crumbs
¾ cup salad oil

GARNISH
3 medium tomatoes (1¼ lb)
½ teaspoon salt
½ teaspoon dried thyme leaves
2 tablespoons chopped parsley

DO AHEAD

1. In the morning, make Beef in Wine: In a 6-quart heavy kettle, slowly heat about 2 tablespoons oil. Add beef cubes, about one-third at a time, and cook over high heat until well browned on all sides. Remove beef as it browns. Add more oil as needed. Set beef aside.
2. Add onions to kettle; cook, stirring, until lightly browned. Remove onions, and set aside.
3. Remove kettle from heat. Stir in flour, sugar, salt, basil, thyme, pepper and cloves until well blended. Gradually stir in tomatoes and Burgundy. Add bay leaves and the browned beef.
4. Bring to boiling, stirring occasionally. Reduce heat, and simmer, covered, 2½ hours; stir occasionally.
5. Add browned onions; cook 40 minutes longer, or until beef and onions are tender. Remove bay leaves. Let cool in kettle; then refrigerate, covered.
6. Meanwhile, prepare Eggplant: Wash eggplants. Cut crosswise into ½-inch-thick slices.

continued on page 276

continued from page 275

7. In shallow dish, beat eggs with water. Dip eggplant slices first into egg mixture, then into crumbs, coating well.

8. In skillet, heat about 2 tablespoons oil. Add eggplant, a few slices at a time, and sauté until golden-brown on each side. Remove eggplant as it browns. Add more oil as needed.

9. When all eggplant is browned, arrange slices, overlapping, around edge of a 3½-quart shallow baking dish; place remaining slices in bottom. Set aside, covered.

10. Prepare Garnish: Wash tomatoes. Cut each into 6 wedges. Arrange in shallow dish; sprinkle with salt and thyme.

TO SERVE

11. About ½ hour before serving, preheat oven to 350F. Bake eggplant 25 minutes, or until piping hot. At same time, slowly bring beef mixture to boiling; reduce heat, and heat gently until thoroughly hot. Turn into eggplant-lined casserole.

12. Arrange tomato wedges, overlapping, around edge of casserole. Sprinkle with parsley. *Makes 12 servings.*

TOASTED PARMESAN GARLIC BREAD
(pictured)

GARLIC BUTTER
1 cup (2 sticks) butter or margarine, softened
¼ cup chopped parsley
¼ cup grated Parmesan cheese
1 garlic clove, crushed
2 teaspoons dried marjoram leaves
½ teaspoon pepper

2 loaves French or Italian bread, about 14 inches long

DO AHEAD

1. Several hours before dinner, make Garlic Butter: In small bowl, combine butter, parsley, Parmesan, garlic, marjoram and pepper; mix until well blended.

2. Cut each loaf in half lengthwise. Spread cut sides with garlic butter. Cut each half, on the diagonal, not quite all the way through, into 1-inch-thick slices. Set the bread aside on a cookie sheet, loosely covered.

TO SERVE

3. Just before serving, broil bread, buttered side up, 4 inches from heat, about 8 minutes, or until lightly toasted. Cut or pull slices apart. *Makes 3 dozen slices.*

MIXED GREEN SALAD BOWL
(pictured)

1 medium head Boston lettuce
2 or 3 Belgian endives
1 small head romaine
¼ lb fresh young spinach leaves
½ bunch watercress
1 cup thinly sliced celery
2 medium cucumbers, pared and thinly sliced
1 bottle (8 oz) oil-and-vinegar-type salad dressing

DO AHEAD

1. Early in the day, wash salad greens; dry well on paper towels or spin in a salad dryer. Trim ends; remove any discolored leaves and stems. Crisp in crisper.

2. Several hours before serving, break salad greens, except watercress, into bite-size pieces, to measure 3½ quarts. Toss lightly with celery in large salad bowl, to mix well.

3. Arrange cucumber slices, overlapping, in a row around edge of bowl. Place watercress in center. Cover with plastic wrap or foil, and refrigerate, along with salad dressing, until serving.

TO SERVE

4. Toss with dressing, to coat salad greens. *Makes 12 servings.*

APRICOT-RUM CAKE WITH WHIPPED CREAM
(pictured)

1 pkg (1 lb, 2.5oz) lemon-chiffon cake mix
1 tablespoon grated orange peel
1 tablespoon grated lemon peel
Eggs, water

APRICOT-RUM SYRUP
1 can (12 oz) apricot nectar
¾ cup sugar
1 cup water
1 cup golden rum
¼ cup lemon juice

APRICOT GLAZE
¾ cup apricot preserves
1 tablespoon orange juice

Clusters of seedless green grapes
1½ cups heavy cream, whipped

DO AHEAD

1. In the morning, preheat oven to 350F.

2. Prepare cake mix as package label directs, adding orange and lemon peel with eggs and water. Turn into ungreased 10-inch tube pan. Bake 45 to 55 minutes, or until surface springs back when gently pressed with fingertip.

3. Invert pan immediately, hanging tube over neck of bottle. Let the cake cool completely—about 1½ hours.

4. Meanwhile, make Apricot-Rum Syrup: In medium saucepan, combine apricot nectar, sugar and water; bring to boiling, stirring until sugar is dissolved. Boil gently, uncovered, 10 minutes, or until syrup measures about 2 cups. Remove from heat. Add rum and lemon juice.

5. With cake tester, make holes, 1 inch apart, in top of cake in pan. Pour warm syrup over cake, ¼ cup at a time, until all is used. Let stand at room temperature 2 hours, or until all syrup is absorbed.

6. Make Apricot Glaze: Melt preserves in small saucepan over low heat. Stir in orange juice. Then strain.

7. Carefully loosen cake from pan; invert onto wire rack; then turn, top side up, onto serving plate. Brush glaze over top and side of cake. Refrigerate.

TO SERVE

8. Garnish plate with grapes and, if desired, leaves, as pictured. Cut cake into wedges. Pass whipped cream, for guests to spoon over cake. *Makes 12 servings.*

COCKTAILS
ASSORTED STUFFED CELERY★
DEVILED EGGS   SALTED NUTS
CASSEROLE OF CHICKEN TETRAZZINI★
TOSSED GREEN SALAD
WARM BUTTERED ITALIAN BREAD
BAKED FRUIT COMPOTE★
SPONGE-CAKE FINGERS★
COFFEE

★Recipes given for starred dishes.

ASSORTED STUFFED CELERY

1 bunch Pascal celery, separated into stalks, trimmed, washed and crisped (2½ lb)

HAM-PEANUT FILLING
1 can (2½ oz) deviled ham
¼ cup chunk-style peanut butter
1 teaspoon bottled salad dressing
2 tablespoons chopped peanuts

AVOCADO FILLING
1 medium-size ripe avocado (about ½ lb)
¼ teaspoon onion salt
¼ teaspoon garlic salt
2 teaspoons chili sauce
1 teaspoon lemon juice
Few drops hot red-pepper sauce

CHEESE FILLING

1 jar (5 oz) sharp-cheese spread
4 slices crisp-cooked bacon, crumbled

DO AHEAD

1. Cut celery into 2-inch lengths.
2. Make Ham-Peanut Filling: In small bowl, combine deviled ham, peanut butter and salad dressing; mix until well combined. Use to stuff celery—about 18 pieces. Garnish with peanuts.
3. Make Avocado Filling: Cut avocado in half lengthwise; remove pit and peel. Slice into small bowl; mash well with fork. Add onion and garlic salts, chili sauce, lemon juice and red-pepper sauce; mix well. Use to stuff celery—about 18 pieces.
4. For Cheese Filling: Fill remaining celery with sharp-cheese spread. Garnish with bacon bits.
5. Refrigerate, covered, until well chilled—at least 1 hour.

TO SERVE

6. Arrange on serving platter. *Makes 12 servings (about 50 celery pieces).*

CHICKEN TETRAZZINI

2 lb whole chicken breasts, split
3 lb chicken legs and thighs
3 celery tops
3 parsley sprigs
2 medium carrots, pared and sliced
1 onion, quartered
2 teaspoons salt
10 black peppercorns
1 bay leaf

SAUCE

¾ cup (1½ sticks) butter or margarine
¾ cup all-purpose flour
3 teaspoons salt
⅛ teaspoon ground nutmeg
Dash ground red pepper
1 quart milk
4 egg yolks
1 cup heavy cream
½ cup dry sherry

1 pkg (1 lb) thin spaghetti
2 cans (6-oz size) whole mushrooms, drained
2 pkg (8-oz size) sharp Cheddar cheese, grated (4 cups)

DO AHEAD

1. In the morning, wash chicken. Place in 6-quart kettle with 3 cups water, the celery, parsley, carrot, onion, salt, peppercorns and bay leaf. Bring to boiling; reduce heat, and simmer, covered, 1 hour, or until chicken is tender.
2. Remove chicken from stock to bowl; set aside. Strain stock; return to kettle. Bring to boiling; boil gently, uncovered, until reduced to 2 cups—about 30 minutes.
3. Remove chicken meat from bones

in large pieces—there should be about 6 cups. Set the chicken meat aside.

4. Make Sauce: Melt butter in large saucepan. Remove from heat. Stir in flour, salt, nutmeg and red pepper until smooth. Gradually stir in milk and the 2 cups stock; bring to boiling, stirring constantly. Boil gently, stirring constantly; 2 minutes, or until slightly thickened.
5. In small bowl, beat egg yolks with cream. Gently beat in a little of the hot mixture. Return to saucepan; cook over low heat, stirring constantly, until sauce is hot—do not let it boil. Remove from heat. Add sherry.
6. Cook spaghetti as package label directs; drain. Return spaghetti to kettle. Add 2 cups sauce, and toss until well blended.
7. Remove another 2 cups sauce and refrigerate, covered. To remaining sauce, add cut-up chicken and the mushrooms.
8. Divide spaghetti into two 12-by-8-by-2-inch baking dishes, arranging it around edges. Spoon half of chicken mixture into center of each. Sprinkle 2 cups cheese over spaghetti in each dish. Cover with foil; refrigerate.

TO SERVE

9. About 1 hour before serving, preheat oven to 350F. Bake, covered, 30 to 45 minutes, or until piping hot.
10. Just before serving, reheat reserved sauce, and spoon over spaghetti in baking dishes. *Makes 12 servings.*

BAKED FRUIT COMPOTE

2 cans (1-lb, 1-oz size) peach halves
2 cans (1-lb, 1-oz size) pear halves
1 can (1 lb, 1 oz) whole figs
¼ lb dried apricots (1 cup)
¼ cup coarsely grated orange peel
¼ cup light-brown sugar, firmly packed
½ cup sliced preserved ginger in syrup, slivered

DO AHEAD

1. Day before serving: Drain all canned fruits in a large colander placed over a large bowl. Reserve all syrup.
2. In medium saucepan, combine apricots and 1 cup reserved syrup. Bring to boiling; reduce heat, and simmer, covered, 15 minutes. Remove from heat, and set aside.
3. Meanwhile, in a large saucepan, combine remaining syrup (it should measure about 3½ cups), the orange peel and brown sugar. Bring to boiling over medium heat; boil, uncovered, to reduce syrup to about 2 cups—takes about 35 minutes. Then add slivered ginger.
4. Preheat oven to 350F.
5. Place a fig in cavity of 7 pear

halves. In a 2½-quart heatproof mixing bowl, arrange pears spoke fashion, fig side down with rounded end at edge of bowl. Pour 1 cup syrup over pears.
6. Arrange some of peach halves around edge, rounded side against bowl. Fill center with remaining pears and peaches and the apricots, along with their cooking liquid. Pour remaining syrup over fruit.
7. Bake, uncovered, 45 minutes, or until hot and bubbly around edge.
8. Let cool slightly; refrigerate, covered, overnight.

TO SERVE

9. Place a shallow glass serving bowl over mixing bowl; carefully invert mixing bowl to preserve the fruit design. *Makes 12 servings.*

SPONGE-CAKE FINGERS

¾ cup milk
1½ cups sifted all-purpose flour
1½ teaspoons baking powder
¼ teaspoon salt
4 eggs
1½ cups granulated sugar
1½ teaspoons vanilla extract

Confectioners' sugar

DO AHEAD

1. In the morning, preheat oven to 350F. Heat milk in small saucepan just until bubbles appear around edge. Remove from heat; let cool until lukewarm—about 15 minutes.
2. Sift flour with baking powder and salt. Set aside.
3. In large bowl, with electric mixer at high speed, beat eggs until thick and lemon-colored. Gradually add granulated sugar, ¼ cup at a time, beating until mixture is thick and smooth. Beat in vanilla.
4. At low speed, blend in flour mixture just until smooth. Add warm milk, beating just until blended. Pour batter immediately into an ungreased 13-by-9-by-2-inch baking pan.
5. Bake 30 to 35 minutes, or until cake tester inserted in center comes out clean.
6. Invert cake by hanging between 2 other pans; let cool completely—about 1 hour. Loosen cake from sides and bottom of pan; remove to serving platter or wooden tray. Sprinkle confectioners' sugar over top; cover loosely until serving.

TO SERVE

7. Cut lengthwise into sixths, then crosswise into quarters, to make 24 finger-shape pieces. *Makes 12 servings.*◆

PERFECT
PARTY STARTERS

Appetizers help set the tone of a meal, and our selection of tantalizing tidbits will keep pace with your party plans. Choose from hot food, cold food, dip-ins, pick-ups, spreads and breads. Many of our delectable appetizers can be prepared hours before party time; some are microwavable. Whatever your taste and whatever your style of entertaining, we have a special appetizer that will make a great first impression for your party. Recipes begin on page 280.

Spicy Crab Cakes (top) are mini morsels rich in Monterey Jack cheese and ricotta cheese and served with a red-pepper mayonnaise. Pear and Brie Purses are a mixture of chopped pears, Brie, almonds and brandy encased in phyllo pastry.

AARON REZNY

Clockwise, starting at top: Shrimp Remoulade is a chilled make-ahead dish of shrimp in a horseradish-mustard marinade. A yellow-pepper cup holds Spinach Dip Provençale, which is a double-cheese blend flavored with onion and pine nuts. Chinese Pot Stickers are do-ahead dumplings filled with pork and cabbage and dipped into a spicy sauce. Jamaican Jerk Wings get their tasty accent from a marinade of herbs and spices.

continued from page 278

SPICY CRAB CAKES

(pictured)

2 eggs
½ lb fresh lump crabmeat
1 cup ricotta cheese
1 cup (4 oz) shredded Monterey Jack
   cheese with jalapeños
3 tablespoons snipped chives
¾ cup fine seasoned dry bread crumbs
¼ cup salad oil
1 jar (7 oz) roasted red peppers, drained
⅓ cup mayonnaise

1. In medium bowl, whisk eggs until blended. Stir in crabmeat, cheeses, chives and ¼ cup bread crumbs. Form heaping tablespoonfuls of crab mixture into ¼-inch-thick cakes. On sheet of waxed paper, coat crab cakes with remaining bread crumbs.

2. Preheat oven to 325F. Line baking sheet with paper towels. In large skillet, heat salad oil over medium-high heat. In hot oil, fry crab cakes, a few at a time, until golden on both sides, about 3 minutes in all. As crab cakes cook, remove from pan, drain on prepared baking sheet and keep warm in oven.

3. In food processor, process red peppers with mayonnaise until smooth. Serve with crab cakes. *Makes 12 servings.*

PEAR AND BRIE PURSES

(pictured)

2 ripe pears, cored and chopped
½ cup chopped almonds
½ cup coarsely chopped bittersweet
   almond-flavored Italian cookies
1 tablespoon brandy
12 phyllo-pastry sheets
½ cup unsalted butter, melted
¾ lb Brie cheese

1. Preheat oven to 425F. In medium bowl, combine pears, almonds, cookies and brandy. Brush 1 phyllo-pastry sheet with butter; fold lengthwise in half. Brush with butter; cut crosswise in half. Repeat with remaining phyllo-pastry sheets.

2. Cut Brie into 24 equal pieces; place 1 piece Brie and 2 tablespoons pear mixture in center of each pastry square. Bring up opposite corners of pastry square; press together to seal. Place on baking sheet. Repeat with remaining pear mixture and pastry squares.

3. Bake purses 10 minutes, or until golden. If desired, tie a chive around top of each purse before serving. *Makes 12 servings.*

SPINACH DIP PROVENCALE

(pictured)

1 tablespoon olive oil
¼ cup pine nuts
1 large red onion, minced
2 medium garlic cloves, crushed
½ teaspoon dried thyme leaves
1 cup low-fat cottage cheese
4 oz cream cheese
⅔ cup milk
1 pkg (10 oz) frozen chopped spinach,
   thawed and squeezed dry
¼ cup chopped calamata or oil-cured
   olives
1 tablespoon lemon juice
¼ teaspoon salt
⅛ teaspoon pepper

Yellow-pepper cup
Pita chips

1. In skillet, heat olive oil; sauté pine nuts 2 minutes, or until golden. Remove nuts to bowl. In same skillet, sauté onion and garlic with thyme leaves 8 minutes, or until onions are tender; cool slightly.

2. In food processor, puree cottage cheese with cream cheese; transfer mixture to bowl with pine nuts. Stir in onion mixture, milk, spinach, olives, lemon juice, salt and pepper; mix well. Spoon mixture into yellow-pepper cup; serve with pita chips. *Makes 10 servings.*

SHRIMP REMOULADE

(pictured)

1½ lb large shrimp, shelled and
   deveined
¼ cup chopped parsley
¼ cup distilled white vinegar
1½ teaspoons paprika
½ teaspoon shrimp or crab boil
   seasoning
2 tablespoons Dijon-style mustard
2 tablespoons prepared white
   horseradish
½ cup olive oil
3 celery stalks, sliced crosswise
3 green onions, minced
1 small red pepper, chopped
Lettuce and radicchio leaves, washed

1. In large saucepan, bring 2 inches water to boiling. Add shrimp; cook 2 or 3 minutes, or until just firm. Drain.

2. In large bowl, combine parsley, vinegar, paprika, shrimp seasoning, mustard and horseradish; whisk in olive oil until well blended; add the shrimp, celery, green onions and red pepper. Mix well; refrigerate, covered, 3 hours or overnight.

3. To serve: Line serving bowl with lettuce; spoon shrimp mixture on top. *Makes 8 servings.*

JAMAICAN JERK WINGS

(pictured)

Jerking is a centuries-old way of preserving and cooking meat. For convenience, we bake these chicken wings after they've been flavored with a Jamaican-style spice-and-herb marinade.

4 lb chicken wings
1 medium onion, quartered
4 green onions, cut into 1-inch pieces
1 jalapeño pepper, seeds removed
3 large garlic cloves
1½ teaspoons ground black pepper
1½ teaspoons salt
1 teaspoon ground allspice
1 teaspoon dried thyme leaves
½ teaspoon ground red pepper
3 tablespoons vegetable oil
1 tablespoon soy sauce

1. Remove and discard tips from chicken wings. Place wings in large glass baking dish.

2. In food processor, combine quartered onion, green onions, jalapeño pepper and garlic; chop. Add remaining ingredients; process until smooth. Pour mixture over chicken wings; stir to coat. Cover with plastic wrap; refrigerate at least 12 hours or overnight, stirring once.

3. Preheat oven to 425F. Place chicken wings in single layer in oiled shallow roasting pan. Bake 40 minutes, or until wings are browned and cooked, turning wings over after 20 minutes. Serve warm, or make ahead and reheat. *Makes 12 servings.*

CHINESE POT STICKERS

(pictured)

The name for these appetizers came about because some Chinese cooks didn't grease their pans well. However, using a nonstick skillet keeps these "wrappers" from sticking as they brown.

FILLING
¾ lb ground pork
1½ cups finely shredded cabbage
4 green onions, minced
3 medium garlic cloves, crushed
¾ teaspoon salt
2 tablespoons soy sauce
1 tablespoon dark sesame oil
2 teaspoons minced gingerroot

¼ cup warm water
1 tablespoon cornstarch
1 pkg (10 oz) Chinese dumpling
   wrappers

DIPPING SAUCE
½ cup soy sauce
¼ cup rice vinegar

¾ teaspoon hot chili oil
6 tablespoons vegetable oil
2¼ cups cold water

1. Make Filling: In medium bowl, combine pork, cabbage, green onions, garlic, salt, soy sauce, sesame oil and gingerroot; mix well. In custard cup, combine the warm water and cornstarch; mix well.

2. Working with several Chinese dumpling wrappers at a time (keep remaining wrappers covered with damp paper towels), place 1 rounded teaspoon filling in center of each wrapper, leaving ¼-inch border. Brush edges with cornstarch mixture. Fold wrapper over filling, pleating and sealing edges. Repeat with remaining wrappers and filling. Place dumplings on jelly-roll pan; cover with plastic wrap. Refrigerate at least 1 hour, or up to 4 hours.

3. Make Dipping Sauce: In bowl, blend all ingredients.

4. Cook Pot Stickers: In 12-inch nonstick skillet, heat 2 tablespoons vegetable oil over high heat. Add one-third of the Pot Stickers; cook 2 or 3 minutes, or until bottoms are browned. Over low heat, add ¾ cup cold water. Bring to boiling; simmer, covered, 5 minutes, or until most of the water has evaporated. Carefully remove Pot Stickers from pan; keep warm. Cook remaining Pot Stickers in 2 batches. Serve with Dipping Sauce. *Makes 25 servings.*

AVOCADO-TOPPED NEW POTATOES

20 small new potatoes, unpared
¼ cup avocado or vegetable oil
½ teaspoon salt
¼ teaspoon ground red pepper

AVOCADO CREAM
1 large garlic clove
¼ cup loosely packed cilantro
2 small ripe avocados (1 lb), peeled and coarsely chopped
½ teaspoon salt
¼ teaspoon ground red pepper
2 tablespoons lime juice
2 tablespoons sour cream

¼ cup chopped roasted red pepper

1. Preheat oven to 375F. Halve potatoes; cut a thin slice from each rounded end so halves will not roll. In bowl, combine avocado oil, salt and red pepper; add potatoes. Toss to coat; arrange potatoes, large cut side up, in broiler pan. Bake 25 minutes, or just until tender.

2. While potatoes bake, make Avocado Cream: In food processor, chop garlic and cilantro. Add remaining ingredients; puree.

3. Spoon Avocado Cream on top of each potato. Top with chopped roasted pepper. *Makes 20 servings.*

TORTELLONI ON A STICK

1 pkg (10 oz) cheese tortelloni
1 cup bottled Caesar-salad dressing
1 jar (10 oz) mild salsa
1 small cucumber, pared, seeded and chopped
½ green pepper, chopped
½ yellow pepper, chopped

1. Cook tortelloni as package label directs. Drain; place in large bowl. Add Caesar-salad dressing; toss to coat. Set aside to cool.

2. In small bowl, combine remaining ingredients. To serve: Arrange tortelloni on skewers; use salsa mixture as dipping sauce. *Makes 12 servings.*

CHILI CON QUESO WITH RAW VEGETABLES

¼ cup (½ stick) butter or margarine
½ cup finely chopped onion
1 can (1 lb) tomatoes, undrained
1½ to 2 cans (4-oz size) green chilies (see Note), drained and chopped
½ teaspoon salt
1 lb Monterey Jack cheese, cubed
½ cup heavy cream

In hot butter, in medium skillet, sauté onion until tender. Add tomatoes, chilies and salt, mashing tomatoes with fork. Simmer, stirring occasionally, 15 minutes. Add cheese cubes, stirring until cheese is melted. Stir in heavy cream. Cook, stirring constantly, 2 minutes. Remove from heat and let stand 15 minutes. Serve warm, in a casserole over a candle warmer, as a dip with carrot sticks, celery hearts, cucumber sticks and large corn chips. *Makes 10 to 12 servings.*

Note: Use a larger amount of green chilies if you prefer the Chili Con Queso really hot.

SAVORY EDAM CHEESE

1 whole Edam cheese (about 1¾ lb)
1 cup beer or ale
¼ cup (½ stick) butter or margarine, softened
1 teaspoon caraway seeds
1 teaspoon dry mustard
½ teaspoon celery salt

1. Let Edam cheese stand at room temperature until soft—about 1 hour.

2. Remove a slice, about 1-inch thick, from top of Edam cheese. With spoon, scoop out cheese from slice and from cheese round, keeping red shell intact. Discard top. Refrigerate shell.

3. Grate scooped-out cheese on fine grater into medium bowl. Let stand at room temperature until very soft.

4. Add beer, butter, caraway seeds, dry mustard and celery salt; mix until well blended. Fill cheese shell with mixture, mounding high.

5. Wrap cheese shell in plastic wrap, then in foil. Store in refrigerator several weeks.

6. To serve: Let stand at room temperature until soft enough to spread. *Makes 3 cups.*

SPRING DIP

¼ cup heavy cream
2 cups creamed cottage cheese
¼ cup grated raw carrot
¼ cup thinly sliced green onion
¼ cup finely chopped green pepper
6 radishes, sliced very thin
Dash freshly ground black pepper
Dash dillweed

Stir heavy cream into cottage cheese. Add remaining ingredients and mix well. Refrigerate. Serve Spring Dip with raw vegetables. *Makes about 3 cups.*

PARMESAN-CHEESE LEAVES

1 cup all-purpose flour
½ cup (1 stick) butter or margarine, cut into small pieces
1 cup grated Parmesan cheese
¼ teaspoon salt
Dash black pepper
Dash ground red pepper
2 tablespoons cold water
1 egg, slightly beaten
Paprika (optional)

1. Make cheese pastry: In medium bowl, combine flour and butter. With pastry blender or 2 knives, used scissors fashion, cut butter into flour until butter particles are the size of small peas. With fork, stir in Parmesan cheese, salt, black and red pepper. Sprinkle evenly with 2 tablespoons cold water. Toss with fork. Form into ball with hands, then flatten slightly.

2. Between sheets of waxed paper, on a slightly damp surface, roll out cheese pastry to ¼-inch thickness.

3. Using leaf-shaped or scalloped cookie cutters (about 2½ inches in diameter), cut out cheese pastry (see Note). Place in plastic freezer container, with waxed paper between layers. Cover; freeze.

continued on page 282

continued from page 281

4. To serve: Preheat oven to 400F. Place frozen Parmesan-Cheese Leaves, about 1 inch apart, on ungreased baking sheets. Brush tops lightly with egg.

5. Sprinkle with a little paprika, if desired. Bake, still frozen, 10 minutes, or until golden. Serve warm. *Makes about 2 dozen.*

Note: Or cut leaves freehand.

CHERRY TOMATOES, SOUR-CREAM DIP

1 pint cherry tomatoes
1 cup sour cream
¼ teaspoon fresh or thawed frozen chopped chives
¼ teaspoon parsley flakes
Dash salt

1. Wash tomatoes, leaving stems on. Drain and refrigerate.

2. In small serving bowl, combine sour cream with rest of ingredients. Refrigerate, covered, about 1 hour, or until well chilled.

3. Place Sour-Cream Dip in center of large tray; surround with cherry tomatoes. *Makes 6 to 8 servings.*

MOUSSE OF CHICKEN LIVERS

½ cup (1 stick) sweet butter
1 large onion, sliced (1 cup)
1¼ lb chicken livers
1 hard-cooked egg, cut in half
1½ tablespoons cognac
½ teaspoon salt
Dash pepper
Chopped green onion
Toast or crackers

1. In 2 tablespoons hot butter in skillet, sauté sliced onion until tender—about 10 minutes. Remove from skillet.

2. Heat remaining butter in same skillet. Add chicken livers and sauté over medium heat 3 to 5 minutes, or until golden-brown. Chicken livers should be pink inside.

3. Put half the sautéed onion, chicken

---

livers, egg and cognac in blender; blend at low speed just until smooth. Turn into crock or bowl. Repeat with rest of sautéed onion, chicken livers, egg and cognac. Stir in salt and pepper. Refrigerate, covered, until well chilled—overnight.

4. To serve: Garnish with chopped green onion; serve with toast or crackers. *Makes 3 cups.*

HOLIDAY CHEESE BALL

4 pkg (3-oz size) cream cheese, softened
6 oz blue cheese, softened
6 oz processed Cheddar-cheese spread
2 tablespoons grated onion
1 teaspoon Worcestershire sauce
⅛ teaspoon monosodium glutamate (optional)
1 cup ground pecans
½ cup finely chopped parsley
Assorted crackers

1. In medium bowl, combine the cheeses, onion, Worcestershire sauce and, if desired, monosodium glutamate. Beat until well blended.

2. Stir in ½ cup pecans and ¼ cup parsley. Shape into a ball. Wrap in waxed paper, then in foil. Refrigerate overnight.

3. About 1 hour before serving, roll cheese ball in remaining pecans and parsley. Place on serving plate and surround with assorted crackers. *Makes about 30 appetizer servings.*

EGGPLANT APPETIZER

1 large eggplant
½ cup plus 2 tablespoons olive or salad oil
2½ cups sliced onion
1 cup diced celery
2 cans (8-oz size) tomato sauce
¼ cup red-wine vinegar
2 tablespoons sugar
2 tablespoons drained capers
½ teaspoon salt
Dash pepper
12 pitted black olives, cut into slivers
Toast rounds

1. Wash eggplant; cut into ½-inch cubes.

2. In ½ cup hot olive oil, in large skillet, sauté eggplant until tender and golden-brown. Remove eggplant and set aside.

3. In 2 tablespoons hot olive oil, in same skillet, sauté onion and celery until tender—about 5 minutes.

4. Return eggplant to skillet. Stir in tomato sauce; bring to boiling. Lower heat and simmer, covered, 15 minutes.

---

5. Add vinegar, sugar, capers, salt, pepper and olives. Simmer, covered, stirring occasionally, 20 minutes longer. Refrigerate, covered, overnight.

6. To serve: Place in serving bowl; surround with toast rounds. *Makes 6 to 8 appetizer servings.*

GARLIC-CHEESE SPREAD

1 head (2 oz) garlic
1 lb ripe Brie cheese, rind removed
½ cup (1 stick) unsalted butter, softened and cut into 1-inch pieces
1 egg yolk
1 teaspoon dried bouquet garni or Italian seasoning
Assorted raw vegetables, bread or crackers

1. Rinse garlic under running water until skins are slightly softened. Enclose garlic head in plastic wrap, leaving a small opening. Microwave at HIGH (100% power) 3 minutes. Let stand until cool. Cut off and discard root ends. Pinch uncut ends of garlic cloves to remove skins.

2. Wrap Brie in plastic wrap; vent; microwave at HIGH (100% power) 1 minute, or until cheese is runny but not hot. Scrape cheese into blender or food processor. Add garlic cloves, butter, egg yolk and bouquet garni. Puree until smooth.

3. Place mixture in crock or serving bowl; refrigerate, covered. Bring to room temperature before serving. Serve with raw vegetables, bread or crackers. *Makes about 1¾ cups.*

ITALIAN FLAT BREAD

1 pkg (10 oz) refrigerated white-bread dough
¼ cup olive oil
4 teaspoons dried rosemary leaves
2 teaspoons coarse (kosher) salt or 1 teaspoon regular salt
1 teaspoon freshly ground black pepper

1. Preheat browning tray for microwave oven at HIGH (100% power), according to manufacturer's directions, about 5 minutes.

2. Meanwhile, remove white-bread dough from package; on board, unroll and brush each side with 2 tablespoons olive oil. Roll dough to 1/16-inch thickness; cut into 8 pieces. Sprinkle each piece with ½ teaspoon rosemary, ¼ teaspoon coarse salt or ⅛ teaspoon regular salt, and ⅛ teaspoon black pepper.

3. With pot holder, remove browning tray from oven. Quickly lay a piece of prepared dough on tray; return to

oven. Microwave at HIGH (100% power) until crust is golden-brown—about 45 seconds. With tongs, turn dough over; microwave at HIGH until second side is golden-brown—about 45 seconds. Remove to wire rack.

4. Repeat with remaining pieces of dough, working quickly so browning tray remains hot. Serve the Italian Flat Bread warm or at room temperature. *Makes 8 servings.*

Note: Recipe was tested in 600- to 700-watt microwave ovens.

CLAMS OREGANATA

1 slice white bread, quartered
¼ cup parsley leaves
1 small garlic clove
2 tablespoons butter or margarine
2 tablespoons grated Parmesan cheese
½ teaspoon dried oregano leaves
1 tablespoon olive oil
1 dozen clams in shells

1. Place bread, parsley and garlic in a blender or a food processor; chop coarsely.

2. In small bowl, melt butter in microwave at HIGH (100% power) 15 seconds. Add the bread mixture, Parmesan cheese, oregano and olive oil; mix lightly with fork.

3. Scrub clams under cold running water to remove any sand. Place clams in microwave-safe pie plate. (If clams are large, open and cook 6 at a time.) Cover with plastic wrap; turn back one corner to vent. Microwave at HIGH (100% power) 1½ minutes, or until clamshells open slightly. Remove clams from oven; discard top shell from each. Reserve liquid for soup, if desired.

4. Return clams in shell to pie plate. Spread bread mixture over clams, dividing evenly; cover with plastic wrap; vent one corner. Microwave at HIGH (100% power) 3 to 4 minutes, rotating dish once, until clams are just firm. *Makes 12 servings.*

ZIPPY CHEDDAR CRISPS

1 cup yellow cornmeal
2 tablespoons butter or margarine
1 tablespoon sugar
½ teaspoon salt
1 cup boiling water
¾ cup (3 oz) shredded Cheddar cheese
3 green onions, minced
1 to 2 jalapeño peppers, seeded and minced
1 tablespoon chopped pimiento

1. Preheat oven to 400F. Generously grease two large baking sheets; set aside.

2. In medium bowl, combine cornmeal, butter, sugar and salt. Stir in boiling water, mixing until blended. Stir in cheese, onions, jalapeño peppers and pimiento.

3. Drop level teaspoonfuls of batter, 1 inch apart, onto prepared baking sheets. With spatula, flatten batter into 2-inch circles. Bake 18 minutes, or until golden and slightly brown around edges. *Makes 6 dozen.*

ALMOND-BUTTER BRIE WITH FRUIT AND CRACKERS

½ cup butter or margarine, softened
¼ cup finely chopped toasted almonds
3 tablespoons light rum
¼ teaspoon lemon juice
⅛ teaspoon garlic salt
⅛ teaspoon paprika
6-inch wheel Brie cheese (about 1 lb)
Whole toasted almonds
Fresh fruits
Assorted crackers

1. In small bowl, beat butter with chopped almonds, rum, lemon juice, garlic salt and paprika.

2. Cut white crust from top of Brie and discard; spread Brie with butter mixture; garnish edge with whole almonds. Cover with plastic wrap; refrigerate until 1 hour before serving. Serve with fruits and crackers. *Makes 16 servings.*

Note: To toast almonds, place in small skillet; heat, shaking the pan frequently, just until nuts turn golden-brown.

HAZELNUT CHEESE SPREAD

2 pkg (3 oz each) cream cheese, softened
½ cup toasted ground hazelnuts
3 tablespoons Marsala wine
1 tablespoon superfine sugar
Belgian-endive leaves, apple slices or pear slices

1. In food processor or electric mixer, combine cream cheese, hazelnuts, wine and sugar; process until smooth. Chill until firm enough to pipe.

2. Spoon mixture into pastry bag fitted with desired tip. Pipe onto endive leaves, apple slices or pear slices. *Makes 1 cup.*

CUCUMBER ROLLS

12-inch European-style cucumber
2 pkg (5 oz-size) garlic-and-herb cheese spread
1 green onion, minced
1 tablespoon minced parsley
1 large carrot, shredded

1. Cut ½ inch from ends of cucumber. Using a vegetable peeler, cut cucumber lengthwise into about 24 thin slices; blot dry with paper towels.

2. In bowl, combine cheese spread, green onion and parsley; spread 2 teaspoons mixture over length of each cucumber slice. Sprinkle with shredded carrot; roll up, jelly-roll fashion. Place rolls, seam sides down, on serving dish. Cover with plastic wrap; refrigerate until serving. *Makes 24.*

ZUCCHINI FRITTERS

3 eggs
¼ cup unsifted all-purpose flour
2 tablespoons grated onion
¼ teaspoon salt
⅛ teaspoon black pepper
1 medium green zucchini, shredded
1 medium yellow zucchini, shredded
1 large carrot, pared and shredded
¼ cup salad oil
Red-Pepper Mayonnaise, recipe follows

1. In large bowl, beat eggs, flour, onion, salt and black pepper; stir in vegetables; mix well.

2. In large skillet, heat salad oil. Drop batter by tablespoons into hot oil. Cook about 1 minute on each side, or until golden. Drain on paper-towel-lined tray. Serve immediately with Red-Pepper Mayonnaise. *Makes 2 dozen fritters.*

RED-PEPPER MAYONNAISE

½ cup mayonnaise
1 jar (7 oz) roasted red peppers, drained
1 teaspoon red-wine vinegar
1 medium garlic clove, crushed

In food processor or blender, puree mayonnaise, red peppers, vinegar and garlic until smooth. Cover and refrigerate. *Makes 1 cup.*   ◆

Party Beverages

If you have a thirst for homemade refreshment, raise your glass to this cool collection of frosty favorites. Fresh lemonade and spiced iced coffee are quick thirst quenchers on a warm day. For a kid's party, serve up some smiles with a frothy root-beer float. A Creamsicle Punch or piña-colada slush will raise spirits at an intimate gathering of adults. And for entertaining on a larger scale, may we suggest one of our chilled fruit punches. Pictured here clockwise starting at top, Choco-Root-Beer Float, Sangria, Sunny Citrus Punch and Creamsicle Punch.

SANGRIA
(pictured)

2 cans (6-oz size) frozen limeade
  concentrate
1 quart dry red wine, chilled
1 bottle (28 oz) club soda, chilled
1 tray ice cubes
Orange peel (optional)

1. Reconstitute limeade according to package directions.
2. Combine limeade, wine and club soda. Pour over ice cubes in small punch bowl.
3. Serve in chilled punch cups; if desired, garnish with orange peel. *Makes about 16 (6-oz) servings.*

SUMMER ICED COFFEE

½ cup instant coffee
¾ teaspoon ground cinnamon
⅛ teaspoon ground cloves
1 cup boiling water
3 cups cold water
2 trays ice cubes
6 twists lemon peel
Sugar and cream (optional)

1. Combine coffee, cinnamon and cloves in a 1-quart measure. Add boiling water; stir until coffee mixture is dissolved.
2. Add cold water; refrigerate, covered, until ready to serve.
3. To serve: Fill 6 tall glasses with ice cubes. Place a lemon twist in each; fill with chilled coffee. Serve with sugar and cream, if desired. *Makes 6 servings.*

CREAMSICLE PUNCH
(pictured)

2 cups cold milk
1 cup (½ pint) vanilla ice cream
½ cup Triple Sec or other orange-
  flavored liqueur

1 can (6 oz) frozen orange-juice
  concentrate

Combine ingredients in blender; puree until frozen orange juice is smooth and well blended. Serve immediately or store in freezer for up to 1 hour, blending again before serving. Pour into chilled punch cups. *Makes 6 (6-ounce) servings.*

SUNNY CITRUS PUNCH
(pictured)

1 quart orange juice
1 can (6 oz) frozen lemonade
  concentrate
1 can (6 oz) frozen limeade concentrate
2 cups water
Orange, lemon and lime slices
1 bottle (1 liter) lemon-lime soda

In punch bowl, combine orange juice, frozen lemonade and limeade and the water; stir until lemonade and limeade are thawed. Stir in fruit slices; chill. To serve: Stir in lemon-lime soda. *Makes 16 (4-ounce) servings.*

FRESH LEMONADE

3 lemons
¾ cup superfine granulated sugar
Ice cubes
2 cups cold water
Mint sprigs

1. Wash lemons well. With sharp knife, slice crosswise into very thin slices.
2. Discard end slices and seeds. Put lemon slices in bottom of large bowl or sturdy pitcher. Add sugar.
3. With potato masher or wooden spoon, pound lemon slices until they are broken and sugar is dissolved.
4. Add 1 tray ice cubes and cold water. Stir until lemonade is very cold.
5. To serve: Pour lemonade, with lemon slices, over ice cubes in tall glasses. Garnish each with a mint sprig. *Makes 4 to 6 servings.*

PINA COLADA

½ cup cream of coconut (see Note)
1 cup unsweetened pineapple juice,
  chilled
⅔ cup light rum
2 cups crushed ice
Pineapple spears (optional)

1. Refrigerate 6 cocktail glasses to chill well—about 1 hour.
2. In electric blender, combine cream of coconut, pineapple juice, rum and ice; cover and blend at high speed ½ minute.
3. Pour into chilled cocktail glasses. If desired, serve with a pineapple spear. *Makes 1 quart; 6 servings.*
Note: Cream of coconut may be purchased as coconut-milk cream.

CHOCO-ROOT-BEER FLOAT
(pictured)

2 cups cold milk
1 cup (½ pint) vanilla ice cream
6 ice cubes
1 cup (½ pint) chocolate ice cream
1 can (12 oz) cold root beer

Combine milk, vanilla ice cream and ice cubes in blender; blend until ice is evenly dispersed. Divide chocolate ice cream among 8 glasses. Pour milk mixture over ice cream, dividing evenly. Add root beer slowly to each glass, pouring it into the center to form a frothy head. *Makes 8 (10-ounce) servings.*

CRANBERRY-CHAMPAGNE PUNCH

1 bottle (32 oz) cranberry-juice cocktail,
  chilled
2 bottles (750 ml each) champagne or
  sparkling white wine, chilled

In large punch bowl, combine cranberry-juice cocktail and champagne; stir gently. Ladle into punch cups. *Makes 20 (½-cup) servings.*   ◆

A BUFFET DINNER

◆

◆

Your guests will gladly line up to sample this bountiful buffet that will turn any gathering—any time of the year—into a celebration. This menu is a happy mix of make-aheads and no-fuss dishes that get you out of the kitchen and into the fun. Now that's entertaining! For recipes see page 288.

Our buffet features (clockwise starting at top left) mugs of make-ahead Spiced Cranberry Punch, served hot or cold; fresh Cranberry-Date Muffins, made with sour cream, cranberries and dates; Marinated Vegetable Ring, a garden of delights flavored with a basil marinade; Glazed Ham With Cumberland Sauce, a smoked sensation basted in apple juice; Lemon-Crunch Drumsticks, crunchy almond-coated chicken drumsticks served with a zesty dipping sauce; and for dessert, Apple Currant Purses, crisp and buttery phyllo packages filled with apples, walnuts and currants seasoned with cinnamon and lemon peel.

continued from page 287

SPICED CRANBERRY PUNCH
(pictured)

1 cup sugar
4 cups water
12 whole cloves
4 (3-inch) cinnamon sticks
2 tablespoons minced gingerroot
8 cups cranberry–apple-juice cocktail
2 cups orange juice
1 cup fresh lemon juice
1½ cups spiced or dark rum (optional)

In large saucepan, combine sugar, the water, cloves, cinnamon sticks and gingerroot; mix until sugar dissolves. Bring to boiling; simmer 10 minutes. Remove from heat, cover; let stand 1 hour. Strain into punch bowl. Stir in cranberry-apple-juice cocktail, orange juice and lemon juice. Punch can be made 2 days ahead of serving and stored, covered, in refrigerator. To serve hot: Reheat; pour into punch bowl. Stir in rum, if desired. To serve cold: Fill ice-cube trays with orange slices, cranberries and additional cranberry-apple-juice cocktail; freeze. Add to chilled punch in punch bowl. Stir in rum, if desired. *Makes 16 servings.*

GLAZED HAM WITH CUMBERLAND SAUCE
(pictured)

8-lb cooked smoked ham on the bone
2 tablespoons Dijon-style mustard
½ cup dark-brown sugar
Whole cloves
1½ cups apple juice

CUMBERLAND SAUCE
1 jar (8 oz) apple jelly
Julienne lemon peel and juice of
    2 lemons
Julienne orange peel and juice of
    1 orange
¼ cup port wine
½ teaspoon ground ginger
¼ teaspoon grated nutmeg
¼ cup water
1 tablespoon cornstarch

1. Preheat oven to 350F. With knife, peel skin from ham; trim fat to ¼-inch thick. Place ham in shallow baking pan; spread with mustard and sprinkle with brown sugar. Score fat in diamond pattern; insert a clove into each diamond. Add apple juice to pan; bake ham 1½ hours, basting frequently.
2. Meanwhile, make Cumberland Sauce: In saucepan, bring jelly, lemon and orange peels and juices, wine and spices to boiling. In cup, blend the water and cornstarch; add to jelly mixture.

Bring to boiling, whisking until thickened. *Makes 14 servings, 1⅓ cups sauce.*

CRANBERRY-DATE MUFFINS
(pictured)

1¾ cups unsifted all-purpose flour
⅓ cup sugar
1 teaspoon baking powder
½ teaspoon baking soda
½ teaspoon salt
1 cup sour cream
1 egg
½ cup cranberries, coarsely chopped
½ cup dates, coarsely chopped

1. Preheat oven to 400F. Grease nine (3-inch) muffin tins.
2. In large bowl, mix flour, sugar, baking powder, baking soda and salt. In small bowl, with fork, blend sour cream with egg. With fork, stir sour-cream mixture into flour mixture just until blended. (Batter will be thick.) With rubber spatula, fold in cranberries and dates just until mixed.
3. Spoon batter into prepared tins. Bake muffins 18 minutes, or until golden. Remove from tins; cool on wire rack. *Makes 9 servings.*

MARINATED VEGETABLE RING
(pictured)

This arrangement of colorful and crunchy vegetables is enhanced by a fragrant and flavorful basil marinade. To bring out the flavor of the dried basil leaves, chop them with 2 tablespoons fresh parsley.

MARINADE
1 teaspoon dried basil leaves, crushed
1 large garlic clove, crushed
¼ teaspoon salt
¼ teaspoon freshly ground pepper
¾ cup olive oil
¼ cup red-wine vinegar

1 cup pearl onions, peeled
3 carrots, pared and sliced crosswise
1 bunch broccoli, broken into flowerets
1 cucumber, scored and sliced crosswise
1 large red pepper, cut into rings
1 large yellow pepper, cut into rings
1 cup cherry tomatoes, halved

1. Make Marinade: In electric blender or food processor, combine marinade ingredients; blend 1 minute, or until smooth.
2. In 5-quart saucepan, bring 4 cups lightly salted water to boiling; add the onions and cook, covered, 1 minute. Add the carrots; cook, covered, 1 minute. Add the broccoli; cook, covered, 1 minute. Drain vegetables; place in large bowl of ice water until chilled.

3. Drain onion mixture; place in large glass baking dish with cucumber, red- and yellow-pepper rings and tomatoes. Pour marinade over vegetables; cover with plastic wrap. Refrigerate at least 2 hours, stirring occasionally.
4. To serve: Drain vegetables and arrange them on a serving dish. *Makes 8 servings.*

LEMON-CRUNCH DRUMSTICKS
(pictured)

½ cup coarsely ground blanched
    almonds
¼ cup fine dry bread crumbs
½ teaspoon garlic powder
½ teaspoon paprika
½ teaspoon ground red pepper
½ teaspoon salt
⅓ cup soy sauce
12 chicken drumsticks (about 3 lb)

LEMON DIPPING SAUCE
1 tablespoon vegetable oil
2 medium garlic cloves, crushed
¼ cup sugar
4 teaspoons cornstarch
1 tablespoon grated lemon peel
½ teaspoon minced gingerroot
½ teaspoon salt
1 cup chicken broth
¼ cup fresh lemon juice
2 tablespoons soy sauce
2 green onions, thinly sliced

1. Preheat oven to 400F. On sheet of waxed paper, combine almonds, bread crumbs, spices and salt; mix well. Pour soy sauce into pie plate. Dip drumsticks into soy sauce; shake off excess. Roll drumsticks in almond mixture. Place on jelly-roll pan. Bake 35 minutes, or until tender and golden-brown.
2. Meanwhile, make Lemon Dipping Sauce: In saucepan, heat vegetable oil over medium-high heat. Add garlic; sauté 2 minutes. Add remaining ingredients except green onions; mix well. Bring mixture to boiling, stirring; simmer 1 minute, or until thickened. Stir in green onions. Serve Lemon Dipping Sauce with drumsticks. *Makes 12 servings, 1½ cups sauce.*

APPLE CURRANT PURSES
(pictured)

Inside these crisp and buttery phyllo packages are crunchy walnuts, juicy apples and currants—all seasoned with cinnamon and lemon peel.

3 lb Golden Delicious apples, peeled,
    cored and coarsely chopped
⅓ cup sugar
¼ cup dried currants

¼ cup chopped walnuts
1 tablespoon all-purpose flour
1 teaspoon ground cinnamon
1 teaspoon grated lemon peel
16 sheets phyllo pastry
⅓ cup butter or margarine, melted

SAUCE
½ cup apple jelly
¼ cup apple cider or juice
2 tablespoons brandy
1 teaspoon cornstarch

3 sheets strawberry-flavor fruit-roll
candy

1. Preheat oven to 350F. Lightly grease large baking sheet.
2. In large bowl, combine apples, sugar, currants, walnuts, flour, cinnamon and lemon peel; mix well. On work surface, place 1 sheet of phyllo pastry with long side nearest you; brush with some butter. Top with second sheet of phyllo pastry; brush with butter. Fold down 2 inches of top of phyllo lengthwise; fold phyllo in half crosswise to make an 8-inch square. Place heaping ½ cup of the apple mixture in center of square; bring ends of phyllo together over filling and tie with kitchen string. Place on prepared baking sheet; brush with melted butter. Repeat with remaining phyllo pastry, butter and filling.
3. Bake purses 30 minutes, or until golden and crisp. (Cover ends of phyllo loosely with foil if edges brown too quickly.) Cool the purses on baking sheet 5 minutes.
4. Meanwhile, make Sauce: In saucepan, combine apple jelly and cider; over medium heat, cook until jelly melts and mixture boils. In cup, blend brandy with cornstarch. Pour into jelly mixture, whisking constantly; cook until sauce is thickened and clear.
5. To serve: Remove string from purses. Cut each fruit roll crosswise into 6 strips. Wrap 1 strip around each purse; form remaining strips into bows. (There will be 2 extra strips.) Press bows onto fruit-roll strips. Spoon 2 tablespoons hot Sauce onto 8 dessert plates; top with a warm Apple-Currant Purse. *Makes 8 servings.*

BREADSTICKS WITH DIPPING SAUCE

BREADSTICKS
⅔ cup warm water (110-115F)
1 env dry yeast
½ teaspoon sugar
1½ cups unsifted all-purpose flour
½ cup unsifted whole-wheat flour
¼ teaspoon salt
2 tablespoons olive oil
¼ cup slivered Calamata olives

1 tablespoon slivered fresh sage leaves
Cornmeal
1 egg white
1 tablespoon water

OLIVE DIPPING SAUCE
5 flat anchovies, rinsed and patted dry
1 small garlic clove, minced
2 tablespoons chopped Italian parsley
¼ cup olive oil
2 tablespoons chicken broth
2 tablespoons olive paste (available at specialty food stores)
2 tablespoons balsamic vinegar
2 teaspoons capers, drained

10 thin slices prosciutto (about ⅓ lb)

1. Make Breadsticks: In glass measure, combine water, yeast and sugar; mix well. Let stand 10 minutes, or until bubbly.
2. In food processor, combine flours and salt. Add 2 tablespoons olive oil to yeast mixture; with processor running, add yeast mixture through feed tube. Process until dough forms; process 60 seconds to knead. Transfer dough to floured pastry board or work surface; knead in olives and sage.
3. Place dough in lightly greased plastic food-storage bag; remove air and seal. Let stand in warm place 1 hour or in refrigerator overnight, until double in bulk.
4. Preheat oven to 400F. With olive oil, grease two large baking sheets; sprinkle with cornmeal.
5. Punch down dough to remove air bubbles; divide in half. With hands, roll each half into a 10-inch-long rope. With kitchen shears, cut dough into 1-inch lengths; roll each piece into a 9-inch rope. Place ropes on prepared baking sheets. In cup, combine egg white and the 1 tablespoon water; mix well. Brush mixture over breadsticks. Bake breadsticks, one sheet at a time, 15 to 17 minutes, or until golden-brown.
6. Make Dipping Sauce: In blender, combine anchovies, garlic, parsley, olive oil, chicken broth, olive paste, vinegar and capers; puree; pour into serving bowl. Place bowl on serving platter.
7. Halve prosciutto slices lengthwise; wrap one slice around one end of each breadstick. Arrange breadsticks on serving platter with dipping sauce. *Makes 20 breadsticks, ¾ cup sauce.*
Note: Breadsticks may be made up to two weeks in advance of serving. After

baking, cool completely; place in airtight container for a few days, or freeze. Thaw; place on baking sheets. Bake in preheated 400F oven 5 minutes before wrapping with prosciutto.

POTATO-PEAR GRATIN

3 tablespoons unsalted butter
3 ripe Bosc pears (6 oz each), peeled, cored and thinly sliced
1½ teaspoons sugar
¼ teaspoon ground nutmeg
2¼ teaspoons salt
1½ teaspoons lemon juice
4 large baking potatoes (2½ lb), peeled
¾ teaspoon freshly ground pepper
1½ cups heavy cream
3 tablespoons freshly grated Parmesan cheese

1. Preheat oven to 325F. In large nonstick skillet, over medium heat, melt butter. Add pears, sugar, nutmeg, ¼ teaspoon salt and the lemon juice; sauté 5 to 8 minutes, or until tender. Set aside.
2. Thinly slice potatoes; place in large bowl of cold water. Drain; pat dry with paper towels. Place in large bowl; add remaining salt and the pepper. Toss to coat.
3. Grease 2-quart gratin dish or oval baking dish. Arrange half the potatoes in dish with slices overlapping. Arrange half the pears over potatoes; repeat with remaining potatoes, pears and any juice from pears. Pour heavy cream over all; sprinkle with cheese. Bake about 1 hour and 5 minutes, or until bubbly and potatoes are tender when tested with a knife. *Makes 8 servings.*

CHOCOLATE-ALMOND-FILLED CREPES

1 pkg (3 oz) cream cheese, softened
1 cup sour cream
1 bar (8 oz) milk chocolate with almonds, coarsely chopped, melted and cooled
1 container (8 oz) frozen whipped topping, thawed
8 prepared 8-inch crêpes
½ cup raspberries

In large bowl, with electric mixer at medium speed, beat cream cheese until smooth. Beat in sour cream and chocolate until well blended. With rubber spatula, fold in 2 cups whipped topping. Spread ½ cup chocolate mixture over each crêpe; roll up, jelly-roll fashion. Place each filled crêpe, seam side down, on dessert plate. Garnish tops of crêpes with remaining whipped topping and raspberries. *Makes 8 servings.* ◆

A Sit-Down
DINNER

Think back to your last dinner party: If you spent more time fussing in the kitchen than enjoying your guests, it's time to take a stand and plan a sit-down dinner that lets everyone—even you, the host—relax. The trick is to select a tempting entrée and build a menu that includes do-ahead accompaniments; that's what we've done here. And any necessary last-minute preparation, such as making gravy and carving, should be kept to a minimum. Then you can sit down to your meal feeling relaxed rather than frazzled.

The centerpiece of our menu is Holiday Goose With Madeira Sauce, roasted with a Bulgur-Fruit Stuffing and served with sugared crab apples and Herbed Fries. Make-ahead accompaniments (clockwise, beginning at top): creamy Carrot Bisque, tangy Pear-and-Apple Chutney, zesty Lemon-Lime Chess Pie and refreshing Mixed Greens With Lemon-Mustard Dressing.

THOM DESANTO

continued from page 291

CARROT BISQUE
(pictured)

¼ cup butter or margarine
3 large leeks, trimmed, washed and sliced
1 large onion, chopped
2 lb carrots, pared and coarsely chopped
1 baking potato, pared and coarsely chopped
1 can (46 oz) chicken broth
¼ teaspoon pepper
½ cup prepared crème fraîche
¼ cup lemon juice
¼ cup chopped parsley
1 teaspoon salt

1. In large Dutch oven, melt butter over medium heat. Add leeks and onion; cook, covered, 10 minutes. Add carrots, potato, chicken broth and pepper; bring to boiling. Simmer, covered, 30 minutes, until tender.

2. In food processor, puree vegetables with some broth, in batches; return to pan. (Carrot Bisque can be made up to this point two days before serving.) Over low heat, whisk in crème fraîche, lemon juice, parsley and salt. Pour into tureen. If desired, garnish with additional crème fraîche and parsley sprig. *Makes 8 servings.*

MIXED GREENS WITH LEMON-MUSTARD DRESSING
(pictured)

DRESSING
1 large shallot, minced
2 tablespoons snipped chives
½ teaspoon salt
⅔ cup olive oil
2 tablespoons lemon juice
1 tablespoon red-wine vinegar
2 teaspoons Dijon-style mustard

3 bunches arugula leaves, washed and crisped
1 large bunch spinach leaves, washed and crisped, large stems discarded
1 bunch watercress, washed and crisped

1 head Boston lettuce leaves, washed and crisped
8 large mushrooms, sliced
2 red peppers, sliced into rings
½ cup ripe sliced and pitted olives

1. Make Dressing: In jar with tight-fitting lid, combine dressing ingredients; shake vigorously until blended. Refrigerate until ready to serve.

2. To serve: In large salad bowl, combine remaining ingredients. Pour dressing over mixture; toss to coat. Serve immediately. *Makes 8 servings.*

HOLIDAY GOOSE WITH MADEIRA SAUCE
(pictured)

16-lb young goose
1 small lemon, halved
¾ teaspoon salt
4 cups water
Bulgur-Fruit Stuffing, recipe follows
Mâche
Sugared crab apples
Herbed Fries, recipe follows
Madeira Sauce, recipe follows

1. Line large roasting pan with aluminum foil; set aside. Prepare goose: About 5 hours before serving, remove neck and giblets from body cavity; set aside. Remove and discard excess fat and neck skin. Rinse goose well; drain. With paper towels, pat dry on inside and outside. Rub inside breast and neck cavities and outside of goose with cut lemon; sprinkle cavities with ¼ teaspoon salt. Place goose, breast side up, on rack in prepared roasting pan; cover loosely with plastic wrap. Refrigerate while cooking giblets and preparing stuffing.

2. In large saucepan, bring 2 cups water and remaining salt to boiling. Add neck and giblets, except liver; simmer, covered, 1½ hours, or until tender, adding liver the last 5 minutes of cooking

time. Drain giblets; cool. Chop coarsely; set aside. Reserve broth for Bulgur-Fruit Stuffing or for another use.

3. Preheat oven to 400F. Make stuffing. Spoon stuffing into breast and neck cavities of goose—do not pack. (Place extra stuffing in greased baking dish; cover and bake last hour goose is in oven.) Close cavities with poultry pins; lace with string. Tie legs together. Pin wings to breast. Insert meat thermometer deep into thigh muscle, away from bone. Pour 2 cups water into roasting pan to prevent grease from spattering.

4. Roast goose, uncovered, 1 hour, spooning or siphoning off accumulated fat every half hour. Reduce oven temperature to 325F. Roast goose until thermometer registers 175F, about 2 hours longer. Cool goose, loosely covered, 15 minutes before carving. Remove legs or slice meat from legs; place on sheet of aluminum foil. Fold over edges of foil to seal. Place foil packet in oven to cook until desired degree of doneness, about 20 minutes. Meanwhile, remove breast from goose; carve crosswise into slices.

5. To serve: Garnish goose on platter with mâche, sugared crab apples and Herbed Fries. Serve with Madeira Sauce. *Makes 16 servings.*

BULGUR-FRUIT STUFFING

Instead of a traditional bread stuffing for the Holiday Goose, we recommend a mixture that combines bulgur (dried cracked wheat that needs only to be soaked to soften) with bacon, onions and an assortment of dried and fresh fruits.

3 cups (1 lb) bulgur
6 cups boiling water
½ cup dried apricots, quartered
½ cup pitted prunes, quartered
¾ cup chicken or goose broth
½ lb bacon, coarsely chopped

3 medium onions, chopped
2 Golden Delicious apples, peeled, cored and coarsely chopped
1 large pink grapefruit, peeled, seeded and cut into 1-inch pieces
2½ teaspoons salt
1 teaspoon dried rosemary leaves, crushed
¼ teaspoon pepper

1. Place bulgur in large heat-proof bowl. Add the boiling water; stir. Let stand 40 minutes, or until most of the water is absorbed and bulgur is softened.

2. Place the apricots and prunes in a medium heat-proof bowl. In a small saucepan, bring chicken broth to boiling; pour over apricot mixture. Let stand 30 minutes, or until fruit is softened.

3. In medium skillet, over medium-high heat, sauté the bacon until crisp. Remove bacon from pan; drain on paper towels. Spoon off and discard all but 3 tablespoons bacon drippings from pan. To drippings in pan, add onions; sauté 5 minutes, or until golden and tender-crisp. When bacon is cool enough to handle, crumble.

4. Drain bulgur; return to large bowl. Add apricot mixture and its liquid, bacon, onions, apples, grapefruit, salt, rosemary and pepper; mix well. *Makes 16 servings.*

HERBED FRIES
(pictured)

4 medium baking potatoes (2 lb)
Vegetable oil for deep-fat frying
½ teaspoon dried thyme leaves, crushed
½ teaspoon seasoned salt
¼ teaspoon seasoned pepper

1. Cut potatoes into long, ¼-inch-thick strips, or use a potato curler to make curly fries. Line jelly-roll pan with paper towels. Preheat oven to 300F. In deep-fat fryer or large saucepan, heat 2 inches of vegetable oil to 375F. Gently drop a handful of potato strips into the oil; cook 3 minutes, or until golden. With slotted spoon, remove fries from oil; drain on paper-towel-lined pan. Repeat with remaining potato strips.

2. In a cup, combine thyme, salt and pepper; mix well. Place the cooked potatoes in brown paper bag; sprinkle with the thyme mixture. Close bag; shake to coat potatoes with thyme mixture. Place potatoes in single layer on baking sheet; keep warm in oven until ready to serve. *Makes 8 servings.*

MADEIRA SAUCE

1½ cups chicken broth
¾ cup Madeira
2 shallots, minced
1 tablespoon mixed black, green and white dried peppercorns, crushed
1 tablespoon cornstarch
½ cup water
½ teaspoon salt

Skim off and discard fat from roasting pan used to cook Holiday Goose; scrape brown bits in pan into medium saucepan. To saucepan, add chicken broth, Madeira, shallots and peppercorns. Bring to boiling; simmer, covered, 5 minutes. In cup, blend cornstarch with the water; pour into broth mixture, whisking constantly. Bring to boiling, whisking until mixture thickens. Add salt; simmer 5 minutes. Serve hot with goose. *Makes 2¼ cups sauce.*

PEAR-AND-APPLE CHUTNEY
(pictured)

This sweet and tangy relish complements the rich Holiday Goose and Bulgur-Fruit Stuffing. One batch will make enough for one meal plus a jarful or two for gift giving.

3 medium Granny Smith apples
3 medium firm, ripe pears
1 medium onion, coarsely chopped
1 medium red pepper, chopped
1 cup firmly packed light-brown sugar
½ cup raisins
2 medium garlic cloves, crushed
1 tablespoon chopped crystallized ginger
1½ teaspoons mustard seeds
3-inch cinnamon stick

1. In large saucepan, combine ingredients; mix well. Bring to boiling; simmer 1 hour, stirring frequently, until mixture thickens and fruit is tender.

2. Remove and discard cinnamon stick. Store chutney, covered, in nonaluminum container in refrigerator. (Chutney will keep up to 2 weeks.) *Makes 16 servings (1 quart).*

LEMON-LIME CHESS PIE
(pictured)

Here's a pie that's a Southern holiday tradition. Just a sliver will satisfy any sweet tooth.

2 cups sugar
2 tablespoons cornmeal
1 tablespoon grated lemon peel
1 tablespoon grated lime peel
⅛ teaspoon salt
4 eggs, beaten
¼ cup butter or margarine, melted
3 tablespoons lemon juice
3 tablespoons lime juice
9-inch unbaked pie shell
1 cup heavy cream, whipped

1. Preheat oven to 350F. In large bowl, combine sugar, cornmeal, lemon and lime peels, and salt; mix well. Add eggs, butter, and lemon and lime juices; mix well. Pour into pie shell; bake 40 to 45 minutes, or until filling is set around edges but wobbly in center. (Filling will set completely upon cooling.) Cool on wire rack.

2. With whipped cream in pastry bag fitted with star tip, decorate pie. If desired, garnish pie with lemon and lime slices. *Makes 8 servings.* ◆

BARBECUING:
Entertainment That Sizzles

Fire up the grill and get ready to sample some exciting and sumptuous barbecue fare that goes a tasty step beyond plain burgers and hot dogs. We've cooked up a hot selection of unique grill food, each with a flair for flavor and fun, not fuss! You'll find marvelous menus, too, and pages of easy-to-fix accompaniments from breads to salads to desserts. So fire up your taste buds and get grilling! Recipes begin on page 300.

This barbecue has a taste for style. A bourbon-flavored marinade gives Grilled Herb Steak a spirited lift; serve it with a creamy horseradish sauce. Oyster-And-Clam Bar is a half-shell spectacle fully dressed with sauces and citrus. Pepper Slaw combines color and spice into a salad that's so nice. Steeped Berries With English Cream is a dessert of mixed berries and orange flavors that make every spoonful a delight.

Surprise your guests with an international grill, beginning at center, with fast-fix Portuguese Gazpacho With Garlic Toast. Proceeding, clockwise, is Grilled Turkey Cassis, an all-American turkey breast flavored with a sauce of plums, ginger and crème de cassis liqueur. Salmon-Cheese "Pear" is a soft-sculpture appetizer of herbed cream cheese and smoked salmon. Pineapple spears, zucchini and lime-marinated chicken go over the coals, then join papaya and starfruit on this platter of Polynesian Grilled Chicken Salad. Rounding out the menu is Apricot Cloud Pie and hearty Barbecued Beans.

A bold new mix of flavors awaits your barbecue guests. Clockwise, starting at top left: *Cajun Kebabs With Fire-And-Ice Sauce* are grilled skewers of spiced chicken, scallops, shrimp and vegetables served with a hot and zesty cream sauce. A platter of *Plantain Nachos* is piled high with fried plantains, beans, melted cheese, salsa and sour cream. Dig in to *Three-Rice Walnut Salad*, a cool and tasty toss of rice, grapes, raisins and walnut halves. *Salmon au Poivre* is grilled to perfection and served with a lemony cucumber sauce. *Summer Pork Salad* is an artful arrangement of sliced grilled pork, potatoes, red cabbage, beans and peppers served with a blue cheese–Dijon dressing. Dessert is a delightfully delicious *Strawberry-Rhubarb Tart* glazed with orange marmalade.

BETH GALTON

continued from page 295

GRILLED HERB STEAK
(pictured)

MARINADE
1 teaspoon dried summer savory, crushed
½ teaspoon pepper
2 large garlic cloves, crushed
2 tablespoons bourbon whiskey
2 tablespoons soy sauce
1 tablespoon catsup
½ teaspoon liquid smoke

2-lb flank steak

HORSERADISH SAUCE
½ cup heavy cream
½ teaspoon salt
3 tablespoons well-drained prepared horseradish

1. Eight hours ahead or day before serving, in small bowl, combine marinade ingredients. Score steak ¼-inch deep in crisscross pattern on each side; rub with marinade. Place steak in shallow glass baking dish; cover with plastic wrap. Refrigerate 8 hours or overnight.

2. Prepare outdoor grill for barbecue. Make Horseradish Sauce: In small bowl of electric mixer, beat heavy cream until stiff peaks form when beaters are raised; fold in salt and prepared horseradish.

3. Using Direct Method, grill steak over medium-hot coals 5 to 7 minutes on each side (for medium-rare). To serve: Thinly slice steak on the diagonal; pass sauce separately. *Makes 8 servings, 1 cup Horseradish Sauce.*

OYSTER-AND-CLAM BAR
(pictured)

TOMATO-CAPER SAUCE
⅓ cup olive or salad oil
¼ cup red-wine vinegar
1 small plum tomato, finely chopped
1 small shallot, minced
1 teaspoon grated lemon peel
1 tablespoon small capers, drained

Crushed ice
Fresh seaweed
Parsley and dill sprigs
12 oysters, shucked and on the half-shell
12 clams, shucked and on the half-shell
½ cup prepared cocktail sauce
¼ cup prepared horseradish
Lemon and lime wedges

1. Make Tomato-Caper Sauce: In small bowl, whisk olive oil and vinegar until blended. Whisk in remaining sauce ingredients.

2. With crushed ice, line large platter; place seaweed, parsley and dill on top of ice. Arrange oysters and clams on top. Fill small bowls or empty oyster shells and clamshells with Tomato-Caper Sauce, cocktail sauce and horseradish. Tuck bowls and lemon and lime wedges around seafood. *Makes 6 appetizer servings, 1 cup sauce.*

PEPPER SLAW
(pictured)

2 lb assorted colored peppers, julienne
1-lb red cabbage, shredded (about 4½ cups)
1 small red onion, thinly sliced
1 cup sliced black olives
¾ cup olive oil
⅓ cup red-wine vinegar
1 tablespoon Dijon-style mustard
2 medium garlic cloves, crushed

In large bowl, mix peppers, cabbage, onion and olives. In jar with tight-fitting lid, combine remaining ingredients; shake to blend. Pour dressing over Pepper Slaw; toss. If desired, serve in lettuce-lined bowl. *Makes 12 servings.*

STEEPED BERRIES WITH ENGLISH CREAM
(pictured)

1 orange-and-spice-flavored tea bag
⅓ cup boiling water
½ cup orange marmalade
2 tablespoons orange-flavored liqueur
4 cups mixed berries
16 chocolate-and-pecan-topped cookies

ENGLISH CREAM
1 cup heavy cream, chilled
2 tablespoons sugar
¼ cup sour cream
1 teaspoon lemon juice

1. In small bowl, steep tea bag in the boiling water 5 minutes; discard tea bag. Stir in the marmalade until melted; stir in the liqueur and berries. Let stand 1 hour, stirring occasionally.

2. Meanwhile, on jelly-roll pan, arrange cookies with chocolate sides down; spoon 1 teaspoon juice from berry mixture over each cookie.

3. Make English Cream: In small bowl of electric mixer, beat heavy cream and sugar until stiff peaks form when beaters are raised; whisk in sour cream and lemon juice. Spoon berry mixture into 8 sherbet glasses, reserving some berries; tuck cookies into berry mixture

---

in glasses. Top with English Cream and reserved berries. *Makes 8 servings, 2½ cups English Cream.*

PORTUGUESE GAZPACHO WITH GARLIC TOAST
(pictured)

¼ cup olive oil
¼ cup red-wine vinegar
2 large garlic cloves, crushed
2 tablespoons chopped cilantro
½ teaspoon dried oregano leaves, crushed
½ teaspoon freshly ground pepper
½ teaspoon salt
1 can (28 oz) whole peeled tomatoes or 1 lb fresh tomatoes, seeds removed, chopped
1 seedless cucumber, pared and diced
1 yellow pepper, finely chopped
1½ cups cubed Portuguese or Italian bread
2 cups ice-cold water

GARLIC TOAST
8 (½-inch-thick) slices Portuguese or Italian bread
1 large garlic clove, crushed
1 tablespoon chopped cilantro
3 tablespoons olive oil

1. In large bowl, whisk ¼ cup olive oil, the vinegar, 2 garlic cloves, 2 tablespoons cilantro, the oregano, pepper and salt until combined. Whisk in tomatoes, cucumber and chopped pepper; stir in bread cubes. Add the water; stir until blended.

2. Make Garlic Toast: Place bread on baking sheet. In cup, combine remaining ingredients; brush over tops of bread. Broil until golden-brown. Serve with gazpacho. *Makes 8 servings.*

GRILLED TURKEY CASSIS

(pictured)

1 can (30 oz) whole plums in heavy
    syrup
½ cup crème de cassis (black-currant-
    flavored liqueur)
1 medium clove garlic
1 teaspoon ground ginger
5-lb boneless turkey breast, split
½ cup orange marmalade
¼ teaspoon salt
⅛ teaspoon pepper

1. Prepare outdoor grill for barbecue. Drain plums, pouring ½ cup syrup into a small saucepan; remove the pits from the plums. In food processor, puree plums with liqueur, garlic and ginger.

2. Place 1 cup puree in saucepan with syrup; set aside. Remove fillets from turkey breast; brush turkey pieces with some of remaining puree. Using Indirect Method, cook breast halves, skin side up, over medium-hot coals with grill covered, 30 to 40 minutes. Turn breast halves; baste with puree. Cook 30 to 40 minutes, or until juices run clear and meat thermometer registers 160F. Place fillets on grill last 10 minutes of cooking time, turning once; and baste all turkey pieces with puree.

3. Make sauce: To syrup and puree in saucepan, add marmalade, salt and pepper. Over medium heat, cook, stirring, until marmalade melts. Cut turkey pieces crosswise on the diagonal into ¼-inch-thick slices; place on platter. If desired, garnish with mâche (lamb's lettuce) and orange slices. Serve with sauce. *Makes 10 servings, 1¾ cups sauce.*

SALMON-CHEESE "PEAR"

(pictured)

1 pkg (8 oz) cream cheese, softened
1 tablespoon heavy cream
1 teaspoon lemon juice
2 oz sliced smoked salmon, chopped
2 green onions, chopped
2 tablespoons finely chopped cucumber
1 tablespoon chopped fresh dill
¼ cup cornflake crumbs, bread crumbs
    or cracker crumbs
2 bay leaves
Paprika
Assorted crackers
Grapes

1. In small bowl of electric mixer, at medium speed, beat cream cheese, heavy cream and lemon juice until blended. With rubber spatula, fold in salmon, green onions, cucumber and dill. Cover; refrigerate until mixture is firm, about 1 hour.

2. Spoon mixture onto serving dish;

with metal spatula, spread into pear shape. Pat cornflake crumbs over "pear." Arrange bay leaves in "stem" end; sprinkle "pear" with paprika for "blush." Serve with crackers and grapes. *Makes 8 servings.*

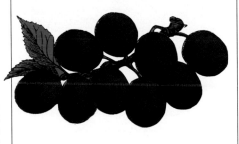

POLYNESIAN GRILLED CHICKEN SALAD

(pictured)

½ teaspoon ground ginger
½ cup frozen limeade concentrate,
    thawed
½ cup lime juice
3 whole chicken breasts (1 lb each),
    skinned, split and boned
Salad oil
1 medium pineapple, peeled, cored and
    cut into ½-inch-thick spears
2 large zucchini, quartered lengthwise
1 teaspoon grated lime peel
2 tablespoons Dijon-style mustard
1 cup olive oil
1 large head Boston lettuce
1 head radicchio
1 papaya, peeled and sliced
1 starfruit, sliced crosswise

1. In shallow glass baking dish, mix ginger, ¼ cup limeade concentrate and ¼ cup lime juice. Add chicken; turn to coat. Cover; refrigerate up to 3 hours.

2. Prepare outdoor grill for barbecue. With salad oil, grease grill rack. Using Direct Method, cook the chicken and the pineapple spears over hot coals 10 to 12 minutes, turning once. After 5 minutes, add zucchini; cook 5 minutes, turning once.

3. Meanwhile, make dressing: In a food processor or blender, blend the remaining limeade concentrate and lime juice, the lime peel and the mustard. With motor running, gradually blend in olive oil in a thin stream; process until mixture is creamy.

4. Arrange lettuce and radicchio leaves on 6 salad plates. Cut pineapple spears and zucchini crosswise in half; cut each chicken breast crosswise into 4 slices. On prepared plates, arrange pineapple, zucchini, chicken, papaya and starfruit, dividing evenly; spoon ¼ cup dressing over each salad. *Makes 6 servings, 1½ cups dressing.*

APRICOT CLOUD PIE

(pictured)

PASTRY
½ cup toasted whole blanched almonds
1 can (8 oz) almond paste
¾ cup unsifted all-purpose flour
¼ cup butter or margarine
¼ teaspoon salt
2 tablespoons cold water

Nonstick cooking spray
½ cup whole blanched almonds

FILLING
1 pkg (3 oz) orange-flavored gelatine
3 cups boiling water
1 pkg (11 oz) dried apricots (1¾ cups)
⅓ cup sugar
2 tablespoons apricot brandy
2 cups heavy cream, chilled

Mint sprigs

1. Make Pastry: In food processor, grind the toasted almonds; add ½ cup almond paste, the flour, butter and salt. Process until mixture resembles coarse crumbs. With motor running, gradually add the water. Process until mixture forms a ball. Remove from processor; form into a disk. Wrap in plastic wrap; refrigerate 1 hour.

2. Make crust: With nonstick cooking spray, grease 9-inch pie plate. Place dough between two sheets of waxed paper; on dampened surface, roll to a 12-inch circle. Remove top sheet of waxed paper; carefully invert dough over prepared plate. Remove waxed paper; pressing gently, fit dough in plate. Fold over edge of dough to form a rim. Reserve 6 whole almonds; using photograph as a guide, press remaining whole almonds into rim. Freeze crust ½ hour.

3. Preheat oven to 350F. Bake crust 20 minutes, or until golden-brown. Cool completely on wire rack.

4. On dampened surface, between 2 sheets of waxed paper, roll remaining almond paste to a 6-inch circle. Remove top sheet of waxed paper; carefully invert almond paste over baked crust. Remove waxed paper.

continued on page 302

continued from page 301

5. Make Filling: In small bowl, dissolve gelatine in 1 cup boiling water; cool. Meanwhile, in medium saucepan, combine apricots with remaining boiling water. Simmer, covered, until apricots are tender, about 30 minutes. Drain apricots; reserve 6 halves for garnish. Place remainder in food processor. Add sugar and brandy; puree. Whisk puree into cooled gelatine; set bowl in larger bowl of ice water. Set aside, stirring frequently, until mixture is consistency of unbeaten egg whites.

6. Meanwhile, in large bowl of electric mixer, at high speed, beat heavy cream until stiff peaks form when beaters are raised. Fold half the whipped cream into the apricot mixture until blended; fold in remaining whipped cream just until swirled throughout.

7. Spoon apricot mixture into crust, piling lightly. Using photograph as a guide, arrange reserved apricot halves in groups of three to resemble flowers; place 3 reserved whole almonds in center of each flower. Garnish with mint sprigs, if desired. Refrigerate pie 1 hour before serving. *Makes 12 servings.*

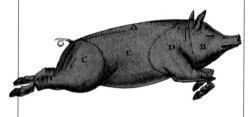

BARBECUED BEANS
(pictured)

4-oz slab bacon, diced
2 medium onions, chopped
2 large garlic cloves, crushed
2 tablespoons dark-brown sugar
2 teaspoons chili powder
1 cup bottled chili sauce
2 tablespoons soy sauce
2 tablespoons balsamic vinegar
¼ teaspoon hot red-pepper sauce
2 cans (19-oz size) cannellini beans, drained
1 can (19 oz) red kidney beans, drained

1. Preheat oven to 375F. Line plate with paper towels. In 3-quart Dutch oven, over medium heat, brown bacon. With slotted spoon, remove bacon to prepared plate.

2. In drippings in pan, sauté onions and garlic 5 minutes, or until tender. Stir in remaining ingredients except beans; bring to boiling, stirring. Boil 5 minutes. Stir in beans and reserved bacon. Cover; bake 30 minutes. *Makes 8 servings.*

CAJUN KEBABS WITH FIRE-AND-ICE SAUCE
(pictured)

MARINADE
2 tablespoons Maryland-style seafood seasoning (see Note)
3 tablespoons lime juice
2 tablespoons olive or salad oil

1 lb boneless chicken breasts, skinned and cut into 2-inch pieces
¾ lb sea scallops
½ lb large shrimp, shelled and deveined, tails intact

FIRE-AND-ICE SAUCE
3 green onions, quartered crosswise
2 jalapeño peppers, seeds and ribs removed
½ cup loosely packed cilantro
¼ cup loosely packed mint leaves
1 cup plain yogurt
½ cup sour cream
2 teaspoons sugar
¼ teaspoon salt
1 tablespoon lime juice

1 large onion
1 medium zucchini, cut crosswise into 1½-inch-thick pieces
1 red pepper, cut into 1½-inch pieces

1. Several hours before serving, in medium bowl, combine marinade ingredients. Add the chicken, scallops and shrimp; toss to coat. Cover with plastic wrap; refrigerate at least 1 hour or up to 3 hours, tossing mixture occasionally.

2. Meanwhile, make Fire-And-Ice Sauce: In food processor, combine green onions, jalapeño peppers, cilantro and mint; puree. Add remaining sauce ingredients; process until blended. Pour into small bowl. Cover with plastic wrap; refrigerate until ready to serve.

3. In large saucepan of boiling water, boil whole onion 2 minutes. Add zucchini and red-pepper pieces; boil 2 minutes. Drain vegetables in colander. Cut onion lengthwise into 8 wedges.

4. Prepare outdoor grill for barbecue. On each of 6 (12-inch) metal skewers, alternately thread the chicken, scallops,

shrimp and blanched vegetables, reserving marinade.

5. Using Direct Method, cook kebabs over low coals with grill covered, 5 minutes. Turn kebabs; cook 5 minutes, or until done. Place on platter with sauce; if desired, garnish with parsley leaves and lemon wedges. *Makes 6 servings, 2 cups sauce.*

Note: Or use mixture of 2 teaspoons dry mustard, 1 teaspoon salt, ¾ teaspoon celery seeds, ¾ teaspoon paprika, ¾ teaspoon seasoned pepper, ½ teaspoon ground ginger, ⅛ teaspoon ground cardamom and ⅛ teaspoon ground cloves.

PLANTAIN NACHOS
(pictured)

Salad oil for frying
3 plantains (2 lb) peeled and cut crosswise into thirds
1 can (16 oz) black beans, drained and rinsed
¼ cup sliced pickled jalapeños
1 jar (8 oz) Mexican-flavored processed cheese spread
1 jar (12 oz) salsa
1 container (8 oz) sour cream

1. In 3-quart saucepan, heat 2 inches salad oil to 360F.

2. Meanwhile, in food processor fitted with thinnest slicing disk, slice plantain pieces lengthwise. In hot oil, fry plantain slices in batches, turning once, 2 minutes, or until golden-brown. With tongs, remove and drain on paper towels.

3. To serve: Pile fried plantains on large serving platter; sprinkle with beans and jalapeños. Heat cheese spread as package label directs; pour over plantains. Serve immediately with salsa and sour cream. *Makes 8 appetizer servings.*

THREE-RICE WALNUT SALAD
(pictured)

DRESSING
1 teaspoon salt
¼ teaspoon freshly ground black pepper
⅓ cup walnut oil
2 tablespoons white-wine vinegar
1 tablespoon prepared coarse, spicy mustard

SALAD

½ cup wild rice, rinsed
½ teaspoon salt
5 cups water
¼ cup brown rice
¼ cup long-grain white rice
1 medium onion, thinly sliced
1 cup sliced celery
1 cup seedless green grapes, halved
1 cup seedless red grapes, halved
1 cup walnut halves
½ cup raisins
¼ cup chopped parsley

1. In jar with tight-fitting lid, combine dressing ingredients. Shake until blended.

2. In 2½-quart saucepan, combine wild rice, salt and the water. Bring to boiling; simmer, covered, 20 minutes. Add brown rice; bring to boiling. Simmer, covered, 20 minutes. Add white rice; bring to boiling. Simmer, covered, 20 minutes. Remove pan from heat; let stand, covered, 20 minutes. Pour rice mixture through sieve; spread out rice mixture on jelly-roll pan. Freeze 30 minutes, stirring occasionally.

3. In medium salad bowl, combine rice mixture with remaining ingredients. Shake dressing to recombine; pour over rice mixture. Toss to coat. If desired, refrigerate salad, stirring occasionally, 30 minutes before serving. If desired, serve in lettuce-lined bowl. *Makes 10 servings, ½ cup dressing.*

SALMON AU POIVRE

(pictured)

Salad oil
2 tablespoons each crushed black, green, pink and white peppercorns
¼ teaspoon salt
4 (1-inch-thick) salmon steaks (2 lb)
½ cup butter or margarine
1 medium cucumber, pared, seeded and finely chopped
3 tablespoons chopped green onions
1 tablespoon minced shallots
2 teaspoons lemon juice
Dill sprigs
Lemon slices

1. Prepare outdoor grill for barbecue. With salad oil, grease grill rack.

2. In cup, mix peppercorns and salt; sprinkle mixture over both sides of salmon steaks. Using Direct Method, cook salmon steaks over medium-hot coals about 6 minutes on each side. (Do not overcook.) Place steaks on heated platter. Cover; keep warm.

3. In medium saucepan, melt 2 tablespoons butter; sauté cucumber, green onions and shallots 3 minutes. Cut remaining butter into 6 equal pieces. Over very low heat, whisk butter pieces, one at a time, into cucumber mixture,

cooking just until butter melts and sauce is creamy. Stir in lemon juice. Garnish steaks with dill sprigs and lemon slices; serve with sauce. *Makes 4 servings, 1½ cups sauce.*

SUMMER PORK SALAD

(pictured)

2-lb boneless pork loin, trimmed and tied
2 tablespoons plus 1 teaspoon salad oil
½ teaspoon salt
¼ teaspoon pepper
½ lb whole green beans
2 medium red potatoes, cut into ¾-inch cubes
2 tablespoons red-wine vinegar
1 carrot, pared and shredded
1 celery stalk, thinly sliced
2 tablespoons finely chopped red onion
4 cups thinly sliced red cabbage (10 oz)
1 tablespoon chopped parsley
½ cup coarsely chopped walnuts

DRESSING

½ cup mayonnaise
½ cup sour cream
¼ cup (1 oz) crumbled blue cheese
¼ cup milk
2 tablespoons prepared coarse-grain Dijon-style mustard
1 tablespoon finely chopped sweet gherkins

1 yellow pepper, cut into ¼-inch-wide strips

1. If desired, pork can be prepared a day ahead of serving. Prepare outdoor grill for barbecue. Brush pork loin with 1 teaspoon salad oil; sprinkle with ¼ teaspoon salt and ⅛ teaspoon pepper. Using Indirect Method, grill pork, fat side up, over medium-hot coals 45 minutes. Turn pork and cook 45 minutes, or until meat thermometer inserted into center of meat registers 160F. Remove to platter; cool slightly. Refrigerate, covered, until cold.

2. In medium saucepan, in 3 inches boiling salted water, cook green beans until tender-crisp, about 4 minutes. With slotted spoon, remove to bowl of ice water. In water in pan, cook potatoes until tender but not soft, about 4 minutes. Drain; place potatoes in another bowl of ice water. Let vegetables stand until cold; drain well.

3. Meanwhile, in small bowl, whisk ¼ teaspoon salt, ⅛ teaspoon pepper, 2 tablespoons salad oil and the vinegar until blended. Place potatoes, carrot, celery and onion in medium bowl; add half the vinegar mixture. Toss until coated.

4. In another medium bowl, combine cabbage, parsley, walnuts and remaining vinegar mixture. Toss until coated.

5. In small bowl, mix dressing ingredients until blended. Place in small serving dish.

6. Assemble salad: Thinly slice pork. Using photograph as a guide, arrange on platter with potato mixture, cabbage mixture, green beans and pepper slices. Pass dressing separately. *Makes 6 servings, 1⅔ cups dressing.*

STRAWBERRY-RHUBARB TART

(pictured)

1½ cups sliced rhubarb (7 oz trimmed)
⅓ cup granulated sugar
3 tablespoons orange-flavored liqueur
½ cup butter or margarine, softened
½ cup packed light-brown sugar
1 egg yolk
½ teaspoon vanilla extract
1½ cups unsifted all-purpose flour
¾ cup heavy cream, chilled
2 pints strawberries, hulled and sliced lengthwise
¼ cup orange marmalade

1. In small saucepan, over medium heat, cook rhubarb, granulated sugar and 2 tablespoons liqueur, stirring occasionally, until the rhubarb is soft and the mixture is thickened. Cool the mixture at room temperature; refrigerate, covered, until cold.

2. Preheat oven to 350F. In large bowl of electric mixer, beat butter, brown sugar, egg yolk and vanilla until fluffy. Beat in flour just until blended. Press mixture over bottom and up sides of 11-by-8-inch tart pan with removable bottom. Prick with fork; bake 20 minutes, or until golden. Cool on wire rack.

3. In small bowl of electric mixer, at high speed, beat heavy cream until stiff peaks form when the beaters are raised. With rubber spatula, fold in cold rhubarb mixture until blended; spread over bottom of tart shell. Using photograph as a guide, arrange sliced strawberries on top.

4. In small saucepan, melt marmalade with remaining liqueur. Brush glaze over strawberries. Refrigerate until ready to serve. *Makes 12 servings.*

continued on page 310

Super Salads For Entertaining

The traditional ingredients of an ordinary chef's salad are combined on this tempting cold platter—julienne strips of ham, plus cheese, lettuce and vegetables. We've given it airs with such delicacies as hearts of palm, white asparagus and raw mushrooms. This salad is a meal all by itself, or it could be a generous appetizer for two. Serve it with a creamy Russian or Roquefort dressing.

This special salad is a delicious combination of artichoke hearts, avocado and mushrooms on a bed of crisp spinach. It can be served as a first course, or it would be perfect as the main course of a luncheon—especially if you're entertaining friends who are on a vegetarian diet. Serve it with a simple oil-and-vinegar dressing.

It may seem unusual to add pine-apple and orange slices to a cold ham-and-asparagus salad, but why not? They are, after all, fruits that are traditionally used to garnish baked ham—the flavors are compatible. This cold platter combines ham and asparagus and fruit with thin-sliced red onion and is garnished with water-cress and black olives. Serve it with our Best French Dressing.

Here is one more colorful salad that is easy to assemble and great for entertaining. This one combines paper-thin slices of cucumber, ripe tomato, canned artichoke hearts and chilled cooked shrimp. Caution: Overcooking can make shrimp tough. Five minutes in gently boiling, salted water will do it. Drain, cool and devein before refrigerating. We like it with Russian Dressing. Recipes for these and more salads, and dressings to go with them, begin on page 306.

GEORGE RATKAI

continued from page 305

SUPER CHEF'S SALAD

(pictured)

4 scallions, trimmed
8 to 10 canned asparagus stalks
8 to 10 cooked whole green beans
4 medium mushrooms, sliced, dipped in
   lemon juice
1 large carrot, pared, cut into julienne
   strips
6 slices hard-cooked egg
1 canned heart of palm, cut in 4 vertical
   slices
About 8 spinach leaves, shredded
About 12 mandarin-orange sections
2 slices Swiss cheese, cut into julienne
   strips
2 leaves Boston lettuce, shredded
2 thin slices boiled ham, cut into julienne
   strips
1 slice black olive and end of egg, cut with
   small fancy cutter
One of salad dressings, page 307, or use a
   prepared dressing, chilled

1. Cut green ends of scallions very
thin; place in ice water about ½ hour to
curl up.
2. On large platter, arrange asparagus, green beans, mushrooms, carrot,
scallions, sliced egg, heart of palm, spinach, mandarin oranges and cheese strips,
radiating from center of platter, as
pictured.
3. Arrange mound of shredded lettuce in center; top with ham. Garnish
with black olive and egg, as pictured.
4. Refrigerate to chill well—about 1
hour. Serve with dressing. *Makes 1 large
serving or 2 small servings.*

SALADE REGINE

(pictured)

About 1 cup curly endive in small pieces
¼ lb fresh young spinach leaves
1 very large mushroom, washed
2 large canned artichoke bottoms
   (see Note)
⅓ medium-size ripe avocado
2 teaspoons lemon juice
4 cherry tomatoes, washed
1 tablespoon chopped parsley
Vinaigrette Dressing, page 307

1. Wash endive; drain; cut into bite-
size pieces.
2. Wash spinach; drain; remove
stems.
3. In center of large round platter,
mound endive. Arrange spinach leaves,
overlapping, around endive.
4. Slice mushroom into five slices,
right through stem. Arrange, overlapping, on spinach, as pictured.

5. Cut each artichoke bottom, on the
diagonal, into thirds. Arrange, overlapping, on spinach, as pictured.
6. Peel avocado; cut in six slices;
brush with lemon juice. Arrange, overlapping, on spinach, as pictured.
7. Slice tops off 3 cherry tomatoes.
Cut one into four parts, not all the way
through. Sprinkle tomatoes with
chopped parsley. Place on spinach, as
pictured.
8. Refrigerate to chill well—about 1
hour. Serve with Vinaigrette Dressing.
Makes 1 large serving or 2 small servings.
Note: You may use fresh artichoke
bottoms and cook them until tender.

HAM-AND-FRESH-FRUIT SALAD

(pictured)

2 thick slices boiled ham (about 6 by 4 by
   ¼ inch)
8 slices large navel orange, ¼ inch thick
½ large red onion, sliced vertically into
   5 wedges
8 canned green-asparagus tips
2 large pitted black olives, halved
2 slices pineapple
Watercress sprigs
One of salad dressings, page 307

1. Cut each slice of ham in half diagonally, to make four triangles; then
cut each triangle in half.
2. On large round platter, arrange
the four smaller triangles of ham alternately with four orange slices, as pictured. Place a wedge of onion on each
orange slice.
3. Roll each of the remaining ham
triangles around two asparagus tips; place
on ham on plate.
4. Top onion slices with orange slices
and halves of black olives, as pictured.
Place pineapple rings in center; top with
a small bunch of watercress. Take a few
onion strips from remaining wedge of
onion to decorate watercress. Garnish
edge of platter with more watercress, as
pictured.
5. Refrigerate to chill well—about 1
hour. Serve with dressing. *Makes 1 large
salad or 2 small salads.*

SALADE McCALL'S
(Shrimp-and-Vegetable-Salad Platter)

(pictured)

12 thin slices cucumber
1 large tomato, sliced vertically into
   5 slices
5 canned artichoke hearts
10 cooked medium-size shrimp (peeled and
   deveined; leave shell on tail)

Watercress
Lemon wedges
One of salad dressings, page 307

1. Arrange cucumber slices, slightly
overlapping, around the edge of a large
round plate.
2. Arrange tomato slices, slightly
overlapping, in circle, as pictured.
3. Arrange artichoke hearts inside
tomato slices. Stand two shrimp between artichoke hearts, as pictured. Place
small bunches of watercress between
shrimp and in center of platter.
4. Refrigerate to chill well—about 1
hour. Serve with lemon wedges and salad
dressing. *Makes 1 large serving or 2 small
servings.*

GREEN-GODDESS SALAD

GREEN-GODDESS DRESSING
1 cup mayonnaise or cooked salad dressing
¼ cup tarragon vinegar
6 anchovy fillets, chopped
¼ cup finely chopped parsely
2 tablespoons finely chopped green onion
2 tablespoons snipped chives
½ teaspoon dry mustard
¼ teaspoon salt
⅛ teaspoon pepper

SALAD
2 quarts bite-size pieces crisp salad greens
3 cups cubed cooked chicken, chilled
2 medium tomatoes, sliced

1. Make Green-Goddess Dressing: In
small bowl, combine all dressing ingredients; mix well. Refrigerate, covered,
several hours or overnight, to let flavors
blend. (Or use bottled green-goddess
dressing.)
2. Just before serving, make Salad:
Place greens in salad bowl.
3. Place chicken in center of greens.
Add dressing; toss to coat chicken and
greens well.
4. Garnish with tomato slices. *Makes
8 servings.*

FRESH-FRUIT SALAD

DRESSING
1 cup sour cream
3 tablespoons maple-blended syrup
Dash salt

2 navel oranges
2 bananas
1 medium pear, unpeeled
1 medium apple, unpeeled
½ lb grapes
1 can (1 lb, 4 oz) pineapple slices
½ cup pitted date halves

1. Make Dressing; In small bowl,

combine sour cream, syrup and salt; mix well. Refrigerate until ready to use. Also refrigerate all fruits until well chilled.

2. Just before serving, peel oranges and cut into 1/4-inch-thick slices. Peel bananas; cut in half crosswise, then lengthwise. Cut pear and apple into wedges; core. Cut grapes into small clusters. Drain pineapple well.

3. Place dressing in attractive bowl in center of large, round platter. Arrange banana, pear, apple, grapes and orange and pineapple slices in groups around dressing. Garnish platter with date halves. *Makes 8 servings.*

VINAIGRETTE DRESSING

1 cup olive oil or salad oil
1/3 cup red-wine vinegar
1 teaspoon salt
1/8 teaspoon pepper
2 tablespoons chopped capers
2 tablespoons chopped chives

1. Combine all ingredients in jar with tight-fitting lid. Shake vigorously.

2. Refrigerate dressing until ready to use. Shake again just before using. *Makes 1 1/2 cups.*

ROQUEFORT SALAD DRESSING

1/4 lb Roquefort cheese
1 cup sour cream
1/4 cup mayonnaise or cooked salad
**   dressing**
1/4 cup dry sherry
1/4 cup wine vinegar
1 tablespoon grated onion
1/2 teaspoon salt
1/2 teaspoon garlic salt
1/4 teaspoon paprika
Generous sprinkle freshly ground
**   pepper**

1. Coarsely crumble cheese into a medium bowl. Add remaining ingredients, stirring until well blended.

2. Refrigerate, covered, until well chilled—at least 1 hour. *Makes about 2 cups.*

BEST FRENCH DRESSING

1 cup salad oil
1/2 cup olive oil
1/4 cup dry white wine
1/2 cup red-wine vinegar
2 teaspoons salt
1/2 teaspoon pepper
1/2 teaspoon dry mustard
1/2 teaspoon dried basil leaves
1/2 cup chopped parsley
1 garlic clove, finely chopped

1. Combine all ingredients in medium bowl; beat with rotary beater until well blended.

2. Pour into jar with tight-fitting lid. Refrigerate at least 2 hours. Shake well just before serving. *Makes 2 1/2 cups.*

COBB SALAD

2 cups crisp iceberg lettuce in bite-size
**   pieces**
2 cups crisp romaine in bite-size pieces
2 cups crisp chicory in bite-size pieces
2 medium tomatoes, cut in eighths
2 medium avocados, peeled and sliced
3 cups slivered cooked chicken, chilled
6 crisp-cooked slices bacon, cut in
**   1/2-inch pieces**
1 hard-cooked egg
2 tablespoons snipped chives
Watercress
Russian Dressing, recipe follows

1. Just before serving, assemble salad: Place iceberg lettuce, romaine and chicory in salad bowl. Arrange tomato and avocado around edge of bowl. Mound chicken in center and sprinkle with bacon. Chop egg white and egg yolk separately; sprinkle, with chives, over top of salad. Garnish with watercress.

2. To serve: At the table, pour half the dressing over salad; toss well. Pass rest of dressing. *Makes 8 to 10 servings.*

RUSSIAN DRESSING

1/2 cup mayonnaise or cooked salad
**   dressing**
1 tablespoon chili sauce
2 tablespoons milk
2 tablespoons finely chopped stuffed
**   olives**
1 tablespoon finely chopped onion
1 tablespoon finely chopped green
**   pepper**
2 tablespoons lemon juice
1/4 teaspoon salt
1 tablespoon prepared horseradish

1. In small bowl, combine mayonnaise with rest of ingredients; mix well.

2. Refrigerate, covered. *Makes 3/4 cup.*

TANGY SPINACH SALAD

1/2 lb spinach leaves, washed
3 cups sliced mushrooms
6 slices bacon
2 tablespoons brown sugar
2 tablespoons Dijon-style mustard
3 tablespoons lemon juice

1. Remove and discard stems from spinach; tear spinach into bite-size pieces. Place in salad bowl. Add mushroom slices; refrigerate.

2. In medium skillet, cook bacon until crisp. Remove from pan; drain on paper towels. Crumble; set aside.

3. To drippings in pan, add brown sugar, mustard and lemon juice. Cook, stirring, 1 minute. Pour onto salad; toss to coat. Sprinkle bacon over salad. Serve immediately. *Makes 4 servings.*

HOLIDAY SALAD VINAIGRETTE

1 lb green beans, trimmed
1 medium red apple, cored
1 ripe avocado, pitted and peeled
1 medium red Bartlett pear, cored
2 tablespoons lemon juice
Red-leaf lettuce leaves
Boston lettuce leaves
2 naval oranges, peeled and sectioned
Champagne grapes
Honey-Mustard Vinaigrette, recipe
**   follows**

1. In 1/2 inch boiling, salted water in saucepan, cook green beans 3 minutes, or until tender-crisp. Drain; place in bowl of ice water until cool. Drain; pat dry.

2. Cut apple, avocado and pear lengthwise into thin wedges; brush with lemon juice. On platter, arrange lettuce leaves, green beans and fruits. Pass dressing separately. *Makes 8 servings.*

HONEY-MUSTARD VINAIGRETTE

1 tablespoon minced parsley
1 teaspoon salt
1/8 teaspoon freshly ground pepper
3/4 cup salad oil
1/4 cup red-wine vinegar
2 tablespoons honey
1 tablespoon prepared mustard

In jar with tight-fitting lid, combine ingredients. Shake until blended. *Makes about 1 1/4 cups.* ◆

Marinated Beef For a Picnic

W e call it Beef 'n' Brew and just wait until you taste it! Tender slices of beer-marinated roast beef are marinated for a second time in an herbed beer, red wine and sherry sauce and then served on thick slices of fresh pumpernickel bread—it's just perfect to take along for a picnic in the park. This is truly a "do-ahead" meal with literally nothing to finish on the day of the picnic. To complete the menu, make a salad of cucumbers and sour cream, slice some fresh tomatoes and take along plenty of beer and wine. For dessert make or buy chunky brownies or blondies! See opposite page for step-by-step directions.

A STEP-BY-STEP RECIPE

BEEF 'N' BREW

BEEF
5-lb sirloin-tip roast of beef
2 cups beer
¼ cup unsifted all-purpose flour
¼ teaspoon salt
½ teaspoon garlic salt
½ teaspoon onion salt
⅛ teaspoon pepper
½ cup vegetable oil

MARINADE
½ cup vegetable oil
¼ cup red-wine vinegar
½ cup tomato purée
½ cup prepared marinara sauce
¼ cup red Burgundy wine
½ cup dry sherry wine
½ teaspoon salt
¼ teaspoon onion salt

¼ teaspoon garlic salt
⅛ teaspoon pepper

Pumpernickel bread
Cold beer or red wine

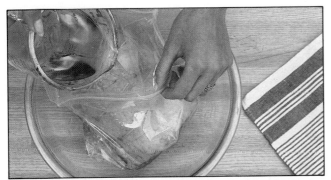

1. Two days before picnic: Place beef in a zip-lock plastic bag; add beer. Zip bag closed while squeezing out all air in bag. Place in bowl; refrigerate overnight or for at least 12 hours. (Or use a regular plastic bag being careful to seal tightly with a rubber band.)

2. The next day: Preheat oven to 325F. Remove roast from bag; reserve beer. Combine flour, salt, ½ teaspoon each garlic and onion salt, ⅛ teaspoon pepper and ¼ cup oil. Rub flour mixture over roast; insert meat thermometer in center of meat being sure it does not rest in fat.

3. Place roast on rack in a shallow roasting pan and place on center rack in oven. Roast, uncovered, for 1 hour and 50 minutes to 2 hours, basting roast every 10 to 15 minutes with ¼ cup vegetable oil mixed with ½ cup of the reserved beer.

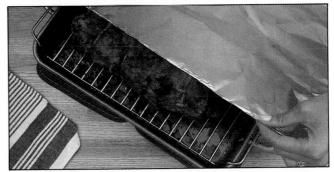

4. When meat thermometer registers 140F for rare, remove from the oven; cover with aluminum foil and let cool. (Meat should be rare to medium-rare for more complete absorption of the marinade.) While the meat cools, prepare the Marinade.

5. In a large casserole, combine ½ cup oil, vinegar, tomato purée, marinara sauce, Burgundy and sherry wines, ½ teaspoon salt, ¼ teaspoon each onion and garlic salt and ⅛ teaspoon pepper; mix well. Place cooled roast on a wooden board and cut into thin slices.

6. Place beef slices in marinade, turning each to coat thoroughly. Cover casserole and refrigerate overnight or for at least 12 hours. The next day, take beef to the picnic right in the casserole. Serve on pumpernickel bread along with cold beer or red wine. Makes 12 servings.

continued from page 303

APPETIZERS

◆

HUMMUS BI TAHINI WITH FRESH GRILLED VEGETABLES

1 can (15 to 19 oz) chick-peas
1 large garlic clove
3 tablespoons tahini (sesame paste)
2 tablespoons lemon juice
½ teaspoon salt
Paprika

GRILLED VEGETABLES
1 small eggplant
1 medium yellow squash
1 medium zucchini
1 green pepper
1 red pepper
Salad oil

1. Drain chick-peas, reserving liquid; set aside. In blender or food processor, finely chop garlic. Add tahini; process until blended. Add 3 tablespoons chick-pea liquid, the lemon juice and salt; puree.

2. Add chick-peas and process until smooth; add more chick-pea liquid, if necessary, to blend smoothly. Turn into serving bowl; dust with paprika.

3. Make Grilled Vegetables: Cut eggplant, yellow squash and zucchini into ½-inch-thick slices. (If the eggplant is over 2 inches in diameter, halve or quarter the slices.) Cut each pepper into 1-inch-wide lengthwise strips. Brush vegetables on one side with salad oil.

4. Grill or broil vegetables. To grill: Place vegetables, oiled side down, in a metal barbecue basket in a single layer; grill just until vegetables start to brown. Serve with Hummus Bi Tahini. To broil: Place vegetables, oiled side down, on foil-covered jelly-roll pan. Broil, at least 4 inches from heat source, 3 to 5 minutes. (Do not overcook, or vegetables will be too limp to use as dippers.) *Makes 8 servings, about 2 cups hummus.*

MARINATED AVOCADOS AND TOMATOES

DRESSING
2 garlic cloves, crushed
1 teaspoon salt
1 teaspoon dry mustard
1 tablespoon prepared horseradish
½ teaspoon paprika
1 teaspoon dried basil leaves
⅓ cup catsup
½ cup lemon juice
1 cup salad oil

3 medium tomatoes (about 1½ lb)

2 large ripe avocados (about 1½ lb)
Salad greens

1. Make Dressing: Combine all the dressing ingredients in a jar with a tight-fitting lid; shake to mix well.

2. Core tomatoes and slice thinly. Cut avocados in half lengthwise; remove pits and peel. Slice lengthwise.

3. Arrange tomato and avocado slices in large, shallow glass dish. Shake dressing; pour over tomato and avocado slices, covering completely. Refrigerate, covered, about 2 hours. Drain slightly and serve on salad greens. *Makes 6 to 8 servings.*

BREADS

◆

BASIL-GRILLED BREAD

1 medium garlic clove, crushed
½ cup unsalted butter or margarine
2 tablespoons sun-dried tomatoes
1 cup (4 oz) shredded provolone cheese
¼ cup chopped fresh basil leaves
1 loaf (1 lb) Italian bread

1. Prepare outdoor grill for barbecue. In food processor, mince garlic. Add butter and tomatoes; process until smooth. Transfer to bowl; stir in provolone cheese and basil.

2. With serrated knife, slice bread diagonally almost all the way through 12 times, at 1½-inch intervals. Spread 1 rounded tablespoon butter mixture between sections, using half of butter mixture. Turn bread so that ends are reversed; slice bread diagonally almost all the way through 12 times, making diamond patterns of 1½-inch sections of bread. Spread with remaining butter mixture.

3. Wrap bread with heavy-duty foil. Place bread, right side up, 5 to 6 inches from medium coals. Using Indirect Method, heat bread with grill covered, 8 minutes, or until bread is heated through. *Makes 6 servings.*

RUSSIAN RYE BREAD

MUSTARD-HORSERADISH BUTTER
½ cup (1 stick) butter or margarine, softened
1 garlic clove, crushed
1 tablespoon prepared mustard
1 tablespoon prepared horseradish, drained
Dash salt

1 loaf (1 lb) round unsliced rye bread

1. Make Mustard-Horseradish Butter: Combine all ingredients in bowl.

2. Cut rye bread into ½-inch-thick slices, being careful not to cut all the way through. Spread butter mixture between bread slices. Wrap loaf in foil.

3. Adjust grill 3 inches from prepared coals. Heat bread on grill 15 to 20 minutes, or until heated through. *Makes 10 servings.*

TO COOK INDOORS

Bake foil-wrapped bread in a 375F preheated oven 20 minutes, or until heated through.

ENTREES

◆

ITALIAN-SAUSAGE KEBABS

4 sweet Italian sausages
4 hot Italian sausages
12 small onions, peeled
1 large red pepper, cut into eighths
2 large green peppers, cut into eighths
Bottled barbecue sauce
Parsley sprigs
6 crusty dinner rolls or 2 small loaves Italian bread

1. In large saucepan, bring 1 cup water to boiling. Add sausages; reduce heat and simmer gently, covered, ½ hour. Drain.

2. In another saucepan, in 1 cup boiling water, simmer onions 5 minutes. Add red and green peppers; simmer 2 minutes longer; drain; cool.

3. Cut sausages diagonally into thirds. On 6 skewers, thread sausage alternately with peppers and onions.

4. Adjust grill 4 to 6 inches from prepared coals. Place kebabs on grill. (Lower hood, if grill has one.) Over low coals, grill kebabs 5 minutes on each side, turning once and brushing frequently with barbecue sauce.

5. Serve in roll, split, or in Italian bread, heated in foil on grill. Garnish each with parsley sprig, if desired. *Makes 6 servings.*

TO COOK INDOORS

Broil kebabs on broiler rack, 4 inches from heat, 10 minutes, turning and basting with barbecue sauce.

PINEAPPLE-HONEY-GLAZED RIBS

4 to 5 lb pork spareribs (2 racks)
1 medium pineapple
½ teaspoon ground ginger
1½ cups pineapple juice
⅓ cup honey
⅓ cup cider vinegar
1 tablespoon soy sauce
3 tablespoons cornstarch

1. Cut each rack into 2- or 3-rib portions. In 13-by-9-by-2-inch microwave-safe baking dish, place ribs with meaty side down and thickest sections toward side of dish. Cover with waxed paper; cook on MEDIUM (50% power) 30 minutes.

2. Turn ribs over and rearrange, placing less-cooked sections toward edge of dish. Cover with waxed paper; cook on MEDIUM 35 minutes.

3. Meanwhile, peel pineapple. Cut crosswise into ½-inch-thick slices.

4. In glass bowl, mix ginger, 1 cup pineapple juice, the honey, cider vinegar and soy sauce. Cook on HIGH (100% power) 3 minutes. In cup, blend remaining pineapple juice with cornstarch; stir into honey mixture. Cook on HIGH 1 minute, or until mixture boils, stirring once.

5. Prepare outdoor grill for barbecue. Place ribs, meaty side up, 4 inches from low coals. Place pineapple slices around ribs; baste with honey mixture. Using Indirect Method, cook ribs, covered, 5 minutes. Turn ribs and pineapple slices; baste with honey mixture. Cover, cook 5 minutes longer. Remove to serving platter. If desired, garnish ribs with rosemary sprigs. *Makes 6 servings.*

PORTUGUESE-STYLE HENS

PORTUGUESE MARINADE
1¼ cups packed fresh cilantro
1 tablespoon ground coriander
2 teaspoons grated lemon peel
½ teaspoon freshly ground black pepper
½ teaspoon crushed red-pepper flakes
8 garlic cloves
6 tablespoons lemon juice
¼ cup olive oil

2 Cornish hens, cut through breast bone, flattened
½ teaspoon coarse (kosher) salt

1. Make Portuguese Marinade: In food processor, combine ingredients; puree. In glass baking dish, spread half the marinade over Cornish hens; reserve remainder. Marinate hens overnight in refrigerator.

2. Prepare outdoor grill for barbecue. Sprinkle hens with the salt. Grill 3 to 4 inches from prepared coals 10 to 13 minutes on each side, until done. Serve with reserved marinade as a dipping sauce. *Makes 4 servings.*

TURKEY BURGERS

BURGERS
3 scallions, cut into 2-inch pieces
1 celery stalk, cut into 2-inch pieces
1 garlic clove
1 lb ground turkey
½ lb turkey sausage, casings removed
½ cup finely grated zucchini, squeezed until dry
1 tablespoon chopped fresh oregano leaves
1 tablespoon sugar
1 teaspoon pepper
¾ teaspoon salt
2 teaspoons soy sauce

3 tomatoes, cut into ½-inch-thick slices

1. Prepare outdoor grill for barbecue. Make Burgers: In food processor, combine scallions, celery and garlic; using pulsing motion, finely chop. Place

in medium bowl; add remaining burger ingredients; mix gently until combined. With wet hands, shape into 6 (½-inch-thick) patties.

2. Grill burgers 4 inches from prepared coals 8 to 9 minutes, turning after 5 minutes. Grill tomatoes 5 minutes, turning once. Serve burgers with tomatoes. *Makes 6 servings.*

SIDE DISHES

ALL-AMERICAN POTATO SALAD

3 lb red new potatoes, scrubbed

DRESSING
1 tablespoon sugar
¾ cup mayonnaise
1 teaspoon salt
⅛ teaspoon pepper
2 tablespoons light cream
1 tablespoon cider vinegar
2 tablespoons Dijon-style mustard

1 celery stalk, thinly sliced
1 small onion, minced
1 small red pepper, cut into ¼-inch-thick strips

1. Cut potatoes in half; in 3 quarts of boiling, salted water in Dutch oven, cook potatoes 12 minutes, or until easily pierced with a fork. Drain; place in large bowl of ice and water to stop cooking. When cool, place in colander; set aside until well drained.

2. In large bowl, combine dressing ingredients. Add potatoes, celery, onion and pepper; toss gently to coat. Cover with plastic wrap; refrigerate at least 1 hour to blend flavors. *Makes 8 servings.*

COLORFUL COLESLAW

DRESSING
¾ cup sour cream
½ cup mayonnaise
¼ cup red-wine vinegar
1 teaspoon celery seeds
1 teaspoon salt
½ teaspoon freshly ground pepper

½ medium head red cabbage, cored
2 medium carrots, trimmed and peeled
2 celery stalks
½ lb snow pea pods, trimmed
2 scallions, thinly sliced diagonally

1. Make Dressing: In large bowl, combine ingredients; mix well.

2. In a food processor, with the medium slicing disk, shred the cabbage. With medium shredding disk, shred carrots. With thin slicing blade, slice celery. Place vegetables in bowl with dressing.

continued on page 315

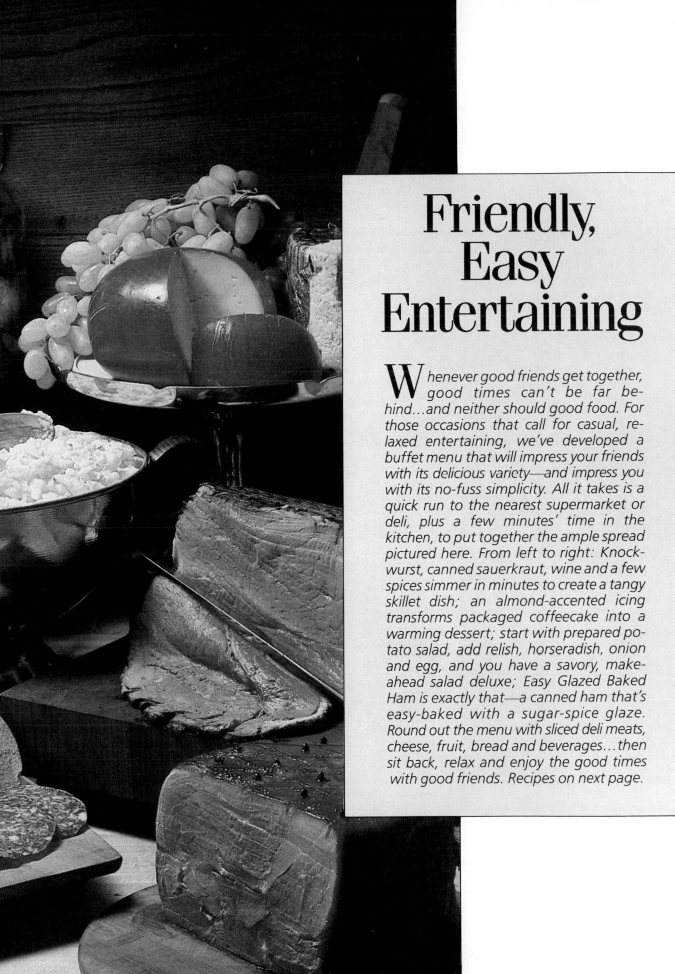

Friendly, Easy Entertaining

Whenever good friends get together, good times can't be far behind…and neither should good food. For those occasions that call for casual, relaxed entertaining, we've developed a buffet menu that will impress your friends with its delicious variety—and impress you with its no-fuss simplicity. All it takes is a quick run to the nearest supermarket or deli, plus a few minutes' time in the kitchen, to put together the ample spread pictured here. From left to right: Knockwurst, canned sauerkraut, wine and a few spices simmer in minutes to create a tangy skillet dish; an almond-accented icing transforms packaged coffeecake into a warming dessert; start with prepared potato salad, add relish, horseradish, onion and egg, and you have a savory, make-ahead salad deluxe; Easy Glazed Baked Ham is exactly that—a canned ham that's easy-baked with a sugar-spice glaze. Round out the menu with sliced deli meats, cheese, fruit, bread and beverages…then sit back, relax and enjoy the good times with good friends. Recipes on next page.

continued from page 313

**RARE ROAST SIRLOIN OF BEEF
PLATTER OF SLICED SALAMI,
BOLOGNA AND LIVERWURST
KNOCKWURST AND SAUERKRAUT★
EASY GLAZED BAKED HAM★
MACARONI SALAD
IN RED-PEPPER SHELLS★
SAVORY POTATO SALAD★
ALL KINDS OF GREAT
DELICATESSEN BREADS
KOSHER DILL PICKLES
MUSTARDS
ICED COFFEECAKE★
FRUIT SALAD IN SHERRY★
RICE PUDDING WITH CARAMEL
CRUNCH★
ASSORTED CHEESE
GREEN GRAPES
BOTTLES OF COLD BEER
BIG POT OF HOT COFFEE**

★Recipes given for starred dishes.

KNOCKWURST AND SAUERKRAUT

(pictured)

**1 pkg (2 lb) sauerkraut, or 2 cans (1-lb size) sauerkraut
2 pkg (1-lb size) knockwurst (8 links)
¼ cup (½ stick) butter or margarine
¼ cup chopped onion
½ teaspoon caraway seed
1¼ cups dry white wine
½ cup water**

1. Place sauerkraut in a colander; rinse with cold water; let drain.
2. In large saucepan, heat 2 quarts water to boiling. Add knockwurst; cover; remove from heat. Let stand 5 to 8 minutes.
3. Meanwhile, in hot butter in large skillet, sauté onion until golden. Add drained sauerkraut, caraway seed, white wine and ½ cup water; toss to combine.
4. Arrange knockwurst on sauerkraut; cook, covered, 30 minutes. *Makes 8 servings.*

EASY GLAZED BAKED HAM

(pictured)

**1 canned ham (3 lb)
Whole cloves
½ cup brown sugar, firmly packed
1 tablespoon prepared mustard
1 teaspoon cider vinegar
¼ teaspoon ground cinnamon**

1. Preheat oven to 350F.

2. Place ham in a 9-by-9-by-2-inch pan. Discard any liquid. With sharp knife, score top of ham into a diamond pattern. Insert a clove in center of each diamond.
3. In small bowl, combine brown sugar, mustard, vinegar and cinnamon. Spoon mixture evenly over the ham.
4. Bake ham, uncovered, 40 minutes. Baste with glaze in pan; bake 20 minutes longer.
5. Remove ham to carving board. Slice thinly. *Makes 8 servings.*

MACARONI SALAD IN RED-PEPPER SHELLS

**½ cup mayonnaise or cooked salad dressing
1 cup finely chopped cucumber
¼ cup sliced green onion
½ teaspoon salt
1 lb delicatessen macaroni salad
6 large roasted sweet red peppers**

1. In medium bowl, combine mayonnaise, cucumber, onion and salt; mix well. Add macaroni salad; mix gently until well combined. Refrigerate, covered, at least 2 hours.
2. Meanwhile, cut peppers in half crosswise. Scoop out seeds; drain. Refrigerate.
3. To serve: Set pepper cups on large platter; fill each with some of salad mixture. *Makes 8 to 12 servings.*

SAVORY POTATO SALAD

(pictured)

**2½ lb delicatessen potato salad
¼ cup sweet-pickle relish, drained
1 tablespoon prepared horseradish, well drained
1 teaspoon instant minced onion
2 hard-cooked eggs, shelled and chopped**

1. In large bowl, combine potato salad, pickle relish, horseradish and on-

ion; stir gently until well blended.
2. Refrigerate, covered, until well chilled—about 2 hours.
3. Spoon into serving bowl. Sprinkle hard-cooked egg over top. *Makes 8 servings.*

ICED COFFEECAKE

(pictured)

**1 8- or 9-inch-square bakery, streusel-topped coffeecake
½ cup unsifted confectioners' sugar
2 teaspoons hot water
2 drops almond extract**

1. Preheat oven to 350F.
2. Place coffeecake on cookie sheet; heat 10 minutes.
3. Meanwhile, combine sugar, hot water and almond extract; stir until smooth.
4. Remove coffeecake from oven. Drizzle with sugar mixture. Serve warm. *Makes 8 servings.*

FRUIT SALAD IN SHERRY

**1 cup dates
2 medium red apples
1 jar (2 lb) fruit salad
½ cup orange juice
¼ cup cream sherry
2 teaspoons grated orange peel**

1. Pit dates and cut in half lengthwise.
2. Wash, quarter and core apples. Slice thinly into a large bowl. Add dates, fruit salad, orange juice, sherry and orange peel; mix gently.
3. Refrigerate, covered, 2 hours. *Makes 8 to 10 servings.*

RICE PUDDING WITH CARAMEL CRUNCH

**2 lb rice pudding from the delicatessen, or 2 cans (15 ¾-oz size) rice pudding
½ cup sugar
8 blanched whole almonds
Sweetened whipped cream**

1. Turn rice pudding into an attractive shallow serving dish. Refrigerate until very well chilled.
2. In medium, heavy skillet, combine sugar with almonds; cook over medium heat, stirring frequently, until sugar melts and forms a golden-amber syrup.
3. Immediately drizzle over rice pudding, to cover as much of surface as possible. Serve with whipped cream. *Makes 8 servings.* ◆

continued from page 311

3. In small saucepan of boiling water, cook snow pea pods 1 minute. Drain; rinse with cold water to stop cooking. Julienne; place in bowl with vegetables. Add sliced scallions. Toss to coat with dressing. Refrigerate until ready to serve. *Makes 8 servings.*

CHEESE-AND-CHILI-BEAN CASSEROLE

6 slices bacon
1 env dried onion-soup mix
2 cans (1-lb size) barbecue beans
¼ cup chili sauce
¼ cup dry red wine
1 cup cubed sharp Cheddar cheese
¼ teaspoon salt

1. Preheat oven to 350F. Lightly grease a 1½-quart casserole.
2. In medium skillet, sauté bacon until crisp. Drain well on paper towels; crumble.
3. In prepared casserole, combine bacon with rest of ingredients, mixing well.
4. Bake, uncovered, 20 minutes, or until cheese is melted and mixture is bubbly. *Makes 6 servings.*

GRILLED CORN WITH DILL BUTTER

8 ears fresh corn in husks

DILL BUTTER
½ cup butter, at room temperature
1 roasted red pepper, chopped
2 tablespoons snipped fresh dill
½ teaspoon salt
⅛ teaspoon pepper

1. Prepare outdoor grill for barbecue. Peel husks from corn to within 2 inches of stem. Do not break husks off ears. Remove silk; pull husks back over ears to cover. Soak corn in cold water 20 minutes.
2. Make Dill Butter: Place butter in food processor; process until smooth. Add red pepper; process until smooth. Add dill, salt and pepper; process until blended. Place butter mixture in serving dish.
3. Remove corn from water; shake to remove excess water. Secure husk over each ear of corn with long strip of husk tied at the top of each ear. Using Direct Method, grill corn over hot coals, turning every 5 minutes until a kernel pulls away from ear cleanly and easily. Serve with Dill Butter. *Makes 8 servings.*

GREEN BEANS PROVENCALE

1 lb fresh green beans
1 medium tomato, peeled and chopped
½ cup chopped green onion
1 teaspoon salt
Dash pepper
½ teaspoon dried basil leaves
2 tablespoons butter or margarine

1. Wash beans; drain. Trim ends; cut on the diagonal into 1-inch pieces.
2. Place beans in center of an 18-by-16-inch rectangle of heavy-duty foil.
3. Add tomato, onion, salt, pepper and basil to beans. Dot top with butter.
4. Bring long sides of foil together; fold over twice to seal securely. Also fold over ends of foil twice to seal.
5. Adjust grill 5 inches from prepared coals. Place foil package, seam side down, at edge of grill. Grill 20 minutes. Using tongs, turn foil package seam side up. Grill 20 minutes longer, or until beans are tender. To serve: Turn back foil; toss vegetables with fork to combine. *Makes 4 servings.*

TO COOK INDOORS

Combine all ingredients in medium skillet. Cook, covered, over low heat, stirring occasionally, 10 to 15 minutes, or until beans are tender.

GOLDEN POTATOES AND ONIONS IN FOIL

4 medium baking potatoes, pared
4 medium onions, thinly sliced
½ cup (1 stick) butter or margarine, softened
2 teaspoons seasoned salt
Paprika

1. Cut 4 (18-by-12-inch) rectangles of heavy-duty foil.
2. To prepare each foil package: Cut a potato crosswise into ¼-inch-thick slices. Place slices of one potato in center of a foil rectangle, keeping original shape of potato.
3. Insert an onion slice between every two potato slices. Spread top with 2 tablespoons butter; sprinkle with ½ teaspoon salt and a little paprika.
4. Bring long sides of foil together; fold over twice to seal securely. Also fold over ends of foil twice to seal. Repeat with rest of ingredients to make three more foil packages.
5. Lay foil packages directly on prepared coals. Roast 20 minutes. Using tongs, turn foil packages. Roast 20 minutes longer, or until potatoes are tender. To serve, turn back foil. *Makes 4 servings.*

SPANISH SQUASH

1½ lb yellow summer squash or zucchini
1 teaspoon instant minced onion
1 teaspoon seasoned salt
¼ teaspoon dried tarragon leaves
Dash pepper
½ cup finely chopped green pepper
¼ cup (½ stick) butter or margarine

1. Wash squash; cut in half lengthwise. Cut crosswise into 1-inch slices. Arrange squash in center of an 18-by-20-inch rectangle of heavy-duty foil. Sprinkle squash with onion, salt, tarragon, pepper and chopped green pepper; dot with butter. Bring long sides of foil together; fold over twice to seal securely. Also fold over ends of foil twice to seal.

continued on page 325

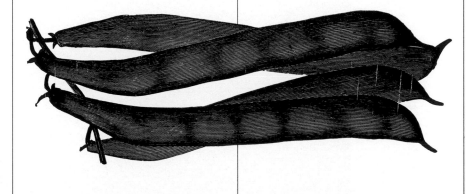

Speedy Gourmet Entertaining

*I*t's easy to be a gourmet cook when you can plan your dinner party weeks ahead. But the test comes when you have to produce a meal at a moment's notice—and you haven't even shopped yet! For those emergencies, here are nine speedy-gourmet menus you can shop for in a late-afternoon trip to the supermarket or on the way home from work, and put together in an hour or less. For example, this impressive feast: Poached Chicken and Winter Vegetables, a lemon-dressed green salad, French bread and a spectacular Raspberry Crème Parfait. The speedy-gourmet sleight of hand behind it: Use two small chickens instead of one large one—they look prettier and cook faster. While they're poaching (60 minutes), steam the vegetables (for better texture and better flavor) in a covered skillet—15 minutes. Prepare a quick raspberry sauce with frozen berries, and layer into a family-size parfait glass with ready-made custard dessert. Pop the bread into the oven, prepare the salad, and you're finished—with perhaps time left in your hour to set the table.

GEORGE RATKAI

*T*he star of this speedy-gourmet spectacular is a thick sirloin steak, baked instead of broiled, so that, after a quick browning, it can cook in the oven to just the right degree of rareness while you go about your other tasks. The very professional-looking Rum-And-Fruit Torte is accomplished in minimum time. Canned fruits are piled atop a rum-sprinkled packaged sponge-cake layer, glazed with melted apple jelly, sprinkled with toasted almond slivers. Then the whole thing is put in the refrigerator to mellow and chill until it's time to serve. That out of the way, you can turn your attention to the savory Baked Tomato Halves. They're spread with mustard and other seasonings, topped with bread cubes, and then put into the oven with the steak. The elegant Pâté-Stuffed Mushrooms that garnish the steak don't look quick and easy, but they are. The secret: The caps, sautéed in wine and butter, are filled with swirls of canned liver pâté forced through a pastry tube. Chilled Asparagus, served with Mustard Dressing, and heated poppy-seed rolls (not shown) complete the menu. For recipes, and for more speedy-gourmet dinners, turn to page 320.

continued from page 319

POACHED CHICKEN AND WINTER VEGETABLES* (POTATOES, CARROTS, CABBAGE AND LEEKS) HORSERADISH SAUCE* GREEN SALAD WITH FRESH-LEMON DRESSING* CRUSTY FRENCH BREAD RASPBERRY CREME PARFAIT* CHILLED WHITE WINE COFFEE

*Recipes given for starred dishes.

POACHED CHICKEN AND WINTER VEGETABLES
(pictured)

2 (2-lb size) ready-to-cook whole
    broiler-fryers
Salt
Pepper
½ cup (1 stick) butter or margarine
8 leeks
1 head (1 lb) green cabbage
1 can (10¾ oz) condensed chicken broth,
    undiluted
½ cup dry white wine
½ teaspoon dried thyme leaves
1 lb small new potatoes, scrubbed
1 can (1 lb) whole carrots, drained
1 tablespoon snipped chives

1. Rinse chickens well; dry with paper towels. Sprinkle inside of each with ½ teaspoon salt and ⅛ teaspoon pepper. Tuck wings under body; fasten skin at neck with skewer. Tie legs together at ends of drumsticks.

2. In ¼ cup hot butter in Dutch oven, over medium heat, brown chicken well all over—takes about 10 minutes. Turn carefully with two wooden spoons; do not break skin.

3. Meanwhile, trim leeks. Cut off root ends and green stems—leeks should be 7 inches long after trimming. Wash thoroughly. Wash cabbage; remove core. Cut cabbage into sixths; set aside.

4. Turn chickens breast side up. Add chicken broth and wine. Sprinkle each chicken with ¼ teaspoon salt and ¼ teaspoon thyme. Bring to boiling; reduce heat; simmer, covered, 60 minutes, or until chicken is tender.

5. Meanwhile, in 1 inch boiling salted water in medium saucepan, cook potatoes, covered, 20 minutes, or until tender. Drain; keep covered in saucepan.

6. In 1 inch boiling salted water in a large skillet, simmer leeks, cabbage and carrots, covered, 15 minutes, or just until cabbage is tender. Drain; return to skillet. Keep covered.

7. To serve: Carefully remove chickens to heated platter; remove skewers and strings. Arrange potatoes, leeks, cabbage and carrots around chickens. Dot vegetables with remaining ¼ cup butter; sprinkle with chives. Pass Horseradish Sauce, below. *Makes 6 servings.*

HORSERADISH SAUCE

¼ cup (½ stick) butter or margarine
2 tablespoons all-purpose flour
1 teaspoon salt
⅛ teaspoon black pepper
Dash ground red pepper
1½ cups milk
½ cup prepared horseradish, drained

1. Melt butter in medium saucepan; remove from heat. Stir in flour, salt and peppers until smooth.

2. Gradually stir in milk; bring to boiling, stirring. Add horseradish; reduce heat, and simmer 3 minutes, or until slightly thickened. Serve hot, with chicken. *Makes 2 cups.*

GREEN SALAD WITH FRESH-LEMON DRESSING
(pictured)

¼ cup bottled herb-and-garlic salad
    dressing
2 tablespoons fresh lemon juice
1 small head Boston lettuce
½ head romaine
¼ teaspoon salt
⅛ teaspoon pepper
Lemon quarters (optional)

1. Pour dressing and lemon juice into a 1-cup measuring cup; refrigerate.

2. Wash Boston lettuce and romaine; remove cores; separate leaves; dry on paper towels or spin in a salad dryer.

3. To serve: Line salad bowl with some of romaine leaves. Tear rest of romaine and the lettuce into bite-size pieces. Turn into salad bowl; sprinkle with salt and pepper.

4. Mix dressing and lemon juice well. Pour over greens; toss lightly. Garnish with lemon quarters if desired. *Makes 6 servings.*

RASPBERRY CREME PARFAIT
(pictured)

1 pkg (10 oz) quick-thaw frozen raspberries
Water
1 tablespoon cornstarch
¼ cup currant jelly
2 tablespoons kirsch
1 pkg (3½ or 4 oz) instant vanilla pudding
    and pie filling

1. Thaw raspberries as package label directs; drain liquid and set aside. Add water to liquid to measure ¾ cup.

2. In small saucepan, blend raspberry liquid with cornstarch; bring to boiling over medium heat, stirring. Reduce heat, and simmer until translucent and slightly thickened—about 1 minute. Add jelly, kirsch and drained raspberries.

3. Cool sauce quickly by setting it in a bowl of ice cubes. Stir until cool—about 5 minutes.

4. Meanwhile, make vanilla pudding as package label directs.

5. Assemble parfait: In a large parfait glass or pretty 2-quart serving bowl, layer ½ cup raspberry sauce, then 1 cup vanilla pudding; repeat layering, ending with sauce. Place in refrigerator or freezer until serving time. *Makes 4 to 6 servings.*

SIRLOIN STEAK WITH RED WINE* PATE-STUFFED MUSHROOMS* BAKED TOMATO HALVES* CHILLED ASPARAGUS WITH MUSTARD DRESSING* POPPY-SEED ROLLS RUM-AND-FRUIT TORTE* RED WINE   COFFEE

*Recipes given for starred dishes.
This menu is pictured on pages 318 and 319.

SIRLOIN STEAK WITH RED WINE
(pictured)

4½- to 5-lb sirloin steak (see Note), about
    1½ inches thick
1 garlic clove, split
⅓ cup olive or salad oil
1½ teaspoons salt
½ teaspoon coarsely cracked pepper
1¼ teaspoons dried rosemary leaves
½ cup dry red wine
1 tablespoon butter or margarine

1. Preheat oven to 350F.

2. Wipe steak with damp paper towels. Rub each side with garlic; reserve garlic.

3. Heat oil in a large, heavy skillet until very hot.

4. Over high heat, brown steak very well on both sides—3 to 5 minutes per side.

5. Place steak on rack in shallow roasting pan. Sprinkle with salt, pepper and rosemary; add garlic. Insert meat thermometer in side of steak, making sure point is as close to center of meat as possible.

6. Bake in top part of oven 25 to 30

minutes, or until meat thermometer registers 130F, for medium rare. Remove thermometer; place steak on hot platter.

7. Pour fat from roasting pan; discard garlic. Add wine to pan, and bring to boiling, stirring to loosen brown particles. Stir in butter. Pour 2 tablespoons sauce over steak; pass the rest.

8. To serve, slice thinly on the diagonal. *Makes 6 to 8 servings.*

Note: Have steak at room temperature.

BAKED TOMATO HALVES
(pictured)

6 medium tomatoes
6 teaspoons prepared brown mustard
3 cups small, fresh bread cubes
4 tablespoons (½ stick) butter or
   margarine, melted
¼ teaspoon salt
⅛ teaspoon pepper
1½ teaspoons Worcestershire sauce
2 dashes hot red-pepper sauce

1. Preheat oven to 375F.
2. Wash tomatoes; halve crosswise. Place in shallow baking dish. Spread each half with ½ teaspoon mustard.
3. In small bowl, toss bread cubes with butter, salt, pepper, Worcestershire and pepper sauce. Spoon about 2 tablespoons evenly over each tomato half.
4. Bake 20 to 25 minutes, or until just tender and crumbs are golden. *Makes 6 servings.*

PATE-STUFFED MUSHROOMS
(pictured)

½ lb large fresh mushrooms
4 tablespoons (½ stick) butter or
   margarine
2 tablespoons dry sherry
2 cans (4¾-oz size) liver pâté

Dash pepper
1 tablespoon chopped parsley

1. Wipe mushrooms with damp paper towels. Remove stems; refrigerate to use another time.
2. In hot butter in skillet, over medium heat, sauté mushroom caps just until tender—2 or 3 minutes. Sprinkle with 1 tablespoon sherry; set skillet aside.
3. In small bowl, combine pâté, 1 tablespoon sherry, the pepper and half of parsley; mix well.
4. Spoon pâté mixture, or press through pastry bag with a number-5 star tip into mushroom caps, mounding high.
5. Reheat slightly in skillet just before serving. Arrange around steak; pour drippings from skillet over mushrooms. Sprinkle with remaining parsley. *Makes 6 servings.*

CHILLED ASPARAGUS WITH MUSTARD DRESSING

1 can (15 oz) green asparagus spears,
   drained
1 can (15 oz) white asparagus spears,
   drained
½ cup bottled herb-garlic dressing
2 tablespoons prepared brown mustard

1. Place asparagus in freezer, to chill quickly.
2. Combine dressing and mustard; mix well. Refrigerate.
3. To serve: Arrange asparagus on small platter. Spoon dressing over it. *Makes 6 servings.*

RUM-AND-FRUIT TORTE
(pictured)

8-inch packaged spongecake layer
Light rum
¾ cup whipped cream cheese
1 tablespoon confectioners' sugar
1 can (1 lb, 14 oz) cling-peach halves,
   drained
1 can (1 lb, 1 oz) pear halves, drained
1 can (3¼ oz) mandarin-orange sections,
   drained
1 tablespoon fruit preserves
¼ cup frozen blueberries
2 fresh strawberries or maraschino
   cherries with stems (optional)
¾ cup apple jelly
¼ cup chopped toasted almonds

1. Place cake layer on strips of waxed paper placed around edge of serving plate (to keep plate clean). Sprinkle cake with 2 or 3 tablespoons rum, to moisten.
2. In small bowl, beat cream cheese with confectioners' sugar until smooth. Spread on cake.
3. Dry all fruit well on paper towels.

Place a peach half, rounded side up, in center of cake. Arrange other peach halves, rounded sides up, around it. Place a pear half between each two peach halves. Arrange mandarin-orange sections between peaches and pears.

4. Top center peach with preserves. Mound slightly thawed berries on preserves. Top with a strawberry or cherry. If desired, decorate with pieces of fresh strawberry.
5. Melt jelly over low heat. Brush over fruit and around side of cake. Press chopped nuts around side of cake.
6. Carefully remove waxed-paper strips. Refrigerate cake (or place in freezer 10 minutes) until serving. *Makes 8 servings.*

PINEAPPLE-GLAZED BAKED HAM*
SCALLOPED-POTATO CASSEROLE*
ASPARAGUS WITH BROWNED BUTTER
ONION-TWIST ROLLS*
CHILLED MELON WITH PORT
THIN CHOCOLATE COOKIES
WHITE WINE   COFFEE

*Recipes given for starred dishes.

PINEAPPLE-GLAZED BAKED HAM

1 can (2 lb) boneless ham
¼ cup dry white wine

PINEAPPLE GLAZE
½ cup pineapple preserves
½ teaspoon dry mustard
Dash ground cloves

1. Preheat oven to 350F.
2. Place ham in small, shallow baking pan. Bake 10 minutes. Pour wine over ham; bake 20 minutes longer. Remove from oven.
3. Increase oven temperature to 450F.
4. Meanwhile, make Pineapple Glaze: In small bowl, combine preserves, mustard and cloves; mix well. Spread on top and sides of ham.
5. Bake ham 15 to 20 minutes, or until glaze is slightly browned. Remove to serving platter. *Makes 6 servings.*

SCALLOPED-POTATO CASSEROLE

1 pkg (5.25 oz) scalloped potatoes
¼ cup ready-to-use crumbled bacon
¼ cup chopped green onion

continued on page 322

continued from page 321

1. Preheat oven to 350F.
2. Prepare potatoes as package label directs, adding bacon and onion; mix.
3. Bake, uncovered, 50 minutes. *Makes 6 servings.*

ONION-TWIST ROLLS

½ cup sour cream
½ env (1⅜-oz size) dry onion-soup mix
1 pkg (8 oz) refrigerator crescent rolls

1. Preheat oven to 375F.
2. In small bowl, combine sour cream and onion-soup mix.
3. Spread out one rectangular section of roll dough. Cut in half crosswise. Cut each half lengthwise into four strips. Repeat with other section of dough.
4. Spread each strip evenly with 1 teaspoon sour-cream mixture. Twist each strip loosely 5 times. Place on ungreased cookie sheet.
5. Bake 10 to 12 minutes, or until golden-brown. Serve hot. *Makes 16.*

**HOT CRANBERRY BOUILLON
CARAWAY CHEESE TRIANGLES
CHICKEN LIVERS
EN BROCHETTE★
MUSHROOM RICE PILAF★
BUTTERED WHOLE GREEN BEANS
MAPLE-WALNUT SUNDAES
(VANILLA ICE CREAM,
MAPLE SYRUP, WALNUTS)
CHILLED WHITE WINE
COFFEE**

★Recipes given for starred dishes.

MUSHROOM RICE PILAF

¼ cup (½ stick) butter or margarine
1½ cups converted white rice
2 chicken-bouillon cubes, crumbled
¾ teaspoon salt
¼ teaspoon pepper
1 cup chopped mushroom stems
3½ cups boiling water
Chopped parsley

1. Preheat oven to 375F.
2. Melt butter in flameproof casserole. Add rice, and sauté, stirring, until lightly browned—about 10 minutes.
3. Add bouillon cubes, salt, pepper, chopped mushroom and boiling water; mix well. (Use mushroom caps for Chicken Livers en Brochette.)
4. Bake, tightly covered, 40 min-

---

utes, or until rice is tender and liquid is absorbed.
5. To serve: Fluff up pilaf with a fork, and turn out on serving platter. Sprinkle with the chopped parsley. *Makes 6 servings.*

CHICKEN LIVERS EN BROCHETTE

1½ lb chicken livers (about 18)
¾ teaspoon dried marjoram leaves
¾ teaspoon dried thyme leaves
¾ teaspoon salt
⅛ teaspoon pepper
12 large fresh mushrooms
9 slices bacon, halved crosswise
6 tablespoons (¾ stick) butter or margarine, melted
¼ cup dry white wine

1. Rinse chicken livers; pat dry with paper towels.
2. In medium bowl, combine the marjoram, thyme, salt and pepper. Add livers; toss to combine.
3. Remove stems from mushrooms; reserve for Rice Pilaf. Wipe mushroom caps with damp towels.
4. Wrap each liver in bacon. On each of 6 skewers, alternate 3 livers and 2 mushrooms. Arrange skewers on rack in broiling pan. Brush with half of butter.
5. Broil, 4 inches from heat, 5 minutes. Turn skewers; brush with remaining butter and the wine. Broil 5 to 7 minutes longer, or until bacon is crisp (livers should still be pink on inside).
6. Serve skewers on platter of Mushroom Rice Pilaf, above. *Makes 6 servings.*

**CUCUMBER CANAPES★
LEMON CHICKEN★
RICE AND VERMICELLI PARMESAN★
TOSSED GREEN SALAD
CRUSTY SALT STICKS
BAKED PEACHES★
ITALIAN RED WINE
COFFEE**

★Recipes given for starred dishes.

CUCUMBER CANAPES

2 medium cucumbers
1 jar (4 oz) red caviar
Parsley sprigs

1. Wash cucumbers well. Slice crosswise into rounds ¼ inch thick, making about 50 rounds.
2. Arrange on tray; spoon ¼ tea-

---

spoon red caviar in center of each round; top each with parsley sprig. *Makes 50.*

LEMON CHICKEN

2 chicken breasts (1½ lb), boned and skinned
1½ tablespoons plus ¼ cup salad oil
1 teaspoon salt
Dash pepper
6 medium-size dried Chinese mushrooms
1 large red pepper
2 whole lemons
6 green onions
½ teaspoon grated fresh ginger
2 teaspoons cornstarch
1½ teaspoons sugar
½ cup chicken broth
¼ cup dry sherry
2 tablespoons soy sauce
6 lemon slices
Hot rice (optional)
Soy sauce (optional)

1. Slice chicken into ¼-inch-wide strips. In small bowl, combine 1½ tablespoons oil, the salt and pepper. Add chicken; mix well. Set aside for 30 minutes.

2. In small bowl, soak mushrooms in 1½ cups warm water for 30 minutes.

3. Wash pepper; cut in half and remove ribs and seeds. Cut into thin julienne strips.

4. With sharp paring knife, remove peel from whole lemon in strips; cut into pieces ⅛ inch wide. Squeeze lemon to make 3 tablespoons juice; set aside.

5. Wash green onions; cut into ½-inch diagonal slices. Drain mushrooms; remove and discard stems. Slice caps into ⅛-inch-wide strips.

6. In large heavy skillet or wok, heat ¼ cup salad oil. Add chicken, and stir-fry 2 minutes. Remove from skillet; keep warm.

7. Add ginger, mushrooms and red pepper. Stir-fry 1 minute. Add lemon peel and green onions. Stir-fry 1 minute longer.

8. In small bowl, combine cornstarch, sugar, chicken broth, sherry, soy sauce and reserved lemon juice; mix until smooth. Add to vegetables, and cook, stirring, until thickened.

9. Return chicken to skillet; stir 1 minute, or until vegetables and chicken are well coated. Turn out into warm serving dish. Garnish with lemon slices. Serve with rice and more soy sauce, if desired. *Makes 6 servings.*

RICE AND VERMICELLI PARMESAN

1 pkg (8 oz) chicken-flavored rice-and-vermicelli mix
3 tablespoons butter or margarine
½ cup grated Parmesan cheese

1. Cook rice as label directs.
2. Just before serving, toss with butter and cheese. *Makes 6 servings.*

BAKED PEACHES

1 can (1 lb, 14 oz) cling-peach halves
16 macaroons
½ cup dry sherry

1. Preheat oven to 350F.
2. Drain peach halves, reserving ½ cup syrup. Arrange, rounded side down, in a single layer in shallow baking dish.
3. Crumble macaroons into medium bowl; toss with 2 tablespoons syrup from peaches.
4. Fill peach halves with macaroon mixture.
5. Combine remaining syrup with sherry; pour over peaches. Bake 20 minutes. Serve warm. *Makes 6 servings.*

ANTIPASTO PLATTER
SHRIMP IN SHELL★
SPAGHETTI WITH BUTTER AND CHEESE
BROCCOLI WITH LEMON
BREAD STICKS
QUICK SICILIAN CHEESECAKE★
ITALIAN WHITE WINE
COFFEE

★Recipes given for starred dishes.

SHRIMP IN SHELL

2½ lb unshelled shrimp
1 cup (2 sticks) butter or margarine, melted
2 tablespoons lemon juice
3 garlic cloves, crushed
2 tablespoons white wine
½ cup olive or salad oil
1 teaspoon salt
1 tablespoon cracked black pepper
Chopped parsley

1. Rinse shrimp and pat dry with paper towels. Place in shallow broiling pan.
2. In small bowl, mix butter, lemon juice, garlic, white wine and oil. Pour over shrimp; sprinkle with some of salt and cracked black pepper.
3. Broil, 6 inches from heat, 6 minutes. Turn shrimp. Sprinkle with salt and pepper; broil 6 minutes. Serve in shells, sprinkled with chopped parsley. *Makes 4 to 6 servings.*

QUICK SICILIAN CHEESECAKE

⅓ cup light rum
¾ cup candied mixed fruit
2 pkg (11-oz size) cheesecake mix
¼ cup sugar
⅔ cup (1⅓ sticks) butter or margarine, melted
2 cups milk
1 teaspoon grated lemon peel
¾ cup ricotta cheese, well drained

1. In small bowl, combine rum and ½ cup candied fruit; let stand.
2. In medium bowl, combine graham-cracker crumbs from both packages of cheesecake mix, the sugar and butter; mix well. Turn into 8-inch springform pan, patting evenly on bottom and 2 inches up side of pan. Refrigerate.
3. In small bowl, combine 2 envelopes cheesecake mix, the milk and lemon peel. Drain rum from fruit; add

rum to cheesecake mixture. With electric mixer, beat at low speed 1 minute, to blend; then at high speed 1 minute.

4. With mixer at low speed, gradually beat in ricotta; then beat at high speed 30 seconds, to blend.

5. Stir in rum-flavored candied fruit. Spoon cheesecake mixture into crumb-lined pan. Decorate cake with remaining candied fruit.

6. Chill in freezer 30 minutes before serving. (May also be chilled in refrigerator 1½ hours before serving.) *Makes 8 to 10 servings.*

HOT CLAM BROTH
FILLET OF SOLE WITH LOBSTER SAUCE★
POTATO PUFFS
BUTTERED SQUASH CREOLE
ASSORTED HOT ROLLS
ORANGE SHERBET WITH FRESH-RASPBERRY SAUCE
WHITE WINE   COFFEE

★Recipes given for starred dishes.

FILLET OF SOLE WITH LOBSTER SAUCE

2 cans (10¾-oz size) semi-condensed lobster bisque (see Note)
2½ lb fresh sole fillets or thawed frozen fillets
½ teaspoon salt
⅛ teaspoon pepper
¼ teaspoon dried tarragon leaves
2 tablespoons lemon juice
¼ cup plus 2 tablespoons dry white wine
3 tablespoons butter or margarine
2 tablespoons light cream
¼ cup grated Parmesan cheese

1. Preheat oven to 425F.
2. Place cans of bisque in a bowl; cover with hot water, and let stand 20 minutes, to partially thaw.
3. Meanwhile, prepare fillets: Wipe fillets with paper towels. Spread flat on waxed paper; sprinkle with ¼ teaspoon salt and dash pepper. Roll up each fillet, and place in shallow baking dish, seam side down. Sprinkle with remaining salt and pepper, the tarragon, lemon juice and ¼ cup wine. Dot with butter.
4. Bake, uncovered, 20 minutes. Remove from oven; pour broth into small saucepan. Cover fish rolls with foil, to keep warm.
5. Bring broth to a boil; let boil, uncovered, about 10 minutes, to reduce to ⅓ cup.

continued on page 324

continued from page 323

6. Meanwhile, in medium saucepan, combine bisque with remaining wine and the cream. Bring just to boiling, stirring to blend smoothly. Stir in broth.

7. Pour lobster sauce over fillets, covering them completely. Sprinkle with cheese. Place pan on broiler rack 4 inches from heat, and broil 3 to 5 minutes, or until browned. *Makes 6 servings.*

Note: If lobster bisque is not available, you may substitute 2 cans (10¾-oz size) condensed cream of shrimp soup and increase cream to ¼ cup. If desired, before adding sauce, top fish rolls with 1 can (4¼ oz) medium shrimp (rinsed and drained).

PATE MAISON
QUICK CASSOULET★
FRENCH BREAD
TOSSED GREEN SALAD
FRUIT COMPOTE WITH KIRSCH★
ALMOND WAFERS
WHITE WINE   COFFEE

★Recipes given for starred dishes.

QUICK CASSOULET

4 slices bacon, coarsely chopped
2-lb broiler-fryer, cut up
6 Italian sweet sausages, or 6 brown-and-serve sausages
1½ cups chopped onion
1 garlic clove, finely chopped
½ cup chopped parsley
2 cans (8-oz size) tomato sauce
1 cup dry white wine
1 teaspoon salt
½ teaspoon cracked black pepper
1 bay leaf
3 cans (20-oz size) white kidney beans, drained

1. Preheat oven to 375F.
2. In 5-quart, flameproof casserole or Dutch oven, cook bacon until crisp. Remove with slotted spoon; drain on paper towels.
3. In hot bacon drippings, brown chicken and sausages, turning to brown evenly. Remove to baking pan as they brown. Bake, uncovered, about 10 minutes.
4. Meanwhile, to remaining drippings in casserole, add onion, garlic and parsley; cook over medium heat till onion is golden—about 5 minutes.
5. Add tomato sauce, wine, salt, pepper and bay leaf; bring to boiling. Reduce heat; add beans; mix well. Remove chicken and sausages from oven,

and add to casserole. Sprinkle with bacon.

6. Bake, uncovered, 30 minutes, or until chicken is tender. *Makes 6 to 8 servings.*

FRUIT COMPOTE WITH KIRSCH

3 pkg (10-oz size) frozen quick-thaw mixed fruit
¼ cup kirsch
3 bananas, sliced on diagonal
1 can (1 lb) whole peeled apricots, drained

1. Thaw frozen fruit 10 minutes, as package label directs.
2. In a 2- or 3-quart compote, combine mixed fruit, kirsch, banana and apricots; toss lightly to combine. Refrigerate until serving. *Makes 6 servings.*

GALA FRUIT CUP★
FLANK STEAK STROGANOFF★
PARSLEY-BUTTERED
GREEN NOODLES
SLICED MARINATED CUCUMBERS
CRUSTY WHOLE-WHEAT BREAD
MOCHA-NUT PIE★
RED WINE   COFFEE

★Recipes given for starred dishes.

GALA FRUIT CUP

1 pkg (12 oz) frozen melon balls
1 can (13¼ oz) frozen pineapple chunks
1 pint lemon sherbet
1 split (6½ oz) champagne, chilled

1. Put melon balls and pineapple chunks in a bowl of cold water to thaw partially—about 30 minutes.
2. To serve: Arrange fruit in 6 sherbet dishes, dividing evenly. Using small scoop or tablespoon, spoon sherbet over fruit, dividing evenly. Add champagne. Serve at once. *Makes 6 servings.*

FLANK STEAK STROGANOFF

2¼-lb flank steak
6 tablespoons (¾ stick) butter or margarine
1 garlic clove, halved
1 cup chopped onion
2 cans (6-oz size) button mushrooms, drained
3 tablespoons all-purpose flour
½ teaspoon salt
⅛ teaspoon pepper
3 beef-bouillon cubes, crumbled

1 can (10½ oz) condensed beef broth, undiluted
¼ cup dry white wine
1 tablespoon snipped fresh dill, or
**   1½ teaspoons dried dillweed**
1 cup sour cream

1. Place steak in freezer 15 minutes; it will be easier to slice.
2. Trim off excess fat. Slice steak, ¼ inch thick, across the grain. Cut long strips into 2½-inch pieces.
3. In large skillet, heat 2 tablespoons butter until very hot. Add sliced steak (just enough to cover bottom of pan); brown quickly on both sides. Remove from pan as it browns; continue browning the rest of the beef.
4. Add remaining butter to skillet. Sauté garlic, onion and mushrooms 5 minutes. Remove from heat. Discard garlic.
5. Stir in flour, salt and pepper until smooth; add bouillon cubes. Gradually stir in broth. Bring to boiling, stirring until thickened; reduce heat; simmer 5 minutes.
6. Over low heat, stir in wine, dill and sour cream. Add the browned beef; heat slowly until thoroughly hot. *Makes 6 to 8 servings.*

MOCHA-NUT PIE

1¼ cups packaged graham-cracker crumbs
¼ cup sugar
¼ cup (½ stick) butter or margarine, softened
1 pkg (2.8-oz size) whipped-topping mix
1 tablespoon instant coffee
1 teaspoon vanilla extract
Butter or margarine
1 pkg (14.3 oz) creamy-fudge-frosting mix
⅓ cup chopped walnuts

1. Mix crumbs, sugar and ¼ cup butter until well combined. Press evenly into bottom and side of 9-inch pie plate—not on rim.
2. Prepare both envelopes of whipped topping as package label directs. Refrigerate, covered.
3. In large bowl, using electric mixer, make frosting mix as package label directs, adding coffee and vanilla to the liquid and butter called for. Beat at medium speed until smooth and creamy—about 1 minute.
4. With a rubber spatula, gently fold half of chilled whipped topping into frosting until smooth. Fold in remaining topping until blended.
5. Pour into prepared crust, mounding high in center.
6. Place in freezer 45 minutes, or until chilled. Or refrigerate overnight.
7. To serve, sprinkle chopped nuts in a ring over pie. *Makes 8 servings.* ◆

continued from page 315

2. Adjust grill 5 inches from prepared coals. Place foil package, seam side down, at edge of grill. Grill 20 minutes. Using tongs, turn foil package. Grill 10 minutes longer, or just until squash is tender. To serve: Fold back foil; mix vegetables lightly. *Makes 4 to 6 servings.*

TO COOK INDOORS

Combine all ingredients with ¼ cup water in medium skillet. Cook, covered, over medium heat, stirring occasionally, 10 to 15 minutes, or until squash is tender.

DESSERTS

BUTTERED-RUM PINEAPPLE

½ cup finely chopped macadamia nuts
1 large pineapple
½ cup butter or margarine
½ cup honey
¼ cup rum
1 quart vanilla ice cream

1. Preheat oven to 400F. Spread macadamia nuts, in a single layer, on baking sheet; bake until golden-brown— about 5 minutes; set aside. Peel and cut pineapple crosswise into 8 (1-inch-thick) slices. Score edges at 1½-inch intervals.

2. In small saucepan, over medium heat, stir butter with honey and rum until butter melts. Remove pan from heat; with fork, dip each pineapple slice into butter mixture. Turn to coat both sides; drain off excess; reserve.

3. Prepare outdoor grill for barbecue, or preheat broiler. Place pineapple on lightly oiled grill or broiler rack. Using Direct Method, grill slices, 6 inches from prepared coals, turning once, until browned slightly on both sides.

4. When pineapple slices are cool enough to handle, coat edges with toasted nuts. Place on eight serving plates; top each slice with a scoop of vanilla ice cream. Top with reserved butter mixture and garnish with remaining nuts. *Makes 8 servings.*

CRUNCH-TOPPED PEACH-ORANGE PIE

FILLING

8 cups peeled, pitted and sliced peaches (about 9 medium peaches)
1 cup granulated sugar
3 tablespoons quick-cooking tapioca
2 tablespoons grated orange peel
1 tablespoon orange juice

9-inch unbaked pie shell

TOPPING

⅓ cup firmly packed light-brown sugar
⅓ cup unsifted all-purpose flour
2 tablespoons unsalted butter or margarine, softened
1 cup coarsely chopped pecans

Whipped cream (optional)
Fresh peach slices (optional)

1. Preheat oven to 425F. Make Filling: In large bowl, combine 8 cups peaches, the granulated sugar, tapioca, orange peel and orange juice; toss to mix well. Spoon into unbaked pie shell; set aside.

2. Make Topping: In small bowl, combine brown sugar and flour. With a pastry blender or two forks, cut in butter until mixture is crumbly; stir in chopped pecans. Sprinkle over peaches in pie shell.

3. Place pie on rimmed baking sheet. Bake 15 minutes; cover loosely with foil; reduce heat to 400F. Bake 35 to 40 minutes longer, or until peaches are tender. Serve with whipped cream and fresh peach slices, if desired. *Makes 8 servings.*

STRAWBERRY-RHUBARB SORBET

½ cup sugar
½ cup water
5 cups chopped fresh rhubarb
1 pint strawberries, hulled
¾ cup unsweetened pink grapefruit juice
2 tablespoons framboise liqueur

1. In medium saucepan, bring sugar and water to boiling. Add rhubarb; return to boiling. Reduce heat; cover and simmer until soft, 5 minutes.

2. Place the strawberries in a food processor. Add rhubarb; puree. Add grapefruit juice and framboise; process to combine.

3. Pour into 13-by-9-by-2-inch pan. Refrigerate until cold. Freeze until edges are firm; stir. Freeze until solid. Cut into 1-inch pieces. Process in food processor until smooth and creamy but still frozen. (Process in batches, if necessary. Do not overprocess.) Serve immediately or place in containers and freeze until ready to serve. If frozen, let soften slightly before serving. *Makes 8 to 10 servings.*

TIRAMI SU

1 container (8 oz) low-fat cottage cheese
1 container (8 oz) low-fat vanilla-flavored yogurt
3 tablespoons sugar
½ teaspoon vanilla extract
½ pkg (10 oz) fat-free poundcake
3 tablespoons very strong coffee
2 tablespoons dark rum
1 square (1 oz) semisweet chocolate, grated
¼ teaspoon unsweetened cocoa powder

1. In food processor, puree cottage cheese. Add yogurt, sugar and vanilla; process until blended.

2. Cut the poundcake into 8 slices; arrange on baking sheet. In cup, combine coffee and rum; brush over cake slices.

3. In each of 4 goblets, layer 3 tablespoons cheese mixture, 1 cake slice and 1 tablespoon grated chocolate. Top with 1 cake slice and 3 tablespoons cheese mixture; sprinkle with cocoa powder. Serve immediately or refrigerate until ready to serve. If desired, serve with milk-chocolate twig-shaped candies. *Makes 4 servings.* ◆

NINE

HOLIDAY CELEBRATIONS

◆

The holidays are a wonderfully joyous time when we all love to entertain friends and family. But the hectic pace of this festive season can make even the most organized and efficient host or hostess weary. So that you can relax a bit and really enjoy the holidays, we offer this section of special make-ahead, make-it-easy beverages, appetizers, main dishes and desserts. Add some sparkle to your holiday get-togethers with party-pleasing punches and finger foods that actually get you out of the kitchen and into the fun. Feast your eyes—and taste buds—on our marvelous do-ahead cookies, cakes, candies and pies that can be prepared days or even weeks before you serve them (or give them away as much-appreciated gifts). We've also included recipes for last-minute cakes in case a party catches you by surprise. And when the feasting is all over, you'll discover new ways to turn leftovers into delightfully easy post-holiday dishes.

INSTANT HOSPITALITY

Entertaining during the holidays should be relaxed and full of good cheer, not laden with the chore of hurried, last-minute food preparation. Whether your holiday plans include a get-together for fifty or just a few, the same principle applies—do it with flair, but do it ahead. For your next party, invite our festive collection of make-ahead beverages and hors d'oeuvres that sparkle with excitement—and ease. Pictured from left to right, some punches with pizzazz: piping-hot Wassail; icy Whiskey-Sour Punch; fruited Champagne Punch; and a fern-trimmed Daiquiri Punch. Recipes for these and other party beverages and food begin on the following page.

continued from page 329

VODKA WASSAIL BOWL

(pictured)

Whole cloves
3 large oranges
1 gallon apple juice
½ cup lemon juice
10 (2-inch) cinnamon sticks
2 cups vodka
¼ cup brandy

1. Preheat oven to 350F.
2. Insert cloves, ½ inch apart, in unpeeled oranges. Place in shallow pan; bake, uncovered, 30 minutes.
3. Meanwhile, heat apple juice in large kettle until bubbles form around edge of kettle.
4. Add lemon juice, cinnamon sticks and baked oranges. Heat, covered, over low heat, 30 minutes. Remove from heat.
5. Add vodka, brandy; mix well. Pour into punch bowl. Serve warm. *Makes about 36 (4-oz) servings.*

CRANBERRY FLOAT

1 quart cranberry juice, chilled
½ cup orange juice, chilled
1 tablespoon lemon juice
2 cups ginger ale, chilled
1 pint orange sherbet

1. Combine juices in punch bowl. Pour in ginger ale.
2. Top with small scoops of sherbet. Serve at once. *Makes 14 servings.*

WHISKEY-SOUR PUNCH

(pictured)

1 can (6 oz) frozen orange-juice
 concentrate, undiluted
1 can (6 oz) frozen lemon-juice
 concentrate, undiluted
1 tablespoon angostura bitters
2 tablespoons sugar
1 jar (8 oz) maraschino cherries
1 bottle (¾ quart) whisky-sour cocktail,
 chilled
1 bottle (1 pint, 12 oz) club soda, chilled
Ice Block, recipe follows
1 large navel orange, thinly sliced
1 lemon, thinly sliced

1. In pitcher or bowl, combine frozen fruit-juice concentrates, bitters, sugar and syrup drained from maraschino cherries. When juices are thawed, stir until well blended. Refrigerate, with cherries, until well chilled—several hours or overnight.
2. To serve: In punch bowl, combine fruit-juice mixture, whisky-sour cocktail and club soda; mix well.
3. Float Ice Block in punch. Place cherries, orange and lemon slices around ice, as pictured. *Makes about 18 (4-oz) servings.*

ICE BLOCK

Day before using, make Ice Block: Fill a bowl with 2 quarts water, and let stand at room temperature 1 hour. Stir occasionally to release air bubbles. Mound 2 trayfuls of ice cubes in a 2-quart, fancy round mold; fill with the water. Freeze until firm. To unmold: Dip mold in warm water until ice loosens; turn out on waxed paper. Return to freezer if not using at once.

FROSTY DAIQUIRI PUNCH

(pictured)

Fern Ice Block, recipe follows
Frosted Punch Bowl, recipe follows
1 bottle (16 oz) daiquiri mix
6 tablespoons superfine sugar
2½ cups light rum
½ cup orange-flavored liqueur
2 dozen ice cubes
1 bottle (1 pint, 12 oz) club soda, chilled

1. Day ahead, prepare Fern Ice Block and Frosted Punch Bowl.
2. In pitcher or bowl, combine daiquiri mix and sugar, and stir until sugar is dissolved. Add rum and orange-flavored liqueur.
3. Refrigerate, stirring occasionally, until well chilled—about 3 hours.
4. To serve: Place Fern Ice Block in Frosted Punch Bowl, as pictured. Place half of daiquiri mixture and 1 dozen ice cubes in electric blender; blend, at high speed, 15 to 20 seconds. Pour into punch bowl. Repeat with remaining mixture and ice. Stir in club soda. *Makes about 20 (4-oz) servings.*

Note: You may use 2 (6-ounce) cans frozen daiquiri mix. If blender is not available, crush ice cubes very fine. Place with daiquiri mixture in jar with tight-fitting lid. Shake vigorously 1 minute.

FERN ICE BLOCK

1. Day before using, make Ice Block: Pour 2 cups cold water into a 2½-quart bowl. Freeze until thin coating of ice forms on top—about 2 hours.
2. Meanwhile, wash 5 fern tips and trim to 5 inches long. Also, wash 1 bunch (1½ lb) green grapes. Break ice in bowl, and arrange ferns against side of bowl, tip ends up. Arrange grapes in center.
3. Place in freezer until grapes and water are frozen. Then fill bowl with water. Freeze overnight.
4. To unmold: Dip bowl in warm water until ice loosens. Turn out on waxed paper. Return to freezer if not using at once.

FROSTED PUNCH BOWL

Beat 1 egg white with 1 tablespoon water. Use to brush a band about 1½ inches wide on outside of punch bowl, at top. Sprinkle sheet of waxed paper with granulated sugar. Roll edge of bowl in sugar, to frost it. Let stand at room temperature about 20 minutes; then roll in sugar again. Set aside to dry—3 to 4 hours or overnight.

ORANGE BLOSSOMS

3 cups orange juice
½ cup lemon juice
½ cup grenadine
1 bottle (¾ quart) martini cocktail, chilled
1 bottle (1 pint, 12 oz) club soda, chilled

1. In large pitcher or bowl, combine orange juice, lemon juice and grenadine; stir until well blended. Refrigerate until well chilled—several hours.
2. To serve: Add martini cocktail and club soda to fruit-juice mixture; mix well. Pour over ice in old-fashioned glasses. *Makes about 20 (4-oz) servings.*

CHAMPAGNE PUNCH BOWL

(pictured)

1 large bunch seedless green grapes (about
 1½ lb)
2 cups sauterne
1 cup cognac
2 tablespoons sugar
2 bottles (7-oz size) club soda, chilled
6 strawberries, hulls on, washed (optional)
1 bottle (⅘ quart) champagne, chilled

1. Day ahead: Wash grapes; place on small tray. Place in freezer.
2. Several hours before serving: In pitcher or bowl, combine sauterne, cognac and sugar; stir until sugar is dissolved. Refrigerate.
3. To serve: Pour sauterne mixture into punch bowl. Stir in soda. Add frozen grapes and the strawberries.
4. Pour champagne into punch just before serving. *Makes about 16 (4-oz) servings.*

CHRISTMAS PUNCH

1 bottle (6 oz) frozen lemon juice, undiluted
1 can (6 oz) frozen orange-juice concentrate, undiluted
1 cup sugar
¼ cup angostura bitters
3 egg whites
1 bottle (¾ quart) daiquiri cocktail, chilled
1 bottle (1 pint, 12 oz) club soda, chilled
1 tray ice cubes
1 bottle (⅘ quart) champagne, chilled

1. In pitcher or bowl, combine frozen concentrates, sugar and bitters. When juices are thawed, stir until they are well blended and sugar is dissolved.
2. Refrigerate the fruit-juice mixture, covered, until it is well chilled—several hours or overnight.
3. Just before serving, beat egg whites until stiff.
4. In punch bowl, combine fruit-juice mixture, daiquiri cocktail and club soda. With wire whisk or rotary beater, gently beat in egg whites. Add ice cubes.
5. Pour champagne into punch at table. *Makes about 24 (4-oz) servings.*

OLD ENGLISH EGGNOG

6 egg yolks
1 cup granulated sugar
2 quarts light cream
1 pint cognac
1 cup light rum
6 egg whites
½ cup confectioners' sugar

1. In large bowl, beat egg yolks until thick. Gradually add granulated sugar, beating until light.
2. Add cream; beat until very well combined. Slowly stir in cognac and rum. Refrigerate, covered, until well chilled.
3. About 1 hour before serving, beat the egg whites until they are foamy. Gradually add the confectioners' sugar, beating well after each addition. Continue beating until soft peaks form when the beaters are slowly raised. Gently fold into egg-yolk mixture.
4. Refrigerate, covered, until serving time. *Makes about 28 (4-oz) servings.*

COCKTAIL FOOD

HOT AND SWEET SAUSAGE

2 lb hot Italian link sausage
2 lb sweet Italian link sausage
¼ lb onion, cut into ¼-inch-thick slices

1. Wash sausage and dry with paper towels. Separate into links.
2. In skillet with tight-fitting cover, brown sausage, a single layer at a time, on all sides. Remove sausage as it browns.
3. When all sausage is browned, return to skillet with onion slices. Reduce heat and simmer, covered, 30 minutes.
4. Remove sausage from pan and drain well. Drain onion slices. With sharp knife, cut each sausage link, on the diagonal, into ½-inch-thick slices.
5. Place sausage and onion slices in a heated serving dish or chafing dish and serve immediately. *Makes 20 servings.*

BAKED COCKTAIL FRANKS

2 tablespoons butter or margarine, softened
2 teaspoons prepared mustard
1 pkg (8 oz) refrigerator crescent rolls
24 cocktail frankfurters, plain or smoked (about ½ lb)
1 egg yolk
1 tablespoon water
1 tablespoon caraway seeds

1. Preheat oven to 375F. Grease a cookie sheet.
2. In small bowl, combine butter with mustard; mix well.
3. Unroll dough from package of crescent rolls. Separate into 4 rectangular pieces; pinch each piece together at perforations to make dough solid. Spread with mustard-butter mixture. Cut each piece crosswise into 6 strips.
4. Place a frankfurter on end of each strip. Roll up and pinch dough together to secure. Place, seam side down, on prepared cookie sheet.
5. Beat egg yolk with water. Brush over top of rolls. Sprinkle with caraway seeds and press seeds lightly into rolls.
6. Bake 10 to 12 minutes, or until golden-brown. Serve hot. *Makes 24.*

Note: To make ahead: Prepare Steps 1 through 5. Refrigerate, covered, about 2 hours. Bake as directed.

CREAM CHEESE WITH RED CAVIAR

2 pkg (8-oz size) cream cheese
1 jar (4 oz) red caviar, slightly drained
Pumpernickel slices

1. Let cream cheese stand at room temperature to soften—about 1 hour. Then, on serving tray, shape into a mound about 5 inches in diameter; flatten top. Refrigerate, covered.
2. To serve: Spoon caviar over top of cream cheese, letting a little drizzle over side. Surround Cream Cheese With Red Caviar with pumpernickel slices. *Makes 30 servings.*

PARSLEY-TRIMMED SWEET-ONION SANDWICHES

48 slices thin-sliced white bread
½ cup (1 stick) butter or margarine, softened
Seasoned salt
Seasoned pepper
2 lb sweet onions
½ cup mayonnaise or cooked salad dressing
2 cups chopped parsley

1. With 2-inch round cookie cutter, cut 2 rounds from each bread slice. Spread rounds lightly with butter, then sprinkle lightly with salt and pepper. Arrange rounds on tray and cover loosely with damp paper towels. Set aside.
2. Peel onions and cut into ⅛-inch-thick slices. Cut with 2-inch cookie cutter to make 48 rounds.
3. Make sandwiches: Place 1 onion round between 2 prepared bread rounds and press together gently.
4. With small spatula, lightly spread mayonnaise around edge of each sandwich (about ½ teaspoon per sandwich). Then roll edge in parsley.
5. Cover; refrigerate, to develop flavor, about 2 hours.
6. To serve: Stack sandwiches, pyramid fashion, on serving plate. *Makes 4 dozen.* ◆

NO TIME TO LOSE

*H*omemade cookies, candies and cakes are as much a part of Christmas as Santa Claus. Besides gracing your own holiday table, such sweet delights make wonderfully delicious gifts for hard-to-buy-for friends, neighbors and acquaintances. This season, in addition to your traditional family favorites, why not include a few of our marvelous make-ahead goodies in your baking plans? They can all be made several weeks in advance, and each recipe gives simple storage directions to ensure just-made freshness in every bite. Among the treats spilling from Santa's sack: almond-studded Danish Spice Cookies, Candied-Grapefruit Baskets and a Cardamom Wreath festively decorated with candied cherries and citron. Turn the page for a collection of make-ahead sweets that say, "Happy Holidays."

continued from page 333

LEBKUCHEN ROUNDS
(pictured)

3 cups sifted all-purpose flour
½ teaspoon baking soda
½ teaspoon salt
1 teaspoon ground allspice
1 teaspoon ground nutmeg
1 teaspoon ground cinnamon
1 teaspoon ground cloves
1 jar (4 oz) citron,* finely chopped
1 can (4 oz) walnuts, finely chopped
1 cup honey
¾ cup light-brown sugar, firmly packed
1 egg
1 tablespoon lemon juice
2 teaspoons grated lemon peel

GLAZE
2 cups sifted confectioners' sugar
3 tablespoons water
Candied cherries (optional)
Angelica (optional)
Blanched almonds

DO AHEAD

1. Sift flour with baking soda, salt and spices; set aside. Toss citron with walnuts; set aside.

2. Warm honey in small saucepan. Remove from heat.

3. In large bowl, using portable electric mixer at medium speed, beat brown sugar and egg until smooth and fluffy.

4. Add lemon juice and honey; beat well. Beat in lemon peel and 1 cup flour mixture; beat until smooth.

5. Using wooden spoon, stir in rest of flour mixture until well combined. Stir in citron-nut mixture.

6. Refrigerate dough, covered, overnight.

NEXT DAY

7. Preheat oven to 375F. Lightly grease 2 cookie sheets.

8. On lightly floured surface, roll out dough, one-half at a time, ¼ inch thick. (Refrigerate remaining half until ready to roll out.)

9. Using floured 2-inch round cookie cutter, cut out cookies. Place, 2 inches apart, on prepared cookie sheets; bake 15 minutes. Remove to wire rack; cool slightly.

10. Meanwhile, make Glaze: Combine confectioners' sugar with water; stir until smooth.

11. Brush glaze on warm cookies. Decorate with candied-cherry, angelica bits and blanched almonds, if desired. Let cookies cool completely.

TO STORE

12. Store, tightly covered, in a cool, dry place 2 to 3 weeks before using. (To keep cookies moist, keep a slice of bread in container, changing bread from time-to-time, to prevent molding.) *Makes 3 dozen.*

*Or use ½ cup mixed candied fruit, finely chopped.

SPICED PEAR BUTTER
(pictured)

12 fresh pears (about 6 lb)
¼ cup cider vinegar
¼ cup water
4 cups sugar
½ cup orange juice
¼ cup lemon juice
1½ teaspoons whole allspice, tied in a cheesecloth bag
Hot paraffin for sealing

DO AHEAD

1. Pare and core pears; cut into 1-inch cubes, to make 3 quarts. Place in 5-quart kettle with vinegar and water; cook, covered, until soft—about 30 minutes.

2. Mash with potato masher, or put through food mill. Measure pulp—there should be about 7 cups. Return to kettle.

3. Add sugar, orange juice, lemon juice and allspice; cook over medium heat, stirring frequently, until mixture is very thick—about 60 minutes. Remove allspice.

4. Meanwhile, sterilize 6 or 7 (8-oz) jelly glasses by boiling 10 minutes. Leave in hot water until ready to fill. Lift out with tongs.

5. Ladle pear butter into hot, sterilized jars, filling to within ½ inch of top. Cover immediately with about ⅛-inch hot paraffin; cool. Cover with metal lids.

TO STORE

6. When jars are cool enough to move, store in a dark, dry, cool place where temperature holds at about 60F. *Makes 6 or 7 (8-oz) glasses.*

DANISH SPICE COOKIES
(pictured)

3½ cups sifted cake flour
1 teaspoon ground cinnamon
½ teaspoon ground allspice
½ teaspoon ground cloves
½ teaspoon ground cardamom
¾ cup (1½ sticks) butter or margarine
½ cup light-brown sugar, firmly packed
½ cup dark corn syrup
1 teaspoon baking soda
1 tablespoon boiling water
½ cup finely chopped blanched almonds
1 teaspoon grated orange peel

Blanched almonds or candied cherries, for decoration

DO AHEAD

1. Sift flour with cinnamon, allspice, cloves and cardamom. Set aside.

2. In medium saucepan, combine butter, sugar and corn syrup; cook over medium heat, stirring constantly, until sugar is melted and mixture is hot, but not boiling. Remove from heat.

3. Dissolve soda in boiling water; stir into hot mixture. Pour into large bowl; let cool to lukewarm.

4. Stir in chopped almonds and orange peel. Add flour mixture, half at a time, stirring after each addition until well blended.

5. Refrigerate, covered, overnight.

NEXT DAY

6. Preheat oven to 375F. Lightly grease cookie sheets. Divide dough in fourths. Refrigerate until ready to roll out.

7. On lightly floured surface, roll out one-fourth of dough to about a 10-inch square—dough will be thin. Cut with 3½-inch diamond or 2½-inch round, fluted cookie cutter. Reroll scraps, and cut. Place on prepared cookie sheets. Decorate each with almond half or candied cherry. Repeat with rest of dough.

8. Bake 6 to 8 minutes, or until lightly browned. Remove to wire rack; cool completely.

TO STORE

9. Store cookies in an airtight container. *Makes about 8 dozen.*

McCALL'S BEST BLACK FRUITCAKE
(pictured)

FRUIT MIXTURE
2 cups coarsely chopped walnuts or pecans
2 cans (4½-oz size) blanched almonds, coarsely chopped
1 lb candied pineapple slices, cut into thin wedges
1 pkg (15 oz) light raisins
1½ cups seeded dark raisins
1 cup currants
1 jar (8 oz) candied red cherries, halved
1 jar (4 oz) diced candied citron
¼ cup diced candied lemon peel
¼ cup diced candied orange peel
½ cup golden rum

CAKE BATTER
2 cups all-purpose flour
½ teaspoon baking soda

½ teaspoon ground mace
½ teaspoon ground cinnamon
½ cup (1 stick) butter or margarine,
    softened
1 cup granulated sugar
1 cup light-brown sugar, firmly packed
5 eggs
1 teaspoon almond extract

Golden rum
1 can (8 oz) almond paste
Frosting Glaze, recipe follows

DO AHEAD

1. Prepare Fruit Mixture: In large kettle, combine walnuts, almonds, pineapple, light raisins, dark raisins, currants, cherries, citron, lemon peel, orange peel and ½ cup rum; using hands, mix well. Let stand at room temperature, covered, overnight.

NEXT DAY

2. Line a 10-inch tube pan. On heavy brown paper, draw a 16½-inch circle, and cut out. Set pan in center of circle; draw around base of pan and tube. (See sketch, this page.) With pencil lines outside, fold paper into eighths; snip off tip. Unfold circle; cut along folds to circle drawn around base of pan. Grease both tube pan and paper well; fit paper, greased side up, into pan.

3. Make Cake Batter: Preheat oven to 275F. Sift flour with baking soda, mace and cinnamon; set aside.

4. In large bowl, with electric mixer at high speed, beat butter, sugars, eggs and almond extract until smooth and fluffy—about 5 minutes.

5. At low speed, beat in flour mixture just until combined.

6. Add batter to fruit mixture; with hands, mix until well combined. Turn into prepared pan, packing firmly and evenly.

7. Bake 3 to 3½ hours, or until cake tester inserted in center comes out clean. Let cool completely in pan on wire rack. Turn out of pan; peel off paper.

TO STORE

8. Wrap cooled cake in cheesecloth that has been soaked in ⅓ cup rum. Then wrap very tightly in plastic wrap or foil. Store in refrigerator. Resoak cheesecloth with rum as it dries out—about once a week. Store cake 6 to 8 weeks, to develop flavor.

TO SERVE

9. Roll almond paste, between 2 sheets of waxed paper, into an 8-inch circle. Remove top sheet of paper. Invert paste onto top of cake; remove paper. With sharp knife, trim edge of paste; then press paste to cake. Spread paste with Frosting Glaze, letting it run down side of cake. If desired, decorate with candied cherries and angelica. *Makes a 7-pound tube cake.*

FROSTING GLAZE

1½ cups confectioners' sugar
2 tablespoons light cream
¼ teaspoon almond extract

In small bowl, combine sugar, cream and extract; beat until smooth.

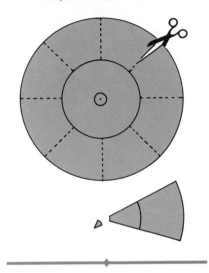

SPRINGERLE
(pictured)

4 cups sifted all-purpose flour
1 teaspoon baking powder
½ teaspoon salt
4 eggs
2 cups granulated sugar
2 teaspoons grated lemon peel
2 tablespoons anise seed
Confectioners' sugar

DO AHEAD

1. Sift flour with baking powder and salt twice; set aside.

2. In large bowl of electric mixer at high speed, beat eggs until thick and lemon-colored about 5 minutes.

3. At medium speed, gradually beat in granulated sugar, 2 tablespoons at a time, beating after each addition. Continue to beat until mixture is thick and smooth—about 10 minutes—occasionally cleaning side of bowl with rubber spatula.

4. Add flour mixture and lemon peel to egg mixture; with a wooden spoon, mix well until mixture is smooth.

5. Refrigerate dough, covered, overnight. Also, refrigerate springerle rolling pin.

6. Lightly grease 2 large cookie sheets; sprinkle each with 1 tablespoon anise seed.

7. Divide dough into 3 parts. Refrigerate until ready to roll out.

8. Sprinkle pastry cloth or wooden board lightly with confectioners' sugar.

9. Roll one part of dough on pastry cloth, to coat with sugar; then roll out to

an 8-by-5½-inch rectangle. Repeat with remaining dough.

10. Remove springerle pin from refrigerator. Coat surface lightly with confectioners' sugar. Starting from long side, slowly roll pin once, firmly and evenly, over dough to make designs. (If dough sticks to springerle pin, peel off with a spatula.)

11. With floured sharp knife, carefully cut along straight lines in dough, to make individual cookies.

12. With wide spatula, transfer cookies to prepared cookie sheets, placing them ½ inch apart. Let stand, uncovered, at room temperature overnight.

NEXT DAY

13. Preheat oven to 325F. Bake cookies 15 minutes, or just until light golden. Remove to wire rack; cool completely.

TO STORE

14. Store springerle in tightly covered container in a cool, dry place 2 to 3 weeks before serving. *Makes about 4½ dozen.*

UPSALA HOLIDAY COOKIES
(pictured)

½ cup (1 stick) butter, softened
7½ tablespoons sugar
1 tablespoon sherry
1½ cups all-purpose flour
3 tablespoons finely chopped blanched
    almonds
1 egg yolk
1 teaspoon water

DO AHEAD

1. In medium bowl, with electric mixer at medium speed, beat butter with 6 tablespoons of the sugar until light and fluffy. Beat in sherry.

2. With wooden spoon, stir in flour until well blended.

3. Refrigerate, covered, 30 minutes.

4. Preheat oven to 375F.

5. On lightly floured surface, roll out dough, one-half at a time, to ¼-inch thickness. Cut with 1½-inch round cookie cutter. Place, 1 inch apart, on ungreased cookie sheets.

6. Mix almonds with remaining 1½ tablespoons sugar. Beat egg yolk with water; brush lightly on cookies. Sprinkle with almond mixture.

7. Bake 15 to 20 minutes, or until lightly browned. Remove to wire rack; let cool completely.

TO STORE

8. Store in tightly covered container in a cool, dry place. (Will keep several weeks.) *Makes about 3 dozen.*

continued on page 336

continued from page 335

CARDAMOM WREATH
(pictured)

1 cup warm water (105 to 115F)
2 pkg active dry yeast
½ cup granulated sugar
1 teaspoon salt
¾ cup (1½ sticks) butter or margarine,
    softened
2 eggs
4¾ cups all-purpose flour
½ cup finely cut-up citron
½ cup finely cut-up candied cherries
½ cup dark raisins
½ cup coarsely chopped walnuts
¾ teaspoon ground cardamom seed
2 tablespoons butter or margarine, melted

GLAZE

1½ cups confectioners' sugar
3 tablespoons milk
½ teaspoon vanilla extract
Candied cherries, halved
Citron

DO AHEAD

1. If possible, check temperature of warm water with thermometer. Sprinkle yeast over water in large bowl; stir until dissolved. Add granulated sugar and salt, stirring until dissolved.

2. Add soft butter, eggs and 2½ cups flour; with electric mixer at medium speed, or vigorously with wooden spoon, beat until smooth—about 2 minutes.

3. Stir in ½ cup citron, ½ cup cherries, the raisins, nuts and cardamom until well combined. Gradually add remaining flour, mixing with a wooden spoon or hands until dough is smooth and stiff enough to leave side of bowl.

4. Turn out dough onto lightly floured surface; roll to coat with flour. Cover with bowl; let rest 10 minutes; then knead until smooth—about 5 minutes.

5. Place in lightly greased large bowl; turn to bring greased side up. Cover with towel; let rise in warm place (85F), free from drafts, until double in bulk—about 2 hours.

6. Punch down dough; turn out onto lightly floured surface. Divide in thirds; with hands, roll each piece into a 24-inch-long strip.

7. Braid the 3 strips together. Place on a greased cookie sheet; form into a ring; pinch ends together to seal.

8. Cover with towel; let rise in warm place (85F), free from drafts, until double in bulk—about 1 hour.

9. Preheat oven to 375F. Brush top of ring with 2 tablespoons melted butter.

10. Bake 40 to 45 minutes, or until nicely browned. Remove to wire rack, and let cool completely.

TO STORE

11. Wrap ring in foil; seal, and label. Place in freezer.

TO SERVE

12. Preheat oven to 400F. Heat foil-wrapped frozen ring 30 to 35 minutes, or just until heated through.

13. Meanwhile, make Glaze: In small bowl, mix sugar, milk and vanilla; mix until smooth. Unwrap ring, and place on wire rack. Brush with glaze, and decorate with candied cherries and citron. *Makes 12 servings.*

OLD-FASHIONED
MINCEMEAT-FILLED COOKIES
(pictured)

3 cups all-purpose flour
1 teaspoon baking powder
½ teaspoon salt
¾ cup (1½ sticks) butter or margarine,
    softened
1½ cups sugar
2 eggs
1 tablespoon grated lemon peel

FILLING

1 cup prepared mincemeat
¼ cup coarsely chopped walnuts
1 teaspoon lemon juice

1 egg yolk
1 teaspoon water
Granulated sugar

DO AHEAD

1. Sift flour with baking powder and salt; set aside.

2. In large bowl, with electric mixer at medium speed, beat butter, 1½ cups sugar, 2 eggs and the lemon peel until light and fluffy.

3. With wooden spoon, beat in flour mixture until smooth and well combined. Using rubber spatula, form dough into a ball on waxed paper or foil. Wrap closely.

4. Refrigerate several hours or overnight.

NEXT DAY

5. Make Filling: In small bowl, combine mincemeat, walnuts and lemon juice; mix well.

6. Preheat oven to 375F. Lightly grease cookie sheets.

7. On lightly floured surface, roll out one-fourth of dough at a time to ⅛-inch thickness (keep dough refrigerated until ready to roll). With floured 2½-inch round, scalloped or heart-shape cookie cutter, cut out cookies. Reroll trimmings, and cut.

8. Using spatula, place half the cookies, 1 inch apart, on prepared cookie sheets. Spread 1 teaspoon filling over each cookie; cover with another cookie. With floured fork, seal edges firmly. Beat egg yolk with water; use to brush tops of cookies. Then sprinkle lightly with sugar.

9. Bake 12 minutes, or until lightly browned. Remove to wire rack; let cool completely.

TO STORE

10. Pack in freezer containers; seal, and label. Place in freezer.

TO SERVE

11. Arrange frozen cookies on serving plate. Let stand at room temperature about 1 hour. *Makes about 3½ dozen.*

CANDIED LEMON PEEL
(pictured)

5 large lemons (2 lb)
1 cup water
3 cups sugar
¼ cup light corn syrup
6 drops yellow food color

DO AHEAD

1. Cut lemons in half lengthwise; squeeze out as much juice as possible. Refrigerate juice to use as desired.

2. In heavy, 3-quart saucepan, place peel and 2 quarts water; bring to boiling. Reduce heat, and simmer, covered, 30 to 40 minutes, or until peel is tender.

3. Drain; cool slightly. Carefully scrape excess pulp from peel.

4. In same saucepan, combine 1 cup water, 2 cups of the sugar, the corn syrup and food color. Cook over medium heat, stirring constantly, until sugar is dissolved and syrup comes to boiling. Continue cooking, without stirring, to 235F on candy thermometer, or until a little syrup forms a soft ball in cold water.

5. Add lemon peel; simmer gently, stirring frequently, 30 to 40 minutes, or until peel becomes translucent. (To prevent scorching during cooking, lift peel off bottom of pan several times.)

6. Turn peel and syrup into bowl. Let stand in a cool, dry place, covered, overnight.

NEXT DAY

7. Remove peel from syrup to wire rack, and let drain 3 hours. Then, with scissors, cut into ¼-inch-wide strips. Roll in remaining sugar, coating well. Place on rack to partially dry—about 3 hours. Roll in sugar again.

TO STORE

8. Store peel in a tightly covered container. *Makes about 1 pound.*

CHRISTMAS-CAKE COOKIES
(pictured)

2 pkg (8-oz size) pitted dates, coarsely chopped
3 colored candied pineapple slices (4 oz), cut into thick wedges
1 jar (4 oz) candied red cherries, quartered
1 can (5 oz) toasted slivered almonds
½ cup whole Brazil nuts, thinly sliced
2 tablespoons sherry
1¼ cups all-purpose flour
½ teaspoon baking soda
½ teaspoon salt
½ cup (1 stick) butter or margarine, softened
¾ cup sugar
1 egg
Candied peel (optional)

DO AHEAD

1. In medium bowl, combine dates, pineapple, cherries, almonds, Brazil nuts and sherry; mix well. Let stand at room temperature 1 hour.

2. Sift flour with baking soda and salt; set aside.

3. In large bowl, with electric mixer at medium speed, beat butter, sugar and egg until light and fluffy.

4. With spoon, stir in flour mixture until well combined; then stir in fruit mixture.

5. Refrigerate, covered, 1 hour.

6. Preheat oven to 375F. Lightly grease cookie sheets.

7. Drop dough by level tablespoons, 2 inches apart, onto prepared cookie sheets. If desired, decorate with bits of candied peel.

8. Bake 12 to 15 minutes, or just until golden-brown. Remove cookies to wire rack; cool completely.

TO STORE

9. Store cookies in an airtight container. A slice of bread in the container helps keep cookies moist. Replace bread often, to prevent mold. *Makes about 6 dozen.*

DATE-NUT LOAVES
(pictured)

4 cups pitted dates
2 cups coarsely chopped walnuts

2 cups boiling water
3 cups all-purpose flour
1½ teaspoons baking soda
1 teaspoon salt
½ cup (1 stick) butter or margarine, softened
1¼ cups light-brown sugar, firmly packed
2 eggs
1 teaspoon vanilla extract

DO AHEAD

1. With scissors, cut dates into thirds into medium bowl. Add nuts and boiling water. Let cool to room temperature—about 45 minutes.

2. Meanwhile, grease four 5¾-by-3¼-by-2¼-inch loaf pans. Sift flour with baking soda and salt; set aside.

3. Preheat oven to 350F.

4. In large bowl, with electric mixer at high speed, beat butter with sugar, eggs and vanilla until ingredients are smooth.

5. Add cooled date mixture; mix well. Add flour mixture; beat with wooden spoon until well combined. Turn into prepared pans, dividing evenly.

6. Bake 1 hour, or until cake tester inserted in center comes out clean. Cool in pans 10 minutes; remove to wire rack, and let cool completely.

TO STORE

7. Wrap each loaf in foil, plastic wrap or moisture-vapor-proof freezer paper; seal, and label. Place in freezer.

TO SERVE

8. Remove number of loaves desired from freezer. Let thaw, still in wrapping, at room temperature several hours, or until loaves are at room temperature. *Makes 4 small loaves.*

Note: One of these loaves, Christmas-wrapped, makes a welcome hostess gift.

CANDIED-GRAPEFRUIT BASKETS
(pictured)

2 large grapefruit, thick-skinned and free from blemishes
1 cup water
2½ cups sugar
¼ cup light corn syrup

DO AHEAD

1. Cut a 1-inch-thick slice from stem end of each grapefruit. With a curved grapefruit knife, remove fruit, being careful to keep whole thick peel intact, forming a shell. Scrape fruit from slices.

2. In 3½-quart saucepan, place grapefruit shells and slices and 2 quarts water; bring to boiling. Reduce heat, and simmer, covered, 30 to 40 minutes, or until peel is tender.

3. Drain; cool slightly. Carefully scrape excess pulp from shells and slices.

4. In same saucepan, combine 1 cup water, 2 cups of the sugar and the corn syrup. Cook over medium heat, stirring constantly, until sugar is dissolved and syrup comes to boiling. Continue cooking, without stirring, to 230F on candy thermometer, or until a little syrup forms a soft ball in cold water.

5. Add the shells and slices; simmer gently, turning frequently, 30 to 40 minutes, or until peel becomes translucent.

6. Turn into medium bowl. Let stand in a cool, dry place, covered, overnight. Turn shells over in syrup several times.

NEXT DAY

7. Remove shells and slices from syrup. Invert each shell over a tumbler. Place slices on wire rack. Let stand at room temperature, uncovered, to drain and dry—about 12 hours.

8. Sprinkle shells and slices with remaining sugar.

TO STORE

9. Place crushed waxed paper in each shell; place slice on top for lid; wrap loosely in waxed paper. Store in tightly covered container.

10. For a gift, remove paper from shells, and fill with candied lemon peel; set lid on top. Wrap in plastic wrap, and decorate. *Makes 2 baskets.*

Note: Or use basket to serve hard sauce for holiday pudding.

SWISS BIBERLI COOKIES
(pictured)

DOUGH
1 cup honey
⅔ cup sugar
2 tablespoons water
1½ teaspoons grated lemon peel
2 tablespoons brandy, rum or kirsch
4 cups all-purpose flour
2 teaspoons baking soda
1 teaspoon ground anise seed
¼ teaspoon ground cinnamon
¼ teaspoon ground ginger
¼ teaspoon ground cloves
¼ teaspoon ground coriander seed

FILLING
3 cups blanched almonds
1 cup sugar
½ cup apricot jam
⅓ cup honey
1 tablespoon grated lemon peel
3 tablespoons lemon juice
1½ teaspoons almond extract

GLAZE
1½ cups sugar
½ cup water

DO AHEAD

1. Make Dough: In small saucepan,
continued on page 338

continued from page 337

combine 1 cup honey, ⅔ cup sugar and 2 tablespoons water. Heat, stirring, just until sugar dissolves—do not boil.

2. Let cool until lukewarm—about 20 minutes. Stir in 1½ teaspoons lemon peel and the brandy.

3. Into large bowl, sift flour with baking soda, anise, cinnamon, ginger, cloves and coriander. Add honey mixture; mix with wooden spoon to a stiff dough. Shape the dough into a ball.

4. Refrigerate, covered, 2 days.

2 DAYS LATER

5. Make Filling: Grind almonds, using fine blade, or use electric blender, or food processor fitted with the steel blade. In medium bowl, combine almonds, 1 cup sugar, the jam, ⅓ cup honey, 1 tablespoon lemon peel, juice, almond extract; mix until well blended. Set aside.

6. Preheat oven to 350F. Lightly grease cookie sheets.

7. Divide dough in half. On lightly floured surface, roll out half of dough into a 16-by-10-inch rectangle. Cut crosswise into quarters, to make 4 strips.

8. Place 5 to 6 tablespoons filling in a 1-inch band down center of each strip of dough. Bring edges of dough over filling to overlap; press gently to seal. Repeat with remaining dough and filling.

9. Cut filled rolls into 1-inch pieces. Place, seam side down, on prepared cookie sheets.

10. Bake 20 minutes, or until light brown.

11. Meanwhile, make Glaze: In small saucepan, combine sugar with ½ cup water. Bring to boiling, stirring until sugar is dissolved. Boil 5 to 7 minutes, or until the mixture is syrupy.

12. Remove cookies to wire rack while hot, and brush with glaze. Cool completely.

TO STORE

13. Pack in airtight containers, with waxed paper between layers, to mellow for several weeks. *Makes about 80.*

OLD-FASHIONED PENUCHE

(pictured)

3 cups light-brown sugar, firmly packed
1 cup light cream
1 tablespoon butter or margarine
1½ teaspoons vanilla extract
⅔ cup chopped pecans or walnuts

DO AHEAD

1. Lightly butter a 9-by-5-by-3-inch loaf pan; set aside.

2. In heavy, 3-quart saucepan, cook sugar and cream over low heat, stirring

constantly with a wooden spoon, until sugar dissolves and mixture comes to boiling.

3. Cook, stirring occasionally, until candy thermometer registers 234F, or until a little syrup forms a soft ball in cold water.

4. Remove from heat, and add butter. Set aside, without stirring, to cool to lukewarm (110F).

5. Add vanilla. With wooden spoon, beat until thick and creamy. Stir in nuts.

6. Quickly turn into prepared loaf pan, and let cool completely.

7. Wrap pan with foil. Let stand overnight at room temperature.

TO STORE

8. Turn out of pan in one piece. With sharp knife, cut into squares (about 1 inch). Wrap each square in waxed paper. Will keep for several weeks in the refrigerator. Wrapped squares may also be stored in a freezer container in freezer.

TO SERVE

9. Unwrap squares. Place on serving plate; let come to room temperature before serving. *Makes about 1¾ pounds.*

CHOCOLATE-WALNUT CARAMELS

(pictured)

2 cups sugar
1 cup light corn syrup
1 cup light cream
2 squares unsweetened chocolate, cut up
2 tablespoons butter or margarine
1 teaspoon vanilla extract
1½ cups coarsely chopped walnuts

DO AHEAD

1. Line an 8-by-8-by-2-inch pan with foil; lightly butter foil.

2. In a heavy, 3½-quart saucepan, combine sugar, corn syrup, cream,

chocolate and butter. Cook over medium heat, stirring with wooden spoon, until sugar is dissolved.

3. Continue cooking, stirring often, to 245F on candy thermometer, or until a little of the mixture forms a firm ball in cold water.

4. Remove from heat. Add vanilla and walnuts. Turn into prepared pan; let cool 1 hour.

TO STORE

5. Turn candy out of pan; peel off foil. With a sharp knife, cut into 36 pieces. Wrap individually in plastic wrap. Refrigerated, these caramels will keep several weeks.

TO SERVE

6. Let stand at room temperature 30 minutes. *Makes 2 pounds.*

SPRITZ WREATHS

(pictured)

2 cups sifted all-purpose flour
¼ teaspoon salt
¾ cup (1½ sticks) butter or margarine, softened
½ cup sugar
1 egg yolk
1 teaspoon vanilla extract or ½ teaspoon almond extract
Cinnamon candies, angelica, miniature multicolored nonpareils

DO AHEAD

1. Refrigerate 2 ungreased cookie sheets until ready to use.

2. Preheat oven to 375F. Sift flour with salt; set aside.

3. In large bowl, using portable electric mixer at medium speed, or wooden spoon, beat butter, sugar, egg yolk and vanilla until smooth and fluffy.

4. Add flour mixture, stirring with wooden spoon until smooth and well combined. With a star disk in cookie press, fill cookie press with dough.

5. Force dough onto cold cookie sheet in 12-inch strip. Cut strip into 3 parts; form each part into a circle. Wreaths should be about 1½ inches apart. Decorate with cinnamon candies, bits of angelica, and nonpareils. Repeat with rest of dough. Bake cookies 8 to 10 minutes, or until light golden. Remove to wire rack; cool completely.

TO STORE

6. Pack in freezer container or coffee cans. Seal; label; freeze.

TO SERVE

7. Take out as many cookies as needed. (Return remaining cookies to freezer, sealed.) Let stand at room temperature about 15 minutes. *Makes 3 dozen.*

SHORTBREAD STARS

1 cup (2 sticks) butter or margarine,
  softened
½ cup sugar
2½ cups sifted all-purpose flour

DO AHEAD

1. In large bowl, with portable electric mixer at medium speed, or wooden spoon, beat butter with sugar until light and fluffy.

2. With wooden spoon, stir in flour until smooth and well combined. Dough will be stiff.

3. Refrigerate dough, covered, several hours.

4. Preheat oven to 300F.

5. Divide dough into 2 parts. Refrigerate until ready to roll out.

6. On lightly floured surface, roll out dough, one part at a time, ⅓ inch thick.

7. Using 1½- or 2-inch star-shape cookie cutters, cut out cookies. Place, 1 inch apart, on ungreased cookie sheets.

8. Bake cookies 25 minutes, or until light golden. Remove to wire rack; cool.

TO STORE

9. When completely cool, pack in freezer containers; seal; label, and freeze.

TO SERVE

10. Take out as many cookies as needed. (Return remaining cookies to freezer, sealed.) Let stand at room temperature about 15 minutes before serving. *Makes about 5 dozen.*

APRICOT SUGARPLUMS

1 pkg (11 oz) dried apricots
3 cups sugar
1 cup water
2 tablespoons light corn syrup
Walnut halves

DO AHEAD

1. In 3-quart saucepan, place apricots and 2 cups water; cover, and bring to boiling. Remove from heat; let stand 10 minutes; then drain.

2. In 10-inch skillet, combine 2 cups of the sugar, 1 cup water and the corn syrup. Bring to boiling over medium heat, stirring until sugar is dissolved. Continue cooking, without stirring, 15 minutes.

3. Add drained apricots, stirring gently to separate. Simmer, uncovered, 20 minutes, or until apricots are translucent. Remove from heat.

4. Let stand in skillet, uncovered, until cooled to room temperature—about 1½ hours.

5. Remove each apricot half from syrup to wire rack. Let stand, at room temperature, uncovered, to drain and dry—about 12 hours.

6. Fill each apricot half with a walnut half, pressing apricot snugly around walnut. Roll in remaining sugar.

TO STORE

7. Place filled apricots in single layer in shallow dish. Cover with foil or plastic wrap. Refrigerate until needed.

TO SERVE

8. Roll apricots in sugar again. *Makes about 6 dozen.*

HARVEST FRUITCAKE

FRUIT MIXTURE

1½ cups currants
1 pkg (10 oz) light raisins
½ lb dried figs, cut in eighths
2 cans (4-oz size) blanched whole almonds
2 cans (4½-oz size) flaked coconut
1 can (8 oz) pecan halves
1 jar (4 oz) diced candied citron
1 jar (4 oz) diced candied orange peel
½ cup sherry

CAKE BATTER

½ cup (1 stick) butter or margarine,
  softened
2 cups sugar
6 eggs
2 cups all-purpose flour
¼ cup orange juice

Sherry
Fruitcake Glaze, recipe follows
Raisin clusters
Dried apricot halves
Blanched almonds

DO AHEAD

1. Prepare Fruit Mixture: In large kettle, combine currants, raisins, figs, almonds, coconut, pecans, citron, orange peel and ½ cup sherry; using hands, mix well. Let stand at room temperature, covered, overnight.

NEXT DAY

2. Line a 10-inch tube pan: On heavy brown paper, draw a 16½-inch circle, and cut out. Set pan in center of circle; draw around base of pan and tube. With pencil lines outside, fold paper into eighths; snip off tip. Unfold circle; cut along folds to circle drawn around base of pan. (See sketch, page 335.) Grease both tube pan and paper well. Fit paper, greased side up, into pan.

3. Make Cake Batter: Preheat oven to 275F.

4. In large bowl, with electric mixer at high speed, beat butter, sugar and 1 egg until smooth and fluffy. Add remaining eggs, one at a time, beating after each addition until light and fluffy.

5. At low speed, beat in flour (in fourths) alternately with orange juice (in thirds), beginning and ending with flour.

6. Add batter to fruit mixture; with rubber spatula or hands, mix until well combined. Turn into prepared pan, packing lightly.

7. Bake about 3½ hours, or until cake tester inserted in center comes out clean. Let cool completely in pan on wire rack. Turn out of pan; peel off paper.

TO STORE

8. Wrap cooled cake in cheesecloth that has been soaked in ⅓ cup sherry. Then wrap very tightly in plastic wrap or foil. Store in refrigerator or in an airtight container. Resoak cheesecloth with sherry as it dries out—about once a week. Store cake 5 to 6 weeks, to develop flavor.

TO SERVE

9. Brush cake with Fruitcake Glaze. Then decorate with raisins, apricot halves and blanched almonds. *Makes a 6½-pound tube cake.*

FRUITCAKE GLAZE

⅓ cup light corn syrup
1 tablespoon lemon juice
1 tablespoon water

1. In small saucepan, combine corn syrup, lemon juice and water.

2. Bring to boiling; reduce heat, and simmer, stirring, 5 minutes, or until mixture is reduced to ⅓ cup. Let cool completely.

CHOCOLATE-NUT BALLS

1 can (6 oz) evaporated milk
1 pkg (6 oz) semisweet-chocolate pieces
2½ cups crushed vanilla wafers (about 64 wafers)
½ cup sifted confectioners' sugar
1¼ cups chopped walnuts or pecans
⅓ cup brandy or orange juice

DO AHEAD

1. In heavy, 2-quart saucepan, cook undiluted milk and chocolate, over medium heat, stirring, until chocolate is melted and the mixture is smooth.

2. Remove from heat. Add crushed wafers, sugar, ½ cup nuts, the brandy or orange juice, mixing well. Let stand at room temperature for 30 minutes.

3. Shape into balls 1 inch in diameter. Roll in remaining nuts. Refrigerate 1 hour, or until firm.

TO STORE

4. When firm, store balls in a freezer container; seal, label and freeze. *Makes 4 dozen.*

◆

This Fresh-Cranberry-Raisin Pie comes out of the freezer fully baked. All you do is pop it into the oven to heat before serving. It's simply delicious with a scoop of vanilla ice cream melting into it.

Rich, dark Plum Pudding, full of that old-fashioned flavor, can be made ahead and refrigerated at least a week. Then, while dinner's cooking, steam it to serve with its made-ahead hard sauce.

This smooth, fragrant Pumpkin Pie is one of the best we know. Bake it in its fluted shell, and freeze it till the day it's needed. To serve: Thaw; then give it a fancy ruffle of whipped cream.

SWEETS
♥ TO ♥
STORE
♥

Days or even weeks before you need them, prepare these favorites at your leisure and store in the refrigerator or freezer. Then, when ready to serve, heat or thaw as directed. When your guests ask, tell them you had a little help from the elves.

Frozen Nesselrode Mousse, elegant and absolutely unlike anything you've ever tasted (we know; we invented it), is frozen right in its serving dish. Trim it with candied cherries and angelica; then serve it proudly.

These Mincemeat Turnovers can be baked weeks ahead and frozen. On the day of your feast, heat them in a hot oven for a mere matter of minutes and serve, spectacularly, with flaming rum sauce. Recipes for these five desserts, plus a Frozen Eggnog Pie in a chocolate-walnut crust and an Icelandic Torte, begin on page 342.

DRAWING BY MILTON GLASER

continued from page 341

PUMPKIN PIE
(pictured)

6 eggs
2 cans (1-lb size) pumpkin
1 cup light-brown sugar, firmly packed
1 cup granulated sugar
2 teaspoons ground cinnamon
1 teaspoon ground ginger
1 teaspoon salt
½ teaspoon ground nutmeg
¼ teaspoon ground cloves
1½ cups milk
1 cup heavy cream
2 (9-inch) unbaked pie shells, with high, fluted edges
1 cup heavy cream, whipped

DO AHEAD

1. Preheat oven to 350F.
2. In 4-quart bowl, beat eggs slightly. Add pumpkin, sugars, cinnamon, ginger, salt, nutmeg and cloves; beat until well blended.
3. Slowly beat in milk and 1 cup cream.
4. Place pie shells on oven rack. Pour in custard mixture, dividing evenly.
5. Bake 60 to 70 minutes, or until knife inserted in center comes out clean. Let cool completely on wire rack—about 2 hours.

TO STORE

6. Freeze until firm. Then wrap in foil, plastic wrap or moisture-vapor-proof freezer paper; seal; label, and return to freezer.

TO SERVE

7. Unwrap frozen pies; let thaw at room temperature—3½ to 4 hours. Place whipped cream in pastry bag with star tip, and decorate top of each pie. *Makes 2 (9-inch) pies.*

FRESH-CRANBERRY-RAISIN PIE
(pictured)

1 pkg (11 oz) piecrust mix
3 cups fresh cranberries
2 cups sugar
2 tablespoons all-purpose flour
¼ teaspoon salt
⅔ cup boiling water
1 cup dark raisins
2 teaspoons grated lemon peel
2 tablespoons butter or margarine
1 egg, beaten
1 tablespoon sugar

DO AHEAD

1. Prepare piecrust mix as package label directs. Shape into a ball; divide in half.
2. On lightly floured surface, roll out one-half of pastry into an 11-inch circle. Use to line 9-inch pie plate. Refrigerate pie shell and remaining pastry until ready to use.
3. Rinse cranberries with cold water, removing any stems.
4. Preheat oven to 425F.
5. In 3-quart saucepan, combine 2 cups sugar, the flour, salt and boiling water; bring to boiling, stirring constantly. Stir in cranberries, raisins and lemon peel. Cook over medium heat, covered, until cranberries start to pop—about 10 minutes. Remove from heat.
6. Add butter; let cool about 5 minutes.
7. Meanwhile, roll out remaining pastry into an 11-inch circle. Cut, with pastry wheel or knife, into 8 strips ½ inch wide.
8. Turn cranberry mixture into pie shell. Moisten edge of shell slightly with cold water. Arrange 4 pastry strips, 1 inch apart, across filling; press ends to rim of shell. Place 4 pastry strips across first ones, at right angle, to make lattice; press ends to rim of shell. Fold overhang of lower crust over ends of strips, to make a rim; crimp.
9. Lightly brush pastry strips with egg. Sprinkle pie with 1 tablespoon sugar. Bake 25 minutes, or until filling in center bubbles slightly. Remove to wire rack; cool completely.

TO STORE

10. Wrap pie in foil, plastic wrap or moisture-vaporproof freezer paper; seal; label, and place in freezer.

TO SERVE

11. To heat: Preheat oven to 350F. Unwrap pie. Place a square of foil loosely over top. Bake 30 minutes, or until heated through. *Makes 6 to 8 servings.*

PLUM PUDDING
(pictured)

1½ cups dark raisins
1½ cups currants
1 jar (4 oz) diced candied citron, finely chopped
½ cup finely chopped walnuts
1 tablespoon grated lemon peel
1¼ cups sifted all-purpose flour
1 teaspoon baking soda
1 teaspoon salt
1 teaspoon ground cinnamon
¼ teaspoon ground cloves
½ teaspoon ground allspice
½ teaspoon ground nutmeg
2 eggs
½ cup sugar
¾ cup finely grated suet (2 oz)
1 cup light molasses
1 cup buttermilk
¼ cup brandy
1¼ cups packaged dry bread crumbs
¼ cup brandy
Hard Sauce, recipe follows

DO AHEAD

1. Grease well a 2-quart pudding mold with tight-fitting cover. In large bowl, combine fruits, nuts, lemon peel and ½ cup of the flour.
2. Sift remaining ¾ cup flour with baking soda, salt and spices.
3. In small bowl, with rotary beater, beat eggs well. Add to fruit mixture, along with sugar, suet, molasses, buttermilk, ¼ cup brandy, the bread crumbs and flour mixture; mix until well combined.
4. Turn into prepared mold; cover. Place mold on trivet in large kettle; pour in enough boiling water to come halfway up side of mold; cover kettle.
5. Steam pudding 3 hours. (Water in kettle should boil gently; add more water as needed.)
6. Cool, uncovered, 10 minutes. Then unmold onto wire rack; let cool completely.

TO STORE

7. Wrap in plastic wrap or foil. Store in refrigerator several weeks.

TO SERVE

8. Replace pudding in mold; cover, and steam, as directed above, 50 minutes, or until hot.
9. To flame: In small saucepan, gently heat ¼ cup brandy; ignite. Pour, flaming, over pudding. Serve with Hard Sauce. *Makes 12 servings.*

HARD SAUCE

⅔ cup (1⅓ sticks) butter or margarine, softened
2 teaspoons vanilla extract
2 cups confectioners' sugar

1. In small bowl of electric mixer, at high speed, cream butter until light.
2. Add vanilla extract and confectioners' sugar; beat until smooth and fluffy. *Makes about 1½ cups.*

FROZEN NESSELRODE MOUSSE
(pictured)

5 egg whites
¼ teaspoon cream of tartar
1 cup sugar
5 egg yolks
⅛ teaspoon salt
⅓ cup golden rum
2 teaspoons lemon juice
2 cups heavy cream
4 oz chopped mixed candied fruit
Candied cherries (optional for garnish)
Angelica leaves (optional for garnish)

DO AHEAD

1. In a large bowl, let the egg whites

warm to room temperature—will take about 1 hour.

2. Add cream of tartar to egg whites. With electric mixer at high speed, beat until soft peaks form when beaters are slowly raised.

3. Gradually add ¾ cup sugar, 2 tablespoons at a time, beating well after each addition. Continue to beat until stiff peaks form.

4. In small bowl, with same beaters, beat egg yolks and salt until thick and lemon-colored.

5. Gradually add remaining ¼ cup sugar, beating well after each addition.

6. Gradually add golden rum and lemon juice; beat until they are well combined.

7. Beat heavy cream until stiff.

8. Gently fold rum mixture, candied fruit and whipped cream into egg-white mixture. Turn evenly and gently into a large serving bowl (about 2-quart).

TO STORE

9. Freeze until firm. Then freezer-wrap; seal; label; return to freezer.

TO SERVE

10. Garnish with candied cherries and angelica leaves, if desired. Let stand 5 to 10 minutes before serving. *Makes 10 to 12 servings.*

FROZEN EGGNOG PIE
(pictured)

CRUST
1 pkg (11 oz) piecrust mix
1½ cups finely chopped walnuts
½ cup light-brown sugar, firmly packed
2 squares unsweetened chocolate, coarsely grated
2 tablespoons water
2 teaspoons vanilla extract

FILLING
4 eggs
1⅓ cups granulated sugar
¼ teaspoon salt
2 env unflavored gelatine
⅔ cup light or golden rum
4 cups heavy cream
1⅓ cups confectioners' sugar

Whipped cream
Chocolate curls

DO AHEAD

1. Make Crust: Preheat oven to 375F. Line 2 (9-inch) pie plates with foil, letting it extend over rims of the plates.

2. In medium bowl, combine piecrust mix, nuts, brown sugar and chocolate. With fork, stir in water and the vanilla.

3. Turn into foil-lined plates, dividing evenly. Press crust mixture against bottoms and sides and up on rims. Edge on rim should be ¼-inch high, as filling is generous.

4. Bake 15 minutes, or until lightly browned. Let cool completely on wire racks.

5. Meanwhile, make Filling: In large bowl, with electric mixer at high speed, beat eggs with granulated sugar and salt until they are well combined.

6. Set bowl in pan of boiling water; continue beating at high speed until mixture is very thick—6 to 8 minutes. Remove bowl from water; cool in refrigerator, stirring occasionally—about 20 minutes.

7. Meanwhile, sprinkle gelatine over rum in small bowl, to soften. Set in pan of boiling water; stir until gelatine is dissolved. Remove bowl from water; let stand at room temperature until cool—about 15 minutes.

8. Gradually beat gelatine into cooled egg mixture until well blended. Refrigerate while beating heavy cream.

9. In large bowl, beat cream with confectioners' sugar just until stiff. With wire whisk or rubber spatula, fold in egg-gelatine mixture until well combined. Refrigerate until mixture is stiff enough to mound.

10. Spoon filling into pie shells, dividing evenly.

TO STORE

11. Freeze until firm—4 to 5 hours. Lift pies, foil and all, from pie plates. Then overwrap each in foil, plastic wrap or moisture-vaporproof freezer paper; seal; label, and return to freezer.

TO SERVE

12. Unwrap pies; peel foil from piecrusts. Place pies on serving plates, and let stand at room temperature until they are soft enough to cut—takes about 10 minutes. Garnish with whipped cream and chocolate curls. *Makes 2 (9-inch) pies.*

MINCEMEAT TURNOVERS WITH RUM SAUCE
(pictured)

PASTRY
2 pkg (11-oz size) piecrust mix
Ice water

FILLING
1¾ cups prepared mincemeat, with brandy and rum
½ cup applesauce
½ cup coarsely chopped walnuts
12 tablespoons (1½ sticks) butter or margarine, softened

1 egg yolk
1 teaspoon water
Granulated sugar

Rum Sauce, recipe follows

DO AHEAD

1. Make Pastry: Place piecrust mix in medium bowl. Blend in ice water as package label directs. Shape into a ball; divide in half. Refrigerate 30 minutes.

2. Make Filling: In medium bowl, combine mincemeat, applesauce and walnuts; mix well.

3. Place half of pastry between two sheets of waxed paper; roll out to 12-inch square. (To keep waxed paper from slipping, place it on a damp cloth.) Remove top sheet of waxed paper. Cut pastry into four 6-inch circles. Reroll trimmings, and cut, to make 6 circles in all. Repeat with remaining dough.

4. Spread each circle, not quite to edge, with 1 tablespoon butter.

5. Place about 3 tablespoons filling on half of each circle. Moisten edge of circle lightly. Fold other half over filling, and press edge with fork, to seal or flute.

6. Preheat oven to 425F. Beat egg yolk with water. Place turnovers on ungreased cookie sheet. Brush with egg yolk mixture; sprinkle each with ¼ teaspoon sugar, and cut a small slit in each for steam vent. Bake 30 minutes, or until they are golden-brown. Let turnovers cool completely.

TO STORE

7. Wrap individually, in foil, and place in shallow plastic freezer containers with tight-fitting lids. Seal; label; place in freezer.

TO SERVE

8. Preheat oven to 400F. Reheat, unwrapped, on cookie sheet 10 to 12 minutes, or until hot. Serve warm, with Rum Sauce. *Makes 12 turnovers.*

RUM SAUCE
(pictured)

⅔ cup granulated sugar
⅔ cup light-brown sugar, firmly packed
2 cups water
1 lemon wedge
1 orange wedge
½ cup dark rum

1. In medium saucepan, combine sugars and water. Cook over medium

continued on page 367

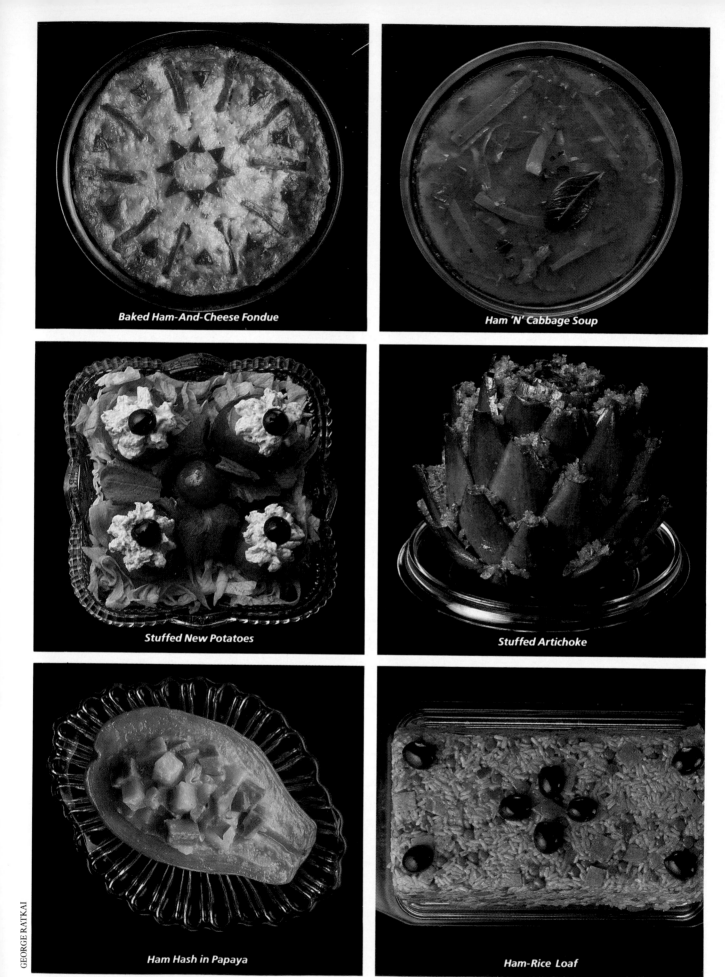

Baked Ham-And-Cheese Fondue

Ham 'N' Cabbage Soup

Stuffed New Potatoes

Stuffed Artichoke

Ham Hash in Papaya

Ham-Rice Loaf

GEORGE RATKAI

Ham-And-Cheese Roulade

Ham Mousse

Banana-Ham Fritters

PLAY IT AGAIN, HAM!

Y*our holiday-dinner ham received rave reviews from the family, but now what's to become of the leftovers? There are always good old ham sandwiches, but we'd like to suggest something better—much better! Pictured here are nine scrumptious ways to turn leftover ham into terrific, timesaving dishes—and isn't that just what you want after cooking a big holiday meal? With only one to one-and-a-half cups of cooked ham, you can create any of these savory "seconds" to serve as appetizers or main courses. For example, Baked Ham-And-Cheese Fondue is an appealing combination of ham slivers, cream-style corn and pimiento with eggs; Ham Hash in Papaya, a light 30-minute meal, tosses cubed ham, potatoes and spices in a cream sauce to bake in papaya shells; and bananas, ham and cheese team up for some deep-fried fun in Banana-Ham Fritters. For all of these fantastic recipes, plus three more, turn the page.*

GEORGE RATKAI

LUSCIOUS
LAST-MINUTE
C·A·K·E·S

*I*f you're too busy to prepare
pastry treats in advance, here's a
medley of Christmas cakes that
require only last-minute baking—
with the help of mixes, molds
and other shortcuts. Glazed
Holiday Loaf Cake, center.
Counterclockwise, from lower
right: Grandma's Fruitcakes;
Lemon-Coconut Cake; molded
Christmas Kuchen, Italian Wine
Cake; Caraway-Seed Cake;
Scottish Dundee Cake. For
recipes, see page 350.

continued from page 349

All recipes are pictured on pages 348 and 349.

CHRISTMAS KUCHEN

½ cup milk
1 cup granulated sugar
1 teaspoon salt
½ cup (1 stick) butter or margarine
2 pkg active dry yeast
½ cup warm water (105 to 115F)
4 eggs, well beaten
1 tablespoon grated lemon peel
4 cups all-purpose flour
½ cup mixed candied peel
½ cup raisins
Confectioners' sugar

1. Heat milk until bubbles form around edge of pan. Add granulated sugar, salt and butter; stir until sugar is dissolved and butter is melted. Let cool to lukewarm.

2. Meanwhile, sprinkle yeast over warm water in large bowl of electric mixer; stir until dissolved.

3. Add lukewarm milk mixture, eggs, lemon peel and 2 cups flour; beat at medium speed until smooth—2 minutes. Stir in rest of flour; beat vigorously with wooden spoon 1 to 2 minutes.

4. Cover with damp towel; let rise in warm place (85F), free from drafts, until light and bubbly—about 1 hour.

5. Stir down with spoon. Stir in candied peel and raisins. Turn into lightly greased 10-inch decorative pan or tube pan. Cover with towel; let rise until 1 inch from top of pan—about 1¼ hours.

6. Meanwhile, preheat oven to 350F.

7. Bake Kuchen 35 to 40 minutes, or until golden-brown. Let cool in pan on wire rack.

8. Loosen from pan, and invert on serving plate. Sprinkle with confectioners' sugar. *Makes 1 Kuchen.*

DUNDEE CAKE

2¼ cups all-purpose flour
½ teaspoon salt
1 cup (2 sticks) butter or margarine
¾ cup sugar
5 eggs
½ cup currants
½ cup raisins
½ cup mixed candied peel
10 candied cherries, cut in half
1 cup ground almonds
1 tablespoon grated orange peel
½ cup sliced almonds

1. Lightly grease a 9-inch springform pan. Preheat oven to 325F.

2. Sift flour with salt.

3. In large bowl of electric mixer, at medium speed, cream butter with sugar until very light and fluffy. Add eggs, one at a time, beating well after each addition.

4. At low speed, beat flour mixture into butter mixture. Mix together currants, raisins, candied peel and cherries. Stir into batter. Add ground almonds and grated orange peel; mix well. Turn into prepared pan.

5. Arrange sliced almonds in a circular pattern on top of batter. Bake on middle shelf of oven 1½ hours, or until cake tester inserted in center comes out clean.

6. Let cake cool on wire rack 15 minutes; then loosen edge of cake from side of pan. Remove side. Let cool completely.

TO STORE

7. Cake will keep well stored in cake tin or wrapped in foil and refrigerated.

8. Serve thinly sliced. *Makes 2½-pound cake.*

GRANDMA'S FRUITCAKE

1 jar (8 oz) diced mixed candied fruit
1 jar (8 oz) candied cherries, halved
1 cup seedless raisins
1 cup currants
1 cup coarsely chopped walnuts
¼ cup brandy
3¾ cups all-purpose flour
2 teaspoons ground allspice
2 teaspoons ground cinnamon
1½ teaspoons baking powder
1 teaspoon salt
1 cup (2 sticks) butter or margarine, softened
1½ cups light-brown sugar, packed
4 eggs
1 cup milk

Frosting Glaze, recipe follows
Candied red cherries, halved
Angelica or citron
Whole blanched almonds

1. Line a 10-inch tube pan: On heavy brown paper, draw a circle 18 inches in diameter, and cut out. Set pan in center of circle: draw around base of pan and tube. (See sketch, page 335.) With pencil lines outside, fold paper into eighths; snip off tip. Unfold circle; cut along folds to inside circle. Grease both pan and paper well; fit paper, greased side up, into pan.

2. In medium bowl, combine candied fruit, cherries, raisins, currants, walnuts and brandy; mix well. Set aside.

3. Preheat oven to 275F. Sift flour with spices, baking powder and salt; set aside.

4. In large bowl of electric mixer, at high speed, beat butter with brown sugar until light and fluffy. Add eggs; continue beating until smooth and light.

5. At low speed, beat in flour mixture (in fourths) alternately with milk (in thirds), beginning and ending with flour mixture; beat just until combined.

6. Add prepared fruit mixture; with spoon or hands, mix until well combined. Turn into prepared pan; press down well with rubber spatula, to make top smooth.

7. Bake 2½ to 3 hours, or until cake tester inserted in center comes out clean. Let cool in pan on wire rack 30 minutes.

8. Turn out of pan: peel off paper. Let cool completely on wire rack.

TO STORE

9. Wrap in foil or plastic wrap, and refrigerate. This is excellent soon after baking but will keep well 3 or 4 weeks stored in the refrigerator. Just before serving, make Frosting Glaze. Spread over top of cake, letting glaze drip unevenly down side. Decorate, as pictured, with cherries, angelica and almonds. *Makes a 5-pound tube cake.*

GIFT FRUITCAKES

1. Prepare pans: Line five (5¾-by-3-by-2-inch) greased loaf pans with strips of greased brown paper.

2. Preheat oven to 275F.

3. Turn Grandma's Fruitcake batter, above, into prepared pans, dividing evenly: pack lightly.

4. Bake 2 hours, or until cake tester inserted in center comes out clean.

5. Cool completely in pans on wire rack. Turn out of pans gently; peel off paper.

6. To decorate before serving or giving as gift, make Frosting Glaze, below. Spread over top of cake. Decorate with candied cherries, angelica and pecans. *Makes 5 (1-pound) loaves.*

FROSTING GLAZE

2 cups confectioners' sugar
3 tablespoons light cream

In small bowl, combine sugar and cream; mix well.

FESTIVE LEMON-COCONUT CAKE

1 pkg (18.25 oz) yellow-cake mix
Lemon Filling, recipe follows
2 cups heavy cream, whipped
1 cup flaked coconut
Citron slices
Candied red cherries, halved

1. Preheat oven to 350F. Grease and flour two 8-by-1½-inch round layer-cake pans.
2. Make and bake cake mix according to package directions. Remove to rack; cool 10 minutes before removing from pans.
3. Meanwhile, make Lemon Filling. Remove ¾ cup filling for top. Combine rest of filling with 1 cup whipped cream; with wire whisk, mix until smooth. Slice layers in half horizontally, to make four layers.
4. To assemble: Place a layer, cut side up, on cake plate. Spread with a third of whipped-cream mixture. Repeat with remaining layers, ending with top layer, cut side down.
5. Spread top layer, 1 inch from edge, with reserved lemon filling. Frost side with rest of whipped cream; sprinkle with coconut. Decorate top of cake, as pictured, with citron and candied cherries. Refrigerate until ready to serve. *Makes 12 servings.*

LEMON FILLING

2 tablespoons cornstarch
1 tablespoon all-purpose flour
½ cup sugar
⅔ cup water
1 egg yolk, slightly beaten
3 tablespoons lemon juice
1 teaspoon grated lemon peel
1 tablespoon butter or margarine

1. In small saucepan, combine cornstarch, flour and sugar, mixing well. Gradually add water, stirring until smooth.
2. Over medium heat, bring to boiling, stirring occasionally; boil 1 minute.
3. Remove from heat. Quickly stir some of hot mixture into egg yolk. Return to hot mixture; stir to blend.
4. Return to heat; cook over low heat, stirring occasionally, 5 minutes. Mixture will be stiff.
5. Remove from heat. Stir in lemon juice, lemon peel and butter.
6. Turn into a small bowl; place in bowl of ice water, stirring occasionally, until chilled and stiff—about 30 minutes—or until ready to assemble cake. *Makes 1¾ cups.*

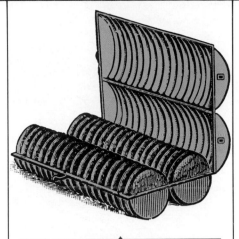

HOLIDAY LOAF CAKE

1 pkg (1 lb, 1 oz) poundcake mix
½ cup milk
1 cup grated tart apple (1 large)
2 eggs
½ cup mixed candied peel
½ cup chopped walnuts or pecans
¼ cup raisins
2 tablespoons light corn syrup
Walnut halves
Candied red cherries, halved

1. Preheat oven to 325F. Lightly grease 9-by-5-by-3-inch loaf pan.
2. Turn cake mix into large bowl. Add milk; blend just until dry ingredients are moistened; with electric beater at medium speed, beat 1 minute. Add grated apple and eggs; beat 2 minutes, scraping bowl frequently.
3. Add candied peel, nuts and raisins; mix with wooden spoon just until blended.
4. Turn into prepared pan. Bake 1 hour and 15 minutes, or until cake tester inserted in center comes out clean. Cool in pan on wire rack 10 minutes. Turn out of pan.
5. Brush warm loaf with corn syrup; decorate, as pictured, with walnuts and candied cherries. Cool completely before serving. *Makes 1 loaf.*

CARAWAY-SEED CAKE

4 cups all-purpose flour
1 teaspoon baking powder
1 teaspoon salt
2 tablespoons caraway seed
2 cups (4 sticks) butter, softened
1½ cups granulated sugar
1 teaspoon vanilla extract
6 eggs
Confectioners' sugar

1. Preheat oven to 350F. Grease and flour 10-inch tube pan or Turk's-head mold. Sift flour with baking powder and salt. Add caraway seed; set aside.

2. In large bowl of electric mixer, at medium speed, beat butter, granulated sugar and vanilla until light.
3. Add eggs, one at a time, beating well after each addition; then beat until light and fluffy—2 minutes.
4. At low speed, gradually beat in flour mixture; beat just until well combined. Turn into prepared pan.
5. Bake 1¼ hours, or until cake tester inserted near center comes out clean.
6. Cool cake in pan on wire rack 15 minutes. Remove from pan to rack; cool completely.
7. To decorate, dust with confectioners' sugar. To serve, cut in thin slices. *Makes 16 servings.*

ITALIAN WINE CAKE

1 cup raisins
1 cup cold water
2 cups all-purpose flour
2 teaspoons unsweetened cocoa
2 teaspoons baking soda
1 teaspoon ground cinnamon
½ teaspoon ground nutmeg
½ cup (1 stick) butter or margarine
½ cup shortening
1 cup granulated sugar
2 eggs
1¼ cups Burgundy wine
1 cup chopped walnuts or pecans

FROSTING
1 cup confectioners' sugar
1 to 1½ tablespoons milk
½ cup chopped mixed candied fruit

1. In small saucepan, cover raisins with cold water. Bring to boiling. Remove from heat; drain well; set aside to cool.
2. Preheat oven to 350F. Sift together flour, cocoa, baking soda, cinnamon and nutmeg. Lightly grease two 8½-by-4½-by-2¾-inch pans.
3. In large bowl of electric mixer, combine butter, shortening and granulated sugar; beat at medium speed until smooth and fluffy. Add eggs, one at a time, beating well after each addition.
4. At low speed, add flour mixture alternately with wine, beginning and ending with flour mixture. Stir in raisins and nuts.
5. Turn batter into prepared pans, dividing evenly. Bake 40 to 50 minutes, or until cake tester inserted in center comes out clean.
6. Cool on rack 10 minutes; turn out of pans. Cool completely before decorating.
7. Make Frosting: In small bowl, combine confectioners' sugar and milk; mix well. Spread in center of cakes, as pictured; sprinkle with candied fruit. *Makes 2 loaves.* ◆

COOKING AHEAD
FOR THE
♥ HOLIDAYS ♥

Homemade treats are a wonderfully delicious part of every holiday, especially when they can be prepared several weeks in advance of the big celebration. Throughout the next few pages, you'll discover make-ahead recipes for taste-tantalizing cakes, cookies and candies—complete with storage directions that ensure just-made freshness. One luscious example is our Old-Fashioned Nut Cake pictured here. Solid with walnuts or pecans, and spirited with rum or brandy, it mellows and improves with age. This five-pound cake will stay fresh for several days when wrapped and stored in a cool, dry place. When refrigerated or frozen, it will keep for several weeks.

Turn plain ice cream into a fabulous dessert flambéed
with Brandied-Date-And-Walnut Sauce. Store in the
refrigerator several weeks—the longer this spirited
sauce stands, the better blended the flavor.

Here's a honey of a do-ahead trio that can be stored for a few weeks: above at left, glazed Austrian Honey Cakes, festively shaped and decorated; at center are Tyrolean Honey Cookies (Leckerli) filled with almonds and candied fruits. Store each in airtight containers. The skillet-baked Honey-Nut Kuchen at right is a terrific do-ahead treat for a busy holiday breakfast or brunch. Once baked and cooled, simply wrap tightly in foil and freeze—then reheat before serving.

Lemon Curd, a traditional English holiday favorite, is a tangy yet sweet custard that makes a heavenly filling for tarts, as well as a tasty toast spread. It keeps several days in the refrigerator, or several weeks in the freezer.

Here are two gift ideas for nut lovers. Above at left, Marzipan Crescents, moist with almond paste and rolled in pine nuts, can be frozen for several weeks. Pecan Pralines, above at right, are rich and crisp pecan-laden cookies that keep for several weeks in an airtight container.

Studded with almonds, sweetened with raisins and currants and dusted with confectioners' sugar, this delectable Kugelhopf, above, is a must for the holidays. Bake it in a tube pan 10½ inches in diameter, then wrap and store in the refrigerator for up to two weeks, or longer in the freezer.

Like sparkling pieces of glass, these Glacéed Cherries and Nuts, at left, are wondrous to behold. A sugar syrup is poured over warmed cherries and nuts to harden like candy. After breaking into pieces, store covered, up to several weeks. Our recipe makes almost two pounds.

Our Orange-Cranberry Jelly, above, made the easy way with cranberry juice instead of whole cranberries, is a great do-ahead gift idea, especially when ladled into decorative glasses with hand-printed labels. Keep a few on hand for last-minute gift giving.

What would the holidays be without fruitcake? Here are our two favorites that can be made weeks in advance. At far left, Tropical Fruitcake, a superb confection of Brazil nuts, dates and cherries with a lemon-accented glaze. At near left, a five-pound beauty we modestly call the Best of All Fruitcakes. It contains eight different fruits and two kinds of nuts— baked in the least possible amount of batter.

Speculaas, spiced almond cookies, are served in Holland and Belgium on Saint Nicholas Day, December 6. Traditionally, special molds are used—Santa Claus, a Christmas tree, a wreath or windmill. We used an antique butter mold, but you can use any 5-inch decorative cookie cutter or mold. These cookies will keep in a tightly covered glass jar or cookie tin for several weeks. For this recipe and more, turn to page 360.

Festive Cookies From Sweden

*I*n Sweden, the cookies traditionally served at Christmastime are called Pepparkakor: firm and crisp, lightly spiced with ginger, cinnamon and cloves. Children all over the country help to make them in their favorite shapes early in December, but they hold off eating them until the 13th, when they celebrate Lucia Day, the start of the holiday season. The cookies can be stored in an airtight container and decorated a few days before serving. See opposite page for our step-by-step directions.

PEPPARKAKOR

COOKIE DOUGH
3½ cups all-purpose flour
1 teaspoon baking soda
¼ teaspoon salt
1½ teaspoons ground ginger
1½ teaspoons ground cinnamon

1 teaspoon ground cloves
½ cup (1 stick) butter or margarine, softened
¾ cup granulated sugar
1 egg
¾ cup light molasses
1 teaspoon grated lemon peel

FROSTING
⅓ cup egg whites (2 to 3 eggs, depending on size)
3¾ cups sifted confectioners' sugar

1. Make Cookie Dough: Measure unsifted flour, and sift with baking soda, salt, and spices onto a large sheet of waxed paper. In large bowl of electric mixer, with the mixer at high speed, beat the butter, granulated sugar and 1 egg until light and fluffy.

2. Add molasses and lemon peel; beat until well blended. With wooden spoon, stir in flour mixture; mix with hands until well blended and smooth. Divide the dough into four parts. Wrap each part separately in waxed paper or foil, and refrigerate overnight.

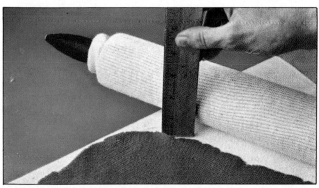

3. Next day, lightly grease several cookie sheets. Preheat oven to 375F. Roll one part of cookie dough at a time; keep rest refrigerated until ready to roll out. With a stockinette-covered rolling pin, roll out the dough ⅛ inch thick on lightly floured pastry cloth.

4. Use various cutters, 2 to 3 inches in diameter, to cut out cookies. Place cookies, 1 inch apart on cookie sheets. Bake 6 to 8 minutes, or until lightly browned. Remove to wire rack to cool. Store, if desired, before decorating, in a tightly covered tin.

5. When you choose to decorate, make Frosting: In medium bowl, with portable electric mixer at medium speed, beat the egg whites with the confectioners' sugar to make a smooth, stiff frosting. Cover with a damp cloth until ready to use, to prevent drying out.

6. To decorate: Fill pastry bag with a number-3 or -4 small tip for writing with frosting. Pipe on frosting, following outline of cookies. Decorate cookies as pictured. Let frosting dry. Store in covered tin at room temperature. *Makes about 7 to 10 dozen.*

continued from page 357

OLD-FASHIONED NUT CAKE
(pictured)

4 cans (8-oz size) walnuts, or 4 cans (6-oz size) pecans, coarsely chopped (8 cups)
3½ cups sifted all-purpose flour
2 teaspoons baking powder
½ teaspoon salt
¾ cup milk
¼ cup rum or brandy
1½ cups (3 sticks) butter or margarine, softened
2 cups sugar
6 eggs
Sherry

DO AHEAD

1. Lightly grease bottom and side of a 10-inch tube pan. Line with brown paper as in recipe for McCall's Best Black Fruitcake, page 334; grease paper.

2. Turn nuts into a large bowl. On sheet of waxed paper, sift flour with baking powder and salt. Set aside.

3. Combine milk with rum. Preheat oven to 275F.

4. In large bowl of electric mixer, at medium speed, beat butter with sugar until very light and fluffy.

5. Add eggs, one at a time, beating at high speed after each addition and scraping down the side of bowl with rubber spatula, as needed. Beat until very light and fluffy.

6. At low speed, beat in flour mixture (in fourths) alternately with milk mixture (in thirds), beginning and ending with flour mixture.

7. Pour batter over nuts in large bowl. Mix well with large spoon or rubber spatula.

8. Turn batter into prepared pan, spreading evenly.

9. Bake 2½ hours, or until a cake tester inserted near center comes out clean.

10. Let cake cool in pan, on wire rack, 30 minutes. Turn out on rack; gently remove paper; let cool completely.

TO STORE

11. Wrap cake in waxed paper, plastic wrap or cheesecloth soaked in sherry; then wrap in foil, or place in a cake tin with a tight-fitting cover. Store in a cool place three or four days, to mellow, before serving. If storing for several weeks, store in refrigerator or freezer.

12. Cut cake into very thin slices. Let slices warm to room temperature. *Makes 5¼-pound cake.*

BRANDIED-DATE-AND-WALNUT SAUCE FOR ICE CREAM
(pictured)

2 cups light-brown sugar, packed
1 cup water
¼ cup brandy
1 pkg (8 oz) pitted dates
1 cup walnut halves
¼ cup brandy

DO AHEAD

1. In medium saucepan, combine brown sugar with 1 cup water. Cook, stirring occasionally, over medium heat 20 minutes.

2. Add ¼ cup brandy, the dates and walnut halves. Let cool.

TO STORE

3. Turn into glass jar or plastic refrigerator container. Store, tightly covered, in refrigerator several weeks. Sauce improves in flavor as it mellows.

TO SERVE

4. Heat sauce over low heat. Turn into serving dish. Heat ¼ cup brandy in small saucepan just until vapor starts to rise; ignite. At the table, pour flaming brandy over sauce. While sauce is still flaming, serve over ice cream. *Makes 3 cups.*

LEMON CURD
(pictured)

6 eggs
2 egg yolks
2 cups sugar
¼ cup grated lemon peel
¾ cup lemon juice
1 cup (2 sticks) butter or margarine

DO AHEAD

1. In top of double boiler, combine eggs, egg yolks and sugar; mix well.

2. Add lemon peel, lemon juice and butter. Cook over gently boiling water, stirring frequently, until the mixture is smooth and thickened. Remove from heat at once, and let cool.

TO STORE

3. Turn into glass jars or plastic

freezer containers. To keep for several days, store, tightly covered, in refrigerator. If keeping for several weeks, store in freezer.

TO SERVE

4. Before using, let stand at room temperature several hours, to thaw. Makes a delicious filling for tarts or a spread for toast. *Makes 2 pints.*

AUSTRIAN HONEY CAKES
(pictured)

3 cups all-purpose flour
½ teaspoon baking soda
½ teaspoon salt
1 teaspoon ground cinnamon
½ teaspoon ground nutmeg
½ teaspoon ground ginger
½ teaspoon ground cloves
1 jar (8 oz) chopped candied orange peel
1 jar (8 oz) chopped candied lemon peel
½ cup ground unblanched almonds
2 tablespoons grated fresh lemon peel
½ cup honey
1 cup light-brown sugar, packed
2 eggs

2 cups confectioners' sugar
3 tablespoons water
Candied red cherries
Angelica

DO AHEAD

1. On sheet of waxed paper, sift flour with baking soda, salt and spices. Set aside.

2. Toss candied peels with almonds and grated fresh lemon peel, to mix well. Set aside.

3. In small saucepan, warm honey; remove from heat.

4. In large bowl of electric mixer, at high speed, beat brown sugar and eggs until smooth and fluffy. Add honey; beat well. Add 1 cup flour mixture; beat, at low speed, just until smooth.

5. Using a wooden spoon, stir in rest of flour mixture until well combined. Then stir in peel-and-nut mixture.

6. Refrigerate dough, covered, overnight.

NEXT DAY

7. Preheat oven to 375F. Lightly grease several cookie sheets.

8. On lightly floured pastry cloth, roll out dough, one half at a time, ¼ inch thick. (Refrigerate remaining half until ready to roll out.)

9. Using floured, 2-inch cookie cutters, cut out cookies. Place, 2 inches apart, on prepared cookie sheets. Bake 10 to 12 minutes. Remove cookies to wire rack.

10. Make glaze: In small bowl, combine confectioners' sugar with water; stir until smooth.

11. Brush glaze on warm cookies. Decorate at once with bits of candied cherries and angelica. Let cool completely.

TO STORE

12. Store in a glass jar or crock or cookie tin, tightly covered, in a cool, dry place for several weeks. Store cookies with a piece of apple, to make them more moist. *Makes about 7 dozen.*

LECKERLI
(Tyrolean Honey Cookies)
(pictured)

¼ cup candied orange peel
¼ cup candied lemon peel
1½ cups whole unblanched almonds
¾ cup honey
1¼ cups granulated sugar
1 tablespoon grated fresh lemon peel
¼ cup lemon juice
1½ tablespoons kirsch or brandy
4 cups sifted all-purpose flour
Dash salt
1 teaspoon baking soda
1 teaspoon ground cinnamon
Dash ground cloves
Dash ground nutmeg

1 cup confectioners' sugar
3 tablespoons water
Candied red cherries

DO AHEAD

1. Put candied orange and lemon peel and almonds through fine blade of food grinder. Or grind in blender or food processor until very fine.

2. In medium saucepan, bring honey and granulated sugar just to boiling, stirring (do not boil). Add fresh lemon peel and lemon juice. Set aside to cool—10 minutes. Then add ground peel and almonds and the kirsch.

3. Into a large bowl, sift flour with salt, baking soda, cinnamon, cloves and nutmeg. Make well in center of flour mixture; pour in fruit-and-honey mixture. Work together, with a kneading motion, until well combined. Dough will be quite stiff.

4. Preheat oven to 350F.

5. Divide dough into 4 parts. Refrigerate 3 parts until ready to use. Between 2 sheets of waxed paper, on slightly dampened surface, roll out one part to form a rectangle 6 by 8 inches, ¼ inch thick. Cut into 16 rectangles. Place about

1 inch apart, on ungreased cookie sheets.

6. Bake about 10 minutes, or just until golden.

7. Repeat with rest of dough.

8. In small bowl, combine confectioners' sugar with water; stir to mix well. Brush over cookies while they are still warm. Decorate with bits of candied cherries.

TO STORE

9. Store in a tightly covered jar or plastic container in a cool, dry place several weeks. *Makes 64.*

HONEY-NUT KUCHEN
(pictured)

¾ cup warm water (105 to 155F)
2 pkg active dry yeast
½ cup sugar
1 teaspoon salt
½ cup (1 stick) butter or margarine, softened
3 eggs
4¼ cups all-purpose flour
¼ teaspoon ground nutmeg

HONEY GLAZE
2 tablespoons sugar
¼ cup all-purpose flour
⅓ cup honey
¼ cup orange marmalade
¼ cup (½ stick) butter or margarine, softened

½ cup pecan halves

DO AHEAD

1. If possible, check temperature of warm water with thermometer. Sprinkle yeast over water in large bowl, stirring until yeast is dissolved. Add ½ cup sugar and the salt, stirring until dissolved.

2. Add ½ cup butter, the eggs, 3 cups flour, and the nutmeg. Beat vigorously with wooden spoon, or with electric mixer at medium speed, until smooth—about 2 minutes.

3. Gradually add remaining 1¼ cups flour, mixing with a wooden spoon, then with hands until dough is smooth and stiff enough to leave side of bowl.

4. Turn out dough onto lightly floured surface. Knead until smooth and blisters appear on surface—about 5 minutes.

5. Place in lightly greased large bowl; turn to bring greased side up. Cover with towel; let rise in warm place (85F), free from drafts, until double in bulk—1 to 1½ hours.

6. Butter generously bottom and side of a 10½-inch skillet with a heat-resistant handle. (Wrap foil around handle to protect it, if necessary.)

7. Turn out dough onto a lightly floured pastry cloth. With palms of hands, roll dough into a rope 36 inches

long. Into prepared skillet, beginning at outside edge, turn dough into a coil, twisting dough at same time (see picture, page 354).

8. Cover with towel; let rise in warm place until double in bulk (dough should rise to top of skillet)—50 to 60 minutes.

9. Meanwhile, make Honey Glaze: In small bowl, combine sugar and flour; mix well. Add rest of ingredients, mixing until well combined.

10. Preheat oven to 375F.

11. Bake 20 minutes. Then spoon half of honey glaze over top of dough, not on outer edge; bake 10 minutes. Spoon rest of glaze over top. Arrange pecans on top—in grooves. Bake 5 minutes longer, or until kuchen is a rich golden-brown.

12. Let cool in pan on wire rack 15 minutes. Remove from pan. Serve at once, or let cool completely.

TO STORE

13. Wrap in foil; seal, label and store in freezer several weeks.

TO SERVE

14. Preheat oven to 400F. Heat foil-wrapped frozen kuchen (loosen foil slightly) 30 to 35 minutes, or just until heated through. *Makes 1 large kuchen.*

MARZIPAN CRESCENTS
(pictured)

2 cans (8-oz size) almond paste (see Note)
1 cup granulated sugar
¼ cup egg white (2 eggs)
¼ cup confectioners' sugar
1 egg white, lightly beaten
Pine nuts or slivered almonds

DO AHEAD

1. In top of double boiler, combine almond paste, granulated sugar and ¼ cup egg white.

2. Place over hot water; stir constantly with a wooden spoon until mixture is smooth and slightly warm—about 5 minutes. Remove top of double boiler; let cool for about 10 minutes.

3. Lightly grease and flour several cookie sheets. Preheat oven to 350F.

4. Turn almond mixture onto board sprinkled lightly with confectioners' sugar. Knead 2 or 3 minutes, or until smooth.

5. Divide dough in half. Shape each half into a 10-inch-long roll. Cut each roll into 10 parts.

6. Shape each part into a thin roll about 4 inches long. Dip in egg white. Then roll in pine nuts, placed on sheet of waxed paper, covering generously and pressing nuts into surface.

7. Curve into crescent shape. Place, *continued on page 362*

continued from page 361

1½ inches apart, on prepared cookie sheets. Bake 15 to 20 minutes, or until a light-golden color.

8. With spatula, remove to wire racks; let cool completely.

TO STORE

9. Place in a plastic, airtight container; freeze for several weeks.

TO SERVE

10. Let thaw at room temperature. *Makes 20 crescents.*

Note: Do not use prepared almond filling.

PECAN PRALINES
(pictured)

1 cup granulated sugar
1 cup light-brown sugar, packed
½ cup light cream
1½ cups pecan halves
2 tablespoons butter or margarine

DO AHEAD

1. In 2-quart heavy saucepan, combine sugars and cream. Over medium heat, bring to boiling, stirring occasionally with wooden spoon. Continue cooking, stirring occasionally, to 228F on candy thermometer, or until syrup spins a 2-inch thread when dropped from spoon.

2. Add pecans and butter. Cook over medium heat, stirring frequently, to 236F on candy thermometer, or until a little syrup forms a soft ball in cold water.

3. Remove pan to wire rack. Let cool 10 minutes—to 200F. Stir about 1 minute, or until slightly thick but still glossy.

4. Drop by rounded tablespoonfuls, 3 inches apart, onto sheet of foil or dou-

ble thickness of waxed paper. Pralines will spread into large patties. If mixture becomes too stiff, stir in a drop or two of cold water.

TO STORE

5. Arrange in layers in plastic refrigerator container or tin with tight-fitting lid, with waxed paper between layers. Store in a cool, dry place several weeks. *Makes 1 dozen.*

KUGELHOPF
(pictured)

½ cup light or dark raisins
½ cup currants
1 can (4½ oz) blanched almonds, finely chopped
1 tablespoon grated fresh lemon peel
1 tablespoon brandy
1 cup milk
1 cup granulated sugar
½ cup warm water (105 to 115F)
1 pkg active dry yeast
5 cups all-purpose flour
14 to 16 whole blanched almonds
1 cup (2 sticks) butter or margarine, softened
1 teaspoon salt
6 eggs
¼ cup (½ stick) butter or margarine, melted

Confectioners' sugar

DO AHEAD

1. In medium bowl, combine raisins, currants, chopped almonds (reserve ¼ cup for later use), lemon peel and brandy; toss lightly to mix well. Set aside.

2. In small saucepan, heat milk until bubbles form around edge of pan; remove from heat. Stir in ¼ cup granulated sugar; let cool to lukewarm.

3. If possible check temperature of warm water with thermometer. Sprinkle yeast over water in large bowl; stir until dissolved. Stir in lukewarm milk mixture and 3 cups flour; with wooden spoon, beat until smooth—about 2 minutes.

4. Cover bowl with towel; let rise in warm place (85F), free from drafts, until double in bulk—about 1 hour. Batter will be light and spongy.

5. Meanwhile, butter generously a 4-quart Turk's-head tube mold, 10½ inches in diameter. Sprinkle inside of mold evenly with reserved chopped almonds. Place a whole almond in each indentation in the bottom of the mold.

6. In large bowl, with electric mixer at medium speed, beat softened butter with remaining ¾ cup granulated sugar and the salt until light and fluffy. Beat in eggs, one at a time, beating until smooth.

7. At low speed, beat in 1 cup flour

and the risen batter until smooth and well blended.

8. With wooden spoon, stir in the remaining flour and the fruit-nut mixture, beating until well combined.

9. Pour batter into prepared mold. Cover with towel; let rise in warm place (85F), free from drafts, 1 hour, or until batter rises almost to top of pan.

10. Meanwhile, preheat oven to 350F.

11. Bake Kugelhopf 50 to 60 minutes, or until a cake tester inserted near the center comes out clean. Let cool in pan on wire rack about 20 minutes.

12. Run spatula around sides of pan to loosen; turn out on wire rack. Brush with melted butter. Let cool completely.

TO STORE

13. Wrap in waxed paper, then in foil. Seal, label and store in a cool, dry place or in the refrigerator if storing for a week or two. Store in freezer if keeping longer.

TO SERVE

14. Let warm to room temperature. Sprinkle lightly with confectioners' sugar. Slice thinly. *Makes 1 large Kugelhopf.*

GLACEED CHERRIES AND NUTS
(pictured)

1½ cups sugar
1 cup light corn syrup
⅓ cup water
1 jar (13 oz) salted mixed nuts
1 jar (4 oz) candied red cherries
2 tablespoons butter or margarine
1 teaspoon vanilla extract

DO AHEAD

1. In a 2½-quart saucepan, combine sugar, corn syrup and water. Stir over medium heat until sugar is dissolved.

2. Continue cooking, without stirring, to 300F on candy thermometer, or until a little syrup separates into hard but not brittle threads, when dropped into cold water.

3. Preheat oven to 350F.

4. Arrange nuts and cherries in a 9-by-9-by-1¾-inch baking pan. Heat in oven 10 minutes; keep warm.

5. Generously butter a 17-by-14-inch cookie sheet.

6. Remove syrup from heat as soon as temperature is reached. Quickly add warm nuts and cherries, butter and vanilla. Stir rapidly just until butter melts. Immediately pour onto buttered cookie sheet, and quickly spread to edge with the back of a wooden spoon.

7. Cool completely on wire rack—about 1½ hours. Loosen from pan with spatula (if candy sticks, warm bottom of

pan over very low heat), and remove candy immediately. Then break into irregular pieces.

TO STORE

8. Store in an airtight container in a cool, dry place several weeks. Separate layers with waxed paper or foil. *Makes about 1¾ pounds.*

ORANGE-CRANBERRY JELLY
(pictured)

4 large navel oranges
6 cups sugar
1 cup fresh orange juice
¼ cup lemon juice
3 cups cranberry juice
1 bottle (6 oz) liquid pectin
6 drops red food color
Hot paraffin for sealing

DO AHEAD

1. Sterilize (see Note) 8 (8-oz) jelly glasses; leave in hot water until you are ready to fill them.

2. Remove peel from each orange in one long spiral.

3. In heavy, deep saucepan, combine orange peel, sugar, orange juice and lemon juice. Bring to boiling, stirring. Remove from heat; let stand, covered, 30 minutes.

4. Add cranberry juice. Then stir, over high heat, until sugar is dissolved and mixture is brought to a full, rolling boil (the boil cannot be stirred down). Stir in pectin.

5. Again bring to a full, rolling boil; boil 1 minute, stirring constantly.

6. Remove saucepan from heat. Remove orange peel to strainer; using wooden spoon, press out juice into saucepan. Discard orange peel. Skim off any foam from liquid. Stir in food color.

7. Ladle jelly into hot, sterilized jelly

glasses. Immediately cover with ⅛ inch hot paraffin.

8. Let cool; then cover with lids.

TO STORE

9. Store in a dark, dry, cool place. *Makes 8 (8-oz) jelly glasses.*

Note: To sterilize jars, wash jars and lids in hot, soapy water; rinse. Place on rack in large kettle; add water to cover. Bring water to boiling; reduce heat; simmer 10 minutes. When ready to fill jars, remove from water with tongs.

TROPICAL FRUITCAKE
(pictured)

Fine dry bread crumbs
1½ cups shelled whole Brazil nuts
2 pkg (8-oz size) pitted dates
1 jar (14 oz) maraschino cherries, drained
1 teaspoon vanilla extract
¾ cup all-purpose flour
¾ cup sugar
½ teaspoon baking powder
½ teaspoon salt
3 eggs

Fruitcake Glaze, recipe follows

DO AHEAD

1. Grease 5-cup ring mold, and line with foil strips. Lightly grease foil, and sprinkle with bread crumbs. Preheat oven to 300F.

2. In large bowl, combine nuts, dates, cherries and vanilla; toss to mix well.

3. Sift flour with sugar, baking powder and salt onto sheet of waxed paper. Add to fruit-nut mixture. With wooden spoon, mix until well combined.

4. In small bowl, with electric mixer at high speed, beat eggs until frothy. Turn into fruit-nut mixture; mix until well combined.

5. Turn into prepared mold. Bake about 1 hour and 10 minutes, or until cake tester inserted in center comes out clean.

6. Remove to wire rack. Let cake cool in mold 20 minutes. Remove from mold, leaving foil on cake.

TO STORE

7. Wrap in plastic wrap or waxed paper, then in foil. Store in a tightly covered tin in a cool, dry place or refrigerator several weeks.

TO SERVE

8. Glaze with Fruitcake Glaze. *Makes 2½-pound cake.*

FRUITCAKE GLAZE

⅓ cup light corn syrup
1 tablespoon lemon juice
1 tablespoon water

In small saucepan, combine corn syrup, lemon juice and water. Bring to boiling; reduce heat; simmer, stirring, 5 minutes, or until reduced to ⅓ cup. Cool completely.

SPECULAAS
(Saint Nicholas Cookies)
(pictured)

3 cups all-purpose flour
1½ teaspoons ground cinnamon
1 teaspoon ground cloves
1 teaspoon ground ginger
⅛ teaspoon baking powder
⅛ teaspoon salt
1 cup (2 sticks) butter or margarine, softened
1¼ cups light-brown sugar, packed
1 egg
½ cup sliced blanched almonds

DO AHEAD

1. On sheet of waxed paper, sift flour with spices, baking powder and salt. Set aside.

2. In large bowl of electric mixer, at high speed, beat butter with sugar and egg until mixture is very light and fluffy.

3. With wooden spoon, stir in half of flour mixture and the almonds, mixing with hands if necessary.

4. Refrigerate dough, covered, several hours. Also, refrigerate a 5-inch wooden butter mold (see picture, page 357).

5. Preheat oven to 350F. Lightly grease several cookie sheets. Remove one fourth of dough at a time from refrigerator. With hand, flatten dough to make a 4-inch rectangle.

6. Between 2 sheets of waxed paper,

continued on page 364

continued from page 363

on slightly dampened surface, roll out dough into a 9-by-5-inch rectangle. Press butter mold, lightly floured, firmly into dough to make design.

7. Cut around mold; remove mold. With wide spatula, transfer to prepared cookie sheet. Reroll trimmings, and repeat.

8. Repeat with rest of dough, one fourth at a time.

9. Bake 20 to 25 minutes, or until golden-brown around edges. Remove cookies to wire rack; cool completely.

TO STORE

10. Keep in a tightly covered glass jar or cookie tin in a cool, dry place several weeks. *Makes 14 to 15 (5-inch) cookies.*

BEST OF ALL FRUITCAKES
(pictured)

1 lb golden raisins
½ lb seeded raisins
¼ lb currants
½ cup dark rum or brandy
1 lb candied pineapple
½ lb candied red cherries
¼ lb candied citron
⅛ lb candied lemon peel
⅛ lb candied orange peel
2 cups all-purpose flour
½ teaspoon ground mace
½ teaspoon ground cinnamon
½ teaspoon baking soda
¼ lb almonds, shelled, blanched, and
    coarsely chopped
¼ lb walnuts or pecans, shelled and
    coarsely chopped
½ cup (1 stick) butter or margarine,
    softened
1 cup granulated sugar
1 cup brown sugar, tightly packed
5 eggs, slightly beaten
1 tablespoon milk
1 teaspoon almond extract

Rum or brandy
1 can (8 oz) almond paste
Frosting Glaze, recipe follows
Angelica
Candied red cherries

DO AHEAD

1. In large bowl, combine raisins and currants. Add ½ cup rum; toss to combine. Let stand, covered, overnight.

NEXT DAY

2. Line a 10-inch tube pan. On heavy brown paper, draw a 16½-inch circle, and cut out. Set pan in center of circle; draw around base of pan and tube. (See sketch, page 335.) With pencil lines outside, fold paper into eighths; snip off tip. Unfold circle; cut along folds to second circle. Grease both the tube pan and un-penciled side of paper well. Fit paper,

greased side up, into pan.

3. Prepare fruits: With sharp knife, cut pineapple in thin wedges; cut ½ pound cherries in half; cut citron and lemon and orange peels into very thin strips. Add to raisins and currants; mix well.

4. On sheet of waxed paper, sift 1½ cups flour with spices and baking soda. Set aside. Preheat oven to 275F.

5. Combine remaining ½ cup flour with nuts and fruits; toss lightly.

6. In large bowl of electric mixer, at medium speed, beat butter until light. Gradually beat in granulated sugar, then brown sugar, beating until very light and fluffy.

7. Beat in eggs, milk and almond extract until thoroughly combined.

8. At low speed, beat in flour mixture, mixing just until combined. Turn batter into fruit and nuts. Mix well with hands.

9. Turn into prepared pan, pressing batter down in pan evenly all around.

10. Bake 3 hours and 15 minutes, or until a cake tester inserted near center comes out dry.

11. Let cake stand in pan on wire rack 30 minutes to cool slightly. Turn out of pan; gently remove paper. Let cool completely.

TO STORE:

12. Wrap cake in cheesecloth soaked in rum or brandy. Place in a cake tin with a tight-fitting cover. Add a few

pieces of raw, unpeeled apple. (As cheesecloth dries out, resoak in rum or brandy.) Store in a cool place several weeks.

TO SERVE

13. To decorate cake for serving: Roll almond paste between 2 sheets of waxed paper into an 8-inch circle. Remove top sheet of paper. Invert paste onto cake; remove paper. With sharp knife, trim edge of paste; then press paste to cake. Spread paste with Frosting Glaze, letting it run down side of cake. Cut angelica into thin slices. Cut cherries in half. Decorate cake as pictured, page 356. *Makes a 5-pound fruitcake.*

FROSTING GLAZE

1½ cups confectioners' sugar
2 tablespoons light cream
¼ teaspoon almond extract

In small bowl, combine sugar, cream and almond extract; beat until smooth.

BABKA

1 cup warm water (105 to 115F)
2 pkg active dry yeast
½ cup granulated sugar
1 teaspoon salt
6 egg yolks
4½ cups sifted all-purpose flour
½ cup (1 stick) butter or margarine,
    softened
1 cup light or dark seedless raisins
½ cup finely chopped candied lemon or
    orange peel
1 tablespoon grated lemon peel
½ cup finely chopped walnuts
1 tablespoon butter or margarine, melted

GLAZE

2 cups sifted confectioners' sugar
1 tablespoon golden rum
2½ tablespoons light cream

Colored sugar crystals

DO AHEAD

1. If possible, check temperature of warm water with thermometer. Sprinkle yeast over water in large bowl, stirring until dissolved.

2. Add granulated sugar, salt, egg yolks and 2 cups flour; beat, with portable electric mixer, at high speed, until smooth—about 4 minutes.

3. Add ½ cup butter; beat until blended.

4. Gradually add remaining flour. Mix in last of it with a rubber spatula or by hand until dough leaves side of bowl.

5. Turn out dough onto lightly floured surface. Cover with bowl; let stand 10 minutes. Knead dough until it

is smooth and no longer sticky—about 10 minutes.

6. Place in lightly greased large bowl; turn dough to bring greased side up. Cover with towel; let rise in warm place (85F), free from drafts, until double in bulk—about 1½ hours.

7. Punch down dough. Add raisins, peels and walnuts; mix in well with hand.

8. Turn out dough onto lightly floured pastry cloth. Shape into a round, smooth ball; with finger, poke 1-inch hole in center of dough. Place in lightly greased 9-by-4-inch tube pan.

9. Brush top with the melted butter. Cover with towel; let rise in warm place (85F), free from drafts, until Babka has more than doubled in bulk and is rounded over top of pan—about 1½ hours.

10. Meanwhile, preheat oven to 350F.

11. Bake 40 to 45 minutes, or until golden.

12. Let stand, in pan, on wire rack 5 minutes. Remove from pan; cool on wire rack.

TO STORE

13. Wrap cooled Babka tightly in foil; seal, label and freeze.

TO SERVE

14. Preheat oven to 400F. Heat foil-wrapped Babka 30 to 35 minutes, or just until heated through.

15. Meanwhile, make Glaze: Combine confectioners' sugar, rum and cream in small bowl, mixing until smooth. Unwrap Babka and place on wire rack. Pour glaze over warm Babka, letting it run down side. Sprinkle with colored sugar. *Makes 1 loaf.*

SCOTCH APPLE TARTES

2 pkg (9½- to 11-oz size) piecrust mix

FILLING
6 cups diced, pared tart green apples (4 to 6)
¾ cup (1½ sticks) butter or margarine
3¼ cups currants
¾ cup light-brown sugar, packed
¾ cup granulated sugar
1¾ teaspoons ground cinnamon
½ teaspoon ground nutmeg
¾ teaspoon salt
¾ cup water
½ cup light or dark rum
1½ tablespoons cornstarch
1 egg yolk
2 teaspoons water

DO AHEAD

1. For 2 tartes: Prepare 1 package at a time of piecrust mix as package label directs. Shape each into 2 balls. Refrigerate until ready to roll out.

2. Between 2 sheets of waxed paper,

on a slightly dampened surface, roll out one ball of pastry to an 11-inch circle. Use to line an 8¾-inch quiche pan (with removable bottom). Fold over extra inch of pastry; press two layers of pastry together to make double thickness around edge.

3. Roll out second ball of pastry to a 9-inch circle. Place quiche pan on pastry. Using edge of pan as guide, with serrated pastry wheel or sharp knife, cut around pan. Remove pan. With pastry wheel, cut circle into 8 triangles. From center, cut out and remove a circle 2 inches in diameter; discard, along with one triangle. (Or sprinkle leftovers with cinnamon-sugar and bake 8 to 10 minutes in a 400F oven. Nice to nibble with a cup of tea.) Refrigerate 7 triangles and pastry-lined pan. Repeat with remaining pastry.

4. Make Filling: Pare, core, and dice apples. In a 3-quart saucepan, combine apples, butter, currants, brown sugar, granulated sugar, cinnamon, nutmeg, salt and ¾ cup water.

5. Bring to boiling, reduce heat, and cook, covered and stirring occasionally, until apples are tender but not mushy—takes about 15 minutes.

6. Mix rum with cornstarch until smooth. Add to filling; bring to boiling, stirring constantly. Remove from heat; let cool completely.

7. Divide filling evenly between the pastry-lined pans. On top of fruit in each, place 7 pastry triangles, spoke fashion.

8. In custard cup, with a fork, beat egg yolk and 2 teaspoons water. Use to brush pastry triangles.

TO STORE

9. Freeze in freezer. When frozen, wrap well in foil; seal, label and store in freezer several weeks, until ready to use.

TO SERVE

10. Preheat oven to 400F. Unwrap

one or both tartes; bake, frozen, in lower part of oven 40 to 45 minutes, or until crust is golden-brown. During last 5 minutes, place a 12-inch sheet of foil loosely over tarte to prevent over-browning.

11. Serve with vanilla ice cream. *Makes 2 tartes, 7 servings each.*

AVA'S HOLIDAY COOKIES

4 cups sifted all-purpose flour
1 teaspoon baking powder
½ teaspoon salt
1 teaspoon ground nutmeg
¾ cup (1½ sticks) butter or margarine, softened
1¼ cups granulated sugar
2 eggs
1 teaspoon vanilla extract

Decorating Frosting, recipe follows
Colored sugar, colored dragées, nonpareils, chocolate pieces

DO AHEAD

1. On sheet of waxed paper, sift flour with baking powder, salt and nutmeg. Set aside.

2. In large bowl of electric mixer, at high speed; beat butter, granulated sugar, eggs and vanilla until light and fluffy.

3. With wooden spoon, stir in half of flour mixture. Then add rest of flour mixture, mixing with hands if necessary.

4. Refrigerate dough, covered, several hours or overnight.

5. Preheat oven to 400F. Divide dough into 4 parts; refrigerate until ready to roll out.

6. Between 2 sheets of waxed paper, on slightly dampened surface, roll out dough, one part at a time, ⅛ inch thick.

7. With floured, assorted cookie cutters, cut out cookies, Place, 2 inches apart, on ungreased cookie sheets.

continued on page 366

continued from page 365

8. Bake 8 minutes, or just until set and lightly brown around the edges. Remove to wire rack; cool completely.

9. Spread cookies evenly with Decorating Frosting. Decorate with colored sugar, dragées, nonpareils and chocolate pieces. Let dry on wire rack about 1 hour.

TO STORE

10. Store in airtight cookie jar or tin, in a cool, dry place, several weeks. *Makes 3 to 4 dozen.*

DECORATING FROSTING

2 egg whites
⅛ teaspoon cream of tartar
1¾ cups sifted confectioners' sugar
1 to 2 tablespoons water
Food colors

In medium bowl, with electric mixer at high speed, beat egg whites with cream of tartar until stiff peaks form when beaters are slowly raised. Gradually add confectioners' sugar, beating until frosting is smooth and thin enough to spread. (If necessary, add 1 to 2 tablespoons water to thin it.) Divide into 3 parts. Tint each with 1 or 2 drops of different food colors. Cover with a damp cloth.

MINIATURE BABAS

¼ cup warm water (105 to 115F)
1 pkg active dry yeast
2 tablespoons sugar
½ teaspoon salt
3 eggs
1¾ cups sifted all-purpose flour
¼ cup (½ stick) butter or margarine, softened

APRICOT-RUM SYRUP
1 can (12 oz) apricot nectar
1 cup water
¾ cup sugar
¼ cup lemon juice
¾ to 1 cup golden rum

Whipped cream (optional)

DO AHEAD

1. Lightly grease 16 (2½-inch) muffin-pan cups. If possible, check temperature of warm water with thermometer.

2. Sprinkle yeast over water in small bowl of electric mixer, stirring until dissolved.

3. Add 2 tablespoons sugar, salt, eggs and 1¼ cups flour. At medium speed, beat 4 minutes, or until smooth, scraping side of bowl and guiding mixture into beaters, with rubber spatula.

4. Add butter; beat 2 minutes, or until very well blended.

5. At low speed, beat in rest of flour; beat until smooth—about 2 minutes. Batter will be thick.

6. Turn batter into prepared muffin cups, using 1 rounded tablespoon batter for each cup; cover with towel.

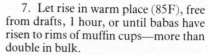

7. Let rise in warm place (85F), free from drafts, 1 hour, or until babas have risen to rims of muffin cups—more than double in bulk.

8. Preheat oven to 400F. Bake babas 15 to 18 minutes, or until deep golden-brown. Let cool several minutes in pan, on wire rack.

9. Meanwhile, make Apricot-Rum Syrup: In medium saucepan, combine apricot nectar with 1 cup water and the ¾ cup sugar. Bring to boiling, stirring until sugar is dissolved.

10. Reduce heat; simmer, uncovered, 15 minutes. Remove from heat; add lemon juice and rum.

11. Turn out babas; arrange in a 13-by-9-by-2-inch pan, tops up. Poke holes in babas, at ½-inch intervals, with cake tester.

12. Pour hot syrup over babas; let stand, basting occasionally, 1 hour, or until all syrup is absorbed.

TO STORE

13. Cool completely. Freezer-wrap, pan and all; label, and freeze.

TO SERVE

14. Let stand at room temperature 1 hour; then reheat, foil-wrapped, 20 minutes at 350F. Serve slightly warm, with sweetened whipped cream, if desired. *Makes 16 servings.*

APRICOT-DATE BALLS

½ cup dried apricot halves (about 12)
1½ cups pitted dates (about 18)
1 can (3½ oz) flaked coconut
½ cup sugar
1 tablespoon grated orange peel
1 tablespoon orange juice

DO AHEAD

1. Rinse apricots in cold water. Combine with ½ cup water in small saucepan; bring to boiling. Reduce heat, and simmer, uncovered, 30 minutes. Drain.

2. Put apricots and dates through coarse blade of food grinder.

3. In medium bowl, combine with the coconut, ¼ cup sugar, orange peel and orange juice; mix very well.

4. Shape into 28 balls, each 1¼ inches in diameter.

TO STORE

5. Refrigerate, covered, on waxed paper placed on cookie sheet, 24 hours or longer. (Flavor improves with age.) These will keep several weeks if they are stored, wrapped, in refrigerator.

TO SERVE

6. Just before using, roll in ¼ cup sugar to coat well. Serve as a confection; nice on the tea table. *Makes 28.* ◆

continued from page 347

1½ cups ground cooked ham
½ cup mayonnaise
2 tablespoons Madeira
2 tablespoons tomato sauce
¼ teaspoon salt
Dash ground red pepper
1 egg white, beaten stiff
½ cup heavy cream, whipped

1 cucumber, thinly sliced

1. Prepare Garnish: Sprinkle ½ envelope gelatine over white wine in measuring cup; let stand until softened. In small saucepan, bring to boiling ¼ cup water. Add gelatine, stirring until dissolved. Set in bowl of ice cubes to cool. Lightly oil bottom and sides of 1-quart decorative mold.

2. Cut hard-cooked egg in half lengthwise. Remove yolk. Slice each half into 4 lengthwise pieces to resemble petals. Dip each petal in gelatine; arrange, rounded side down, in bottom of prepared mold.

3. With paring knife, cut seven ½-inch pimiento rounds and one round from egg yolk (for center of flower). Dip in gelatine mixture. Arrange pimiento rounds around edge. Refrigerate.

4. Make Mousse: Soften gelatine in ½ cup chicken broth; let stand 5 minutes. In small saucepan, bring remaining broth to boiling. Add gelatine mixture, stirring until dissolved. Set aside to cool.

5. In medium bowl, combine ham, mayonnaise, Madeira, tomato sauce, salt and red pepper. With wire whisk, mix until well combined. Add cooled gelatine mixture; mix well.

6. Turn into medium bowl; set in bowl of ice cubes; let stand, stirring occasionally, until consistency of unbeaten egg white—15 minutes.

7. Combine chilled ham mixture with beaten egg white and whipped cream. With wire whisk, mix until well combined. Turn into prepared mold, spreading evenly. Refrigerate until

firm—several hours or overnight.

8. To unmold: Run a spatula around edge of mold. Invert onto a chilled serving plate. Place a hot, damp dishcloth over mold; shake gently to release. Repeat if necessary; lift off. *Makes 8 servings.*

CORNMEAL-HAM MUFFINS

1 cup all-purpose flour
2 teaspoons baking powder
1 teaspoon sugar
⅛ teaspoon salt
¾ cup cornmeal
2 eggs
¼ cup salad oil
¾ cup milk
1 cup ground cooked ham

1. Preheat oven to 400F. Grease bottoms of 8 (2½-inch) muffin-pan cups.

2. On sheet of waxed paper, sift together flour, baking powder, sugar and salt. Add cornmeal, mixing well; set aside.

3. In medium bowl, beat together eggs, salad oil and milk. Add flour mixture and ham, stirring only until mixture is moistened.

4. Spoon batter into prepared pan. Bake 15 to 20 minutes, until golden.

5. Loosen edge of each muffin with spatula; turn out. Serve hot. *Makes 8.* ♦

SWEETS TO STORE

continued from page 343

heat, stirring, until sugars are dissolved.

2. Add lemon and orange wedges; bring to boiling. Boil, uncovered, 20 minutes. Discard fruit.

3. Just before serving, add rum; heat, over very low heat, just until vapor rises. Remove from heat. Ignite with match, and serve sauce flaming over Mincemeat Turnovers.

ICELANDIC TORTE

FILLING
2 pkg (12-oz size) pitted prunes
2 cups water
¾ cup granulated sugar
1 teaspoon vanilla extract
¾ teaspoon ground cardamom seed
¼ teaspoon salt

TORTE LAYERS
4 cups sifted all-purpose flour
2 teaspoons baking powder
½ teaspoon salt
1 cup (2 sticks) butter or margarine,
**   softened**
1 cup granulated sugar
1 teaspoon vanilla extract

2 eggs
¼ cup milk

Confectioners' sugar
Whipped cream

DO AHEAD
1. Make Filling: In 3-quart saucepan, place prunes and 2 cups water; bring to boiling. Reduce heat, and simmer, covered, 30 minutes, or until prunes are very tender.

2. Drain prunes, reserving liquid. Chop prunes finely. Add ¾ cup granulated sugar, 1 teaspoon vanilla, the cardamom, ¼ teaspoon salt and ½ cup reserved cooking liquid; mix until ingredients are well blended. Set aside to cool.

3. Make Torte Layers: Sift flour with baking powder and salt.

4. In large bowl, with electric mixer at high speed, beat butter with granulated sugar and vanilla until light and fluffy.

5. Add eggs, one at a time, beating well after each addition.

6. At low speed, add flour mixture alternately with milk, beginning and ending with flour mixture.

7. Refrigerate dough until chilled and easy to handle—about 20 minutes.

8. Preheat oven to 350F. Divide dough into 7 equal pieces.

9. For each layer, invert an 8-inch round layer-cake pan. Flatten a piece of dough with hands; place on pan; pat to fit. Then gently roll to make layer even; trim edge if necessary. Keep pieces of dough refrigerated until ready to use.

10. Bake 15 to 20 minutes, or until edge is golden-brown. Carefully remove baked layer to wire rack; let cool. Continue until all 7 layers are baked and cooled.

11. To assemble: Place one layer on serving plate; spread with about ½ cup filling. Repeat with 5 more layers and remaining filling. Set last layer on top. Cover completely with plastic wrap or foil.

TO STORE
12. Refrigerate at least 24 hours, to mellow. If longer storage is desired, seal, label and place cake in freezer. Set it in refrigerator overnight to defrost before serving.

TO SERVE
13. Sprinkle top with confectioners' sugar. Cut in thin slices. Pass whipped cream. Return unused portion to refrigerator. *Makes 16 servings.* ♦

COOKIES
IN NO TIME

*F*or your favorite holiday-party hostess (and/or your own family),
bake an assortment of mouth-melting cookies that can easily be prepared
ahead of time. Shape them with your hands or drop from a spoon.
Peanut-Butter Balls, Holiday Macaroons, Fruitcake Bars, Pecan Crescents,
Christmas Logs, Pinwheel Cookies and more. For recipes, see page 370.

continued from page 369

PEANUT-BUTTER BALLS
(pictured)

1 cup peanut butter
½ cup honey
1 cup quick-cooking oats
1 cup chopped mixed dried fruit
½ cup wheat germ
Coconut
Red and green food color
Chopped peanuts

1. In large bowl, combine peanut butter, honey, oats, dried fruit and wheat germ; mix well with wooden spoon until well combined.

2. Shape into 1-inch balls. Roll in plain coconut or coconut tinted with red or green food color or chopped peanuts.

TO STORE
3. Arrange in layers in a plastic refrigerator container or a tin with a tight-fitting lid, with waxed paper between layers. Store in refrigerator; do not freeze. *Makes 46 balls.*

HOLIDAY MACAROONS
(pictured)

2 eggs
¾ cup sugar
⅓ cup all-purpose flour
¼ teaspoon baking powder
Dash salt
1 tablespoon butter or margarine, melted, cooled
1 teaspoon vanilla extract
2⅔ cups flaked coconut
¼ teaspoon ground cinnamon
½ teaspoon grated lemon peel

Pecan halves (optional)
Red or green candied cherries, halved (optional)

1. Preheat oven to 325F. Lightly grease and flour two cookie sheets.

2. In small bowl of electric mixer, beat eggs until foamy. Gradually add sugar, beating until thick and lemon-colored—5 minutes.

3. Fold in flour, baking powder and salt. Then add butter, vanilla and coconut; mix well.

4. Divide batter in half. Add cinnamon to one half, lemon peel to the other. Drop by teaspoonfuls onto prepared cookie sheets.

5. Bake 12 to 15 minutes, or until edges are golden. Let stand a few seconds; remove from sheets to rack.

6. If desired, before baking, decorate with pecan halves or red or green candied cherry halves.

TO STORE
7. Arange in layers in a plastic refrigerator container or a tin with a tight-fitting lid, with waxed paper between layers. Store in a cool, dry place. *Makes about 3 dozen.*

PECAN CRESCENTS
(pictured)

2 cups unsifted all-purpose flour
1 cup (2 sticks) butter or margarine, softened
1 cup ground pecans or hazelnuts
½ cup confectioners' sugar
⅛ teaspoon salt
1 teaspoon vanilla extract
¼ teaspoon almond extract

VANILLA SUGAR
3-inch strip vanilla bean, cut up
2 cups sifted confectioners' sugar

DO AHEAD
1. In large bowl, combine flour, butter, nuts, ½ cup confectioners' sugar, the salt and extracts. Mix with hands until thoroughly combined. Refrigerate, covered, 30 minutes.

2. Make Vanilla Sugar: In electric blender, combine cut-up vanilla bean and ¼ cup sifted confectioners' sugar; cover; blend at high speed about 8 seconds. On a large sheet of foil, combine with remaining 1¾ cups sifted confectioners' sugar.

3. Preheat oven to 375F.

4. Shape cookies: Form dough into balls, using 1 tablespoon dough for each. Then, with palms of hands, form each ball into a roll 3 inches long.

5. Place rolls 2 inches apart, on ungreased cookie sheets. Curve each to make a crescent. Bake 12 to 15 minutes, or until set but not brown.

6. Let stand 1 minute before removing. With spatula, place hot cookies in Vanilla Sugar; turn gently to coat both sides. Cool completely.

TO STORE
7. Store in a tightly covered crock or cookie tin in a cool, dry place.

TO SERVE
8. Just before serving, coat with additional Vanilla Sugar, if desired. *Makes about 3½ dozen.*

DUTCH COOKIES
(pictured)

1¾ cups all-purpose flour
1½ teaspoons baking powder
⅛ teaspoon salt
¾ cup (1½ sticks) butter or margarine, softened
¾ cup sugar
1 teaspoon vanilla extract
¼ teaspoon almond extract
Blanched whole almonds, halved
Red and green candied cherries, cut in bits

DO AHEAD
1. Preheat oven to 375F. On sheet of waxed paper, sift flour with baking powder and salt; set aside.

2. In large bowl, with wooden spoon, beat butter with sugar and vanilla and almond extracts until smooth. Gradually add flour mixture, stirring until well combined. Dough will be stiff. Divide in half.

3. On slightly dampened surface, between two sheets of waxed paper, roll out half of dough into a 7½-inch square. Cut into 25 (1½-inch) squares or diamonds. Decorate each with a nut half and bits of cherry. Place, 2 inches apart, on ungreased cookie sheets.

4. Bake 10 to 12 minutes, or just until lightly browned. Remove to wire rack; cool completely. Repeat with remaining dough.

TO STORE
5. When completely cool, place in tightly covered jar or tin container. Store in cool, dry place. *Makes 50 cookies.*

PISTACHIO COOKIES
(pictured)

2 cups all-purpose flour
1½ teaspoons baking powder
½ teaspoon salt
⅔ cup (1⅓ sticks) butter or margarine, softened
1 cup sugar
1 egg
1 teaspoon vanilla extract
Red or green food color
¼ cup finely chopped pistachio nuts
Multicolor nonpareils

1. Sift flour with baking powder and salt; set aside.

2. In large bowl, combine butter, sugar, egg and vanilla. With wooden spoon or electric mixer, beat until smooth.

3. Add flour mixture, beating at low speed, just until combined.

4. Turn 1 cup batter into small bowl; add 2 or 3 drops food color; mix well. Add nuts. On waxed paper, with hands, shape into a roll 10 inches long; place in

freezer 10 minutes.

5. Roll remaining dough between two sheets of waxed paper into a 10-by-6-inch rectangle. Place in freezer 10 minutes. Then remove top sheet of waxed paper.

6. To shape: Place colored roll lengthwise in center of rectangle of dough. With hands, mold white dough around roll, covering completely. Roll in nonpareils. Wrap in waxed paper; place in freezer 20 to 30 minutes, until firm enough to slice.

7. Preheat oven to 375F. With sharp knife, cut into slices ⅛ inch thick. Place 2 inches apart on ungreased cookie sheets.

8. Bake 8 to 10 minutes, or until lightly browned. Remove cookies to wire rack; cool completely.

TO STORE

9. Place in tightly covered jar or tin container. Store in a cool, dry place. *Makes about 6 dozen.*

EASY PINWHEEL COOKIES
(pictured)

FILLING
1 cup raisins, chopped
½ cup dates, chopped
½ cup candied red cherries, chopped
½ cup walnuts, chopped
2 tablespoons flour
½ cup cold water

1 pkg (17 oz) refrigerated sugar cookies

1. Make Filling: In small saucepan, combine filling ingredients; mix well.

2. Cook over medium heat, stirring, about 2 minutes. Remove from heat. Place pan in bowl of ice water to cool completely. Makes 2 cups.

3. Meanwhile, remove wrapper from sugar-cookie dough. Let stand at room temperature to soften.

4. Preheat oven to 325F. Lightly grease cookie sheets.

5. Cut roll in half. Between two pieces of waxed paper placed on a damp surface, roll each half to a rectangle, 9 by 7 inches.

6. Spread 1 cup filling over each rectangle. From long side, roll each rectangle, jelly-roll fashion. If too soft to slice, wrap in waxed paper; place in freezer 10 minutes, or until firm.

7. Slice cookies ¼ inch thick. Bake, one inch apart on prepared cookie sheet, 8 to 10 minutes, or until golden. Remove to rack; cool completely.

TO STORE

8. Place in tightly covered jar or tin container. Store in a cool, dry place. *Makes 44 cookies.*

CHRISTMAS LOGS
(pictured)

¾ cup (1½ sticks) butter or margarine, softened
⅓ cup granulated sugar
1 teaspoon vanilla extract
2 cups all-purpose flour
¼ teaspoon salt

FROSTING
1 cup confectioners' sugar
1 to 1½ tablespoons milk

Colored sugar
Chopped walnuts

1. Preheat oven to 350F. Lightly grease cookie sheets.

2. In large bowl, with wooden spoon, beat butter, granulated sugar and vanilla until light and fluffy.

3. Add flour and salt; mix well with hands.

4. Turn out dough onto lightly floured surface. With hands, shape into a roll 6 inches long. With sharp knife, cut roll crosswise into six parts.

5. Shape each part into a roll 12 inches long and ¾ inch in diameter. Cut each roll into six (3-inch) pieces.

6. Place rolls, 1 inch apart, on cookie sheets.

7. Bake 15 to 20 minutes, or until delicately brown. Remove to wire rack; cool.

8. Make Frosting: In small bowl, combine ingredients; mix well. Dip ends of cookies in frosting; sprinkle with colored sugar or chopped nuts.

TO STORE

9. Arrange in a plastic or tin container with a tight-fitting lid; separate layers with waxed paper. Store in a cool place. *Makes 24 cookies.*

CHRISTMAS AMARETTI
(pictured)

COOKIE DOUGH
½ cup granulated sugar
½ cup confectioners' sugar
¼ cup all-purpose flour
⅛ teaspoon salt
1 can (8 oz) almond paste
2 egg whites

⅓ cup finely chopped blanched almonds
Candied red or green cherries, halved

DO AHEAD

1. Preheat oven to 300F. Lightly grease two large cookie sheets.

2. Make Cookie Dough: Sift both sugars with flour and salt; set aside.

3. Using a fork, break almond paste into small pieces in medium bowl. Add

egg whites; beat with electric mixer at medium speed until well blended.

4. Using slightly rounded teaspoonfuls, roll dough between hands into balls about 1 inch in diameter; then roll in chopped almonds.

5. Place 2 inches apart on prepared cookie sheets. Lightly press into rounds 1½ inches in diameter. Press a candied-cherry half into top of each.

6. Bake 20 to 25 minutes, or until golden. Remove to wire rack; cool.

TO STORE

7. Store several days in tightly covered container, to mellow. *Makes about 2½ dozen.*

FRUITCAKE BARS
(pictured)

1 cup all-purpose flour
½ teaspoon baking soda
½ teaspoon salt
½ teaspoon ground cinnamon
½ cup (1 stick) butter or margarine, softened
¾ cup granulated sugar
2 eggs
1 pkg (8 oz) pitted dates, coarsely chopped
¼ cup mixed candied fruit
½ cup candied cherries, quartered
½ cup chopped walnuts or pecans

GLAZE
1½ cups confectioners' sugar
2 to 3 tablespoons milk

Red and green candied cherries, halved
Red and green candied pineapple

1. Preheat oven to 375F. Grease and flour 13- by- 9- by- 2-inch pan. Sift flour with baking soda, salt and cinnamon.

2. In large bowl, with wooden spoon or electric mixer at medium speed, beat butter, granulated sugar and eggs until light and fluffy.

continued on page 372

continued from page 371

3. Stir in flour mixture until well combined. Add fruits and nuts, mixing well.

4. Spread in prepared pan; bake 30 minutes, or until golden-brown. Let cool in pan on wire rack.

5. Make Glaze: In medium bowl, combine confectioners' sugar and milk; stir until smooth.

6. Spread with glaze. Cut into 30 bars. Decorate, as pictured, with candied cherries and wedges of candied pineapple.

TO STORE

7. Arrange in layers, separated with waxed paper, in a container with a tight-fitting lid. Store in a cool place. *Makes 30.*

GLAZED FRUITCAKE TARTS
(pictured)

Fruitcake Bars, above

GLAZE
⅓ cup light corn syrup
1 teaspoon lemon juice
1 tablespoon water

Red and green candied cherries

1. Preheat oven to 375F.

2. Grease well 2½- to 3-inch tart pans of assorted shapes and sizes. Set pans on cookie sheet.

3. Make batter for Fruitcake Bars. Spoon 1 tablespoonful of dough into each pan. Bake 20 to 25 minutes, or until cake tester comes out dry.

4. Remove to rack; cool 10 minutes before removing from pans.

5. Make Glaze: In small saucepan, combine corn syrup, lemon juice and water. Bring to boiling; cool.

6. Brush tarts with glaze; decorate with green and red candied cherries, as pictured.

TO STORE

7. Store as Fruitcake Bars, above. *Makes 30.*

DATE-AND-WALNUT BARS
(pictured)

¾ cup all-purpose flour
1 teaspoon baking powder
½ teaspoon salt
2 eggs
1 cup light-brown sugar, packed
1 cup sliced dates
1 cup coarsely chopped walnuts
1 teaspoon vanilla extract
Confectioners' sugar

1. Preheat oven to 350F. Lightly grease and line bottom of a 9-by-9-by-2-inch baking pan with waxed paper.

2. Sift flour with baking powder and salt; set aside.

3. In medium bowl, with electric mixer, beat eggs until light.

4. Gradually add brown sugar, beating until smooth and fluffy.

5. Add dates, nuts and vanilla; mix thoroughly. Stir in dry ingredients; mix well. Spread in prepared pan.

6. Bake 25 to 30 minutes, or until surface springs back when lightly pressed with fingertip.

7. Cool slightly. Remove from pan on wire rack; peel off waxed paper.

8. While still warm, with sharp knife, cut into 24 bars. To serve, roll in confectioners' sugar.

TO STORE

9. When bars are completely cool, place in a tin with a tight-fitting lid, with waxed paper between layers. Store in a cool, dry place. *Makes 24.*

HALF-MOONS
(pictured)

2½ cups all-purpose flour
¼ teaspoon salt
1 cup (2 sticks) butter or margarine, softened
⅔ cup granulated sugar
1 egg yolk
1 teaspoon vanilla extract

GLAZE
1½ cups confectioners' sugar
1½ tablespoons milk

Multicolor nonpareils

1. Sift flour with salt; set aside.

2. In large bowl, with wooden spoon, or electric mixer at medium speed, beat

butter, granulated sugar, egg yolk and vanilla until smooth.

3. Gradually stir in flour mixture, mixing until well blended.

4. Divide dough in half; with hands, shape each half into a roll 2 inches in diameter. Wrap in foil or plastic wrap. Freeze 20 to 30 minutes, or until firm.

5. Preheat oven to 350F. Make Glaze: In small bowl, combine confectioners' sugar and milk; mix well.

6. Lightly grease cookie sheets. With sharp knife, cut dough into slices ¼ inch thick. For half-moon, cut each slice in half. Place cookies, 1 inch apart, on prepared cookie sheet.

7. Bake 8 to 10 minutes, or until lightly browned. Remove to rack. Spread glaze over warm cookies; dip edge, as pictured, into nonpareils.

TO STORE

8. Cool cookies completely. Place in a tin with a tight-fitting lid, with waxed paper between layers. Store in a cool, dry place. *Makes about 6 dozen.*

DOUBLE-CHOCOLATE DROPS

1 pkg (6 oz) semisweet chocolate pieces
1 cup sifted all-purpose flour
½ teaspoon baking soda
½ teaspoon salt
½ cup (1 stick) butter or margarine, softened
½ cup sugar
1 egg
¼ cup warm water
½ cup coarsely chopped walnuts or pecans

1. In top of double boiler, over hot, not boiling, water, melt ½ cup chocolate pieces. Let cool.

2. Sift together flour, baking soda and salt; set aside.

3. In large bowl of electric mixer, at medium speed, beat butter, sugar and egg until light and fluffy.

4. At low speed, beat in melted chocolate and warm water.

5. Then beat in flour mixture, just until combined.

6. With spoon, stir in remaining chocolate pieces and the nuts. Refrigerate 30 minutes.

7. Meanwhile, preheat oven to 375F. Lightly grease cookie sheets.

8. Drop batter by teaspoonfuls, 3 inches apart, onto prepared cookie sheets. Decorate, if desired, with additional chopped nuts.

9. Bake 10 to 12 minutes. Remove to wire rack; cool.

TO STORE

10. Store in tightly covered crock or cookie tin in a cool, dry place. *Makes about 3 dozen.* ◆

INDEX